Jeep Wrangler Automotive Repair Manual

by Mike Stubblefield and John H Haynes

Member of the Guild of Motoring Writers

Models covered:
All Jeep Wrangler models
1987 through 2003

(10K22 - 50030)

ABCDE
FGHIJ
KLMNO
P
2

Haynes Publishing Group
Sparkford Nr Yeovil
Somerset BA22 7JJ England

Haynes North America, Inc
861 Lawrence Drive
Newbury Park
California 91320 USA

About this manual

Its purpose

The purpose of this manual is to help you get the best value from your vehicle. It can do so in several ways. It can help you decide what work must be done, even if you choose to have it done by a dealer service department or a repair shop; it provides information and procedures for routine maintenance and servicing; and it offers diagnostic and repair procedures to follow when trouble occurs.

We hope you use the manual to tackle the work yourself. For many simpler jobs, doing it yourself may be quicker than arranging an appointment to get the vehicle into a shop and making the trips to leave it and pick it up. More importantly, a lot of money can be saved by avoiding the expense the shop must pass on to you to cover its labor and overhead costs. An added benefit is the sense of satisfaction and accomplishment that you feel after doing the job yourself.

Using the manual

The manual is divided into Chapters. Each Chapter is divided into numbered Sections, which are headed in bold type between horizontal lines. Each Section consists of consecutively numbered paragraphs.

At the beginning of each numbered Section you will be referred to any illustrations which apply to the procedures in that Section. The reference numbers used in illustration captions pinpoint the pertinent Section and the Step within that Section. That is, illustration 3.2 means the illustration refers to Section 3 and Step (or paragraph) 2 within that Section.

Procedures, once described in the text, are not normally repeated. When it's necessary to refer to another Chapter, the reference will be given as Chapter and Section number. Cross references given without use of the word "Chapter" apply to Sections and/or paragraphs in the same Chapter. For example, "see Section 8" means in the same Chapter.

References to the left or right side of the vehicle assume you are sitting in the driver's seat, facing forward.

Even though we have prepared this manual with extreme care, neither the publisher nor the author can accept responsibility for any errors in, or omissions from, the information given.

NOTE

A **Note** provides information necessary to properly complete a procedure or information which will make the procedure easier to understand.

CAUTION

A **Caution** provides a special procedure or special steps which must be taken while completing the procedure where the Caution is found. Not heeding a Caution can result in damage to the assembly being worked on.

WARNING

A **Warning** provides a special procedure or special steps which must be taken while completing the procedure where the Warning is found. Not heeding a Warning can result in personal injury.

Acknowledgements

We are grateful to the Chrysler Corporation for assistance with technical information, certain illustrations and vehicle photos. Technical writers who contributed to this project include Larry Warren, Robert Maddox and Doug Nelson.

© Haynes North America, Inc. 1992, 1994, 1996, 1999, 2000, 2004
With permission from J.H. Haynes & Co. Ltd.

A book in the Haynes Automotive Repair Manual Series

Printed in the U.S.A.

ISBN 13: 978 1 56392 561 0
ISBN 10: 1 56392 561 3

Library of Congress Catalog Card Number 2004115644

Contents

1991 Jeep Wrangler "S"

Introduction to the Jeep Wrangler

Jeep Wrangler models are all equipped with a roll bar and a removable hard top or soft top. The body style varies slightly with the different models: "S" type, Sahara and Islander.

The 2.4L and 2.5L four cylinder and the 4.0L and 4.2L six-cylinder engines used in these vehicles are equipped with a carburetor or fuel injection system, depending on the model. The engine drives the rear wheels through either a four or five-speed manual or three or four-speed automatic transmission via a driveshaft and solid rear axle. A transfer case and driveshaft are used to drive the front axle when the vehicle is switched into 4WD.

The suspension features solid axles at the front and rear. The front axle on models through 1995 is suspended by leaf springs and shock absorbers and is located by a stabilizer bar and a track bar. 1997 and later models have coil springs at all four corners. The rear axle is suspended by leaf springs and shock absorbers.

The steering box is mounted to the left of the engine and is connected to the steering arms through a series of rods which incorporates a damper. Power assist is optional on most models.

The brakes are disc at the front and drums at the rear, with power assist standard.

Vehicle identification numbers

Modifications are a continuing and unpublicized process in vehicle manufacturing. Since spare parts manuals and lists are compiled on a numerical basis, the individual vehicle numbers are essential to correctly identify the component required.

Vehicle Identification Number (VIN)

This very important identification number is stamped on a plate attached to the left (driver's) side of the dashboard just inside the windshield. The VIN also appears on the Vehicle Certificate of Title and Registration. It contains information such as where and when the vehicle was manufactured, the model year and the body style.

Vehicle Identification/Body Code Plate

This plate is located on the radiator support on the driver's side on 1987 through 1989 models and on the left (driver's) side of the engine compartment on the dash panel on 1990 and later models. On some later models the plate is attached to the floor pan under the driver's seat. It contains information on the vehicle model, emission certification, engine and transmission type as well as the paint code **(see illustration).**

Four-cylinder engine ID number location

Vehicle Identification/Body Code plate

Six-cylinder engine ID number location

The build date and serial number are stamped on the bottom of the AX 4/5 manual transmission case

BA 10/5 manual transmission ID number location

The three-speed automatic transmission numbers are stamped on the edge of the left side of the case

The four-speed automatic transmission ID plate is on the right side of the case

Typical transfer case ID tag

Location of the front axle ID number for models equipped with the Selec-Trac system

Location of the front axle ID number for models equipped with the Command-Trac system

Safety Certification label

The Safety Certification label is affixed to the left front door pillar. The plate contains the name of the manufacturer, the month and year of production, the Gross Vehicle Weight Rating (GVWR) and the certification statement.

Rear axle number location

Engine identification number

The engine ID number on 2.5L four-cylinder engines is located on a machined surface on the right side of the block between the number three and four cylinders (see illustration). On the 2.4L four-cylinder engine, the identification number is located on the left rear of the engine block. On six-cylinder engines, the ID number is located on a machined surface on the right side of the block between the number two and three cylinders (see illustration).

Transmission identification number

On AX 4/5 manual transmissions, there are two identification codes: a model/code shipping date stamped on the shift tower and an eight digit code stamped on the bottom surface of the case (see illustration). On the BA 10/5 manual transmission, the ID plate is attached to the left side of the front case (see illustration). On three-speed automatic transmissions the ID numbers are stamped on the left edge of the case (see illustration). The ID plate on four-speed automatic transmissions is located on the right rear of the case (see illustration).

Transfer case identification number

On most models the transfer case identification plate is located on the left rear side of the case (see illustration).

Axle identification numbers

On most front axles the identification number is located either on the right side (see illustration) or on a plate on the front differential housing cover (see illustration). On rear axles, the identification numbers are stamped on the differential cover (see illustration).

Buying parts

Replacement parts are available from many sources, which generally fall into one of two categories - authorized dealer parts departments and independent retail auto parts stores. Our advice concerning these parts is as follows:

Retail auto parts stores: Good auto parts stores will stock frequently needed components which wear out relatively fast, such as clutch components, exhaust systems, brake parts, tune-up parts, etc. These stores often supply new or reconditioned parts on an exchange basis, which can save a considerable amount of money. Discount auto parts stores are often very good places to buy materials and parts needed for general vehicle maintenance such as oil, grease, filters, spark plugs, belts, touch-up paint, bulbs, etc. They also usually sell tools and general accessories, have convenient hours, charge lower prices and can often be found not far from home.

Authorized dealer parts department: This is the best source for parts which are unique to the vehicle and not generally available elsewhere (such as major engine parts, transmission parts, trim pieces, etc.).

Warranty information: If the vehicle is still covered under warranty, be sure that any replacement parts purchased - regardless of the source - do not invalidate the warranty!

To be sure of obtaining the correct parts, have engine and chassis numbers available and, if possible, take the old parts along for positive identification.

Maintenance techniques, tools and working facilities

Maintenance techniques

There are a number of techniques involved in maintenance and repair that will be referred to throughout this manual. Application of these techniques will enable the home mechanic to be more efficient, better organized and capable of performing the various tasks properly, which will ensure that the repair job is thorough and complete.

Fasteners

Fasteners are nuts, bolts, studs and screws used to hold two or more parts together. There are a few things to keep in mind when working with fasteners. Almost all of them use a locking device of some type, either a lockwasher, locknut, locking tab or thread adhesive. All threaded fasteners should be clean and straight, with undamaged threads and undamaged corners on the hex head where the wrench fits. Develop the habit of replacing all damaged nuts and bolts with new ones. Special locknuts with nylon or fiber inserts can only be used once. If they are removed, they lose their locking ability and must be replaced with new ones.

Rusted nuts and bolts should be treated with a penetrating fluid to ease removal and prevent breakage. Some mechanics use turpentine in a spout-type oil can, which works quite well. After applying the rust penetrant, let it work for a few minutes before trying to loosen the nut or bolt. Badly rusted fasteners may have to be chiseled or sawed off or removed with a special nut breaker, available at tool stores.

If a bolt or stud breaks off in an assembly, it can be drilled and removed with a special tool commonly available for this purpose.

Most automotive machine shops can perform this task, as well as other repair procedures, such as the repair of threaded holes that have been stripped out.

Flat washers and lockwashers, when removed from an assembly, should always be replaced exactly as removed. Replace any damaged washers with new ones. Never use a lockwasher on any soft metal surface (such as aluminum), thin sheet metal or plastic.

Grade 1 or 2   Grade 5   Grade 8

Bolt strength marking (standard/SAE/USS; bottom - metric)

Grade	Identification	Grade	Identification			
Hex Nut Grade 5	3 Dots	Hex Nut Property Class 9	Arabic 9			
Hex Nut Grade 8	6 Dots	Hex Nut Property Class 10	Arabic 10	Class 10.9	Class 9.8	Class 8.8

Standard hex nut strength markings

Metric hex nut strength markings

Metric stud strength markings

00-1 HAYNES

Fastener sizes

For a number of reasons, automobile manufacturers are making wider and wider use of metric fasteners. Therefore, it is important to be able to tell the difference between standard (sometimes called U.S. or SAE) and metric hardware, since they cannot be interchanged.

All bolts, whether standard or metric, are sized according to diameter, thread pitch and length. For example, a standard 1/2 - 13 x 1 bolt is 1/2 inch in diameter, has 13 threads per inch and is 1 inch long. An M12 - 1.75 x 25 metric bolt is 12 mm in diameter, has a thread pitch of 1.75 mm (the distance between threads) and is 25 mm long. The two bolts are nearly identical, and easily confused, but they are not interchangeable.

In addition to the differences in diameter, thread pitch and length, metric and standard bolts can also be distinguished by examining the bolt heads. To begin with, the distance across the flats on a standard bolt head is measured in inches, while the same dimension on a metric bolt is sized in millimeters (the same is true for nuts). As a result, a standard wrench should not be used on a metric bolt and a metric wrench should not be used on a standard bolt. Also, most standard bolts have slashes radiating out from the center of the head to denote the grade or strength of the bolt, which is an indication of the amount of torque that can be applied to it. The greater the number of slashes, the greater the strength of the bolt. Grades 0 through 5 are commonly used on automobiles. Metric bolts have a property class (grade) number, rather than a slash, molded into their heads to indicate bolt strength. In this case, the higher the number, the stronger the bolt. Property class numbers 8.8, 9.8 and 10.9 are commonly used on automobiles.

Strength markings can also be used to distinguish standard hex nuts from metric hex nuts. Many standard nuts have dots stamped into one side, while metric nuts are marked with a number. The greater the number of dots, or the higher the number, the greater the strength of the nut.

Metric studs are also marked on their ends according to property class (grade). Larger studs are numbered (the same as metric bolts), while smaller studs carry a geometric code to denote grade.

It should be noted that many fasteners, especially Grades 0 through 2, have no distinguishing marks on them. When such is the case, the only way to determine whether it is standard or metric is to measure the thread pitch or compare it to a known fastener of the same size.

Standard fasteners are often referred to as SAE, as opposed to metric. However, it should be noted that SAE technically refers to a non-metric fine thread fastener only. Coarse thread non-metric fasteners are referred to as USS sizes.

Since fasteners of the same size (both standard and metric) may have different

Metric thread sizes	Ft-lbs	Nm
M-6	6 to 9	9 to 12
M-8	14 to 21	19 to 28
M-10	28 to 40	38 to 54
M-12	50 to 71	68 to 96
M-14	80 to 140	109 to 154
Pipe thread sizes		
1/8	5 to 8	7 to 10
1/4	12 to 18	17 to 24
3/8	22 to 33	30 to 44
1/2	25 to 35	34 to 47
U.S. thread sizes		
1/4 - 20	6 to 9	9 to 12
5/16 - 18	12 to 18	17 to 24
5/16 - 24	14 to 20	19 to 27
3/8 - 16	22 to 32	30 to 43
3/8 - 24	27 to 38	37 to 51
7/16 - 14	40 to 55	55 to 74
7/16 - 20	40 to 60	55 to 81
1/2 - 13	55 to 80	75 to 108

Standard (SAE and USS) bolt dimensions/grade marks

- **G** Grade marks (bolt strength)
- **L** Length (in inches)
- **T** Thread pitch (number of threads per inch)
- **D** Nominal diameter (in inches)

Metric bolt dimensions/grade marks

- **P** Property class (bolt strength)
- **L** Length (in millimeters)
- **T** Thread pitch (distance between threads in millimeters)
- **D** Diameter

strength ratings, be sure to reinstall any bolts, studs or nuts removed from your vehicle in their original locations. Also, when replacing a fastener with a new one, make sure that the new one has a strength rating equal to or greater than the original.

Tightening sequences and procedures

Most threaded fasteners should be tightened to a specific torque value (torque is the twisting force applied to a threaded component such as a nut or bolt). Overtightening the fastener can weaken it and cause it to break, while undertightening can cause it to eventually come loose. Bolts, screws and studs, depending on the material they are

made of and their thread diameters, have specific torque values, many of which are noted in the Specifications at the beginning of each Chapter. Be sure to follow the torque recommendations closely. For fasteners not assigned a specific torque, a general torque value chart is presented here as a guide. These torque values are for dry (unlubricated) fasteners threaded into steel or cast iron (not aluminum). As was previously mentioned, the size and grade of a fastener determine the amount of torque that can safely be applied to it. The figures listed here are approximate for Grade 2 and Grade 3 fasteners. Higher grades can tolerate higher torque values.

Fasteners laid out in a pattern, such as cylinder head bolts, oil pan bolts, differential cover bolts, etc., must be loosened or tight-

Micrometer set

Dial indicator set

ened in sequence to avoid warping the component. This sequence will normally be shown in the appropriate Chapter. If a specific pattern is not given, the following procedures can be used to prevent warping.

Initially, the bolts or nuts should be assembled finger-tight only. Next, they should be tightened one full turn each, in a criss-cross or diagonal pattern. After each one has been tightened one full turn, return to the first one and tighten them all one-half turn, following the same pattern. Finally, tighten each of them one-quarter turn at a time until each fastener has been tightened to the proper torque. To loosen and remove the fasteners, the procedure would be reversed.

Component disassembly

Component disassembly should be done with care and purpose to help ensure that the parts go back together properly. Always keep track of the sequence in which parts are removed. Make note of special characteristics or marks on parts that can be installed more than one way, such as a grooved thrust washer on a shaft. It is a good idea to lay the disassembled parts out on a clean surface in the order that they were removed. It may also be helpful to make sketches or take instant photos of components before removal.

When removing fasteners from a component, keep track of their locations. Sometimes threading a bolt back in a part, or putting the washers and nut back on a stud, can prevent mix-ups later. If nuts and bolts cannot be returned to their original locations, they should be kept in a compartmented box or a series of small boxes. A cupcake or muffin tin is ideal for this purpose, since each cavity can hold the bolts and nuts from a particular area (i.e. oil pan bolts, valve cover bolts, engine mount bolts, etc.). A pan of this type is especially helpful when working on assemblies with very small parts, such as the carburetor, alternator, valve train or interior dash and trim pieces. The cavities can be marked with paint or tape to identify the contents.

Whenever wiring looms, harnesses or connectors are separated, it is a good idea to

identify the two halves with numbered pieces of masking tape so they can be easily reconnected.

Gasket sealing surfaces

Throughout any vehicle, gaskets are used to seal the mating surfaces between two parts and keep lubricants, fluids, vacuum or pressure contained in an assembly.

Many times these gaskets are coated with a liquid or paste-type gasket sealing compound before assembly. Age, heat and pressure can sometimes cause the two parts to stick together so tightly that they are very difficult to separate. Often, the assembly can be loosened by striking it with a soft-face hammer near the mating surfaces. A regular hammer can be used if a block of wood is placed between the hammer and the part. Do not hammer on cast parts or parts that could be easily damaged. With any particularly stubborn part, always recheck to make sure that every fastener has been removed.

Avoid using a screwdriver or bar to pry apart an assembly, as they can easily mar the gasket sealing surfaces of the parts, which must remain smooth. If prying is absolutely necessary, use an old broom handle, but keep in mind that extra clean up will be necessary if the wood splinters.

After the parts are separated, the old gasket must be carefully scraped off and the gasket surfaces cleaned. Stubborn gasket material can be soaked with rust penetrant or treated with a special chemical to soften it so it can be easily scraped off. A scraper can be fashioned from a piece of copper tubing by flattening and sharpening one end. Copper is recommended because it is usually softer than the surfaces to be scraped, which reduces the chance of gouging the part. Some gaskets can be removed with a wire brush, but regardless of the method used, the mating surfaces must be left clean and smooth. If for some reason the gasket surface is gouged, then a gasket sealer thick enough to fill scratches will have to be used during reassembly of the components. For most applications, a non-drying (or semi-drying) gasket sealer should be used.

Hose removal tips

Warning: *If the vehicle is equipped with air conditioning, do not disconnect any of the A/C hoses without first having the system depressurized by a dealer service department or a service station.*

Hose removal precautions closely parallel gasket removal precautions. Avoid scratching or gouging the surface that the hose mates against or the connection may leak. This is especially true for radiator hoses. Because of various chemical reactions, the rubber in hoses can bond itself to the metal spigot that the hose fits over. To remove a hose, first loosen the hose clamps that secure it to the spigot. Then, with slip-joint pliers, grab the hose at the clamp and rotate it around the spigot. Work it back and forth until it is completely free, then pull it off. Silicone or other lubricants will ease removal if they can be applied between the hose and the outside of the spigot. Apply the same lubricant to the inside of the hose and the outside of the spigot to simplify installation.

As a last resort (and if the hose is to be replaced with a new one anyway), the rubber can be slit with a knife and the hose peeled from the spigot. If this must be done, be careful that the metal connection is not damaged.

If a hose clamp is broken or damaged, do not reuse it. Wire-type clamps usually weaken with age, so it is a good idea to replace them with screw-type clamps whenever a hose is removed.

Tools

A selection of good tools is a basic requirement for anyone who plans to maintain and repair his or her own vehicle. For the owner who has few tools, the initial investment might seem high, but when compared to the spiraling costs of professional auto maintenance and repair, it is a wise one.

To help the owner decide which tools are needed to perform the tasks detailed in this manual, the following tool lists are offered: *Maintenance and minor repair, Repair/overhaul* and *Special*.

The newcomer to practical mechanics

Dial Caliper

Hand-operated vacuum pump

Timing light

Compression gauge with spark plug hole adapter

Damper/steering wheel puller

General purpose puller

Hydraulic lifter removal tool

Valve spring compressor

Valve spring compressor

Ridge reamer

Piston ring groove cleaning tool

Ring removal/installation tool

Ring compressor

Cylinder hone

Brake hold-down tool

Brake cylinder hone

Clutch plate alignment tool

Tap and die set

should start off with the *maintenance and minor repair* tool kit, which is adequate for the simpler jobs performed on a vehicle. Then, as confidence and experience grow, the owner can tackle more difficult tasks, buying additional tools as they are needed. Eventually the basic kit will be expanded into the *repair and overhaul* tool set. Over a period of time, the experienced do-it-yourselfer will assemble a tool set complete enough for most repair and overhaul procedures and will add tools from the special category when it is felt that the expense is justified by the frequency of use.

Maintenance and minor repair tool kit

The tools in this list should be considered the minimum required for performance of routine maintenance, servicing and minor repair work. We recommend the purchase of combination wrenches (box-end and open-end combined in one wrench). While more expensive than open end wrenches, they offer the advantages of both types of wrench.

Combination wrench set (1/4-inch to
    1 inch or 6 mm to 19 mm)
Adjustable wrench, 8 inch
Spark plug wrench with rubber insert
Spark plug gap adjusting tool
Feeler gauge set
Brake bleeder wrench
Standard screwdriver (5/16-inch x
    6 inch)

Phillips screwdriver (No. 2 x 6 inch)
Combination pliers - 6 inch
Hacksaw and assortment of blades
Tire pressure gauge
Grease gun
Oil can
Fine emery cloth
Wire brush
Battery post and cable cleaning tool
Oil filter wrench
Funnel (medium size)
Safety goggles
Jackstands (2)
Drain pan

Note: *If basic tune-ups are going to be part of routine maintenance, it will be necessary to purchase a good quality stroboscopic timing light and combination tachometer/dwell meter. Although they are included in the list of special tools, it is mentioned here because they are absolutely necessary for tuning most vehicles properly.*

Repair and overhaul tool set

These tools are essential for anyone who plans to perform major repairs and are in addition to those in the maintenance and minor repair tool kit. Included is a comprehensive set of sockets which, though expensive, are invaluable because of their versatility, especially when various extensions and drives are available. We recommend the 1/2-inch drive over the 3/8-inch drive. Although the larger drive is bulky and more expensive,

it has the capacity of accepting a very wide range of large sockets. Ideally, however, the mechanic should have a 3/8-inch drive set and a 1/2-inch drive set.

Socket set(s)
Reversible ratchet
Extension - 10 inch
Universal joint
Torque wrench (same size drive as
    sockets)
Ball peen hammer - 8 ounce
Soft-face hammer (plastic/rubber)
Standard screwdriver (1/4-inch x 6 inch)
Standard screwdriver (stubby -
    5/16-inch)
Phillips screwdriver (No. 3 x 8 inch)
Phillips screwdriver (stubby - No. 2)
Pliers - vise grip
Pliers - lineman's
Pliers - needle nose
Pliers - snap-ring (internal and external)
Cold chisel - 1/2-inch
Scribe
Scraper (made from flattened copper
    tubing)
Centerpunch
Pin punches (1/16, 1/8, 3/16-inch)
Steel rule/straightedge - 12 inch
Allen wrench set (1/8 to 3/8-inch or
    4 mm to 10 mm)
A selection of files
Wire brush (large)
Jackstands (second set)
Jack (scissor or hydraulic type)

Note: *Another tool which is often useful is an electric drill with a chuck capacity of 3/8-inch and a set of good quality drill bits.*

Special tools

The tools in this list include those which are not used regularly, are expensive to buy, or which need to be used in accordance with their manufacturer's instructions. Unless these tools will be used frequently, it is not very economical to purchase many of them. A consideration would be to split the cost and use between yourself and a friend or friends. In addition, most of these tools can be obtained from a tool rental shop on a temporary basis.

This list primarily contains only those tools and instruments widely available to the public, and not those special tools produced by the vehicle manufacturer for distribution to dealer service departments. Occasionally, references to the manufacturer's special tools are included in the text of this manual. Generally, an alternative method of doing the job without the special tool is offered. However, sometimes there is no alternative to their use. Where this is the case, and the tool cannot be purchased or borrowed, the work should be turned over to the dealer service department or an automotive repair shop.

Valve spring compressor
Piston ring groove cleaning tool
Piston ring compressor
Piston ring installation tool
Cylinder compression gauge
Cylinder ridge reamer
Cylinder surfacing hone
Cylinder bore gauge
Micrometers and/or dial calipers
Hydraulic lifter removal tool
Balljoint separator
Universal-type puller
Impact screwdriver
Dial indicator set
Stroboscopic timing light (inductive pick-up)
Hand operated vacuum/pressure pump
Tachometer/dwell meter
Universal electrical multimeter
Cable hoist
Brake spring removal and installation tools
Floor jack

Buying tools

For the do-it-yourselfer who is just starting to get involved in vehicle maintenance and repair, there are a number of options available when purchasing tools. If maintenance and minor repair is the extent of the work to be done, the purchase of individual tools is satisfactory. If, on the other hand, extensive work is planned, it would be a good idea to purchase a modest tool set from one of the large retail chain stores. A set can usually be bought at a substantial savings over the individual tool prices, and they often come with a tool box. As additional tools are needed, add-on sets, individual tools and a larger tool box can be purchased to expand the tool selection. Building a tool set gradually allows the cost of the tools to be spread over a longer period of time and gives the mechanic the freedom to choose only those tools that will actually be used.

Tool stores will often be the only source of some of the special tools that are needed, but regardless of where tools are bought, try to avoid cheap ones, especially when buying screwdrivers and sockets, because they won't last very long. The expense involved in replacing cheap tools will eventually be greater than the initial cost of quality tools.

Care and maintenance of tools

Good tools are expensive, so it makes sense to treat them with respect. Keep them clean and in usable condition and store them properly when not in use. Always wipe off any dirt, grease or metal chips before putting them away. Never leave tools lying around in the work area. Upon completion of a job, always check closely under the hood for tools that may have been left there so they won't get lost during a test drive.

Some tools, such as screwdrivers, pliers, wrenches and sockets, can be hung on a panel mounted on the garage or workshop wall, while others should be kept in a tool box or tray. Measuring instruments, gauges, meters, etc. must be carefully stored where they cannot be damaged by weather or impact from other tools.

When tools are used with care and stored properly, they will last a very long time. Even with the best of care, though, tools will wear out if used frequently. When a tool is damaged or worn out, replace it. Subsequent jobs will be safer and more enjoyable if you do.

How to repair damaged threads

Sometimes, the internal threads of a nut or bolt hole can become stripped, usually from overtightening. Stripping threads is an all-too-common occurrence, especially when working with aluminum parts, because aluminum is so soft that it easily strips out.

Usually, external or internal threads are only partially stripped. After they've been cleaned up with a tap or die, they'll still work. Sometimes, however, threads are badly damaged. When this happens, you've got three choices:

1) *Drill and tap the hole to the next suitable oversize and install a larger diameter bolt, screw or stud.*

2) *Drill and tap the hole to accept a threaded plug, then drill and tap the plug to the original screw size. You can also buy a plug already threaded to the original size. Then you simply drill a hole to the specified size, then run the threaded plug into the hole with a bolt and jam nut. Once the plug is fully seated, remove the jam nut and bolt.*

3) *The third method uses a patented thread repair kit like Heli-Coil or Slimsert. These easy-to-use kits are designed to repair damaged threads in straight-through holes and blind holes. Both are available as kits which can handle a variety of sizes and thread patterns. Drill the hole, then tap it with the special included tap. Install the Heli-Coil and the hole is back to its original diameter and thread pitch.*

Regardless of which method you use, be sure to proceed calmly and carefully. A little impatience or carelessness during one of these relatively simple procedures can ruin your whole day's work and cost you a bundle if you wreck an expensive part.

Working facilities

Not to be overlooked when discussing tools is the workshop. If anything more than routine maintenance is to be carried out, some sort of suitable work area is essential.

It is understood, and appreciated, that many home mechanics do not have a good workshop or garage available, and end up removing an engine or doing major repairs outside. It is recommended, however, that the overhaul or repair be completed under the cover of a roof.

A clean, flat workbench or table of comfortable working height is an absolute necessity. The workbench should be equipped with a vise that has a jaw opening of at least four inches.

As mentioned previously, some clean, dry storage space is also required for tools, as well as the lubricants, fluids, cleaning solvents, etc. which soon become necessary.

Sometimes waste oil and fluids, drained from the engine or cooling system during normal maintenance or repairs, present a disposal problem. To avoid pouring them on the ground or into a sewage system, pour the used fluids into large containers, seal them with caps and take them to an authorized disposal site or recycling center. Plastic jugs, such as old antifreeze containers, are ideal for this purpose.

Always keep a supply of old newspapers and clean rags available. Old towels are excellent for mopping up spills. Many mechanics use rolls of paper towels for most work because they are readily available and disposable. To help keep the area under the vehicle clean, a large cardboard box can be cut open and flattened to protect the garage or shop floor.

Whenever working over a painted surface, such as when leaning over a fender to service something under the hood, always cover it with an old blanket or bedspread to protect the finish. Vinyl covered pads, made especially for this purpose, are available at auto parts stores.

Jacking and towing

Jacking

The jack supplied with the vehicle should only be used for raising the vehicle when changing a tire or placing jackstands under the frame. **Warning:** Never work under the vehicle or start the engine while this jack is being used as the only means of support.

The vehicle should be on level ground with the hazard flashers on, the wheels blocked, the parking brake applied and the transmission in Park (automatic) or Reverse (manual). If a tire is being changed, loosen the lug nuts one-half turn and leave them in place until the wheel is raised off the ground.

Place the jack under the vehicle suspension in the indicated position **(see illustration)**. Operate the jack with a slow, smooth motion until the wheel is raised off the ground. Remove the lug nuts, pull off the wheel, install the spare and thread the lug nuts back on with the beveled sides facing in. Tighten them snugly, but wait until the vehicle is lowered to tighten them completely. Note that some spare tires are designed for temporary use only - don't exceed the recommended speed, mileage or other restrictions accompanying the spare.

Lower the vehicle, remove the jack and tighten the lug nuts (if loosened or removed) in a criss-cross pattern.

Towing

As a general rule, vehicles can be towed with all four wheels on the ground, provided that the driveshaft(s) are removed (see Chapter 8).

Equipment specifically designed for towing should be used and should be attached to the main structural members of the vehicle, not the bumper or brackets. Tow hooks are attached to the frame at both ends of the vehicle. However, they are for emergency use only and should not be used for highway towing. Stand clear of vehicles when using the tow hooks - tow straps and chains may break, causing serious injury.

Safety is a major consideration when towing and all applicable state and local laws must be obeyed. A safety chain must be used for all towing (in addition to the tow bar). While towing, the parking brake should be released and the transmission and (if equipped) transfer case must be in Neutral. The steering must be unlocked (ignition switch in the Off position). Remember that power steering and power brakes will not work with the engine off.

Jacking points and procedure

1   Place the transmission in Park (automatic) or Reverse (manual)
2   Turn on the hazard flashers
3   Apply the parking brake
4   Block the wheel diagonally opposite the one being changed
5   Use the jack to raise the vehicle
6   Rear jacking point
7   Front jacking point

Jacking points and procedure

1   Place the transmission in Park (automatic) or Reverse (manual)
2   Turn on the hazard flashers
3   Apply the parking brake
4   Block the wheel diagonally opposite the one being changed
5   Use the jack to raise the vehicle
6   Front jacking point
7   Rear jacking point

Booster battery (jump) starting

Observe these precautions when using a booster battery to start a vehicle:

a) Before connecting the booster battery, make sure the ignition switch is in the Off position.
b) Turn off the lights, heater and other electrical loads.
c) Your eyes should be shielded. Safety goggles are a good idea.
d) Make sure the booster battery is the same voltage as the dead one in the vehicle.
e) The two vehicles MUST NOT TOUCH each other!
f) Make sure the transaxle is in Neutral (manual) or Park (automatic).
g) If the booster battery is not a maintenance-free type, remove the vent caps and lay a cloth over the vent holes.

Connect the red jumper cable to the positive (+) terminals of each battery **(see illustration)**.

Connect one end of the black jumper cable to the negative (-) terminal of the booster battery. The other end of this cable should be connected to a good ground on the vehicle to be started, such as a bolt or bracket on the body.

Start the engine using the booster battery, then, with the engine running at idle speed, disconnect the jumper cables in the reverse order of connection.

Make the booster battery cable connections in the numerical order shown (note that the negative cable of the booster battery is NOT attached to the negative terminal of the dead battery)

Automotive chemicals and lubricants

A number of automotive chemicals and lubricants are available for use during vehicle maintenance and repair. They include a wide variety of products ranging from cleaning solvents and degreasers to lubricants and protective sprays for rubber, plastic and vinyl.

Cleaners

Carburetor cleaner and choke cleaner is a strong solvent for gum, varnish and carbon. Most carburetor cleaners leave a dry-type lubricant film which will not harden or gum up. Because of this film it is not recommended for use on electrical components.

Brake system cleaner is used to remove brake dust, grease and brake fluid from the brake system, where clean surfaces are absolutely necessary. It leaves no residue and often eliminates brake squeal caused by contaminants.

Electrical cleaner removes oxidation, corrosion and carbon deposits from electrical contacts, restoring full current flow. It can also be used to clean spark plugs, carburetor jets, voltage regulators and other parts where an oil-free surface is desired.

Demoisturants remove water and moisture from electrical components such as alternators, voltage regulators, electrical connectors and fuse blocks. They are non-conductive and non-corrosive.

Degreasers are heavy-duty solvents used to remove grease from the outside of the engine and from chassis components. They can be sprayed or brushed on and, depending on the type, are rinsed off either with water or solvent.

Lubricants

Motor oil is the lubricant formulated for use in engines. It normally contains a wide variety of additives to prevent corrosion and reduce foaming and wear. Motor oil comes in various weights (viscosity ratings) from 0 to 50. The recommended weight of the oil depends on the season, temperature and the demands on the engine. Light oil is used in cold climates and under light load conditions. Heavy oil is used in hot climates and where high loads are encountered. Multi-viscosity oils are designed to have characteristics of both light and heavy oils and are available in a number of weights from 5W-20 to 20W-50.

Gear oil is designed to be used in differentials, manual transmissions and other areas where high-temperature lubrication is required.

Chassis and wheel bearing grease is a heavy grease used where increased loads and friction are encountered, such as for wheel bearings, balljoints, tie-rod ends and universal joints.

High-temperature wheel bearing grease is designed to withstand the extreme temperatures encountered by wheel bearings in disc brake equipped vehicles. It usually contains molybdenum disulfide (moly), which is a dry-type lubricant.

White grease is a heavy grease for metal-to-metal applications where water is a problem. White grease stays soft under both low and high temperatures (usually from -100 to +190-degrees F), and will not wash off or dilute in the presence of water.

Assembly lube is a special extreme pressure lubricant, usually containing moly, used to lubricate high-load parts (such as main and rod bearings and cam lobes) for initial start-up of a new engine. The assembly lube lubricates the parts without being squeezed out or washed away until the engine oiling system begins to function.

Silicone lubricants are used to protect rubber, plastic, vinyl and nylon parts.

Graphite lubricants are used where oils cannot be used due to contamination problems, such as in locks. The dry graphite will lubricate metal parts while remaining uncontaminated by dirt, water, oil or acids. It is electrically conductive and will not foul electrical contacts in locks such as the ignition switch.

Moly penetrants loosen and lubricate frozen, rusted and corroded fasteners and prevent future rusting or freezing.

Heat-sink grease is a special electrically non-conductive grease that is used for mounting electronic ignition modules where it is essential that heat is transferred away from the module.

Sealants

RTV sealant is one of the most widely used gasket compounds. Made from silicone, RTV is air curing, it seals, bonds, waterproofs, fills surface irregularities, remains flexible, doesn't shrink, is relatively easy to remove, and is used as a supplementary sealer with almost all low and medium temperature gaskets.

Anaerobic sealant is much like RTV in that it can be used either to seal gaskets or to form gaskets by itself. It remains flexible, is solvent resistant and fills surface imperfections. The difference between an anaerobic sealant and an RTV-type sealant is in the curing. RTV cures when exposed to air, while an anaerobic sealant cures only in the absence of air. This means that an anaerobic sealant cures only after the assembly of parts, sealing them together.

Thread and pipe sealant is used for sealing hydraulic and pneumatic fittings and vacuum lines. It is usually made from a Teflon compound, and comes in a spray, a paint-on liquid and as a wrap-around tape.

Chemicals

Anti-seize compound prevents seizing, galling, cold welding, rust and corrosion in fasteners. High-temperature ant-seize, usually made with copper and graphite lubricants, is used for exhaust system and exhaust manifold bolts.

Anaerobic locking compounds are used to keep fasteners from vibrating or working loose and cure only after installation, in the absence of air. Medium strength locking compound is used for small nuts, bolts and screws that may be removed later. High-strength locking compound is for large nuts, bolts and studs which aren't removed on a regular basis.

Oil additives range from viscosity index improvers to chemical treatments that claim to reduce internal engine friction. It should be noted that most oil manufacturers caution against using additives with their oils.

Gas additives perform several functions, depending on their chemical makeup. They usually contain solvents that help dissolve gum and varnish that build up on carburetor, fuel injection and intake parts. They also serve to break down carbon deposits that form on the inside surfaces of the combustion chambers. Some additives contain upper cylinder lubricants for valves and piston rings, and others contain chemicals to remove condensation from the gas tank.

Miscellaneous

Brake fluid is specially formulated hydraulic fluid that can withstand the heat and pressure encountered in brake systems. Care must be taken so this fluid does not come in contact with painted surfaces or plastics. An opened container should always be resealed to prevent contamination by water or dirt.

Weatherstrip adhesive is used to bond weatherstripping around doors, windows and trunk lids. It is sometimes used to attach trim pieces.

Undercoating is a petroleum-based, tar-like substance that is designed to protect metal surfaces on the underside of the vehicle from corrosion. It also acts as a sound-deadening agent by insulating the bottom of the vehicle.

Waxes and polishes are used to help protect painted and plated surfaces from the weather. Different types of paint may require the use of different types of wax and polish. Some polishes utilize a chemical or abrasive cleaner to help remove the top layer of oxidized (dull) paint on older vehicles. In recent years many non-wax polishes that contain a wide variety of chemicals such as polymers and silicones have been introduced. These non-wax polishes are usually easier to apply and last longer than conventional waxes and polishes.

Conversion factors

Length (distance)

Inches (in)	X	25.4	= Millimetres (mm)	X 0.0394	= Inches (in)
Feet (ft)	X	0.305	= Metres (m)	X 3.281	= Feet (ft)
Miles	X	1.609	= Kilometres (km)	X 0.621	= Miles

Volume (capacity)

Cubic inches (cu in; in³)	X	16.387	= Cubic centimetres (cc; cm³)	X 0.061	= Cubic inches (cu in; in³)
Imperial pints (Imp pt)	X	0.568	= Litres (l)	X 1.76	= Imperial pints (Imp pt)
Imperial quarts (Imp qt)	X	1.137	= Litres (l)	X 0.88	= Imperial quarts (Imp qt)
Imperial quarts (Imp qt)	X	1.201	= US quarts (US qt)	X 0.833	= Imperial quarts (Imp qt)
US quarts (US qt)	X	0.946	= Litres (l)	X 1.057	= US quarts (US qt)
Imperial gallons (Imp gal)	X	4.546	= Litres (l)	X 0.22	= Imperial gallons (Imp gal)
Imperial gallons (Imp gal)	X	1.201	= US gallons (US gal)	X 0.833	= Imperial gallons (Imp gal)
US gallons (US gal)	X	3.785	= Litres (l)	X 0.264	= US gallons (US gal)

Mass (weight)

Ounces (oz)	X	28.35	= Grams (g)	X 0.035	= Ounces (oz)
Pounds (lb)	X	0.454	= Kilograms (kg)	X 2.205	= Pounds (lb)

Force

Ounces-force (ozf; oz)	X	0.278	= Newtons (N)	X 3.6	= Ounces-force (ozf; oz)
Pounds-force (lbf; lb)	X	4.448	= Newtons (N)	X 0.225	= Pounds-force (lbf; lb)
Newtons (N)	X	0.1	= Kilograms-force (kgf; kg)	X 9.81	= Newtons (N)

Pressure

Pounds-force per square inch (psi; lbf/in²; lb/in²)	X	0.070	= Kilograms-force per square centimetre (kgf/cm²; kg/cm²)	X 14.223	= Pounds-force per square inch (psi; lbf/in²; lb/in²)
Pounds-force per square inch (psi; lbf/in²; lb/in²)	X	0.068	= Atmospheres (atm)	X 14.696	= Pounds-force per square inch (psi; lbf/in²; lb/in²)
Pounds-force per square inch (psi; lbf/in²; lb/in²)	X	0.069	= Bars	X 14.5	= Pounds-force per square inch (psi; lbf/in²; lb/in²)
Pounds-force per square inch (psi; lbf/in²; lb/in²)	X	6.895	= Kilopascals (kPa)	X 0.145	= Pounds-force per square inch (psi; lbf/in²; lb/in²)
Kilopascals (kPa)	X	0.01	= Kilograms-force per square centimetre (kgf/cm²; kg/cm²)	X 98.1	= Kilopascals (kPa)

Torque (moment of force)

Pounds-force inches (lbf in; lb in)	X	1.152	= Kilograms-force centimetre (kgf cm; kg cm)	X 0.868	= Pounds-force inches (lbf in; lb in)
Pounds-force inches (lbf in; lb in)	X	0.113	= Newton metres (Nm)	X 8.85	= Pounds-force inches (lbf in; lb in)
Pounds-force inches (lbf in; lb in)	X	0.083	= Pounds-force feet (lbf ft; lb ft)	X 12	= Pounds-force inches (lbf in; lb in)
Pounds-force feet (lbf ft; lb ft)	X	0.138	= Kilograms-force metres (kgf m; kg m)	X 7.233	= Pounds-force feet (lbf ft; lb ft)
Pounds-force feet (lbf ft; lb ft)	X	1.356	= Newton metres (Nm)	X 0.738	= Pounds-force feet (lbf ft; lb ft)
Newton metres (Nm)	X	0.102	= Kilograms-force metres (kgf m; kg m)	X 9.804	= Newton metres (Nm)

Vacuum

Inches mercury (in. Hg)	X	3.377	= Kilopascals (kPa)	X 0.2961	= Inches mercury
Inches mercury (in. Hg)	X	25.4	= Millimeters mercury (mm Hg)	X 0.0394	= Inches mercury

Power

Horsepower (hp)	X	745.7	= Watts (W)	X 0.0013	= Horsepower (hp)

Velocity (speed)

Miles per hour (miles/hr; mph)	X	1.609	= Kilometres per hour (km/hr; kph)	X 0.621	= Miles per hour (miles/hr; mph)

Fuel consumption*

Miles per gallon, Imperial (mpg)	X	0.354	= Kilometres per litre (km/l)	X 2.825	= Miles per gallon, Imperial (mpg)
Miles per gallon, US (mpg)	X	0.425	= Kilometres per litre (km/l)	X 2.352	= Miles per gallon, US (mpg)

Temperature

Degrees Fahrenheit = (°C x 1.8) + 32   Degrees Celsius (Degrees Centigrade; °C) = (°F - 32) x 0.56

*It is common practice to convert from miles per gallon (mpg) to litres/100 kilometres (l/100km),
where mpg (Imperial) x l/100 km = 282 and mpg (US) x l/100 km = 235

Safety first!

Regardless of how enthusiastic you may be about getting on with the job at hand, take the time to ensure that your safety is not jeopardized. A moment's lack of attention can result in an accident, as can failure to observe certain simple safety precautions. The possibility of an accident will always exist, and the following points should not be considered a comprehensive list of all dangers. Rather, they are intended to make you aware of the risks and to encourage a safety conscious approach to all work you carry out on your vehicle.

Essential DOs and DON'Ts

DON'T rely on a jack when working under the vehicle. Always use approved jackstands to support the weight of the vehicle and place them under the recommended lift or support points.

DON'T attempt to loosen extremely tight fasteners (i.e. wheel lug nuts) while the vehicle is on a jack - it may fall.

DON'T start the engine without first making sure that the transmission is in Neutral (or Park where applicable) and the parking brake is set.

DON'T remove the radiator cap from a hot cooling system - let it cool or cover it with a cloth and release the pressure gradually.

DON'T attempt to drain the engine oil until you are sure it has cooled to the point that it will not burn you.

DON'T touch any part of the engine or exhaust system until it has cooled sufficiently to avoid burns.

DON'T siphon toxic liquids such as gasoline, antifreeze and brake fluid by mouth, or allow them to remain on your skin.

DON'T inhale brake lining dust - it is potentially hazardous (see *Asbestos* below).

DON'T allow spilled oil or grease to remain on the floor - wipe it up before someone slips on it.

DON'T use loose fitting wrenches or other tools which may slip and cause injury.

DON'T push on wrenches when loosening or tightening nuts or bolts. Always try to pull the wrench toward you. If the situation calls for pushing the wrench away, push with an open hand to avoid scraped knuckles if the wrench should slip.

DON'T attempt to lift a heavy component alone - get someone to help you.

DON'T rush or take unsafe shortcuts to finish a job.

DON'T allow children or animals in or around the vehicle while you are working on it.

DO wear eye protection when using power tools such as a drill, sander, bench grinder, etc. and when working under a vehicle.

DO keep loose clothing and long hair well out of the way of moving parts.

DO make sure that any hoist used has a safe working load rating adequate for the job.

DO get someone to check on you periodically when working alone on a vehicle.

DO carry out work in a logical sequence and make sure that everything is correctly assembled an   s and fluids tightly capped and out of the reach of children and pets.

DO remember that your vehicle's safety affects that of yourself and others. If in doubt on any point, get professional advice.

Asbestos

Certain friction, insulating, sealing, and other products - such as brake linings, brake bands, clutch linings, torque converters, gaskets, etc. - may contain asbestos. Extreme care must be taken to avoid inhalation of dust from such products, since it is hazardous to health. If in doubt, assume that they do contain asbestos.

Fire

Remember at all times that gasoline is highly flammable. Never smoke or have any kind of open flame around when working on a vehicle. But the risk does not end there. A spark caused by an electrical short circuit, by two metal surfaces contacting each other, or even by static electricity built up in your body under certain conditions, can ignite gasoline vapors, which in a confined space are highly explosive. Do not, under any circumstances, use gasoline for cleaning parts. Use an approved safety solvent.

Always disconnect the battery ground (-) cable at the battery before working on any part of the fuel system or electrical system. Never risk spilling fuel on a hot engine or exhaust component. It is strongly recommended that a fire extinguisher suitable for use on fuel and electrical fires be kept handy in the garage or workshop at all times. Never try to extinguish a fuel or electrical fire with water.

Fumes

Certain fumes are highly toxic and can quickly cause unconsciousness and even death if inhaled to any extent. Gasoline vapor falls into this category, as do the vapors from some cleaning solvents. Any draining or pouring of such volatile fluids should be done in a well ventilated area.

When using cleaning fluids and solvents, read the instructions on the container carefully. Never use materials from unmarked containers.

Never run the engine in an enclosed space, such as a garage. Exhaust fumes contain carbon monoxide, which is extremely poisonous. If you need to run the engine, always do so in the open air, or at least have the rear of the vehicle outside the work area.

If you are fortunate enough to have the use of an inspection pit, never drain or pour gasoline and never run the engine while the vehicle is over the pit. The fumes, being heavier than air, will concentrate in the pit with possibly lethal results.

The battery

Never create a spark or allow a bare light bulb near a battery. They normally give off a certain amount of hydrogen gas, which is highly explosive.

Always disconnect the battery ground (-) cable at the battery before working on the fuel or electrical systems.

If possible, loosen the filler caps or cover when charging the battery from an external source (this does not apply to sealed or maintenance-free batteries). Do not charge at an excessive rate or the battery may burst.

Take care when adding water to a non maintenance-free battery and when carrying a battery. The electrolyte, even when diluted, is very corrosive and should not be allowed to contact clothing or skin.

Always wear eye protection when cleaning the battery to prevent the caustic deposits from entering your eyes.

Household current

When using an electric power tool, inspection light, etc., which operates on household current, always make sure that the tool is correctly connected to its plug and that, where necessary, it is properly grounded. Do not use such items in damp conditions and, again, do not create a spark or apply excessive heat in the vicinity of fuel or fuel vapor.

Secondary ignition system voltage

A severe electric shock can result from touching certain parts of the ignition system (such as the spark plug wires) when the engine is running or being cranked, particularly if components are damp or the insulation is defective. In the case of an electronic ignition system, the secondary system voltage is much higher and could prove fatal.

Troubleshooting

Contents

This section provides an easy reference guide to the more common problems that may occur during the operation of your vehicle. Various symptoms and their probable causes are grouped under headings denoting components or systems, such as Engine, Cooling system, etc. They also refer to the Chapter and/or Section that deals with the problem.

Remember that successful troubleshooting isn't a mysterious "black art" practiced only by professional mechanics, it's simply the result of knowledge combined with an intelligent, systematic approach to a problem. Always use a process of elimination starting with the simplest solution and working through to the most complex - and never overlook the obvious. Anyone can run the gas tank dry or leave the lights on overnight, so don't assume that you're exempt from such oversights.

Finally, always establish a clear idea why a problem has occurred and take steps to ensure that it doesn't happen again. If the electrical system fails because of a poor connection, check all other connections in the system to make sure they don't fail as well. If a particular fuse continues to blow, find out why - don't just go on replacing fuses. Remember, failure of a small component can often be indicative of potential failure or incorrect functioning of a more important component or system.

Engine and performance

1 Engine will not rotate when attempting to start

1 Battery terminal connections loose or corroded. Check the cable terminals at the battery; tighten cable clamp and/or clean off corrosion as necessary (see Chapter 1).
2 Battery discharged or faulty. If the cable ends are clean and tight on the battery posts, turn the key to the On position and switch on the headlights or windshield wipers. If they won't run, the battery is discharged.
3 Automatic transmission not engaged in park (P) or Neutral (N).
4 Broken, loose or disconnected wires in the starting circuit. Inspect all wires and connectors at the battery, starter solenoid and ignition switch (on steering column).
5 Starter motor pinion jammed in flywheel ring gear. If manual transmission, place transmission in gear and rock the vehicle to manually turn the engine. Remove starter (Chapter 5) and inspect pinion and flywheel (Chapter 2) at earliest convenience.
6 Starter solenoid faulty (Chapter 5).
7 Starter motor faulty (Chapter 5).
8 Ignition switch faulty (Chapter 13).
9 Engine seized. Try to turn the crankshaft with a large socket and breaker bar on the pulley bolt.

2 Engine rotates but will not start

1 Fuel tank empty.
2 Battery discharged (engine rotates slowly). Check the operation of electrical components as described in previous Section.
3 Battery terminal connections loose or corroded. See previous Section.
4 Fuel not reaching carburetor or fuel injector. Check for clogged fuel filter or lines and defective fuel pump. Also make sure the tank vent lines aren't clogged (Chapter 4).
5 Choke not operating properly (Chapter 1).
6 Faulty distributor components. Check the cap and rotor (Chapter 1).
7 Low cylinder compression. Check as described in Chapter 2.
8 Water in fuel. Drain tank and fill with new fuel.
9 Defective ignition coil (Chapter 5).
10 Dirty or clogged carburetor jets or fuel injector. Carburetor out of adjustment. Check the float level (Chapter 4). Check the needle valve and its seat (Chapter 4).
11 Wet or damaged ignition components (Chapters 1 and 5).
12 Worn, faulty or incorrectly gapped spark plugs (Chapter 1).
13 Broken, loose or disconnected wires in the starting circuit (see previous Section).
14 Loose distributor (changing ignition timing). Turn the distributor body as necessary to start the engine, then adjust the ignition timing as soon as possible (Chapter 1).
15 Broken, loose or disconnected wires at the ignition coil or faulty coil (Chapter 5).
16 Timing chain failure or wear affecting valve timing (Chapter 2).

3 Starter motor operates without turning engine

1 Starter pinion sticking. Remove the starter (Chapter 5) and inspect.
2 Starter pinion or flywheel/driveplate teeth worn or broken. Remove the inspection cover and inspect.

4 Engine hard to start when cold

1 Battery discharged or low. Check as described in Chapter 1.
2 Fuel not reaching the carburetor or fuel injectors. Check the fuel filter, lines and fuel pump (Chapters 1 and 4).
3 Choke inoperative (Chapters 1 and 4).
4 Defective spark plugs (Chapter 1).

5 Engine hard to start when hot

1 Air filter dirty (Chapter 1).
2 Fuel not reaching carburetor or fuel injectors (see Section 4). Check for a vapor

lock situation, brought about by clogged fuel tank vent lines.
3 Bad engine ground connection.
4 Choke sticking (Chapter 1).
5 Defective pick-up coil in distributor (Chapter 5).
6 Float level too high (Chapter 4).
7 Defective crankshaft position sensor (Chapter 6).

6 Starter motor noisy or engages roughly

1 Pinion or flywheel/driveplate teeth worn or broken. Remove the inspection cover on the left side of the engine and inspect.
2 Starter motor mounting bolts loose or missing.

7 Engine starts but stops immediately

1 Loose or damaged wire harness connections at distributor, coil or alternator.
2 Intake manifold vacuum leaks. Make sure all mounting bolts/nuts are tight and all vacuum hoses connected to the manifold are attached properly and in good condition.
3 Insufficient fuel flow (see Chapter 4).

8 Engine "lopes" while idling or idles erratically

1 Vacuum leaks. Check mounting bolts at the intake manifold for tightness. Make sure that all vacuum hoses are connected and in good condition. Use a stethoscope or a length of fuel hose held against your ear to listen for vacuum leaks while the engine is running. A hissing sound will be heard. A soapy water solution will also detect leaks. Check the intake manifold gasket surfaces.
2 Leaking EGR valve or plugged PCV valve (see Chapters 1 and 6).
3 Air filter clogged (Chapter 1).
4 Fuel pump not delivering sufficient fuel (Chapter 4).
5 Leaking head gasket. Perform a cylinder compression check (Chapter 2).
6 Timing chain worn (Chapter 2).
7 Camshaft lobes worn (Chapter 2).
8 Valves burned or otherwise leaking (Chapter 2).
9 Ignition timing out of adjustment (Chapter 1).
10 Ignition system not operating properly (Chapters 1 and 5).
11 Thermostatic air cleaner not operating properly (Chapter 1).
12 Choke not operating properly (Chapters 1 and 4).
13 Dirty or clogged injectors. Carburetor dirty, clogged or out of adjustment. Check the float level (Chapter 4).
14 Idle speed out of adjustment (Chapter 1).

9 Engine misses at idle speed

1 Spark plugs faulty or not gapped properly (Chapter 1).
2 Faulty spark plug wires (Chapter 1).
3 Wet or damaged distributor components (Chapter 1).
4 Short circuits in ignition, coil or spark plug wires.
5 Sticking or faulty emissions systems (see Chapter 6).
6 Clogged fuel filter and/or foreign matter in fuel. Remove the fuel filter (Chapter 1) and inspect.
7 Vacuum leaks at intake manifold or hose connections. Check as described in Section 8.
8 Incorrect idle speed (Chapter 1) or idle mixture (Chapter 4).
9 Incorrect ignition timing (Chapter 1).
10 Low or uneven cylinder compression. Check as described in Chapter 2.
11 Choke not operating properly (Chapter 1).
12 Clogged or dirty fuel injectors (Chapter 4).

10 Excessively high idle speed

1 Sticking throttle linkage (Chapter 4).
2 Choke opened excessively at idle (Chapter 4).
3 Idle speed incorrectly adjusted (Chapter 1).

11 Battery will not hold a charge

1 Alternator drivebelt defective or not adjusted properly (Chapter 1).
2 Battery cables loose or corroded (Chapter 1).
3 Alternator not charging properly (Chapter 5).
4 Loose, broken or faulty wires in the charging circuit (Chapter 5).
5 Short circuit causing a continuous drain on the battery.
6 Battery defective internally.

12 Alternator light stays on

1 Fault in alternator or charging circuit (Chapter 5).
2 Alternator drivebelt defective or not properly adjusted (Chapter 1).

13 Alternator light fails to come on when key is turned on

1 Faulty bulb (Chapter 12).
2 Defective alternator (Chapter 5).
3 Fault in the printed circuit, dash wiring or bulb holder (Chapter 12).

14 Engine misses throughout driving speed range

1 Fuel filter clogged and/or impurities in the fuel system. Check fuel filter (Chapter 1) or clean system (Chapter 4).
2 Faulty or incorrectly gapped spark plugs (Chapter 1).
3 Incorrect ignition timing (Chapter 1).
4 Cracked distributor cap, disconnected distributor wires or damaged distributor components (Chapter 1).
5 Defective spark plug wires (Chapter 1).
6 Emissions system components faulty (Chapter 6).
7 Low or uneven cylinder compression pressures. Check as described in Chapter 2.
8 Weak or faulty ignition coil (Chapter 5).
9 Weak or faulty ignition system (Chapter 5).
10 Vacuum leaks at intake manifold or vacuum hoses (see Section 8).
11 Dirty or clogged carburetor or fuel injector (Chapter 4).
12 Leaky EGR valve (Chapter 6).
13 Carburetor out of adjustment (Chapter 4).
14 Idle speed out of adjustment (Chapter 1).

15 Hesitation or stumble during acceleration

1 Ignition timing incorrect (Chapter 1).
2 Ignition system not operating properly (Chapter 5).
3 Dirty or clogged carburetor or fuel injector (Chapter 4).
4 Low fuel pressure. Check for proper operation of the fuel pump and for restrictions in the fuel filter and lines (Chapter 4).
5 Carburetor out of adjustment (Chapter 4).

16 Engine stalls

1 Idle speed incorrect (Chapter 1).
2 Fuel filter clogged and/or water and impurities in the fuel system (Chapter 1).
3 Choke not operating properly (Chapter 1).
4 Damaged or wet distributor cap and wires.
5 Emissions system components faulty (Chapter 6).
6 Faulty or incorrectly gapped spark plugs (Chapter 1). Also check the spark plug wires (Chapter 1).
7 Vacuum leak at the carburetor, intake manifold or vacuum hoses. Check as described in Section 8.

17 Engine lacks power

1 Incorrect ignition timing (Chapter 1).

2 Excessive play in distributor shaft. At the same time check for faulty distributor cap, wires, etc. (Chapter 1).
3 Faulty or incorrectly gapped spark plugs (Chapter 1).
4 Air filter dirty (Chapter 1).
5 Faulty ignition coil (Chapter 5).
6 Brakes binding (Chapters 1 and 10).
7 Automatic transmission fluid level incorrect, causing slippage (Chapter 1).
8 Clutch slipping (Chapter 8).
9 Fuel filter clogged and/or impurities in the fuel system (Chapters 1 and 4).
10 EGR system not functioning properly (Chapter 6).
11 Use of sub-standard fuel. Fill tank with proper octane fuel.
12 Low or uneven cylinder compression pressures. Check as described in Chapter 2.
13 Air leak at carburetor or intake manifold (check as described in Section 8).
14 Dirty or clogged carburetor jets or malfunctioning choke (Chapters 1 and 4).
15 Restricted exhaust system or catalytic converter (Chapter 4).

18 Engine backfires

1 EGR system not functioning properly (Chapter 6).
2 Ignition timing incorrect (Chapter 1).
3 Thermostatic air cleaner system not operating properly (Chapter 6).
4 Vacuum leak (refer to Section 8).
5 Damaged valve springs or sticking valves (Chapter 2).
6 Intake air leak (see Section 8).
7 Carburetor float level out of adjustment (Chapter 4).

19 Engine surges while holding accelerator steady

1 Intake air leak (see Section 8).
2 Fuel pump not working properly (Chapter 4).

20 Pinging or knocking engine sounds when engine is under load

1 Incorrect grade of fuel. Fill tank with fuel of the proper octane rating.
2 Ignition timing incorrect (Chapter 1).
3 Carbon build-up in combustion chambers. Remove cylinder head(s) and clean combustion chambers (Chapter 2).
4 Incorrect spark plugs (Chapter 1).

21 Engine diesels (continues to run) after being turned off

1 Idle speed too high (Chapter 1).

2   Ignition timing incorrect (Chapter 1).
3   Incorrect spark plug heat range (Chapter 1).
4   Intake air leak (see Section 8).
5   Carbon build-up in combustion chambers. Remove the cylinder head(s) and clean the combustion chambers (Chapter 2).
6   Valves sticking (Chapter 2).
7   EGR system not operating properly (Chapter 6).
8   Fuel shut-off system not operating properly (Chapter 6).
9   Check for causes of overheating (Section 27).

22   Low oil pressure

1   Improper grade of oil.
2   Oil pump worn or damaged (Chapter 2).
3   Engine overheating (refer to Section 27).
4   Clogged oil filter (Chapter 1).
5   Clogged oil strainer (Chapter 2).
6   Oil pressure gauge not working properly (Chapter 2).

23   Excessive oil consumption

1   Loose oil drain plug.
2   Loose bolts or damaged oil pan gasket (Chapter 2).
3   Loose bolts or damaged front cover gasket (Chapter 2).
4   Front or rear crankshaft oil seal leaking (Chapter 2).
5   Loose bolts or damaged valve cover gasket (Chapter 2).
6   Loose oil filter (Chapter 1).
7   Loose or damaged oil pressure switch (Chapter 2).
8   Pistons and cylinders excessively worn (Chapter 2).
9   Piston rings not installed correctly on pistons (Chapter 2).
10   Worn or damaged piston rings (Chapter 2).
11   Intake and/or exhaust valve oil seals worn or damaged (Chapter 2).
12   Worn valve stems.
13   Worn or damaged valves/guides (Chapter 2).

24   Excessive fuel consumption

1   Dirty or clogged air filter element (Chapter 1).
2   Incorrect ignition timing (Chapter 1).
3   Incorrect idle speed (Chapter 1).
4   Low tire pressure or incorrect tire size (Chapter 11).
5   Fuel leakage. Check all connections, lines and components in the fuel system (Chapter 4).
6   Choke not operating properly (Chapter 1).
7   Dirty or clogged carburetor jets or fuel injectors (Chapter 4).

25   Fuel odor

1   Fuel leakage. Check all connections, lines and components in the fuel system (Chapter 4).
2   Fuel tank overfilled. Fill only to automatic shut-off.
3   Charcoal canister filter in Evaporative Emissions Control system clogged (Chapter 1).
4   Vapor leaks from Evaporative Emissions Control system lines (Chapter 6).

26   Miscellaneous engine noises

1   A strong dull noise that becomes more rapid as the engine accelerates indicates worn or damaged crankshaft bearings or an unevenly worn crankshaft. To pinpoint the trouble spot, remove the spark plug wire from one plug at a time and crank the engine over. If the noise stops, the cylinder with the removed plug wire indicates the problem area. Replace the bearing and/or service or replace the crankshaft (Chapter 2).
2   A similar (yet slightly higher pitched) noise to the crankshaft knocking described in the previous paragraph, that becomes more rapid as the engine accelerates, indicates worn or damaged connecting rod bearings (Chapter 2). The procedure for locating the problem cylinder is the same as described in Paragraph 1.
3   An overlapping metallic noise that increases in intensity as the engine speed increases, yet diminishes as the engine warms up indicates abnormal piston and cylinder wear (Chapter 2).To locate the problem cylinder, use the procedure described in Paragraph 1.
4   A rapid clicking noise that becomes faster as the engine accelerates indicates a worn piston pin or piston pin hole. This sound will happen each time the piston hits the highest and lowest points in the stroke (Chapter 2). The procedure for locating the problem piston is described in Paragraph 1.
5   A metallic clicking noise coming from the water pump indicates worn or damaged water pump bearings or pump. Replace the water pump with a new one (Chapter 3).
6   A rapid tapping sound or clicking sound that becomes faster as the engine speed increases indicates "valve tapping". This can be identified by holding one end of a section of hose to your ear and placing the other end at different spots along the valve cover. The point where the sound is loudest indicates the problem valve. If the problem persists, you likely have a collapsed valve lifter or other damaged valve train component. Changing the engine oil and adding a high viscosity oil treatment will sometimes cure a stuck lifter problem. If the problem still persists, the lifters, pushrods and rocker arms must be removed for inspection (see Chapter 2).

7   A steady metallic rattling or rapping sound coming from the area of the timing chain cover indicates a worn, damaged or out-of-adjustment timing chain. Service or replace the chain and related components (Chapter 2).

Cooling system

27   Overheating

1   Insufficient coolant in system (Chapter 1).
2   Drivebelt defective or not adjusted properly (Chapter 1).
3   Radiator core blocked or radiator grille dirty and restricted (Chapter 3).
4   Thermostat faulty (Chapter 3).
5   Fan not functioning properly (Chapter 3).
6   Radiator cap not maintaining proper pressure. Have cap pressure tested by gas station or repair shop.
7   Ignition timing incorrect (Chapter 1).
8   Defective water pump (Chapter 3).
9   Improper grade of engine oil.
10   Inaccurate temperature gauge (Chapter 12).

28   Overcooling

1   Thermostat faulty (Chapter 3).
2   Inaccurate temperature gauge (Chapter 12).

29   External coolant leakage

1   Deteriorated or damaged hoses. Loose clamps at hose connections (Chapter 1).
2   Water pump seals defective. If this is the case, water will drip from the weep hole in the water pump body (Chapter 3).
3   Leakage from radiator core or header tank. This will require the radiator to be professionally repaired (see Chapter 3 for removal procedures).
4   Engine drain plugs or water jacket freeze plugs leaking (see Chapters 1 and 2).
5   Leak from coolant temperature switch (Chapter 3).
6   Leak from damaged gaskets or small cracks (Chapter 2).
7   Damaged head gasket. This can be verified by checking the condition of the engine oil as noted in Section 30.

30   Internal coolant leakage

Note: *Internal coolant leaks can usually be detected by examining the oil. Check the dipstick and inside the valve cover for water deposits and an oil consistency like that of a milkshake.*
1   Leaking cylinder head gasket. Have the system pressure tested or remove the cylinder head (Chapter 2) and inspect.

2   Cracked cylinder bore or cylinder head. Dismantle engine and inspect (Chapter 2).
3   Loose cylinder head bolts (tighten as described in Chapter 2).

31   Abnormal coolant loss

1   Overfilling system (Chapter 1).
2   Coolant boiling away due to overheating (see causes in Section 27).
3   Internal or external leakage (see Sections 29 and 30).
4   Faulty radiator cap. Have the cap pressure tested.
5   Cooling system being pressurized by engine compression. This could be due to a cracked head or block or leaking head gasket(s).

32   Poor coolant circulation

1   Inoperative water pump. A quick test is to pinch the top radiator hose closed with your hand while the engine is idling, then release it. You should feel a surge of coolant if the pump is working properly (Chapter 3).
2   Restriction in cooling system. Drain, flush and refill the system (Chapter 1). If necessary, remove the radiator (Chapter 3) and have it reverse flushed or professionally cleaned.
3   Loose water pump drivebelt (Chapter 1).
4   Thermostat sticking (Chapter 3).
5   Insufficient coolant (Chapter 1).

33   Corrosion

1   Excessive impurities in the water. Soft, clean water is recommended. Distilled or rainwater is satisfactory.
2   Insufficient antifreeze solution (refer to Chapter 1 for the proper ratio of water to antifreeze).
3   Infrequent flushing and draining of system. Regular flushing of the cooling system should be carried out at the specified intervals as described in (Chapter 1).

Clutch

Note: *All clutch related service information is located in Chapter 8, unless otherwise noted.*

34   Fails to release (pedal pressed to the floor - shift lever does not move freely in and out of Reverse)

1   Clutch contaminated with oil. Remove clutch plate and inspect.
2   Clutch plate warped, distorted or otherwise damaged.
3   Diaphragm spring fatigued. Remove clutch cover/pressure plate assembly and inspect.

4   Leakage of fluid from clutch hydraulic system. Inspect master cylinder, operating cylinder and connecting lines.
5   Air in clutch hydraulic system. Bleed the system.
6   Insufficient pedal stroke. Check and adjust as necessary.
7   Piston seal in operating cylinder deformed or damaged.
8   Lack of grease on pilot bushing.

35   Clutch slips (engine speed increases with no increase in vehicle speed)

1   Worn or oil soaked clutch plate.
2   Clutch plate not broken in. It may take 30 or 40 normal starts for a new clutch to seat.
3   Diaphragm spring weak or damaged. Remove clutch cover/pressure plate assembly and inspect.
4   Flywheel warped (Chapter 2).
5   Debris in master cylinder preventing the piston from returning to its normal position.
6   Clutch hydraulic line damaged.

36   Grabbing (chattering) as clutch is engaged

1   Oil on clutch plate. Remove and inspect. Repair any leaks.
2   Worn or loose engine or transmission mounts. They may move slightly when clutch is released. Inspect mounts and bolts.
3   Worn splines on transmission input shaft. Remove clutch components and inspect.
4   Warped pressure plate or flywheel. Remove clutch components and inspect.
5   Diaphragm spring fatigued. Remove clutch cover/pressure plate assembly and inspect.
6   Clutch linings hardened or warped.
7   Clutch lining rivets loose.

37   Squeal or rumble with clutch engaged (pedal released)

1   Improper pedal adjustment. Adjust pedal free play.
2   Release bearing binding on transmission shaft. Remove clutch components and check bearing. Remove any burrs or nicks, clean and relubricate before reinstallation.
3   Pilot bushing worn or damaged.
4   Clutch rivets loose.
5   Clutch plate cracked.
6   Fatigued clutch plate torsion springs. Replace clutch plate.

38   Squeal or rumble with clutch disengaged (pedal depressed)

1   Worn or damaged release bearing.

2   Worn or broken pressure plate diaphragm fingers.

39   Clutch pedal stays on floor when disengaged

Binding linkage or release bearing. Inspect linkage or remove clutch components as necessary.

Manual transmission

Note: *All manual transmission service information is located in Chapter 7, unless otherwise noted.*

40   Noisy in Neutral with engine running

1   Input shaft bearing worn.
2   Damaged main drive gear bearing.
3   Insufficient transmission oil (Chapter 1).
4   Transmission oil in poor condition. Drain and fill with proper grade oil. Check old oil for water and debris (Chapter 1).
5   Noise can be caused by variations in engine torque. Change the idle speed and see if noise disappears.

41   Noisy in all gears

1   Any of the above causes, and/or:
2   Worn or damaged output gear bearings or shaft.

42   Noisy in one particular gear

1   Worn, damaged or chipped gear teeth.
2   Worn or damaged synchronizer.

43   Slips out of gear

1   Transmission loose on clutch housing.
2   Stiff shift lever seal.
3   Shift linkage binding.
4   Broken or loose input gear bearing retainer.
5   Dirt between clutch lever and engine housing.
6   Worn linkage.
7   Damaged or worn check balls, fork rod ball grooves or check springs.
8   Worn mainshaft or countershaft bearings.
9   Loose engine mounts (Chapter 2).
10   Excessive gear end play.
11   Worn synchronizers.

44   Oil leaks

1   Excessive amount of lubricant in transmission (see Chapter 1 for correct checking procedures). Drain lubricant as required.

2 Rear oil seal or speedometer oil seal damaged.

3 To pinpoint a leak, first remove all built-up dirt and grime from the transmission. Degreasing agents and/or steam cleaning will achieve this. With the underside clean, drive the vehicle at low speeds so the air flow will not blow the leak far from its source. Raise the vehicle and determine where the leak is located.

45 Difficulty engaging gears

1 Clutch not releasing completely.
2 Loose or damaged shift linkage. Make a thorough inspection, replacing parts as necessary.
3 Insufficient transmission oil (Chapter 1).
4 Transmission oil in poor condition. Drain and fill with proper grade oil. Check oil for water and debris (Chapter 1).
5 Worn or damaged striking rod.
6 Sticking or jamming gears.

46 Noise occurs while shifting gears

1 Check for proper operation of the clutch (Chapter 8).
2 Faulty synchronizer assemblies. Measure baulk ring-to-gear clearance. Also, check for wear or damage to baulk rings or any parts of the synchromesh assemblies.

Automatic transmission

Note: *Due to the complexity of the automatic transmission, it's difficult for the home mechanic to properly diagnose and service. For problems other than the following, the vehicle should be taken to a reputable mechanic.*

47 Fluid leakage

1 Automatic transmission fluid is a deep red color, and fluid leaks should not be confused with engine oil which can easily be blown by air flow to the transmission.
2 To pinpoint a leak, first remove all built-up dirt and grime from the transmission. Degreasing agents and/or steam cleaning will achieve this. With the underside clean, drive the vehicle at low speeds so the air flow will not blow the leak far from its source. Raise the vehicle and determine where the leak is located. Common areas of leakage are:
a) **Fluid pan:** *tighten mounting bolts and/or replace pan gasket as necessary (Chapter 1).*
b) **Rear extension:** *tighten bolts and/or replace oil seal as necessary.*
c) **Filler pipe:** *replace the rubber oil seal where pipe enters transmission case..*
d) **Transmission oil lines:** *tighten fittings where lines enter transmission case and/or replace lines.*

e) **Vent pipe:** *transmission overfilled and/or water in fluid (see checking procedures, Chapter 1).*
f) **Speedometer connector:** *replace the O-ring where speedometer cable enters transmission case.*

48 General shift mechanism problems

Chapter 7 deals with checking and adjusting the shift linkage on automatic transmissions. Common problems which may be caused by out of adjustment linkage are:
a) *Engine starting in gears other than P (park) or N (Neutral).*
b) *Indicator pointing to a gear other than the one actually engaged.*
c) *Vehicle moves with transmission in P (Park) position.*

49 Transmission will not downshift with the accelerator pedal pressed to the floor

Chapter 7 deals with adjusting the TV linkage to enable the transmission to downshift properly.

50 Engine will start in gears other than Park or Neutral

Chapter 7 deals with adjusting the Neutral start switch installed on automatic transmissions.

51 Transmission slips, shifts rough, is noisy or has no drive in forward or reverse gears

1 There are many probable causes for the above problems, but the home mechanic should concern himself only with one possibility; fluid level.
2 Before taking the vehicle to a shop, check the fluid level and condition as described in Chapter 1. Add fluid, if necessary, or change the fluid and filter if needed. If problems persist, have a professional diagnose the transmission.

Driveshaft

Note: *Refer to Chapter 8, unless otherwise specified, for service information.*

52 Leaks at front of driveshaft

Defective transmission rear seal. See Chapter 7 for replacement procedure. As this is done, check the splined yoke for burrs or roughness that could damage the new seal. Remove burrs with a fine file or whetstone.

53 Knock or clunk when transmission is under initial load (just after transmission is put into gear)

1 Loose or disconnected rear suspension components. Check all mounting bolts and bushings (Chapters 7 and 10).
2 Loose driveshaft bolts. Inspect all bolts and nuts and tighten them securely.
3 Worn or damaged universal joint bearings. Replace driveshaft (Chapter 8).
4 Worn sleeve yoke and mainshaft spline.

54 Metallic grating sound consistent with vehicle speed

Pronounced wear in the universal joint bearings. Replace U-joints or driveshafts, as necessary.

55 Vibration

Note: Before blaming the driveshaft, make sure the tires are perfectly balanced and perform the following test.
1 Install a tachometer inside the vehicle to monitor engine speed as the vehicle is driven. Drive the vehicle and note the engine speed at which the vibration (roughness) is most pronounced. Now shift the transmission to a different gear and bring the engine speed to the same point.
2 If the vibration occurs at the same engine speed (rpm) regardless of which gear the transmission is in, the driveshaft is NOT at fault since the driveshaft speed varies.
3 If the vibration decreases or is eliminated when the transmission is in a different gear at the same engine speed, refer to the following probable causes.
4 Bent or dented driveshaft. Inspect and replace as necessary.
5 Undercoating or built-up dirt, etc. on the driveshaft. Clean the shaft thoroughly.
6 Worn universal joint bearings. Replace the U-joints or driveshaft as necessary.
7 Driveshaft and/or companion flange out of balance. Check for missing weights on the shaft. Remove driveshaft and reinstall 180-degrees from original position, then recheck. Have the driveshaft balanced if problem persists.
8 Loose driveshaft mounting bolts/nuts.
9 Defective center bearing, if so equipped.
10 Worn transmission rear bushing (Chapter 7).

56 Scraping noise

Make sure the dust cover on the sleeve yoke isn't rubbing on the transmission extension housing.

57 Whining or whistling noise

Defective center bearing, if so equipped.

Rear axle and differential

Note: *For differential servicing information refer to Chapter 8 unless otherwise specified.*

58 Noise - same when in drive as when vehicle is coasting

1   Road noise. No corrective action available.
2   Tire noise. Inspect tires and check tire pressures (Chapter 1).
3   Front wheel bearings loose, worn or damaged (Chapter 1).
4   Insufficient differential oil (Chapter 1).
5   Defective differential.

59 Knocking sound when starting or shifting gears

Defective or incorrectly adjusted differential.

60 Noise when turning

Defective differential.

61 Vibration

See probable causes under Driveshaft. Proceed under the guidelines listed for the driveshaft. If the problem persists, check the rear wheel bearings by raising the rear of the vehicle and spinning the wheels by hand. Listen for evidence of rough (noisy) bearings. Remove and inspect (Chapter 8).

62 Oil leaks

1   Pinion oil seal damaged (Chapter 8).
2   Axleshaft oil seals damaged (Chapter 8).
3   Differential cover leaking. Tighten mounting bolts or replace the gasket as required.
4   Loose filler or drain plug on differential (Chapter 1).
5   Clogged or damaged breather on differential.

Transfer case

Note: *Refer to Chapter 7C for 4WD system service and repair information.*

63 Gear jumping out of mesh

1   Incorrect control lever free play (Chapter 7C).

2   Interference between the control lever and the console.
3   Play or fatigue in the transfer case mounts.
4   Internal wear or incorrect adjustments.

64 Difficult shifting

1   Lack of oil.
2   Internal wear, damage or incorrect adjustment.

65 Noise

1   Lack of oil in transfer case.
2   Noise in 4H and 4L, but not in 2H indicates cause is in the front differential or front axle.
3   Noise in 2H, 4H and 4L indicates cause is in rear differential or rear axle.
4   Noise in 2H and 4H but not in 4L, or in 4L only, indicates internal wear or damage in transfer case.

Brakes

Note: *Before assuming a brake problem exists, make sure the tires are in good condition and inflated properly, the front end alignment is correct and the vehicle is not loaded with weight in an unequal manner. All service procedures for the brakes are included in Chapter 10, unless otherwise noted.*

66 Vehicle pulls to one side during braking

1   Defective, damaged or oil contaminated brake pad on one side. Inspect as described in Chapter 1. Refer to Chapter 10 if replacement is required.
2   Excessive wear of brake pad material or disc on one side. Inspect and repair as necessary.
3   Loose or disconnected front suspension components. Inspect and tighten all bolts securely (Chapters 1 and 11).
4   Defective caliper assembly. Remove caliper and inspect for stuck piston or damage.
5   Brake pad to rotor adjustment needed. Inspect automatic adjusting mechanism for proper operation.
6   Scored or out of round rotor.
7   Loose caliper mounting bolts.
8   Incorrect wheel bearing adjustment (Chapter 8).

67 Noise (high-pitched squeal)

1   Front brake pads worn out. This noise comes from the wear sensor rubbing against the disc. Replace pads with new ones immediately!
2   Glazed or contaminated pads.

3   Dirty or scored rotor.
4   Bent support plate.

68 Excessive brake pedal travel

1   Partial brake system failure. Inspect entire system (Chapter 1) and correct as required.
2   Insufficient fluid in master cylinder. Check (Chapter 1) and add fluid - bleed system if necessary.
3   Air in system. Bleed system.
4   Excessive lateral rotor play.
5   Brakes out of adjustment. Check the operation of the automatic adjusters.
6   Defective proportioning valve. Replace valve and bleed system.

69 Brake pedal feels spongy when depressed

1   Air in brake lines. Bleed the brake system.
2   Deteriorated rubber brake hoses. Inspect all system hoses and lines. Replace parts as necessary.
3   Master cylinder mounting nuts loose. Inspect master cylinder bolts (nuts) and tighten them securely.
4   Master cylinder faulty.
5   Incorrect shoe or pad clearance.
6   Defective check valve. Replace valve and bleed system.
7   Clogged reservoir cap vent hole.
8   Deformed rubber brake lines.
9   Soft or swollen caliper seals.
10 Poor quality brake fluid. Bleed entire system and fill with new approved fluid.

70 Excessive effort required to stop vehicle

1   Power brake booster not operating properly.
2   Excessively worn linings or pads. Check and replace if necessary.
3   One or more caliper pistons seized or sticking. Inspect and rebuild as required.
4   Brake pads or linings contaminated with oil or grease. Inspect and replace as required.
5   New pads or linings installed and not yet seated. It'll take a while for the new material to seat against the rotor or drum.
6   Worn or damaged master cylinder or caliper assemblies. Check particularly for frozen pistons.
7   Also see causes listed under Section 69.

71 Pedal travels to the floor with little resistance

Little or no fluid in the master cylinder

reservoir caused by leaking caliper piston(s) or loose, damaged or disconnected brake lines. Inspect entire system and repair as necessary.

72 Brake pedal pulsates during brake application

1 Wheel bearings damaged, worn or out of adjustment (Chapter 8).
2 Caliper not sliding properly due to improper installation or obstructions. Remove and inspect.
3 Rotor not within specifications. Remove the rotor and check for excessive lateral runout and parallelism. Have the rotors resurfaced or replace them with new ones. Also make sure that all rotors are the same thickness.
4 Out of round rear brake drums. Remove the drums and have them turned or replace them with new ones.

73 Brakes drag (indicated by sluggish engine performance or wheels being very hot after driving)

1 Output rod adjustment incorrect at the brake pedal.
2 Obstructed master cylinder compensator. Disassemble master cylinder and clean.
3 Master cylinder piston seized in bore. Overhaul master cylinder.
4 Caliper assembly in need of overhaul.
5 Brake pads or shoes worn out.
6 Piston cups in master cylinder or caliper assembly deformed. Overhaul master cylinder.
7 Rotor not within specifications (Section 72).
8 Parking brake assembly will not release.
9 Clogged brake lines.
10 Wheel bearings out of adjustment (Chapter 8).
11 Brake pedal height improperly adjusted.
12 Wheel cylinder needs overhaul.
13 Improper shoe to drum clearance. Adjust as necessary.

74 Rear brakes lock up under light brake application

1 Tire pressures too high.
2 Tires excessively worn (Chapter 1).

75 Rear brakes lock up under heavy brake application

1 Tire pressures too high.
2 Tires excessively worn (Chapter 1).
3 Front brake pads contaminated with oil, mud or water. Clean or replace the pads.
4 Front brake pads excessively worn.
5 Defective master cylinder or caliper assembly.

Suspension and steering

Note: *All service procedures for the suspension and steering systems are included in Chapter 10, unless otherwise noted.*

76 Vehicle pulls to one side

1 Tire pressures uneven (Chapter 1).
2 Defective tire (Chapter 1).
3 Excessive wear in suspension or steering components (Chapter 1).
4 Front end alignment incorrect.
5 Front brakes dragging. Inspect as described in Section 73.
6 Wheel bearings improperly adjusted (Chapter 8).
7 Wheel lug nuts loose.

77 Shimmy, shake or vibration

1 Tire or wheel out of balance or out of round. Have them balanced on the vehicle.
2 Loose, worn or out of adjustment wheel bearings (Chapter 8).
3 Shock absorbers and/or suspension components worn or damaged. 4 Wheel lug nuts loose.
5 Incorrect tire pressures.
6 Excessively worn or damaged tire.
7 Loosely mounted steering gear housing.
8 Steering gear improperly adjusted.
9 Loose, worn or damaged steering components.
10 Damaged idler arm.
11 Worn balljoint.

78 Excessive pitching and/or rolling around corners or during braking

1 Defective shock absorbers. Replace as a set.
2 Broken or weak leaf springs and/or suspension components.
3 Worn or damaged stabilizer bar or bushings.

79 Wandering or general instability

1 Improper tire pressures.
2 Worn or out of adjustment wheel bearings (Chapter 8).
3 Incorrect front end alignment.
4 Worn or damaged steering linkage or suspension components.
5 Improperly adjusted steering gear.
6 Out of balance wheels.
7 Loose wheel lug nuts.
8 Worn rear shock absorbers.
9 Fatigued or damaged rear leaf springs.

80 Excessively stiff steering

1 Lack of lubricant in power steering fluid reservoir, where appropriate (Chapter 1).
2 Incorrect tire pressures (Chapter 1).
3 Lack of lubrication at balljoints (Chapter 1).
4 Front end out of alignment.
5 Steering gear out of adjustment or lacking lubrication.
6 Improperly adjusted wheel bearings.
7 Worn or damaged steering gear.
8 Interference of steering column with turn signal switch.
9 Low tire pressures.
10 Worn or damaged balljoints.
11 Worn or damaged steering linkage.
12 See also Section 79.

81 Excessive play in steering

1 Loose wheel bearings (Chapter 8).
2 Excessive wear in suspension bushings (Chapter 1).
3 Steering gear improperly adjusted.
4 Incorrect front end alignment.
5 Steering gear mounting bolts loose.
6 Worn steering linkage.

82 Lack of power assistance

1 Steering pump drivebelt faulty or not adjusted properly (Chapter 1).
2 Fluid level low (Chapter 1).
3 Hoses or pipes restricting the flow. Inspect and replace parts as necessary.
4 Air in power steering system. Bleed system.
5 Defective power steering pump.

83 Steering wheel fails to return to straight-ahead position

1 Incorrect front end alignment.
2 Tire pressures low.
3 Steering gears improperly engaged.
4 Steering column out of alignment.
5 Worn or damaged balljoint.
6 Worn or damaged steering linkage.
7 Improperly lubricated idler arm.
8 Insufficient oil in steering gear.
9 Lack of fluid in power steering pump.

84 Steering effort not the same in both directions (power system)

1 Leaks in steering gear.
2 Clogged fluid passage in steering gear.

85 Noisy power steering pump

1 Insufficient oil in pump.

2   Clogged hoses or oil filter in pump.
3   Loose pulley.
4   Improperly adjusted drivebelt (Chapter 1).
5   Defective pump.

86   Miscellaneous noises

1   Improper tire pressures.
2   Insufficiently lubricated balljoint or steering linkage.
3   Loose or worn steering gear, steering linkage or suspension components.
4   Defective shock absorber.
5   Defective wheel bearing.
6   Worn or damaged suspension bushings.
7   Damaged leaf spring.
8   Loose wheel lug nuts.
9   Worn or damaged rear axleshaft spline.
10 Worn or damaged rear shock absorber mounting bushing.

11 Incorrect rear axle endplay.
12 See also causes of noises at the rear axle and driveshaft.

87   Excessive tire wear (not specific to one area)

1   Incorrect tire pressures.
2   Tires out of balance. Have them balanced on the vehicle.
3   Wheels damaged. Inspect and replace as necessary.
4   Suspension or steering components worn (Chapter 1).

88   Excessive tire wear on outside edge

1   Incorrect tire pressure.

2   Excessive speed in turns.
3   Front end alignment incorrect (excessive toe-in).

89   Excessive tire wear on inside edge

1   Incorrect tire pressure.
2   Front end alignment incorrect (toe-out).
3   Loose or damaged steering components (Chapter 1).

90   Tire tread worn in one place

1   Tires out of balance. Have them balanced on the vehicle.
2   Damaged or buckled wheel. Inspect and replace if necessary.
3   Defective tire.

Notes

Chapter 1
Tune-up and routine maintenance

Contents

Specifications

Recommended lubricants and fluids

Note: *Listed here are manufacturer recommendations at the time this manual was written. Manufacturers occasionally upgrade their fluid and lubricant specifications, so check with your local auto parts store for current recommendations.*

Engine oil
 Type .... API grade "certified for gasoline engines"
 Viscosity .... See accompanying chart

ENGINE OIL VISCOSITY

For best fuel economy and cold starting, select the lowest SAE viscosity grade oil for the expected temperature range

1-a3 HAYNES

Recommended lubricants and fluids (continued)

Engine oil (continued)
    Capacity (with new oil filter)*
        Four-cylinder engines .... 4 qts
        Six-cylinder engines.. 6 qts
Manual transmission lubricant
    Type
        AX-4/5 .... SAE 75/90W GL-5 gear lubricant
        AX-15 .... SAE 75/90W GL-5 gear lubricant
        NV1500 .... Mopar, manual transmission lubricant
        NV3550 .... Mopar, manual transmission lubricant
    Capacity*
        AX-4/5 and AX-15 .... 3.5 qts
        NV1500 .... 4.8 pts
        NV3550 .... 4.2 pts
Automatic transmission fluid
    Type .... Mopar, ATF Plus+4, type 9602 or equivalent fluid
    Capacity (drain and refill**) .... 4 qts
Transfer case lubricant
    Type .... Mopar, ATF Plus+4, type 9602 or equivalent fluid
    Capacity (approximate)*
        NP 207 .... 4.5 pints
        NP 231 .... 3 pints
        NP 241 .... 4 pints
        NP 242 .... 3 pints
Differential lubricant type
    Normal operation... SAE 75W-90 API GL-5 gear lubricant
    Trailer towing or severe service.. SAE 75W-140 synthetic gear lubricant
    Limited-slip differential .... Include 4 oz. (188 ml) of Mopar, Friction Modifier additive
Coolant
    Type
        2000 and earlier models .... 50-percent distilled or deionized water and 50- percent ethylene gly-
col-based antifreeze
        2001 and later models .... 50-percent distilled or deionized water and 50- percent Mopar,
100,000 mile Anti-freeze/coolant with Hybrid Organic technology (HOAT) additives
    Capacity*
        Four-cylinder engines .... 9 qts
        Six-cylinder engines .... 10.5 qts
Brake fluid type... DOT 3 brake fluid
Power steering fluid .... Mopar, ATF +4 Type 9602 or equivalent fluid
Chassis grease type .... NLGI LB or GC-LB chassis grease

All capacities approximate. Add as necessary to bring to appropriate level.
**This is the approximate capacity when draining the transmission pan and replacing the filter. After overhaul, when filling the transmission from "dry," the capacity will be much higher.*

2.4L four-cylinder engine   4-cylinder engine   6-cylinder engine

Cylinder location and distributor rotation

Tune-up information

Spark plug type and gap (1996 and earlier)
  2.5L four cylinder engine
    Type .... Champion RC12LYC or equivalent
    Gap .... 0.033 to 0.038 in
Six-cylinder engine
  Type
    Carbureted models .... Champion RFN14LY or equivalent
    Fuel-injected models .... Champion RC9YC or equivalent
  Gap .... 0.033 to 0.038 in
Spark plug type and gap (1997 and later)
  All except 2.4L 4-cylinder engine
    Type ....
      1997 and 1998.. Champion RC12LYC or equivalent
      1999 on... Champion RC12ECC or equivalent
    Gap .... 0.035 in
  2.4L four-cylinder engine
    Type .... Champion RE14MCC5 or equivalent
    Gap .... 0.048-0.053 in
Firing order
  Four-cylinder engine 1-3-4-2
  Six-cylinder engine.. 1-5-3-6-2-4
Cylinder numbers .... See below
Ignition timing (carbureted models only)* .... 9 to 11-degrees BTDC
Engine idle speed (carbureted models only)*
  Manual transmission .... 680 plus or minus 70 rpm
  Automatic transmission.. 600 plus or minus 70 rpm

*The Vehicle Emission Control Information label in the engine compartment, if different, supersedes this information.

Brakes

Disc brake pad lining thickness (minimum) 1/8-inch
Drum brake shoe lining thickness (minimum)
  Bonded shoes 1/16-inch
  Riveted shoes (thickness above rivets) 1/32-inch

Torque specifications   **Ft-lbs** (unless otherwise indicated)

Automatic transmission
  Filter screws
    30RH and 32RH .... 35 in-lbs
    42RLE .... 45 in-lbs
  Pan bolts 14
Carburetor/throttle body mounting nuts/bolts.................... 14
Transfer case oil drain/fill plug
  NP 231 .... 15 to 25
  NP 241 .... 3.4 pints
Rear differential cover bolts... 30
Front differential cover bolts.. 30
Transfer case fill/drain plug 20
Manual transmission fill/drain plug
  AX-4/5 .... 32.5
  AX-1500... 25
  NV3550.. 14 to 20
Spark plugs
  2.4L four-cylinder engine .... 132 in-lbs
  2.5L four-cylinder engine 27
  6-cylinder engine... 27
Engine oil drain plug 25
Oxygen sensor.. 22
Wheel lug nuts .... 80 to 110

Engine compartment component checking points (2.5L four-cylinder engine shown)

1	Distributor cap and wires	6	Windshield washer fluid reservoir	11	Oil filler cap
2	PVC valve	7	Air cleaner housing	12	Engine drivebelt
3	Brake fluid reservoir	8	Power steering fluid reservoir	13	Radiator hose
4	Clutch fluid reservoir	9	Radiator cap	14	Engine oil dipstick
5	Radiator coolant reservoir	10	Radiator	15	Battery

Typical engine compartment underside components (1987 through 1996 models)

1	Radiator drain fitting	5	Front differential check plug	8	Engine oil drain plug
2	Radiator	6	Front driveshaft grease fitting	9	Steering damper
3	Radiator hose	7	Exhaust pipe	10	Front disc brake caliper
4	Steering grease fitting				

Typical rear underside vehicle components (1987 through 1996 models)

1	Fuel tank skid plate	4	Exhaust system	7	Check plug
2	Rear spring	5	Rear differential check plug	8	Rear drum brake
3	Shock absorber	6	Transfer case		

Typical engine compartment underside component locations (1997 and later models)

1	Steering damper (4WD models)	4	Driveaxle boot (4WD models)	7	Engine oil pan
2	Steering grease fitting	5	Driveshaft grease fitting (4WD models)	8	Exhaust system
3	Front differential check/fill plug	6	Automatic transmission fluid pan	9	Front disc brake

Typical rear underside component locations (1997 and later models)

1	Rear disc brake	4	Exhaust system
2	Differential check/fill plug	5	Driveshaft rear universal joint
3	Rear shock absorber		

1 Jeep Wrangler Maintenance schedule

The following maintenance intervals are based on the assumption that the vehicle owner will be doing the maintenance or service work, as opposed to having a dealer service department do the work. Although the time/mileage intervals are loosely based on factory recommendations, most have been shortened to ensure, for example, that such items as lubricants and fluids are checked/changed at intervals that promote maximum engine/driveline service life. Also, subject to the preference of the individual owner interested in keeping his or her vehicle in peak condition at all times, and with the vehicle's ultimate resale in mind, many of the maintenance procedures may be performed more often than recommended in the following schedule. We encourage such owner initiative.

When the vehicle is new it should be serviced initially by a factory authorized dealer service department to protect the factory warranty. In many cases the initial maintenance check is done at no cost to the owner (check with your dealer service department for more information).

Every 250 miles or weekly, whichever comes first

Check the engine oil level (Section 4)
Check the engine coolant level (Section 4)
Check the windshield washer fluid level (Section 4)
Check the brake and clutch fluid levels (Section 4)
Check the tires and tire pressures (Section 5)

Every 3000 miles or 3 months, whichever comes first

All items listed above plus:
Check the automatic transmission fluid level (Section 6)
Check the power steering fluid level (Section 7)
Check and service the battery (Section 8)
Check the cooling system (Section 9)
Inspect and replace, if necessary, all underhood hoses (Section 10)
Inspect and replace, if necessary, the windshield wiper blades (Section 11)

Every 7500 miles or 12 months, whichever comes first

All items listed above plus:
Change the engine oil and filter (Section 12)*
Lubricate the chassis components (Section 13)
Inspect the suspension and steering components (Section 14)*
Inspect the exhaust system (Section 15)*
Check the manual transmission lubricant level (Section 16)*
Check the differential lubricant level (Section 17)*
Check the transfer case lubricant level (Section 18)
Rotate the tires (Section 19)
Check the brakes (Section 20)*
Inspect the fuel system (Section 21)
Check the carburetor choke operation (Section 22)
Check the carburetor/throttle body mounting nut torque (Section 23)
Check the throttle linkage (Section 24)
Check the thermostatically-controlled air cleaner (Section 25)
Check the engine drivebelts (Section 26)
Check the seatbelts (Section 27)
Check the starter safety switch (Section 28)
Check the spare tire and jack (Section 29)

Every 30,000 miles or 24 months, whichever comes first

All items listed above plus:
Check and adjust, if necessary, the engine idle speed (Section 30)
Replace the fuel filter (1987 through 1995 models only) (Section 31)
Replace the air and PCV filters (Section 32)
Check and adjust, if necessary, the ignition timing (Section 33)
Change the automatic transmission fluid (Section 34)**
Change the manual transmission lubricant (Section 35)
Change the differential lubricant (Section 36)
Change the transfer case lubricant (Section 37)
Service the cooling system (drain, flush and refill) (Section 38)
Inspect and replace, if necessary, the PCV valve (Section 39)
Inspect the evaporative emissions control system (Section 40)
Replace the spark plugs (Section 41)
Inspect the spark plug wires, distributor cap and rotor (Section 42)

Every 82,500 miles or 82 months, whichever comes first

Replace the oxygen sensor and emissions timer (49-state models) (Section 43)
Inspect and replace, if necessary, all underhood hoses

* This item is affected by "severe" operating conditions as described below. If your vehicle is operated under severe conditions, perform all maintenance indicated with an asterisk (*) at 3000 miles/3 month intervals.
In dusty areas
Off road use
Towing a trailer
Idling for extended periods and/or low speed operation
When outside temperatures remain below freezing and most trips are less than four miles

** If operated under one or more of the following conditions, change the automatic transmission fluid every 12,000 miles:
In heavy city traffic where the outside temperature regularly reaches 90-degrees F (32-degrees C) or higher
In hilly or mountainous terrain
Frequent trailer pulling
Frequent off road use

2   Introduction

This Chapter is designed to help the home mechanic maintain the Jeep Wrangler with the goals of maximum performance, economy, safety and reliability in mind. Included is a master maintenance schedule (see the previous page) followed by procedures dealing specifically with each item on the schedule. Visual checks, adjustments, component replacement and other helpful items are included. Refer to the accompanying illustrations of the engine compartment and the underside of the vehicle for the locations of various components.

Servicing your vehicle in accordance with the mileage/time maintenance schedule and the step-by-step procedures will result in a planned maintenance program that should produce a long and reliable service life. Keep in mind that it is a comprehensive plan, so maintaining some items but not others at the specified intervals will not produce the same results.

As you service your vehicle, you will discover that many of the procedures can - and should - be grouped together because of the nature of the particular procedure you're performing or because of the close proximity of two otherwise unrelated components to one another.

For example, if the vehicle is raised for chassis lubrication, you should inspect the exhaust, suspension, steering and fuel systems while you're under the vehicle. When you're rotating the tires, it makes good sense to check the brakes since the wheels are already removed. Finally, let's suppose you have to borrow or rent a torque wrench. Even if you only need it to tighten the spark plugs, you might as well check the torque of as many critical fasteners as time allows.

The first step in this maintenance program is to prepare yourself before the actual work begins. Read through all the procedures you're planning to do, then gather up all the parts and tools needed. If it looks like you might run into problems during a particular job, seek advice from a mechanic or an experienced do-it-yourselfer.

3   Tune-up general information

The term tune-up is used in this manual to represent a combination of individual operations rather than one specific procedure.

If, from the time the vehicle is new, the routine maintenance schedule is followed closely and frequent checks are made of fluid levels and high wear items, as suggested throughout this manual, the engine will be kept in relatively good running condition and the need for additional work will be minimized.

More likely than not, however, there will be times when the engine is running poorly due to lack of regular maintenance. This is even more likely if a used vehicle, which has not received regular and frequent maintenance checks, is purchased. In such cases, an engine tune-up will be needed outside of the regular routine maintenance intervals.

The first step in any tune-up or diagnostic procedure to help correct a poor running engine is a cylinder compression check. A compression check (see Chapter 2 Part C) will help determine the condition of internal engine components and should be used as a guide for tune-up and repair procedures. If, for instance, a compression check indicates serious internal engine wear, a conventional tune-up will not improve the performance of the engine and would be a waste of time and money. Because of its importance, the compression check should be done by someone with the right equipment and the knowledge to use it properly.

The following procedures are those most often needed to bring a generally poor running engine back into a proper state of tune.

Minor tune-up

Check all engine related fluids (Section 4)
Clean, inspect and test the battery (Section 8)
Check and adjust the drivebelts (Section 26)
Replace the spark plugs (Section 41)
Inspect the distributor cap and rotor (Section 42)
Inspect the spark plug and coil wires (Section 42)
Check and adjust the ignition timing (Section 33)
Check the PCV valve (Section 40)
Check the air and PCV filters (Section 32)
Check the cooling system (Section 9)
Check all underhood hoses (Section 10)

Major tune-up

All items listed under Minor tune-up plus . . .
Check the ignition system (Chapter 5)
Check the charging system (Chapter 5)
Check the fuel system (Section 21)

Replace the air and PCV filters (Section 32)
Replace the distributor cap and rotor (Section 42)
Replace the spark plug wires (Section 42)

4   Fluid level checks

Note: *The following are fluid level checks to be done on a 250 mile or weekly basis. Additional fluid level checks can be found in specific maintenance procedures which follow. Regardless of intervals, be alert to fluid leaks under the vehicle which would indicate a fault to be corrected immediately.*

1   Fluids are an essential part of the lubrication, cooling, brake, clutch and windshield washer systems. Because the fluids gradually become depleted and/or contaminated during normal operation of the vehicle, they must be periodically replenished. See *Recommended lubricants and fluids* at the beginning of this Chapter before adding fluid to any of the following components. **Note:** *The vehicle must be on level ground when fluid levels are checked.*

Engine oil

Refer to illustrations 4.4 and 4.6

2   The engine oil level is checked with a dipstick on the passenger's side of the engine compartment that extends through a tube and into the oil pan at the bottom of the engine.

3   The oil level should be checked before the vehicle has been driven, or about 15 minutes after the engine has been shut off. If the oil is checked immediately after driving the vehicle, some of the oil will remain in the upper engine components, resulting in an inaccurate reading on the dipstick.

4   Pull the dipstick from the tube and wipe all the oil from the end with a clean rag or paper towel. Insert the clean dipstick all the way back into the tube, then pull it out again. Note the oil at the end of the dipstick. Add oil as necessary to keep the level between the ADD mark and the FULL mark on the dipstick **(see illustration)**.

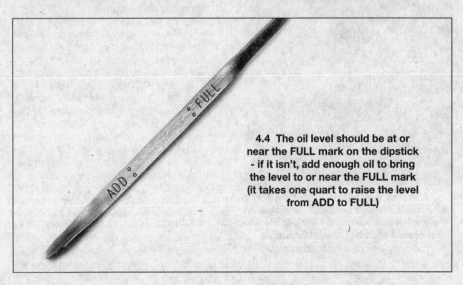

4.4 The oil level should be at or near the FULL mark on the dipstick - if it isn't, add enough oil to bring the level to or near the FULL mark (it takes one quart to raise the level from ADD to FULL)

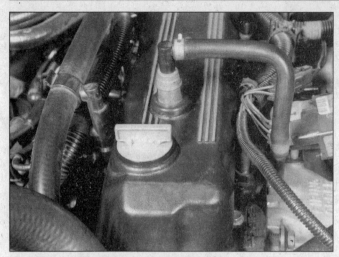

4.6 The twist-off oil filter cap is located on the valve cover - always makes sure the area around this opening is clean before unscrewing the cap to prevent dirt from contaminating the engine

4.8 The coolant reserve bottle allows for contraction and expansion of the coolant - it can be checked visually with the engine hot or cold

5   Do not overfill the engine by adding too much oil since this may result in oil fouled spark plugs, oil leaks or oil seal failures.

6   Oil is added to the engine after removing a cap **(see illustration)**. An oil can spout or funnel may help to reduce spills.

7   Checking the oil level is an important preventive maintenance step. A consistently low oil level indicates oil leakage through damaged seals, defective gaskets or past worn rings or valve guides. If the oil looks milky in color or has water droplets in it, the cylinder head gasket(s) may be blown or the head(s) or block may be cracked. The engine should be checked immediately. The condition of the oil should also be checked. Whenever you check the oil level, slide your thumb and index finger up the dipstick before wiping off the oil. If you see small dirt or metal particles clinging to the dipstick, the oil should be changed (see Section 12).

4.14 The windshield washer fluid reservoir is located on the driver's side of the engine compartment - keep the level at or near the FULL line; fluid can be added after flipping up the cap

Engine coolant

Refer to illustration 4.8

Warning: *Do not allow antifreeze to come in contact with your skin or painted surfaces of the vehicle. Rinse off spills immediately with plenty of water. Antifreeze is highly toxic if ingested. Never leave antifreeze lying around in open containers or in puddles on the floor; children and pets are attracted by its sweet smell and may drink it. Check with local authorities about disposing of used antifreeze. Many communities have collection centers which will see that antifreeze is disposed of safely.*

8   All vehicles covered by this manual are equipped with a pressurized coolant recovery system. A white plastic coolant reserve or pressure bottle located on the driver's side of the engine compartment is connected by a hose to the radiator or radiator filler neck **(see illustration)**. If the engine overheats, coolant escapes through a valve in the radiator cap and travels through the hose into the reservoir. As the engine cools, the coolant is automatically drawn back into the cooling system to maintain the correct level.

9   The coolant level in the reservoir should be checked regularly. **Warning:** *Do not remove the radiator cap to check the coolant level when the engine is warm. The coolant level in the reservoir should be kept between the FULL and ADD marks on the side of the reservoir. If it is necessary to add coolant, allow the engine to cool, then remove the cap from the reservoir and add a 50/50 mixture of ethylene glycol-based antifreeze and water.*

10   Drive the vehicle and recheck the coolant level. If only a small amount of coolant is required to bring the system up to the proper level, water can be used. However, repeated additions of water will dilute the antifreeze and water solution. In order to maintain the proper ratio of antifreeze and water, always top up the coolant level with the correct mixture. An empty plastic milk jug or bleach bottle makes an excellent container

for mixing coolant. Do not use rust inhibitors or additives.

11   If the coolant level drops consistently, there may be a leak in the system. Inspect the radiator, hoses, filler cap, drain plugs and water pump (see Section 9). If no leaks are noted, have the radiator cap pressure tested by a service station.

12   If you have to remove the radiator cap, wait until the engine has cooled, then wrap a thick cloth around the cap and turn it to the first stop. If coolant or steam escapes, let the engine cool down longer, then remove the cap.

13   Check the condition of the coolant as well. It should be relatively clear. If it's brown or rust colored, the system should be drained, flushed and refilled. Even if the coolant appears to be normal, the corrosion inhibitors wear out, so it must be replaced at the specified intervals.

Windshield washer fluid

Refer to illustration 4.14

14   Fluid for the windshield washer system is located in a plastic reservoir in the engine compartment **(see illustration)**.

15   In milder climates, plain water can be used in the reservoir, but it should be kept no more than 2/3 full to allow for expansion if the water freezes. In colder climates, use windshield washer system antifreeze, available at any auto parts store, to lower the freezing point of the fluid. Mix the antifreeze with water in accordance with the manufacturer's directions on the container. **Caution:** *Don't use cooling system antifreeze - it will damage the vehicle's paint.*

16   To help prevent icing in cold weather, warm the windshield with the defroster before using the washer.

Battery electrolyte

17   All vehicles with which this manual is concerned are equipped with a battery which is permanently sealed (except for vent holes)

4.18a The clutch master cylinder is located next to the brake booster - maintain the fluid level between the MAX and MIN marks; you'll have to move the grille support rod to add fluid by first loosening the bolt (arrow) . . .

4.18b . . . then these nuts and swing the radiator grille support rod out of the way . . .

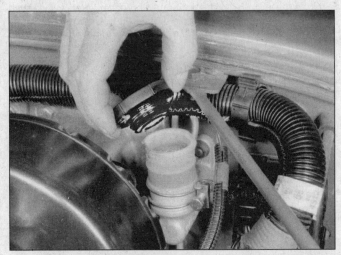

4.18c . . . so you can remove the cap and add fluid to the clutch reservoir - be sure to tighten everything securely afterward

4.19a Pry the clip off the brake master cylinder cover with a screwdriver (non-ABS models)

4.19b The brake fluid level should be kept 1/4-inch below the top edge of the reservoir

and has no filler caps. Water doesn't have to be added to these batteries at any time. If a maintenance-type battery is installed, the caps on the top of the battery should be removed periodically to check for a low water level. This check is most critical during the warm summer months.

Brake and clutch fluid

Refer to illustrations 4.18a, 4.18b, 4.18c, 4.19a and 4.19b

18 The brake master cylinder is mounted on the front of the power booster unit in the engine compartment. The clutch master cylinder used on manual transmissions is mounted adjacent to it on the firewall **(see illustration)**. The reservoir is translucent plastic so the fluid level can be checked visually. To add fluid, you'll have to loosen the nuts and swing the radiator grille support rod out of the way **(see illustrations)**. Be sure to tighten the bolt and nuts securely when you are finished.

19 On ABS-equipped models, unscrew both caps from the brake fluid reservoir. On non-ABS models, use a screwdriver to pry the brake fluid reservoir clip free; then remove the cover **(see illustrations)**. Be sure to wipe the top of the reservoir caps or cover with a clean rag to prevent contamination of the brake and/or clutch system before removing the caps or cover.

20 When adding fluid, pour it carefully into the reservoir to avoid spilling it onto surrounding painted surfaces. Be sure the specified fluid is used, since mixing different types of brake fluid can cause damage to the system. See *Recommended lubricants and fluids* at the front of this Chapter or your owner's manual. **Warning:** *Brake fluid can harm your eyes and damage painted surfaces, so use extreme caution when handling or pouring it. Do not use brake fluid that has been standing open or is more than one year old. Brake fluid absorbs moisture from the air. Excess moisture can cause a dangerous loss of braking effectiveness.*

21 At this time the fluid and master cylinder can be inspected for contamination. The sys-

5.2 Use a tire tread depth indicator to monitor tire wear - they are available at auto parts stores and service stations and cost very little

tem should be drained and refilled if deposits, dirt particles or water droplets are seen in the fluid.

22 After filling the reservoir to the proper level, make sure the cover or cap is on tight to prevent fluid leakage. Push the rubber gasket on the brake fluid cover up before reinstalling it so it doesn't hang down and cause the fluid to gush out.

23 The brake fluid level in the brake master cylinder will drop slightly as the pads and the brake shoes at each wheel wear down during normal operation. If the master cylinder requires repeated additions to keep it at the proper level, it's an indication of leakage in the brake system, which should be corrected immediately. Check all brake lines and connections (see Section 20 for more information).

24 If, upon checking the master cylinder fluid level, you discover one or both reservoirs empty or nearly empty, the brake system should be bled (see Chapter 9).

5   Tire and tire pressure checks

Refer to illustrations 5.2, 5.3, 5.4a, 5.4b and 5.8

1 Periodic inspection of the tires may spare you the inconvenience of being stranded with a flat tire. It can also provide you with vital information regarding possible problems in the steering and suspension systems before major damage occurs.

2 The original tires on this vehicle are equipped with 1/2-inch wide bands that will appear when tread depth reaches 1/16-inch, at which point the tires can be considered worn out. Tread wear can be monitored with a simple, inexpensive device known as a tread depth indicator **(see illustration)**.

3 Note any abnormal tread wear **(see illustration)**. Tread pattern irregularities such as cupping, flat spots and more wear on one side than the other are indications of front end alignment and/or balance problems. If any of these conditions are noted, take the

UNDERINFLATION

CUPPING

Cupping may be caused by:
- Underinflation and/or mechanical irregularities such as out-of-balance condition of wheel and/or tire, and bent or damaged wheel.
- Loose or worn steering tie-rod or steering idler arm.
- Loose, damaged or worn front suspension parts.

OVERINFLATION

INCORRECT TOE-IN OR EXTREME CAMBER

FEATHERING DUE TO MISALIGNMENT

5.3 This chart will help you determine the condition of the tires, the probable cause(s) of abnormal wear and the corrective action necessary

5.4a If a tire loses air on a steady basis, check the valve core first to make sure it's snug (special inexpensive wrenches are commonly available at auto parts stores)

5.4b If the valve core is tight, raise the corner of the vehicle with the low tire and spray a soapy solution onto the tread as the tire is turned slowly - leaks will cause small bubbles to appear

5.8 To extend the life of the tires, check the air pressure at least once a week with an accurate gauge (don't forget the spare!)

vehicle to a tire shop or service station to correct the problem.

4   Look closely for cuts, punctures and embedded nails or tacks. Sometimes a tire will hold air pressure for a short time or leak down very slowly after a nail has embedded itself in the tread. If a slow leak persists, check the valve stem core to make sure it's tight **(see illustration)**. Examine the tread for an object that may have embedded itself in the tire or for a "plug" that may have begun to leak (radial tire punctures are repaired with a plug that's installed in a puncture). If a puncture is suspected, it can be easily verified by spraying a solution of soapy water onto the puncture area **(see illustration)**. The soapy solution will bubble if there's a leak. Unless the puncture is unusually large, a tire shop or service station can usually repair the tire.

5   Carefully inspect the inner sidewall of each tire for evidence of brake fluid leakage. If you see any, inspect the brakes immediately.

6   Correct air pressure adds miles to the lifespan of the tires, improves mileage and enhances overall ride quality. Tire pressure cannot be accurately estimated by looking at a tire, especially if it's a radial. The correct tire pressures are located on a label on the inside of the glove box door. A tire pressure gauge is essential. Keep an accurate gauge in the vehicle. The pressure gauges attached to the nozzles of air hoses at gas stations are often inaccurate.

7   Always check tire pressure when the tires are cold. Cold, in this case, means the vehicle has not been driven over a mile in the three hours preceding a tire pressure check. A pressure rise of four to eight pounds is not uncommon once the tires are warm.

8   Unscrew the valve cap protruding from the wheel or hubcap and push the gauge firmly onto the valve stem **(see illustration)**. Note the reading on the gauge and compare the figure to the recommended tire pressure shown on the placard on the driver's side

door pillar. Be sure to reinstall the valve cap to keep dirt and moisture out of the valve stem mechanism. Check all four tires and, if necessary, add enough air to bring them up to the recommended pressure.

9   Don't forget to keep the spare tire inflated to the specified pressure (refer to your owner's manual or the tire sidewall). Note that the pressure recommended for the compact spare is higher than for the tires on the vehicle.

6   Automatic transmission fluid level check

Refer to illustration 6.6

1   The automatic transmission fluid level should be carefully maintained. Low fluid level can lead to slipping or loss of drive, while overfilling can cause foaming and loss of fluid.

2   Warm the transmission by driving the vehicle at least 15 miles. With the parking brake set, start the engine, then move the shift lever through all the gear ranges, ending in Neutral. The fluid level must be checked with the vehicle level and the engine running at idle.

3   With the transmission at normal operating temperature, remove the dipstick from the filler tube. The dipstick is located at the rear of the engine compartment, near the firewall on the passenger's side.

4   Wipe the fluid from the dipstick with a clean rag and push it back into the filler tube until the cap seats.

5   Pull the dipstick out again and note the fluid level.

6   The level should be between the ADD and FULL marks **(see illustration)**. If additional fluid is required, add it directly into the tube using a funnel. It takes about one pint to raise the level from the ADD mark to the FULL mark with a warm transmission, so add the fluid a little at a time and keep checking the level until it's correct.

6.6 The automatic transmission dipstick is located in the long tube at the rear of the engine compartment on the passenger's side

**7.5 Twist the cap counterclockwise and
lift it out of the reservoir**

**7.6 The power steering fluid dipstick is
marked on both sides so the level can be
checked with the fluid hot or cold**

7   The condition of the fluid should also be
checked along with the level. If the fluid at the
end of the dipstick is a dark reddish-brown
color, or if it smells burned, it should be
changed. If you are in doubt about the condition of the fluid, purchase some new fluid and
compare the two for color and smell.

7   Power steering fluid level check

Refer to illustrations 7.5 and 7.6
1   Unlike manual steering, the power steering system relies on fluid which may, over a
period of time, require replenishing.
2   The fluid reservoir for the power steering
pump is located on the pump body at the
front of the engine.
3   For the check, the front wheels should
be pointed straight ahead and the engine
should be off.
4   Use a clean rag to wipe off the reservoir
cap and the area around the cap. This will
help prevent any foreign matter from entering
the reservoir during the check.
5   Twist off the cap and check the temperature of the fluid at the end of the dipstick
with your finger **(see illustration)**.

6   Wipe off the fluid with a clean rag, rein-
sert the dipstick, then withdraw it and read
the fluid level. The level should be at the
FULL HOT mark if the fluid was hot to the
touch **(see illustrations)**. It should be at the
FULL COLD mark if the fluid was cool to the
touch. Never allow the fluid level to drop
below the ADD mark.
7   If additional fluid is required, pour the
specified type directly into the reservoir,
using a funnel to prevent spills.
8   If the reservoir requires frequent fluid
additions, all power steering hoses, hose
connections and the power steering pump
should be carefully checked for leaks.

8   Battery check, maintenance and charging

*Refer to illustrations 8.1, 8.8a, 8.8b, 8.8c and
8.8d*
Warning: *Certain precautions must be followed when checking and servicing the battery. Hydrogen gas, which is highly
flammable, is always present in the battery
cells, so keep lighted tobacco and all other
open flames and sparks away from the battery. The electrolyte in the battery cells is
actually dilute sulfuric acid, which will cause
injury if splashed on your skin or in your eyes.
It will also ruin clothes and painted surfaces.
When removing the battery cables, always
detach the negative cable first and hook it up
last!*
1   Battery maintenance is an important
procedure which will help ensure that you're
not stranded because of a dead battery. Several tools are required for this procedure **(see
illustration)**.
2   Before servicing the battery, always turn
the engine and all accessories off and disconnect the cable from the negative terminal.
3   A sealed (sometimes called maintenance-free) battery is standard equipment on
these vehicles. The cell caps cannot be
removed, no electrolyte checks are required
and water cannot be added to the cells.
However, if an aftermarket battery that
requires regular maintenance has been
installed, the following procedure can be
used.
4   Check the electrolyte level in each of the
battery cells. It must be above the plates.
There's usually a split-ring indicator in each
cell to indicate the correct level. If the level is
low, add distilled water only, then install the
cell caps. **Caution:** *Overfilling the cells may
cause electrolyte to spill over during periods
of heavy charging, causing corrosion and
damage to nearby components.*
5   If the positive terminal and cable clamp
on your vehicle's battery is equipped with a
rubber protector, make sure that it's not torn
or damaged. It should completely cover the
terminal.
6   The external condition of the battery
should be checked periodically. Look for
damage such as a cracked case.

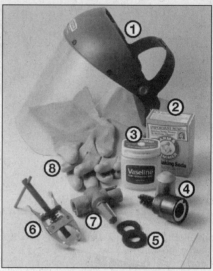

**8.1 Tools and materials required for
battery maintenance**

1   *Face shield/safety goggles - When
removing corrosion with a brush, the
acidic particles can easily fly up into
your eyes*
2   *Baking soda - A solution of baking
soda and water can be used to
neutralize corrosion*
3   *Petroleum jelly - A layer of this on the
battery posts will help prevent
corrosion*
4   *Battery post/cable cleaner - This
wire brush cleaning tool will remove all
traces of corrosion from the battery
posts and cable clamps*
5   *Treated felt washers - Placing one of
these on each post, directly under the
cable clamps, will help prevent
corrosion*
6   *Puller - Sometimes the cable clamps
are very difficult to pull off the posts,
even after the nut/bolt has been
completely loosened. This tool pulls
the clamps straight up and off the post
without damage*
7   *Battery post/cable cleaner - Here is
another cleaning tool which is a
slightly different version of number 4
above, but it does the same thing*
8   *Rubber gloves - Another safety item
to consider when servicing the battery;
remember that's acid inside the
battery!*

7   Check the tightness of the battery cable
clamps to ensure good electrical connections
and inspect the entire length of each cable,
looking for cracked or abraded insulation and
frayed conductors.
8   If corrosion (visible as white, fluffy
deposits) is evident, remove the cables from
the terminals, clean them with a battery brush
and reinstall them **(see illustrations)**. Corrosion can be kept to a minimum by installing
specially treated washers available at auto
parts stores or by applying a layer of

8.8a Battery terminal corrosion usually appears as light fluffy powder

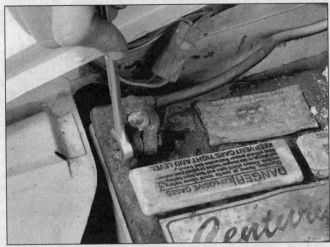

8.8b Removing the cable from a battery post with a wrench - sometimes special battery pliers are required for this procedure if corrosion has caused deterioration of the hex nut (always remove the ground cable first and hook it up last!)

8.8c Regardless of the type of tool used on the battery posts, a clean, shiny surface should be the result

8.8d When cleaning the cable clamps, all corrosion must be removed (the inside of the clamp is tapered to match the taper on the post, so don't remove too much material)

petroleum jelly or grease to the terminals and cable clamps after they are assembled.

9   Make sure that the battery carrier is in good condition and that the hold-down clamp bolt is tight. If the battery is removed (see Chapter 5 for the removal and installation procedure), make sure that no parts remain in the bottom of the carrier when it's reinstalled. When reinstalling the hold-down clamp, don't overtighten the bolt.

10   Corrosion on the carrier, battery case and surrounding areas can be removed with a solution of water and baking soda. Apply the mixture with a small brush, let it work, then rinse it off with plenty of clean water.

11   Any metal parts of the vehicle damaged by corrosion should be coated with a zinc-based primer, then painted.

Charging

12   Remove all of the cell caps (if equipped) and cover the holes with a clean cloth to prevent spattering electrolyte. Disconnect the negative battery cable and hook the battery charger leads to the battery posts (positive to positive, negative to negative), then plug in the charger. Make sure it is set at 12 volts if it has a selector switch.

13   If you're using a charger with a rate higher than two amps, check the battery regularly during charging to make sure it doesn't overheat. If you're using a trickle charger, you can safely let the battery charge overnight after you've checked it regularly for the first couple of hours.

14   If the battery has removable cell caps, measure the specific gravity with a hydrometer every hour during the last few hours of the charging cycle. Hydrometers are available inexpensively from auto parts stores - follow the instructions that come with the hydrometer. Consider the battery charged when there's no change in the specific gravity read-

ing for two hours and the electrolyte in the cells is gassing (bubbling) freely. The specific gravity reading from each cell should be very close to the others. If not, the battery probably has a bad cell(s).

15   Some batteries with sealed tops have built-in hydrometers on the top that indicate the state of charge by the color displayed in the hydrometer window. Normally, a bright-colored hydrometer indicates a full charge and a dark hydrometer indicates the battery still needs charging. Check the battery manufacturer's instructions to be sure you know what the colors mean.

16   If the battery has a sealed top and no built-in hydrometer, you can hook up a digital voltmeter across the battery terminals to check the charge. A fully charged battery should read 12.6 volts or higher.

17   Further information on the battery and jump starting can be found in Chapter 5 and at the front of this manual.

Check for a chafed area that could fail prematurely.

Check for a soft area indicating the hose has deteriorated inside.

Overtightening the clamp on a hardened hose will damage the hose and cause a leak.

Check each hose for swelling and oil-soaked ends. Cracks and breaks can be located by squeezing the hose.

9.4 Hoses, like drivebelts, have a habit of failing at the worst possible time - to prevent the inconvenience of a blown radiator or heater hose, inspect them carefully as shown here

9   Cooling system check

Refer to illustration 9.4

1   Many major engine failures can be attributed to a faulty cooling system. If the vehicle is equipped with an automatic transmission, the cooling system also cools the transmission fluid and thus plays an important role in prolonging transmission life.

2   The cooling system should be checked with the engine cold. Do this before the vehicle is driven for the day or after it has been shut off for at least three hours.

3   Remove the radiator cap by turning it to the left until it reaches a stop. If you hear a hissing sound (indicating there is still pressure in the system), wait until this stops. Now press down on the cap with the palm of your hand and continue turning to the left until the cap can be pulled off. Thoroughly clean the

cap, inside and out, with clean water. Also clean the filler neck on the radiator. All traces of corrosion should be removed. On inline six-cylinder engines, unscrew the cap on the coolant pressure bottle and clean the cap. The coolant inside the radiator or pressure bottle should be relatively transparent. If it is rust colored, the system should be drained and refilled (see Section 38). If the coolant level is not up to the top, add additional antifreeze/coolant mixture (see Section 4).

4   Carefully check the large upper and lower radiator hoses along with the smaller diameter heater hoses which run from the engine to the firewall. On some models the heater return hose runs directly to the radiator. Inspect each hose along its entire length, replacing any hose which is cracked, swollen or shows signs of deterioration. Cracks may become more apparent if the hose is squeezed **(see illustration)**. Regardless of condition, it's a good idea to replace hoses with new ones every two years.

5   Make sure that all hose connections are tight. A leak in the cooling system will usually show up as white or rust colored deposits on the areas adjoining the leak. If wire-type clamps are used at the ends of the hoses, it may be a good idea to replace them with more secure screw-type clamps.

6   Use compressed air or a soft brush to remove bugs, leaves, etc. from the front of the radiator or air conditioning condenser. Be careful not to damage the delicate cooling fins or cut yourself on them.

7   Every other inspection, or at the first indication of cooling system problems, have the cap and system pressure tested. If you don't have a pressure tester, most gas stations and repair shops will do this for a minimal charge.

10   Underhood hose check and replacement

General

1   **Caution:** *Replacement of air conditioning hoses must be left to a dealer service department or air conditioning shop that has the equipment to depressurize the system safely. Never remove air conditioning components or hoses until the system has been depressurized.*

2   High temperatures in the engine compartment can cause the deterioration of the rubber and plastic hoses used for engine, accessory and emission systems operation. Periodic inspection should be made for cracks, loose clamps, material hardening and leaks. Information specific to the cooling system hoses can be found in Section 9.

3   Some, but not all, hoses are secured to the fittings with clamps. Where clamps are used, check to be sure they haven't lost their tension, allowing the hose to leak. If clamps aren't used, make sure the hose has not expanded and/or hardened where it slips over the fitting, allowing it to leak.

Vacuum hoses

4   It's quite common for vacuum hoses, especially those in the emissions system, to be color coded or identified by colored stripes molded into them. Various systems require hoses with different wall thicknesses, collapse resistance and temperature resistance. When replacing hoses, be sure the new ones are made of the same material.

5   Often the only effective way to check a hose is to remove it completely from the vehicle. If more than one hose is removed, be sure to label the hoses and fittings to ensure correct installation.

6   When checking vacuum hoses, be sure to include any plastic T-fittings in the check. Inspect the fittings for cracks and the hose where it fits over the fitting for distortion, which could cause leakage.

7   A small piece of vacuum hose (1/4-inch inside diameter) can be used as a stethoscope to detect vacuum leaks. Hold one end of the hose to your ear and probe around vacuum hoses and fittings, listening for the "hissing" sound characteristic of a vacuum leak. **Warning:** *When probing with the vacuum hose stethoscope, be very careful not to come into contact with moving engine components such as the drivebelt, cooling fan, etc.*

Fuel hoses

Warning: *There are certain precautions which must be taken when inspecting or servicing fuel system components. Work in a well ventilated area and do not allow open flames (cigarettes, appliance pilot lights, etc.) or bare light bulbs near the work area. Mop up any spills immediately and do not store fuel soaked rags where they could ignite. On vehicles equipped with fuel injection, the fuel system is under pressure, so if any fuel lines are to be disconnected, the pressure in the system must be relieved first (see Chapter 4 for more information).*

8   Check all rubber fuel lines for deterioration and chafing. Check especially for cracks in areas where the hose bends and just before fittings, such as where a hose attaches to the fuel filter.

9   High quality fuel line, usually identified by the word *Fluroelastomer* printed on the hose, should be used for fuel line replacement. Never, under any circumstances, use unreinforced vacuum line, clear plastic tubing or water hose for fuel lines.

10   Spring-type clamps are commonly used on fuel lines. These clamps often lose their tension over a period of time, and can be "sprung" during removal. Replace all spring-type clamps with screw clamps whenever a hose is replaced.

Metal lines

11   Sections of metal line are often used for fuel line between the fuel pump and carburetor or fuel injection unit. Check carefully to be sure the line has not been bent or crimped and that cracks have not started in the line.

11.6 Lift the release lever up (arrow) and slide the wiper off the stud on the arm

12   If a section of metal fuel line must be replaced, only seamless steel tubing should be used, since copper and aluminum tubing don't have the strength necessary to withstand normal engine vibration.

13   Check the metal brake lines where they enter the master cylinder and brake proportioning unit (if used) for cracks in the lines or loose fittings. Any sign of brake fluid leakage calls for an immediate thorough inspection of the brake system.

11 Wiper blade inspection and replacement

Refer to illustration 11.6

1   The windshield wiper and blade assembly should be inspected periodically for damage, loose components and cracked or worn blade elements.

2   Road film can build up on the wiper blades and affect their efficiency, so they should be washed regularly with a mild detergent solution.

3   The action of the wiping mechanism can loosen the bolts, nuts and fasteners, so they should be checked and tightened, as necessary, at the same time the wiper blades are checked.

4   If the wiper blade elements (sometimes called inserts) are cracked, worn or warped, the blade assemblies should be replaced with new ones.

5   Pull the wiper blade/arm assembly away from the glass.

6   Lift the release lever and slide the blade assembly off the wiper arm and over the retaining stud **(see illustration)**. The blade/element assembly must be replaced as a unit.

7   Compare the new blade assembly to the old one for length, design, etc.

8   Reinstall the blade assembly on the arm, wet the windshield and check for proper operation.

12 Engine oil and filter change

Refer to illustrations 12.3, 12.9, 12.14, 12.16 and 12.18

1   Frequent oil changes are the most important preventive maintenance procedures that can be done by the home mechanic. As engine oil ages, it becomes diluted and contaminated, which leads to premature engine wear.

2   Although some sources recommend oil filter changes every other oil change, we feel that the minimal cost of an oil filter and the relative ease with which it is installed dictate that a new filter be installed every time the oil is changed.

3   Gather together all necessary tools and materials before beginning this procedure **(see illustration)**.

4   You should have plenty of clean rags and newspapers handy to mop up any spills. Access to the underside of the vehicle is greatly improved if the vehicle can be lifted on a hoist, driven onto ramps or supported by jackstands. **Warning:** *Do not work under a vehicle which is supported only by a bumper, hydraulic or scissors-type jack.*

5   If this is your first oil change, get under the vehicle and familiarize yourself with the locations of the oil drain plug and the oil filter. The engine and exhaust components will be warm during the actual work, so note how they are situated to avoid touching them when working under the vehicle.

6   Warm the engine to normal operating temperature. If the new oil or any tools are needed, use this warm-up time to gather everything necessary for the job. The correct type of oil for your application can be found in *Recommended lubricants and fluids* at the beginning of this Chapter.

7   With the engine oil warm (warm engine oil will drain better and more built-up sludge will be removed with it), raise and support the vehicle. Make sure it's safely supported!

8   Move all necessary tools, rags and newspapers under the vehicle. Set the drain pan under the drain plug. Keep in mind that the oil will initially flow from the pan with some force; position the pan accordingly.

9   Being careful not to touch any of the hot exhaust components, use a wrench to remove the drain plug near the bottom of the oil pan **(see illustration)**. Depending on how hot the oil is, you may want to wear gloves while unscrewing the plug the final few turns.

10   Allow the old oil to drain into the pan. It may be necessary to move the pan as the oil flow slows to a trickle.

11   After all the oil has drained, wipe off the drain plug with a clean rag. Small metal particles may cling to the plug and would immediately contaminate the new oil.

12   Clean the area around the drain plug opening and reinstall the plug. Tighten the plug securely with the wrench. If a torque wrench is available, use it to tighten the plug.

13   Move the drain pan into position under the oil filter.

12.3 These tools are required when changing the engine oil and filter

1   *Drain pan - It should be fairly shallow in depth, but wide to prevent spills*

2   *Rubber gloves - When removing the drain plug and filter, you will get oil on your hands (the gloves will prevent burns)*

3   *Breaker bar - Sometime the oil drain plug is tight and a long breaker bar is needed to loosen it*

4   *Socket - To be used with the breaker bar or a ratchet (must be the correct size to fit the drain plug - six-point preferred)*

5   *Filter wrench - This is a metal band-type wrench, which requires clearance around the filter to be effective*

6   *Filter wrench - This type fits on the bottom of the filter and can be turned with a ratchet or breaker bar (different size wrenches are available for different types of filters)*

12.9 Use the correct size box-end wrench or six-point socket to avoid rounding off the drain plug when removing or installing it

12.14 The oil filter is on very tight and will require a special wrench for removal - DO NOT use the wrench to tighten the new filter

12.16 Some six-cylinder engines use a metric 20 mm filter - if the old filter is so marked, make sure the new one is too

12.18 Lubricate the oil filter gasket with clean engine oil before installing the filter on the engine

14   Use the filter wrench to loosen the oil filter **(see illustration)**. Chain or metal band filter wrenches may distort the filter canister, but it doesn't matter since the filter will be discarded anyway.

15   Completely unscrew the old filter. Be careful; it's full of oil. Empty the oil inside the filter into the drain pan.

16   Compare the old filter with the new one to make sure they're the same type **(see illustration)**.

17   Use a clean rag to remove all oil, dirt and sludge from the area where the oil filter mounts to the engine. Check the old filter to make sure the rubber gasket isn't stuck to the engine. If the gasket is stuck to the engine (use a flashlight if necessary), remove it.

18   Apply a light coat of clean oil to the rubber gasket on the new oil filter **(see illustration)**.

19   Attach the new filter to the engine, following the tightening directions printed on the filter canister or packing box. Most filter manufacturers recommend against using a filter wrench due to the possibility of overtightening and damage to the seal.

20   Remove all tools, rags, etc. from under the vehicle, being careful not to spill the oil in the drain pan, then lower the vehicle.

21   Move to the engine compartment and locate the oil filler cap.

22   If an oil can spout is used, push the spout into the top of the oil can and pour the fresh oil through the filler opening. A funnel may also be used.

23   On four-cylinder engines, pour four quarts of fresh oil into the engine. On inline six-cylinder engines, pour in five quarts. Wait a few minutes to allow the oil to drain into the pan, then check the level on the oil dipstick (see Section 4 if necessary). If the oil level is above the ADD mark, start the engine and allow the new oil to circulate.

24   Run the engine for only about a minute checking the pressure gauge or indicator light to make sure normal oil pressure is achieved. Shut off the engine. Immediately

look under the vehicle and check for leaks at the oil pan drain plug and around the oil filter. If either is leaking, tighten with a bit more force.

25   With the new oil circulated and the filter now completely full, recheck the level on the dipstick and add more oil as necessary.

26   During the first few trips after an oil change, make it a point to check frequently for leaks and proper oil level.

27   The old oil drained from the engine cannot be reused in its present state and should be disposed of. Oil reclamation centers, and some recycling centers will accept the oil, which can be refined and used again. After the oil has cooled it can be drained into a suitable container (capped plastic jugs, topped bottles, milk cartons, etc.) for transport to one of these disposal sites.

13   Chassis lubrication

Refer to illustrations 13.1, 13.6, 13.9 and 13.10

1   Refer to *Recommended lubricants and fluids* at the front of this Chapter to obtain the necessary grease, etc. You will also need a grease gun **(see illustration)**. Occasionally plugs will be installed rather than grease fittings. If so, grease fittings will have to be purchased and installed.

2   Look under the vehicle for grease fittings or plugs on the steering, suspension, and driveline components. They are normally found on the balljoints, tie-rod ends and universal joints. If there are plugs, remove them and buy grease fittings, which will thread into the component. A dealer or auto parts store will be able to supply the correct fittings. Straight, as well as angled, fittings are available.

3   For easier access under the vehicle, raise it with a jack and place jackstands under the frame. Make sure it is safely supported by the stands. If the wheels are to be removed at this interval for tire rotation or brake inspection, loosen the lug nuts slightly while the vehicle is still on the ground.

13.1 Materials required for chassis and body lubrication

1   **Engine oil -** *Light engine oil in a can like this can be used for door and hood hinges*

2   **Graphite spray -** *Used to lubricate lock cylinders*

3   **Grease -** *Grease, in a variety of types and weights, is available for use in a grease gun, check the Specifications for your requirements*

4   **Grease gun -** *A common grease gun, shown here with a detachable hose and nozzle, is needed for chassis lubrication. After use, clean it thoroughly!*

4   Before beginning, force a little grease out of the nozzle to remove any dirt from the end of the gun. Wipe the nozzle clean with a rag.

5   With the grease gun and plenty of clean rags, crawl under the vehicle and begin lubricating the components.

6   Wipe the balljoint grease fitting nipple clean and push the nozzle firmly over it.

13.6 Pump grease into the steering end fittings until the boot is firm

13.9 The slip joint grease fitting is located on the collar - pump grease into it until it comes out of the collar

13.10 You may have to rotate the Driveshaft for access to the universal joint grease fitting - pump grease into it until grease can be seen coming out of the contact surfaces

Squeeze the trigger on the grease gun to force grease into the component. The balljoints should be lubricated until the rubber seal is firm to the touch. Do not pump too much grease into the fittings as it could rupture the seal. For all other suspension and steering components, continue pumping grease into the fitting until it oozes out of the joint between the two components (see illustration). If it escapes around the grease gun nozzle, the nipple is clogged or the nozzle is not completely seated on the fitting. Resecure the gun nozzle to the fitting and try again. If necessary, replace the fitting with a new one.

7   Wipe the excess grease from the components and the grease fitting. Repeat the procedure for the remaining fittings.

8   Lubricate the transfer case shift mechanism contact surfaces with clean engine oil.

9   Lubricate the driveshaft slip joint by pumping grease into the fitting until it can be seen coming out of the slip joint seal (see illustration)

10   Lubricate conventional universal joints until grease can be seen coming out of the contact points (see illustration).

11   While you are under the vehicle, clean and lubricate the parking brake cable along with the cable guides and levers. This can be done by smearing some chassis grease onto the cable and its related parts with your fingers.

12   The manual steering gear seldom requires the addition of lubricant, but if there is obvious leakage of grease at the seals, remove the plug or cover and check the lubricant level. If the level is low, add the specified lubricant.

13   Lubricate the contact points on the steering knuckle and adjustment bolt.

14   Open the hood and smear a little chassis grease on the hood latch mechanism. Have an assistant pull the hood release lever from inside the vehicle as you lubricate the cable at the latch.

15   Lubricate all the hinges (door, hood, etc.) with engine oil to keep them in proper working order.

16   The key lock cylinders can be lubricated with spray-on graphite or silicone lubricant, which is available at auto parts stores.

17   Lubricate the door weatherstripping with silicone spray. This will reduce chafing and retard wear.

14   Suspension and steering check

1   Indications of a fault in these systems are excessive play in the steering wheel before the front wheels react, excessive sway around corners, body movement over rough roads, noise from the axle or wheel areas or binding at some point as the steering wheel is turned.

2   Raise the front of the vehicle periodically and visually check the suspension and steering components for wear. Because of the work to be done, make sure the vehicle cannot fall from the stands.

3   Check the wheel bearings. Do this by spinning the front wheels. Listen for any abnormal noises and watch to make sure the wheel spins true (doesn't wobble). Grab the top and bottom of the tire and pull in-and-out on it. Notice any movement which would indicate a loose wheel bearing assembly. If the bearings are suspect, refer to Chapter 10 for more information.

4   From under the vehicle, check for loose bolts, broken or disconnected parts and deteriorated rubber bushings on all suspension and steering components. Look for grease or fluid leaking from the steering assembly. Check the power steering hoses and connections for leaks.

5   Have an assistant turn the steering wheel from side-to-side and check the steering components for free movement, chafing and binding. If the steering doesn't react simultaneously with the movement of the steering wheel, try to determine where the slack is located.

15   Exhaust system check

1   With the engine cold (at least three hours after the vehicle has been driven), check the complete exhaust system from the manifold to the end of the tailpipe. Be careful around the catalytic converter, which may be hot even after three hours. The inspection should be done with the vehicle on a hoist to permit unrestricted access. If a hoist isn't available, raise the vehicle and support it securely on jackstands.

2   Check the exhaust pipes and connections for signs of leakage and/or corrosion indicating a potential failure. Make sure that all brackets and hangers are in good condition and tight.

3   Inspect the underside of the body for holes, corrosion, open seams, etc. which may allow exhaust gases to enter the passenger compartment. Seal all body openings with silicone or body putty.

4   Rattles and other noises can often be traced to the exhaust system, especially the hangers, mounts and heat shields. Try to move the pipes, mufflers and catalytic converter. If the components can come in contact with the body or suspension parts, secure the exhaust system with new brackets and hangers.

16   Manual transmission lubricant level check

Refer to illustration 16.1

1   The manual transmission has a fill plug which must be removed to check the lubricant level (see illustration). If the vehicle is raised to gain access to the plug, be sure to support it safely on jackstands - DO NOT crawl under a vehicle which is supported only by a jack!

2   Remove the fill plug from the transmission and use your little finger to reach inside the housing to feel the oil level. The level

16.1 The manual transmission fill plug (arrow) is mounted high on the passenger's side of the case - you'll need a hand pump to add oil

17.2a Front differentials use a screw-in check/fill plug - use a 3/8 inch drive ratchet and extension to remove it

17.2b The rear differential check/fill plug is rubber, pry it out with a screwdriver

17.3 Some axle housings have a tag (arrow) which contains information on the differential

18.1 The transfer case drain and fill plugs (arrows) are located on the front face of the housing - the upper one is the check/fill plug and the lower one is the drain plug

RADIAL TIRE ROTATION

1-AJ HAYNES

19.2 The recommended tire rotation pattern for these vehicles

---

should be at or near the bottom of the plug hole.

3   If it isn't, add the recommended oil through the plug hole with a syringe or squeeze bottle.

4   Install and tighten the plug and check for leaks after the first few miles of driving.

17   Differential lubricant level check

Refer to illustrations 17.2a, 17.2b and 17.3
Note: *4WD vehicles have two differentials - one in the center of each axle. Be sure to check the lubricant level in both differentials.*

1   The differential has a check/fill plug which must be removed to check the lubricant level. If the vehicle must be raised to gain access to the plug, be sure to support it safely on jackstands - DO NOT crawl under the vehicle when it's supported only by the jack.

2   Remove the oil check/fill plug from the back of the rear differential or the front of the

front differential **(see illustrations)**.

3   The oil level should be at the bottom of the plug opening. If it isn't, use a syringe to add the specified lubricant until it just starts to run out of the opening. On some models a tag is located in the area of the plug which gives information regarding lubricant type, particularly on models equipped with a limited slip differential **(see illustration)**.

4   Install the plug and tighten it securely.

18   Transfer case lubricant level check

Refer to illustration 18.1

1   The transfer case lubricant level is checked by removing the upper plug located in the side of the case **(see illustration)**.

2   After removing the plug, reach inside the hole. The lubricant level should be just at the bottom of the hole. If not, add the appropriate lubricant through the opening.

19   Tire rotation

Refer to illustration 19.2

1   The tires should be rotated at the specified intervals and whenever uneven wear is noticed.

2   Refer to the accompanying illustration for the preferred tire rotation pattern **(see illustration)**.

3   Refer to the information in *Jacking and towing* at the front of this manual for the proper procedures to follow when raising the vehicle and changing a tire. If the brakes are to be checked, don't apply the parking brake as stated. Make sure the tires are blocked to prevent the vehicle from rolling as it's raised.

4   Preferably, the entire vehicle should be raised at the same time. This can be done on a hoist or by jacking up each corner and then lowering the vehicle onto jackstands placed under the frame rails. Always use four jackstands and make sure the vehicle is safely supported.

20.6 You will find an inspection hole like this in each caliper - placing a steel ruler across the window should enable you to determine the thickness of remaining pad materials for both the inner and outer pads (arrows)

20.12 If the lining is bonded to the brake shoe, measure the lining thickness from the outer surface to the metal shoe, as show here; if the lining is riveted to the shoe, measure from the lining outer surface to the rivet head

20.14 Peel the wheel cylinder boot back carefully and check for leaking fluid - any leakage indicates the cylinder must be replaced or rebuilt

5   After rotation, check and adjust the tire pressures as necessary and be sure to check the lug nut tightness.

6   For additional information on the wheels and tires, refer to Chapter 10.

20 Brake check

Refer to illustrations 20.6, 20.12 and 20.14
Note: *For detailed photographs of the brake system, refer to Chapter 9.*
Warning: *Brake system dust may contain asbestos, which is hazardous to your health. DO NOT blow it out with compressed air and DO NOT inhale it. DO NOT use gasoline or solvents to remove the dust. Use brake system cleaner or denatured alcohol only.*

1   In addition to the specified intervals, the brakes should be inspected every time the wheels are removed or whenever a defect is suspected.

2   To check the brakes, raise the vehicle and place it securely on jackstands. Remove the wheels (see *Jacking and towing* at the front of the manual, if necessary).

Disc brakes

3   Disc brakes are used on the front wheels. Extensive rotor damage can occur if the pads are not replaced when needed.

4   These vehicles are equipped with a wear sensor attached to the inner pad. This is a small, bent piece of metal which is visible from the inner side of the brake caliper. When the pad wears to the specified limit, the metal sensor rubs against the rotor and makes a squealing sound.

5   The disc brake calipers, which contain the pads, are visible with the wheels removed. There is an outer pad and an inner pad in each caliper. All pads should be inspected.

6   Each caliper has an inspection hole to inspect the pads. Check the thickness of the pad lining by looking into the caliper at each end and down through the inspection hole at the top of the housing **(see illustration)**. If the wear sensor is very close to the rotor or the pad material has worn to about 1/8-inch or less, the pads should be replaced.

7   If you're unsure about the exact thickness of the remaining lining material, remove the pads for further inspection or replacement (refer to Chapter 9).

8   Before installing the wheels, check for leakage and/or damage (cracks, splitting, etc.) around the brake hose connections. Replace the hose or fittings as necessary, referring to Chapter 9.

9   Check the condition of the disc. Look for score marks, deep scratches and burned spots. If any of these conditions exist, the hub/disc assembly should be removed for servicing (see Chapter 9).

Drum brakes

10   On rear brakes, remove the drum by pulling it off the axle and brake assembly (see Chapter 9).

11   With the drum removed, do not touch any brake dust (see the Warning at the beginning of this Section).

12   Note the thickness of the lining material on both the front and rear brake shoes. If the material has worn away to within 1/16-inch of the recessed rivets or metal backing, the shoes should be replaced **(see illustration)**. The shoes should also be replaced if they're cracked, glazed (shiny surface) or contaminated with brake fluid.

13   Make sure that all the brake assembly springs are connected and in good condition.

14   Check the brake components for any signs of fluid leakage. With your finger or a small screwdriver, carefully pry back the rubber cups on the wheel cylinders located at the top of the brake shoes **(see illustration)**. Any leakage is an indication that the wheel cylinders should be overhauled immediately (see Chapter 9). Also check brake hoses and connections for signs of leakage.

15   Wipe the inside of the drum with a clean rag and brake cleaner or denatured alcohol. Again, be careful not to breath the dangerous asbestos dust.

16   Check the inside of the drum for cracks, score marks, deep scratches and hard spots, which will appear as small discolorations. If these imperfections cannot be removed with fine emery cloth, the drum must be taken to a machine shop equipped to turn the drums.

17   If after the inspection process all parts are in good working condition, reinstall the brake drum (see Chapter 9).

18   Install the wheels and lower the vehicle.

Parking brake

19   The parking brake operates from a foot pedal and locks the rear brake system. The easiest, and perhaps most obvious method of periodically checking the operation of the parking brake assembly is to park the vehicle on a steep hill with the parking brake set and the transmission in Neutral. If the parking brake cannot prevent the vehicle from rolling, it's in need of adjustment (see Chapter 9).

21 Fuel system check

Warning: *Take certain precautions when inspecting or servicing the fuel system components. Work in a well ventilated area and don't allow open flames (cigarettes, appliance pilot lights, etc.) in the work area. Mop up spills immediately and don't store fuel soaked rags where they could ignite. On fuel-injected models the fuel system is under pressure. No components should be disconnected until the pressure has been relieved (see Chapter 4).*

1   On all models, the fuel tank is located under the rear of the vehicle, covered by a shield.

2   The fuel system is most easily checked with the vehicle raised on a hoist so the components underneath the vehicle are readily

visible and accessible.

3   If the smell of gasoline is noticed while driving or after the vehicle has been in the sun, the system should be thoroughly inspected immediately.

4   Remove the gas tank cap and check it for damage, corrosion and an unbroken sealing imprint on the gasket. Replace the cap with a new one if necessary.

5   With the vehicle raised, check the gas tank and filler neck for punctures, cracks and other damage. The connection between the filler neck and the tank is especially critical. Sometimes a rubber filler neck will leak due to loose clamps or deteriorated rubber; these are problems a home mechanic can usually rectify. **Warning:** *Do not, under any circumstances, try to repair a fuel tank yourself (except rubber components). A welding torch or any open flame can easily cause the fuel vapors to explode if the proper precautions are not taken!*

6   Carefully check all rubber hoses and metal lines attached to the fuel tank. Look for loose connections, deteriorated hoses, crimped lines and other damage. Follow the lines to the front of the vehicle, carefully inspecting them all the way. Repair or replace damaged sections as necessary.

7   If a fuel odor is still evident after the inspection, refer to Section 40.

22   Carburetor choke check

1   The choke operates only when the engine is cold, so this check should be performed before the engine has been started for the day.

2   Remove the top plate of the air cleaner assembly. It's usually held in place by a wing nut at the center. If any vacuum hoses must be disconnected, make sure you tag the hoses for reinstallation in their original positions. Place the top plate and wing nut aside, out of the way of moving engine components.

3   Look at the center of the air cleaner housing. You will notice a flat plate at the carburetor opening. This is the choke plate.

4   Press the accelerator pedal to the floor. The plate should close completely. Start the engine while you watch the choke plate. Don't position your face near the carburetor, as the engine could backfire, causing serious burns. When the engine starts, the choke plate should open slightly.

5   Allow the engine to continue running at an idle speed. As the engine warms up to operating temperature, the plate should slowly open, allowing more air to enter through the top of the carburetor.

6   After a few minutes, the choke plate should be fully open to the vertical position. Tap the accelerator to make sure the fast idle cam disengages.

7   You'll notice that the engine speed corresponds to the plate opening. With the plate fully closed, the engine should run at a fast idle speed. As the plate opens and the throttle is moved to disengage the fast idle cam, the engine speed will decrease.

8   Refer to Chapter 4 for specific information on adjusting and servicing the choke components.

23   Carburetor/throttle body mounting nut torque check

1   The carburetor or Throttle Body Injection (TBI) unit is attached to the top of the intake manifold by several bolts or nuts. These fasteners can sometimes work loose from vibration and temperature changes during normal engine operation and cause a vacuum leak.

2   If you suspect that a vacuum leak exists at the bottom of the carburetor or throttle body, obtain a length of hose. Start the engine and place one end of the hose next to your ear as you probe around the base with the other end. You will hear a hissing sound if a leak exists (be careful of hot or moving engine components when performing this check).

3   Remove the air cleaner assembly, tagging each hose to be disconnected with a piece of numbered tape to make reassembly easier.

4   Locate the mounting nuts or bolts at the base of the carburetor or throttle body. Decide what special tools or adapters will be necessary, if any, to tighten the fasteners.

5   Tighten the nuts to the specified torque. Don't overtighten them, as the threads could strip.

6   If, after the nuts or bolts are properly tightened, a vacuum leak still exists, the carburetor or throttle body must be removed and a new gasket installed. See Chapter 4 for more information.

7   After tightening the fasteners, reinstall the air cleaner and return all hoses to their original positions.

24   Throttle linkage inspection

1   Inspect the throttle linkage for damage and missing parts and for binding and interference when the accelerator pedal is depressed.

2   Lubricate the various linkage pivot points with engine oil.

25   Thermostatic air cleaner check

Refer to illustration 25.3

1   Some engines are equipped with a thermostatically controlled air cleaner which draws air to the carburetor from different locations, depending on engine temperature.

2   This is a visual check. If access is limited, a small mirror may have to be used.

3   Locate the air valve inside the air cleaner assembly. It's inside the snorkel of the air cleaner housing **(see illustration)**.

4   If there is a flexible air duct attached to the end of the snorkel, leading to an area behind the grille, disconnect it at the snorkel. This will enable you to look through the end of the snorkel and see the air valve inside.

5   The check should be done when the engine is cold. Start the engine and look through the snorkel at the air valve, which should move to a closed position. With the valve closed, air cannot enter through the end of the snorkel, but instead enters the air cleaner through the flexible duct attached to the exhaust manifold and the heat stove passage.

6   As the engine warms up to operating temperature, the air valve should open to allow air through the snorkel end. Depending on outside temperature, this may take 10-to-15 minutes. To speed up this check, you can reconnect the snorkel air duct, drive the vehicle until it reaches normal operating temperature, then check to see if the air valve is completely open.

7   If the thermostatically controlled air cleaner isn't operating properly, see Chapter 6 for more information.

25.3 Thermostatic air cleaner operation (air valve shown open) - when the engine is cold, the air valve (1) should close off the snorkel end (2) allowing warm air to flow through the flexible duct (3), which is attached to the exhaust manifold and heat stove passage - when the engine is at normal operating temperature, the air valve should be open, allowing cool air to flow through the snorkel end (2)

STREAKED SIDEWALL

FRAYING

CRACKS

SEPARATION

GLAZING

OIL SOAKED

TENSILE BREAK

26.3 Here are some of the more common problems associated with drivebelts (check the belts very carefully to prevent an untimely breakdown)

26.4a Measuring drivebelt deflection with a straightedge and ruler

RULER

STRAIGHT EDGE

BELT DEFLECTION

MAKE SURE RULER IS PERPENDICULAR TO STRAIGHT EDGE

NIPPONDENSO   BURROUGHS

26.4b If you are able to borrow either a Nippondenso or Burroughs belt tension gauge, this is how it's installed on the belt - compare the reading on the scale with the specified drivebelt tension

26 Drivebelt check, adjustment and replacement

Refer to illustrations 26.3,, 26.4a, 26.4b, 26.7 and 26.12

1   The drivebelts, or V-belts as they are often called, are located at the front of the engine and play an important role in the overall operation of the engine and accessories. Due to their function and material makeup, the belts are prone to failure after a period of time and should be inspected and adjusted periodically to prevent major engine damage.
2   The number of belts used on a particular vehicle depends on the accessories installed. Drivebelts are used to turn the alternator, power steering pump, water pump and air conditioning compressor. Depending on the pulley arrangement, more than one of these components may be driven by a single belt. Six-cylinder and later four-cylinder models are equipped with one serpentine drivebelt that runs all engine accessories.
3   With the engine off, locate the drivebelts at the front of the engine. Using your fingers

(and a flashlight, if necessary), move along the belts checking for cracks and separation of the belt plies. Also check for fraying and glazing, which gives the belt a shiny appearance **(see illustration)**. Both sides of each belt should be inspected, which means you will have to twist the belt to check the underside. Check the pulleys for nicks, cracks, distortion and corrosion.
4   The tension of each V-belt is checked by pushing on it at a distance halfway between the pulleys. Push firmly and see how much the belt moves (deflects) **(see illustration)**. A rule of thumb is that if the distance from pulley center-to-pulley center is between 7 and 11-inches, the belt should deflect 1/4-inch. If the belt travels between pulleys spaced 12-to-16 inches apart, the belt should deflect 1/2-inch. The tension on serpentine belts can only be checked using a belt tension gauge, available at auto parts stores **(see illustration)**.
5   If adjustment is needed, either to make the belt tighter or looser, it's done by moving the belt-driven accessory on the bracket.
6   For each component there will be an adjusting bolt and a pivot bolt. Both bolts must be loosened slightly to enable you to move the component. On later models with a serpentine belt, belt tension is adjusted at the power steering pump or idler pulley (if not equipped with power steering).
7   After the bolts have been loosened, move the component away from the engine to tighten the belt or toward the engine to

loosen the belt. Hold the accessory in position and check the belt tension **(see illustration)**. If it's correct, tighten the bolts until just snug, then recheck the tension. If the tension is all right, tighten the bolts.
8   On models without a serpentine belt, it will often be necessary to use some sort of pry bar to move the accessory while the belt is adjusted. If this must be done to gain the proper leverage, be very careful not to damage the component being moved or the part being pried against.
9   To replace a belt, follow the above procedures for drivebelt adjustment, but slip the

26.7 Loosen the adjusting bolt (arrow), then move the alternator in-or-out to adjust the drivebelt tension

26.12 Typical serpentine drivebelt routing

30.7 Disconnect the sole-vac vacuum hose and plug it

belt off the pulleys and remove it. Since belts tend to wear out more or less at the same time, it's a good idea to replace all of them at the same time. Mark each belt and the corresponding pulley grooves so the replacement belts can be installed properly.

10   Take the old belts with you when purchasing new ones in order to make a direct comparison for length, width and design.

11   Adjust the belts as described earlier in this Section.

12   When replacing a serpentine drivebelt (used on later models), make sure the new belt is routed correctly or the water pump could turn backwards, causing overheating **(see illustration)**. A belt routing diagram is usually located in the engine compartment. Also, the belt must completely engage the grooves in the pulleys.

27   Seatbelt check

1   Check the seatbelts, buckles, latch plates and guide loops for any obvious damage or signs of wear.

2   Make sure the seatbelt reminder light comes on when the key is turned on.

3   The seatbelts are designed to lock up during a sudden stop or impact, yet allow free movement during normal driving. The retractors should hold the belt against your chest while driving and rewind the belt when the buckle is unlatched.

4   If any of the above checks reveal problems with the seatbelt system, replace parts as necessary.

28   Neutral start switch check

Warning: *During the following checks there is a chance that the vehicle could lunge forward, possibly causing damage or injuries. Allow plenty of room around the vehicle, apply the parking brake firmly and hold down the regular brake pedal during the checks.*

1   Automatic transmission equipped models have a Neutral start switch which prevents the engine from starting unless the shift lever is in Neutral or Park.

2   Try to start the vehicle in each gear. The engine should crank only in Park or Neutral.

3   Make sure the steering column lock allows the key to go into the Lock position only when the shift lever is in Park.

4   The ignition key should come out only in the Lock position.

5   Refer to Chapter 7, Part B for further information on the Neutral start switch.

30.8 Unplug the electrical connector from the sole-vac solenoid

29   Spare tire and jack check

1   Check the spare tire to make sure it's securely fastened so it cannot come loose when the vehicle is in motion.

2   Make sure the jack and components are secured in place.

30   Idle speed check and adjustment (1987 and 1988 carbureted models only)

Refer to illustrations 30.7, 30.8 and 30.12

Note: *Idle speed check and adjustment are not routine maintenance procedures on vehicles other than those identified in the heading above.*

1   Engine idle speed is the speed at which the engine operates when no throttle pedal pressure is applied. The idle speed is critical to the performance of the engine itself, as well as many engine sub-systems.

2   A hand-held tachometer must be used when adjusting idle speed to get an accurate reading. The exact hook-up for these meters varies with the manufacturer, so follow the particular directions included.

3   Set the parking brake and block the wheels. Be sure the transmission is in Neutral (manual transmission) or Park (automatic transmission).

4   Turn off the air conditioner (if equipped), the headlights and any other accessories during this procedure.

5   Start the engine and allow it to reach normal operating temperature.

6   Shut off the engine.

7   Disconnect and plug the vacuum hose on the sole-vac vacuum actuator **(see illustration)**.

8   Unplug the sole-vac holding solenoid electrical connector **(see illustration)**.

9   On automatic transmission equipped vehicles, have an assistant shift to Drive while keeping the brake pedal firmly depressed. Place the manual transmission equipped vehicles in Neutral.

10   Increase the engine speed to 1200 rpm

30.12 Be sure to turn only the idle speed screw (arrow)

31.3 Remove the shield, then unscrew the fuel hose clamps, pull off the hoses and remove the securing strap bolt (arrow)

for three to five seconds, then let it return to idle.

11   Check the engine idle speed reading on the tachometer and compare this to the one in the Specifications Section at the beginning of this Chapter. If your vehicle has a VECI label located in the engine compartment refer instead to the idle speed there.

12   If the idle speed is not correct, turn the idle speed adjusting screw until the idle speed is correct **(see illustration)**.

13   After adjustment, reconnect the sole-vac hose, shift the automatic transmission into Park and turn the engine off.

31   Fuel filter replacement (1987 through 1995 models)

Refer to illustration 31.3

Note: *Only 1987 through 1995 models use a replaceable in-line fuel filter. The manufacturer does not suggest periodic fuel filter*

replacement on 1997 and later models. Since the fuel filter is part of the fuel pump assembly inside the fuel tank on 1997 and later models, refer to Chapter 4 if fuel contamination makes it necessary to replace the fuel filter.

1   1995 and earlier models employ an in-line fuel filter. The filter is located on the left side frame rail, near the fuel tank. On port fuel injected engines, the system is under pressure even when the engine is off. **Warning:** *On port fuel injected engines, the system must be depressurized (see Chapter 4) before any work is performed.*

2   With the engine cold, place a container, newspapers or rags under the fuel filter.

3   Remove the metal shield, disconnect the fuel hoses and detach the filter from the frame **(see illustration)**.

4   Install the new filter by reversing the removal procedure. Make sure the arrow or the word "OUT" on the filter points toward the engine, not the fuel tank. Tighten the screw clamps securely, but not to the point where the rubber hose is badly distorted.

32   Air filter and PCV filter replacement

Refer to illustrations 32.2a, 32.2b, 32.4 and 32.6

1   At the specified intervals, the air filter and (if equipped) PCV filter should be replaced with new ones. The engine air cleaner also supplies filtered air to the PCV system.

2   The filter on carburetor-equipped models is located on top of the carburetor and is replaced by unscrewing the wing nut from the top of the filter housing body, disconnecting the clips and lifting off the cover **(see illustration)**. On most fuel-injected models, the filter is located in a housing in the engine compartment. It can be replaced after disengaging the clips holding the top plate in place **(see illustration)**.

3   While the top plate is off, be careful not to drop anything into the carburetor or air cleaner assembly.

32.2a On carburetor models, remove the air cleaner wing nut, disconnect the clips, lift the cover off and remove the filter element

32.2b On fuel-injected models, clips on the sides hold the cover on the air cleaner housing - they can be pried loose with a screwdriver

32.4 Hold the cover up out of the way and lift the filter element out of the housing (fuel-injected model shown)

32.6 The PCV filter used on some carburetor models

4   Lift the air filter element out **(see illustration)** and wipe out the inside of the air cleaner housing with a clean rag.

5   Place the new filter in the air cleaner housing. Make sure it seats properly in the bottom of the housing.

6   The PCV filter is also located inside the air cleaner housing on some models **(see illustration)**. Remove the cover and air filter as previously described, then locate the PCV filter on the inside of the housing.

7   Remove the old filter.

8   Install the new PCV filter and the new air filter.

9   Install the cover and any hoses which were disconnected.

33   Ignition timing check and adjustment (carbureted models only)

Refer to illustrations 33.1 and 33.4

Note: *Ignition timing check and adjustment are not required on vehicles other than those identified in the heading above. If the information in this Section differs from the Vehicle Emission Control Information label (located in*

33.1 Tools needed to check and adjust the ignition timing

1   *Vacuum plugs - Vacuum hoses will, in most cases, have to be disconnected and plugged. Molded plugs in various shapes and sizes are available for this.*

2   *Inductive pick-up timing light - Flashes a bright concentrated beam of light when the number one spark plug fires. Connect the leads according to the instructions supplied with the light.*

3   *Distributor wrench - On some models, the hold-down bolt for the distributor is difficult to reach and turn with conventional wrenches or sockets. A special wrench like this must be used.*

33.4 The ignition timing marks are located at the front of the engine

the engine compartment of your vehicle), the label should be considered correct.

1   The engine must be at normal operating temperature and the air conditioner must be Off. Make sure the idle speed is correct (see Section 30).

Some special tools will be required for this procedure **(see illustration)**.

2   Apply the parking brake and block the wheels to prevent movement of the vehicle. The transmission must be in Park (automatic) or Neutral (manual).

3   Disconnect and plug the hose connected to the vacuum advance unit on the distributor and unplug the electrical connector from the CEC system switch assembly on top of the valve cover.

4   Locate the timing marks at the front of the engine (they should be visible from above after the hood is opened) **(see illustration)**. The crankshaft pulley or vibration damper has a groove in it and a scale with notches and numbers is either molded into or attached to the engine's timing cover. Clean the scale with solvent so the numbers are visible.

5   Use chalk or white paint to mark the groove in the pulley/vibration damper.

6   Highlight the notch or point on the scale that corresponds to the ignition timing specification on the Vehicle Emission Control Information label.

7   Hook up the timing light, following the manufacturer's instructions (an inductive pick-up timing light is preferred). Generally, the power leads are attached to the battery terminals and the pick-up lead is attached to the number one spark plug wire. The number one spark plug is the very front one. **Caution:** *If an inductive pick-up timing light isn't available, don't puncture the spark plug wire to attach the timing light pick-up lead. Instead, use an adapter between the spark plug and plug wire. If the insulation on the plug wire is damaged, the secondary voltage will jump to ground at the damaged point and the engine will misfire.*

34.10 The automatic transmission fluid filter is held in place by three screws

SCREWS   FILTER

35.3 The transmission drain plug (arrow) is located at the bottom of the case

8   Connect a tachometer, following the manufacturer's instructions.

9   Make sure the timing light and tachometer wires are routed away from the drivebelts and fan, then start the engine.

10   Allow the idle speed to stabilize, then point the flashing timing light at the timing marks - be very careful of moving engine components!

11   Increase the engine speed to 1600 rpm. The mark on the pulley/vibration damper will appear stationary. If it's aligned with the specified point on the scale, the ignition timing is correct.

12   If the marks aren't aligned, adjustment is required. Loosen the distributor hold-down bolt and turn the distributor very slowly until the marks are aligned. Since access to the bolt is tight, a special distributor wrench may be needed.

13   Tighten the bolt and recheck the timing.

14   Turn off the engine and remove the timing light (and adapter, if used).

15   Reconnect any components which were disconnected.

34 Automatic transmission fluid and filter change

Refer to illustration 34.10

1   At the specified time intervals, the transmission fluid should be drained and replaced. Since the fluid will remain hot long after driving, perform this procedure only after the engine has cooled down completely.

2   Before beginning work, purchase the specified transmission fluid (see *Recommended lubricants and fluids* at the front of this Chapter) and a new filter.

3   Other tools necessary for this job include jackstands to support the vehicle in a raised position, a drain pan capable of holding at least eight pints, newspapers and clean rags.

4   Raise the vehicle and support it securely on jackstands.

5   With a drain pan in place, remove the front and side pan mounting bolts.

6   Loosen the rear pan bolts approximately one turn.

7   If the pan does not loosen and fluid does not begin to drain, carefully pry the transmission pan loose with a putty knife.

8   Remove the remaining bolts, pan and gasket. Carefully clean the gasket surface of the transmission to remove all traces of the old gasket and sealant.

9   Drain the fluid from the transmission pan, clean it with solvent and dry it with compressed air.

10   Remove the filter from the transmission valve body **(see illustration)**. With the vehicle raised and the pan off, this is a good time to adjust the transmission bands (see Chapter 7B).

11   Install a new filter.

12   Make sure the gasket surface on the transmission pan is clean, then install a new gasket. Put the pan in place against the transmission and, working around the pan, tighten each bolt a little at a time until the final torque figure is reached.

13   Lower the vehicle and add the specified amount of automatic transmission fluid through the filler tube (see Section 6).

14   With the transmission in Park and the parking brake set, run the engine at a fast idle, but don't race it.

15   Move the gear selector through each range and back to Neutral. Check the fluid level.

16   Check under the vehicle for leaks during the first few trips.

35 Manual transmission lubricant change

Refer to illustration 35.3

1   Raise the vehicle and support it securely on jackstands.

2   Move a drain pan, rags, newspapers and wrenches under the transmission.

3   Remove the transmission drain plug at the bottom of the case **(see illustration)** and allow the oil to drain into the pan.

4   After the oil has drained completely, reinstall the plug and tighten it securely.

5   Remove the fill plug from the side of the transmission case. Using a hand pump, syringe or funnel, fill the transmission with the correct amount of the specified lubricant. Reinstall the plug and tighten it securely.

6   Lower the vehicle.

7   Drive the vehicle for a short distance then check the drain and fill plugs for leakage.

36 Differential lubricant change

Refer to illustrations 36.4a, 36.4b, 36.4c and 36.6

1   These models don't have a drain plug so a hand suction pump is used to remove the differential lubricant through the filler hole. If the cover plate is leaking and/or a suction pump isn't available, the lubricant can be drained by removing the cover plate, so be sure to obtain a tube of gasket sealant when the lubricant is purchased. On models equipped with a limited slip differential (denoted by a tag attached to the differential cover), a packet of special additive will be required (Section 17).

2   Raise the vehicle and support it securely on jackstands. Move a drain pan, rags, newspapers and wrenches under the vehicle.

3   If a suction pump is being used, insert the flexible hose. Work the hose down to the bottom of the differential housing and pump the lubricant out.

4   If the differential is being drained by removing the cover, remove the bolts on the lower half of the cover **(see illustration)**. Loosen the bolts on the upper half and use them to keep the cover loosely attached **(see illustration)**. Allow the lubricant to drain into the pan, then completely remove the cover **(see illustration)**.

5   Using a lint-free rag, clean the inside of the cover and the accessible areas of the differential housing. As this is done, check for chipped gears and metal particles in the

36.4a Remove the bolts from the lower edge of the cover . . .

36.4b . . . then loosen the top bolts and let the lubricant drain out

36.4c After the lubricant has completely drained, remove the cover

36.6 Carefully scrape the old sealant material off to ensure a clean surface

lubricant, indicating that the differential should be more thoroughly inspected and/or repaired.

6   Thoroughly clean the gasket mating surfaces of the differential housing and the cover plate. Use a gasket scraper or putty knife to remove all traces of the old sealant **(see illustration)**.

7   Apply a thin layer of sealant to the cover flange, then place the cover on the differential

38.3 The drain plug is located at the bottom of the radiator - you might need a pair of pliers to turn it

housing and install the bolts. Tighten the bolts securely.

8   On all models, use a hand pump, syringe or funnel to fill the differential housing with the specified lubricant until it's level with the bottom of the plug hole. On limited slip-equipped differentials, add the packet of additive first, before filling the housing.

9   Install the filler plug and tighten it securely.

10   On limited slip differential-equipped models, drive the vehicle slowly in a figure-8 pattern seven or eight times to work the lubricant into the clutch packs.

37   Transfer case lubricant change

1   Drive the vehicle for at least 15 minutes in stop and go traffic to warm the lubricant in the case. Perform this warm-up procedure in 4WD. Use all gears, including Reverse, to ensure the lubricant is sufficiently warm to drain completely.

2   Raise the vehicle and support it securely on jackstands.

3   Remove the filler plug from the case **(see illustration 18.1)**.

4   Remove the drain plug from the lower part of the case and allow the old lubricant to drain completely.

38.5 The block drain plug holes are located on the driver's side of the engine block (some, like this six-cylinder, may have coolant temperature sensors screwed into the plug hole)

5   Carefully clean and install the drain plug after the case is completely drained. Tighten the plug to the torque listed in the Specifications Section at the beginning of this Chapter.

6   Fill the case with the specified lubricant until it is level with the lower edge of the filler hole.

7   Install the filler plug and tighten it securely.

8   Drive the vehicle for a short distance and recheck the lubricant level. In some instances a small amount of additional lubricant will have to be added.

38   Cooling system servicing (draining, flushing and refilling)

Refer to illustrations 38.3 and 38.5
Warning: *Do not allow antifreeze to come in contact with your skin or painted surfaces of the vehicle. Rinse off spills immediately with plenty of water. Antifreeze is highly toxic if ingested. Never leave antifreeze lying around in an open container or in puddles on the floor; children and pets are attracted by it's sweet smell and may drink it. Check with local authorities about disposing of used antifreeze. Many communities have collection centers which will see that antifreeze is disposed of safely.*

1   Periodically, the cooling system should be drained, flushed and refilled to replenish the antifreeze mixture and prevent formation of rust and corrosion, which can impair the performance of the cooling system and cause engine damage. When the cooling system is serviced, all hoses and the radiator cap should be checked and replaced if necessary.

Draining

2   Apply the parking brake and block the wheels. If the vehicle has just been driven, wait several hours to allow the engine to cool down before beginning this procedure.

3   Move a large container under the radiator drain fitting to catch the coolant. Once the

39.3 Place your thumb over the end of the PCV valve - with the engine running you should feel friction

39.4 Shake the PCV valve to make sure it rattles, indicating that it isn't clogged

39.11 A paper clip can be used to clean the CCV system orifice

engine is completely cool, open the drain fitting (a pair of pliers may be required to turn it) **(see illustration)**.

4   Once the coolant reserve bottle has drained, remove the radiator cap.

5   After the coolant stops flowing out of the radiator, move the container under the engine block drain plug(s) on the engine **(see illustration)**. On four-cylinder engines, the drain plug is located at the left rear side of the block. Six-cylinder engines have two drain plugs located on the left side of the block (on some models there may be a coolant temperature sensor). Loosen the plug(s) and allow the coolant in the block to drain.

6   While the coolant is draining, check the condition of the radiator hoses, heater hoses and clamps (refer to Section 10 if necessary).

7   Replace any damaged clamps or hoses (refer to Chapter 3 for detailed replacement procedures).

Flushing

8   Once the system is completely drained, flush the radiator with fresh water from a garden hose until water runs clear at the drain.

The flushing action of the water will remove sediments from the radiator but will not remove rust and scale from the engine and cooling tube surfaces.

9   These deposits can be removed by the chemical action of a cleaner. Follow the procedure outlined in the manufacturer's instructions. If the radiator is severely corroded, damaged or leaking, it should be removed (see Chapter 3) and taken to a radiator repair shop.

Refilling

10   Close and tighten the radiator drain. Install and tighten the block drain plug(s).

11   Place the heater temperature control in the maximum heat position.

12   Slowly add new coolant (a 50/50 mixture of water and antifreeze) to the radiator until it's full. Add coolant to the reservoir bottle until the level is at the upper mark.

13   Leave the radiator cap off and run the engine in a well-ventilated area until the thermostat opens (coolant will begin flowing through the radiator and the upper radiator hose will become hot).

14   Turn the engine off and let it cool. Add more coolant mixture to bring the level back up to the lip on the radiator filler neck.

15   Squeeze the upper radiator hose to expel air, then add more coolant mixture if necessary. Replace the radiator cap.

16   Start the engine, allow it to reach normal operating temperature and check for leaks.

---

39   Positive Crankcase Ventilation (PCV) valve or Crankcase Ventilation (CCV) hose check, cleaning and replacement

Refer to illustrations 39.3, 39.4 and 39.11

Check

1   The PCV valve or CCV hose is located in the valve cover.

2   With the engine idling at normal operating temperature, pull the valve (with hose attached) or CCV hose from the rubber grommet in the cover.

3   Place your thumb over the valve or hose opening **(see illustration)**. If there's no vacuum, check for a plugged hose, manifold port, or valve. Replace any plugged or deteriorated hoses.

4   Turn off the engine and shake the PCV valve, listening for a rattle **(see illustration)**. If the valve doesn't rattle, replace it with a new one.

PCV valve replacement

5   To replace the valve, pull it from the end of the hose, noting its installed position and direction.

6   When purchasing a replacement PCV valve, make sure it's for your particular vehicle and engine size. Compare the old valve with the new one to make sure they're the same.

7   Push the valve into the end of the hose until it's seated.

8   Inspect the rubber grommet for damage and replace it with a new one if necessary.

9   Push the PCV valve and hose securely into position.

CCV hose and orifice cleaning

10   Later models are equipped with a CCV system which performs the same function as the PCV system but uses a rubber fitting with a molded-in orifice which is pressed into a hole in the valve cover. The fitting is connected to the intake manifold by a plastic hose.

11   If there is no vacuum at the end of the hose (Step 3), turn off the engine, remove the fitting and clean the hose with solvent. Clean the fitting orifice **(see illustration)** if it's plugged. If the fitting or hose are cracked or deteriorated, replace them with new ones.

12   Install the fitting and hose securely in the valve cover.

40.2 The evaporative emissions canister (arrow) is located on the passenger's side firewall - check the housing and hoses for damage

40   Evaporative emissions control system check

Refer to illustration 40.2

1   The function of the evaporative emissions control system is to draw fuel vapors from the gas tank and fuel system, store them in a charcoal canister and route them to the intake manifold during normal engine operation.

2   The most common symptom of a fault in the evaporative emissions system is a strong fuel odor in the engine compartment. If a fuel odor is detected, inspect the charcoal canister, located in the right rear corner of the engine compartment **(see illustration)**. Check the canister and all hoses for damage and deterioration.

3   The evaporative emissions control system is explained in more detail in Chapter 6.

41   Spark plug replacement

Refer to illustrations 41.2, 41.5a, 41.5b, 41.6, 41.8 and 41.10

1   Open the hood.

2   In most cases, the tools necessary for spark plug replacement include a spark plug socket which fits onto a ratchet (spark plug sockets are padded inside to prevent damage to the porcelain insulators on the new plugs), various extensions and a gap gauge to check and adjust the gaps on the new plugs **(see illustration)**. A special plug wire removal tool is available for separating the wire boots from the spark plugs, but it isn't absolutely necessary. A torque wrench should be used to tighten the new plugs.

3   The best approach when replacing the spark plugs is to purchase the new ones in advance, adjust them to the proper gap and replace them one at a time. When buying the new spark plugs, be sure to obtain the correct plug type for your particular engine. This information can be found in the Specifica-

41.2 Tools required for changing spark plugs

1   **Spark plug socket -** *This will have special padding inside to protect the spark plug's porcelain insulator*

2   **Torque wrench -** *Although not mandatory, using this tool is the best way to ensure the plugs are tightened properly*

3   **Ratchet -** *Standard hand tool to fit the spark plug socket*

4   **Extension -** *Depending on model and accessories, you may need special extensions and universal joints o reach one or more of the plugs*

5   **Spark plug gap gauge -** *This gauge for checking the gap comes in a variety of styles. Make sure the gap for your engine is included.*

tions Section at the beginning of this Chapter, or on the *Vehicle Emission Control Information* label located on the underside of the hood on the driver's side or in the vehicle owner's manual. The plug specified on the emissions label is assumed to be correct if it is different from that in the Specifications or owner's manual.

4   Allow the engine to cool completely before attempting to remove any of the plugs. While you're waiting for the engine to cool, check the new plugs for defects and adjust the gaps.

5   The gap is checked by inserting the proper thickness gauge between the electrodes at the tip of the plug **(see illustration)**. The gap between the electrodes should be the same as the one specified. The wire should just slide between the electrodes with a slight amount of drag. If the gap is incorrect, use the adjuster on the gauge body to bend the curved side electrode slightly until the proper gap is obtained **(see illustration)**. If the side electrode is not exactly over the center electrode, bend it with the adjuster until it is. Check for cracks in the porcelain insulator (if any are found, the plug should not be used).

6   With the engine cool, remove the spark plug wire from one spark plug. Pull only on the boot at the end of the wire - do not pull on the wire. A plug wire removal tool should be used if available **(see illustration)**.

41.5a Spark plug manufacturers recommend using a wire type gauge when checking the gap - if the wire does not slide between the electrodes with a slight drag, adjustment is required

41.5b To change the gap, bend the *side* **electrode only, as indicated by the arrows, and be very careful not to crack or chip the porcelain insulator surrounding the center electrodes**

41.6 Grasp the spark plug wire boot and use a twisting/pulling motion - it's a good idea to use a tool such as the one shown here to get a good grip

7   If compressed air is available, use it to blow any dirt or foreign material away from the spark plug hole. A common bicycle pump will also work. The idea here is to eliminate the possibility of debris falling into the cylinder as the spark plug is removed.

8   Place the spark plug socket over the plug and remove it from the engine by turning it in a counterclockwise direction (see illustration).

9   Compare the spark plug to those shown in the photos on the inside back cover of this manual to get an indication of the general running condition of the engine.

10   Thread one of the new plugs into the hole until you can no longer turn it with your fingers, then tighten it with a torque wrench (if available) or the ratchet. It is a good idea to slip a short length of rubber hose over the end of the plug to use as a tool to thread it into place (see illustration). The hose will grip the plug well enough to turn it, but will start to slip if the plug begins to cross-thread in the hole - this will prevent damaged threads and the accompanying repair costs.

11   Before pushing the spark plug wire onto the end of the plug, inspect it following the procedures outlined in Section 42.

12   Attach the plug wire to the new spark plug, again using a twisting motion on the boot until it's seated on the spark plug.

13   Repeat the procedure for the remaining spark plugs, replacing them one at a time to prevent mixing up the spark plug wires.

---

42   Spark plug wire, distributor cap and rotor check and replacement

Refer to illustrations 42.11 and 42.12

1   The spark plug wires should be checked whenever new spark plugs are installed.

2   Begin this procedure by making a visual check of the spark plug wires while the engine is running. In a darkened garage (make sure there is ventilation) start the engine and observe each plug wire. Be careful not to come into contact with any moving engine parts. If there is a break in the wire, you will see arcing or a small spark at the damaged area. If arcing is noticed, make a note to obtain new wires, then allow the engine to cool and check the distributor cap and rotor.

3   The spark plug wires should be inspected one at a time to prevent mixing up the order, which is essential for proper engine operation. Each original plug wire should be numbered to help identify its location. If the number is illegible, a piece of tape can be marked with the correct number and wrapped around the plug wire.

4   Disconnect the plug wire from the spark plug. A removal tool can be used for this purpose or you can grasp the rubber boot, twist the boot half a turn and pull the boot free. Do not pull on the wire itself.

5   Check inside the boot for corrosion, which will look like a white crusty powder.

41.8 A socket with an extension makes it easier to remove the spark plug

41.10 A length of snug-fitting rubber hose will save time and prevent damaged threads when installing the spark plug

6   Push the wire and boot back onto the end of the spark plug. It should fit tightly onto the end of the plug. If it doesn't, remove the wire and use pliers to carefully crimp the metal connector inside the wire boot until the fit is snug.

7   Using a clean rag, wipe the entire length of the wire to remove built-up dirt and grease. Once the wire is clean, check for burns, cracks and other damage. Do not bend the wire sharply, because the conductor might break.

8   Disconnect the wire from the distributor. Again, pull only on the rubber boot. Check for corrosion and a tight fit. Replace the wire in the distributor.

9   Inspect the remaining spark plug wires, making sure that each one is securely fastened at the distributor and spark plug when the check is complete.

10   If new spark plug wires are required, purchase a set for your specific engine model. Pre-cut wire sets with the boots already installed are avail- able. Remove and replace the wires one at a time to avoid mix-ups in the firing order.

11   Detach the distributor cap by removing the two cap retaining bolts. Look inside it for cracks, carbon tracks and worn, burned or loose contacts (see illustration).

BROKEN OR
CRACKED
TOWER

CRACKS

CARBON
TRACK

CARBON TRACK

CHARRED OR
ERODED TERMINALS

WORN OR DAMAGED
ROTOR BUTTON

42.11 Shown here are some of the common defects to look for when inspecting the distributor cap (if In doubt about its condition, install a new one)

42.12 The ignition rotor should be checked for wear and corrosion as indicated here (if in doubt about its condition, buy a new one)

43.3 The oxygen sensor (arrow) is screwed into the exhaust pipe, just below where the pipe and exhaust manifold meet

12   Pull the rotor off the distributor shaft and examine it for cracks and carbon tracks **(see illustration)**. Replace the cap and rotor if any damage or defects are noted.

13   It is common practice to install a new cap and rotor whenever new spark plug wires are installed, but if you wish to continue using the old cap, check the resistance between the spark plug wires and the cap first. If the indicated resistance is more than the specified maximum value, replace the cap and/or wires.

14   When installing a new cap, remove the wires from the old cap one at a time and attach them to the new cap in the exact same location - do not simultaneously remove all the wires from the old cap or firing order mix-ups may occur.

43   Oxygen sensor and emission maintenance timer replacement

Refer to illustrations 43.3 and 43.8
Note: *Special care must be taken when handling the oxygen sensor - it's very sensitive:*

  a) The oxygen sensor has a permanently
  attached pigtail and connector, which
  should not be removed. Damage or
  removal of the pigtail or connector can
  adversely affect sensor operation.
  b) Grease, dirt and other contaminants
  should be kept away from the electrical
  connector and the louvered end of the
  sensor.
  c) Do not use cleaning solvents of any kind
  on the oxygen sensor.
  d) Do not drop or roughly handle the
  sensor.

1   The sensor is located in the exhaust manifold or exhaust pipe and is accessible from under the vehicle.

2   Since the oxygen sensor may be difficult to remove with the engine cold, begin by operating the engine until it has warmed to at least 120-degrees F (48-degrees C).

3   Disconnect the electrical wire from the oxygen sensor and carefully unscrew the oxygen sensor from the exhaust pipe **(see illustration)**. Be advised that excessive force may damage the threads. Inspect the oxygen sensor for damage.

4   A special anti-seize compound must be used on the threads of the oxygen sensor to aid in future removal. New or service sensors will have this compound already applied, but if for any reason an oxygen sensor is removed and then reinstalled, the threads must be coated before reinstallation.

5   Install the sensor and tighten it securely.

6   Connect the electrical wire.

7   On 1990 and earlier models an emission maintenance timer (mounted under the right side of the dashboard) activates the emissions maintenance indicator light on the instrument panel when the oxygen sensor is scheduled for replacement (approximately 82,500 miles). The timer cannot be reset and must be replaced or disconnected to turn out the indicator light.

8   The timer is located under the instrument panel, to the right of the steering column **(see illustration)**. Unplug the electrical connector, remove the screws and lower the timer from the instrument panel. Installation is the reverse of removal.

9   On 1991 and later models, the emissions maintenance indicator light can only be reset with a special tool available at most auto parts stores. After replacing the oxygen sensor, take the vehicle to a dealer service department or other properly equipped repair facility and have the light reset.

43.8 The emissions timer details (1990 and earlier models)

A   Retaining screws
B   Electrical connectors

Chapter 2 Part A
2.4L four-cylinder engine

Contents

Specifications

General

Bore	3.445 inches (87.5 mm)
Stroke	3.976 inches (101 mm)
Compression ratio	9.5:1
Displacement	2.4 liters (148 cubic inches)
Firing order	1-3-4-2

Camshaft

Bearing bore diameter	1.024 to 1.025 inches (26.020 to 26.041 mm)
Bearing journal diameter	1.021 to 1.022 inches (25.951 to 25.970 mm)
Bearing clearance	0.0027 to 0.003 inch (0.0691 to 0.071 mm)
Endplay	0.0019 to 0.0066 inch (0.05 to 0.17 mm)
Lobe lift	
Intake	0.324 inch (8.25 mm)
Exhaust	0.259 inch (6.60 mm)

**Cylinder locations
(2.4L four-cylinder)**

Front

50035-1-A HAYNES

Cylinder head

Head gasket surface warpage limit	0.004 inch maximum (0.1 mm)
Intake and Exhaust manifold mounting surface warpage limit	0.006 inch per foot maximum (0.15 mm per 300 mm)

Intake and exhaust manifolds

Warpage limit	0.006 inch per foot maximum (0.15 mm per 300 mm)

Oil pump

Cover warpage limit	0.001 inch (0.025 mm)
Inner rotor thickness (minimum)	0.370 inch (9.40 mm)
Outer rotor thickness (minimum)	0.370 inch (9.40 mm)
Outer rotor diameter (minimum)	3.148 inch (79.95 mm)
Rotor-to-pump cover clearance (maximum)	0.004 inch (0.10 mm)
Outer rotor-to-housing clearance (maximum)	0.015 inch (0.039 mm)
Inner rotor-to-outer rotor lobe clearance (maximum)	0.008 inch (0.20 mm)
Pressure relief spring free length	2.39 inches (approximate)

Torque specifications

	Ft-lbs (unless otherwise indicated)	Nm
Camshaft bearing cap bolts **(see illustration 11.5 for bolt tightening sequence)**		
M6 bolts	105 in-lbs	12
M8 bolts	250 in-lbs	28
Camshaft timing belt sprocket bolt	75	101
Crankshaft damper bolt	100	136
Cylinder head bolts **(in sequence - see illustration 15.18)**		
Step 1	25	34
Step 2	50	68
Step 3	50	68
Step 4	Tighten an additional 1/4-turn (90-degrees)	
Driveplate-to-crankshaft bolts	70	95
Exhaust manifold-to-cylinder head bolts	200 in-lbs	23
Exhaust manifold-to-exhaust pipe bolts	21	28
Intake manifold bolts	250 in-lbs	28
Oil pan bolts	105 in-lbs	12
Oil pump		
Attaching bolts	250 in-lbs	28
Cover screws	105 in-lbs	12
Pick-up tube bolt	20	27
Relief valve cap bolt	30	41
Timing belt		
Cover bolts	105 in-lbs	12
Idler pulley bolt	45	61
Tensioner assembly		
Tensioner pulley bolt	45	61
Tensioner assembly mounting bolt	45	61
Valve cover bolts		
Step 1	40 in-lbs	4.5
Step 2	80 in-lbs	9.0
Step 3	105 in-lbs	12

*Refer to Part C for additional torque specifications

1 General information

This Part of Chapter 2 is devoted to in-vehicle engine repair procedures for the 2.4L four-cylinder engine. Information concerning engine removal and installation can be found in Part D of this Chapter.

The following repair procedures are based on the assumption that the engine is installed in the vehicle. If the engine has been removed from the vehicle and mounted on a stand, many of the steps outlined in this Part of Chapter 2 will not apply.

The Specifications included in this Part of Chapter 2 apply only to the procedures contained in this Part.

2 Repair operations possible with the engine in the vehicle

Many major repair operations can be accomplished without removing the engine from the vehicle.

Clean the engine compartment and the exterior of the engine with some type of degreaser before any work is done. It will make the job easier and help keep dirt out of the internal areas of the engine.

Depending on the components involved, it may be helpful to remove the hood to improve access to the engine as repairs are performed (refer to Chapter 11 if necessary). Cover the fenders to prevent damage to the paint. Special pads are available, but an old bedspread or blanket will also work.

If vacuum, exhaust, oil or coolant leaks develop, indicating a need for gasket or seal replacement, the repairs can generally be made with the engine in the vehicle. The intake and exhaust manifold gaskets, oil pan gasket, camshaft and crankshaft oil seals and cylinder head gasket are all accessible with the engine in place.

Exterior engine components, such as the intake and exhaust manifolds, the oil pan, the oil pump, the water pump, the starter motor, the alternator, the distributor and the fuel system components can be removed for repair with the engine in place.

Since the camshafts and cylinder head can be removed without pulling the engine, valve component servicing can also be accomplished with the engine in the vehicle. Replacement of the timing belt and sprockets is also possible with the engine in the vehicle.

In extreme cases caused by a lack of necessary equipment, repair or replacement of piston rings, pistons, connecting rods and rod bearings is possible with the engine in the vehicle. However, this practice is not recommended because of the cleaning and preparation work that must be done to the components involved.

3 Top Dead Center (TDC) for number one piston - locating

1 Top Dead Center (TDC) is the highest point in the cylinder that each piston reaches as it travels up-and-down when the crankshaft turns. Each piston reaches TDC on the compression stroke and again on the exhaust stroke, but TDC generally refers to piston position on the compression stroke. The cast-in timing mark arrow on the crankshaft timing belt pulley (installed on the front of the crankshaft) refers to the number one piston at TDC - when the arrow is straight up, or at "12 o'clock," and aligned with the cast-in timing mark arrow on the oil pump housing (see Section 7).

2 Positioning a specific piston at TDC is an essential part of many procedures such as camshaft(s) removal, rocker arm removal, timing belt and sprocket replacement.

3 In order to bring any piston to TDC, the crankshaft must be turned using one of the methods outlined below. When looking at the front of the engine, normal crankshaft rotation is clockwise. **Warning:** *Before beginning this procedure, be sure to set the emergency brake, place the transmission in Park or Neutral and disable the ignition system by disconnecting the primary electrical connector from the ignition coil pack.*

a) *The preferred method is to turn the crankshaft with a large socket and breaker bar attached to the crankshaft balancer hub bolt that is threaded into the front of the crankshaft.*

b) *A remote starter switch, which may save some time, can also be used. Attach the switch leads to the S (switch) and B (battery) terminals on the starter solenoid. Once the piston is close to TDC, discontinue with the remote switch and use a socket and breaker bar as described in the previous paragraph.*

c) *If an assistant is available to turn the ignition switch to the Start position in short bursts, you can get the piston close to TDC without a remote starter switch. Use a socket and breaker bar as described in Paragraph a) to complete the procedure.*

4 Remove all of the spark plugs as this will make it easier to rotate the engine by hand.

5 Insert a compression gauge (screw-in type with a hose) in the number 1 spark plug hole. Place the gauge dial where you can see it while turning the crankshaft pulley hub bolt. **Note:** *The number one cylinder is located at the front of the engine.*

6 Turn the crankshaft clockwise until you see compression building up on the gauge - you are on the compression stroke for that cylinder. If you did not see compression build up, continue with one more complete revolution to achieve TDC for the number one cylinder.

7 Remove the compression gauge. Through the number one cylinder spark plug hole insert a length of wooden dowel or plastic rod and slowly push it down until it reaches the top of the piston. **Caution:** *Don't insert a metal or sharp object into the spark plug hole as the piston crown may be damaged.*

8 With the dowel or rod in place on top of the piston crown, slowly rotate the crankshaft clockwise until the dowel or rod is pushed upward, stops, and then starts to move back down. At this point, rotate the crankshaft slightly counterclockwise until the dowel or rod has reached it uppermost travel. At this point the number one piston is at the TDC position.

9 Remove the upper timing belt cover (see Section 7). Then check the alignment of the camshaft timing marks **(see illustration 7.11a)**. At this point, the camshafts' timing marks should be aligned. If not repeat this procedure until alignment is correct.

10 After the number one piston has been positioned at TDC on the compression stroke, TDC for any of the remaining cylinders can be located by turning the crankshaft 180-degrees (1/2-turn) at a time and following the firing order (refer to the Specifications).

4 Valve cover - removal and installation

Removal

1 Disconnect the cable from the negative terminal of the battery (see Chapter 5).

2 Remove the upper intake manifold (see Section 5).

3 Remove the ignition coil pack from the valve cover (see Chapter 5).

4 Clearly label and detach any electrical wiring harnesses which connect to or cross over the valve cover.

5 Disconnect the PCV valve hose and breather hose from the valve cover.

6 Remove the valve cover bolts in the reverse order of the tightening sequence **(see illustration 4.9)**, then lift off the cover. If the cover sticks to the cylinder head, tap on it with a soft-face hammer or place a wood block against the cover and tap on the wood with a hammer. **Caution:** *If you have to pry between the valve cover and the cylinder head, be extremely careful not to gouge or nick the gasket surfaces of either part - which could cause a leak to develop after reassembly.*

7 Remove the valve gaskets and spark plug well seals. Thoroughly clean the valve cover and remove all traces of old gasket material. Gasket removal solvents are available from auto parts stores and may prove helpful. After cleaning the surfaces, degrease them with a rag soaked in lacquer thinner or acetone.

Installation

Refer to illustration 4.9

8 Install a new gasket and spark plug well

FRONT

←

50035-2A-4.9 HAYNES

4.9 Valve cover bolt tightening sequence

seals on the cover, using RTV sealant to hold them in place. Apply RTV sealant to the camshaft cap corners and the top edges of the half-round seal. Place the cover on the engine and install the cover bolts. **Note:** *Make sure the two bolts with the sealing washers are in their proper locations.*

9   Tighten the valve cover bolts in three stages in the proper sequence to the torque listed in this Chapter's Specifications **(see illustration).**

10   The remaining steps are the reverse of removal. When finished, run the engine and check for oil leaks.

5   Intake manifold - removal and installation

1   The intake manifold is a two-piece aluminum design. **Note:** *If you are removing the intake manifold simply to access the spark plugs or valve cover, it's not necessary to remove the entire intake manifold unit - only remove the upper intake manifold. Otherwise, the intake manifold can be removed as a complete unit (upper and lower plenum sections bolted together).*

2   If removing the complete intake manifold, relieve the fuel system pressure (see Chapter 4). If only removing the upper intake manifold, this step may be skipped.

3   Disconnect the cable from the negative terminal of the battery (see Chapter 5).

4   Disconnect the electrical connector at the Intake Air Temperature (IAT) sensor and remove the air intake tube and air filter upper housing.

5   Disconnect the electrical connectors at the Idle Air Control (IAC) motor, Throttle Position Sensor (TPS) and Manifold absolute Pressure (MAP) sensor.

6   Disconnect the vacuum hoses at the intake manifold from the PCV valve, Leak Detection Pump (LDP), evaporative system purge solenoid, EGR transducer, power brake booster and, if equipped, the cruise control vacuum reservoir.

7   Disconnect the accelerator cable from its bracket and lever and, if equipped, remove the cruise control and transmission control cables.

8   Remove the EGR pipe bolts at the EGR valve and at the intake manifold, then remove the EGR pipe.

9   Remove the oil dipstick.

10   **Note:** *If the upper and lower intake manifolds are being removed as a unit, skip to step 11. If only the upper intake manifold is being removed, proceed as follows:*

a) *Remove the bolt from the manifold support bracket at the front of the upper intake manifold.*

b) *Remove the upper intake manifold attaching bolts and lift the upper manifold off.*

c) *Refer to Step 17 for the inspection procedure.*

d) *Use a new manifold gasket and install the upper intake manifold and tighten the upper intake manifold bolts gradually and evenly, starting with the center bolts and working outward, to the torque listed in this Chapter's Specifications.*

e) *The remainder of the Installation is the reverse of removal.*

11   If you are removing the complete intake manifold unit, remove the electrical connector at the Coolant Temperature Sensor (CTS) and proceed with the remaining steps.

12   Remove the fuel injector harness connectors.

13   Remove the fuel rail, fuel pressure regulator and fuel injectors as a single assembly (see Chapter 4).

14   If you're planning to *replace* or *service* the intake manifold plenum, remove the throttle body (see Chapter 4). If you're simply removing the intake manifold plenum to remove or service the cylinder head, it's not necessary to remove the throttle body from the intake manifold plenum.

15   Remove the bolts from the intake manifold support bracket.

16   Remove the intake manifold bolts and washers, then remove the intake manifold and the manifold gasket.

Inspection

17   Using a straightedge and feeler gauge, check the intake manifold mating surface for warpage.

18   Check the intake manifold surface on the cylinder head also.

19   If the warpage on either surface exceeds the limit listed in this Chapter's Specifications, the intake manifold and/or the cylinder head must be resurfaced at an automotive machine shop or, if the warpage is too excessive for resurfacing, it should be replaced.

Installation

20   Using a new manifold gasket, install the intake manifold and tighten the intake manifold-to-cylinder head bolts gradually and evenly, starting with the inner bolts and working outward, to the torque listed in this Chapter's Specifications.

21   The remainder of the installation is the reverse of removal.

6   Exhaust manifold - removal and installation

Warning: *Allow the engine to cool completely before beginning this procedure.*

Removal

1   Raise the front of the vehicle and place it securely on jackstands.

2   Disconnect the exhaust pipe from the exhaust manifold and lower the vehicle.

3   Remove the air filter housing and bracket (see Chapter 4).

4   Remove the exhaust manifold heat shield.

5   Unplug the electrical connector for the oxygen sensor, then remove the oxygen sensor from the exhaust manifold (see Chapter 6).

6   Unscrew the mounting bolts and remove the exhaust manifold and the old manifold gasket.

Inspection

7   Inspect the exhaust manifold for cracks and any other obvious damage. If the manifold is cracked or damaged in any way, replace it.

8   Using a wire brush, clean up the threads of the exhaust manifold bolts and inspect the threads for damage. Replace any bolts that have thread damage.

9   Using a scraper, remove all traces of gasket material from the mating surfaces and inspect them for wear and cracks. **Caution:** *When removing gasket material from any surface, especially aluminum, be very careful not to scratch or gouge the gasket surface. Any damage to the surface may result in a leak after reassembly. Gasket removal solvents are available from auto parts stores and may prove helpful.*

10   Using a straightedge and feeler gauge, inspect the exhaust manifold mating surface for warpage. Check the exhaust manifold surface on the cylinder head also. If the warpage on any surface exceeds the limits listed in this Chapter's Specifications, the exhaust manifold and/or cylinder head must be replaced or resurfaced at an automotive machine shop.

Installation

11   Using a new exhaust manifold gasket, install the exhaust manifold and hand-tighten the mounting bolts.

12   Raise the front of the vehicle and place it securely on jackstands.

13   Hand-tighten the exhaust pipe bolts.

14   Starting in the center and working your way outward, tighten the exhaust manifold mounting bolts to the torque listed in this Chapter's Specifications.

15   Tighten the exhaust pipe bolts to the torque listed in this Chapter's Specifications.

16   The remainder of installation is the reverse of removal.

7.7 Insert a large screwdriver or bar through the opening in the pulley and wedge it against the engine block, then loosen the bolt with a socket and breaker bar

7 Timing belt - removal, inspection and installation

Refer to illustrations 7.7, 7.8, 7.11a and 7.11b
Caution 1: *Do not try to turn the crankshaft with a camshaft sprocket bolt and do not rotate the crankshaft counterclockwise.*
Caution 2: *Do not turn the camshafts after the timing belt has been removed. Doing so will damage the valves from contact with other valves and/or the piston(s).*

Removal

1   Position the number one piston at Top Dead Center (see Section 3).
2   Disconnect the cable from the negative terminal of the battery (see Chapter 5).
3   Remove the air filter housing and tube (see Chapter 4).
4   Remove the drivebelt (see Chapter 1).
5   Set the parking brake and block the rear wheels. Raise the front of the vehicle and support it securely on jackstands.
6   Remove the drivebelt splash shield from underneath the vehicle.
7   Loosen the large bolt in the center of the crankshaft damper pulley. It might be very tight; to break it loose, insert a large screwdriver or bar through the opening in the pulley to keep the pulley stationary and loosen the bolt with a socket and breaker bar **(see illustration)**.
8   Install a 3-jaw puller onto the damper pulley and remove the pulley from the crankshaft **(see illustration)**. Use the proper insert to keep the puller from damaging the crankshaft bolt threads. If the pulley is difficult to remove, tap the center bolt of the puller with a brass mallet to break it loose. Reinstall the bolt with a spacer so you can rotate the crankshaft later.
9   Remove the drivebelt tensioner and pulley assembly (right below the alternator).
10   Remove the lower timing belt cover and remove the cover. Remove the upper timing belt cover bolts and remove the

7.8 Install a 3-jaw puller onto the damper pulley, position the center post of the puller on the crankshaft end (use the proper insert to keep from damaging the crankshaft threads), tighten the puller and remove the pulley from the crankshaft

cover. **Note:** *Lower the vehicle, if necessary.*
11   Before removing the timing belt, make sure that the camshaft timing marks are aligned and that the TDC mark on the crankshaft timing belt sprocket is aligned with the stationary index mark on the oil pump housing **(see illustrations)**. Note that the crankshaft sprocket TDC mark is located on the trailing edge of the sprocket tooth. If you don't align the trailing edge of the sprocket tooth with the TDC mark on the oil pump housing, the camshaft timing marks won't be aligned.
12   Insert a 6 mm Allen wrench into the belt tensioner and insert the long end of a 1/8-inch or a 3 mm Allen wrench into the small hole located on the front of the tensioner. Then, using the 6 mm Allen wrench as a lever, rotate the tensioner counterclockwise and simultaneously and lightly push in your 1/8-inch or 3 mm Allen wrench until it slides into the hole in the tensioner.
13   Remove the timing belt.

50035-2A-7.11b HAYNES

7.11b ...and that the TDC mark on the crankshaft timing belt sprocket is aligned with the stationary index mark on the oil pump housing

50035-2A-7.11a HAYNES

7.11a Before removing the timing belt, make sure that the camshaft timing marks are aligned . . .

Inspection

Refer to illustration 7.15
14   Rotate the tensioner pulley and idler pulley by hand and move them side-to-side to detect roughness and excess play. Replace parts as necessary (see Section 8). Visually inspect the sprockets for any signs of damage and wear.
15   Inspect the timing belt for cracks, separation, wear, missing teeth and oil contamination. Replace the belt if it's in questionable condition **(see illustration)**. If the timing belt is excessively worn or damaged on one side, it might be due to incorrect tracking (misalignment). If the belt looks like it was misaligned, be sure to replace the belt tensioner assembly.
16   Check the automatic tensioner for leaks or any obvious damage to the body.

Installation

Refer to illustration 7.18
17   Make sure that the TDC mark on the crankshaft timing belt sprocket is still aligned with the stationary index mark on the oil pump housing **(see illustrations 7.11a and 7.11b)**.

7.15 Carefully inspect the timing belt; bending it backwards wear or damage more c

7.18 Before installing the timing belt, turn the exhaust camshaft sprocket clockwise so that the timing mark on the exhaust sprocket is slightly (1/2-notch) below the timing mark on the intake camshaft sprocket

Camshaft sprocket timing marks

50035-2A-7.18 HAYNES

18   Turn the exhaust camshaft sprocket clockwise so that the timing mark on the exhaust sprocket is slightly below the timing mark on the intake camshaft sprocket **(see illustration)**.

19   Install the timing belt as follows: Start at the crankshaft sprocket, then thread the belt onto the water pump sprocket, the idler pulley, the camshaft sprockets and then finally the tensioner **(see illustration)**. Now take up tension by moving the exhaust camshaft sprocket counterclockwise until the timing marks on the two cam sprockets are realigned.

20   Remove the Allen wrench from the ten-

50035-2A-7.19 HAYNES

7.19 When installing the belt, start at the crankshaft sprocket and thread the belt around the water pump sprocket, the idler pulley, the cam sprockets and the tensioner pulley

A   Crankshaft TDC marks aligned
B   Exhaust camshaft mark 1/2-notch below the intake camshaft mark
C   Install the belt in a counterclockwise direction (looking at the front of the engine)
D   Rotate the exhaust camshaft counterclockwise to remove the timing belt slack

sioner. If you have installed a new tensioner assembly, remove the pull pin (new tensioners are locked in the "wound" position by a pull pin).

21   Rotate the crankshaft 720-degrees (two complete revolutions) and verify that the TDC marks on the crankshaft sprocket and the oil pump housing are still aligned and that the timing marks on the camshaft sprockets are still aligned. If they're not, stop right here, go back to Step 17 and install the belt again.

22   Install the upper and lower timing belt covers and tighten the fasteners to the torque listed in this Chapter's Specifications.

23   Install the drivebelt idler pulley and tighten the idler pulley bolt to the torque listed in this Chapter's Specifications.

24   Install the crankshaft vibration damper, the washer and pulley bolt. Tighten the pulley bolt to the torque listed in this Chapter's Specifications.

25   The remainder of installation is the reverse of removal.

8   Timing belt tensioner and pulley - removal and installation

Removal

1   Remove the timing belt (see Section 7).
2   Remove the timing belt idler pulley bolt,

8.9 When installing a camshaft sprocket, make sure the pin in the camshaft is aligned with the hole in the sprocket

then remove the timing belt idler pulley.

3   Using a suitable holding tool, remove the camshaft sprocket bolts. **Caution:** *Don't allow the camshafts to turn as the bolts are loosened.* Then, using two large screwdrivers, lever the sprockets off the camshafts.

4   Remove the bolts for the rear timing belt cover and then remove the rear cover.

5   Remove the lower timing belt tensioner bolt and remove the tensioner assembly.

Installation

Refer to illustration 8.9

6   Place the timing belt tensioner in position on the front of the engine and then install the lower mounting bolt to hold it in place, but don't tighten the lower bolt yet. Install an engine bracket mounting bolt (M10) in the upper tensioner bolt hole **(see illustration 8.5)** and then screw it in five to seven turns. Tighten the lower tensioner bolt to the torque listed in this Chapter's Specifications and then remove the upper bolt.

7   Install the rear timing belt cover and tighten the cover fasteners securely.

8   Install the timing belt idler pulley and tighten the bolt to the torque listed in this Chapter's Specifications.

9   Install each camshaft sprocket, aligning the pin in the camshaft with the hole in the sprocket **(see illustration)**. Use an appropriate tool to hold the camshaft sprocket while tightening the bolt to the torque listed in this Chapter's Specifications.

10   Install the timing belt (see Section 7).

9   Crankshaft front oil seal - replacement

Refer to illustrations 9.2, 9.3, 9.5 and 9.6
Caution: *Do not rotate the camshafts when the timing belt is removed or damage to the engine may occur.*

1   Remove the timing belt and timing belt covers (see Sections 7 and 8).

2   **Caution:** *When installing the crankshaft sprocket, it must be positioned in its original position to ensure proper timing belt alignment. Before removing the sprocket, measure the distance between the end of the crankshaft and the sprocket and record this distance. When installing the sprocket, be sure to return it to the same position on the crankshaft.* Pull the crankshaft sprocket from the crankshaft with a bolt-type gear puller **(see illustration)**. Remove the Woodruff key.

3   Use a screwdriver or seal removal tool to pry the seal out of its bore **(see illustration)**. Take care to prevent damaging the oil pump assembly, the crankshaft and the seal bore.

4   Thoroughly clean and inspect the seal bore and sealing surface on the crankshaft. Minor imperfections can be removed with emery cloth. If there is a groove worn in the crankshaft sealing surface (from contact with the seal), installing a new seal will probably not stop the leak.

9.2 Attach a bolt-type gear puller to the crankshaft sprocket and remove the sprocket from the crankshaft

9.3 Carefully pry the seal out of its bore

5   Lubricate the new seal with engine oil and drive the seal into place with a hammer and an appropriate size socket **(see illustration)**.

6   **Caution:** *Position the crankshaft sprocket with the arrow mark or "FRONT" facing out and in its original position on the*

9.5 Lubricate the new seal with engine oil and drive the seal into place with a hammer and seal driver or a socket

9.6 Position the crankshaft sprocket with the mark facing out, and install it onto the crankshaft in its original position

crankshaft (as discussed in Step 2) **(see illustration)**. Use a hammer and socket to install the sprocket.

7   The remaining steps are the reverse of removal. Reinstall the timing belt (see Section 7).

8   Run the engine and check for oil leaks.

10 Camshaft oil seal - replacement

Refer to illustrations 10.3 and 10.5

Caution: *Do not rotate the camshafts when the timing belt is removed or damage to the engine may occur.*

1   Remove the timing belt (see Section 7)

2   Remove the camshaft sprockets and rear timing belt cover (see Section 8). Remove the exhaust camshaft target ring and sensor.

3   Note how far the seal is seated in the bore, then carefully pry it out with a small screwdriver **(see illustration)**. Don't scratch the bore or damage the camshaft in the process (if the camshaft is damaged, the new seal will end up leaking).

10.3 Carefully pry the camshaft seal out of the bore - DO NOT nick or scratch the camshaft or seal bore

4   Clean the bore and coat the outer edge of the new seal with engine oil or multi-purpose grease. Also lubricate the seal lip.

5   Using a socket with an outside diameter slightly smaller than the outside diameter of the seal **(see illustration)**, carefully drive the new seal into place with a hammer. Make sure it's installed squarely and driven in to the same depth as the original. If a socket isn't available, a short section of pipe will also work.

6   Install the rear timing belt cover part and camshaft sprockets (see Section 8).

7   Install the timing belt (see Section 7).

8   Run the engine and check for oil leaks at the camshaft seal.

11 Camshafts - removal, inspection and installation

Removal

Refer to illustration 11.5

1   Remove the valve cover (see Section 4).

2   Remove the Camshaft Position Sensor (CMP) (see Chapter 6) and the camshaft target magnet.

10.5 Gently tap the new seal into place with the spring side toward the engine

FRONT

50035-2A-11.5 HAYNES

11.5 First, remove the outside bearing caps (A), then loosen the remaining camshaft bearing cap bolts a little at a time in the sequence shown

11.9 Measure the camshaft bearing journal diameters with a micrometer

3   Remove the timing belt (see Section 7).
4   Remove the camshaft sprockets and the rear timing belt cover (see Section 8).
5   The camshaft bearing caps are identified with their numbered location in the cylinder head. They must be returned to their original locations. Remove the front and rear bearing caps at each end of the camshafts. Remove the remaining camshaft bearing caps. Loosen the bolts a little at a time to prevent distorting the camshafts, in the sequence shown **(see illustration)**. When the bearing caps have all been loosened enough for removal, they may still be difficult to remove. Use the bearing cap bolts for leverage and move the cap back and forth to loosen the cap from the cylinder head. If they are still difficult to remove you can tap them gently with a soft face mallet until they can be lifted off. **Caution:** *Store them in order so they can be returned to their original locations, with the same side facing forward.*
6   Carefully lift the camshafts out of the cylinder head. Mark the camshafts INTAKE and EXHAUST. They cannot be interchanged.
7   Remove the front seal from each camshaft. **Note:** *It would be a good idea to inspect the rocker arms and lash adjusters at this time (see Section 12).*

Inspection

Refer to illustration 11.9
8   Clean the camshaft(s) and the gasket surface. Inspect the camshaft for wear and/or damage to the lobe surfaces, bearing journals, and seal contact surfaces. Inspect the camshaft bearing surfaces in the cylinder head and bearing caps for scoring and other damage.
9   Measure the camshaft bearing journal diameters **(see illustration)**. Measure the inside diameter of the camshaft bearing surfaces in the cylinder head, using a telescoping gauge (temporarily install the bearing caps). Subtract the journal measurement from the bearing measurement to obtain the camshaft bearing oil clearance. Compare this

clearance with the value listed this Chapter's Specifications. Replace worn components as required.
10   Replace the camshaft if it fails any of the above inspections. **Note:** *If the lobes are worn, replace the rocker arms and lash adjusters along with the camshaft.* The cylinder head may need to be replaced, if the camshaft bearing surfaces in the head are damaged or excessively worn.
11   Clean and inspect the cylinder head (see Chapter 2D).

Camshaft endplay measurement

12   Lubricate the camshaft(s) and cylinder head bearing journals with clean engine oil.
13   Place the camshaft in its original location in the cylinder head. **Note:** *Do not install the rocker arms for this check.* Install the rear bearing cap and tighten the bolts to the torque listed in this Chapter's Specifications.
14   Install a dial indicator on the cylinder head and place the indicator tip on the camshaft at the sprocket end.

15   Use a screwdriver to carefully pry the camshaft fully to the rear until it stops. Zero the dial indicator and pry the camshaft fully to the front. The amount of indicator travel is the camshaft endplay. Compare the endplay with the tolerance given in this Chapter's Specifications. If the endplay is excessive, check the camshaft and cylinder head bearing journals for wear. Replace as necessary.

Installation

Refer to illustrations 11.17 and 11.20
16   Install the valve lash adjusters and rocker arms (see Section 11).
17   Clean the camshaft and bearing journals and caps. Liberally coat the journals, lobes, and thrust portions of the camshaft with assembly lube or engine oil **(see illustration)**.
18   Carefully install the camshafts in the cylinder head in their original location. Temporarily install the camshaft sprockets and rotate the camshafts so that their timing marks align **(see illustration 7.11a)**. Make sure the crankshaft is positioned with the

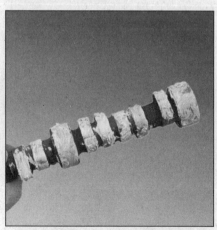

11.17 Prior to installing each camshaft, lubricate the bearing journals, thrust surfaces and lobes with assembly lube or clean engine oil

50035-2A-11.20 HAYNES

11.20 Apply a bead of anaerobic sealant to the indicated areas on the No. 1 and No. 6 bearing caps, then install these bearing caps

crankshaft sprocket timing mark at three teeth BTDC. **Caution:** *If the pistons are at TDC when tightening the camshaft bearing caps, damage to the engine may occur.*

19   Install the bearing caps, except for the No. 1 and No. 6 (left side) end caps. Tighten the bolts in several steps, in the proper sequence **(see illustration 11.5)** to the torque listed in this Chapter's Specifications.

20   Apply a small bead of anaerobic sealant (approximately 1/8-inch) to the No. 1 and No. 6 (left side) bearing caps **(see illustration)**. Install the bearing caps and tighten the bolts to the torque listed in this Chapter's Specifications.

21   Install new camshaft oil seals (see Section 10).

22   Install the timing belt, covers, and related components (see Sections 7 and 8).

23   Install the valve cover (see Section 4).

12 Rocker arms - removal, inspection and installation

Removal

1   Remove the valve cover (see Section 4).
2   Remove both camshafts (see Section 11).
3   Once the camshafts have been removed, the rocker arms can be lifted off. **Caution:** *Each rocker arm must be placed back in the same location it was removed from, so mark each rocker arm or place them in a container (such as an egg carton) so they won't get mixed up. The lash adjusters can remain in the head at this time, unless they are being replaced (see Section 13).*

Inspection

4   Inspect the rocker arm tip, roller and lash adjuster pocket for wear. Replace them if evidence of wear or damage is found.
5   Carefully inspect each lash adjuster for signs of wear and damage, particularly on the ball tip that contacts the rocker arm. The lash adjusters become clogged as they age, so it's a good idea to replace them if you're concerned about their condition or if the engine is making valve "tapping" noises.

Installation

6   Installation is the reverse of removal. When reinstalling the rocker arms, make sure that you install them at the same locations from which they were removed.

13 Valve lash adjusters - removal, inspection and installation

1   Remove the rocker arms (see Section 12).
2   If the lash adjusters aren't already removed from the head, lift them out now. **Caution:** *Be sure to keep the adjusters in order so they can be placed back in the same location in the cylinder head it was removed from.*
3   Inspect each adjuster carefully for signs

14.4 This is what the air hose adapter that threads into the spark plug hole looks like - they're generally available from auto parts stores

of wear and damage, particularly on the ball tip that contacts the rocker arm. Since the lash adjusters can become clogged, we recommend replacing them if you're concerned about their condition or if the engine is exhibiting valve "tapping" noises.

4   The lash adjusters must be partially full of engine oil - indicated by little or no plunger action when the adjuster is depressed. If there's excessive plunger travel, place the lash adjuster into clean engine oil and pump the plunger until the plunger travel is eliminated. **Note:** *If the plunger still travels within the lash adjuster when full of oil it's defective and the lash adjuster must be replaced.*

5   When re-starting the engine after replacing the adjusters, the adjusters will normally make "tapping" noises. After warm-up, raise the speed of the engine from idle to 3,000 rpm for one minute. If the adjuster(s) do not become silent, replace the defective ones.

14 Valve springs, retainers and seals - replacement

Refer to illustrations 14.4, 14.7, 14.8, 14.13 and 14.15

Note: *Broken valve springs and defective valve stem seals can be replaced without removing the cylinder heads. Two special tools and a compressed air source are normally required to perform this operation, so read through this Section carefully and rent or buy the tools before beginning the job.*

1   Remove the rocker arms (see Section 13).
2   Remove the spark plug from the cylinder that has the defective component. If all of the valve stem seals are being replaced, all of the spark plugs should be removed.
3   Turn the crankshaft until the piston in the affected cylinder is at top dead center on the compression stroke (refer to Section 3). If you're replacing all of the valve stem seals, begin with cylinder number one and work on the valves for one cylinder at a time. Move from cylinder-to-cylinder following the firing

14.7 Use needle-nose pliers (shown) or a small magnet to remove the valve spring keepers - be careful not to drop them down into the engine!

order sequence (see this Chapter's Specifications).

4   Thread an adapter into the spark plug hole **(see illustration)** and connect an air hose from a compressed air source to it. Most auto parts stores can supply the air hose adapter. **Note:** *Many cylinder compression gauges utilize a screw-in fitting that may work with your air hose quick-disconnect fitting.*

5   Remove the camshaft(s) and the rocker arm(s) (see Sections 11 and 12).

6   Apply compressed air to the cylinder. **Warning:** *The piston may be forced down by compressed air, causing the crankshaft to turn suddenly. If the wrench used when positioning the number one piston at TDC is still attached to the bolt in the crankshaft nose, remove it as it could cause damage or injury when the crankshaft moves.*

7   Stuff clean shop rags into the various oil-drain holes in the cylinder head, to prevent parts and tools from falling into the engine. Use a valve spring compressor to compress the spring. Remove the keepers with small needle-nose pliers or a magnet **(see illustration)**.

8   Remove the spring retainer and valve spring, then remove the valve guide seal/spring seat assembly **(see illustration)**.

14.8 Remove the valve guide seal with a pair of pliers

Caution: *If air pressure fails to hold the valve in the closed position during this operation, the valve face and/or seat is probably damaged. If so, the cylinder head will have to be removed for additional repair operations.*

9   Wrap a rubber band or tape around the top of the valve stem so the valve won't fall into the combustion chamber, then release the air pressure.

10   Inspect the valve stem for damage. Rotate the valve in the guide and check the end for eccentric movement, which would indicate that the valve is bent.

11   Move the valve up-and-down in the guide and make sure it doesn't bind. If the valve stem binds, either the valve is bent or the guide is damaged. In either case, the head will have to be removed for repair.

12   Pull up on the valve stem to close the valve, reapply air pressure to the cylinder to retain the valve in the closed position, then remove the tape or rubber band from the valve stem.

13   Lubricate the valve stem with engine oil and install a new valve guide seal/spring seat assembly. Tap into place with a deep socket **(see illustration)**.

14   Install the spring in position over the valve.

15   Install the valve spring retainer. Compress the valve spring and carefully position the keepers in the groove. Apply a small dab of grease to the inside of each keeper to hold it in place if necessary **(see illustration)**.

16   Remove the pressure from the spring tool and make sure the keepers are seated.

17   Disconnect the air hose and remove the adapter from the spark plug hole.

18   The remainder of the installation is the reverse of removal.

19   Start and run the engine, then check for oil leaks and unusual sounds coming from the valve cover area.

14.13 Gently tap the new seal into place with a hammer and a deep socket

15   Cylinder head - removal and installation

Warning: *Allow the engine to cool completely before beginning this procedure.*

Removal

Refer to illustrations 15.4 and 15.12

1   Position the number one piston at Top Dead Center (see Section 3).

2   Disconnect the cable from the negative terminal of the battery (see Chapter 5).

3   Drain the cooling system (see Chapter 1).

4   Remove the intake manifold (see Section 5). Cover the intake ports with duct tape to keep out debris **(see illustration)**.

5   Remove the spark plug wires, spark plugs and ignition coil (see Chapters 1 and 5).

6   Remove the upper radiator and heater hoses (see Chapter 1). Remove the heater tube support bracket.

7   Detach the power steering pump bolts

14.15 Apply a small dab of grease to each keeper before installation to hold it in place on the valve stem until the spring is released

from the engine (leaving the hoses attached) and set the pump aside (see Chapter 10). Remove the accessory bracket(s).

8   Raise the front of the vehicle and place it securely on jackstands. Disconnect the exhaust pipe from the exhaust manifold (see Chapter 4) and lower the vehicle.

9   Remove the timing belt (see Section 7).

10   Remove the valve cover, camshafts and rocker arms (see Sections 4, 11 and 12).

11   Loosen the cylinder head bolts 1/4-turn at a time, in the reverse of the tightening sequence **(see illustration 15.18)** until they can be removed by hand. **Note:** *Write down the location of the different length bolts so they will be reinstalled in the correct location.*

12   Carefully lift the cylinder head straight up and place the head on wood blocks to prevent damage to the sealing surfaces. If the head sticks to the engine block, dislodge it by placing a wood block against the head casting and tapping the wood with a hammer or by prying the head with a prybar placed

15.4 Cover the intake ports with duct tape to keep out debris before removing the cylinder head (typical)

15.12 If the head sticks to the engine block, dislodge it by placing a wood block against the head casting and tapping the wood with a hammer or by prying the head with a prybar placed carefully on a casting protrusion (typical)

15.18 Cylinder head bolt TIGHTENING sequence

50035-2A-15.18 HAYNES

16.11a Using a criss-cross pattern, loosen and remove the oil pan bolts (typical) . . .

◄ — **Front**

carefully on a casting protrusion **(see illustration). Caution:** *The cylinder head is aluminum, so you must be very careful not to gouge the sealing surfaces.*

Inspection

13   Special gasket removal solvents that soften gaskets and make removal much easier are available at auto parts stores. Remove all traces of old gasket material from the block and head. Do not allow anything to fall into the engine.
14   Using a straightedge and feeler gauge, check the gasket mating surfaces for warpage. If the warpage on either surface exceeds the limit listed in this Chapter's Specifications, the cylinder head must be resurfaced at an automotive machine shop. The machine shop can also clean and inspect the cylinder head components.
15   Clean and inspect all threaded bolts and be sure the threaded holes in the block are clean and dry. Inspect the threads on the cylinder head bolts with a straight edge. If any of the threads don't touch the straight edge, the bolts are stretched, and should be replaced.

Installation

Refer to illustrations 15.18

16   Place a new gasket and the cylinder head in position on the engine block.
17   Apply clean engine oil to the cylinder head bolt threads prior to installation. The four short bolts (4.33 inch long) are to be installed in each corner of the cylinder head.
18   Tighten the cylinder head bolts in several stages in the recommended sequence **(see illustration)** to the torque listed in this Chapter's Specifications.
19   Reinstall the timing belt (see Section 7).
20   Reinstall the remaining parts in the reverse order of removal.
21   Refill the cooling system and change the engine oil and filter (see Chapter 1). Rotate the crankshaft clockwise slowly by hand

through six complete revolutions. Recheck the camshaft timing marks (see Section 7).
22   Start the engine and run it until normal operating temperature is reached. Check for leaks and proper operation.

16   Oil pan - removal and installation

Removal

Refer to illustrations 16.11a, 16.11b, 16.11c, 16.12a, 16.12b and 16.13

1   Disconnect the cable from the negative terminal of the battery (see Chapter 5).
2   Remove the air filter housing (see Chapter 4).
3   Raise the vehicle and support it securely on jackstands.
4   Drain the engine oil (see Chapter 1).
5   Disconnect the exhaust pipe at the exhaust manifold (see Chapter 4).
6   Remove the structural collar.
7   On 4WD models, support the front axle

assembly with a floor jack, remove the front axle assembly mounting bolts (see Chapter 8), then lower the axle housing as much as possible.
8   Remove nuts from the engine mounts.
9   Support the engine from above with an engine hoist (but not on the intake manifold), take the weight off the engine mounts with the hoist and remove the engine mount through-bolts (see Section 19).
10   Raise the engine sufficiently to allow access for oil pan removal.
11   Remove the mounting bolts and lower the oil pan from the vehicle **(see illustrations)**. If the pan is stuck, tap it with a soft-face hammer **(see illustration)** or place a wood block against the pan and tap the wood block with a hammer. **Caution:** *If you're wedging something between the oil pan and the engine block to separate the two, be extremely careful not to gouge or nick the gasket surface of either part; an oil leak could result.*
12   Remove the oil pump pickup tube and

16.11b . . . then lower the pan carefully (there might still be some residual oil in the pan) (typical)

16.11c If the pan is stuck, tap it with a soft-face hammer or place a wood block against the pan and tap the wood block with a hammer (typical)

16.12a Remove the bolt and remove the oil pump pick-up tube and screen assembly - clean both the tube and screen thoroughly before reassembly

16.12b Replace the seal at the oil pump pick-up tube mounting flange with a new one

screen assembly **(see illustration)** and clean both the tube and screen thoroughly. Install the pick-up tube and screen with a new seal **(see illustration)**.

13   Thoroughly clean the oil pan and sealing surfaces on the block and pan **(see illustration)**. Use a scraper to remove all traces of old gasket material. Gasket removal solvents are available at auto parts stores and may prove helpful. Check the oil pan sealing surface for distortion. Straighten or replace as necessary. After cleaning and straightening (if necessary), wipe the gasket surfaces of the pan and block clean with a rag soaked in lacquer thinner or acetone.

Installation

14   Apply a 1/8-inch bead of RTV sealant at the cylinder block-to-oil pump assembly joint at the oil pan flange. Install a new oil pan gasket.

15   Place the oil pan into position and install the bolts finger-tight. Working side-to-side from the center out, tighten the bolts to the torque listed in this Chapter's Specifications.

16   Lower the engine and install the through-bolts in the engine mounts (see Section 19). Tighten them securely.

17   Install the structural collar as follows:

   a) *Place the collar in position between the transmission and the oil pan and then hand-start the collar-to-transmission bolts.*
   b) *Install and then hand-tighten the collar-to-oil pan bolts.*
   c) *Tighten the collar-to-transmission bolts.*
   d) *Tighten the collar-to-oil pan bolts.*

18   The remainder of installation is the reverse of removal.

19   Refill the crankcase with the correct quantity and grade of oil, run the engine and check for leaks.

20   Road test the vehicle and check for leaks again.

17   Oil pump - removal, inspection and installation

Removal

Refer to illustrations 17.3a, 17.3b, 17.5a, 17.5b and 17.5c

1   Remove the timing belt, timing belt covers and the crankshaft front seal (see Sections 7, 8 and 9).

2   Remove the oil pan and pick-up tube/screen assembly (see Section 16).

3   Remove the bolts and detach the oil pump assembly from the engine **(see illustration)**. **Caution:** *If the pump doesn't come off by hand, tap it gently with a soft-faced hammer or pry on a casting boss* **(see illustration)**.

4   Remove the crankshaft oil seal from the oil pump, by prying it out with a screwdriver wrapped in a rag. **Caution:** *To prevent an oil leak after the new seal is installed, be very*

16.13 Thoroughly clean the oil pan and sealing surfaces on the engine block and oil pan (arrow) with a scraper to remove all traces of old gasket material (typical)

17.3a Remove the oil pump assembly mounting bolts and remove the assembly (typical)

17.3b If the pump doesn't come off by hand, tap it gently with a soft-faced hammer or pry gently on a casting protrusion (typical)

17.5a Remove the cover mounting screws (typical) . . .

17.5b . . . and the cover (typical)

17.5c Arrangement of oil pump components (typical)

A Cover	C Inner rotor
B Outer rotor	D Oil pump body

17.7 Oil pressure relief valve components (typical)

A Cap	C Spring	E Oil pump
B Gasket	D Relief valve	body

careful not to scratch or otherwise damage the seal-bore in the pump body.

5   Remove the mounting screws and remove the cover **(see illustration)**. Remove the inner and outer rotor from the body **(see illustration)**. **Caution:** *Be very careful with these parts. Close tolerances are critical in creating the correct oil pressure. Any nicks or other damage will require replacement of the complete pump assembly.*

Inspection

Refer to illustrations 17.7, 17.8a, 17.8b, 17.8c, 17.8d and 17.8e

6   Clean all components including the block surfaces with solvent, then inspect all surfaces for excessive wear and/or damage.

7   To disassemble the relief valve, remove the cap bolt, washer, spring and relief valve **(see illustration)**. Check the oil pressure relief valve piston sliding surface and valve spring. If either the spring or the valve is damaged, they must be replaced as a set. If no damage is found reassemble the relief valve

parts. **Caution:** *Make sure to install the relief valve into the pump body with the grooved end going in first - otherwise engine damage may occur. Coat the parts with oil and reinstall them in the oil pump body. Tighten the*

cap bolt to this Chapter's Specifications.

8   Check the clearance of the oil pump components with a micrometer and a feeler gauge **(see illustrations)** and compare the results to this Chapter's Specifications.

17.8a Measure the outer rotor thickness

17.8b Measure the inner rotor thickness

17.8c Use a caliper and measure the outer diameter of the outer rotor

17.8d Use a feeler gauge and measure the outer rotor-to-case clearance

17.8e Place a precision straightedge over the rotors and measure the clearance between the rotors and the cover

Installation

Refer to illustrations 17.10a and 17.10b

9   Lubricate the housing and the inner and outer rotors with clean engine oil and install both rotors in the body. **Caution:** *When installing the inner rotor, the chamfer faces the pump cover.* Prime the oil pump by filling the rotor cavities with clean engine oil. Install the cover and tighten the cover screws to the torque listed in this Chapter's Specifications.

10   Install a new O-ring in the oil discharge passage **(see illustration)**. Apply sealant to the oil pump body **(see illustration)**, and raise the pump assembly to the block. Align the flat parts of the rotor with the flat parts of the crankshaft. Tighten the bolts to the torque listed in this Chapter's Specifications.

11   Install the crankshaft seal (see Section 9).

12   Install the pick-up tube/strainer assembly and oil pan (see Section 16).

13   Install the crankshaft sprocket (see Section 9).

14   Install the rear timing belt cover (see Section 8).

15   Install the timing belt (see Section 7).

16   Install a new oil filter and engine oil (see

Chapter 1).

17   Start the engine and check for oil pressure and leaks.

18   Recheck the engine oil level.

18 Flywheel/driveplate - removal and installation

Removal

Refer to illustration 18.5

1   Raise the vehicle and support it securely on jackstands.

2   Remove the transmission assembly (see Chapter 7).

3   If the vehicle has a manual transmission, remove the pressure plate and clutch disc (see Chapter 8). Now is a good time to check/replace the clutch components.

4   To ensure correct alignment during reinstallation, mark the position of the flywheel/driveplate to the crankshaft before removal.

5   Remove the bolts that secure the flywheel/driveplate to the crankshaft **(see illustration)**. A tool is available at most auto parts

17.10a Replace the O-ring seal in the oil pump body - apply clean engine oil to the seal

stores to hold the flywheel/driveplate while loosening the bolts. If the tool is not available, wedge a screwdriver in the ring gear teeth to jam the flywheel.

6   Remove the flywheel/driveplate from the crankshaft. Since the flywheel is fairly heavy,

17.10b Apply a bead of anaerobic sealant to the housing sealing surface as shown

18.5 Mark the relative position of the flywheel or driveplate to the crankshaft and, using an appropriate tool to hold the flywheel, remove the bolts (typical)

19.5 Carefully pry the crankshaft seal out of the bore - DO NOT nick or scratch the crankshaft or seal bore

be sure to support it while removing the last bolt.

7   Clean the flywheel to remove grease and oil. Inspect the flywheel (see Chapter 8).

8   Clean and inspect the mating surfaces of the flywheel/driveplate and the crankshaft. If the crankshaft rear main seal is leaking, replace it before reinstalling the flywheel/driveplate (see Section 19).

Installation

9   Position the flywheel/driveplate against the crankshaft. Align the previously applied match marks. Before installing the bolts, apply thread locking compound to the threads.

10   Hold the flywheel/driveplate with the holding tool, or wedge a screwdriver in the ring gear teeth to keep the flywheel/driveplate from turning as you tighten the bolts to the torque listed in this Chapter's Specifications.

11   The remainder of installation is the reverse of the removal procedure.

19   Rear main oil seal - replacement

Refer to illustrations 19.5 and 19.7

1   The one-piece rear main oil seal is pressed into a bore machined into the rear main bearing cap and engine block.

2   Remove the transmission (see Chapter 7)

3   If equipped, remove the clutch components (see Chapter 8)

4   Remove the flywheel or driveplate (see Section 18).

5   **Note:** *Observe that the oil seal is installed flush with the outer surface of the*

block. Using the chamfered edge on the crankshaft, pry out the old seal with a 3/16-inch flat blade screwdriver (see illustration). Caution: To prevent an oil leak after the new seal is installed, be very careful not to scratch or otherwise damage the crankshaft sealing surface or the bore in the engine block.

6   Clean the crankshaft and seal bore in the block thoroughly and de-grease these areas by wiping them with a rag soaked in lacquer thinner or acetone. If there is a burr or scratch on the crankshaft chamfer edge, sand it with 400-grit sandpaper. Do not lubricate the lip or outer diameter of the new seal - it must be installed as it comes from the manufacturer.

7   Position the new seal onto the crankshaft. **Note:** *When installing the new seal, the words THIS SIDE OUT on the seal must face out, toward the rear of the vehicle. If the seal is not marked, the seal lip (that seals against the crankshaft) must face in.* Using an appropriate size driver and pilot tool, gently and gradually drive the seal into the cylinder block until it is flush with the outer surface of the block **(see illustration)**. Caution: *If the seal is driven-in past the flush-position, there will be an oil leak.*

8   The remainder of installation is the reverse of removal.

20   Engine mounts - check and replacement

1   Engine mounts seldom require attention, but broken or deteriorated mounts should be replaced immediately or the added strain placed on the driveline components may cause damage or wear.

Check

2   During the check, the engine must be raised slightly to remove the weight from the mounts.

3   Raise the vehicle and support it securely on jackstands, then position a jack under the engine oil pan. Place a large wood block between the jack head and the oil pan to prevent oil pan damage, then carefully raise the engine just enough to take the weight off the mounts. **Warning:** *DO NOT place any part of your body under the engine when only a jack supports it.*

4   Check the mounts to see if the rubber is cracked, hardened or separated from the metal backing. Sometimes the rubber will split right down the center.

5   Check for relative movement between the mount plates and the engine or frame (use a large screwdriver or pry bar to attempt to move the mounts). If movement is noted,

19.7 Position the new seal with the words THIS SIDE OUT facing out, toward the rear of the engine. If the seal is not marked, the seal lip (that seals against the crankshaft) must face in. Gently and gradually drive the seal into the cylinder block until it is flush with the outer surface of the block. Do not drive it past flush or there will be an oil leak - the seal must be flush

lower the engine and tighten the mount fasteners.

6   Rubber preservative may be applied to the mounts to slow deterioration.

Replacement

7   Disconnect the cable from the negative terminal of the battery, then raise the vehicle and support it securely on jackstands (if not already done).

8   Place a floor jack under the engine (with a wood block between the jack head and oil pan) and raise the engine slightly to relieve the weight from the mounts.

9   Remove the through-bolt from the engine mount.

10   Remove the engine mount from the side of the engine block. **Note:** *Do not disconnect more than one mount at a time, except during engine removal.*

11   Install the new engine mount assembly to the engine block and tighten the bolts securely.

12   Slowly lower the engine, while watching for proper mount-to-frame alignment, and then install the through-bolt. Hand-tighten the nut on the through-bolt.

13   Completely lower the engine and tighten the through-bolt securely.

14   If necessary, repeat the process for the motor mount on the other side of the engine.

15   The remainder of installation is the reverse of removal.

Notes

Chapter 2 Part B
2.5L four-cylinder engine

Contents

Specifications

General

Displacement..	150 cu. in. (2.5 liters)
Cylinder numbers (front-to-rear)...	1-2-3-4
Firing order	1-3-4-2

Camshaft

Lobe lift (intake and exhaust)...	0.265 in
End-play	None
Journal-to-bearing (oil) clearance...	0.001 to 0.003 in
Journal out-of-round limit..	0.002 in
Fuel pump eccentric diameter...	1.615 to 1.625 in
Journal diameter (journals numbered from front-to-rear of engine)	
No. 1	2.029 to 2.030 in
No. 2	2.019 to 2.020 in
No. 3	2.009 to 2.010 in
No. 4	1.999 to 2.000 in

FIRING ORDER:
1 3 4 2
CLOCKWISE
ROTATION

Cylinder location and distributor rotation

Torque specifications

Ft-lbs (unless otherwise indicated)

Camshaft sprocket bolt	80
Crankshaft pulley-to-vibration damper bolts	20
Cylinder head bolts (see illustration 8.15 for tightening sequence)	
1987 and 1988	
Bolts 1 through 7 and 9, 10	85
Bolt 8 only	75
1989 on	
Bolts 1 through 7 and 9, 10	110
Bolt 8 only	100
Driveplate-to-crankshaft bolts	
First step	40
Second step	60 degrees additional turn
Exhaust manifold nuts	23
Flywheel-to-crankshaft bolts	
First step	50
Second step	60 degrees additional turn
Intake manifold-to-cylinder head bolts	23
Oil pan mounting bolts	
1/4 x 20	7
5/16 x 18	11
Oil pump bolts	
Short	10
Long	17
Rocker arm capscrews	19
Valve cover-to-cylinder head bolts	
With RTV	55 in-lbs
With pre-cured permanent gasket	44 in-lbs
Timing chain tensioner-to-block bolt	14
Timing chain cover-to-block	
Bolts	5
Nuts	16
Vibration damper bolt (lubricated)	80

1   General information

This Part of Chapter 2 is devoted to in-vehicle repair procedures for the 2.5 liter four-cylinder engine. Information concerning engine removal and installation, as well as engine block and cylinder head overhaul, is in Part C of this Chapter.

The following repair procedures are based on the assumption that the engine is installed in the vehicle. If the engine has been removed from the vehicle and mounted on a stand, many of the steps included in this Part of Chapter 2 will not apply.

The Specifications included in this Part of Chapter 2 apply only to the engine and procedures in this Part. The Specifications necessary for rebuilding the block and cylinder head are found in Part D.

2   Repair operations possible with the engine in the vehicle

Many major repair operations can be accomplished without removing the engine from the vehicle.

Clean the engine compartment and the exterior of the engine with some type of pressure washer before any work is done. A clean engine will make the job easier and will help keep dirt out of the internal areas of the engine.

If vacuum, exhaust, oil or coolant leaks develop, indicating a need for gasket or seal replacement, the repairs can generally be made with the engine in the vehicle. The intake and exhaust manifold gaskets, oil pan gasket and cylinder head gasket are all accessible with the engine in place.

Exterior engine components such as the intake and exhaust manifolds, the oil pan (and the oil pump), the water pump, the starter motor, the alternator, the distributor and the carburetor or fuel injection components can be removed for repair with the engine in place.

Since the cylinder head can be removed without pulling the engine, valve component servicing can also be accomplished with the engine in the vehicle.

In extreme cases caused by a lack of necessary equipment, repair or replacement of piston rings, pistons, connecting rods and rod bearings is possible with the engine in the vehicle. However, this practice is not recommended because of the cleaning and preparation work that must be done to the components involved.

3   Top Dead Center (TDC) for number one piston - locating

Refer to illustrations 3.6 and 3.8
Note: *The following procedure is based on the assumption that the distributor is cor-*rectly installed. If you are trying to locate TDC to install the distributor correctly, piston position must be determined by feeling for compression at the number one spark plug hole, then aligning the ignition timing marks as described in Step 8.

1　Top Dead Center (TDC) is the highest point in the cylinder that each piston reaches as it travels up-and-down when the crankshaft turns. Each piston reaches TDC on the compression stroke and again on the exhaust stroke, but TDC generally refers to piston position on the compression stroke.

2　Positioning the piston(s) at TDC is an essential part of many procedures such as rocker arm removal, camshaft and timing chain/sprocket removal and distributor removal.

3　Before beginning this procedure, be sure to place the transmission in Neutral and apply the parking brake or block the rear wheels. Also, remove the spark plugs (see Chapter 1) and disable the ignition system. Detach the coil wire from the center terminal of the distributor cap and ground it on the block with a jumper wire.

4　In order to bring any piston to TDC, the crankshaft must be turned using one of the methods outlined below. When looking at the front of the engine, normal crankshaft rotation is clockwise.

a) *The preferred method is to turn the crankshaft with a socket and ratchet attached to the bolt threaded into the front of the crankshaft.*

3.6 Make a mark on the aluminum distributor body directly below the number one spark plug wire terminal on the distributor cap (arrow)

3.8 Turn the crankshaft clockwise until the notch aligns with the 0

b) *A remote starter switch, which may save some time, can also be used. Follow the instructions included with the switch. Once the piston is close to TDC, use a socket and ratchet, as described in the previous paragraph.*

c) *If an assistant is available to turn the ignition switch to the Start position in short bursts, you can get the piston close to TDC without a remote starter switch. Make sure your assistant is out of the vehicle, away from the ignition switch, then use a socket and ratchet (as described in Paragraph a) to complete the procedure.*

5   Note the position of the terminal for the number one spark plug wire on the distributor cap. If the terminal isn't marked, follow the plug wire from the number one cylinder spark plug to the cap.

6   Use a felt-tip pen or chalk to make a mark on the distributor body directly under the terminal **(see illustration)**.

7   Detach the cap from the distributor and set it aside (see Chapter 1 if necessary).

8   Turn the crankshaft (see Paragraph 3 above) until the notch in the crankshaft pulley is aligned with the 0 on the timing plate (located at the front of the engine) **(see illustration)**.

9   Look at the distributor rotor - it should be pointing directly at the mark you made on the distributor body. If it is, go to Step 12.

10   If the rotor is 180 degrees off, the number one piston is at TDC on the exhaust stroke. Go to Step 11.

11   To get the piston to TDC on the compression stroke, turn the crankshaft one complete turn (360 degrees) clockwise. The rotor should now be pointing at the mark on the distributor. When the rotor is pointing at the number one spark plug wire terminal in the distributor cap and the ignition timing marks are aligned, the number one piston is at TDC on the compression stroke.

12   After the number one piston has been positioned at TDC on the compression

stroke, TDC for any of the remaining pistons can be located by turning the crankshaft and following the firing order. Mark the remaining spark plug wire terminal locations on the distributor body just like you did for the number one terminal, then number the marks to correspond with the cylinder numbers. As you turn the crankshaft, the rotor will also turn. When it's pointing directly at one of the marks on the distributor, the piston for that particular cylinder is at TDC on the compression stroke.

4   Valve cover - removal and installation

Refer to illustrations 4.3a, 4.3b, 4.4, 4.5a, 4.5b, 4.7a and 4.7b

1   Disconnect the negative cable from the battery.

2   Remove the air cleaner (see Chapter 4).

3   Label and then remove all hoses and/or wires necessary to provide clearance for valve cover removal **(see illustrations)**.

4.3a Typical valve cover - before removing, disconnect the vacuum and crankcase ventilating hoses (arrows)

4.3b Remove the nut (arrow) and clamp from the valve cover and place the heater hose toward the rear of the engine compartment

4 Remove the valve cover retaining bolts and lift off the cover. The cover may stick. Detach the cover by breaking the seal with a putty knife or razor blade. Locations for prying have been provided **(see illustration)**. **Caution:** *To avoid damaging the cover, do not pry up until the seal has been broken.*

5 Prior to installation, remove all traces of dirt, oil and old gasket material from the cover and cylinder head with a scraper **(see illustrations)**. Clean the mating surfaces with lacquer thinner or acetone and a clean rag.

6 Inspect the mating surface on the cover for damage and warpage. Correct or replace as necessary.

7 On models which use RTV, apply a continuous 1/8-inch (3mm) bead of sealant (Jeep Gasket-In-a-Tube or equivalent) to the cover flange. Be sure the sealant is applied to the inside of the bolt holes **(see illustrations)**. **Note:** *On models with plastic valve covers* **(see illustration)**, *RTV or a gasket may be*

4.4 If the valve cover is specifically marked, carefully pry the cover loose after breaking the seal with a putty knife or razor blade

4.5a Remove the old sealant from the valve cover flange and the cylinder head with a gasket scraper, then clean the mating surfaces with lacquer thinner or acetone

4.5b On engines equipped with plastic valve covers, pry the rubber gasket from the groove along the perimeter

4.7a On engines equipped with plastic valve covers, the rubber gasket may not be available for replacement. Instead, apply a continuous 3/16-inch diameter bead of the sealant (arrow) to the valve cover flange

4.7b Make sure the sealant is applied to the INSIDE of the bolt holes or oil will leak out around the bolt threads

ROCKER ARM
CAPSCREW

BRIDGE

PIVOT

ROCKER ARM

CYLINDER
HEAD
PEDESTAL

HOLLOW
PUSH ROD

5.3 Rocker arm mounts - exploded view

5.4 If more than one pushrod is being removed, store them in a perforated cardboard box to prevent mix-ups during installation - note the label indicating the front of the engine

6.4 This is what the air hose adapter that threads into the spark plug holes looks like - they're commonly available from auto parts stores

6.9 Once the spring is depressed, the keepers can be removed with a small magnet or needle-nose pliers (a magnet is preferred to prevent dropping the keepers)

used. Check with an automotive parts department. On models equipped with an aluminum valve cover, RTV must be used. Later models use a pre-cured reusable gasket - install these without sealant.

8   Place the valve cover on the cylinder head while the sealant (if used) is still wet and install the mounting bolts. Tighten the bolts a little at a time until the torque listed in this Chapter's Specifications is reached.

9   Complete the installation procedure by reversing the removal procedure.

10   Start the engine and check for oil leaks.

5   Rocker arms and pushrods - removal, inspection and installation

Refer to illustrations 5.3 and 5.4

Removal

1   Detach the valve cover from the cylinder head, referring to Section 4.

2   Beginning at the front of the cylinder head, loosen the rocker arm bolts.

3   Remove the capscrews, bridges, pivots and rocker arms (see illustration). Store them in marked containers (they must be reinstalled in their original locations).

4   Remove the pushrods and store them separately to make sure they don't get mixed up during installation (see illustration).

Inspection

5   Check each rocker arm for wear, cracks and other damage, especially where the pushrods and valve stems contact the rocker arm faces.

6   Make sure the hole at the pushrod end of each rocker arm is open.

7   Check each rocker arm pivot area for wear, cracks and galling. If the rocker arms are worn or damaged, replace them with new ones and use new pivots as well.

8   Inspect the pushrods for cracks and excessive wear at the ends. Roll each

pushrod across a piece of plate glass to see if it's bent (if it wobbles, it's bent).

Installation

9   Lubricate the lower ends of the pushrods with clean engine oil or moly-base grease and install them in their original locations. Make sure each pushrod seats completely in the lifter socket.

10   Apply moly-base grease to the ends of the valve stems and the upper ends of the pushrods before positioning the rocker arms and installing the capscrews.

11   Set the rocker arms in place, then install the pivots, bridges and capscrews. Apply moly-base grease to the pivots to prevent damage to the mating surfaces before engine oil pressure builds up. Tighten the bolts to the torque listed in this Chapter's Specifications.

12   Reinstall the valve cover and run the engine. Check for oil leaks and unusual valve train noises.

6   Valve spring, retainer and seals - replacement

Refer to illustrations 6.4, 6.9 and 6.17

Note: Broken valve springs and defective valve stem seals can be replaced without removing the cylinder heads. Two special tools and a compressed air source are normally required to perform this operation, so read through this Section carefully and rent or buy the tools before beginning the job. If compressed air isn't available, a length of nylon rope can be used to keep the valves from falling into the cylinder during this procedure.

1   Remove the valve cover referring to Section 4.

2   Remove the spark plug from the cylinder which has the defective component. If all of the valve stem seals are being replaced, all of the spark plugs should be removed.

3   Turn the crankshaft until the piston in

the affected cylinder is at top dead center (TDC) on the compression stroke (see Section 3 for instructions). If you're replacing all of the valve stem seals, begin with cylinder number one and work on the valves for one cylinder at a time. Move from cylinder-to-cylinder following the firing order sequence (see the Specifications listed at the beginning of this Chapter).

4   Thread an adapter into the spark plug hole (see illustration) and connect an air hose from a compressed air source to it. Most auto parts stores can supply the air hose adapter. **Note:** Many cylinder compression gauges utilize a screw-in fitting that may work with your air hose quick-disconnect fitting.

5   Remove the rocker arm and pivot for the valve with the defective part and pull out the pushrod. If all of the valve stem seals are being replaced, all of the rocker arms and pushrods should be removed (see Section 5).

6   Apply compressed air to the cylinder. **Warning:** The piston may be forced down by compressed air, causing the crankshaft to turn suddenly. If the wrench used when positioning the number one piston at TDC is still attached to the bolt in the crankshaft nose, it could cause damage or injury when the crankshaft moves.

7   The valves should be held in place by the air pressure. If the valve faces or seats are in poor condition, leaks may prevent air pressure from retaining the valves - refer to the alternative procedure below.

8   If you don't have access to compressed air, an alternative method can be used. Position the piston at a point just before TDC on the compression stroke, then feed a long piece of nylon rope through the spark plug hole until it fills the combustion chamber. Be sure to leave the end of the rope hanging out of the engine so it can be removed easily. Use a large ratchet and socket to rotate the crankshaft in the normal direction of rotation until slight resistance is felt.

9   Stuff shop rags into the cylinder head holes above and below the valves to prevent

6.17 Apply a small dab if grease to the keepers before installation - it will hold them in place on the valve stem as the spring is released

7.2 Disconnect any coolant lines from the intake manifold

press the valve spring and carefully position the keepers in the groove. Apply a small dab of grease to the inside of each keeper to hold it in place **(see illustration)**.

18   Remove the pressure from the spring tool and make sure the keepers are seated.

19   Disconnect the air hose and remove the adapter from the spark plug hole. If a rope was used in place of air pressure, pull it out of the cylinder.

20   Refer to Section 5 and install the rocker arm(s) and pushrod(s).

21   Install the spark plug(s) and hook up the wire(s).

22   Refer to Section 4 and install the valve cover.

23   Start and run the engine, then check for oil leaks and unusual sounds coming from the valve cover area.

---

7   Intake and exhaust manifold - removal and installation

Intake manifold

Refer to illustrations 7.2, 7.4, 7.5, 7.6, 7.7, 7.11a, 7.11b, 7.12a, 7.12b, and 7.15

Warning: *Allow the engine to cool to room temperature before following this procedure.*

1   Disconnect the negative cable from the battery.

2   Drain the cooling system (see Chapter 1). Disconnect any coolant hoses that connect to the intake manifold **(see illustration)**.

3   Remove the throttle body (see Chapter 4).

4   Label and then disconnect any wiring, hoses **(see illustration)** and control cables still connected to the intake manifold.

5   Disconnect the bolt **(see illustration)** that retains the vacuum tubing bracket to the intake manifold.

parts and tools from falling into the engine, then use a valve spring compressor to compress the spring. Remove the keepers with small needle-nose pliers or a magnet **(see illustration)**. **Note:** *A couple of different types of tools are available for compressing the valve springs with the head in place. One type grips the lower spring coils and presses on the retainer as the knob is turned, while the other type, shown here, utilizes the rocker arm capscrews for leverage. Both types work very well, although the lever type is usually less expensive.*

10   Remove the spring retainer, oil shield and valve spring, then remove the guide seal. **Note:** *If air pressure fails to hold the valve in the closed position during this operation, the valve face and/or seat is probably damaged. If so, the cylinder head will have to be removed for additional repair operations.*

11   Wrap a rubber band or tape around the top of the valve stem so the valve won't fall into the combustion chamber, then release the air pressure. **Note:** *If a rope was used*

instead of air pressure, turn the crankshaft slightly in the direction opposite normal rotation.

12   Inspect the valve stem for damage. Rotate the valve in the guide and check the end for eccentric movement, which would indicate that the valve is bent.

13   Move the valve up-and-down in the guide and make sure it doesn't bind. If the valve stem binds, either the valve is bent or the guide is damaged. In either case, the head will have to be removed for repair.

14   Reapply air pressure to the cylinder to retain the valve in the closed position, then remove the tape or rubber band from the valve stem. If a rope was used instead of air pressure, rotate the crankshaft in the normal direction of rotation until slight resistance is felt.

15   Lubricate the valve stem with engine oil and install a new guide seal.

16   Install the spring and shield in position over the valve.

17   Install the valve spring retainer. Com-

7.4 Use paint or masking tape to mark each hose for proper installation

7.5 Remove the bolt (arrow) that retains the vacuum assembly to the intake manifold

7.6 Disconnect the multiple vacuum connector (arrow) from the main assembly

7.7 Lift the vacuum assembly off the engine

6   Reach around the back of the cylinder head and disconnect the multiple vacuum connector (see illustration).

7   Carefully lift the vacuum tube assembly from the engine compartment (see illustration).

8   Unbolt the power steering pump (if equipped), and set it aside without disconnecting the hoses (see Chapter 10).

9   Disconnect the throttle valve (TV) linkage, if equipped with an automatic transmission (see Chapter 7, Part B).

10   Disconnect the EGR tube from the intake manifold (see Chapter 6).

11   Remove the intake manifold bolts (see illustrations). Pull the manifold away from the engine slightly to disengage it from the dowel pins in the cylinder head, then lift the manifold from the engine. If the manifold sticks to the engine after all the bolts are removed, tap it with a softface hammer or a block of wood and a hammer while supporting the manifold.

12   Thoroughly clean the mating surfaces, removing all traces of gasket material (see illustration). Note: Some early engines are

7.11a Remove the bolts (1), pull the manifold away from the engine slightly to disengage it from the dowel pins (2), then lift the manifold from the engine

equipped with a gasket that covers both the intake and exhaust manifold surfaces while later engines are equipped with an intake manifold gasket only (see illustration). On the early type, it is necessary to remove the exhaust manifold in order to replace the gasket properly (see Steps 18 through 26).

13   If the manifold is being replaced, transfer all fittings to the new one.

14   Position the replacement gasket on the cylinder head and install the manifold.

15   Install the intake manifold bolts and tighten them (along with the exhaust manifold nuts and EGR tube nut and bolts) in several

7.11b Use an extension to reach the two lower bolts on the intake manifold

7.12a Remove the old intake manifold gasket with a scraper - don't leave any material on the mating surfaces

7.12b The intake manifold gasket can be removed without removing the exhaust manifold on the later engines

7.15 Intake and exhaust manifold bolt tightening sequence

7.22 Exhaust manifold mounting details

stages, following the sequence shown to the torque listed in this Chapter's Specifications **(see illustration)**.

16   Reinstall the remaining parts in the reverse order of removal.

17   Run the engine and check for vacuum leaks and proper operation.

Exhaust manifold

Refer to illustration 7.22

Warning: *Allow the engine to cool to room temperature before following this procedure.*

18   Remove the intake manifold (see Steps 1 through 17).

19   Disconnect the EGR tube (see Chapter 6).

20   Remove the two nuts and bolts that secure the exhaust pipe to the exhaust manifold. It may be necessary to apply penetrating oil to the threads.

21   Unplug the oxygen sensor wire connector (see Chapter 1, if necessary).

22   Remove the mounting nuts and spacers **(see illustration)** and detach the exhaust manifold from the engine.

23   Clean the mating surfaces and, if the manifold is being replaced, transfer the oxygen sensor to the new manifold.

24   Reinstall the exhaust manifold and finger tighten the nuts on the end studs.

25   Reinstall the intake manifold (see Steps 1 through 17) and tighten all mounting fasteners to the torque listed in this Chapter's Specifications, following the sequence shown in **illustration 7.15**. Reinstall the remaining components in the reverse order of removal.

26   Run the engine and check for exhaust leaks.

---

8   Cylinder head - removal and installation

Refer to illustrations 8.8, 8.9, 8.12, 8.14, 8.15, and 8.15

Warning: *Allow the engine to cool to room temperature before following this procedure.*

1   Remove the rocker arms and pushrods (see Section 5).

2   Remove the intake and exhaust manifolds (see Section 7).

3   Remove the drivebelt(s) as described in Chapter 1.

4   Unbolt the power steering pump (if equipped) and set it aside without disconnecting the hoses.

5   On air conditioned models, remove the bolt that secures the air conditioning compressor/alternator bracket to the cylinder head, then unbolt the compressor/alternator bracket from the engine. Set the compressor aside without disconnecting the hoses.

6   Label, then disconnect the wire from the coolant temperature sending unit on the cylinder head.

7   Label the spark plug wires and remove the spark plugs.

8   Remove the ten bolts that secure the cylinder head and lift it off the engine **(see illustration)**. If the head is stuck to the engine block, it may be necessary to tap it with a soft-face hammer or a block of wood and a hammer to break the seal.

9   Stuff clean shop towels into the cylin-

8.8 If necessary, use a prybar to separate the cylinder head from the block. Be sure not to damage any gasket surfaces while applying pressure on the tool.

8.9 A die should be used to remove sealant and corrosion from the head bolt threads

8.12 Use a sealant appropriate for steel gaskets on the surface of the metal head gasket.

8.14 Be sure the designation on the head gasket - Top - faces up

8.15 Cylinder head bolt/nut tightening sequence

ders. Thoroughly clean the gasket surfaces, removing all traces of gasket material. Run an appropriate sized tap into the bolt holes in the cylinder head and run a die over the bolt threads **(see illustration)**. Ensure all bolt holes are clean and dry.

10   Inspect the cylinder head for cracks and check it for warpage. Refer to Chapter 2, Part D, for cylinder head servicing procedures.

11   1987 and 1988 four-cylinder engines use different head gaskets than 1989 and later models. The two types of gaskets are NOT interchangeable and require different tightening torques.

1987 and 1988 models

12   These engines use stamped steel gaskets. Apply an even coat of gasket sealing compound suitable for steel gaskets, available at most auto parts stores, to both sides of the new gasket **(see illustration)**.

1989 and later models

13   These engines use a composition gasket. Install it dry (without any sealing compound).

All models

14   Install the new gasket with the word TOP **(see illustration)** on the cylinder head

side. Place the cylinder head on the engine.

15   Coat the threads of the stud bolt (no. 8 in the tightening sequence) with Loctite Pipe Sealant with Teflon no. 592 (or equivalent). Install the bolts and tighten them in the sequence shown **(see illustration)**. Tighten them in the steps and to the torque listed in this Chapter's Specifications. **Caution:** *During the final tightening step, bolt no. 8 is tightened to a lower torque than the other bolts.*

16   Install the remaining components in the reverse order of removal.

17   Change the oil and filter (see Chapter 1).

18   Refill the cooling system and run the engine, checking for leaks and proper operation.

9   Hydraulic lifters - removal, inspection and installation

Removal

Refer to illustrations 9.5 and 9.6

1   A noisy valve lifter can be isolated when the engine is idling. Place a length of hose or tubing on the valve cover near the position of each valve while listening at the other end. Or remove the valve cover and, with the engine idling, place a finger on each of the valve spring retainers, one at a time. If a valve lifter is defective, it'll be evident from the shock felt at the retainer as the valve opens.

2   The most likely cause of a noisy valve lifter is a piece of dirt trapped between the plunger and the lifter body.

3   Remove the valve cover (see Section 4).

4   Remove both rocker arms and both pushrods at the cylinder with the noisy lifter (see Section 5).

5   Remove the lifters through the pushrod openings in the cylinder head.
A special removal tool is available **(see illustration)**, but isn't always necessary. On newer engines without a lot of varnish buildup, lifters can often be removed with a magnet attached to a long handle.

6   Store the lifters in a clearly labeled box to insure their reinstallation in the same lifter bores **(see illustration)**.

9.5 Removing lifters with special tool

9.6 If you're removing more than one lifter, keep them in order in a clearly labeled box

9.8a If the bottom (foot) of any lifter is worn concave (shown here), scratched or galled, replace the entire set with new lifters

Inspection

Refer to illustrations 9.8a, 9.8b, 9.8c and 9.8d

7   Clean the lifters with solvent and dry them thoroughly. Do this one lifter at a time to avoid mixing them up.

8   Check each lifter wall, pushrod seat and foot for scuffing, score marks and uneven wear. Each lifter foot (the surface that rides on the cam lobe) must be slightly convex, although this can be difficult to determine by eye. If the base of the lifter is concave or rough **(see illustrations)**, the lifters and camshaft must be replaced. If the lifter walls are damaged or worn (which isn't very likely), inspect the lifter bores in the engine block as well. If the pushrod seats **(see illustration)** are worn, check the pushrod ends.

9   If new lifters are being installed, a new camshaft must also be installed. If a new camshaft is installed, then use new lifters as well. Never install used lifters unless the original camshaft is used and the lifters can be installed in their original locations!

Installation

10   The used lifters must be installed in their original bores. Coat them with moly-base grease or engine assembly lube.

11   Lubricate the bearing surfaces of the lifter bores with engine oil.

12   Install the lifter(s) in the lifter bore(s).

13   Install the pushrods and rocker arms (see Section 5). **Caution:** *Make sure that each pair of lifters is on the base circle of the camshaft; that is, with both valves closed, before tightening the rocker arm bolts.*

14   Tighten the rocker arm capscrews to the torque listed in this Chapter's Specifications.

15   Install the valve cover (see Section 4).

---

10   Vibration damper - removal and installation

Refer to illustration 10.6

1   Remove the cable from the negative battery terminal.

2   Remove the drivebelts (see Chapter 1). Tag each belt as it's removed to simplify reinstallation. If the vehicle is equipped with a fan shroud, unscrew the mounting bolts and position the shroud out of the way.

3   Raise the vehicle and place it securely on jackstands.

4   If the vehicle is equipped with a manual transmission, apply the parking brake and put the transmission in gear to prevent the crankshaft from turning, then remove the crankshaft pulley bolts. If your vehicle is equipped with an automatic transmission, it may be necessary to remove the starter motor (see Chapter 5) and immobilize the starter ring gear with a large screwdriver while an assistant loosens the pulley bolts. **Note:** *On vehicles with serpentine belts, the pulley and vibration damper are combined as one piece - there are no pulley bolts to remove.*

5   To loosen the vibration damper retaining bolt, install a bolt in one of the pulley bolt holes. Attach a breaker bar, extension and socket to the vibration damper retaining bolt and immobilize the crankshaft by wedging a large screwdriver between the bolt and the socket. Remove the retaining bolt.

6   Remove the vibration damper. Use a puller if necessary **(see illustration)**.

7   Refer to Section 11 for the front oil seal

9.8b The foot of each lifter should be slightly convex - the side of another lifter can be used as a straightedge to check it; if it appears flat, it's worn and must not be used

9.8c Check the pushrod seal (arrow) in the top of each lifter for wear

9.8d If the lifters are pitted or rough, they shouldn't be reused

10.6 To remove the vibration damper, use a puller which attaches to the bolt holes

11.2 The front crankshaft seal can be removed with a seal removal tool or a large screwdriver

replacement procedure.

8 Apply a thin layer of multi-purpose grease to the seal contact surface of the vibration damper.

9 Slide the vibration damper onto the crankshaft. Note that the slot in the hub must be aligned with the Woodruff key in the end of the crankshaft. Once the key is aligned with the slot, tap the damper onto the crankshaft with a soft-face hammer. The retaining bolt can also be used to press the damper into position.

10 Tighten the vibration damper-to-crankshaft bolt to the torque listed in this Chapter's Specifications.

11 Install the crankshaft pulley (if equipped) on the hub and tighten the bolts to the specified torque. Use Locktite on the bolt threads.

12 Install the drivebelt(s) (see Chapter 1) and replace the fan shroud (if equipped).

---

11 Front crankshaft oil seal - replacement

Note: *The front crankshaft oil seal can be replaced with the timing chain cover in place. However, due to the limited amount of room available, you may conclude that the procedure would be easier if the cover were removed from the engine first. If so, refer to Section 12 for the cover removal and installation procedure.*

Timing chain cover in place

Refer to illustration 11.2

1 Disconnect the negative battery cable from the battery, then remove the vibration damper (see Section 10).

2 Note how the seal is installed - the new one must face the same direction! Carefully pry the oil seal out of the cover with a seal puller or a large screwdriver **(see illustration)**. Be very careful not to distort the cover or scratch the crankshaft!

3 Apply clean engine oil or multi-purpose grease to the outer edge of the new seal, then install it in the cover with the lip (open

end) facing in. Drive the seal into place with a large socket and a hammer (if a large socket isn't available, a piece of pipe will also work). Make sure the seal enters the bore squarely and stop when the front face is flush with the cover.

4 Install the vibration damper (see Section 10).

Timing chain cover removed

Refer to illustrations 11.6, 11.8a and 11.8b

5 Remove the timing chain cover as described in Section 12.

6 Using a large screwdriver, pry the old seal out of the cover **(see illustration)**. Be careful not to distort the cover or scratch the wall of the seal bore. If the engine has accumulated a lot of miles, apply penetrating oil to the seal-to-cover joint and allow it to soak in before attempting to remove the seal.

7 Clean the bore to remove any old seal material and corrosion. Support the cover on a block of wood and position the new seal in the bore with the lip (open end) of the seal facing in. A small amount of oil applied to the outer edge of the new seal will make installation easier - don't overdo it!

8 Drive the seal into the bore with a large

11.6 Once the timing chain cover is removed, place it on a flat surface and gently pry the old seal out with a large screwdriver

socket and hammer until it's completely seated **(see illustration)**. Select a socket that's the same outside diameter as the seal. A section of pipe or even a block of wood can be used if a socket isn't available **(see illustration)**.

9 Reinstall the timing chain cover.

11.8a Clean the bore, then apply a small amount of oil to the outer edge of the new seal and drive it squarely into the opening with a large socket . . .

11.8b . . . or a block of wood and a hammer - don't damage the seal in the process!

12.6 Cut the end tabs (1) flush with the block and trim the end seal tabs (2)

12.7 Inside view of timing chain cover

A *Cutout for driving out oil seal*
B *Timing chain guide*

12.13 Use paint (arrows) to mark the locations of the studs in the timing cover

12 Timing chain cover - removal and installation

Refer to illustrations 12.6, 12.7 and 12.13

1   Remove the vibration damper (see Section 10).
2   Remove the fan and hub assembly (see Chapter 3).
3   Remove the air conditioning compressor (if equipped) and the alternator bracket assembly from the cylinder head and set it aside.

4   Remove the oil pan-to-timing chain cover bolts and the timing chain cover-to-block bolts and stud nuts. Mark the locations of the studs to ensure correct reassembly **(see illustration 12.13)**.
5   Separate the timing chain cover from the engine. Avoid damaging the sealing surfaces; do not force tools between the cover and block.
6   Cut off the oil pan gasket end tabs flush with the front face of the cylinder block and trim off the end seal tabs **(see illustration)**.
7   Thoroughly clean the cover and all sealing surfaces, removing any traces of gasket material. Drive the old oil seal out from the rear of the timing chain cover and replace it with a new one (see Section 11). Also replace the chain guide, if necessary **(see illustration)**.
8   Apply sealing compound (Perfect Seal or equivalent) to both sides of the new timing cover gasket and position the gasket on the engine block.
9   Trim the end tabs off the new oil pan gaskets to correspond with those cut off the original gasket. Attach the new end tabs to the oil pan with cement.
10   Coat the timing chain cover-to-oil pan seal tab recesses generously with RTV sealant (Jeep Gasket-In-A-Tube or equivalent) and position the seal onto the timing chain cover. Then apply a film of oil to the seal-to-oil pan contact surface.

11   Position the timing chain cover on the engine block.
12   Install the vibration damper to center the timing chain cover.
13   Install the cover-to-block nuts and bolts and the oil pan-to-cover bolts and tighten them to the torque listed in this Chapter's Specifications **(see illustration)**.
14   Reinstall the remaining parts in the reverse order of removal.
15   Run the engine and check for oil leaks.

13 Timing chain and sprockets - removal, inspection and installation

Refer to illustrations 13.3, 13.5a, 13.5b, 13.6, 13.7, and 13.11

1   Set the number one piston at Top Dead Center (TDC) (see Section 3).
2   Remove the timing chain cover (see Section 12).
3   Reinstall the vibration damper bolt and rotate the crankshaft until the zero timing mark on the crankshaft sprocket is lined up with the timing mark on the camshaft sprocket **(see illustration)**.
4   Slide the oil slinger off the crankshaft.
5   Turn the tensioner lever to the unlock position. Pull the tensioner block toward the tensioner lever to compress the spring. Hold

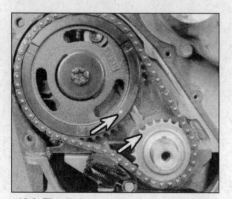

13.3 The timing marks on the sprockets (arrows) should be lined up as shown

13.5a The timing chain tensioner is locked or unlocked with the tensioner lever

LOCK
UNLOCK
TENSIONER LEVER
TENSIONER BLOCK PULL FORWARD

13.5b While compressing the tensioner with one screwdriver, lock the mechanism with the other screwdriver

13.6 Use a small screwdriver to remove to remove the clip from the tensioner mount

13.7 The timing chain and sprockets are removed and installed as an assembly

13.11 On 1996 and earlier models, with the camshaft sprocket timing mark at one o'clock, count the chain pins between the two timing marks - there must be 20 pins

CAMSHAFT SPROCKET

20 PINS

TIMING MARKS

CRANKSHAFT SPROCKET

the block and turn the tensioner lever to the lock position (**see illustrations**).

6   If necessary, use a small screwdriver to remove the retaining clip (**see illustration**) and remove the tensioner from the block.

7   Remove the camshaft retaining bolt and slip both sprockets and the chain off as an assembly (**see illustration**).

8   Clean the components and inspect for wear and damage. Excessive chain slack and teeth that are deformed, chipped, pitted or discolored call for replacement. Always replace the sprockets and chain as a set. Inspect the tensioner for excessive wear and replace it, if necessary.

9   Install the tensioner, crankshaft camshaft sprockets and timing chain. Ensure the marks on the sprockets are still properly aligned (**see illustration 13.3**).

10   Install the camshaft sprocket retaining bolt and washer and tighten to the torque listed in this Chapter's Specifications.

11   On 1996 and earlier models, verify correct installation of the timing chain by turning the crankshaft to place the camshaft sprocket timing mark at approximately the one o'clock position. This positions the crankshaft timing mark where the adjacent tooth meshes with

the chain at the three o'clock position. Count the number of chain pins between the timing marks of both sprockets. There must be 20 pins (**see illustration**).

12   Release the tensioner by turning the lever to the unlock position. Be sure the tensioner is released before installing the timing cover.

13   Install the oil slinger and the remaining parts in the reverse order of removal. Refer to the appropriate sections for instructions.

14   Camshaft and bearings - removal, inspection and installation

Camshaft lobe lift check

Refer to illustration 14.3

1   To determine the extent of cam lobe wear, the lobe lift should be checked prior to camshaft removal. Refer to Section 4 and remove the valve cover.

2   Position the number one piston at TDC on the compression stroke (see Section 3).

3   Beginning with the number one cylinder

valves, mount a dial indicator on the engine and position the plunger against the top surface of the first rocker arm. The plunger should be directly above and in line with the pushrod (**see illustration**).

4   Zero the dial indicator, then very slowly turn the crankshaft in the normal direction of

14.3 When checking the camshaft lobe lift, the dial indicator plunger must be positioned directly above the pushrod

14.19 Support the camshaft near the block

14.21 The camshaft bearing journal diameters are checked to pinpoint excessive wear and out-of-round conditions

rotation until the indicator needle stops and begins to move in the opposite direction. The point at which it stops indicates maximum cam lobe lift.

5   Record this figure for future reference, then reposition the piston at TDC on the compression stroke.

6   Move the dial indicator to the remaining number one cylinder rocker arm and repeat the check. Be sure to record the results for each valve.

7   Repeat the check for the remaining valves. Since each piston must be at TDC on the compression stroke for this procedure, work from cylinder-to-cylinder following the firing order sequence.

8   After the check is complete, compare the results to the specifications. If camshaft lobe lift is less than specified, cam lobe wear has occurred and a new camshaft should be installed.

Removal

Refer to illustration 14.19

9   Set the number one piston at Top Dead Center (see Section 3).

10   Disconnect the negative cable from the battery.

11   Remove the radiator (see Chapter 3).

12   On models equipped with air conditioning, unbolt the air conditioning compressor and set it aside without disconnecting the refrigerant lines.

13   On carburetor equipped models, remove the fuel pump (see Chapter 4).

14   Remove the distributor (see Chapter 5).

15   If not removed already, detach the valve cover (see Section 4).

16   Remove the rocker arms and pushrods (see Section 5).

17   Remove the hydraulic lifters (see Section 9).

18   Remove the timing chain and sprockets (see Section 13). **Note:** *If the camshaft appears to have been rubbing against the timing chain cover, examine the oil pressure relief holes in the rear cam journal and ensure they are free of debris.*

19   Install a bolt in the end of the camshaft to use as a handle. Carefully slide the camshaft out of the block. **Caution:** *To avoid damage to the camshaft bearings as the lobes pass over them, support the camshaft near the block as it is withdrawn* **(see illustration).**

Inspection

Refer to illustration 14.21

20   After the camshaft has been removed from the engine, cleaned with solvent and dried, inspect the bearing journals for uneven wear, pitting and evidence of seizure. If the journals are damaged, the bearing inserts in the block are probably damaged also. Both the camshaft and bearings will have to be replaced.

21   If the bearing journals are in good condition, measure them with a micrometer and record the measurements **(see illustration).** Measure each journal at several locations around its circumference. If you get different measurements at different locations, the journal is out of round.

22   Check the inside diameter of each camshaft bearing with a telescoping gauge and measure the gauge with a micrometer. Subtract each cam journal diameter from the corresponding camshaft bearing inside diameter to obtain the bearing oil clearance.

23   Compare the clearance for each bearing to the specifications. If it is excessive, for any of the bearings, have new bearings installed by an automotive machine shop.

24   Inspect the distributor drive gear for wear. Replace the camshaft if the gear is worn.

25   Inspect the camshaft lobes (including the fuel pump lobe on carburetor equipped models) for heat discoloration, score marks, chipped areas, pitting and uneven wear. If the lobes are in good condition and if the lobe lift measurements are as specified, the camshaft can be reused.

Bearing replacement

26   Camshaft bearing replacement requires special tools and expertise that place it outside the scope of the home mechanic. Take the engine block (see Part D of this Chapter) to an automotive machine shop to ensure the job is done correctly.

Installation

Refer to illustration 14.27

27   Lubricate the camshaft bearing journals and lobes with moly-base grease or engine assembly lube **(see illustration).**

14.27 Be sure to apply moly-base grease or engine assembly lube to the cam lobes and bearing journals before installing the camshaft

15.6 Remove the bolts from the perimeter of the oil pan

15.8a Oil pan components - exploded view

28   Slide the camshaft into the engine. Support the cam near the block and be careful not to scrape or nick the bearings.
29   Temporarily place the camshaft sprocket onto the camshaft and turn the camshaft until the timing mark is aligned with the centerline of the crankshaft (see Section 13). Remove the sprocket.
30   Install the timing chain and sprockets and the remaining components in the reverse order of removal. Refer to the appropriate Sections for installation instructions. **Note:** *If the original cam and lifters are being reinstalled, be sure to install the lifters in their original locations. If a new camshaft was installed, be sure to install new lifters also.*
31   Add coolant and change the oil and filter (see Chapter 1).
32   Start the engine and check the ignition timing. Check for leaks and unusual noises.

15 Oil pan - removal and installation

Refer to illustrations 15.6, 15.8a, 15.8b and 15.8c
1   Disconnect the cable from the negative battery terminal.
2   Raise the vehicle and support it securely on jackstands.

3   Drain the engine oil and remove the oil filter (Chapter 1).
4   Disconnect the exhaust pipe at the manifold (see Section 7) and hangers and tie the system aside.
5   Remove the starter (see Chapter 5) and the bellhousing dust cover.
6   Remove the bolts **(see illustration)** and detach the oil pan. Don't pry between the block and pan or damage to the sealing surfaces may result and oil leaks could develop. If the pan is stuck, dislodge it with a soft-face hammer or a block of wood and a hammer.
7   Use a scraper to remove all traces of sealant from the pan and block, then clean the mating surfaces with lacquer thinner or acetone.
8   Using gasket adhesive, position new oil pan seals and gaskets on the engine **(see illustrations)**.
9   Install the oil pan and tighten the mounting bolts to the torque listed in this Chapter's Specifications. Note that the 1/4-inch diameter and 5/16-inch diameter bolts have different torques. Start at the center of the pan and work out toward the ends in a spiral pattern.
10   Install the bellhousing dust cover and the starter, then reconnect the exhaust pipe to the manifold and hanger brackets.
11   Lower the vehicle.

12   Install a new filter and add oil to the engine.
13   Reconnect the negative battery cable.
14   Start the engine and check for leaks.

16 Oil pump - removal and installation

Refer to illustration 16.2
1   Remove the oil pan (see Section 15).
2   Remove the two oil pump attaching bolts from the engine block **(see illustration)**.
3   Detach the oil pump and strainer assembly from the block.
4   If the pump is defective, replace it with a new one. If the engine is being completely overhauled, install a new oil pump - don't reuse the original or attempt to rebuild it.
5   On four-cylinder engines, to install the oil pump, turn the shaft so the gear tang mates with the slot on the lower end of the distributor shaft. The oil pump should slide easily into place. If it doesn't, pull it off and turn the tang until it's aligned with the lower end of the shaft.
6   On six-cylinder engines, to install the oil pump, turn the shaft so the gear tang mates with the slot on the lower end of the distribu-

15.8b Be sure to apply RTV sealant to the corners of the gasket over the rear main bearing cap . . .

15.8c . . . and in the corners and seams over the timing cover

16.2 Oil pump and components

17.3 Before removing the flywheel, index it to the crankshaft (arrow)

17.4 To prevent the flywheel from turning, hold a pry bar against two bolts or wedge a large screwdriver into the flywheel ring gear

tor shaft on 1987 through 1999 models, or the camshaft position sensor drive shaft on 2000 models. The oil pump should slide easily into place. If it doesn't, pull it off and turn the tang until it's aligned with the lower end of the shaft.

7   Install the pump attaching bolts. Tighten them to the torque listed in this Chapter's Specifications.

8   Reinstall the oil pan (see Section 15).

9   Add oil, run the engine and check for leaks.

17   Flywheel/driveplate - removal and installation

Refer to illustrations 17.3, 17.4, 17.8 and 17.10

1   Raise the vehicle and support it securely on jackstands, then refer to Chapter 7 and remove the transmission. If it's leaking, now would be a very good time to replace the front pump seal/O-ring (automatic transmission only).

2   Remove the pressure plate and clutch disc (see Chapter 8) (manual transmission equipped vehicles). Now is a good time to check/replace the clutch components and pilot bearing.

3   Use paint or a center-punch to make alignment marks on the flywheel/driveplate and crankshaft to ensure correct alignment during reinstallation **(see illustration)**.

4   Remove the bolts that secure the flywheel/driveplate to the crankshaft **(see illustration)**. If the crankshaft turns, hold the flywheel with a pry bar or wedge a screwdriver into the ring gear teeth to jam the flywheel.

5   Remove the flywheel/driveplate from the crankshaft. Since the flywheel is fairly heavy, be sure to support it while removing the last bolt.

6   Clean the flywheel to remove grease and oil. Inspect the surface for cracks, rivet grooves, burned areas and score marks. Light scoring can be removed with emery cloth. Check for cracked and broken ring

17.8 The driveplate on a four-cylinder engine with an automatic transmission has a trigger wheel - check the inner surface (A) for excessive runout with a dial indicator - inspect the timing slot separators (B) for dents, distortion and cracks

gear teeth or a loose ring gear. Lay the flywheel on a flat surface and use a straight-edge to check for warpage.

7   Clean and inspect the mating surfaces of the flywheel/driveplate and the crankshaft. If the crankshaft rear seal is leaking, replace it before reinstalling the flywheel/driveplate.

8   On certain models equipped with a four-cylinder engine and an automatic transmission, the trigger wheel portion of the driveplate assembly provides the timing signal for the fuel and ignition systems. If the trigger wheel becomes damaged when removing/installing the engine, transmission or torque converter, ignition performance will be affected. The general result is either rough engine operation and backfire, or a no-start

17.10 Make marks every 60 degrees on the socket to indicate how much you have turned the bolt

condition. Check for suspected trigger wheel damage as follows:

a) *Check the trigger wheel radial runout on the inner surface (A) with a dial indicator* **(see illustration)**. *Replace the driveplate assembly if runout is excessive.*

b) *Inspect the timing slot separators (B) in the trigger wheel. Replace the driveplate assembly if the separators are dented, distorted, or cracked. Do not attempt to repair the wheel as the results are usually not satisfactory.*

9   Position the flywheel/driveplate against the crankshaft. Be sure to align the marks made during removal. Note that some engines have an alignment dowel or staggered bolt holes to ensure correct installation. Before installing the bolts, apply thread locking compound to the threads.

10   Wedge a screwdriver into the ring gear teeth to keep the flywheel/driveplate from turning as you tighten the bolts to the torque listed in this Chapter's Specifications. After the initial torque has been reached, turn each bolt an additional 60 degrees as outlined in the specifications. **Note:** *A 3/4-inch socket should be marked every 60 degrees on the outside* **(see illustration)**. *After reaching the specified torque, make a reference mark below one of the marks on the socket. Turn the bolt until the next 60 degrees mark is reached.*

11   The remainder of installation is the reverse of the removal procedure.

18.5 Carefully pry the oil seal out with a removal tool or a screwdriver - don't nick or scratch the crankshaft or the new seal will be damaged and leaks will develop

18.8 If the socket isn't available, tap around the outer edge of the new seal with a hammer and punch to seat it squarely in the bore

18   Rear main oil seal - replacement

Refer to illustrations 18.5 and 18.8

1   The rear main bearing oil seal can be replaced without removing the oil pan or crankshaft.

2   Remove the transmission (see Chapter 7).

3   If equipped with a manual transmission, remove the pressure plate and clutch disc (see Chapter 8).

4   Remove the flywheel or driveplate (see Section 17).

5   Using a seal removal tool or a large screwdriver, carefully pry the seal out of the block **(see illustration)**. Don't scratch or nick the crankshaft in the process.

6   Clean the bore in the block and the seal contact surface on the crankshaft. Check the crankshaft surface for scratches and nicks that could damage the new seal lip and cause oil leaks. If the crankshaft is damaged, the only alternative is a new or different crankshaft.

7   Apply a light coat of engine oil or multi-purpose grease to the outer edge of the new seal. Lubricate the seal lip with multi-purpose grease.

8   Carefully work the seal lip over the end of the crankshaft, then tap the new seal into place with a hammer and a large socket (if available) or a rounded punch **(see illustration)**. The seal lip must face toward the front of the engine.

9   Install the flywheel or driveplate.

10   If equipped with a manual transmission, reinstall the clutch disc and pressure plate.

11   Reinstall the transmission as described in Chapter 7.

19   Engine mounts - check and replacement

Refer to illustration 19.8

1   Engine mounts seldom require attention, but broken or deteriorated mounts should be replaced immediately or the added strain placed on the driveline components may cause damage or wear.

Check

2   During the check, the engine must be raised slightly to remove the weight from the mounts.

3   Raise the vehicle and support it securely on jackstands, then position a jack under the engine oil pan. Place a large block of wood between the jack head and the oil pan, then carefully raise the engine just enough to take the weight off the mounts. **Warning:** *DO NOT place any part of your body under the engine when it's supported only by a jack!*

4   Check the mounts to see if the rubber is cracked, hardened or separated from the metal plates. Sometimes the rubber will split right down the center.

5   Check for relative movement between the mount plates and the engine or frame (use a large screwdriver or pry bar to attempt to move the mounts). If movement is noted, lower the engine and tighten the mount fasteners.

6   Rubber preservative should be applied to the mounts to slow deterioration.

Replacement

7   Disconnect the negative battery cable from the battery, then raise the vehicle and support it securely on jackstands (if not already done).

8   Loosen the nut on the through bolt and remove the bolt and nut that secure the mount to the frame bracket **(see illustration)**.

9   Raise the engine slightly with a jack or hoist (make sure the fan doesn't hit the radiator or shroud). Remove the through bolt and nut and detach the mount.

10   Installation is the reverse of removal. Use thread locking compound on the mount bolts and be sure to tighten them securely.

19.8 Remove the through-bolt and nut (A) and mount bolt (B), then remove the mount nut (not visible in this photo) from beneath the frame bracket

Notes

Chapter 2 Part C
4.0L and 4.2L six-cylinder engines

Contents

Specifications

General

Displacement	
4.0L engine	243 cubic inches
4.2L engine	258 cubic inches
Cylinder numbers (front-to-rear)	1-2-3-4-5-6
Firing order	1-5-3-6-2-4

Camshaft

Lobe lift (intake and exhaust)	0.253 inch
Endplay	None
Journal diameter	
No. 1	2.029 to 2.030 inches
No. 2	2.019 to 2.020 inches
No. 3	2.009 to 2.010 inches
No. 4	1.999 to 2.000 inches
Journal-to-bearing (oil) clearance	0.001 to 0.003 inch

Torque specifications

	Ft-lbs (unless otherwise indicated)
Camshaft sprocket bolt	50
Crankshaft pulley-to-vibration damper bolts	20
Cylinder head bolts (see illustration 9.21 for tightening sequence)	
4.2L engine	85
4.0L engine	
Step A	22
Step B	45
Step C	45
Step D	
Bolt no. 11	100
All other bolts	110
Flywheel/driveplate bolts	105
Intake and exhaust manifold retaining bolts and nuts (all except 1989 models)	
Nos. 1 through 5 and 8 through 11	23
Nos. 6 and 7	17
1989 models	
Nos. 1 and 2	30
Nos. 3 through 12	23
Oil pan mounting bolts	
1/4 x 20	84 in-lbs
5/16 x 18	132 in-lbs
Oil pump mounting bolt	
Short	120 in-lbs
Long	17

FIRING ORDER:
1 5 3 6 2 4
CLOCKWISE
ROTATION

Cylinder location and distributor rotation

Torque specifications (continued)   Ft-lbs (unless otherwise indicated)

Rear main bearing cap bolts	80
Rocker arm bolts	19
Tensioner bracket-to-block bolts	14
Timing chain cover-to-block	
Bolts	60 in-lbs
Studs	16
Valve cover-to-cylinder head bolts	
With RTV	28 in-lbs
With permanent gasket	55 in-lbs
Vibration damper center bolt (lubricated)	80

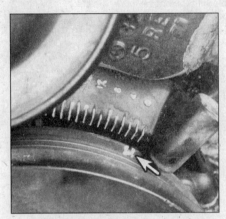

3.1a Align the notch (arrow) on the vibration damper with the "0" on the timing cover

3.1b Locate the number one spark plug terminal on the distributor cap, make a mark on the distributor housing, directly under the number one plug terminal . . .

3.1c . . . then remove the distributor cap and verify that the rotor is pointing at the mark (arrow)

1   General information

This Part of Chapter 2 is devoted to in-vehicle repair procedures for the inline six-cylinder engine. All information concerning engine removal and installation and engine block and cylinder head overhaul can be found in Part D of this Chapter.

The following repair procedures are based on the assumption that the engine is installed in the vehicle. If the engine has been removed from the vehicle and mounted on a stand, many of the steps outlined in this Part of Chapter 2 will not apply.

The Specifications included in this Part of Chapter 2 apply only to the procedures contained in this Part. Part D of Chapter 2 contains the Specifications necessary for cylinder head and engine block rebuilding.

2   Repair operations possible with the engine in the vehicle

Many major repair operations can be accomplished without removing the engine from the vehicle.

Clean the engine compartment and the exterior of the engine with some type of pressure washer before any work is done. It will make the job easier and help keep dirt out of the internal areas of the engine.

Remove the hood, if necessary, to

improve access to the engine as repairs are performed (refer to Chapter 11 if necessary).

If vacuum, exhaust, oil or coolant leaks develop, indicating a need for gasket or seal replacement, the repairs can generally be made with the engine in the vehicle. The intake and exhaust manifold gaskets, timing cover gasket, oil pan gasket, crankshaft oil seals and cylinder head gaskets are all accessible with the engine in place.

Exterior engine components, such as the intake and exhaust manifolds, the oil pan (and the oil pump), the water pump, the starter motor, the alternator, the distributor and the fuel system components can be

4.1 View from above shows locations of crankcase breather tube and hose (arrows)

removed for repair with the engine in place.

Since the cylinder heads can be removed without pulling the engine, valve component servicing can also be accomplished with the engine in the vehicle. Replacement of the camshaft and timing chain and sprockets is also possible with the engine in the vehicle.

In extreme cases caused by a lack of necessary equipment, repair or replacement of piston rings, pistons, connecting rods and rod bearings is possible with the engine in the vehicle. However, this practice is not recommended because of the cleaning and preparation work that must be done to the components involved.

3   Top Dead Center (TDC) for number one piston - locating

Refer to illustrations 3.1a, 3.1b and 3.1c

See Chapter 2, Part A, Section 3 for this procedure, but refer to the illustrations included in this Section **(see illustrations)**.

4   Valve cover - removal and installation

Refer to illustrations 4.1, 4.3 and 4.4

1   Pull the crankcase breather tube and hose off the valve cover **(see illustration)**.

4.3 Pull off the wire harness clips

4.4 Use a soft-face mallet to break the cover loose - DO NOT pry between the cover and head

5.2 Go back and forth between the intake and exhaust rocker arms, loosening each bolt 1/4-turn at a time

5.3 Rocker arm components - exploded view

A	Bolt	C	Fulcrum
B	Bridge	D	Rocker arm

2   Remove the cruise control servo, if equipped.

3   Remove the wire harness clips **(see illustration)**, noting the locations of their studs for reinstallation.

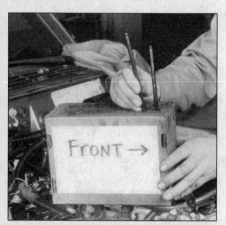

5.4 Store the pushrods in a box like this to ensure reinstallation in the same location

4   Remove the valve cover retaining bolts and lift the cover off. If the cover is stuck, tap on it gently with a soft-face mallet **(see illustration)**. Do not pry on the gasket flange. **Note:** *These covers have a reusable pre-cured gasket that is attached to the cover.*

5   Clean the sealing surfaces, removing any traces of oil with lacquer thinner or acetone and a clean rag.

6   Small cracks in the pre-cured gasket are allowable and can be repaired by applying RTV sealant to the cracked area before the cover is installed.

7   Install the cover and bolts. Tighten the bolts to the torque listed in this Chapter's Specifications.

8   Reinstall the crankcase breather hoses and cruise control servo, if equipped.

9   Run the engine and check for oil leaks.

5   Rocker arms and pushrods - removal, inspection and installation

Refer to illustrations 5.2, 5.3 and 5.4

Removal

1   Remove the valve cover (see Section 4).

2   Beginning at the front of the cylinder head, loosen and remove the rocker arm mounting bolts in pairs **(see illustration)**.

3   Remove the rocker arms, bridges and fulcrums **(see illustration)** and store them with their respective mounting bolts. Store each set of rocker arm components separately in a marked plastic bag to ensure they are reinstalled in their original locations. The bridges may be reinstalled in any location.

4   Remove the pushrods and store them separately to make sure they don't get mixed up during installation **(see illustration)**.

Inspection

5   Check each rocker arm for wear, cracks and other damage, especially where the pushrods and valve stems contact the rocker

arm faces. Check the fulcrum seat in each rocker arm and the fulcrum faces. Look for galling, stress cracks and unusual wear patterns. If the rocker arms are worn or damaged, replace them with new ones and install new fulcrums as well.

6   Make sure the oil hole at the pushrod end of each rocker arm is open.

7   Inspect the pushrods for cracks and excessive wear at the ends. Roll each pushrod across a piece of plate glass to see if it's bent (if it wobbles, it's bent).

Installation

8   Lubricate the lower end of each pushrod with clean engine oil or moly-base grease and install it in its original location. Make sure each pushrod seats completely in the lifter socket.

9   Bring the number one piston to Top Dead Center (TDC) on the compression stroke (see Section 3).

10   Apply moly-base grease to the ends of the valve stems and the upper ends of the pushrods before placing the rocker arms in position.

11   Apply moly-base grease to the fulcrums to prevent damage to the mating surfaces before engine oil pressure builds up. Install the rocker arms, fulcrums, bridges and bolts in their original locations. Tighten the bolts to the torque listed in this Chapter's Specifications.

12   Install the valve cover (see Section 4).

13   Start the engine, listen for unusual valvetrain noises and check for oil leaks at the valve cover joint.

6   Valve spring, retainer and seals - replacement

See Chapter 2, Part B, Section 6 for this procedure, but be sure to follow the valve cover and rocker arm/pushrod procedures outlined in this Part.

7.5 Lift the vacuum connector from its bracket and pull it apart

7.6 Label the connections before detaching them

7   Intake manifold - removal and installation

Refer to illustrations 7.5, 7.6, 7.11, 7.12, 7.20a, 7.20b and 7.20c

Note 1: *Since the intake and exhaust manifolds share a common gasket, they must be removed and replaced at the same time.*

Note 2: *If you are working on a carbureted model (4.2L engine), simply ignore all references to the fuel injection system.*

1   Disconnect the negative cable from the battery.

2   Remove the air cleaner assembly and the accelerator cable (see Chapter 4).

3   On automatic transmission equipped models, disconnect the transmission line pressure (TV) cable (see Chapter 7, Part B).

4   Detach the cruise control cable, if equipped.

5   Disconnect the vacuum connector on the intake manifold by lifting the connector assembly up and out of the bracket and then pulling it apart **(see illustration)**.

6   Label and disconnect all vacuum and electrical connectors on the intake manifold **(see illustration)**.

7   Relieve the fuel pressure and then disconnect the fuel supply and return lines from the fuel rail assembly (see Chapter 4). Cap the open ends.

8   Loosen the serpentine drivebelt (see Chapter 1).

9   Remove the power steering pump and bracket from the intake manifold and set it aside without disconnecting the hoses. Be sure to leave the pump in an upright position so fluid won't spill.

10   Remove the fuel rail and injectors (see Chapter 4).

11   Remove the intake manifold heat shield **(see illustration)**.

12   Unscrew the intake manifold bolts **(see illustration)**.

13   Remove the EGR tube from the intake manifold (see Chapter 6). Pull the manifold away from the engine slightly to disengage it from the locating dowels in the cylinder head, then lift the manifold out of the engine compartment.

14   Remove the exhaust manifold (see Section 8). This is necessary because the intake and exhaust manifolds share a common gasket.

15   Thoroughly clean the gasket mating surfaces, removing all traces of old gasket material.

16   If the manifold is being replaced, make sure all the fittings, etc. are transferred to the replacement manifold.

17   Position a new gasket on the cylinder head, using the locating dowels to hold it in place. Install the exhaust manifold and hand

tighten the nuts.

18   Position the intake manifold loosely on the cylinder head.

19   Install the EGR tube between the manifolds.

20   Install the manifold retaining bolts and tighten all fasteners in sequence **(see illustrations)** to the torque listed in this Chapter's Specifications.

21   Reinstall the remaining parts in the reverse order of removal. **Caution:** *Before connecting the fuel lines to the fuel rail, replace the O-rings in the quick-connect fuel line couplings (see Chapter 4).*

22   Run the engine and check for leaks.

8   Exhaust manifold - removal and installation

Warning: *Allow the engine to cool completely before following this procedure.*

1   Remove the intake manifold (see Section 7).

2   Apply penetrating oil to the threads of the exhaust manifold attaching studs and the exhaust pipe-to-manifold attaching bolts.

3   On 1987 through 1999 models, remove the nuts that secure the exhaust pipe to the exhaust manifold and detach the pipe from the manifold. On models since 2000, remove the nuts that secure the exhaust pipe assembly to the exhaust manifolds.

4   On 1987 through 1999 models, remove the three nuts that secure the exhaust manifold to the cylinder head and pull the manifold off the engine. On 2000 models, remove the remaining nuts that secure the exhaust manifolds to the cylinder head and pull both manifolds off the engine.

5   Remove all traces of old gasket material from the mating surfaces.

6   If the manifold gasket was blown out, have the manifold checked for warpage by an automotive machine shop and repaired if necessary.

7   Position a new gasket on the locating dowels and slide the manifold over the studs.

8   Install the attaching nuts on the studs finger tight.

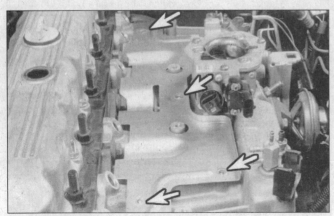

7.11 Remove the bolts (arrows) and lift the heat shield off

7.12 Four of the intake manifold mounting bolts (arrows) can be accessed from the top - you must reach below the manifold to remove the remaining four, which are visible in illustration 7.20 (1987 through 1999 shown)

7.20a Intake/exhaust manifold bolt/nut tightening sequence. Note that the EGR tube (#12 and #13) should be finger tight at first but properly torqued very last (1987 through 1999)

7.20b Intake/exhaust manifold bolt/nut tightening sequence 1989 models only

9   Reinstall the intake manifold (see Section 7) and tighten all fasteners, in the sequence shown in **illustration 7.20**, to the torque listed in this Chapter's Specifications.
10   Reconnect the exhaust pipe, run the engine and check for leaks.

9   Cylinder head - removal and installation

Refer to illustrations 9.11, 9.15, 9.19 and 9.21
Caution: *Allow the engine to cool completely before following this procedure.*

Removal

1   Disconnect the negative cable from the battery.
2   Drain the coolant from the radiator and the engine block (see Chapter 1).
3   Remove the air cleaner assembly (see Chapter 4).
4   Detach the fuel pipe and vacuum advance hose.
5   Remove the valve cover (see Section 4).
6   Remove the rocker arms and pushrods (see Section 5).
7   Unbolt the power steering pump bracket (if equipped) and set the pump aside without disconnecting the hoses. Leave the pump upright so fluid doesn't spill.

7.20c Intake and exhaust manifold bolt/nut tightening sequence (2000 4.0L)

8   Remove the intake and exhaust manifolds (see Sections 7 and 8).

Air-conditioned models

9   Remove the bracket on the cylinder head that supports the idler pulley for the air conditioning compressor drivebelt (see Chapter 1).
10   Loosen the alternator drivebelt and remove the alternator bracket-to-cylinder head mounting bolt.
11   Unplug the wiring and unbolt the air conditioning compressor (see Chapter 3) without disconnecting the refrigerant hoses. Set the compressor aside and remove the upper two bolts from the bracket **(see illustration)**.

All models

12   Label the spark plug wires and remove the distributor cap with the wires attached to it. Remove the spark plugs as described in Chapter 1.
13   Disconnect the wire from the temperature sending unit, which is on the top left rear corner of the cylinder head. Also disconnect the battery ground cable, which is on the right side of the engine.
14   Remove the ignition coil and bracket assembly (see Chapter 5).
15   Remove the heater hose bracket, if equipped **(see illustration)**.
16   Remove the cylinder head bolts and lift the head off the engine. **Note 1:** *Bolt number 14* **(see illustration 9.21)** *cannot be removed until the cylinder head is moved forward enabling the bolt to clear the firewall.* **Note 2:** *If the head sticks to the engine, insert a prybar into an exhaust port and pry gently to break the seal.*
17   Thoroughly clean the gasket mating surfaces, removing all traces of old gasket material. Stuff shop towels into each cylinder so scraped material doesn't fall in.
18   Inspect the head for cracks and warpage. See Chapter 2, Part D, for cylinder head servicing information. If you are replacing the cylinder head, be sure to transfer all fittings, etc. to the new head.

9.11 Set the compressor aside with the refrigerant lines still attached - then remove the upper bracket bolts (arrows)

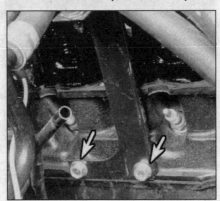

9.15 Remove the two bolts (arrows) to disconnect the heater hose bracket

9.19 Install the head gasket with the TOP mark facing up

9.21 Cylinder head bolt tightening sequence - be sure to coat the threads of bolt no. 11 (arrow) with Loctite 592 sealant (or equivalent)

Installation

19   On models equipped with the 4.2L engine, apply an even coat of Perfect Seal sealing compound (or equivalent) to both sides of the replacement head gasket (metal type). On models equipped with the 4.0L engine, it is not necessary to use any type of sealant on the head gasket (composition type). Position the new head gasket on the engine block with the word TOP facing up **(see illustration)**.

20   Install the cylinder head on the engine block.

21   Coat the threads of bolt number 11 **(see illustration)** with Loctite 592 sealant (or equivalent) and install the head bolts hand tight. **Note:** *Clean each bolt and mark it with a dab of paint. Replace any bolts which were painted and reused during an earlier servicing operation.*

22   Tighten the cylinder head bolts in sequence **(see illustration 9.21)** to the torque values listed in this Chapter's Specifications.

23   Reinstall the remaining components in the reverse order of removal.

24   Add coolant and run the engine, checking for proper operation and coolant and oil leaks.

10   Vibration damper - removal and installation

Refer to illustrations 10.6 and 10.7

1   Disconnect the negative cable from the battery.

2   Raise the front of the vehicle and support it securely on jackstands.

3   Remove the splash pan which is mounted below the front of the engine.

4   Remove the drivebelts (see Chapter 1).

5   Remove the radiator and cooling fan(s) as described in Chapter 3.

6   Remove the vibration damper retaining bolt and washer. **Note:** *To prevent the crankshaft from rotating, place two 5/16 x 1-1/2-inch long bolts into the damper holes and hold a pry bar between them* **(see illustration)**. Rotate the crankshaft until the bar contacts the frame.

7   Using a vibration damper removal tool **(see illustration)**, pull the damper off the crankshaft.

8   Clean and inspect the area on the center hub of the damper where the front oil seal contacts it. Minor imperfections can be cleaned up with fine emery cloth. If there is a groove worn in the hub, replace the vibration

damper or have a special sleeve installed on the hub to restore the contact surface.

9   Apply clean engine oil to the seal contact surface of the damper hub.

10   Align the key slot of the vibration damper hub with the crankshaft key and tap the damper onto the crankshaft with a soft-face mallet.

11   Install the vibration damper bolt and tighten it to the torque listed in this Chapter's Specifications.

12   Reinstall the remaining parts in the reverse order of removal.

11   Crankshaft front oil seal - replacement

Refer to illustrations 11.2 and 11.3

1   Remove the vibration damper (see Section 10).

2   Carefully pry the oil seal out of the timing chain cover with a seal removal tool or screwdriver **(see illustration)**. Don't scratch the cover bore or damage the crankshaft in the process (if the crankshaft is damaged the new seal will end up leaking).

3   Clean the bore in the cover and coat the outer edge of the new seal with engine oil or

10.6 Install two bolts in the damper and use them to keep the crankshaft from rotating

10.7 Use a vibration damper removal tool such as this one - do not use a gear puller with jaws; it will damage the damper

11.2 Pry the old seal out with a seal removal tool (shown here) or a screwdriver

11.3 Gently drive the new seal into place with a hammer and large socket

12.4 Once the alternator has been removed, remove the bracket retaining nuts (arrows), then unbolt the timing chain cover

12.7 Cut off the end tabs at both sides where the oil pan and engine block meet

multi-purpose grease. Using a socket with an outside diameter slightly smaller than the outside diameter of the seal, carefully drive the new seal into place with a hammer **(see illustration)**. If a socket isn't available, a short section of large diameter pipe will work. Check the seal after installation to be sure that the spring didn't pop out of place.

4   Reinstall the vibration damper.
5   The parts removed to gain access to the damper can now be reinstalled.
6   Run the engine and check for leaks.

12   Timing chain cover - removal and installation

Refer to illustrations 12.4, 12.7 and 12.13

Removal

1   Disconnect the negative cable from the battery.
2   Remove the fan, fan shroud, radiator and water pump pulley (see Chapter 3).
3   Remove the vibration damper (see Section 10).
4   Unbolt the alternator and bracket assembly **(see illustration)**.
5   Remove the oil pan-to-timing chain cover bolts and timing chain cover-to-engine block bolts.
6   Separate the timing chain cover from the engine. If necessary, tap on it gently with a soft-face mallet to break the seal. Temporarily stuff a rag into the oil pan opening to prevent entry of debris.
7   Cut off the oil pan side gasket end tabs flush with the front face of the engine block **(see illustration)**. Save the cut off gasket tabs for reference later.
8   Clean the mating surfaces of the timing chain cover, oil pan and engine block, removing all traces of oil and old gasket material.

Installation

9   Apply RTV sealant to both sides of the new timing chain cover-to-engine block gasket and position the gasket on the engine.

10   Using the end tabs you cut off as guides, trim the replacement oil pan side gasket ends to the appropriate sizes. Apply RTV sealant to the gasket ends and install them on the exposed portions of the oil pan side rails.
11   Using RTV sealant, generously coat the timing chain cover end tab recesses of the new timing chain cover-to-oil pan seal. Position the seal on the timing chain cover. Apply engine oil to the seal-to-oil pan contact surface.
12   Position the timing chain cover on the engine block.
13   Use the vibration damper to center the timing chain cover **(see illustration)**. Be sure the old oil seal (not the new one) is in place, as it may be damaged.
14   Install the timing chain cover-to-block and oil pan-to-cover bolts and tighten them to the torque listed in this Chapter's Specifications.
15   Replace the crankshaft front oil seal (see Section 11).
16   With the key inserted in the crankshaft,

install the vibration damper as described in Section 10.
17   Reinstall the remaining components in the reverse order of removal.
18   Run the engine and check for oil leaks.

13   Timing chain and sprockets - inspection, removal and installation

Refer to illustrations 13.3, 13.7, 13.8, 13.9, 13.10a, 13.10b and 13.13

1   Set the number one piston at Top Dead Center (see Section 3).
2   Remove the timing chain cover (see Section 12).

Inspection

3   Slip the oil slinger off the crankshaft **(see illustration)** and reinstall the vibration damper bolt. Using this bolt, rotate the crankshaft clockwise just enough to take up the slack on one side of the chain.

12.13 Use the vibration damper to center the timing chain cover during installation

13.3 Slip the oil slinger off the crankshaft, noting that the cupped side faces away from the engine

13.7 Install the timing chain with the sprocket index dots (arrows) directly opposite each other

13.8 Remove the thrust pin and spring (arrow), then remove the bolt in the center of the camshaft sprocket - put a large screwdriver through one of the holes in the sprocket to keep it from turning

13.9 Remove and install the chain and sprockets as an assembly

4   Count the pins on the timing chain. The correct timing chain has 48 pins. A chain with more pins will cause excessive slack.

5   Establish a reference point on the block. Move the slack side of the chain from side-to-side with your fingers and measure the movement. The difference between the two measurements is the deflection.

6   If the deflection exceeds 1/2-inch, replace the timing chain and sprockets.

13.10a Note that the engine side of the camshaft sprocket has a hole (arrow) . . .

13.10b . . . for the camshaft locating dowel (arrow) - be sure they are aligned properly during installation

Removal

7   Align the sprocket timing marks **(see illustration)**.

8   Remove the camshaft thrust pin and spring and the sprocket retaining bolt and washer **(see illustration)**.

9   Pull the crankshaft sprocket, camshaft sprocket and timing chain off as an assembly **(see illustration)**. **Caution:** *Do not turn the crankshaft or camshaft while the timing chain is removed.*

Installation

10   Be sure the crankshaft key is still pointing up. Note the locations of the locating dowel on the camshaft and the corresponding hole in the cam sprocket **(see illustrations)**.

11   Pre-assemble the timing chain, crankshaft sprocket and camshaft sprocket with the timing marks aligned and facing out. Slip the assembly onto the engine in such a way that a line drawn through the timing marks will also pass through the centers of the sprockets.

12   Install the camshaft sprocket bolt and tighten it to the torque listed in this Chapter's Specifications. Reinstall the thrust pin and spring.

13   To verify the correct installation of the

timing chain, turn the crankshaft clockwise until the camshaft sprocket timing mark is at the one o'clock position. This positions the crankshaft sprocket timing mark where the adjacent tooth meshes with the chain at the three o'clock position. There must be 15 chain pins between the sprocket timing marks **(see illustration)**.

14   Install the crankshaft oil slinger on the crankshaft with the cupped side facing out.

15   Install the timing chain cover and vibration damper as described in Sections 10 and 12.

16   Reinstall the remaining parts in the reverse order of removal.

17   Run the engine and check for oil leaks and proper operation.

14   Camshaft, bearings and lifters - removal, inspection and installation

Refer to illustrations 14.9 and 14.11

1   The extent of camshaft wear can be determined by measuring the lobe lift. This procedure does not involve removing the camshaft. Refer to Chapter 2, Part A, Section 14 for the lobe lift measuring procedure, but use the specifications provided in this Part of Chapter 2.

13.13 To verify correct installation, turn the crankshaft clockwise until the timing marks are positioned as shown and count the pins between the marks

14.9 Remove the lifters with a magnetic pick-up tool (shown here) or a special lifter removal tool

2   To remove the lifters only, follow steps 7 through 9, 12, 16 and 17 of this procedure.
3   Remove the radiator, fan and fan shroud (see Chapter 3).
4   On air-conditioned models, unbolt the condenser assembly (see Chapter 3) WITHOUT disconnecting the refrigerant lines. Set the condenser aside. It may be necessary to remove the battery case (see Chapter 5).
5   Remove the distributor (see Chapter 5).
6   Remove the front bumper and/or grille

as necessary for the camshaft to be slid out the front of the engine (see Chapter 11).
7   Label and then remove the spark plug wires from the spark plugs.
8   Remove the cylinder head (see Section 9).
9   Remove the valve lifters **(see illustration)** and store them separately so they can be reinstalled in the same bores.
10   Remove the timing chain and sprockets (see Section 13).
11   Carefully pull the camshaft out. Temporarily install the sprocket bolt, if necessary, to use as a handle. Support the cam so the lobes don't nick or gouge the bearings as it's withdrawn **(see illustration)**.
12   See Chapter 2, Part A, Section 9 for the lifter inspection procedure. Camshaft and bearing inspection are covered in Chapter 2, Part A, Section 14. Be sure to use the specifications provided in this Part of Chapter 2.
13   Camshaft bearing replacement requires special tools and expertise that place it outside the scope of the home mechanic. Remove the engine and take the block to an automotive machine shop to ensure the job is done correctly. **Note:** *If the camshaft appears to have been rubbing hard against the timing chain cover, first check the camshaft thrust pin and spring and then examine the oil pressure relief holes in the rear cam journal to make sure they are open.*

14   Lubricate the camshaft journals and lobes with moly-base grease or engine assembly lube.
15   Slide the camshaft into the engine. Support the cam near the block and be careful not to scrape or nick the bearings.
16   The rest of the installation procedure is the reverse of removal.
17   Before starting and running the engine, change the oil and filter (see Chapter 1).

15   Oil pan - removal and installation

Refer to illustrations 15.10, 15.12, 15.13 and 15.16

Removal

1   Disconnect the negative cable from the battery.
2   Raise the vehicle and support it securely on jackstands.
3   Remove the belly pan from under the front of the engine.
4   Drain the oil and replace the oil filter (see Chapter 1).
5   Remove the starter motor (see Chapter 5).
6   Remove the bellhousing inspection cover from the front of the transmission.
7   Detach the steering damper from the center steering link (see Chapter 10).
8   Support the front axle with a jack and remove the lower shock absorber bolts.
9   Lower the jack and allow the axle to hang free.
10   Mark the locations of the oil pan mounting studs **(see illustration)**.
11   Remove the oil pan mounting bolts/studs and carefully separate the pan from the engine block. If the pan sticks to the block, tap the side of the pan gently with a soft-face mallet.
12   If necessary, set the oil pan on the axle and remove the oil pump and pick-up tube **(see illustration)**.
13   Remove the oil pan by sliding it out to the rear **(see illustration)**.
14   Thoroughly clean the mating surfaces, removing all traces of oil and old gasket material.

14.11 Support the camshaft as you slowly withdraw it from the block

CAMSHAFT

CRANKSHAFT

15.10 Mark the location of the studs with paint to ensure proper reassembly

15.12 The oil pick-up tube interferes with pan removal - remove the two attaching bolts and detach the oil pump (arrow) . . .

15.13 . . . then remove the oil pan from the rear by sliding it out between the axle and bellhousing

OIL PAN-TO-BEARING CAP SEAL   OIL PAN GASKET SET   OIL PAN TIMING CASE COVER SEAL

OIL PAN

15.16 Oil pan gaskets - exploded view

18.3a Drive one side of the upper seal in

Installation

15   Check the oil pan flange for distortion and warpage. Straighten the flange by placing the distorted area on a block of wood and pounding it flat with a hammer.

16   Position new gaskets **(see illustration)** on the pan with Jeep Spraya-Gasket (or equivalent). Apply a generous amount of RTV sealant at the corners where the gaskets join. Coat the inside curved surface of the replacement rear gasket section (where it contacts the bearing cap) with soap.

17   Slide the oil pan up under the engine and reinstall the oil pump and pick-up tube, tightening the oil pump mounting bolts to the torque listed in this Chapter's Specifications. Install the oil pan and tighten the bolts to the specified torque, working from the center out in several steps.

18   Reinstall the remaining parts in the reverse order of removal.

19   Check that the drain plug is tight and then add the amount of oil specified in Chapter 1.

20   Run the engine and check for oil leaks.

16   Oil pump - removal and installation

See Chapter 2, Part B, Section 16 for this procedure, but be sure to use the torque specifications and illustration 15.12 in this Part of Chapter 2.

17   Flywheel/driveplate - removal and installation

Refer to Chapter 2, Part B, Section 17 for this procedure, but be sure to use the torque specifications in this Part of Chapter 2.

18   Rear main oil seal - replacement

Refer to illustrations 18.3a, 18.3b and 18.5

1   Remove the oil pan (see Section 15).

2   Remove the rear main bearing cap and pry the old seal half out of the bearing cap with a small screwdriver.

3   Carefully drive the old upper main seal out with a small brass punch and a hammer until it protrudes sufficiently from the engine block to be gripped with needle-nose pliers and removed **(see illustrations)**. Use great care to avoid damaging the crankshaft.

4   Thoroughly clean the main bearing cap and the rear of the block/crankshaft, removing all traces of oil and old sealant.

5   Coat the lip of the new upper seal with engine oil. Coat the outside surface with liquid soap **(see illustration)**.

6   Insert the seal into the groove in the engine block with the lip facing forward.

7   Coat both sides of the lower seal ends with RTV sealant and put liquid soap on the outside of the seal **(see illustration 18.5)**. Do not apply RTV or soap to the seal lip. Press the seal into place in the cap and apply a film of engine oil to the seal lip. **Caution:** *Do not apply sealant to the cylinder block mating surfaces of the rear main bearing cap. Doing this would alter the bearing-to-journal clearance.*

8   Apply RTV sealant to the chamfered edges of the rear main bearing cap **(see illustration 18.5)** and install the cap. Tighten the bolts to the torque listed in this Chapter's Specifications.

9   Reinstall the remaining components in the reverse order of removal.

10   Add the amount of oil specified in Chapter 1, run the engine and check for oil leaks.

18.3b . . . until the other side protrudes far enough to grasp it with needle-nose pliers and pull it out

19   Engine mounts - check and replacement

Refer to Chapter 2, Part B, Section 19. The inline six-cylinder engine mounts are slightly different, but this doesn't affect the check and replacement procedures.

ENGINE OIL ON LIP   LIQUID SOAP ON OUTSIDE

RTV SEALER ON TOP AND BOTTOM OF BOTH SIDES OF SEAL

RTV SEALER ON CHAMFERED EDGES

RTV SEALER ON CHAMFERED EDGES

18.5 Rear main seal components - exploded view

Chapter 2 Part D
General engine overhaul procedures

Contents

Specifications

2.4L four-cylinder engine

Note: *Many clearances and overhaul specifications for the 2.4L engine were not available at the time of publication. Check with your automotive machine shop for advice concerning overhaul.*

General

Displacement	2.4 liters (148 cubic inches)
Bore and Stroke	3.445 x 3.976 inches (87.5 x 101.0 mm)
Cylinder compression pressure (minimum)	100 psi (690 kPa)
Maximum variation between cylinders	25 percent
Oil pressure (engine warmed-up)	
At idle	4 psi* (25 kPa)
At 3000 rpm	25 to 80 psi (170 to 550 kPa)

* Note: *If the oil pressure at idle is less than the specified minimum, don't run the engine at 3000 rpm.*

Torque specifications

Ft-lbs (unless otherwise indicated)

Balance shaft assembly	
Chain cover	105 in-lbs
Carrier-to-block bolts	40
Gear cover bolt/stud	105 in-lbs
Sprocket bolt	250 in-lbs
Tensioner bolts	105 in-lbs
Connecting rod cap bolts	
Step 1	20
Step 2	Tighten an additional 1/4-turn
Main bearing/bedplate bolts	
Step one	
Tighten bolts 11, 17 and 20	Hand-tighten until bedplate contacts block mating surface
Step two	
Tighten bolts 1 through 10	30
Step three	
Tighten bolts 1 through 10	Tighten an additional 1/4-turn
Step four	
Tighten bolts 11 through 20	20

Note: *Many clearances and overhaul specifications for the 2.4L engine were not available at the time of publication. Check with your automotive machine shop for advice concerning overhaul.*

2.5L four-cylinder engine

General

Cylinder compression pressure	155 to 185 psi
Maximum allowable variation between cylinders	30 psi
Oil pressure	
At idle	25 to 35 psi
Above 1600 rpm	37 to 75 psi

Engine block

Cylinder bore diameter (standard)	3.8751 to 3.8775 inches
Maximum allowable taper and out-of-round	0.001 inch
Warpage limit	0.002 inch per 6 inches
Valve lifter bore diameter	0.9055 to 0.9065 inch

Cylinder head and valves

Cylinder head warpage limit	0.002 inch per 6 inches (0.006 inch overall)
Minimum valve margin	1/32-inch
Valve stem diameter	0.311 to 0.312 inch
Valve stem-to-guide clearance	0.001 to 0.003 inch
Valve spring pressure	
Valve closed	80 to 90 lbs at 1.64 inch
Valve open	200 lbs at 1.216 inch
Valve spring free length	1.967 inch
Valve spring installed height	Not available
Valve lifter	
Diameter	0.904 to 0.9045 inch
Lifter-to-bore clearance	0.001 to 0.0025 inch

Crankshaft and connecting rods

Connecting rod journal	
Diameter	02.0934 to 2.0955 inches
Bearing oil clearance	
Desired	0.0015 to 0.0020 inch
Allowable	0.001 to 0.0025 inch
Connecting rod side clearance (endplay)	0.0010 to 0.0019 inch
Main bearing journal	
Diameter	2.4996 to 2.5001 inches
Bearing oil clearance	
Desired	0.002 inch
Allowable	0.001 to 0.0025 inch
Crankshaft endplay	0.0015 to 0.0065 inch
Maximum taper and out-of-round (all journals)	0.0005 inch

Pistons and rings

Piston-to-bore clearance	0.0013 to 0.0021 inch
Piston ring end gap	
Compression rings	0.0010 to 0.020 inch
Oil control ring (steel rail)	0.015 to 0.055 inch
Piston ring side clearance	
Compression rings	0.001 to 0.0032 inch
Oil control ring	0.001 to 0.0085 inch

Torque specifications *

	Ft-lbs
Connecting rod cap nuts	33
Main bearing cap bolts	80

* **Note:** *Refer to Part A for additional torque specifications.*

4.0L and 4.2L six-cylinder engines

General

Cylinder compression pressure	120 to 150 psi
Maximum variation between cylinders	30 psi
Oil pressure	
At idle (600 rpm)	13 psi
Above 1600 rpm	37 to 75 psi

Cylinder head and valves

Warpage limit	0.002 inch per 6 inches
Minimum valve margin	1/32-inch

Valve stem diameter
  4.2L engine.. 0.372 inch
  4.0L engine.. 0.312 inch
  Valve stem-to-guide clearance .... 0.001 to 0.003 inch
Valve spring pressure
  Valve open.. 205 to 220 lbs at 1.2 inch
  Valve closed .... 64 to 74 lbs at 1.625 inch
Valve lifter
  Diameter... 0.904 to 0.9045 inch
  Lifter-to-bore clearance .... 0.001 to 0.0025 inch

Crankshaft and connecting rods

Connecting rod journal
  Diameter... 2.0934 to 2.0955 inches
  Bearing oil clearance
    Desired.. 0.0015 to 0.002 inch
    Allowable... 0.001 to 0.003 inch
  Connecting rod side clearance (endplay)................................... 0.010 to 0.019 inch
Main bearing
  Journal diameter .... 2.4996 to 2.5001 inches
  Bearing oil clearance
    Desired.. 0.002 inch
    Allowable... 0.001 to 0.0025 inch
  Crankshaft endplay (at thrust bearing) .... 0.0015 to 0.0065 inch
  Maximum taper and out-of-round (all journals)......................... 0.0005 inch

Pistons and rings

Piston-to-bore clearance
  4.2L engine
    Desired.. 0.0012 to 0.0013 inch
    Allowable... 0.0009 to 0.0017 inch
  4.0L engine
    Desired.. 0.0013 to 0.0021 inch
    Allowable... 0.0013 to 0.0015 inch
Piston ring end gap
  Compression rings .... 0.010 to 0.020 inch
  Oil control ring (steel rails).. 0.010 to 0.025 inch
Piston ring side clearance
  4.2L engine
    Compression rings
      Desired .... 0.0017 inch
      Allowable .... 0.0017 to 0.0032 inch
    Oil control ring
      Desired .... 0.003 inch
      Allowable .... 0.001 to 0.008 inch
  4.0L engine
    Compression rings
      Desired .... 0.001 inch
      Allowable .... 0.001 to 0.0032 inch
    Oil control ring
      Desired .... 0.003 inch
      Allowable .... 0.001 to 0.0095 inch

Engine block

Maximum warpage... 0.002 inch per 6 inches (0.008 inch overall)
Cylinder bore diameter (standard)
  4.0L engine... 3.8751 to 3.8775 inches
  4.2L engine... 3.7501 to 3.7533 inches
Maximum taper and out-of-round.. 0.001 inch

Torque specifications*   Ft-lbs
Main bearing cap bolts.. 80
Connecting rod cap nuts 33

* **Note:** *Refer to Part B for additional torque specifications.*

1   General information

Included in this portion of Chapter 2 are the general overhaul procedures for the cylinder head(s) and internal engine components.

The information ranges from advice concerning preparation for an overhaul and the purchase of replacement parts to detailed, step-by-step procedures covering removal and installation of internal engine components and the inspection of parts.

The following Sections have been written based on the assumption that the engine has been removed from the vehicle. For information concerning in-vehicle engine repair, as well as removal and installation of the external components necessary for the overhaul, see Part A, B or C of this Chapter and Section 7 of this Part.

The Specifications included in this Part are only those necessary for the inspection and overhaul procedures which follow. Refer to Parts A, B and C for additional Specifications.

2   Engine overhaul - general information

Refer to illustrations 2.4a and 2.4b

It's not always easy to determine when, or if, an engine should be completely overhauled, as a number of factors must be considered.

High mileage is not necessarily an indication that an overhaul is needed, while low mileage doesn't preclude the need for an overhaul. Frequency of servicing is probably the most important consideration. An engine that's had regular and frequent oil and filter changes, as well as other required maintenance, will most likely give many thousands of miles of reliable service. Conversely, a neglected engine may require an overhaul very early in its life.

Excessive oil consumption is an indication that piston rings, valve seals and/or valve guides are in need of attention. Make sure that oil leaks aren't responsible before deciding that the rings and/or guides are bad. Perform a cylinder compression check to determine the extent of the work required (see Section 3).

Check the oil pressure with a gauge installed in place of the oil pressure sending unit **(see illustrations)** and compare it to the Specifications. If it's extremely low, the bearings and/or oil pump are probably worn out.

Loss of power, rough running, knocking or metallic engine noises, excessive valve train noise and high fuel consumption rates may also point to the need for an overhaul, especially if they're all present at the same time. If a complete tune-up doesn't remedy the situation, major mechanical work is the only solution.

An engine overhaul involves restoring the internal parts to the specifications of a new engine. During an overhaul, the piston rings are replaced and the cylinder walls are

2.4a Remove the oil pressure sending unit (arrow) (2.5L engine shown) . . .

2.4b . . . and connect a gauge to check oil pressure (4.0L engine shown) - the sending unit is located near the oil filter on all models

reconditioned (rebored and/or honed). If a rebore is done by an automotive machine shop, new oversize pistons will also be installed. The main bearings, connecting rod bearings and camshaft bearings are generally replaced with new ones and, if necessary, the crankshaft may be reground to restore the journals. Generally, the valves are serviced as well, since they're usually in less than-perfect condition at this point. While the engine is being overhauled, other components, such as the distributor, starter and alternator, can be rebuilt as well. The end result should be a like new engine that will give many thousands of trouble free miles. **Note:** *Critical cooling system components such as the hoses, drivebelts, thermostat and water pump MUST be replaced with new parts when an engine is overhauled. The radiator should be checked carefully to ensure that it isn't clogged or leaking (see Chapter 3). Also, we don't recommend overhauling the oil pump - always install a new one when an engine is rebuilt.*

Before beginning the engine overhaul, read through the entire procedure to familiarize yourself with the scope and requirements of the job. Overhauling an engine isn't difficult if you have the right equipment and follow the instructions carefully, but it is time consuming. Plan on the vehicle being tied up for a minimum of two weeks, especially if parts must be taken to an automotive machine shop for repair or reconditioning. Check on availability of parts and make sure that any necessary special tools and equipment are obtained in advance. Most work can be done with typical hand tools, although a number of precision measuring tools are required for inspecting parts to determine if they must be replaced. Often an automotive machine shop will handle the inspection of parts and offer advice concerning reconditioning and replacement. **Note:** *Always wait until the engine has been completely disassembled and all components, especially the engine block, have been inspected before deciding what service and repair operations must be performed by an automotive machine shop. Since the block's condition will be the major factor to consider when determining whether to overhaul the original engine or buy a rebuilt*

one, *never purchase parts or have machine work done on other components until the block has been thoroughly inspected. As a general rule, time is the primary cost of an overhaul, so it doesn't pay to install worn or substandard parts.*

As a final note, to ensure maximum life and minimum trouble from a rebuilt engine, everything must be assembled with care in a spotlessly clean environment.

3   Cylinder compression check

Refer to illustration 3.6

1   A compression check will tell you what mechanical condition the upper end (pistons, rings, valves, head gaskets) of your engine is in. Specifically, it can tell you if the compression is down due to leakage caused by worn piston rings, defective valves and seats or a blown head gasket. **Note:** *The engine must be at normal operating temperature and the battery must be fully charged for this check. Also, if the engine is equipped with a carburetor, the choke valve must be all the way open to get an accurate compression reading (if the engine's warm, the choke should be open).*

2   Begin by cleaning the area around the spark plugs before you remove them (compressed air should be used, if available, otherwise a small brush or even a bicycle tire pump will work). The idea is to prevent dirt from getting into the cylinders as the compression check is being done.

3   Remove all of the spark plugs from the engine (see Chapter 1).

4   Block the throttle wide open.

5   Detach the coil wire from the center of the distributor cap and ground it on the engine block. Use a jumper wire with alligator clips on each end to ensure a good ground. On fuel-injected models, the fuel pump circuit should also be disabled (see Chapter 4).

6   Install the compression gauge in the number one spark plug hole **(see illustration)**.

7   Crank the engine over at least seven

3.6 A compression gauge with a threaded fitting for the spark plug hole is preferred over the type that requires hand pressure to maintain the seal

5.5a Label both ends of each wire before unplugging the connector

5.5b Remove the nut on the engine stud and disconnect the ground strap (arrow)

compression strokes and watch the gauge. The compression should build up quickly in a healthy engine. Low compression on the first stroke, followed by gradually increasing pressure on successive strokes, indicates worn piston rings. A low compression reading on the first stroke, which doesn't build up during successive strokes, indicates leaking valves or a blown head gasket (a cracked head could also be the cause). Deposits on the undersides of the valve heads can also cause low compression. Record the highest gauge reading obtained.

8   Repeat the procedure for the remaining cylinders and compare the results to the Specifications.

9   Add some engine oil (about three squirts from a plunger-type oil can) to each cylinder, through the spark plug hole, and repeat the test.

10   If the compression increases after the oil is added, the piston rings are definitely worn. If the compression doesn't increase significantly, the leakage is occurring at the valves or head gasket. Leakage past the valves may be caused by burned valve seats and/or faces or warped, cracked or bent valves.

11   If two adjacent cylinders have equally low compression, there's a strong possibility that the head gasket between them is blown. The appearance of coolant in the combustion chambers or the crankcase would verify this condition.

12   If one cylinder is about 20-percent lower than the others, and the engine has a slightly rough idle, a worn exhaust lobe on the camshaft could be the cause.

13   If the compression is unusually high, the combustion chambers are probably coated with carbon deposits. If that's the case, the cylinder head should be removed and decarbonized.

14   If compression is way down or varies greatly between cylinders, it would be a good idea to have a leak-down test performed by an automotive repair shop. This test will pinpoint exactly where the leakage is occurring and how severe it is.

4   Engine removal - methods and precautions

If you've decided that an engine must be removed for overhaul or major repair work, several preliminary steps should be taken.

Locating a suitable place to work is extremely important. Adequate work space, along with storage space for the vehicle, will be needed. If a shop or garage isn't available, at the very least a flat, level, clean work surface made of concrete or asphalt is required.

Cleaning the engine compartment and engine before beginning the removal procedure will help keep your tools and your hands clean.

An engine hoist or A-frame will also be necessary. Make sure the equipment is rated in excess of the combined weight of the engine and accessories. Safety is of primary importance, considering the potential hazards involved in lifting the engine out of the vehicle.

If the engine is being removed by a novice, a helper should be available. Advice and aid from someone more experienced would also be helpful. There are many instances when one person cannot simultaneously perform all of the operations required when lifting the engine out of the vehicle.

Plan the operation ahead of time. Arrange for or obtain all of the tools and equipment you'll need prior to beginning the job. Some of the equipment necessary to perform engine removal and installation safely and with relative ease are (in addition to an engine hoist) a heavy duty floor jack, complete sets of wrenches and sockets as described in the front of this manual, wooden blocks and plenty of rags and cleaning solvent for mopping up spilled oil, coolant and gasoline. If the hoist must be rented, make sure that you arrange for it in advance and perform all of the operations possible without it beforehand. This will save you money and time.

Plan for the vehicle to be out of use for quite a while. A machine shop will be required to perform some of the work which the do-it-yourselfer can't accomplish without special equipment. These shops often have a

busy schedule, so it would be a good idea to consult them before removing the engine in order to accurately estimate the amount of time required to rebuild or repair components that may need work.

Always be extremely careful when removing and installing the engine. Serious injury can result from careless actions. Plan ahead, take your time and a job of this nature, although major, can be accomplished successfully.

5   Engine - removal and installation

Refer to illustrations 5.5a, 5.5b, 5.11, 5.19, 5.20 and 5.24

Warning: *The air conditioning system is under high pressure! Have a dealer service department or service station discharge the system before disconnecting any system hoses or fittings.*

Removal

1   Refer to Chapter 4 and relieve the fuel system pressure (fuel-injected models only), then disconnect the negative cable from the battery.

2   Cover the fenders and cowl (see Chapter 11). Special pads are available to protect the fenders, but an old bedspread or blanket will also work.

3   Remove the air cleaner assembly (see Chapter 4).

4   Drain the cooling system (see Chapter 1).

5   Label the vacuum lines, emissions system hoses, wiring connectors, ground strap and fuel lines, to ensure correct reinstallation **(see illustration)**, then detach them **(see illustration)**. If there's any possibility of confusion, make a sketch of the engine compartment and clearly label the lines, hoses and wires.

6   Label and detach all coolant hoses from the engine.

7   Remove the cooling fan, shroud and radiator (see Chapter 3).

8   Remove the drivebelt(s) (see Chapter 1).

9   **Warning:** *Gasoline is extremely flammable, so extra precautions must be taken when working on any part of the fuel*

5.11 Set the power steering pump aside with the lines still connected - be sure it's upright so fluid won't spill

5.19 Attach the chain to the lifting brackets (4.0L shown)

system. DO NOT smoke or allow open flames or bare light bulbs near the vehicle. Also, don't work in a garage if a natural gas appliance with a pilot light is present. Disconnect the fuel lines running from the engine to the chassis (see Chapter 4). Plug or cap all open fittings/lines.

10   Disconnect the throttle linkage (and TV linkage/cruise control cable, if equipped) from the engine (see Chapter 4).

11   On power steering equipped vehicles, unbolt the power steering pump (see Chapter 10). Leave the lines/hoses attached **(see illustration)** and make sure the pump is kept in an upright position in the engine compartment (use wire or rope to restrain it out of the way).

12   On air conditioned vehicles, unbolt the compressor (see Chapter 3) and set it aside. Do not disconnect the hoses.

13   Drain the engine oil (see Chapter 1) and remove the oil filter.

14   Remove the starter motor (see Chapter 5).

15   Remove the alternator (see Chapter 5).

16   Unbolt the exhaust system from the engine (see Chapter 4).

17   If you're working on a vehicle with an automatic transmission, refer to Chapter 7, Part B and remove the torque converter-to-

driveplate bolts.

18   Support the transmission with a jack. Position a block of wood between the jack and transmission to prevent damage to the transmission. Special transmission jacks with safety chains are available - use one if possible.

19   Attach an engine sling or a length of chain to the lifting brackets on the engine **(see illustration)**.

20   Roll the hoist into position and connect the sling to it **(see illustration)**. Take up the slack in the sling or chain, but don't lift the engine. **Warning:** *DO NOT place any part of your body under the engine when it's supported only by a hoist or other lifting device.*

21   Remove the transmission-to-engine block bolts.

22   Remove the engine mount-to-frame bolts.

23   Recheck to be sure nothing is still connecting the engine to the transmission or vehicle. Disconnect anything still remaining.

24   Raise the engine slightly. Carefully work it forward to separate it from the transmission. If you're working on a vehicle with an automatic transmission, be sure the torque converter stays in the transmission (clamp a pair of vise-grips to the housing to keep the converter from sliding out). If you're working

on a vehicle with a manual transmission, the input shaft must be completely disengaged from the clutch. Slowly raise the engine out of the engine compartment **(see illustration)**. Check carefully to make sure nothing is hanging up.

25   Remove the flywheel/driveplate and mount the engine on an engine stand.

Installation

26   Check the engine and transmission mounts. If they're worn or damaged, replace them.

27   If you're working on a vehicle with a manual transmission, install the clutch and pressure plate (see Chapter 8). Now is a good time to install a new clutch.

28   Carefully lower the engine into the engine compartment - make sure the engine mounts line up.

29   If you're working on a vehicle with an automatic transmission, guide the torque converter into the crankshaft following the procedure outlined in Chapter 7, Part B.

30   If you're working on a vehicle with a manual transmission, apply a dab of high-temperature grease to the input shaft and guide it into the crankshaft pilot bearing until the bellhousing is flush with the engine block.

5.20 If possible, use the adjustable-angle type lifting sling (2.5L shown)

5.24 Pull the engine forward as far as possible to clear the transmission and then lift the engine high enough to clear the body

7.3a 2.5L four-cylinder engine - front view

7.3b 2.5L four-cylinder engine - left side view

31   Install the transmission-to-engine bolts and tighten them securely. **Caution:** *DO NOT use the bolts to force the transmission and engine together!*

32   Reinstall the remaining components in the reverse order of removal.

33   Add coolant, oil, power steering and transmission fluid as needed.

34   Run the engine and check for leaks and proper operation of all accessories, then install the hood and test drive the vehicle.

35   Have the air conditioning system recharged and leak tested.

6   Engine rebuilding alternatives

The do-it-yourselfer is faced with a number of options when performing an engine overhaul. The decision to replace the engine block, piston/connecting rod assemblies and crankshaft depends on a number of factors, with the number one consideration being the condition of the block. Other considerations are cost, access to machine shop facilities, parts availability, time required to complete the project and the extent of prior mechanical experience on the part of the do-it-yourselfer.

Some of the rebuilding alternatives include:

Individual parts - If the inspection procedures reveal that the engine block and most engine components are in reusable condition, purchasing individual parts may be the most economical alternative. The block, crankshaft and piston/connecting rod assemblies should all be inspected carefully. Even if the block shows little wear, the cylinder bores should be surface honed.

Short block - A short block consists of an engine block with a crankshaft, camshaft and piston/connecting rod assemblies already installed. All new bearings are incorporated and all clearances will be correct. The existing valve train components, cylinder head and external parts can be bolted to the short block with little or no machine shop work necessary.

Long block - A long block consists of a short block plus an oil pump, oil pan, cylinder head, valve cover and valve train components, timing sprockets and chain or gears and timing cover. All components are installed with new bearings, seals and gaskets incorporated throughout. The installation of manifolds and external parts is all that's necessary.

Give careful thought to which alternative is best for you and discuss the situation with local automotive machine shops, auto parts dealers and experienced rebuilders before ordering or purchasing replacement parts.

7   Engine overhaul - disassembly sequence

Refer to illustrations 7.3a, 7.3b, 7.3c, 7.3d, 7.3e, 7.3f, 7.5a and 7.5b

1   It's much easier to disassemble and work on the engine if it's mounted on a portable engine stand. A stand can often be rented quite cheaply from an equipment rental yard. Before the engine is mounted on a stand, the flywheel/driveplate should be removed from the engine.

2   If a stand isn't available, it's possible to disassemble the engine with it blocked up on the floor. Be extra careful not to tip or drop the engine when working without a stand.

3   If you're going to obtain a rebuilt engine, all external components must come off first **(see illustrations)**, to be transferred to the replacement engine, just as they will if you're doing a complete engine overhaul yourself.

7.3c 2.5L four-cylinder engine - right side view

7.3d Inline six-cylinder engine - front view

7.3e Inline six-cylinder engine - left side view (typical)

7.3f Inline six-cylinder engine - right side view

These include:

    Alternator and brackets
    Emissions control components
    Distributor, spark plug wires and spark
      plugs
    Thermostat and housing cover
    Water pump
    Fuel injection components or carburetor
    Intake/exhaust manifolds
    Oil filter
    Engine mounts

    Clutch and flywheel/driveplate
    Engine rear plate

Note: *When removing the external components from the engine, pay close attention to details that may be helpful or important during installation. Note the installed position of gaskets, seals, spacers, pins, brackets, washers, bolts and other small items.*

4   If you're obtaining a short block, which consists of the engine block, crankshaft, pistons and connecting rods all assembled, then

the cylinder head(s), oil pan and oil pump will have to be removed as well. See *Engine rebuilding alternatives* for additional information regarding the different possibilities to be considered.

5   If you're planning a complete overhaul, the engine must be disassembled and the internal components **(see illustrations)** removed in the following order:

    Valve cover
    Intake and exhaust manifolds

7.5a Internal engine components - exploded view (2.5L four-cylinder engine)

1	Engine oil dipstick and tube	21	Main bearing caps
2	Ring set	22	Main bearings
3	Piston	23	Crankshaft sprocket
4	Pin set	24	Oil shedder (slinger)
5	Connecting rod	25	Washer
6	Plug	26	Timing chain
7	Engine block	27	Camshaft sprocket
8	Flywheel and ring gear	28	Timing chain tensioner
9	Pilot bushing	29	Keys
10	Bushing oil wick	30	Crankshaft
11	Rear main oil seal	31	Pin
12	Main bearing cap	32	Camshaft
13	Connecting rod bearing	33	Oil channel plug
14	Connecting rod bearing cap		
15	Gasket		
16	Timing case cover		
17	Seal		
18	Vibration damper		
19	Vibration damper pulley		
20	Washer		

7.5b Internal engine components - exploded view (4.0L inline six-cylinder engine shown, 4.2L engine similar)

1	Engine oil dipstick and tube	21	Connecting rod bearing cap
2	Oil filter by-pass plug	22	Main bearings
3	Build date code location	23	Vibration damper pulley
4	Ring set	24	Washer
5	Piston	25	Vibration damper
6	Pin set	26	Seal
7	Plug	27	Timing chain cover
8	Engine block	28	Gasket
9	Oil channel plug	29	Main bearing cap (rear)
10	Camshaft	30	Main bearing cap seal kit (rear)
11	Connecting rod	31	Pilot bushing (with manual transmission)
12	Pin		
13	Camshaft sprocket	32	Bushing oil wick (with manual transmission)
14	Keys		
15	Washer	33	Flywheel and ring gear (with manual transmission)
16	Timing chain		
17	Oil shedder (slinger)		
18	Crankshaft sprocket	34	Bearing set
19	Crankshaft	35	Dowel
20	Connecting rod bearing	36	Plug

Rocker arms and pushrods
Cylinder head
Valve lifters
Timing cover
Timing chain and sprockets
Camshaft
Oil pan
Oil pump
Piston/connecting rod assemblies
Crankshaft and main bearings

6   Before beginning the disassembly and overhaul procedures, make sure the following items are available. Also, refer to *Engine overhaul - reassembly sequence* for a list of tools and materials needed for engine reassembly.

Common hand tools
Small cardboard boxes or plastic bags for storing parts
Gasket scraper
Ridge reamer
Vibration damper puller
Micrometers
Telescoping gauges
Dial indicator set
Valve spring compressor
Cylinder surfacing hone
Piston ring groove cleaning tool
Electric drill motor
Tap and die set
Wire brushes
Oil gallery brushes
Cleaning solvent

8   Cylinder head - disassembly

Refer to illustrations 8.2, 8.3 and 8.4

Note: *New and rebuilt cylinder heads are commonly available for most engines at dealerships and auto parts stores. Due to the fact that some specialized tools are necessary for the disassembly and inspection procedures, and replacement parts may not be readily available, it may be more practical and economical for the home mechanic to purchase a replacement head rather than taking the time to disassemble, inspect and recondition the original.*

1   Cylinder head disassembly involves removal of the intake and exhaust valves and related components. If they're still in place, remove the rocker arm bolts or nuts, pivot and rocker arms from the cylinder head studs. Label the parts or store them separately so they can be reinstalled in their original locations.

2   Before the valves are removed, arrange to label and store them, along with their related components, so they can be kept separate and reinstalled in the same valve guides they were removed from **(see illustration)**.

3   Compress the springs on the first valve with a spring compressor and remove the keepers **(see illustration)**. Carefully release the valve spring compressor and remove the

8.2 A small plastic bag, with an appropriate label, can be used to store the valve train components so they can be kept together and reinstalled in their original locations

8.3 Use a valve spring compressor to compress the spring, then remove the keepers from the stem

8.4 If the valve won't pull through the guide, deburr the edge of the stem end and the area around the top of the keeper groove with a file or whetstone

9.12 Check the cylinder head gasket for warpage by trying to slip a feeler gauge under the straightedge (see this Chapter's Specifications for the maximum warpage allowed and use a feeler gauge of that thickness)

9.14 A dial indicator can be used to determine the valve stem-to-guide clearance (move the valve stem as indicated by the arrows)

retainer, the spring and the spring seat (if used).

4   Pull the valve out of the head, then remove the oil seal from the guide. If the valve binds in the guide (won't pull through), push it back into the head and deburr the area around the keeper groove with a fine file or whetstone **(see illustration)**.

5   Repeat the procedure for the remaining valves. Remember to keep all the parts for each valve together so they can be reinstalled in the same locations.

6   Once the valves and related components have been removed and stored in an organized manner, the head should be thoroughly cleaned and inspected. If a complete engine overhaul is being done, finish the engine disassembly procedures before beginning the cylinder head cleaning and inspection process.

9   Cylinder head - cleaning and inspection

Refer to illustrations 9.12, 9.14, 9.15a, 9.15b, 9.16, 9.17 and 9.18

1   Thorough cleaning of the cylinder head and related valve train components, followed by a detailed inspection, will enable you to decide how much valve service work must be done during the engine overhaul. **Note:** *If the engine was severely overheated, the cylinder head is probably warped (see Step 12).*

Cleaning

2   Scrape all traces of old gasket material and sealing compound off the head gasket, intake manifold and exhaust manifold sealing surfaces. Be very careful not to gouge the cylinder head. Special gasket removal solvents that soften gaskets and make removal much easier are available at auto parts stores.

3   Remove all built up scale from the coolant passages.

4   Run a stiff wire brush through the various holes to remove deposits that may have formed in them.

5   Run an appropriate size tap into each of the threaded holes to remove corrosion and thread sealant that may be present. If compressed air is available, use it to clear the holes of debris produced by this operation. **Warning:** *Wear eye protection when using compressed air!*

6   Clean the rocker arm pivot bolt or stud threads with a wire brush.

7   Clean the cylinder head with solvent and dry it thoroughly. Compressed air will speed the drying process and ensure that all holes and recessed areas are clean. **Note:** *Decarbonizing chemicals are available and may prove very useful when cleaning cylinder heads and valve train components. They are very caustic and should be used with caution. Be sure to follow the instructions on the container.*

8   Clean the rocker arms, pivot balls or fulcrums, nuts or bolts and pushrods with solvent and dry them thoroughly (don't mix them up during the cleaning process). Compressed air will speed the drying process and can be used to clean out the oil passages.

9   Clean all the valve springs, spring seats, keepers and retainers (or rotators) with solvent and dry them thoroughly. Do the components from one valve at a time to avoid mixing up the parts.

10   Scrape off any heavy deposits that may have formed on the valves, then use a motorized wire brush to remove deposits from the valve heads and stems. Again, make sure the valves don't get mixed up.

Inspection

Note: *Be sure to perform all of the following inspection procedures before concluding that machine shop work is required. Make a list of the items that need attention.*

Cylinder head

11   Inspect the head very carefully for cracks, evidence of coolant leakage and other damage. If cracks are found, check with an automotive machine shop concerning repair. If repair isn't possible, a new cylinder head should be obtained.

12   Using a straightedge and feeler gauge, check the head gasket mating surface for warpage **(see illustration)**. If the warpage exceeds the specified limit, it can be resurfaced at an automotive machine shop.

13   Examine the valve seats in each of the combustion chambers. If they're pitted, cracked or burned, the head will require valve service that's beyond the scope of the home mechanic.

14   Check the valve stem-to-guide clearance by measuring the lateral movement of the valve stem with a dial indicator attached securely to the head **(see illustration)**. The valve must be in the guide and approximately 1/16-inch off the seat. The total valve stem movement indicated by the gauge needle

9.15a Check for valve wear at the points shown here

9.15b Valve stem tip wear patterns

1   *Proper tip pattern (rotator functioning properly)*
2   *No rotation pattern (replace rotator and check rotation)*
3   *Partial rotation pattern (replace rotation and check rotation)*

9.16 The margin width on each valve must be as specified (if no margin exists, the valve cannot be reused)

must be divided by two to obtain the actual clearance. After this is done, if there's still some doubt regarding the condition of the valve guides they should be checked by an automotive machine shop (the cost should be minimal).

Valves

15   Carefully inspect each valve for uneven wear, deformation, cracks, pits and burned areas **(see illustrations)**. Check the valve stem for scuffing and galling and the neck for cracks. Rotate the valve and check for any obvious indication that it's bent. Look for pits and excessive wear on the end of the stem. The presence of any of these conditions indicates the need for valve service by an automotive machine shop.
16   Measure the margin width on each valve **(see illustration)**. Any valve with a margin narrower than specified will have to be replaced with a new one.

Valve components

17   Check each valve spring for wear (on the ends) and pits. Measure the free length and compare it to the Specifications **(see illustration)**. Any springs that are shorter than specified have sagged and should not be reused. The tension of all springs should be checked with a special fixture before deciding that they're suitable for use in a rebuilt engine (take the springs to an automotive machine shop for this check).
18   Stand each spring on a flat surface and check it for squareness **(see illustration)**. If any of the springs are distorted or sagged, replace all of them with new parts.
19   Check the spring retainers and keepers for obvious wear and cracks. Any questionable parts should be replaced with new ones, as extensive damage will occur if they fail during engine operation.

Rocker arm components

20   Check the rocker arm faces (the areas that contact the pushrod ends and valve stems) for pits, wear, galling, score marks and rough spots. Check the rocker arm pivot contact areas and pivot balls or fulcrums as well. Look for cracks in each rocker arm and nut or bolt.
21   Inspect the pushrod ends for scuffing and excessive wear. Roll each pushrod on a

flat surface, like a piece of plate glass, to determine if it's bent.
22   Check the rocker arm bolt holes or studs in the cylinder heads for damaged threads and secure installation.
23   Any damaged or excessively worn parts must be replaced with new ones.
24   If the inspection process indicates that the valve components are in generally poor condition and worn beyond the limits specified, which is usually the case in an engine that's being overhauled, reassemble the valves in the cylinder head and refer to Section 10 for valve servicing recommendations.

10   Valves - servicing

1   Because of the complex nature of the job and the special tools and equipment needed, servicing of the valves, the valve seats and the valve guides, commonly known as a valve job, should be done by a professional.
2   The home mechanic can remove and disassemble the head, do the initial cleaning and inspection, then reassemble and deliver it to a dealer service department or an automotive machine shop for the actual service work. Doing the inspection will enable you to see what condition the head and valvetrain components are in and will ensure that you know what work and new parts are required when dealing with an automotive machine shop.

3   The dealer service department, or automotive machine shop, will remove the valves and springs, recondition or replace the valves and valve seats, recondition the valve guides, check and replace the valve springs, spring retainers or rotators and keepers (as necessary), replace the valve seals with new ones, reassemble the valve components and make sure the installed spring height is correct. The cylinder head gasket surface will also be resurfaced if it's warped.
4   After the valve job has been performed by a professional, the head will be in like-new condition. When the head is returned, be sure to clean it again before installation on the engine to remove any metal particles and abrasive grit that may still be present from the valve service or head resurfacing operations. Use compressed air, if available, to blow out all the oil holes and passages.

11   Cylinder head - reassembly

Refer to illustrations 11.3, 11.5a, 11.5b, 11.6 and 11.8

1   Regardless of whether or not a head was sent to an automotive repair shop for valve servicing, make sure it's clean before

9.17 Measure the free length of each valve spring with a dial or vernier caliper

9.18 Check each valve spring for squareness

11.3 Make sure the new valve stem seals are seated against the tops of the valve guides

1   Valve seated in tool
2   End of valve stem - be sure to deburr this area before installing the seal
3   Seal
4   Valve seal installation tool (if you don't have this tool, a deep socket also will work)

11.5a Valve and related components for four and six-cylinder engines - exploded view

1   Keepers
2   Retainers
3   Springs
4   Umbrella-type oil seals
5   Valves

11.5b Later model four-cylinder engines have progressively wound valve springs - install them with the closely wound coils toward the cylinder head

11.6 Apply a small dab of grease to each keeper as shown here before installation - it'll hold them in place on the valve stem as the spring is released

beginning reassembly.

2   If a head was sent out for valve servicing, the valves and related components will already be in place. Begin the reassembly procedure with Step 8.

3   Install new seals on each of the intake valve guides. Using a hammer and a deep socket or seal installation tool, gently tap each seal into place until it's completely seated on the guide **(see illustration)**. Don't twist or cock the seals during installation or they won't seal properly on the valve stems. The umbrella-type seals (if used) are installed

over the valves after the valves are in place.

4   Beginning at one end of the head, lubricate and install the first valve. Apply moly-base grease or clean engine oil to the valve stem.

5   Drop the spring seat or shim(s) over the valve guide and set the valve springs, shield and retainer in place **(see illustrations)**.

6   Compress the springs with a valve spring compressor. Position the keepers in the upper groove, then slowly release the compressor and make sure the keepers seat properly. Add a small dab of grease to each

keeper to hold it in place if necessary **(see illustration)**.

7   Repeat the procedure for the remaining valves. Be sure to return the components to their original locations - don't mix them up!

8   Check the installed valve spring height with a ruler graduated in 1/32-inch increments or a dial caliper. If the head was sent out for service work, the installed height should be correct (but don't automatically assume that it is). The measurement is taken from the top of each spring seat or shim(s) to the top of the oil shield (or the bottom of the retainer, the two points are the same) **(see illustration)**. If the height is greater than specified, shims can be added under the springs to correct it. **Caution:** *Don't, under any circumstances, shim the springs to the point where the installed height is less than specified.*

12 Pistons/connecting rods - removal

Refer to illustrations 12.1, 12.3 and 12.6
Note 1: *Prior to removing the piston/connecting rod assemblies, remove the cylinder head, the oil pan and the oil pump by referring to the appropriate Sections in Chapter 2.*
Note 2: *On 2.4L four-cylinder engines, the balance shaft carrier assembly must be removed before the piston/connecting rod assembly can be removed (see Section 25).*

1   Use your fingernail to feel if a ridge has formed at the upper limit of ring travel (about 1/4-inch down from the top of each cylinder).

11.8 Be sure to check the valve spring installed height (the distance from the top of the seat/shims to the top of the shield or the bottom of the retainer)

12.1 A ridge reamer is required to remove the ridge from the top of each cylinder - do this before removing the pistons!

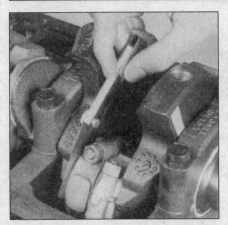

12.3 Check the connecting rod side clearance with a feeler gauge as shown

12.6 To prevent damage to the crankshaft journals and cylinder walls, slip sections of rubber or plastic hose over the rod bolts before removing the pistons

If carbon deposits or cylinder wear have produced ridges, they must be completely removed with a special tool **(see illustration)**. Follow the manufacturer's instructions provided with the tool. Failure to remove the ridges before attempting to remove the piston/connecting rod assemblies may result in piston breakage.

2 After the cylinder ridges have been removed, turn the engine upside-down so the crankshaft is facing up.

3 Before the connecting rods are removed, check the endplay with feeler gauges. Slide them between the first connecting rod and the crankshaft throw until the play is removed **(see illustration)**. The endplay is equal to the thickness of the feeler gauge(s). If the end-play exceeds the service limit, new connecting rods will be required. If new rods (or a new crankshaft) are installed, the endplay may fall under the specified minimum (if it does, the rods will have to be machined to restore it - consult an automotive machine shop for advice if necessary). Repeat the procedure for the remaining connecting rods.

4 Check the connecting rods and caps for

identification marks. If they aren't plainly marked, use a small center-punch to make the appropriate number of indentations on each rod and cap (1, 2, 3, etc., depending on the engine type and cylinder they're associated with).

5 Loosen each of the connecting rod cap nuts 1/2-turn at a time until they can be removed by hand. Remove the number one connecting rod cap and bearing insert. Don't drop the bearing insert out of the cap.

6 Slip a short length of plastic or rubber hose over each connecting rod cap bolt to protect the crankshaft journal and cylinder wall as the piston is removed **(see illustration)**.

7 Remove the bearing insert and push the connecting rod/piston assembly out through the top of the engine. Use a wooden hammer handle to push on the upper bearing surface in the connecting rod. If resistance is felt, double-check to make sure that all of the ridge was removed from the cylinder.

8 Repeat the procedure for the remaining cylinders.

9 After removal, reassemble the connecting rod caps and bearing inserts in their respective connecting rods and install the cap nuts finger tight. Leaving the old bearing inserts in place until reassembly will help prevent the connecting rod bearing surfaces from being accidentally nicked or gouged.

10 Don't separate the pistons from the connecting rods (see Section 17 for additional information).

13 Crankshaft

Refer to illustrations 13.1, 13.3, 13.4a and 13.4b

Note: *The crankshaft can be removed only after the engine has been removed from the vehicle. It's assumed that the flywheel or driveplate, crankshaft pulley, timing chain(s), oil pan, oil pump body, oil filter and piston/connecting rod assemblies have already been removed. On 2.4L four-cylinder engines, the balance shaft carrier assembly must be removed (see Section 25). The rear main oil seal retainer must be unbolted and separated from the block before proceeding with crankshaft removal.*

1 before the crankshaft is removed, measure the endplay. Mount a dial indicator with the indicator in line with the crankshaft and touching the end of the crankshaft as shown **(see illustration)**.

2 Pry the crankshaft all the way to the rear and zero the dial indicator. Next, pry the crankshaft to the front as far as possible and check the reading on the dial indicator. The distance traveled is the endplay. A typical crankshaft endplay will fall between 0.003 and 0.010-inch (0.076 to 0.254 mm). If it's greater than that, check the crankshaft thrust surfaces for wear after its removed. If no wear is evident, new main bearings should correct the endplay.

3 If a dial indicator isn't available, feeler gauges can be used. Gently pry the crankshaft all the way to the front of the

13.1 Checking crankshaft endplay with a dial indicator

13.3 Checking crankshaft endplay with a feeler gauge

13.4a Use a center punch or number stamping dies to mark the main bearing caps to ensure installation in their original locations on the block (make the punch marks near one of the bolt heads)

13.4b The arrow on the main cap indicates the direction to the front of the engine while the stamped numbers indicate the specific journal (2.5L engine shown)

engine. Slip feeler gauges between the crankshaft and the front face of the thrust bearing or washer to determine the clearance **(see illustration)**.

4   On 2.5L four-cylinder and six-cylinder engines, check the main bearing caps to see if they're marked to indicate their locations. They should be numbered consecutively from the front of the engine to the rear. If they aren't, mark them with number stamping dies or a center-punch **(see illustrations)**. Main bearing caps generally have a cast-in arrow, which points to the front of the engine.

5   On 2.4L four-cylinder engines, loosen the main bearing cap/bedplate fasteners 1/4-turn at a time each, until they can be removed by hand. Carefully and evenly pry the main bearing caps/bedplate off of the engine. **Caution:** *Use the cast-in pry points on the bedplate. Do not pry on the block or bedplate mating surfaces, because damage to those surfaces can occur.* Try not to drop the bearing inserts if they come out with the caps.

6   On all other engines, tap the caps with a soft-face hammer, then separate them from the engine block. If necessary, use the bolts

as levers to remove the caps. Try not to drop the bearing inserts if they come out with the caps.

7   On all models, carefully lift the crankshaft out of the engine. It may be a good idea to have an assistant available, since the crankshaft is quite heavy and awkward to handle. With the bearing inserts in place inside the engine block and main bearing caps/bedplate, reinstall the main bearing caps/bedplate onto the engine block and tighten the fasteners finger tight.

14 Engine block - cleaning

Refer to illustrations 14.1, 14.8 and 14.10

1   Remove the core plugs from the engine block. To do this, knock one side of the plug into the block with a hammer and a punch, then grasp them with large pliers and pull them out **(see illustrations)**.

2   Using a gasket scraper, remove all traces of gasket material from the engine block. Be very careful not to nick or gouge the gasket sealing surfaces.

3   Remove the main bearing caps and separate the bearing inserts from the caps and the engine block. Tag the bearings, indicating which cylinder they were removed from and whether they were in the cap or the block,

then set them aside.

4   Remove all of the threaded oil gallery plugs from the block. The plugs are usually very tight - they may have to be drilled out and the holes retapped. Use new plugs when the engine is reassembled.

5   If the engine is extremely dirty it should be taken to an automotive machine shop to be steam cleaned or hot tanked.

6   After the block is returned, clean all oil holes and oil galleries one more time. Brushes specifically designed for this purpose are available at most auto parts stores. Flush the passages with warm water until the water runs clear, dry the block thoroughly and wipe all machined surfaces with a light, rust preventive oil. If you have access to compressed air, use it to speed the drying process and to blow out all the oil holes and galleries. **Warning:** *Wear eye protection when using compressed air!*

7   If the block isn't extremely dirty or sludged up, you can do an adequate cleaning job with hot soapy water and a stiff brush. Take plenty of time and do a thorough job. Regardless of the cleaning method used, be sure to clean all oil holes and galleries very thoroughly, dry the block completely and coat all machined surfaces with light oil.

14.1a A hammer and a large punch can be used to knock the core plugs sideways in their bores

14.1b Pull the core plugs form the block with pliers

14.8 All bolt holes in the block - particularly the main bearing cap and head bolt holes - should be cleaned and restored with a tap (be sure to remove debris from the holes after this is done)

14.10 A large socket on an extension can be used to drive the new core plugs into the bores

← CENTERLINE OF ENGINE →

15.4a Measure the diameter of each cylinder at a right angle to the engine centerline (A), and parallel to the engine centerline (B) - out-of-round is the difference between A and B; taper is the difference between A and B at the top of the cylinder and A and B at the bottom of the cylinder

8   The threaded holes in the block must be clean to ensure accurate torque readings during reassembly. Run the proper size tap into each of the holes to remove rust, corrosion, thread sealant or sludge and restore damaged threads **(see illustration)**. If possible, use compressed air to clear the holes of debris produced by this operation. Now is a good time to clean the threads on the head bolts and the main bearing cap bolts as well.

9   Reinstall the main bearing caps and tighten the bolts finger tight.

10   After coating the sealing surfaces of the new core plugs with Permatex no. 2 sealant, install them in the engine block **(see illustration)**. Make sure they're driven in straight and seated properly or leakage could result. Special tools are available for this purpose, but a large socket, with an outside diameter that will just slip into the core plug, a 1/2-inch drive extension and a hammer will work just as well.

11   Apply non-hardening sealant (such as Permatex no. 2 or Teflon pipe sealant) to the new oil gallery plugs and thread them into the holes in the block. Make sure they're tightened securely.

12   If the engine isn't going to be reassembled right away, cover it with a large plastic trash bag to keep it clean.

15   Engine block - inspection

Refer to illustrations 15.4a, 15.4b, 15.4c, 15.14a and 15.14b

1   Before the block is inspected, it should be cleaned as described in Section 14.

2   Visually check the block for cracks, rust and corrosion. Look for stripped threads in the threaded holes. It's also a good idea to have the block checked for hidden cracks by an automotive machine shop that has the special equipment to do this type of work. If defects are found, have the block repaired, if possible, or replaced.

3   Check the cylinder bores for scuffing and scoring.

4   Measure the diameter of each cylinder at the top (just under the ridge area), center and bottom of the cylinder bore, parallel to the crankshaft axis **(see illustrations)**.

5   Next, measure each cylinder's diameter at the same three locations across the crankshaft axis. Compare the results to the specifications.

6   If the required precision measuring tools aren't available, the piston-to-cylinder clearances can be obtained, though not quite as accurately, using feeler gauge stock. Feeler gauge stock comes in 12-inch lengths and various thicknesses and is generally available at auto parts stores.

7   To check the clearance, select a feeler gauge and slip it into the cylinder along with the matching piston. The piston must be positioned exactly as it normally would be. The feeler gauge must be between the piston

15.4b The ability to "feel" when the telescoping gauge is at the correct point will be developed over time, so work slowly and repeat the check until you're satisfied the bore measurement is accurate

15.4c The gauge is then measured with a micrometer to determine the bore size

LETTER CODE

PM

OIL FILTER BOSS

DISTRIBUTOR

15.14a The engine component letter code is located on the oil filter boss between the fuel pump and the distributor

CODE	COMPONENT	UNDERSIZE
P	One or more connecting rod bearing journals	0.254 mm (0.010 in)
M	All crankshaft main bearing journals	0.254 mm (0.010 in)
PM	All crankshaft main bearing journals and one or more connecting rod journals	0.254 mm (0.010 in)

CODE	COMPONENT	OVERSIZE
B	All cylinder bores	0.254 mm (0.010 in)
C	All camshaft bearing bores	0.254 mm (0.010 in)

15.14b Engine component codes

and cylinder on one of the thrust faces (90 degrees to the piston pin bore).

8   The piston should slip through the cylinder (with the feeler gauge in place) with moderate pressure.

9   If it falls through or slides through easily, the clearance is excessive and a new piston will be required. If the piston binds at the lower end of the cylinder and is loose toward the top, the cylinder is tapered. If tight spots are encountered as the piston/feeler gauge is rotated in the cylinder, the cylinder is out-of-round.

10   Repeat the procedure for the remaining pistons and cylinders.

11   If the cylinder walls are badly scuffed or scored, or if they're out-of-round or tapered beyond the limits given in the specifications, have the engine block rebored and honed at an automotive machine shop. If a rebore is done, oversize pistons and rings will be required.

12   If the cylinders are in reasonably good condition and not worn to the outside of the limits, and if the piston-to-cylinder clearances can be maintained properly, then they don't have to be rebored. Honing is all that's necessary (see Section 16).

13   Many different engines are produced with oversize or undersize components, such as oversize cylinder bores, undersize main bearing and connecting rod journals, or oversize camshaft bearing bores.

14   These engines are identified by a letter code stamped on the engine block (see illustrations).

16 Cylinder honing

Refer to illustrations 16.3a and 16.3b

1   Prior to engine reassembly, the cylinder bores must be honed so the new piston rings will seat correctly and provide the best possible combustion chamber seal. **Note:** *If you don't have the tools or don't want to tackle the honing operation, most automotive machine shops will do it for a reasonable fee.*

2   Before honing the cylinders, install the main bearing caps and tighten the bolts to the torque listed in this Chapter's Specifications.

3   Two types of cylinder hones are commonly available - the flex hone or "bottle brush" type and the more traditional surfacing hone with spring-loaded stones. Both will do the job, but for the less experienced mechanic the "bottle brush" hone will probably be easier to use. You'll also need some kerosene or honing oil, rags and an electric drill motor. Proceed as follows:

a)   *Mount the hone in the drill motor, compress the stones (if applicable) and slip it into the first cylinder* **(see illustration).** *Be sure to wear safety goggles or a face shield!*

b)   *Lubricate the cylinder with plenty of honing oil or kerosene, turn on the drill and move the hone up-and-down in the cylinder at a pace that will produce a fine crosshatch pattern on the cylinder walls. Ideally, the crosshatch lines should intersect at approximately a 60-degree*

angle **(see illustration).** *Be sure to use plenty of lubricant and don't take off any more material than is absolutely necessary to produce the desired finish.* **Note:** *Piston ring manufacturers may specify a smaller crosshatch angle than the traditional 60-degrees - read and follow any instructions included with the new rings.*

c)   *Don't withdraw the hone from the cylinder while it's running. Instead, shut off the drill and continue moving the hone up-and-down in the cylinder until it comes to a complete stop, then compress the stones and withdraw the hone. If you're using a "bottle brush" type hone, stop the drill motor, then turn the*

16.3a A "bottle brush" hone will produce better results if you've never honed cylinders before

16.3b The cylinder hone should leave a smooth, crosshatch pattern with the lines intersecting at approximately a 60-degree angle

17.4a The piston ring grooves can be cleaned with a special tool, as shown here

17.4b . . . or a section of a broken ring

chuck in the normal direction of rotation while withdrawing the hone from the cylinder.

d) *Wipe the oil out of the cylinder and repeat the procedure for the remaining cylinders.*

4   After the honing job is complete, chamfer the top edges of the cylinder bores with a small file so the rings won't catch when the pistons are installed. Be very careful not to nick the cylinder walls with the end of the file.

5   The entire engine block must be washed again very thoroughly with warm, soapy water to remove all traces of the abrasive grit produced during the honing operation. **Note:** *The bores can be considered clean when a lint-free white cloth - dampened with clean engine oil - used to wipe them out doesn't pick up any more honing residue, which will show up as gray areas on the cloth. Be sure to run a brush through all oil holes and galleries and flush them with running water.*

6   After rinsing, dry the block and apply a coat of light rust preventive oil to all machined surfaces. Wrap the block in a plastic trash bag to keep it clean and set it aside until reassembly.

17 Pistons/connecting rods - inspection

Refer to illustrations 17.4a, 17.4b, 17.10 and 17.11

1   Before the inspection process can be carried out, the piston/connecting rod assemblies must be cleaned and the original piston rings removed from the pistons. **Note:** *Always use new piston rings when the engine is reassembled.*

2   Using a piston ring installation tool, carefully remove the rings from the pistons. Be careful not to nick or gouge the pistons in the process.

3   Scrape all traces of carbon from the top of the piston. A handheld wire brush or a piece of fine emery cloth can be used once

the majority of the deposits have been scraped away. Do not, under any circumstances, use a wire brush mounted in a drill motor to remove deposits from the pistons. The piston material is soft and may be eroded away by the wire brush.

4   Use a piston ring groove cleaning tool to remove carbon deposits from the ring grooves. If a tool isn't available, a piece broken off the old ring will do the job. Be very careful to remove only the carbon deposits - don't remove any metal and do not nick or scratch the sides of the ring grooves **(see illustrations)**.

5   Once the deposits have been removed, clean the piston/rod assemblies with solvent and dry them with compressed air (if available). Make sure the oil return holes in the back sides of the ring grooves are clear.

6   If the pistons and cylinder walls aren't damaged or worn excessively, and if the engine block is not rebored, new pistons won't be necessary. Normal piston wear appears as even vertical wear on the piston thrust surfaces and slight looseness of the top ring in its groove. New piston rings, however, should always be used when an engine is rebuilt.

7   Carefully inspect each piston for cracks

around the skirt, at the pin bosses and at the ring lands.

8   Look for scoring and scuffing on the thrust faces of the skirt, holes in the piston crown and burned areas at the edge of the crown. If the skirt is scored or scuffed, the engine may have been suffering from overheating and/or abnormal combustion, which caused excessively high operating temperatures. The cooling and lubrication systems should be checked thoroughly. A hole in the piston crown is an indication that abnormal combustion (preignition) was occurring. Burned areas at the edge of the piston crown are usually evidence of spark knock (detonation). If any of the above problems exist, the causes must be corrected or the damage will occur again. The causes may include intake air leaks, incorrect fuel/air mixture, incorrect ignition timing and EGR system malfunctions.

9   Corrosion of the piston, in the form of small pits, indicates that coolant is leaking into the combustion chamber and/or the crankcase. Again, the cause must be corrected or the problem may persist in the rebuilt engine.

10   Measure the piston ring side clearance by laying a new piston ring in each ring groove and slipping a feeler gauge in beside

17.10 Check the ring side clearance with a feeler gauge at several points around the groove

17.11 Measure the piston diameter at a 90-degree angle to the piston pin and in line with it

18.6 Measure the diameter of each crankshaft journal at several points to detect taper and out-of-round conditions

it **(see illustration)**. Check the clearance at three or four locations around each groove. Be sure to use the correct ring for each groove - they are different. If the side clearance is greater than specified, new pistons will have to be used.

11   Check the piston-to-bore clearance by measuring the bore (see Section 15) and the piston diameter. Make sure the pistons and bores are correctly matched. Measure the piston across the skirt, at a 90 degree angle to and in line with the piston pin **(see illustration)**. Subtract the piston diameter from the bore diameter to obtain the clearance. If it's greater than specified, the block will have to be rebored and new pistons and rings installed.

12   Check the piston-to-rod clearance by twisting the piston and rod in opposite directions. Any noticeable play indicates exces-sive wear, which must be corrected. The pis-ton/connecting rod assemblies should be taken to an automotive machine shop to have the pistons and rods resized and new pins installed.

13   If the pistons must be removed from the connecting rods for any reason, they should be taken to an automotive machine shop. While they are there have the connecting rods checked for bend and twist, since auto-motive machine shops have special equip-ment for this purpose. **Note:** *Unless new pis-tons and/or connecting rods must be installed, do not disassemble the pistons and connecting rods.*

14   Check the connecting rods for cracks and other damage. Temporarily remove the rod caps, lift out the old bearing inserts, wipe the rod and cap bearing surfaces clean and inspect them for nicks, gouges and scratches. After checking the rods, replace the old bearings, slip the caps into place and tighten the nuts finger tight. **Note:** *If the engine is being rebuilt because of a connect-ing rod knock, be sure to install new rods.*

18   Crankshaft - inspection

Refer to illustration 18.6

1   Remove all burrs from the crankshaft oil holes with a stone, file or scraper.

2   Clean the crankshaft with solvent and dry it with compressed air (if available). Be sure to clean the oil holes with a stiff brush and flush them with solvent.

3   Check the main and connecting rod bearing journals for uneven wear, scoring, pits and cracks.

4   Rub a penny across each journal several times. If a journal picks up copper from the penny, it's too rough and must be reground.

5   Check the rest of the crankshaft for cracks and other damage. It should be mag-nafluxed to reveal hidden cracks - an auto-motive machine shop will handle the pro-cedure.

CRATERS OR POCKETS

FATIGUE FAILURE

BRIGHT (POLISHED) SECTIONS

IMPROPER SEATING

SCRATCHES

DIRT IMBEDDED INTO BEARING MATERIAL

SCRATCHED BY DIRT

OVERLAY WIPED OUT

LACK OF OIL

OVERLAY GONE FROM ENTIRE SURFACE

EXCESSIVE WEAR

RADIUS RIDE

TAPERED JOURNAL

19.1 Typical bearing failures

Crankshaft Main Bearing Journal 2-3-4-5 Color Code and Diameter in Inches (Journal Size)	Bearing Insert Color Code	
	Upper Insert Size	Lower Insert Size
Yellow — 2.0955 to 2.0948 (53.2257 - 53.2079 mm) (Standard) Orange —2.0948 to 2.0941 (53.2079 - 53.1901 mm) (0.0007 Undersize) Black — 2.0941 to 2.0943 (53.1901 to 53.1723 mm) (0.0014 Undersize) Red — 2.0855 to 2.0848 (53.9717 to 53.9539 mm) (0.010 Undersize)	Yellow — Standard Yellow — Standard Black — 0.001-Inch (0.025 mm) Undersize Red — 0.010-Inch (0.254 mm) Undersize	Yellow — Standard Black — 0.001-Inch (0.025 mm) Undersize Black — 0.001-Inch (0.025 mm) Undersize Red — 0.010-Inch (0.245 mm) Undersize

19.8a Connecting rod bearing section chart - four-cylinder engines (1993 and earlier)

Crankshaft Journal		Corresponding Connecting Rod Bearing Insert	
Color Code	Diameter	Upper Insert Size	Lower Insert Size
Yellow	53.2257-53.2079 mm (2.0955-2.0948 in.)	Yellow - Standard	Yellow - Standard
Orange	53.2079-53.1901 mm (2.0948-2.0941 in.) 0.0178 mm (0.0007 in.) Undersize	Yellow - Standard	Blue - Undersize 0.025 mm (0.001 in.)
Blue	53.1901-53.1724 mm (2.0941-2.0934 in.) 0.0356 mm (0.0014 in.) Undersize	Blue - Undersize 0.025 mm (0.001 in.)	Blue - Undersize 0.025 mm (0.001 in.)
Red	52.9717-52.9539 mm (2.0855-2.0848 in.) 0.254 mm (0.010 in.) Undersize	Red - Undersize 0.254 mm (0.010 in.)	Red - Undersize 0.254 mm (0.010 in.)

19.8b Connecting rod bearing selection chart - four-cylinder engines (1994 models)

19 Main and connecting rod bearings - inspection

Inspection

Refer to illustration 19.1

1   Even though the main and connecting rod bearings should be replaced with new ones during the engine overhaul, the old bearings should be retained for close examination, as they may reveal valuable information about the condition of the engine **(see illustration)**.

2   Bearing failure occurs because of lack of lubrication, the presence of dirt or other foreign particles, overloading the engine and corrosion. Regardless of the cause of bearing failure, it must be corrected before the engine is reassembled to prevent it from happening again.

3   When examining the bearings, remove them from the engine block, the main bearing caps, the connecting rods and the rod caps and lay them out on a clean surface in the same general position as their location in the engine. This will enable you to match any bearing problems with the corresponding crankshaft journal.

4   Dirt and other foreign particles get into the engine in a variety of ways. It may be left in the engine during assembly, or it may pass through filters or the PCV system. It may get

6   Using a micrometer, measure the diameter of the main and connecting rod journals and compare the results to the specifications **(see illustration)**. By measuring the diameter at a number of points around each journal's circumference, you'll be able to determine whether or not the journal is out-of-round. Take the measurement at each end of the journal, near the crank throws, to determine if the journal is tapered.

7   If the crankshaft journals are damaged, tapered, out-of-round or worn beyond the limits given in the specifications, have the crankshaft reground by an automotive machine shop. Be sure to use the correct size bearing inserts if the crankshaft is reconditioned.

8   Check the oil seal journals at each end of the crankshaft for wear and damage. If the seal has worn a groove in the journal, or if it's nicked or scratched, the new seal may leak when the engine is reassembled. In some cases, an automotive machine shop may be able to repair the journal by pressing on a thin sleeve. If repair isn't feasible, a new or different crankshaft should be installed.

9   Refer to Section 19 and examine the main and rod bearing inserts.

Connecting Rod Bearing Journal Color Code and Diameter (Journal Size)	Bearing Insert Color Code	
	Upper Insert Size	Lower Insert Size
Yellow – 53.2257 - 53.2079 mm (2.0955 - 2.0948 in.) (Standard)	Yellow – Standard	Yellow – Standard
Orange – 53.2079 - 53.1901 mm (2.0948 - 2.0941 in.) (0.0007 Undersize)	Yellow – Standard	Black – 0.025 mm (0.001 in.) Undersize
Black – 53.1901 - 53.1723 mm (2.0941 - 2.0933 in.) (0.0014 Undersize)	Black – 0.025 mm (0.001 in.) Undersize	Black – 0.025 mm (0.001 in.) Undersize
Red – 53.9717 - 53.9539 mm (2.0855 - 2.0848 in.) (0.010 Undersize)	Red – 0.254 mm (0.010 in.) Undersize	Red – 0.245 mm (0.010 in.) Undersize

19.8c Connecting rod bearing selection chart - inline six-cylinder engines (1993 and earlier)

Crankshaft Journal		Corresponding Connecting Rod Bearing Insert	
Color Code	Diameter	Upper Insert Size	Lower Insert Size
Yellow	53.2257-53.2079 mm (2.0955-2.0948 in.)	Yellow - Standard	Yellow - Standard
Orange	53.2079-53.1901 mm (2.0948-2.0941 in.) 0.0178 mm (0.0007 in.) Undersize	Yellow - Standard	Blue - Undersize 0.025 mm (0.001 in.)
Blue	53.1901-53.1724 mm (2.0941-2.0934 in.) 0.0356 mm (0.0014 in.) Undersize	Blue - Undersize 0.025 mm (0.001 in.)	Blue - Undersize 0.025 mm (0.001 in.)
Red	52.9717-52.9539 mm (2.0855-2.0848 in.) 0.254 mm (0.010 in.) Undersize	Red - Undersize 0.254 mm (0.010 in.)	Red - Undersize 0.254 mm (0.010 in.)

19.8d Connecting rod bearing selection chart - inline six-cylinder engines (1994 models)

into the oil, and from there into the bearings. Metal chips from machining operations and normal engine wear are often present. Abrasives are sometimes left in engine components after reconditioning, especially when parts are not thoroughly cleaned using the proper cleaning methods. Whatever the source, these foreign objects often end up embedded in the soft bearing material and are easily recognized. Large particles will not embed in the bearing and will score or gouge the bearing and journal. The best prevention for this cause of bearing failure is to clean all parts thoroughly and keep everything spotlessly clean during engine assembly. Frequent and regular engine oil and filter changes are also recommended.

5   Lack of lubrication (or lubrication breakdown) has a number of interrelated causes.

Crankshaft No. 1 Main Bearing Journal Color Codes and Diameter in Inches (mm)	Cylinder Block No. 1 Main Bearing Bore Color Code and Size in Inches (mm)		Bearing Insert Color Code	
			Upper Insert Size	Lower Insert Size
Yellow — 2.5001 to 2.4996 (Standard) (63.5025 to 63.4898 mm)	Yellow —	2.6910 to 2.6915 (68.3514 to 68.3641 mm)	Yellow — Standard	Yellow — Standard
	Black —	2.6915 to 2.6920 (68.3641 to 68.3768 mm)	Yellow — Standard	Black — 0.001-inch Undersize (0.025 mm)
Orange — 2.4996 to 2.4991 (0.0005 Undersize) (63.4898 to 63.4771 mm)	Yellow —	2.6910 to 2.6915 (68.3514 to 68.3641 mm)	Yellow — Standard	Black — 0.001-inch Undersize — (0.001 mm)
	Black —	2.6915 to 2.6920 (68.3461 to 68.3768 mm)	Black — 0.001-inch Undersize (0.025 mm)	Black — 0.001-inch Undersize (0.025 mm)
Black — 2.4991 to 2.4986 (0.001 Undersize) (63.4771 to 63.4644 mm)	Yellow —	2.6910 to 2.6915 (68.3514 to 68.3641 mm)	Black — 0.001-inch Undersize — (0.025 mm)	Black — 0.001-inch Undersize — (0.025 mm)
	Black —	2.6915 to 2.6920 (68.3461 to 68.3768 mm)	Black — 0.001-inch Undersize (0.025 mm)	Green — 0.002-inch Undersize (0.051 mm)
Green — 2.4986 to 2.4981 (0.0015 Undersize) (63.4644 to 63.4517 mm)	Yellow —	2.6910 to 2.6915 (68.3514 to 68.3641 mm)	Black — 0.001-inch Undersize — (0.025 mm)	Green — 0.002-inch Undersize — (0.051 mm)
Red — 2.4901 to 2.4896 (0.010 Undersize) (63.2485 to 63.2358 mm)	Yellow —	2.6910 to 2.6915 (68.3514 to 68.3641 mm)	Red — 0.010-inch Undersize (0.254 mm)	Red — 0.010-inch Undersize — (0.254 mm)

NOTE: With Green and Red Coded Crankshaft Journals, Use Yellow Coded Cylinder Block Bores Only.

Crankshaft Main Bearing Journal 2-3-4-5 Color Code and Diameter in Inches (Journal Size)	Bearing Insert Color Code	
	Upper Insert Size	Lower Insert Size
Yellow — 2.5001 to 2.4996 (Standard) (63.5025 to 63.4898 mm)	Yellow — Standard	Yellow — Standard
Orange — 2.4996 to 2.4991 (0.0005 Undersize) (63.4898 to 63.4771 mm)	Yellow — Standard	Black — 0.001-inch Undersize (0.025mm)
Black — 2.4991 to 2.4986 (0.001 Undersize) (63.4771 to 63.4644 mm)	Black — 0.001-inch Undersize (0.025 mm)	Black — 0.001-inch Undersize (0.025 mm)
Green — 2.4986 to 2.4981 (0.0015 Undersize) (63.4644 to 63.4517 mm)	Black — 0.001-inch Undersize (0.025 mm)	Green — 0.002-inch Undersize (0.051 mm)
Red — 2.4901 to 2.4896 (0.010 Undersize) (63.2485 to 63.2358 mm)	Red — 0.010-inch Undersize (0.254 mm)	Red — 0.010-inch Undersize (0.254 mm)

19.8e Main bearing selection chart (four-cylinder engines 1993 and earlier models) - note that on all 1992 and 1993 2.5L engines, the specifications listed on the upper chart include the number 1 main bearing journal

Crankshaft No. 1 Main Bearing Journal Color Code and Diameter	Cylinder Block No. 1 Main Bearing Bore Color Code and Size	Bearing Insert Color Code	
		Upper Insert Size	Lower Insert Size
Yellow – 63.5025-63.4898 mm (2.5001-2.4996 in.) (Standard)	Yellow – 68.3514-68.3641 mm (2.6910-2.6915 in.)	Yellow – Standard	Yellow – Standard
	Black – 68.3641-68.3768 mm (2.6915-2.6920 in.)	Yellow – Standard	Black – 0.025 mm Undersize (0.001 in.)
Orange – 63.4898-63.4771 mm (2.4996-2.4991 in.) (0.0005 Undersize)	Yellow – 68.3514-68.3641 mm (2.6910-2.6915 in.)	Yellow – Standard	Black – 0.025 mm Undersize (0.001 in.)
	Black – 68.3641-68.3768 mm (2.6915-2.6920 in.)	Black – 0.025 mm Undersize (0.001 in.)	Black – 0.025 mm Undersize (0.001 in.)
Black – 63.4771-63.4644 mm (2.4991-2.4986 in.) (0.001 Undersize)	Yellow – 68.3514-68.3641 mm (2.6910-2.6915 in.)	Black – 0.025 mm Undersize (0.001 in.)	Black – 0.025 mm Undersize (0.001 in.)
	Black – 68.3641-68.3768 mm (2.6915-2.6920 in.)	Black – 0.025 mm Undersize (0.001 in.)	Green – 0.051 mm Undersize (0.002 in.)
Green – 63.4644-63.4517 mm (2.4986-2.4981 in.) (0.0015 Undersize)	Yellow – 68.3514-68.3641 mm (2.6910-2.6915 in.)	Black – 0.025 mm Undersize (0.001 in.)	Green – 0.051 mm Undersize (0.002 in.)
Red – 63.2485-63.2358 mm (2.4901-2.4986 in.) (0.010 Undersize)	Yellow – 68.3514-68.3641 mm (2.6910-2.6915 in.)	Red – 0.254 mm Undersize (0.010 in.)	Red – 0.254 mm Undersize (0.010 in.)

NOTE: With Green and Red Coded Crankshaft Journals, Use Yellow Coded Cylinder Block Bores Only.

Crankshaft Main Bearing Journals 2-6 Color Code and Diameter (Journal Size)	Bearing Insert Color Code	
	Upper Insert Size	Lower Insert Size
Yellow – 63.5025-63.4898 mm (2.5001-2.4996 in.) (Standard)	Yellow – Standard	Yellow – Standard
Orange – 63.4898-63.4771 mm (2.4996-2.4991 in.) (0.0005 Undersize)	Yellow – Standard	Black – 0.025 mm Undersize (0.001 in.)
Black – 63.4771-63.4644 mm (2.4991-2.4986 in.) (0.001 Undersize)	Black – 0.025 mm Undersize (0.001 in.)	Black – 0.025 mm Undersize (0.001 in.)
Green – 63.4644-63.4517 mm (2.4986-2.4981 in.) (0.0015 Undersize)	Black – 0.025 mm Undersize (0.001 in.)	Green – 0.051 mm Undersize (0.002 in.)
Red – 63.2485-63.2358 mm (2.4901-2.4966 in.) (0.010 Undersize)	Red – 0.054 mm Undersize (0.010 in.)	Red – 0.254 mm Undersize (0.010 in.)

Crankshaft Main Bearing Journal 7 Color Code and Diameter (Journal Size)	Bearing Insert Color Code	
	Upper Insert Size	Lower Insert Size
Yellow – 63.4873-63.4746 mm (2.4995-2.4990 in.) (Standard)	Yellow – Standard	Yellow – Standard
Orange – 63.4746-63.4619 mm (2.4990-2.4985 in.) (0.0005 Undersize)	Yellow – Standard	Black – 0.025 mm Undersize (0.001 in.)
Black – 63.4619-63.4492 mm (2.4985-2.4980 in.) (0.001 Undersize)	Black – 0.025 mm Undersize (0.001 in.)	Black – 0.025 mm Undersize (0.001 in.)
Green – 63.4492-63.4365 mm (2.4980-2.4975 in.) (0.0015 Undersize)	Black – 0.025 mm Undersize (0.001 in.)	Green – 0.051 mm Undersize (0.002 in.)
Red – 63.2333-63.2206 mm (2.4895-2.4890 in.) (0.010 Undersize)	Red – 0.254 mm Undersize (0.010 in.)	Red – 0.254 mm Undersize (0.010 in.)

19.8f Main bearing selection chart - 4.0L and 4.2L six-cylinder engines on 1993 and earlier models

Crankshaft Journals #1 - #4		Corresponding Crankshaft Bearing Insert	
Color Code	Diameter	Upper Insert Size	Lower Insert Size
Yellow	63.5025-63.4898 mm (2.5001-2.4996 in.)	Yellow - Standard	Yellow - Standard
Orange	63.4898-63.4771 mm (2.4996-2.4991 in.) 0.0127 mm (0.0005 in.) Undersize	Blue - Undersize 0.025 mm (0.001 in.)	Yellow - Standard
Blue	63.4771-63.4644 mm (2.4991-2.4986 in.) 0.0254 mm (0.001 in.) Undersize	Blue - Undersize 0.025 mm (0.001 in.)	Blue - Undersize 0.025 mm (0.001 in.)
Green	63.4644-63.4517 mm (2.4986-2.4981 in.) 0.0381 mm (0.0015 in.) Undersize	Blue - Undersize 0.025 mm (0.001 in.)	Green - Undersize 0.051 mm (0.002 in.)
Red	63.2485-63.2358 mm (2.4901-2.4896 in.) 0.254 mm (0.010 in.) Undersize	Red - Undersize 0.254 mm (0.010 in.)	Red - Undersize 0.254 mm (0.010 in.)

Crankshaft Journals #1 - #6		Corresponding Crankshaft Bearing Insert	
Color Code	Diameter	Upper Insert Size	Lower Insert Size
Yellow	63.5025-63.4898 mm (2.5001-2.4996 in.)	Yellow - Standard	Yellow - Standard
Orange	63.4898-63.4771 mm (2.4996-2.4991 in.) 0.0127 mm (0.0005 in.) Undersize	Blue - Undersize 0.025 mm (0.001 in.)	Yellow - Standard
Blue	63.4771-63.4644 mm (2.4991-2.4986 in.) 0.0254 mm (0.001 in.) Undersize	Blue - Undersize 0.025 mm (0.001 in.)	Blue - Undersize 0.025 mm (0.001 in.)
Green	63.4644-63.4517 mm (2.4986-2.4981 in.) 0.0381 mm (0.0015 in.) Undersize	Blue - Undersize 0.025 mm (0.001 in.)	Green - Undersize 0.051 mm (0.002 in.)
Red	63.2485-63.2358 mm (2.4901-2.4896 in.) 0.254 mm (0.010 in.) Undersize	Red - Undersize 0.254 mm (0.010 in.)	Red - Undersize 0.254 mm (0.010 in.)

Crankshaft Journals #5 Only		Corresponding Crankshaft Bearing Insert	
Color Code	Diameter	Upper Insert Size	Lower Insert Size
Yellow	63.4873-63.4746 mm (2.4995-2.4990 in.)	Yellow - Standard	Yellow - Standard
Orange	63.4746-63.4619 mm (2.4990-2.4985 in.) 0.0127 mm (0.0005 in.) Undersize	Blue - Undersize 0.025 mm (0.001 in.)	Yellow - Standard
Blue	63.4619-63.4492 mm (2.4985-2.4980 in.) 0.0254 mm (0.001 in.) Undersize	Blue - Undersize 0.025 mm (0.001 in.)	Blue - Undersize 0.025 mm (0.001 in.)
Green	63.4492-63.4365 mm (2.4980-2.4975 in.) 0.0381 mm (0.0015 in.) Undersize	Blue - Undersize 0.025 mm (0.001 in.)	Green - Undersize 0.051 mm (0.002 in.)
Red	63.2333-63.2206 mm (2.4895-2.4890 in.) 0.254 mm (0.010 in.) Undersize	Red - Undersize 0.254 mm (0.010 in.)	Red - Undersize 0.254 mm (0.010 in.)

Crankshaft Journals #7 Only		Corresponding Crankshaft Bearing Insert	
Color Code	Diameter	Upper Insert Size	Lower Insert Size
Yellow	63.4873-63.4746 mm (2.4995-2.4990 in.)	Yellow - Standard	Yellow - Standard
Orange	63.4746-63.4619 mm (2.4990-2.4985 in.) 0.0127 mm (0.0005 in.) Undersize	Blue - Undersize 0.025 mm (0.001 in.)	Yellow - Standard
Blue	63.4619-63.4492 mm (2.4985-2.4980 in.) 0.0254 mm (0.001 in.) Undersize	Blue - Undersize 0.025 mm (0.001 in.)	Blue - Undersize 0.025 mm (0.001 in.)
Green	63.4492-63.4365 mm (2.4980-2.4975 in.) 0.0381 mm (0.0015 in.) Undersize	Blue - Undersize 0.025 mm (0.001 in.)	Green - Undersize 0.051 mm (0.002 in.)
Red	63.2333-63.2206 mm (2.4895-2.4890 in.) 0.254 mm (0.010 in.) Undersize	Red - Undersize 0.254 mm (0.010 in.)	Red - Undersize 0.254 mm (0.010 in.)

19.8g Main bearing selection chart - four-cylinder engines (1994 and later models)

19.8h Main bearing selection chart - inline six-cylinder engines (1994 and later models)

Excessive heat (which thins the oil), overloading (which squeezes the oil from the bearing face) and oil leakage or throw off (from excessive bearing clearances, worn oil pump or high engine speeds) all contribute to lubrication breakdown. Blocked oil passages, which usually are the result of misaligned oil holes in a bearing shell, will also oil starve a bearing and destroy it. When lack of lubrication is the cause of bearing failure, the bearing material is wiped or extruded from the steel backing of the bearing. Temperatures may increase to the point where the steel backing turns blue from overheating.

6   Driving habits can have a definite effect on bearing life. Full throttle, low speed operation (lugging the engine) puts very high loads on bearings, which tends to squeeze out the oil film. These loads cause the bearings to flex, which produces fine cracks in the bearing face (fatigue failure). Eventually the bearing material will loosen in pieces and tear away from the steel backing. Short trip driving leads to corrosion of bearings because insufficient engine heat is produced to drive off the condensed water and corrosive gases. These products collect in the engine oil, forming acid and sludge. As the oil is carried to the engine bearings, the acid attacks and corrodes the bearing material.

7   Incorrect bearing installation during engine assembly will lead to bearing failure as well. Tight fitting bearings leave insufficient bearing oil clearance and will result in oil starvation. Dirt or foreign particles trapped behind a bearing insert result in high spots on the bearing which lead to failure.

Bearing selection

Refer to illustrations 19.8a, 19.8b, 19.8c. 19.8d, 19.8e, 19.8f, and 19.8g

8   If the oil clearances are incorrect (see Section 22) or you are replacing the original bearings, refer to the accompanying charts to select the correct new bearings **(see illustrations)**.

9   If the crankshaft has been reground, new undersize bearings must be installed. Disregard steps 11 through 13 and consult the automotive machine shop that reground the crankshaft. They will provide or help you select the correct size bearings.

10   Regardless of how the bearing sizes are determined, use the oil clearance measured with Plastigage (see Section 22) as a guide to ensure the proper size bearings are installed.

11   Engines are assembled at the factory with various sizes of color-coded bearing inserts as listed in **illustrations 19.8a through 19.8d**. The color code appears on the edge of the bearing insert.

12   The journal size codes are generally painted on the adjacent cheek toward the flanged end (rear) of the crankshaft, except for the rear main bearing journal, which is marked on the crankshaft rear flange.

13   To obtain a select fit, upper and lower bearing inserts of different sizes may be used as a pair. For example, a standard insert is sometimes used in combination with a 0.001-inch undersize insert to reduce clearance by 0.0005-inch. **Caution:** *Never use a pair of bearing inserts with a greater size difference than 0.001-inch. When replacing inserts, the odd sized inserts must be either all on the top or all on the bottom.*

20   Engine overhaul - reassembly sequence

1   Before beginning engine reassembly, make sure you have all the necessary new parts, gaskets and seals as well as the following items on hand:

Common hand tools
3/8-inch and 1/2-inch drive torque wrenches
Piston ring installation tool
Piston ring compressor
Vibration damper installation tool
Short lengths of rubber or plastic hose to fit over connecting rod bolts

21.3 When checking piston ring end gap, the ring must be square in the cylinder bore (this is done by pushing the ring down with the top of a piston as shown)

21.4 With the ring square in the cylinder, measure the end gap with a feeler gauge

21.5 If the end gap is too small, clamp a file in a vise and file the ring ends (from the outside in only) to enlarge the gap slightly

Plastigage
Feeler gauges
A fine-tooth file
New engine oil
Engine assembly lube or moly-base grease
Gasket sealant
Thread locking compound

2   In order to save time and avoid problems, engine reassembly must be done in the following general order:

New camshaft bearings (must be done by automotive machine shop)
Piston rings
Crankshaft and main bearings
Piston/connecting rod assemblies
Oil pump
Camshaft and lifters
Oil pan
Timing chain and sprockets
Cylinder head, pushrods and rocker arms
Timing cover
Intake and exhaust manifolds
Valve cover
Engine rear plate
Flywheel/driveplate

21 Piston rings - installation

Refer to illustrations 21.3, 21.4, 21.5, 21.9a, 21.9b and 21.12

1   Before installing the new piston rings, the ring end gaps must be checked. It's assumed that the piston ring side clearance has been checked and verified correct (see Section 17).

2   Lay out the piston/connecting rod assemblies and the new ring sets so the ring sets will be matched with the same piston and cylinder during the end gap measurement and engine assembly.

3   Insert the top (number one) ring into the first cylinder and square it up with the cylinder walls by pushing it in with the top of the piston **(see illustration)**. The ring should be near the bottom of the cylinder, at the lower limit of ring travel.

4   To measure the end gap, slip feeler gauges between the ends of the ring until a gauge equal to the gap width is found **(see illustration)**. The feeler gauge should slide between the ring ends with a slight amount of drag. Compare the measurement to the

Specifications. If the gap is larger or smaller than specified, double-check to make sure you have the correct rings before proceeding.

5   If the gap is too small, it must be enlarged or the ring ends may come in contact with each other during engine operation, which can cause serious damage to the engine. The end gap can be increased by filing the ring ends very carefully with a fine file. Mount the file in a vise equipped with soft jaws, slip the ring over the file with the ends contacting the file face and slowly move the ring to remove material from the ends. When performing this operation, file only from the outside in **(see illustration)**.

6   Excess end gap isn't critical unless it's greater than 0.040-inch. Again, double-check to make sure you have the correct rings for your engine.

7   Repeat the procedure for each ring that will be installed in the first cylinder and for each ring in the remaining cylinders. Remember to keep rings, pistons and cylinders matched up.

8   Once the ring end gaps have been checked/corrected, the rings can be installed on the pistons.

9   The oil control ring (lowest one on the piston) is usually installed first. It's normally composed of three separate components. Slip the spacer/expander into the groove **(see illustration)**. If an anti-rotation tang is used, make sure it's inserted into the drilled hole in the ring groove. Next, install the lower side rail. Don't use a piston ring installation tool on the oil ring side rails, as they may be damaged. Instead, place one end of the side rail into the groove between the spacer/expander and the ring land, hold it firmly in place and slide a finger around the piston while pushing the rail into the groove **(see illustration)**. Next, install the upper side rail in the same manner.

10   After the three oil ring components have been installed, check to make sure that both the upper and lower side rails can be turned smoothly in the ring groove.

11   The number two (middle) ring is installed

21.9a Installing the spacer/expander in the oil control ring groove

21.9b DO NOT use a piston ring installation tool when installing the oil ring side rails

next. It's usually stamped with a mark which must face up, toward the top of the piston. **Note:** *Always follow the instructions printed on the ring package or box - different manufacturers may require different approaches. Do not mix up the top and middle rings, as they have different cross sections.*

12   Use a piston ring installation tool and make sure the identification mark is facing the top of the piston, then slip the ring into the middle groove on the piston **(see illustration)**. Don't expand the ring any more than necessary to slide it over the piston.

13   Install the number one (top) ring in the same manner. Make sure the mark is facing up. Be careful not to confuse the number one and number two rings.

14   Repeat the procedure for the remaining pistons and rings.

22   Crankshaft - Installation and main bearing oil clearance check

Refer to illustrations 22.11 and 22.15

1   Crankshaft installation is the first step in engine reassembly. It's assumed at this point that the engine block and crankshaft have been cleaned, inspected and repaired or reconditioned.

2   Position the engine block with the bottom facing up.

3   Remove the main bearing cap bolts and lift out the caps (all but 2.4L) or remove the mounting fasteners and lift off the main bearing caps/bedplate (2.4L). Lay the caps out in proper order.

4   If they're still in place, remove the original bearing inserts from the block and from the main bearing caps/bedplate. Wipe the bearing surfaces of the block and main bearing caps/bedplate with a clean, lint-free cloth. They must be kept spotlessly clean. This is critical for determining the correct bearing oil clearance.

Main bearing oil clearance check

5   Without mixing them up, clean the back sides of the new upper main bearing inserts (with grooves and oil holes) and lay one in each main bearing saddle in the block or bedplate. Each upper bearing has an oil groove and oil hole in it. **Caution:** *The oil holes in the block must line up with the oil holes in the upper bearing inserts.* On 2.4L four-cylinder engines, install the grooved thrust bearing into the block saddle that has the machined surface. Clean the back sides of the lower main bearing inserts (without grooves) and lay them in the main bearing cap/bedplate saddles. Make sure the tab on the bearing insert fits into the recess in the block or main bearing caps/bedplate. **Caution:** *Do not hammer the bearing insert into place and don't nick or gouge the bearing faces. DO NOT apply any lubrication at this time.*

21.12 Installing the compression rings with a ring expander - the mark (arrow) must face up

6   On 2.5L four-cylinder and all six-cylinder engines the flanged thrust bearing must be installed in the proper gap and saddle. On 2.5L four cylinder engines it is number two, counting from the front of the engine); on six-cylinder engines its number three.

7   Clean the faces of the bearing inserts in the block and the crankshaft main bearing journals with a clean, lint-free cloth.

8   Check or clean the oil holes in the crankshaft, as any dirt here can go only one way - straight through the new bearings.

9   Once you're certain the crankshaft is clean, carefully lay it in position in the cylinder block.

10   Before the crankshaft can be permanently installed, the main bearing oil clearance must be checked.

11   Cut several strips of the appropriate size of Plastigage (they must be slightly shorter than the width of the main bearing journal) and place one piece on each crankshaft main bearing journal, parallel with the journal axis, as shown **(see illustration)**.

12   Clean the faces of the bearing inserts in the main bearing caps or bedplate. On 2.4L four-cylinder engines, hold the bearing inserts in place and install the main bearing cap/bedplate assembly onto the crankshaft and cylinder block. On all other engines install the caps in their respective positions (be careful not to mix them up! DO NOT disturb the Plastigage.

13   Apply clean engine oil to all bolt threads prior to installation, then install all bolts finger-tight. On 2.4L engines tighten the bedplate fasteners in the sequence shown **(see illustration)**, progressing in several steps, to the torque listed in this Chapter's Specifications. On all other engines, tighten the main bearing cap bolts by starting with the center main and working out towards the ends, tighten the main bearing cap bolts in three steps, to the torque listed in this Chapter's Specifications. DO NOT rotate the crankshaft at any time during this operation.

14   Remove the bolts in the reverse order of the tightening sequence and carefully lift the

22.11 Lay the plastigage stripe (arrow) on the main bearing journals, parallel to the crankshaft centerline

main bearing caps/bedplate straight up and off the block. Do not disturb the Plastigage or rotate the crankshaft. If any of the main bearing caps are difficult to remove, tap them gently from side-too-side with a soft-face hammer to loosen them.

15   Compare the width of the crushed Plastigage on each journal to the scale printed on the Plastigage envelope to determine the main bearing oil clearance **(see illustration)**. A typical main bearing oil clearance should fall between 0.0015 to 0.0023-inch (0.038 to 0.058 mm). Check the Specifications Section in this Chapter to make sure it's correct. You can also check with an automotive machine shop for the oil clearance for your engine.

16   If the clearance is not acceptable, the bearing inserts may be the wrong size (which means different ones will be required). Before deciding if different inserts are needed, make sure that no dirt or oil was between the bearing inserts and the main bearing caps/bedplate or block when the clearances were measured. If the Plastigage was wider at one

22.15 Compare the width of the crushed Plastigage to the scale on the envelope to determine the main bearing oil clearance (always take the measurements at the widest point of the Plastigage); be sure to use the correct scale - standard and metric ones are included

22.22a On 2.5L four-cylinder engines, apply a thin coat of sealant to the chamfered areas (arrows) of the rear bearing cap

end than the other, the crankshaft journal may be tapered (refer to Section 18). If the clearance still exceeds the limit specified, the bearing insert(s) will have to be replaced with an undersize bearing insert(s). **Caution:** *When installing a new crankshaft, always install a standard bearing insert set.*

17   Carefully scrape all traces of the Plastigage material off the main bearing journals and/or the bearing insert faces. Be sure to remove all residue from the oil holes. Use your fingernail or the edge of a plastic card - don't nick or scratch the bearing faces.

18   Carefully lift the crankshaft out of the engine.

19   Clean the bearing insert faces in the cylinder block, then apply a thin, uniform layer of moly-base grease or engine assembly lube to each of the bearing surfaces. Be sure to coat the thrust faces of the thrust bearing/washers as well. (See Steps 5 and 6 for thrust washer/bearing locations.) On six cylinder engines, install the rear main oil seal sections in the block and rear main bearing cap.

Final crankshaft installation

Refer to illustrations 22.2a and 22.22b

20   Make sure the crankshaft journals are clean, then lay the crankshaft back in place in the cylinder block.

21   Clean the bearing insert faces and then apply the same lubricant to them.

22   On 2.5L four-cylinder engines, apply Loctite 515 sealant or equivalent to the chamfered area of the rear main bearing cap **(see illustration)**. On 2.4L four-cylinder engines, apply Mopar Bedplate Sealant or equivalent to the bedplate sealing area on the block **(see illustration)**. Hold the bearing inserts in place and install the main bearing caps/bedplate on the crankshaft and cylinder block. Tap the main bearing caps/bedplate into place with a brass or a soft-face hammer.

23   Using NEW main bearing cap bolts, apply clean engine oil to the bolt threads, wipe off any excess oil and then install the fasteners finger-tight.

2.5L four-cylinder and six-cylinder engines

24   Tighten all except the thrust bearing cap bolts to the specified torque (work from the center out and approach the final torque in three steps).

25   Tighten the thrust bearing cap bolts to 10-to-12 ft-lbs.

26   Tap the ends of the crankshaft forward and backward with a lead or brass hammer to line up the main bearing and crankshaft thrust surfaces.

27   Retighten all main bearing cap bolts to the specified torque, starting with the center main and working out toward the ends.

28   On manual transmission equipped models, install a new pilot bearing in the end of the crankshaft (see Chapter 8).

29   Rotate the crankshaft a number of times by hand to check for obvious binding.

30   The final step is to check the crankshaft endplay with a feeler gauge or a dial indicator as described in Section 13. The endplay

should be correct if the crankshaft thrust faces aren't worn or damaged and new bearings have been installed.

31   If you are working on an engine with a one-piece rear main oil seal, refer to Section 23 and install a new seal.

2.4L four-cylinder engines

Refer to illustration 22.34

32   Push the crankshaft forward using a screwdriver or prybar to seat the thrust bearing. Once the crankshaft is pushed fully forward to seat the thrust bearing, leave the screwdriver in position so that pressure stays on the crankshaft until after all main bearing cap/bedplate fasteners have been tightened.

33   Tighten the main bearing cap/bedplate fasteners in the indicated sequence, to the torque listed in Step 1 of this Chapter's Specifications. Remove the screwdriver or prybar.

34   Tighten the main bearing bedplate fasteners in the indicated sequence to the torque and angle listed in the remaining steps of this Chapter's Specifications **(see illustration)**.

35   Recheck crankshaft endplay with a feeler gauge or a dial indicator. The endplay should be correct if the crankshaft thrust faces aren't worn or damaged and if new bearings have been installed.

36   Rotate the crankshaft a number of times by hand to check for any obvious binding.

37   Install the new rear main oil seal (see Chapter 2A or 2B).

38   Reinstall the balance shaft carrier assembly (see Section 25).

23   Rear main oil seal installation

Note: *Refer to Chapter 2, Part B, Section 19 for the 2.4L four-cylinder engine rear main oil seal replacement procedure.*

2.5L engine

Refer to illustration 23.3

1   Clean the bore in the block/cap and the

22.22b On 2.4L four-cylinder engines, apply Mopar Bedplate sealant or equivalent to the block-to-bedplate mating surface as shown

22.34 2.4L four cylinder main bearing cap/bedplate tightening sequence

seal contact surface on the crankshaft. Check the crankshaft surface for scratches and nicks that could damage the new seal lip and cause oil leaks. If the crankshaft is damaged, the only alternative is a new or different crankshaft.

2   Apply a light coat of engine oil or multipurpose grease to the outer edge of the new seal, and to the seal lip.

3   Carefully work the seal lip over the end of the crankshaft and tap the seal in with a hammer and punch until it's seated in the bore **(see illustration)**.

4.0L and 4.2L engines

Refer to illustrations 23.5 and 23.7

4   Inspect the rear main bearing cap and engine block mating surfaces, as well as the seal grooves, for nicks, burrs and scratches. Remove any defects with a fine file or deburring tool.

5   Install the semi-circular seal section in the block with the lip facing the front of the engine **(see illustration)**.

6   Repeat the procedure to install the other seal half in the rear main bearing cap.

7   During final installation of the crankshaft (after the main bearing oil clearances have been checked with Plastigage) as described in Section 22, apply a thin, even coat of anaerobic type gasket sealant to the chamfered areas of the cap or block **(see illustration)**. Don't get any sealant on the bearing face, crankshaft journal, seal ends or seal lips. Also, lubricate the seal lips with multipurpose grease or engine assembly lube.

---

24   Pistons/connecting rods - installation and rod bearing oil clearance check

Refer to illustrations 24.5, 24.9, 24.11, 24.13, 24.17 and 24.21

1   Before installing the piston/connecting rod assemblies, the cylinder walls must be perfectly clean, the top edge of each cylinder must be chamfered, and the crankshaft must be in place.

2   Remove the cap from the end of the

23.3 Tap around the circumference of the oil seal with a hammer and a punch to seat it squarely in the bore

number one connecting rod (refer to the marks made during removal). Remove the original bearing inserts and wipe the bearing surfaces of the connecting rod and cap with a clean, lint-free cloth. They must be kept spotlessly clean.

Connecting rod bearing oil clearance check

3   Clean the back side of the new upper bearing insert, then lay it in place in the connecting rod. Make sure the tab on the bearing fits into the recess in the rod. Don't hammer the bearing insert into place and be very careful not to nick or gouge the bearing face. Don't lubricate the bearing at this time.

4   Clean the back side of the other bearing insert and install it in the rod cap. Again,

23.5 Rear main oil seal installation details - 4.0L and 4.2L engine

make sure the tab on the bearing fits into the recess in the cap, and don't apply any lubricant. It's critically important that the mating surfaces of the bearing and connecting rod are perfectly clean and oil free when they're assembled.

5   Position the piston ring gaps at intervals around the piston **(see illustration)**.

6   Slip a section of plastic or rubber hose over each connecting rod cap bolt.

7   Lubricate the piston and rings with clean engine oil and attach a piston ring compressor to the piston. Leave the skirt protruding about 1/4-inch to guide the piston into the cylinder. The rings must be compressed until they're flush with the piston.

8   Rotate the crankshaft until the number one connecting rod journal is at BDC (bottom dead center) and apply a coat of engine oil to the cylinder walls.

9   With the arrow or notch on top of the piston **(see illustration)** facing the front of the engine, gently insert the piston/connecting rod assembly into the number one cylinder bore and rest the bottom edge of the ring compressor on the engine block.

10   Tap the top edge of the ring compressor to make sure it's contacting the block around its entire circumference.

23.7 Apply anaerobic sealant to the areas shown on the rear main bearing cap prior to installation (don't get sealant in the grooves or on the seal)

24.5 Position the piston ring gaps as shown here before installing the piston/connecting rod assemblies in the engine

24.9 The arrow must point towards the front of the engine

24.11 Drive the piston gently into the cylinder bore with the end of a wooden or plastic hammer handle

24.13 Lay the Plastigage strips on each rod bearing journal, parallel to the crankshaft centerline

24.17 Measuring the width of the crushed Plastigage to determine the rod bearing oil clearance (be sure to use the correct scale - standard and metric ones are included)

11   Gently tap on the top of the piston with the end of a wooden hammer handle **(see illustration)** while guiding the end of the connecting rod into place on the crankshaft journal. The piston rings may try to pop out of the ring compressor just before entering the cylinder bore, so keep some down pressure on the ring compressor. Work slowly, and if any resistance is felt as the piston enters the cylinder, stop immediately. Find out what's hanging up and fix it before proceeding. Do not, for any reason, force the piston into the cylinder - you might break a ring and/or the piston.

12   Once the piston/connecting rod assembly is installed, the connecting rod bearing oil clearance must be checked before the rod cap is permanently bolted in place.

13   Cut a piece of the appropriate size Plastigage slightly shorter than the width of the connecting rod bearing and lay it in place on the number one connecting rod journal, parallel with the journal axis **(see illustration)**.

14   Clean the connecting rod cap bearing face, remove the protective hoses from the connecting rod bolts and install the rod cap. Make sure the mating mark on the cap is on the same side as the mark on the connecting rod.

15   Install the nuts and tighten them to the torque listed in this Chapter's Specifications, working up to it in three steps. **Note:** *Use a thin-wall socket to avoid erroneous torque readings that can result if the socket is wedged between the rod cap and nut. If the socket tends to wedge itself between the nut and the cap, lift up on it slightly until it no longer contacts the cap. Do not rotate the crankshaft at any time during this operation.*

16   Remove the nuts and detach the rod cap, being very careful not to disturb the Plastigage.

17   Compare the width of the crushed Plastigage to the scale printed on the Plastigage envelope to obtain the oil clearance **(see illustration)**. Compare it to the Specifications to make sure the clearance is correct.

18   If the clearance is not as specified, the bearing inserts may be the wrong size (which means different ones will be required). Before

deciding that different inserts are needed, make sure that no dirt or oil was between the bearing inserts and the connecting rod or cap when the clearance was measured. Also, recheck the journal diameter. If the Plastigage was wider at one end than the other, the journal may be tapered (refer to Section 18).

Final connecting rod installation

19   Carefully scrape all traces of the Plastigage material off the rod journal and/or bearing face. Be very careful not to scratch the bearing - use your fingernail or the edge of a credit card.

20   Make sure the bearing faces are perfectly clean, then apply a uniform layer of clean moly-base grease or engine assembly lube to both of them. You'll have to push the piston into the cylinder to expose the face of the bearing insert in the connecting rod - be sure to slip the protective hoses over the rod bolts first.

21   Slide the connecting rod back into place on the journal, remove the protective hoses from the rod cap bolts, install the rod cap and tighten the nuts to the torque listed in this Chapter's Specifications. Again, work up to the torque in three steps **(see illustration)**.

22   Repeat the entire procedure for the remaining pistons/connecting rods.

23   The important points to remember are:

a) *Keep the back sides of the bearing inserts and the insides of the connecting rods and caps perfectly clean when assembling them.*

b) *Make sure you have the correct piston/rod assembly for each cylinder.*

c) *The notch or mark on the piston must face the front of the engine.*

d) *Lubricate the cylinder walls with clean oil.*

e) *Lubricate the bearing faces when installing the rod caps after the oil clearance has been checked.*

24   After all the piston/connecting rod assemblies have been properly installed,

24.21 Be sure the numbers (arrow) on the connecting rod match before tightening the cap nuts

rotate the crankshaft a number of times by hand to check for any obvious binding.

25   As a final step, the connecting rod endplay must be checked. Refer to Section 12 for this procedure.

26   Compare the measured endplay to the Specifications to make sure it's correct. If it was correct before disassembly and the original crankshaft and rods were reinstalled, it should still be right. If new rods or a new crankshaft were installed, the endplay may be inadequate. If so, the rods will have to be removed and taken to an automotive machine shop for resizing.

---

25   Balance shaft assembly - removal and installation (2.4L four-cylinder engine)

Removal

1   Remove the balance shaft assembly chain cover.

2   Remove the balance shaft sprocket bolt.

3   Loosen the balance shaft chain tensioner bolts.

25.8 Align the balance shaft keyways and balance shaft gear marks as shown

A   *Balance shaft keyways pointing up*
B   *Alignment marks on balance shaft gears*

25.7 Rotate the crankshaft so that the No. 1 TDC mark on the crankshaft sprocket is aligned with the parting line of the main bearing cap/bedplate. When the balance shaft chain and balance shaft driven-sprocket are installed, they must also be aligned as shown

A   *Mark on crankshaft sprocket*
B   *Balance shaft keyways pointing up*
C   *Alignment marks on counter balance sprocket and counter balance carrier case*
D   *Plated link on balance shaft chain*
E   *Parting line of main bearing cap/bedplate*
F   *Plated link on balance shaft chain*

4   Push the balance shaft inward, and pull or pry the balance shaft sprocket off of the shaft, so that the sprocket hangs freely. Remove the chain and sprocket.
5   Remove the balance shaft carrier-to-block bolts and remove the carrier assembly.

Installation

Refer to illustrations 25.7, 25.8 and 25.11

6   Install the carrier assembly and tighten the bolts to the torque listed in this Chapter's Specifications.
7   Remove the bolt from the other balance shaft and remove the gear cover. Rotate the crankshaft to the No. 1 top-dead-center (TDC) position, so that the No. 1 TDC timing mark on the crankshaft sprocket is aligned with the parting line of the main bearing cap (see illustration).
8   Align both balance shaft keyways at the 12 o'clock position (pointing toward the top of the engine) so that both balance shaft gear timing dots are pointed to each other (see illustration). Install the gear cover and tighten the bolt/stud to the torque listed in this Chapter's Specifications.

9   Install the chain so that the each of the plated links are aligned with each of the timing marks on the crankshaft and balance shaft sprockets, then slide the sprocket onto the balance shaft (see illustration 9.7).
10   Check the timing marks, plated links and keyways for correct alignment, then install both of the balance bolts and tighten to the torque listed in this Chapter's Specifications. **Note:** *To prevent the crankshaft from rotating, wedge a wooden block between a crankshaft counterweight and the block.*
11   Position the chain tensioner and loosely install the tensioner bolts. Install the chain guide, making sure the tab is in the slot. Position a 0.039-inch thick x 2.75-inch long spacer-shim between the tensioner and chain (see illustration). Push firmly on the tensioner, then tighten the top tensioner arm bolt, then tighten the lower tensioner pivot bolt - each to the torque listed in this Chapter's Specifications. Remove the spacer-shim.
12   Install the chain cover and tighten the bolts to the torque listed in this Chapter's Specifications.

26   Initial start-up and break-in after overhaul

Warning: *Have a fire extinguisher handy when starting the engine for the first time.*

1   Once the engine has been installed in the vehicle, double-check the engine oil and coolant levels.
2   With the spark plugs out of the engine and the ignition system disabled (see Section 3), crank the engine until oil pressure registers on the gauge or the light goes out.
3   Install the spark plugs, hook up the plug wires and restore the ignition system functions (see Section 3).
4   Start the engine. It may take a few moments for the fuel system to build up pressure, but the engine should start without a great deal of effort. **Note:** *If backfiring occurs through the carburetor or throttle body, recheck the valve timing and ignition timing.*
5   After the engine starts, it should be allowed to warm up to normal operating temperature. While the engine is warming up, make a thorough check for fuel, oil and coolant leaks.
6   Shut the engine off and recheck the engine oil and coolant levels.

7   Drive the vehicle to an area with minimum traffic, accelerate at full throttle from 30 to 50 mph, then allow the vehicle to slow to 30 mph with the throttle closed. Repeat the procedure 10 or 12 times. This will load the piston rings and cause them to seat properly against the cylinder walls. Check again for oil and coolant leaks.
8   Drive the vehicle gently for the first 500 miles (no sustained high speeds) and keep a constant check on the oil level. It is not unusual for an engine to use oil during the break-in period.
9   At approximately 500 to 600 miles, change the oil and filter.
10   For the next few hundred miles, drive the vehicle normally. Do not pamper it or abuse it.
11   After 2000 miles, change the oil and filter again and consider the engine broken in.

25.11 To adjust the balance shaft chain tensioner, position a .039-inch (1 mm) thick x 2.75-inch (70 mm) long shim spacer between the chain and tensioner, push on the tensioner firmly, then tighten the tensioner arm bolt and tensioner pivot bolt

A   *0.039 (1 mm) thick shim*
B   *Tensioner adjuster bolt*
C   *Tensioner pivot bolt*

Chapter 3
Cooling, heating and air conditioning systems

Contents

Specifications

General

Coolant capacity	See Chapter 1
Drivebelt tension	See Chapter 1
Radiator cap pressure rating	
2.4L engine	18 to 21 psi
2.5L engine	12 to 15 psi
Six-cylinder engine	16 to 18 psi
Thermostat opening temperature	195-degrees F
Refrigerant capacity	38 ounces

Torque specifications

Ft-lbs (unless otherwise indicated)

2.4L engine	
Thermostat housing bolts	15
Water pump attaching bolts	105 in-lbs
2.5L engine	
Fan clutch-to-water pump bolts	15 to 22
Fan-to-fan clutch nuts	18
Thermostat housing bolts	13
Water pump attaching bolts	13
4.0L and 4.2L engines	
Fan clutch-to-water pump bolts	18
Fan-to-fan clutch nuts	18
Thermostat housing bolts	13
Water pump attaching bolts	9 to 18

1.1a Coolant flow 2.5l engine (all)

1.1b Coolant flow 4.2L engine (1987 through 1990)

1   General information

Refer to illustrations 1.1a, 1.1b, 1.1c, 1.2 and 1.3

Engine cooling system

All vehicles covered by this manual employ a pressurized engine cooling system with thermostatically controlled coolant circulation. An impeller type water pump mounted on the front of the block pumps coolant through the engine. The coolant flows around each cylinder and toward the rear of the engine. Cast-in coolant passages direct coolant around the intake and exhaust ports, near the spark plug areas and in close proximity to the exhaust valve guides **(see illustrations)**.

A wax pellet type thermostat is located in a housing near the front of the engine. During warm up, the closed thermostat allows the engine to reach operating temperature quickly, the thermostat maintains the normal operating temperature, at the same time pre-

vents the engine from over heating **(see illustration)**.

The cooling system is sealed by a pressure type radiator cap, which raises the boiling point of the coolant and increases the cooling efficiency of the radiator. If the system pressure exceeds the cap pressure relief value, the excess pressure in the system forces the spring-loaded valve inside the cap off its seat and allows the coolant to escape through the overflow tube into a coolant reservoir. When the system cools the excess coolant is automatically drawn from the reservoir back into the radiator **(see illustration)**.

The coolant reservoir does double duty as both the point at which fresh coolant is added to the cooling system to maintain the proper fluid level and as a holding tank for overheated coolant.

This type of cooling system is known as a closed design because coolant that escapes past the pressure cap is saved and reused.

Heating system

The heating system consists of a blower fan and heater core located in the heater box, the hoses connecting the heater core to the engine cooling system and the heater/air conditioning control head on the dashboard. Hot engine coolant is circulated through the heater core. When the heater mode is activated, a flap door opens to expose the heater box to the passenger compartment. A fan switch on the control head activates the blower motor, which forces air through the core, heating the air.

Air conditioning system

The air conditioning system consists of a condenser mounted in front of the radiator,

1.1c Coolant flow 4.0L engine
(1991 and later)

1.2 The thermostat

1.3 The coolant reserve system

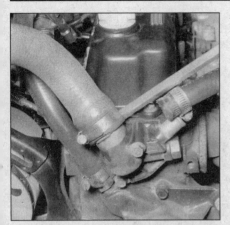

3.8 Loosen the hose clamp, then detach the hose from the thermostat housing

3.10 Remove the thermostat housing bolts

an evaporator mounted adjacent to the heater core, a compressor mounted on the engine, a receiver/drier which contains a high pressure relief valve and the plumbing connecting all of the above components.

A blower fan forces the warmer air of the passenger compartment through the evaporator core (sort of a radiator-in-reverse), transferring the heat from the air to the refrigerant. The liquid refrigerant boils off into low pressure vapor, taking the heat with it when it leaves the evaporator.

3.11 Note how the thermostat is installed

2 Antifreeze - general information

Warning: *Do not allow antifreeze to come in contact with your skin or painted surfaces of the vehicle. Rinse off spills immediately with plenty of water. Never leave antifreeze lying around in an open container or in a puddle in the driveway or on the garage floor. Children and pets are attracted by its sweet smell. Antifreeze is fatal if ingested in sufficient quantity. Check with local authorities before disposing of used antifreeze. Many communities have collection centers which will see that antifreeze is disposed of safely. Antifreeze is also combustible, so don't store or use it near open flames.*

The cooling system should be filled with a water/ethylene glycol based antifreeze solution, which will prevent freezing down to at least negative 20-degrees F, or lower if local climate requires it. It also provides protection against corrosion and increases the coolant boiling point.

The cooling system should be drained, flushed and refilled at the specified intervals (see Chapter 1). Old or contaminated antifreeze solutions are likely to cause damage and encourage the formation of rust and scale in the system. Use distilled water with the antifreeze.

Before adding antifreeze, check all hose connections, because antifreeze tends to search out and leak through very minute openings. Engines don't normally consume coolant, so if the level goes down, find the cause and correct it.

The exact mixture of antifreeze-to-water which you should use depends on the relative weather conditions. The mixture should contain at least 50 percent antifreeze, but should never contain more than 70 percent antifreeze. Consult the mixture ratio chart on the antifreeze container before adding coolant. Hydrometers are available at most auto parts stores to test the coolant. Use antifreeze which meets the vehicle manufacturer's specifications.

3 Thermostat - check and replacement

Warning: *Do not remove the radiator cap, drain the coolant or replace the thermostat until the engine has cooled completely.*

Check

1 Before assuming the thermostat is to blame for a cooling system problem, check the coolant level, drivebelt tension (see Chapter 1) and temperature gauge (or light) operation.

2 If the engine seems to be taking a long time to warm up (based on heater output or temperature gauge operation), the thermostat is probably stuck open. Replace the thermostat with a new one.

3 If the engine runs hot, use your hand to check the temperature of the upper radiator hose. If the hose isn't hot, but the engine is, the thermostat is probably stuck closed, preventing the coolant inside the engine from escaping to the radiator. Replace the thermostat. **Caution:** *Don't drive the vehicle without a thermostat. The computer may stay in open loop and emissions and fuel economy will suffer.*

4 If the upper radiator hose is hot, it means that the coolant is flowing and the thermostat is open. Consult the *Troubleshooting* section at the front of this manual for cooling system diagnosis.

Replacement

Refer to illustrations 3.8, 3.10 and 3.11

5 Disconnect the negative battery cable from the battery.

6 Drain the cooling system (see Chapter 1). If the coolant is relatively new or in good condition, save it and reuse it.

7 Follow the upper radiator hose to the engine to locate the thermostat housing.

8 Loosen the hose clamp, then detach the hose from the fitting **(see illustration)**. If it's stuck, grasp it near the end with a pair of adjustable pliers and twist it to break the seal, then pull it off. If the hose is old or deteriorated, cut it off and install a new one.

9 If the outer surface of the large fitting that mates with the hose is deteriorated (corroded, pitted, etc.) it may be damaged further by hose removal. If it is, the thermostat housing cover will have to be replaced.

10 Remove the bolts and detach the housing cover **(see illustration)**. If the cover is stuck, tap it with a soft-face hammer to jar it loose. Be prepared for some coolant to spill as the gasket seal is broken.

11 Note how it's installed (which end is facing into the cylinder head) **(see illustration)**, then remove the thermostat.

12 Stuff a rag into the engine opening, then remove all traces of old gasket material and sealant from the housing and cover with a gasket scraper. Remove the rag from the opening and clean the gasket mating surfaces with lacquer thinner or acetone.

13 Install the new thermostat in the housing. Make sure the correct end faces up - the spring end is normally directed into the engine **(see illustration 3.11)**.

14 Apply a thin, uniform layer of RTV sealant to both sides of the new gasket and position it on the housing.

15 Install the cover and bolts. Tighten the bolts to the torque listed in this Chapter's Specifications.

16 Reattach the hose to the fitting and tighten the hose clamp securely.

17 Refill the cooling system (see Chapter 1).

18 Start the engine and allow it to reach normal operating temperature, then check for leaks and proper thermostat operation (as described in Steps 2 through 4).

4.3a Loosen the upper radiator hose

4.3b Grasp the hose with adjustable pliers and twist it to break the seal

4.5a Remove the bolts that attach the fan shroud to the radiator

4.5b Lift the fan shroud out of the engine compartment

4.6a Loosen the lower radiator hose clamp

4   Radiator - removal and installation

Refer to illustrations 4.3a, 4.3b, 4.5a, 4.5b, 4.6a, 4.6b, 4.9 and 4.10
Warning: *Wait until the engine is completely cool before beginning this procedure.*

Removal

1   Disconnect the negative battery cable from the battery.
2   Drain the cooling system (see Chapter 1). If the coolant is relatively new or in good condition, save it and reuse it.
3   Loosen the hose clamps, then detach the upper radiator hose from the fitting **(see illustration)**. If it's stuck, grasp the hose near the end with a pair of adjustable pliers and twist it to break the seal **(see illustration)**, then pull it off - be careful not to distort the radiator fittings! If the hose is old or deteriorated, cut it off and install a new one.
4   Disconnect the reservoir hose from the radiator filler neck.
5   Remove the bolts that attach the shroud to the radiator and lift the shroud out of the engine compartment **(see illustrations)**.

6   Loosen the clamp **(see illustration)** and detach the lower hose from the radiator. To ease and speed the removal of the lower radiator hose use retaining ring pliers (if available) to separate the hose from the radiator **(see illustration)**.
7   If the vehicle is equipped with an automatic transmission, disconnect the cooler lines from the radiator. Use a drip pan to

4.6b Use retaining ring pliers to break the seal on the lower radiator hose

catch spilled fluid.
8   Plug the lines and fittings.
9   Remove the radiator mounting bolts **(see illustration)**.
10   Carefully lift out the radiator **(see illustration)**. Don't spill coolant on the vehicle or scratch the paint.
11   With the radiator removed, it can be inspected for leaks and damage. If it needs

4.9 Remove the radiator mounting bolts

4.10 Carefully lift the radiator out of the engine compartment

5.6 Remove the bolts attaching the clutch-fan to the water pump pulley

5.7 Remove the clutch-fan assembly out of the engine compartment

repair, have a radiator shop or dealer service department perform the work as special techniques are required.

12   Bugs and dirt can be removed from the radiator with compressed air and a soft brush. Don't bend the cooling fins as this is done.

13   Check the radiator mounts for deterioration and make sure there's nothing in them when the radiator is installed.

Installation

14   Installation is the reverse of the removal procedure.

15   After installation, fill the cooling system with the proper mixture of antifreeze and water. Refer to Chapter 1 if necessary.

16   Start the engine and check for leaks. Allow the engine to reach normal operating temperature, indicated by the upper radiator hose becoming hot. Recheck the coolant level and add more if required.

17   If you're working on an automatic transmission equipped vehicle, check and add fluid as needed.

---

5   Engine cooling fan and clutch - check, removal and installation

---

Warning: *To avoid possible injury or damage, DO NOT operate the engine with a damaged fan. Do not attempt to repair fan blades - replace a damaged fan with a new one. All the vehicles covered in this manual are equipped with a temperature-controlled viscous fan clutch. It is driven by the water pump pulley and automatically increases or decreases the speed of the fan to provide the radiator proper cooling.*

Check

1   Disconnect the negative battery cable and rock the fan back and forth by hand to check for excessive bearing play.

2   With the engine cold, turn the fan blades by hand. The fan should turn freely.

3   Visually inspect for substantial leakage

5.9 The clutch can now be unbolted from the fan

1   Mounting flange
2   Fan-to-clutch bolt
3   Fan clutch

from the clutch assembly. If problems are noted, replace the clutch assembly.

4   With the engine completely warmed up, turn off the ignition switch and disconnect the negative battery cable from the battery. Turn the fan by hand. Some drag should be evident. If the fan turns easily, replace the fan clutch.

Removal and installation

Refer to illustrations 5.6, 5.7 and 5.9

5   Disconnect the negative battery cable. Remove the fan shroud mounting screws and detach the shroud (see Section 4).

6   Remove the bolts/nuts attaching the fan/clutch assembly to the water pump pulley **(see illustration)**.

7   Lift the fan/clutch assembly (and shroud, if necessary) out of the engine compartment **(see illustration)**.

8   Carefully inspect the fan blades for damage and defects. Replace the fan if it's damaged.

9   At this point, the fan may be unbolted from the clutch, if necessary **(see illustration)**. If the fan clutch is stored, position it with the radiator side facing down.

10   Installation is the reverse of removal. Be sure to tighten the fan and clutch mounting nuts/bolts to the torque listed in this Chapter's Specifications.

6   Coolant temperature sending unit - check and replacement

Refer to illustrations 6.1a and 6.1b
Warning: *Wait until the engine is completely cool before beginning this procedure.*

1   The coolant temperature indicator system is composed of a light or temperature gauge mounted in the instrument panel and a coolant temperature sending unit mounted on the engine **(see illustrations)**. Some vehicles have more than one sending unit, but

6.1a The temperature sending unit for the four-cylinder engine is at the back of the cylinder head

6.1b The temperature sending unit on the six-cylinder engine is at the back of the cylinder head

8.4 The water pump weep hole (arrow) will drip coolant when the seal on the pump shaft fails (pump removed from engine for clarity)

8.5 Grasp the water pump flange and try to rock the shaft back and forth for play (fan and pulley shown removed for clarity)

only one is used for the indicator system.

2   If an overheating indication occurs, check the coolant level in the system and then make sure the wiring between the light or gauge and the sending unit is secure and all fuses are intact.

3   When the ignition switch is turned on and the starter motor is turning, the indicator light should be on (overheated engine indication).

4   If the light is not on, the bulb may be burned out, the ignition switch may be faulty or the circuit may be open. Test the circuit by grounding the wire to the sending unit while the ignition is on (engine not running for safety). If the gauge deflects full scale or the light comes on, replace the sending unit.

5   As soon as the engine starts, the light should go out and remain out unless the engine overheats. Failure of the light to go out may be due to a grounded wire between the light and the sending unit, a defective sending unit or a faulty ignition switch. Check the coolant to make sure it's the proper type. Plain water may have too low a boiling point to activate the sending unit.

6   If the sending unit must be replaced, simply unscrew it from the engine and install the replacement **(see illustration)**. **Warning:** *Make sure the engine is cool before removing the defective sending unit. Use sealant on the threads. There will be some coolant loss as*

the unit is removed, so be prepared to catch it. Check the level after the unit has been installed.

7   Coolant reservoir - removal and installation

Warning: *Wait until the engine is completely cool before beginning this procedure.*

1   Remove the reservoir cap and drain the cooling system (see Chapter 1) until the coolant level is below the bottom of the reservoir.

2   Loosen the hose clamps and detach the hose(s) from the reservoir.

3   Remove the screws or retaining strap and lift the reservoir from the vehicle.

4   Installation is the reverse of removal.

5   Refill the cooling system and check for leaks.

8   Water pump - check

Refer to illustrations 8.4 and 8.5

1   A failure in the water pump can cause serious engine damage due to overheating.

2   There are three ways to check the operation of the water pump while it's installed on the engine. If the pump is defective, it should be replaced with a new or rebuilt unit.

3   With the engine running at normal operating temperature, squeeze the upper radiator hose. If the water pump is working properly, a pressure surge should be felt as the hose is released. **Warning:** *Keep your hands away from the fan blades!*

4   Water pumps are equipped with weep or vent holes. If a failure occurs in the pump seal, coolant will leak from the hole. In most cases you'll need a flashlight to find the hole on the water pump from underneath to check for leaks **(see illustration)**.

5   If the water pump shaft bearings fail there may be a howling sound at the front of the engine while it's running. Shaft wear can be felt if the water pump pulley is rocked up and down **(see illustration)**. Don't mistake

drivebelt slippage, which causes a squealing sound, for water pump bearing failure.

9   Water pump - replacement

Refer to illustrations 9.5, 9.6a, 9.6b, 9.7a, 9.7b, 9.9a and 9.9b

Warning: *Wait until the engine is completely cool before beginning this procedure.*

Caution: *All 4.0L engines and some 2.5L and 4.2L engines have a reverse rotating water pump and viscous fan. This type of water pump can be identified by the words "REVERSE" imprinted on the viscous drive and/or inner side of the fan. On the body of the water pump "REV" is cast, and an "R" is stamped into the water pump impeller. The installation of the wrong pump will cause major engine damage.*

1   Disconnect the negative battery cable from the battery.

2   Drain the cooling system (see Chapter 1). If the coolant is relatively new or in good condition, save it and reuse it.

3   Remove the cooling fan and shroud (see Section 4).

4   Remove the drivebelts (see Chapter 1) and the pulley at the end of the water pump shaft.

5   Loosen the clamps and detach the hoses from the water pump **(see illustration)**. If they're stuck, grasp each hose near the end with a pair of adjustable pliers and twist it to break the seal, then pull it off. If the hoses are deteriorated, cut them off and install new ones.

6   Remove all accessory brackets from the water pump. When removing the power steering pump **(see illustrations)**, and air conditioning compressor, don't disconnect the hoses. Tie the units aside with the hoses attached. On 2.4L four-cylinder engines, remove the timing belt, timing belt idler pulley, camshaft sprockets and rear timing belt cover (see Chapter 2A)

7   Remove the bolts and detach the water pump from the engine. Note the locations of the various lengths and different types of bolts as they're removed to ensure correct

9.5 Loosen the hose clamps and detach the hoses from the water pump

9.6a Remove the power steering pump (2.5L engine shown, 4.2L engine similar)

1 Mounting bolt
2 Adjusting bolt

installation **(see illustrations)**.
8   Clean the bolt threads and the threaded holes in the engine to remove corrosion and sealant.
9   Compare the new pump to the old one to make sure they're identical **(see illustrations)**.
10   Remove all traces of old gasket material from the engine with a gasket scraper.
11   Clean the engine and new water pump mating surfaces with lacquer thinner or acetone.
12   Apply a thin coat of RTV sealant to the engine side of the new gasket.
13   Apply a thin layer of RTV sealant to the gasket mating surface of the new pump, then carefully mate the gasket and the pump. Slip a couple of bolts through the pump mounting holes to hold the gasket in place. On 2.4L four-cylinder engines, apply a thin coat of RTV sealant to the new water pump O-ring and position it in the grove on the back of the water pump. **Caution:** *Make sure the O-ring is correctly seated in the water pump groove to avoid a coolant leak.*
14   Carefully attach the pump and gasket to the engine and thread the bolts into the holes finger tight.
15   Install the remaining bolts. Tighten them to the torque listed in this Chapter's Specifi-

9.6b Loosen the adjusting bolt on the alternator (2.5L engine shown, 4.2L engine similar)

cations in 1/4-turn increments. Don't overtighten them or the pump may be distorted.
16   Reinstall all parts removed for access to the pump.
17   Refill the cooling system and check the drivebelt tension (see Chapter 1). Run the engine and check for leaks.

10   Heater and air conditioner blower motor - removal and installation

Refer to illustration 10.6
Warning: *Some models covered by this manual are equipped with airbags. Always disable the airbag system when working in the vicinity of airbag system components (see Chapter 12).*

Heater blower motor
Removal
1   Disconnect the negative cable from the battery.
2   Remove the heater core housing (see Section 11).
3   Disconnect the blower motor wires.
4   Remove the blower motor screws.
5   Lift the blower motor from the housing. If you are not replacing the motor, you may disregard Steps 6 through 8.

9.7a Remove the bolts and detach the water pump from the engine (four-cylinder engine shown, six-cylinder engines similar)

9.7b Note the location and various lengths and different types of bolts as they're removed (four-cylinder engine shown, six-cylinder engines similar)

6   Detach the fan retainer clip from the fan hub **(see illustration)**.

10.6 Pry the clip ears (1 and 3) off the flat surface (2) of the motor shaft (4) - bend the retaining clip like the original when installing it

9.9a The water pump for the 2.5L and 4.2L engines with the "V" type drivebelts (forward rotating)

9.9b The water pump for the 2.5L, 4.0L and 4.2L engines with the serpentine drivebelt (reverse rotating)

11.3 Disconnect the heater hoses at the heater core

11.4a Disconnect the heater control cable (right side)

11.4b Disconnect the heater control cable (center)

7   Slip the fan off the old motor shaft, remove the motor-to-cover attaching nuts and pull the motor off the cover.

8   Mount the new motor on the cover and slip the fan onto the shaft. Install the retainer clip **(see illustration 10.6)**.

Installation

9   Place the blower motor in position and install the mounting screws.

10   Install the heater core housing (see Section 11).

11   Reconnect the wires and battery cable. Test the motor in operation.

Air conditioner blower motor

Removal

12   Disconnect the negative cable from the battery.

13   Remove the mounting screws and lower the air conditioning evaporator core housing to access the blower motor attaching screws (it's not necessary to discharge the air conditioner system the remove the blower motor) **(see illustration 11.18)**.

14   Disconnect the blower motor wires.

15   Remove the blower motor mounting screws.

16   Lift the blower motor from the vehicle (see Steps 6 through 8 for replacing the blower motor). If you are not replacing the motor, you may disregard Steps 6 through 8.

Installation

17   Place the blower motor in position and install the mounting screws.

18   Raise the air conditioning evaporator core housing and install the mounting screws.

11   Heater core and air conditioner evaporator core - replacement

Warning 1: *Wait until the engine is completely cool before beginning this procedure.*

Warning 2: *The air conditioning system is under high pressure. DO NOT disconnect any refrigerant fittings until after the system has been discharged by a dealer service department or service station.*

Warning 3: *Some models covered by this manual are equipped with airbags. Always disable the airbag system when working in the vicinity of airbag system components (see Chapter 12).*

Heater core

Refer to illustrations 11.3, 11.4a, 11.4b and 11.6

Removal

1   Disconnect the negative cable from the battery.

2   Drain the cooling system (see Chapter 1).

3   Disconnect the heater hoses at the heater core inlet and outlet **(see illustration)**.

4   Disconnect the heater control cables **(see illustrations)** and defroster duct.

5   On 1997 and later models, remove the instrument panel (see Chapter 11).

6   Disconnect the housing attaching nuts from the studs on the engine compartment side of the firewall **(see illustration)**.

7   Tilt the heater housing assembly down and pull it to the rear. You can now remove the heater housing assembly from the vehicle.

8   Remove the retaining screws on the housing assembly and remove the heater core by pulling it straight out of the housing.

Installation

9   Reinstall the parts in the reverse order of removal. **Note:** *Be sure the housing studs are extended through the firewall. Also avoid trapping wires between the housing fresh air inlet and the firewall and the heater housing.*

10   Refill the cooling system.

11   Start the engine and check for proper operation and leaks.

11.6 Heating system assembly (exploded view)

1	Defroster nozzle	5	Hose	8	Heater housing
2	Defroster duct	6	Blower motor	9	Cable
3	Heater core	7	Fan	10	Heater housing cover
4	Seal				

11.16 Location of evaporative housing-to-instrument panel screws

11.18 Evaporative housing assembly (exploded view)

1	Feed wire	13	Drain tube
2	Blower fan	14	Temperature control knob
3	Blower housing	15	Fan control knob
4	Grommet	16	Nut
5	Hose	17	Thermostat
6	Capillary tube	18	Fan control switch
7	Expansion valve	19	Switch harness
8	Insulation	20	Upper housing
9	Evaporative core	21	Bracket
10	Lower housing	22	Insulation
11	Louver panel	23	Blower motor
12	Louver		

Evaporator core

Refer to illustrations 11.16 and 11.18

Removal

Note: *On 1997 and later models, remove the instrument panel (see Chapter 11).*

12   Have the air conditioning system discharged (see the **Warning** at the beginning of this Section).

13   Disconnect the negative cable from the battery.

14   Disconnect the inlet and receiver/drier-to-evaporator hoses.

15   Remove the retaining screws, hose clamps and dash grommet.

16   Remove the attaching screws to the evaporator housing-to-instrument panel **(see illustration)**.

17   Lower the evaporator housing from the dash panel. You can now remove the evaporator housing assembly from the vehicle.

18   Remove the retaining screws **(see illustration)**, and remove the evaporator core by pulling it straight out of the housing.

Installation

19   Position the evaporator core in the housing and install the screws.

20   Reinstall the parts in the reverse order of removal.

21   Have the air conditioning system evacuated, recharged and leak tested.

22   Start the engine and check for proper operation.

12   Air conditioning system - check and maintenance

Refer to illustration 12.7

Warning: *The air conditioning system is under high pressure. Do not loosen any hose fittings or remove any components until after the system has been discharged by a dealer service department or service station. Always wear eye protection when disconnecting air conditioning system fittings.*

Note 1: *The air conditioning system on 1995 and later models uses the non-ozone depleting refrigerant, referred to as R-134a. The R-134a refrigerant and its lubricating oil are not compatible with the R-12 system, and under no circumstances should the two different types of refrigerant and lubricating oil be intermixed. If mixed, it could result in costly compressor failure due to improper lubrication.*

Note 2: *Because of recent EPA regulations, 14-ounce cans of refrigerant may not be available in your area. If you choose to recharge the system yourself, purchase a 20-pound bulk drum of refrigerant, an air conditioning manifold gauge set and refer to the Haynes Automotive Heating and Air Conditioning Manual for recharging instructions.*

1   The following maintenance checks should be performed on a regular basis to ensure that the air conditioner continues to operate at peak efficiency.

12.7 Inspect the sight glass - if the refrigerant looks foamy, it's low

13.3 Unplug the electrical connector (1) and unbolt the mounting bracket (2)

15.5a Disconnect the refrigerant lines from the condenser - be sure to use a back up wrench to avoid bending the line (use a flare nut wrench on the fitting. if available)

a) *Check the compressor drivebelt. If it's worn or deteriorated, replace it (see Chapter 1).*
b) *Check the drivebelt tension and, if necessary, adjust it (see Chapter 1).*
c) *Check the system hoses. Look for cracks, bubbles, hard spots and deterioration. Inspect the hoses and all fittings for oil bubbles and seepage. If there's any evidence of wear, damage or leaks, replace the hose(s).*
d) *Inspect the condenser fins for leaves, bugs and other debris. Use a "fin comb" or compressed air to clean the condenser.*
e) *Make sure the system has the correct refrigerant charge.*

2   It's a good idea to operate the system for about 10 minutes at least once a month, particularly during the winter. Long term non-use can cause hardening, and subsequent failure, of the seals.

3   Because of the complexity of the air conditioning system and the special equipment necessary to service it, in-depth troubleshooting and repairs are not included in this manual. However, simple checks and component replacement procedures are provided in this Chapter. For more complete information on the air conditioning system, refer to the *Haynes Automotive Heating and Air Conditioning Manual.*

4   The most common cause of poor cooling is simply a low system refrigerant charge. If a noticeable drop in cool air output occurs, one of the following quick checks will help you determine if the refrigerant level is low.

Check

5   Warm the engine up to normal operating temperature.

6   Place the air conditioning temperature selector at the coldest setting and put the blower at the highest setting. Open the doors (to make sure the air conditioning system doesn't cycle off as soon as it cools the passenger compartment).

7   With the compressor engaged - the clutch will make an audible click and the center of the clutch will rotate - inspect the sight

glass, if equipped **(see illustration)**. If the refrigerant looks foamy, it's low. Have the air conditioning system charged by an automotive air conditioning specialist or dealer service department.

---

13   Air conditioning receiver/drier - removal and installation

Refer to illustration 13.3
Warning: *The air conditioning system is under high pressure. DO NOT disassemble any part of the system (hoses, compressor, line fittings, etc.) until after the system has been depressurized by a dealer service department or service station.*

1   Have the air conditioning system discharged (see **Warning** above).

2   Disconnect the negative battery cable from the battery.

3   Unplug the electrical connector from the pressure switch near the top of the receiver/drier **(see illustration)**.

4   Disconnect the refrigerant line from the receiver/drier. Use a back-up wrench to prevent twisting the tubing.

5   Plug the open fittings to prevent entry of dirt and moisture.

6   Loosen the mounting bracket bolts and lift the receiver/drier out.

7   If a new receiver/drier is being installed, remove the Schrader valve and pour the oil out into a measuring cup, noting the amount. Add fresh refrigerant oil to the new receiver/drier equal to the amount removed from the old unit plus one ounce.

8   Installation is the reverse of removal.

9   Take the vehicle back to the shop that discharged it. Have the air conditioning system evacuated, charged and leak tested.

---

14   Air conditioning compressor - removal and installation

Warning: *The air conditioning system is under high pressure. DO NOT disassemble any part of the system (hoses, compressor, line fittings, etc.) until after the system has been depressurized by a dealer service*

15.5b The lower fitting can be reached through the grille opening

department or service station.
Note: *The receiver/drier (see Section 13) should be replaced whenever the compressor is replaced.*

1   Have the air conditioning system discharged (see **Warning** above).

2   Disconnect the negative battery cable from the battery.

3   Disconnect the compressor clutch wiring harness.

4   Remove the drivebelt (see Chapter 1).

5   Disconnect the refrigerant lines from the rear of the compressor. Plug the open fittings to prevent entry of dirt and moisture.

6   Unbolt the compressor from the mounting brackets and lift it out of the vehicle.

7   If a new compressor is being installed, follow the directions with the compressor regarding the draining of excess oil prior to installation.

8   The clutch may have to be transferred from the original to the new compressor.

9   Installation is the reverse of removal. Replace all O-rings with new ones specifically made for air conditioning system use and lubricate them with refrigerant oil.

10   Have the system evacuated, recharged and leak tested by the shop that discharged it.

16.4 Remove the instrument panel mounting screws (typical)

16.5 Unplug the electrical connectors and the vacuum lines

15 Air conditioning condenser - removal and installation

Refer to illustrations 15.5a and 15.5b
Warning: *The air conditioning system is under high pressure. DO NOT disassemble any part of the system (hoses, compressor, line fittings, etc.) until after the system has been depressurized by a dealer service department or service station.*

1   Have the air conditioning system discharged (see **Warning** above).
2   Disconnect the negative battery cable from the battery (see Chapter 5).
3   Drain the cooling system (see Chapter 1).
4   Remove the radiator (see Section 4).
5   Disconnect the refrigerant lines from the condenser **(see illustrations)**.
6   Remove the mounting bolts from the condenser brackets.
7   Lift the condenser out of the vehicle and plug the lines to keep dirt and moisture out.
8   If the original condenser will be reinstalled, store it with the line fittings on top to prevent oil from draining out.

9   If a new condenser is being installed, pour one ounce of refrigerant oil into it prior to installation.
10   Reinstall the components in the reverse order of removal. Be sure the rubber pads are in place under the condenser.
11   Have the system evacuated, recharged and leak tested by the shop that discharged it.

16 Air conditioner and heater control assembly - removal and installation

Refer to illustrations 16.4, 16.5, 16.7 and 16.8
Warning: *Some models covered by this manual are equipped with airbags. Always disable the airbag system when working in the vicinity of airbag system components (see Chapter 12).*

1   Disconnect the negative cable from the battery.
2   Detach the instrument panel bezel (see Chapter 11).
3   Remove the radio (see Chapter 12).
4   On 1987 through 1995 models, remove

the mounting screws from the center section of the instrument panel **(see illustration)**. On 1997 and later models, remove the glove box and the center bezel (see Sections 22 and 24 in Chapter 11).
5   On 1987 through 1995 models, slide out the assembly and unplug the electrical connectors **(see illustration)**.
6   On 1997 and later models, remove the four control assembly mounting bolts, pull out the assembly slightly, reach through the glove box opening and disconnect the two halves of the heater/air conditioning vacuum harness connector.
7   On 1987 through 1995 models, release the control cable locking tab with a screwdriver **(see illustration)**.
8   On 1987 through 1995 models, detach the ring on the end of the control cable from the arm on the bottom of the control panel **(see illustration)**.
9   On 1997 and later models, pull out the heater/air conditioning assembly a little more and unplug the three electrical connectors from the backside of the assembly. Remove the heater/air conditioning assembly.
10   Installation is the reverse of removal.

16.7 Release the control cable locking tab with a screwdriver

16.8 Detach the ring on the end of the control cable

Notes

Chapter 4
Fuel and exhaust systems

Contents

Specifications

Fuel pressure (at idle)

TBI systems	14 to 15 psi
MPI systems	
1995 and earlier models	
Vacuum hose connected	31 psi
Vacuum hose disconnected	39 psi
1997 and later models	44 to 54 psi

Torque specifications

Ft-lbs (unless otherwise indicated)

Fuel pump (mechanical) mounting bolts	13 to 19
Carburetor-to-intake manifold mounting nuts	13 to 19
Throttle body mounting nuts	
TBI models	16
MPI models	108 in-lbs

1   General information

Warning: *Gasoline is extremely flammable, so take extra precautions when you work on any part of the fuel system. Don't smoke or allow open flames or bare light bulbs near the work area, and don't work in a garage where a gas-type appliance (such as a water heater or a clothes dryer) is present. Since gasoline is carcinogenic, wear latex gloves when there's a possibility of being exposed to fuel, and, if you spill any fuel on your skin, rinse it off immediately with soap and water. Mop up any spills immediately and do not store fuel-soaked rags where they could ignite. The fuel system is under constant pressure, so, if any fuel lines are to be disconnected, the fuel pressure in the system must be relieved first. When you perform any kind of work on the fuel system, wear safety glasses and have a Class B type fire extinguisher on hand.*

The fuel system consists of the fuel tank, the fuel pump, the fuel filter, an air cleaner assembly and a carburetor or fuel injection system.

The pre-1991 2.5L engine is equipped with throttle body injection (TBI). In 1991, the 2.5L engine became available with Multi Point Injection (MPI). The 2.4L four-cylinder engine is also equipped with multi-point fuel injection.

The 4.2L engine is equipped with a two-barrel model BBD feedback carburetor. Wranglers equipped with this engine were manufactured from 1987 through 1990.

Vehicles with a 4.0L engine are equipped with a Multi-point Injection (MPI) system. Wranglers equipped with this engine are manufactured from 1990 and later.

The fuel pumps of carbureted models use a mechanical pump driven by an eccentric lobe on the camshaft. Fuel injected engines use a gear/rotor type pump driven by

an electric motor. The mechanical pump is mounted on the engine block; electric pumps are installed inside the fuel tank. It should be noted that the electric pumps used with TBI and MPI systems are different and cannot be interchanged. For more information on the fuel feedback systems used on earlier models, refer to Chapter 6

Later models covered by this manual are equipped with a sequential Multi Port Fuel Injection (MPFI) system. This system uses timed impulses to sequentially inject the fuel directly into the intake ports of each cylinder. The injectors are controlled by the Powertrain Control Module (PCM). The PCM monitors various engine parameters and delivers the exact amount of fuel, in the correct sequence, into the intake ports.

The fuel filters on 1995 and later models are extended-life parts and are not replaced during normal scheduled maintenance. The filters will only be replaced when diagnostic

2.5 To relieve the fuel pressure on an MPI-equipped vehicle, remove the cap from the pressure test port, place some shop towels underneath to absorb sprayed fuel . . .

2.7 . . . then depress the valve in the test port with a small screwdriver or pin punch - wear safety goggles during pressure relief to protect your eyes from spraying fuel

3.10 The proper setup for the fuel pump pressure and capacity tests (if you don't have a hose restrictor, a pair of vise grips with padded jaws will work just as well)

testing requires it. The main fuel filter is mounted to the front of the fuel tank. An inlet fuel filter, electric fuel pump and pressure regulator are mounted inside the fuel tank. The fuel level sending unit is an integral component of the fuel pump and it must be removed from the fuel tank in the same manner. On vehicles that are not equipped with an access cover under the carpeting of the rear cargo area, it is necessary to lower the fuel tank for access to these fuel system components.

The exhaust system consists of exhaust manifold(s), a catalytic converter, an exhaust pipe and a muffler. Each of these components is replaceable. For further information regarding the catalytic converter, refer to Chapter 6.

2   Fuel pressure relief (fuel-injected vehicles)

Refer to illustrations 2.5 and 2.7
Warning: *Gasoline is extremely flammable, so take extra precautions when you work on any part of the fuel system. Don't smoke or allow open flames or bare light bulbs near the work area, and don't work in a garage where a gas-type appliance (such as a water heater or a clothes dryer) is present. Since gasoline is carcinogenic, wear latex gloves when there's a possibility of being exposed to fuel, and, if you spill any fuel on your skin, rinse it off immediately with soap and water. Mop up any spills immediately and do not store fuel-soaked rags where they could ignite. The fuel system is under constant pressure, so, if any fuel lines are to be disconnected, the fuel pressure in the system must be relieved first. When you perform any kind of work on the fuel system, wear safety glasses and have a Class B type fire extinguisher on hand.*
Note: *After the fuel pressure has been relieved, it's a good idea to lay a shop towel over any fuel connection to be disassembled, to absorb the residual fuel that may leak out when servicing the fuel system.*

TBI-equipped vehicles

1   The fuel system of vehicles equipped with Throttle Body Injection (TBI) is only under pressure when the fuel pump is operating. As long as the fuel pump is not operating (ignition key in the OFF position), TBI fuel system components can be removed without the need to release system pressure.

MPI-equipped vehicles

2   The MPI system is under a constant fuel pressure. Before attempting to service any fuel supply or return components on vehicles equipped with this system, release the fuel pressure.
3   Detach the cable from the negative battery terminal.
4   Remove the fuel tank filler cap to relieve fuel tank pressure.
5   Remove the cap from the pressure test port on the fuel rail **(see illustration)**.
6   Place shop towels under the pressure test port to absorb fuel when the pressure is released from the fuel rail.
7   Using a small screwdriver or pin punch, push the test port valve in to relieve fuel pressure **(see illustration)**. Absorb the spilled fuel with the shop towels.
8   Remove the shop towels.
9   Disconnect the cable from the negative terminal of the battery before performing any work on the fuel system.
10   Install the cap on the pressure test port.

3   Fuel pump/fuel pressure - check

Warning: *Gasoline is extremely flammable, so take extra precautions when you work on any part of the fuel system. See the* **Warning** *at the beginning of Section 2.*

Mechanical pump (4.2L carbureted engines)
Quick check
1   Detach the cable from the negative battery terminal.

2   Remove the air cleaner assembly (see Section 7).
3   Detach the fuel inlet fitting from the carburetor and place the end of the inlet line in a metal or plastic container.
4   Attach the cable to the negative battery terminal.
5   Hook up a remote starter switch, if available, in accordance with the manufacturer's instructions. If you don't have a remote starter switch, you will need an assistant for the following procedures.
6   Disable the ignition coil by detaching the primary lead wires (see Chapter 5).
7   With the fuel line directed into the container, have an assistant turn the ignition key to Start and crank the engine for about ten seconds.
8   Fuel should be emitted from the fuel line in well-defined spurts. If it isn't, there is a problem somewhere in the fuel delivery system. The following tests will determine where the problem lies.

Pressure test
Refer to illustration 3.10
Note: *You will need a fuel pressure gauge, a hose restrictor and a section of flexible hose to perform the following procedures.*
9   Detach the fuel return hose at the fuel filter (next to the carburetor) and plug the fitting on the filter.
10   Attach a pressure gauge, restrictor and flexible hose between the fuel inlet fitting or the fuel filter and the carburetor **(see illustration)**.
11   Position the flexible hose and restrictor so fuel can be discharged into a graduated container.
12   Reattach the coil primary lead wires (the engine must be operated for the following test).
13   Start the engine (or have your assistant start it), let it run at curb idle rpm, then discharge the fuel into the container by momentarily opening the hose restrictor.
14   Close the hose restrictor, allow the pressure to stabilize and note the pressure. The gauge should indicate 4-to-5 psi.

3.28 All system pressure tests on TBI-equipped vehicles require the removal of the pressure test port from the throttle body - in its place, install a special pressure test fitting (available at most auto parts stores)

3.31 If the TBI system fuel pressure indicated on the test gauge is incorrect, adjust it by turning the regulator adjusting screw - turn the screw in (clockwise) to increase pressure or out (counterclockwise) to decrease pressure

3.35 To test the MPI fuel system pressure, you will need to attach a 0-to-60 psi pressure gauge to the test port pressure fitting on the fuel rail

a) *If the pump pressure is not within specification, and the fuel lines are in satisfactory condition, the pump is defective and should be replaced.*

b) *If the pump pressure is within specifications, perform the following tests for capacity and vacuum.*

Capacity test

15 Operate the engine at curb idle rpm.

16 Open the hose restrictor and allow fuel to discharge into a graduated container for 30 seconds, then close the restrictor. At least one pint of fuel should have been discharged.

a) *If the pump volume is less than one pint, repeat the test with an auxiliary fuel supply and a replacement fuel filter.*

b) *If the pump volume conforms to the specified amount while using the auxiliary fuel supply, look for a restriction in the fuel supply line from the tank and check the tank vent to make sure it's working properly.*

Direct connection vacuum test

17 You will need a vacuum gauge to perform the direct connection vacuum test. In this test, the vacuum test gauge is connected directly to the fuel pump inlet to test the pump's ability to create a vacuum.

18 Detach the fuel inlet line at the fuel pump.

19 Attach a vacuum gauge to the fuel pump inlet.

20 Operate the engine at curb idle speed and note the vacuum gauge reading. It should indicate a vacuum of 10 in-Hg (the gauge will not indicate a vacuum until the fuel in the carburetor float bowl has been consumed and the pump begins to operate at full capacity).

21 If the pump vacuum is not within specification, the pump is defective. Replace it (see Section 4).

Indirect connection vacuum test

22 You will need a vacuum gauge and a T-fitting to perform the indirect connection vacuum test. In this test, a vacuum gauge is con-

nected by a T-fitting into the pump inlet to determine whether an obstruction exists in the fuel line or the in-tank fuel filter.

23 Detach the fuel inlet line at the fuel pump.

24 Install a T-fitting between the disconnected fitting and the fuel pump inlet. Connect a vacuum gauge to the T-fitting.

25 Operate the engine at a speed of 1500 rpm for 30 seconds and note the reading on the vacuum gauge (again, the gauge will not indicate any vacuum until the fuel in the carburetor float bowl has been consumed and the pump begins to operate at full capacity). The indicated vacuum should not exceed 3 in-Hg.

26 If the indicated vacuum exceeds the specified vacuum, check the fuel line for a restriction. A partially clogged in-tank fuel filter can also cause excess vacuum.

Electric pump (1995 and earlier fuel-injected engines)

TBI pressure test

Refer to illustrations 3.28 and 3.31

27 Detach the cable from the negative battery terminal.

28 Remove the pressure test port plug from the throttle body **(see illustration)**.

29 Install a pressure test fitting (available at a Jeep parts department) in place of the test port plug.

30 Attach a 0-to-30 psi fuel pressure gauge to the pressure test fitting (don't use a carburetor type 0-to-15 psi gauge).

31 Start the engine and let it idle. The pressure gauge should read 14-to-15 psi. If the pressure is incorrect, adjust it by turning the regulator adjusting screw **(see illustration)** to obtain the correct fuel pressure. Turn the screw at the bottom of the regulator in (clockwise) to increase pressure or out (counterclockwise) to decrease pressure.

32 If the fuel pressure is considerably higher than specified, and adjusting the regulator fails to lower it to the specified level, inspect the fuel return line for blockage.

33 If the fuel pressure is considerably

below specification and adjusting the regulator fails to raise it to the specified level, momentarily pinch off the fuel return line and recheck the pressure.

a) *If the fuel pressure has risen, replace the pressure regulator (see Section 15).*

b) *If the pressure has not risen, check the fuel filter (see Chapter 1) and fuel supply line for blockage. If they're OK, the fuel pump is probably faulty.*

MPI pressure test

Refer to illustrations 3.35, 3.36 and 3.41

34 The MPI fuel system employs a vacuum-assisted pressure regulator. Fuel pressure should be about 8 to 10 psi higher with the vacuum line attached to the regulator than with the vacuum line disconnected. Fuel system pressure should be 31 psi with the vacuum line attached to the regulator and 39 psi with the line detached.

35 Attach a 0-to-60 psi fuel pressure gauge to the test port pressure fitting on the fuel rail **(see illustration)**.

36 Detach and plug the vacuum tube from the fuel pressure regulator **(see illustration)**.

37 Start the engine.

3.36 Detach he vacuum tube from the fuel pressure regulator, start the vehicle and note the gauge reading - with the vacuum line detached, fuel pressure should be about 30 psi

3.41 If the fuel is below the specified level, momentarily pinch off the hose section of the fuel return line - fuel pressure will rise to 95 psi when the fuel return line is pinched, so turn the engine off immediately after pinching off the fuel return line

38 Note the gauge reading. With the vacuum line detached, fuel pressure should be about 39 psi.
39 Attach the vacuum line to the pressure regulator. Note the gauge reading. Fuel pressure should be about 31 psi.
40 If the indicated fuel pressure is not about 8-to-10 psi higher with the vacuum line removed from the regulator, inspect the pressure regulator vacuum line for leaks, kinks and blockage.
41 If the fuel pressure is below the specified level, momentarily pinch off the hose section of the return line **(see illustration)**. The fuel pressure will rise to 95 psi when the fuel return line is pinched shut, so turn off the engine immediately after pinching off the fuel return line.

a) *If the fuel pressure remains below specifications, inspect the fuel supply line, fuel filter (see Chapter 1) and fuel rail inlet (see Section 14) for blockage.*
b) *If the fuel pressure rises, replace the regulator.*
c) *If the fuel pressure is above specification, inspect the fuel return line for kinks and blockage.*

MPI fuel pressure leak-down test

42 If an abnormally long cranking period is required to restart a hot engine after the vehicle has been shut down for a short period of time, the fuel pressure may be leaking past the fuel pressure regulator or the check valve in the outlet end of the fuel pump.
43 With the engine off, attach a gauge capable of reading 0-to-100 psi to the pressure test port fitting on the fuel rail.
44 Start the vehicle and let the engine idle. Check the fuel pressure reading on the gauge. The fuel pressure should be within the specifications noted above.
45 Shut the engine off. Note the fuel pressure reading on the gauge. Leave the fuel

pressure gauge connected. Allow the engine to sit for 30 minutes, then compare the fuel pressure reading on the gauge to the reading you took when you shut down the engine. A drop of 0-to-20 psi (to the 19-to-39 psi range) is acceptable. If the fuel pressure drop is within specification, the fuel pump outlet check valve and the fuel pressure regulator are both operating normally. If the fuel pressure drop is greater than 20 psi, restart the vehicle, let the engine idle and momentarily pinch off the hose section of the fuel return line. The fuel pressure will rise to 95 psi when the fuel return line is pinched off, so shut the engine down immediately after pinching off the fuel return line. Note the pressure reading on the gauge. Allow the engine to sit for 30 minutes. Take another reading and compare it to the reading you took when you first shut down the engine.

a) *If the fuel pressure has dropped about 20 psi, replace the fuel pressure regulator.*
b) *If the fuel pressure has dropped considerably more than 20 psi, fuel pressure is bleeding off past the outlet check valve in the fuel pump. Replace the pump.*

Capacity test

46 Remove the cap from the pressure test port in the fuel rail **(see illustration 2.5)**.
47 Attach a 0-to-60 psi fuel pressure gauge to the pressure fitting.
48 Start the engine. Pressure should be about 31 psi with the vacuum hose attached to the pressure regulator and 39 psi with the vacuum hose removed from the pressure regulator **(see illustration 3.36)**. If the pressure is not within specifications, one of the following problems exists:

a) *There is a kink or other restriction in a fuel supply or return line hose. Inspect the lines and hoses.*
b) *The fuel pump flow rate is not sufficient. Take the vehicle to a dealer service department for proper checking of the fuel pump flow rate.*
c) *The fuel pressure regulator is malfunctioning. Take the vehicle to a dealer service department for proper checking (See Section 16 to replace the regulator).*

Electric pump (1997 and later models)

Refer to illustration 3.50
Note: *In order to perform the fuel pressure test, you will need a fuel pressure gauge capable of measuring high fuel pressure. The fuel gauge must be equipped with the proper fittings or adapters required to attach it to the fuel rail.*
49 Relieve the fuel pressure (see Section 2).
50 Remove the cap from the fuel pressure test port (if equipped) on the fuel rail and attach a fuel pressure gauge **(see illustration)**. **Note:** *A special adapter with a T-fitting will be required to perform the leakdown test described in Step 54.*
51 Start the engine and check the pressure on the gauge, comparing your reading with

3.50 A special adapter hose with a T-fitting will be required for the fuel pressure checks

the pressure listed in this Chapter's Specifications.
52 If the fuel pressure is lower than specified, check the fuel lines and the fuel filter for restrictions. If no restriction is found, replace the fuel pump (see Section 4).
53 If fuel pressure is higher than specified, replace the fuel pressure regulator/fuel filter (see Section 16).
54 If the fuel pressure is within specifications, turn the engine off and monitor the fuel pressure for five minutes. The fuel pressure should not drop below 30 psi within five minutes. If it does, there is a leak in the fuel line, a fuel injector is leaking or the fuel pump module check valve is defective. To determine the problem area, perform the following:
Note: *A special fuel gauge adapter hose is required for the following tests, the fuel pressure gauge must be connected to the T-fitting* **(see illustration 3.50)**.
55 Install the adapter hose, then turn on the ignition key to power-up the fuel system. Clamp off the adapter hose between the T-fitting and the line to the fuel pump, then turn the ignition key off. If the pressure drops below 30 psi within five minutes, a fuel injector (or injectors) is leaking (or the fuel rail may be leaking, but such a leak would be very apparent).
56 With the adapter hose installed, clamp off the adapter hose between the T-fitting and the fuel rail. Turn the ignition key on to energize the fuel pump, then turn the key off. If the pressure drops below 30 psi within five minutes, the fuel line is leaking, the check valve in the fuel pressure regulator is defective or the fuel pump is defective.

a) *Check the entire length of the fuel line for leaks.*
b) *If no leaks are found in the fuel line and the pressure dropped quickly, replace the fuel pressure regulator/fuel filter.*
c) *If no leaks are found in the fuel line and the pressure dropped slowly, replace the fuel pump.*

4.13 Once the fuel tank is lowered from the chassis, detach the electrical connector from the fuel pump harness

4.15a To loosen the lock ring for the fuel pump/sending unit assembly, turn it counterclockwise (1995 and earlier models)

4.15b On vehicles equipped with a 20-gallon tank, the fuel pump/sending unit assembly is mounted with screws (1995 and earlier models)

4 Fuel pump - removal and installation

Warning: *Gasoline is extremely flammable, so take extra precautions when you work on any part of the fuel system. See the* **Warning** *at the beginning of Section 2.*

Mechanical pump

1   Detach the cable from the negative battery terminal.

2   Remove the fuel tank filler cap to relieve fuel pressure.

3   Wrap shop towels around the fuel pump inlet hose and outlet line fitting to absorb any fuel spilled during fuel pump removal.

4   Detach the fuel inlet hose and outlet line fitting from the fuel pump.

5   Unscrew the fuel pump mounting bolts and remove the fuel pump and gasket.

6   Carefully scrape away any old gasket material from the fuel pump and engine block sealing surfaces.

7   Installation is the reverse of removal. Be sure to use a new gasket and tighten the fuel pump bolts to the torque listed in this Chapter's Specifications.

Electric pump

Removal

Refer to illustrations 4.13, 4.15a, 4.15b, 4.15c, 4.16, 4.20a, 4.20b and 4.29

Note: *The following procedure requires removal of the fuel tank.*

8   Relieve the fuel system pressure (see Section 2).

9   Detach the cable from the negative battery terminal.

10   Raise the vehicle and place it securely on jackstands.

11   Remove the fuel tank (see Section 5).

12   Disconnect the fuel vent, supply and return hoses from the fittings on the fuel pump/sending unit **(see illustrations 4.20a and 4.20b)**.

13   Detach the fuel pump/sending unit electrical harness connector from the main harness **(see illustration)**.

14   The fuel pump/sending unit assembly is located inside the fuel tank. It's held in place by a cam lock ring mechanism consisting of an inner ring with three locking cams and an outer ring with three retaining tangs (1995 and earlier models) or a large plastic locknut (1997and later models).

15   To unlock the fuel pump/sending unit assembly on 1995 and earlier models, turn the inner ring counterclockwise until the locking cams are free of the retaining tangs. If the rings are locked together too tightly to release them by hand, gently knock them loose with a wood dowel or a brass punch and hammer **(see illustration)**. **Warning:** *Do not use a steel punch to knock the lockrings loose. A spark could cause an explosion!* **Note:** *On vehicles equipped with the 20-gallon fuel tank, remove the mounting screws and then lift the fuel pump/sending unit assembly from the tank* **(see illustration)***. On 1997 and later models, use a hammer and punch to turn the lockring counterclockwise until it can be unscrewed by hand* **(see illustration)***.*

16   Extract the fuel pump/sending unit assembly from the fuel tank. The fuel level float and sending unit are delicate **(see illustration)**. Do not bump them during removal or the accuracy of the sending unit may be affected.

17   Inspect the condition of the gasket (O-ring) around the mouth of the lockring mechanism. If it's dried, cracked or deformed, replace it.

18   Inspect the inside of the tank. Have it cleaned by a radiator shop if sediment is present.

4.15c Fuel tank and fuel pump details - 1997 and later models

FUEL SUPPLY TUBE
FRONT
RETAINER CLAMP
FUEL FILTER/ FUEL PRESSURE REGULATOR
FUEL PUMP MODULE
LOCKNUT
ROLLOVER VALVE
ROLLOVER VALVE
ELECTRICAL CONNECTOR
TOP OF FUEL TANK

4.16 Carefully remove the fuel pump/sending unit assembly from the fuel tank

4.20a The TBI fuel pump/sending unit assembly

4.20b The MPI fuel pump/sending unit assembly

4.29 Fuel pump/gauge sender unit installation

19   If you are replacing the fuel pump, make sure you get the right pump. The TBI and MPI pumps look alike, but they're NOT interchangeable.

Disassembly (1995 and earlier models only)

Note: *On 1997 and later models the fuel pump is not serviceable. In the event of failure, the complete assembly must be replaced.*

20   Remove and discard the fuel pump inlet filter **(see illustrations)**.
21   Detach the fuel pump wires (the wire ends are different sizes and cannot be connected to the wrong terminal).
22   Detach the fuel pump outlet hose and clamp. Replace the hose if it shows signs of wear or deterioration.
23   Remove the fuel pump top mounting bracket nut. Remove the fuel pump.

Reassembly

24   Install a new inlet filter.
25   Place the fuel pump top mounting bracket over the top of the pump.
26   Position the fuel pump in the lower bracket. Slide the stud of the top bracket through the hole in the fuel pump side bracket. Tighten the fuel pump top mounting nut.
27   Install the fuel pump outlet hose. Secure it with new clamps.
28   Connect the wire terminals to the motor.

Installation

29   Insert the fuel pump/sending unit assembly into the fuel tank. **Note:** *On some models it is necessary to align the stopper (mounted on the fuel pump/sending unit assembly) with the cup located in the bottom of the fuel tank* **(see illustration)**.
30   On 1995 and earlier models, turn the inner lock ring clockwise until the locking cams are fully engaged by the retaining tangs. If you have installed a new O-ring type rubber gasket, it may be necessary to push down on the inner lock ring until the locking cams slide under the retaining tangs. On 1997 and later models, tighten the locknut securely.
31   Install the fuel tank.

5   Fuel tank - removal and installation

Refer to illustrations 5.6a, 5.6b, 5.6c, 5.9a and 5.9b

Note: *The following procedure is much easier to perform if the fuel tank is empty. Run the engine until the tank is empty.*

Warning: *Gasoline is extremely flammable, so take extra precautions when you work on any part of the fuel system. See the* Warning *at the beginning of Section 2.*

1   Remove the fuel tank filler cap to relieve fuel tank pressure.
2   If the vehicle is fuel-injected, relieve the fuel system pressure (see Section 2).
3   Detach the cable from the negative terminal of the battery.
4   If the tank still has fuel in it, you can drain it at the fuel supply line after raising the vehicle.
5   Raise the vehicle and place it securely on jackstands.
6   Disconnect all hoses **(see illustrations)** and the electrical connector for the fuel gauge sending unit and electric fuel pump (if equipped) (see Section 4). Carefully label all hoses so you can reinstall them in their original locations. **Note:** *On some models it may be necessary to remove the fuel filler neck shroud* **(see illustration)** *from the left rear wheel well in order to access the supply hose. Pull back the stem of the push clips and remove the shroud.*
7   Siphon the fuel from the tank at the fuel feed line, not the return line.
8   Support the fuel tank with a floor jack or jackstands. Position a piece of wood between the jack head and the fuel tank to protect the tank.
9   Remove the nuts from the flanges of the

5.6a Remove the vent lines from the side of the fuel tank

5.6b Remove the fuel supply line (A) and the vent hose (B) from the side of the fuel tank

5.6c Pull the push clips OUT to separate the shroud from the chassis

5.9a Remove the fuel tank mounting nuts on the front section and . . .

5.9b . . . remove the nuts from the rear section of the fuel tank

fuel tank **(see illustrations)** and carefully lower the tank down until it is clear. **Note:** *Do not loosen the nuts from the tank straps.*
10   Remove the tank from the vehicle.
11   Installation is the reverse of removal.

6   Fuel tank cleaning and repair - general information

1   All repairs to the fuel tank or filler neck should be carried out by a professional who has experience in this critical and potentially dangerous work. Even after cleaning and flushing of the fuel system, explosive fumes can remain and ignite during repair of the tank.
2   If the fuel tank is removed from the vehicle, it should not be placed in an area where sparks or open flames could ignite the fumes coming out of the tank. Be especially careful inside garages where a gas type appliance is located, because it could cause an explosion.

7   Air cleaner - removal and installation

2.5L engine

Refer to illustrations 7.3, 7.5 and 7.6
1   Detach the cable from the negative terminal of the battery.

2   Remove the air filter from the housing (see Chapter 1). Inspect the element for contamination by dirt and moisture. Replace it if necessary.
3   Lift up on the clips **(see illustration)** that hold the air intake assembly to the throttle body or remove the band clamp.
4   Remove the clamp that retains the air intake assembly to the housing and lift the air intake tube from the engine compartment.
5   Remove the nut from the bottom of the air cleaner housing **(see illustration)** and partially lift the air cleaner housing up.
6   Detach the warm air hose **(see illustration)** from the bottom of the housing.

7.3 Use a small screwdriver and remove the clips from the air intake cover

7   Label and remove any vacuum hoses from the air cleaner housing.
8   Remove the air cleaner housing assembly.
9   Installation is the reverse of removal.

4.0L engine

Refer to illustrations 7.11a and 7.11b
10   Detach the cable from the negative battery terminal.
11   Loosen the hose clamp at one end and remove the three attaching screws at the other end of the flexible air duct between the air cleaner housing and the throttle body **(see illustrations)**. Remove the duct.

7.5 Remove the mounting bolt located in the lower section of the housing

7.6 The warm air hose is located under the air cleaner housing

7.11a To remove the flexible air duct on a 4.0L MPI engine, loosen the hose clamp at one end (arrow) and remove the three attaching screws (arrows) from the other end - the third attaching screw is hidden by the duct in this photo

7.11b Exploded view of the air cleaner assembly on a 4.0L MPI engine

12   Clearly label, then detach, all vacuum hoses from the air cleaner housing.
13   Detach the heat riser tube from the air cleaner housing.
14   Remove the upper half of the air cleaner housing lid, then remove the air filter element (see Chapter 1).
15   Remove the two bolts and one nut from the floor of the air cleaner housing. Remove the housing.
16   Installation is the reverse of removal.

4.2L engine

Refer to illustration 7.18

17   Detach the cable from the negative terminal of the battery.
18   Detach the flexible ambient air duct from the air cleaner housing snorkel **(see illustration)**.
19   Remove the wing nut from the cover and remove the cover and filter element. Inspect the element for contamination by dirt and moisture. Replace it if necessary (see Chapter 1).
20   Clearly label, then detach, all hoses from the air cleaner housing.
21   Remove the air cleaner housing assembly.
22   Installation is the reverse of removal.

8   Accelerator cable - replacement

Refer to illustrations 8.1, 8.2, 8.3 and 8.4

1   Working inside the engine compartment, carefully pry the cable end from the throttle valve pivoting ball **(see illustration)** with a screwdriver.
2   Depress the cable-to-bracket fitting with a pair of pliers **(see illustration)** and then pull the cable through the bracket from the other side.
3   Working inside of the driver's compartment below the dash area, depress the throt-

7.18 Air cleaner assembly components - exploded view (4.2L engine)

1   Air cleaner cover
2   PCV valve filter
3   Thermal switch
4   Check valve
5   Vacuum motor
6   Heated air tube
7   Ambient air duct
8   Reverse delay valve
9   Trap door assembly
10   Reverse delay valve
11   Thermal vacuum switch
12   Filter element

tle pedal and remove the cable stop through the larger opening **(see illustration)**.
4   Remove the cable from the engine compartment. **Note:** *If the cable is equipped with a plastic retainer in the firewall* **(see illustration)**, *squeeze the tang with a pair of pliers and push the retainer through the opening.*
5   Installation is the reverse of removal.

9   Carburetor - adjustments

1   The carburetors used on the vehicles covered by this manual are protected by a Federally-mandated extended warranty (at the time this manual was written, the warranty was for 5 years/50,000 miles, whichever comes first - see your dealer for details).
2   We don't recommend carburetor adjustments while it's still under warranty. If you are having problems related to fuel delivery - and you have eliminated all other parts of the fuel delivery system as possible causes - take the vehicle to a dealer and have the carburetor professionally serviced.
3   Unless you really know what you're doing, we don't recommend you attempt to adjust an out-of-warranty carburetor either.

The carburetors on these vehicles are expensive, complex and tricky to adjust. The adjustments are also totally interrelated, so it's impossible to do certain adjustments unless you have already done several others. Finally, by the time adjustments become necessary, the carburetor will probably be approaching the end of its service life and will be impossible to adjust to a like-new state of tune. At this point, you're better off buying a rebuilt or new carburetor.

10   Carburetor - removal and installation

Warning: *Gasoline is extremely flammable, so take extra precautions when you work on any part of the fuel system. See the Warning at the beginning of Section 2.*

Removal

Refer to illustration 10.9

1   Detach the cable from the negative battery terminal.
2   Remove the fuel filler cap to relieve fuel tank pressure.

8.1 Use a small screwdriver to pry the cable end off the throttle valve (TBI engine shown)

8.2 The cable is retained by a plastic tang. Use a pair of pliers and first squeeze the tang and then push the cable through the bracket (TBI engine shown)

8.3 First pull the cable stop out and then lift it up and through the opening in the pedal assembly (TBI engine shown)

3   Remove the air cleaner from the carburetor. Be sure to label all vacuum hoses attached to the air cleaner housing.

4   Disconnect the throttle cable from the throttle lever.

5   If the vehicle is equipped with an automatic transmission, disconnect the TV cable from the throttle lever (see Chapter 7, Part B).

6   Clearly label all vacuum hoses and fittings, then disconnect the hoses.

7   Disconnect the fuel line from the carburetor.

8   Label the wires and terminals, then unplug all wire harness connectors.

9   Remove the mounting fasteners **(see illustration)** and detach the carburetor from the intake manifold. Remove the carburetor mounting gasket. Stuff a shop rag into the intake manifold openings.

Installation

10   Use a gasket scraper to remove all traces of gasket material and sealant from the intake manifold (and the carburetor, if it's being reinstalled), then remove the shop rag from the manifold openings. Clean the mating surfaces with lacquer thinner or acetone.

11   Place a new gasket on the intake manifold.

8.4 Squeeze the tang (arrow) with a pair of pliers and push the retainer through the opening

12   Position the carburetor on the gasket and install the mounting fasteners.

13   To prevent carburetor distortion or damage, tighten the fasteners to the torque listed in this Chapter's Specifications in a crisscross pattern, 1/4-turn at a time.

14   The remaining installation steps are the reverse of removal.

15   Check and, if necessary, adjust the idle speed (see Chapter 1).

16   If the vehicle is equipped with an automatic transmission, refer to Chapter 7, Part B for the TV cable adjustment procedure.

17   Attach the negative battery cable.

18   Start the engine and check carefully for fuel leaks.

11 Carburetor - diagnosis and overhaul

Refer to illustration 11.8

Warning: *Gasoline is extremely flammable, so take extra precautions when you work on any part of the fuel system. See the* **Warning** *at the beginning of Section 2.*

10.9 Remove the four mounting nuts from the base of the carburetor

Diagnosis

1   A thorough road test and check of carburetor adjustments should be done before any major carburetor service work. Specifications for some adjustments are listed on the Vehicle Emissions Control Information (VECI) label found in the engine compartment.

2   Carburetor problems usually show up as flooding, hard starting, stalling, severe backfiring and poor acceleration. A carburetor that's leaking fuel and/or covered with wet looking deposits definitely needs attention.

3   Some performance complaints directed at the carburetor are actually a result of loose, out-of-adjustment or malfunctioning engine or electrical components. Others develop when vacuum hoses leak, are disconnected or are incorrectly routed. The proper approach to analyzing carburetor problems should include the following items:

a)   *Inspect all vacuum hoses and actuators for leaks and correct installation (see Chapters 1 and 6).*

b)   *Tighten the intake manifold and carburetor mounting nuts/bolts evenly and securely.*

c)   *Perform a cylinder compression test (see Chapter 2).*

d)   *Clean or replace the spark plugs as necessary (see Chapter 1).*

e)   *Check the spark plug wires (see Chapter 1).*

f)   *Inspect the ignition primary wires.*

g)   *Check the ignition timing (follow the instructions printed on the Emissions Control Information label).*

h)   *Check the fuel pump and fuel pressure (see Section 3).*

i)   *Check the heat control valve in the air cleaner for proper operation (see Chapter 1).*

j)   *Check/replace the air filter element (see Chapter 1).*

k)   *Check the crankcase ventilation system (see Chapter 6).*

l)   *Check/replace the fuel filter (see Chapter 1). Also, the filter in the tank could be restricted.*

m)   *Check for a plugged exhaust system.*

11.8 Exploded view of the model BBD carburetor

1   Rollover check valve and bowl vent
2   Lock
3   Dashpot
4   Solenoid and bracket
5   Cluster screw
6   Idle fuel pick-up tube
7   Gasket
8   Venturi cluster
9   Gasket
10 Check ball (small)
11 Stepper motor (actuator)
12 Clip
13 Screw
14 Fast idle cam
15 Choke link
16 Gasket
17 Screw
18 Pump link
19 Throttle body
20 Flange gasket
21 Idle mixture screw
22 Choke housing
23 Baffle
24 Gasket
25 Choke coil
26 Retainer
27 Lever
28 Wide open throttle switch and bracket
29 Needle and seat assembly
30   Main body
31 Main metering jet
32 Pin
33 Baffle
34 Fulcrum retainer
35 Float
36 Spring and accelerator pump plunger
37 Air horn
38 Accelerator pump lever
39 Choke vacuum diaphragm
40 Hose
41 Metering rod
42 Vacuum piston
43 Pump arm
44 Rod lifter
45 Gasket
46 Spring
47 S-link

n) *Check EGR valve operation (see Chapter 6).*
o) *Check the choke-it should be completely open at normal engine operating temperature (see Chapter 1).*
p) *Check for fuel leaks and kinked or dented fuel lines (see Chapters 1 and 4).*
q) *Check accelerator pump operation with the engine off (remove the air cleaner cover and operate the throttle as you look into the carburetor throat - you should see a stream of gasoline enter the carburetor).*
r) *Check for incorrect fuel or bad gasoline.*
s) *Have a dealer service department or repair shop check the electronic engine and carburetor controls.*

4   Diagnosing carburetor problems may require that the engine be started and run with the air cleaner off. While running the engine without the air cleaner, backfires are possible. This situation is likely to occur if the carburetor is malfunctioning, but just the removal of the air cleaner can lean the fuel/air mixture enough to produce an engine backfire. **Warning:** *Do not position any part of your body, especially your face, directly over the carburetor during inspection and servicing procedures. Wear eye protection!*

Overhaul

5   Once it's determined that the carburetor needs an overhaul, several options are available. If you're going to attempt to overhaul the carburetor yourself, first obtain a good quality carburetor rebuild kit (which will include all necessary gaskets, internal parts, instructions and a parts list). You'll also need some special sol-

vent and a means of blowing out the internal passages of the carburetor with air.

6   An alternative is to obtain a new or rebuilt carburetor. They are readily available from dealers and auto parts stores. Make absolutely sure the exchange carburetor is identical to the original. A tag is usually attached to the top of the carburetor or a number is stamped on the float bowl. It will help determine the exact type of carburetor you have. When obtaining a rebuilt carburetor or a rebuild kit, make sure the kit or carburetor matches your application exactly. Seemingly insignificant differences can make a large difference in engine performance.

7   If you choose to overhaul your own carburetor, allow enough time to disassemble it carefully, soak the necessary parts in the cleaning solvent (usually for at least one-half

13.6 When attaching a section of rubber fuel hose to a metal fuel line, be sure to overlap the hose as shown and secure it to the line with a new hose clamp of the proper type

13.9a Typical under body quick-connect fittings (TBI-equipped vehicle)

13.9b Quick-connect fitting locations (MPI-equipped vehicle)

day or according to the instructions listed on the carburetor cleaner) and reassemble it, which will usually take much longer than disassembly. When disassembling the carburetor, match each part with the illustration in the carburetor kit and lay the parts out in order on a clean work surface. Overhauls by inexperienced mechanics can result in an engine which runs poorly or not at all. To avoid this, use care and patience when disassembling the carburetor so you can reassemble it correctly.

8   Because carburetor designs are constantly modified by the manufacturer in order to meet increasingly more stringent emissions regulations, it isn't feasible to include a step-by-step overhaul of each type. You'll receive a detailed, well illustrated set of instructions with any carburetor overhaul kit; they will apply in a more specific manner to the carburetor on your vehicle. An exploded view of the carburetor is included here **(see illustration)**.

12 Fuel injection system - general information

Fuel-injected vehicles are equipped with either a Throttle Body Injection (TBI) system (2.5L engine) or a Multi-Point Injection (MPI) system (1991 and later 2.5L and all 4.0L engines). Both systems use an Electronic Control Unit (ECU) to control pulse width.

The pulse width is the period of time during which the injector is energized (squirts fuel). The Electronic Control Unit (ECU), opens and closes the injector's ground path to control fuel injector pulse width and thus meter the amount of fuel available to the engine. By continually altering the pulse width, the ECU adjusts the air-fuel ratio for varying operating conditions. For more information about the ECU, see Chapter 6.

Throttle body injection (TBI) is a single-point system that injects fuel through one electrically operated fuel injector into the throttle body above the throttle plate.

Multi-Point Injection (MPI) is a multi-injector, sequential system: Fuel is injected

into the intake manifold upstream of each intake valve in precisely metered amounts through electrically operated injectors. The injectors are energized in a specific sequence by the Electronic Control Unit (ECU). There is no injector in the throttle body itself, as in a TBI system; the injectors are installed in the intake manifold. They receive pressurized fuel from a fuel rail attached to their upper ends.

System fuel pressure on both systems is provided by an in-tank electric fuel pump and is controlled by a fuel pressure regulator.

13 Fuel lines and fittings - inspection and replacement

Warning: *Gasoline is extremely flammable, so take extra precautions when you work on any part of the fuel system. See the* Warning *at the beginning of Section 2.*

Inspection and replacement

Refer to illustration 13.6

1   Check the fuel lines and all fittings and connections for cracks, leakage and deformation.
2   Check the fuel tank vapor vent system hoses and connections for looseness, sharp bends and damage.
3   Check the fuel tank for deformation, cracks, fuel leakage and tank band looseness.
4   Check the filler neck for damage and fuel leakage.
5   Repair or replace any damaged or deteriorated hoses or lines. If your vehicle is equipped with fuel injection, see below for information on replacing fuel line fittings.
6   When attaching hoses to metal lines, overlap them as shown **(see illustration)**.

Two-tab type fuel line fitting replacement (fuel-injected vehicles)

Refer to illustrations 13.9a, 13.9b, 13.10, 13.13 and 13.14

7   Remove the fuel tank filler cap to relieve fuel tank pressure.
8   If the vehicle is equipped with Multi Point Injection (MPI), relieve the system pres-

sure before proceeding (see Section 2). If the vehicle is equipped with Throttle Body Injection (TBI), system pressure is bled off when the fuel pump is not operating - you can disconnect fuel hoses and lines as soon as you have turned off the engine.
9   All fuel injected engines use special quick-connect fuel line fittings. On TBI-equipped vehicles, the fittings are located at the throttle body ends of the nylon reinforced hoses which connect the throttle body to the fuel supply and return lines and under the vehicle along the left frame rail **(see illustration)**. On MPI-equipped engines, they're located at the fuel rail inlet port and at the connection between the fuel return line and the fuel return hose **(see illustration)**.
10   The fittings consist of two O-rings, a spacer between the two O-rings and a retainer **(see illustration)**.
11   Every time you disconnect a quick-connect fitting, you must replace the O-rings, spacer and retainer. These parts are available as a repair kit through any dealer parts department.
12   To disconnect a quick connect fitting, simply pinch the two retainer tabs together and pull the fitting apart. The retainer, O-rings and spacer will come out of the fitting when you pull the fuel lines apart. Discard these parts.
13   The replacement kit (O-rings, spacer and retainer) is installed on a disposable

13.10 Cutaway of quick-connect fitting showing relationship of O-rings, spacer and retainer

13.13 The new O-rings, spacer and retainer are already installed on a disposable plug - to install them in the quick-connect fitting, insert the plug into the fitting until you hear a click, then withdraw and discard the plug

plastic plug. To replace these parts, push the disposable plug assembly into the quick connect fitting until you hear a "click" sound **(see illustration)**. Then grasp the end of the disposable plug and pull it out of the fitting.

14 Push the fuel line into the refurbished quick-connect fitting until you hear a "click" sound **(see illustration)**.

15 Verify that the connection is secure by pulling firmly back on the fuel line. It should be locked in place.

Single-tab type fuel line fitting replacement (fuel-injected models)

Refer to illustrations 13.18a and 13.18b

Caution: *Do not try to repair damaged fittings or fuel lines. If repair is necessary, replace the complete fuel line quick-connect fitting assembly.*

16 Relieve the system pressure before proceeding (see Section 2).

17 The fittings consist of O-rings, spacers and a pull tab. The O-rings and spacers can't be serviced separately, but new pull tabs are available and must be used.

18 To disconnect the fitting, simply press the release tab on the side of the fitting, use a screwdriver to pry up the pull tab and pull the

13.14 Once you've installed the new O-rings, spacer and retainer, push the fuel line into the fitting until you hear a click

fitting apart **(see illustrations)**. Discard the old pull tab.

19 Apply a light coat of clean engine oil to the inner surface of the fitting.

20 Insert the quick-connect fitting into the fuel line until the built-in stop on the fuel line rests on the back of the fitting.

21 Push the new pull tab down until it locks into place in the quick-connect fitting.

22 Verify the connection is secure by pulling firmly back on the fuel line. It should be locked in place. Run the engine and check for fuel leaks.

Plastic retainer ring type fuel line fitting replacement (fuel-injected models)

Refer to illustration 13.25

Caution: *Do not try to repair damaged fittings or fuel lines. If repair is necessary, replace the complete fuel line quick-connect fitting assembly.*

23 Relieve the system pressure before proceeding (see Section2).

24 The fittings consist of O-rings, spacers and a plastic retainer. The O-rings and spacers can't be serviced separately.

25 To disconnect a quick-connect fitting, simply push the fitting toward the component being serviced while pushing the plastic retaining ring squarely into the fitting **(see illustration)**. While the plastic retaining ring is

depressed, pull the fitting from the component.

26 Apply a light coat of clean engine oil to the inner surface of the fitting.

27 Insert the quick-connect fitting into the fuel line until you hear a "click" sound.

28 Verify the connection is secure by pulling firmly back on the fuel line. It should be locked in place. Run the engine and check for fuel leaks.

14   Throttle body (TBI-equipped vehicles) - removal and installation

Refer to illustrations 14.3a, 14.3b, 14.4, 14.5 and 14.8

Warning: *Gasoline is extremely flammable, so take extra precautions when you work on any part of the fuel system. See the Warning at the beginning of Section 2.*

1 Detach the cable from the negative battery terminal.

2 Detach the vacuum hoses from the throttle body upper bonnet. Release the mounting clips and remove the upper bonnet.

3 Remove the three mounting nuts and lift off the lower bonnet **(see illustrations)**.

4 Disconnect the ISA motor harness connector **(see illustration)**.

5 Detach the fuel supply and return lines **(see illustration)** from the throttle body.

6 Remove the accelerator cable and return spring (see Section 8).

7 Detach the wire harness connector from the injector by compressing the lock tabs and lifting up.

8 Identify and label the vacuum tubes at the back of the throttle body so you can install them in their original locations. Detach the vacuum tubes from the throttle body **(see illustration)**.

9 Detach the TPS connector (two connectors on automatics).

10 Remove the throttle body mounting nuts and remove the throttle body.

11 Remove any old gasket material or dirt

13.25 On models with plastic retainer rings, press the ring squarely into the fitting body, making sure the ring doesn't get cocked and, if necessary, use an open-end wrench on the plastic retaining ring shoulder to help pull the fitting free

13.18a On single-tab fittings, use your fingers to press the release tabs on the sides of the fitting . . .

13.18b . . . then, while pressing the tabs, pry up the pull tab with a screwdriver, then pull the fitting apart

14.3a Remove the mounting nuts, then detach the lower bonnet and . . .

14.3b . . . remove the gasket from the rim of the throttle body

14.4 Disconnect the ISA motor connector from the throttle body

from the mating surfaces of the intake manifold and the throttle body.

12   If you are replacing the throttle body assembly, remove the ISA motor and throttle position sensor. Install them on the replacement throttle body and adjust them (see Section 15).

13   Installation is the reverse of removal. Be sure to use a new gasket and tighten the mounting nuts to the torque listed in this Chapter's Specifications.

15   Throttle body injection (TBI) system - component replacement

Warning: *Gasoline is extremely flammable, so take extra precautions when you work on any part of the fuel system. See the* Warning *at the beginning of Section 2.*

Fuel body

Refer to illustration 15.3

1   Detach the cable from the negative battery terminal.

2   Remove the throttle body (see Section 14).

3   Remove the three Torx head screws that

attach the fuel body to the throttle body **(see illustration).**

4   Remove the original gasket and discard it.

5   Installation is the reverse of removal.

Fuel injector

Refer to illustrations 15.8, 15.9 and 15.10

14.5 Use a back-up wrench to keep the fitting on the TBI unit stationary while loosening the fuel line

Removal

6   Remove the throttle body upper bonnet (see Section 14).

7   Remove the throttle body lower bonnet (see Section 14).

8   Detach the injector connector **(see illustration)** by compressing the lock tabs and lifting up.

9   Remove the screws and lift off the

14.8 Identify and tag the vacuum tubes at the back of the throttle body, then detach them

15.3 An exploded view of the fuel body assembly

FUEL BODY

GASKET

MOUNTING SCREWS

THROTTLE BODY

15.8 To remove the injector connector on TBI-equipped vehicles, compress the tabs and lift up

15.9 First remove the screws (Torx 15) from the retainer and . . .

15.10 . . . gently pry the center with a screwdriver and carefully extract the injector by rocking it back and forth while lifting up - do not twist it during removal

15.12 An exploded view of TBI fuel injector components

15.21 Remove the three Torx screws from the fuel pressure regulator housing (TBI unit removed for clarity)

retainer **(see illustration).**

10   Using a small screwdriver, gently pry the center collar of the injector and carefully remove the injector by rocking it back and forth with your fingers while lifting up **(see illustration)** with the screwdriver. **Caution:** *Do not twist the injector during removal or its locating tab will be damaged.*

11   Remove and discard the centering ring and upper and lower O-rings. **Caution:** *Do not re-use these rings or fuel leakage and poor driveability may occur.*

Installation

Refer to illustration 15.12

12   Lubricate the replacement lower O-ring with light oil. Install the replacement lower O-ring in the bottom of the fuel injector housing bore **(see illustration).**

13   Lubricate the replacement upper O-ring with light oil. Install it in the fuel injector housing bore.

14   Install the centering ring on top of the upper O-ring.

15   Align the locating tab on the bottom of the injector **(see illustration 15.12)** with the slot in the bottom of the housing and install the injector.

16   Install the retainer and tighten the screws securely.

17   Attach the injector connector.

18   Install the lower and upper bonnets.

19   Attach the negative battery cable.

Fuel pressure regulator

Refer to illustrations 15.21 and 15.22

20   Remove the throttle body (see Section 14).

21   Remove the pressure regulator mounting screws **(see illustration). Warning:** *The regulator is under spring pressure. To prevent possible injury from the regulator flying off,*

keep the regulator forced against the throttle body while you're removing the screws.

22   Remove the housing, spring, spring seats, diaphragm and pivot **(see illustration).**

23   Remove any foreign material from the housing.

24   Installation is the reverse of removal. Make sure you install the diaphragm so its vent hole is aligned with the vent holes in the throttle body and housing.

25   After you have replaced the regulator and installed the throttle body on the engine, start the engine and check for leaks.

26   Adjust the fuel pressure (see Section 3).

Throttle position sensor (TPS)

Refer to illustrations 15.28 and 15.29

27   Remove the upper and lower air inlet bonnets (see Section 14).

28   Remove the throttle body (see Section 14). This is not absolutely necessary, but it makes it easier to get at the TPS. If you don't remove the throttle body, unplug the TPS connector **(see illustration).** Note that

15.22 An exploded view of the fuel pressure regulator assembly

15.28 To remove the throttle position sensor (TPS), unplug the electrical connector and remove the two mounting screws

15.29 Remove the two Torx screws from the TPS housing (TBI unit removed for clarity)

15.33 Disconnect the ISA motor harness connector; to remove the motor, unscrew the three mounting nuts - use a back-up wrench to avoid damaging the motor

16.4 Idle speed stepper motor connector (left) - TPS connector (right)

the TPS used on vehicles with automatic transmissions has two connectors.

29   Remove the TPS mounting screws **(see illustration)**.

30   Remove the TPS from the throttle shaft lever.

31   Installation is the reverse of removal. Be sure the TPS arm is underneath the throttle shaft lever.

32   Have the TPS adjusted by a dealer service department.

Idle speed actuator (ISA) motor

Refer to illustration 15.33

33   Remove the ISA motor harness connector **(see illustration)**.

34   Detach the throttle return spring.

35   Remove the three ISA motor-to-bracket mounting nuts **(see illustration 15.33)**. Use a back-up wrench to prevent the studs which hold the ISA motor together from turning. **Caution:** *Don't attempt to remove the ISA motor-to-bracket nuts without using a back-up wrench on the stud nuts. ISA motor internal components may be damaged if the studs disengage.*

36   Remove the ISA motor from the bracket.

37   Installation is the reverse of removal.

38   After you have replaced the ISA motor, have it adjusted by a dealer service department.

16   Multi-Point Injection (MPI) - component replacement

Warning: *Gasoline is extremely flammable, so take extra precautions when you work on any part of the fuel system. See the* Warning *at the beginning of Section 2.*

Throttle body

Refer to illustrations 16.4, 16.5, 16.6 and 16.7

1   Detach the cable from the negative battery terminal.

2   Relieve the fuel pressure (see Section 2).

3   Disconnect the flexible air duct from the throttle body (see Section 7).

4   Detach the idle speed stepper motor and throttle position sensor wire connectors **(see illustration)**.

5   Detach the MAP sensor vacuum tube

from the back of the throttle body **(see illustration)**.

6   Detach the throttle linkage at the throttle arm **(see illustration)**.

7   If equipped an with automatic transmission, detach the line pressure cable at the throttle arm **(see illustration)**.

8   Remove the mounting bolts, throttle body and gasket. Discard the old gasket and clean the gasket mating surfaces on the throttle body and intake manifold.

9   Installation is the reverse of removal.

Idle speed stepper motor

10   Detach the cable from the negative battery terminal.

11   Unplug the wire connector from the idle speed stepper motor, remove the retaining screws, then pull off the idle speed stepper motor **(see illustration 16.4)**.

12   Installation is the reverse of removal.

Throttle position sensor

Refer to illustration 16.15

13   Detach the cable from the negative battery terminal.

16.5 Use a small screwdriver to pry the MAP sensor vacuum tube from the back of the throttle body

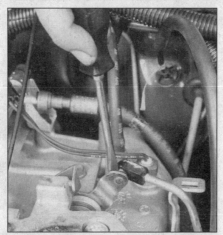

16.6 To detach the linkage from the throttle arm, insert a screwdriver between the linkage and the arm and pop it loose

16.7 If the vehicle is equipped with an automatic transmission, detach the line pressure cable at the throttle arm

16.15 To remove the TPS, remove the retaining screws (arrows), then pull the TPS from the throttle assembly - if the screws are secured by lock tabs (as shown here), bend the tabs back - use new tabs when reinstalling the screws (manual transmission shown)

---

14   Unplug the TPS wire connector **(see illustration 16.4)**.

15   Bend back the TPS lock tabs, if equipped **(see illustration)**. Remove the retaining screws, then detach the TPS from the throttle plate assembly.

16   Installation is the reverse of removal.

16.21a Numerically label the injector harness connectors (arrows) so you don't mix them up during reassembly

17   Have the TPS adjusted by a dealer service department.

Fuel injector rail assembly

Refer to illustrations 16.21a, 16.21b, 16.23a, 16.23b, 16.23c, 16.24 and 16.27

18   Remove the fuel filler cap to relieve fuel tank pressure.

19   Relieve the fuel pressure (see Section 2).

20   Detach the cable from the negative battery terminal.

21   Numerically label, then unplug, the injector harness connectors **(see illustrations)**.

22   Detach the vacuum tube from the fuel pressure regulator **(see illustration 3.36)**.

23   Detach the fuel supply hose from the fuel rail, the fuel return line from the intake manifold, then the fuel return line from the fuel pressure regulator **(see illustrations)**. Refer to Section 13 for information on removing and replacing fuel line fittings.

24   Remove the fuel rail mounting bolts **(see illustration)**.

25   If the vehicle is equipped with an automatic transmission, it may be necessary to remove the automatic transmission line pressure cable and bracket to remove the fuel rail assembly **(see illustration 16.7)**.

16.21b Use a scribe (shown) or a small screwdriver to pop loose the retaining clip that attaches the harness connector to each injector

16.23a Detach the fuel supply hose from the fuel rail

16.23b Remove the nut from the fuel return line bracket and slide the bracket off its mounting stud . . .

16.23c . . . then detach the fuel return line from the fuel pressure regulator

16.24 Remove the fuel rail mounting bolts (typical)

16.27 Before installing the fuel rail mounting bolts, position the tip of each injector over its respective bore in the intake manifold, then push down on the injectors to seat them completely (4.0L engine shown)

16.32 Use a small screwdriver (shown) or scribe to pop loose the clip that secures the injector to the fuel rail assembly

26   Remove the fuel rail by simultaneously rocking and pulling up on it until all injectors are out of the intake manifold. Work slowly and carefully so you don't damage the assembly.

27   Installation is the reverse of removal, but be sure to do the following:

a) *Before attempting to reattach the fuel rail assembly mounting bolts, position the tip of each injector above its corresponding bore in the intake manifold* **(see illustration)**, *then seat the injectors by pushing down on them. You must seat the injectors properly before you tighten the fuel rail mounting bolts.*

b) *When you reattach the fuel lines, be sure to use a new O-ring, spacer and retainer repair kit (see Section 13).*

Fuel injectors

Refer to illustrations 16.32 and 16.33

28   Remove the fuel filler cap to relieve fuel tank pressure.

29   Relieve the system fuel pressure (see Section 2).

30   Detach the cable from the negative battery terminal.

31   Remove the fuel injector rail assembly (see above).

32   Remove the retaining clip(s) that attach the injector(s) to the rail assembly **(see illustration).**

16.33 Be sure to remove the old O-ring and seal from the injector (a replacement kit, available at most auto parts stores, includes O-rings and seals - enough O-rings and seals for all injectors and an extra seal for the fuel pressure regulator)

33   If you are servicing a leaking injector, remove the old O-rings and seals **(see illustration).**

34   An O-ring kit is available from a dealer parts department for both the 2.5L and the 4.0L engines. For example, a kit for a 4.0L engine consists of 6 brown and 7 black seals. The brown seals fit on the injector tips; the

16.40 Remove the fuel pressure regulator retaining screws (arrows)

black seals fit on the rail end of the injectors. Do not switch the brown and black O-rings - they're different in design and composition. The extra black seal is for the fuel pressure regulator - see Step 42.

35   Because the O-ring kit includes enough O-rings for all six injectors (they're not available individually), it's a good idea to replace the upper and lower O-rings on all injectors, even if only one or two are actually leaking at the time you service them. Otherwise, you will probably find yourself repeating this

16.41 Pull the fuel pressure regulator off the end of the fuel rail

16.42 Always install a new O-ring on the pressure regulator

16.48 Fuel pressure regulator/fuel filter details (1997 and later models)

RETAINER CLAMP

FUEL FILTER/FUEL PRESSURE REGULATOR

ALIGNMENT ARROW

FUEL SUPPLY TUBE

17.1a Exploded view of a typical exhaust system for a four-cylinder engine

1	Upper heat shield
2	Tail pipe
3	Muffler
4	Catalytic converter
5	Lower heat shield
6	Exhaust pipe
7	Resonator (Canada only)

17.1b Exploded view of a typical exhaust system for a six-cylinder engine

1	Front exhaust pipe
2	Catalytic converter
3	Resonator (Canada only)
4	Converter heat-shield
5	Tailpipe
6	Muffler
7	Downstream air injection tube port
8	Upstream air injection tube port

entire procedure down the road - to fix other leaky injectors.

36   Installation is the reverse of removal. Be sure to coat the injector O-rings with a little fuel before installing the injectors.

Fuel pressure regulator

1995 and earlier models

Refer to illustrations 16.40, 16.41 and 16.42

37   Remove the fuel filler cap to relieve fuel tank pressure.

38   Relieve the system fuel pressure (see Section 2).

39   Detach the cable from the negative battery terminal.

40   Remove the fuel pressure regulator retaining screws **(see illustration)**.

41   Pull the regulator off the fuel rail **(see illustration)**.

42   Whenever you remove the fuel pressure regulator, always install a new O-ring **(see illustration)**. This O-ring is available as part of an O-ring kit for the injectors (see Step 34 above).

43   Installation is the reverse of removal.

1997 and later models

Refer to illustration 16.48

Note 1: *These models are equipped with a "returnless" fuel system. The fuel pressure regulator is mounted on top of the fuel pump/fuel level sending unit assembly.*

Note 2: *The fuel filter requires service only when a fuel contamination problem is suspected.*

44   Relieve the fuel system pressure (see Section 2).

45   Detach the cable from the negative battery terminal.

46   Remove the fuel tank (see Section 5).

47   Detach the fuel line from the fuel pressure regulator.

48   Unsnap the clamp from the top of the fuel filter/pressure regulator assembly **(see illustration)**.

49   Remove the fuel pressure regulator/fuel filter by gently prying the unit from the fuel pump module. Remove the gasket from under the regulator.

50   Check the regulator to make sure that both O-rings came off with it (there's a small one at the end of the regulator and a larger one up a little higher). If both of them aren't present, retrieve the missing one(s) from the fuel pump module.

51   Installation is the reverse of removal. Lubricate the O-rings with clean engine oil, and be sure to install a new gasket to the top of the fuel pump module. The arrow on the top of the pressure regulator should point to the front of the vehicle. Also, a new regulator retaining clamp should be used.

---

17   Exhaust system servicing - general information

Refer to illustrations 17.1a and 17.1b

Warning: *Inspection and repair of exhaust system components should be done only after enough time has elapsed after driving the vehicle to allow the system components to cool completely. Also, when working under the vehicle, make sure it is securely supported on jackstands.*

1   The exhaust system **(see illustrations)** consists of the exhaust manifold(s), the catalytic converter, the muffler, the tailpipe and all connecting pipes, brackets, hangers and clamps. The exhaust system is attached to the body with mounting brackets and rubber hangers. If any of the parts are improperly installed, excessive noise and vibration will be transmitted to the body.

2   Conduct regular inspections of the exhaust system to keep it safe and quiet.

Look for any damaged or bent parts, open seams, holes, loose connections, excessive corrosion or other defects which could allow exhaust fumes to enter the vehicle. Deteriorated exhaust system components should not be repaired; they should be replaced with new parts.

3   If the exhaust system components are extremely corroded or rusted together, welding equipment will probably be required to remove them. The convenient way to accomplish this is to have a muffler repair shop remove the corroded sections with a cutting torch. If, however, you want to save money by doing it yourself (and you don't have a welding outfit with a cutting torch), simply cut off the old components with a hacksaw. If you have compressed air, special pneumatic cutting chisels can also be used. If you do decide to tackle the job at home, be sure to wear safety goggles to protect your eyes from metal chips and work gloves to protect your hands.

4   Here are some simple guidelines to follow when repairing the exhaust system:

a) *Work from the back to the front when removing exhaust system components.*

b) *Apply penetrating oil to the exhaust system component fasteners to make them easier to remove.*

c) *Use new gaskets, hangers and clamps when installing exhaust systems components.*

d) *Apply anti-seize compound to the threads of all exhaust system fasteners during reassembly.*

e) *Be sure to allow sufficient clearance between newly installed parts and all points on the underbody to avoid overheating the floor pan and possibly damaging the interior carpet and insulation. Pay particularly close attention to the catalytic converter and heat shield.*

Chapter 5
Engine electrical systems

Contents

Specifications

Ignition coil resistance

1987 through 1990 four-cylinder models	
Primary	0.4 to 0.8 ohms
Secondary	2500 to 4000 ohms
Carbureted models	
Primary	1.13 to 1.23 ohms
Secondary	77 to 93 K-ohms
1991 and later models (except 2000 six-cylinder models)	
Diamond	
Primary	0.97 to 1.18 ohms
Secondary	11.3 to 15.3 K-ohms
Toyodenso	
Primary	0.95 to 1.20 ohms
Secondary	11.3 to 13.3 K-ohms
2000 Six-cylinder models (Primary only)	0.71 to 0.88 ohms
Ignition coil wire resistance (all except 2000 six-cylinder models)	3 to 10 k ohms

1   General information

The engine electrical systems include all ignition, charging and starting components. Because of their engine-related functions, these components are discussed separately from chassis electrical devices such as the lights, the instruments, etc. (which are included in Chapter 12).

Always observe the following precautions when working on the electrical systems:

a) *Be extremely careful when servicing engine electrical components. They are easily damaged if checked, connected or handled improperly.*

b) *Never leave the ignition switch on for long periods of time with the engine off.*

c) *Don't disconnect the battery cables while the engine is running.*

d) *Maintain correct polarity when connecting a battery cable from another vehicle during jump starting.*

e) *Always disconnect the negative cable first and hook it up last or the battery may be shorted by the tool being used to loosen the cable clamps.*

It's also a good idea to review the safety-related information regarding engine electrical systems located in the *Safety first* section near the front of this manual before beginning any operation included in this Chapter.

2   Battery - emergency jump starting

Refer to the Booster battery (jump) starting procedure at the front of this manual.

3   Battery - removal and installation

Refer to illustration 3.2

1   **Caution:** *Always disconnect the negative cable first and hook it up last or the battery may be shorted by the tool being used to loosen the cable clamps. Disconnect both cables from the battery terminals.*

3.2 Unscrew the nuts (1) and lift the clamp (2) off the battery

6.1 To use a calibrated ignition tester (available at most auto parts stores), simply disconnect a spark plug wire, attach the wire to the tester and clip the tester to a good ground - if there is enough power to fire the plug, sparks will be clearly visible between the electrode tip and the tester body as the engine is turned over

2   Remove the battery hold down clamp **(see illustration)**.
3   Lift out the battery. Be careful - it's heavy.
4   While the battery is out, inspect the carrier (tray) for corrosion (see Chapter 1).
5   If you are replacing the battery, make sure you get one that's identical, with the same dimensions, amperage rating, cold cranking rating, etc.
6   Installation is the reverse of removal.

4   Battery cables - check and replacement

1   Periodically inspect the entire length of each battery cable for damage, cracked or burned insulation and corrosion. Poor battery connections can cause starting problems and decreased engine performance.
2   Check the cable-to-terminal connections at the ends of the cables for cracks, loose wire strands and corrosion. The presence of white, fluffy deposits under the insulation at the cable terminal connection is a sign that the cable is corroded and should be replaced. Check the terminals for distortion, missing mounting bolts and corrosion.
3   When removing the cables, always disconnect the negative cable first and hook it up last or the battery may be shorted by the tool used to loosen the cable clamps. Even if only the positive cable is being replaced, be sure to disconnect the negative cable from the battery first (see Chapter 1 for further information regarding battery cable removal).
4   Disconnect the old cables from the battery, then trace each of them to their opposite ends and detach them from the starter solenoid and ground terminals. Note the routing of each cable to ensure correct installation.
5   If you are replacing either or both of the old cables, take them with you when buying new cables. It is vitally important that you replace the cables with identical parts. Cables have characteristics that make them

easy to identify: positive cables are usually red, larger in cross-section and have a larger diameter battery post clamp; ground cables are usually black, smaller in cross-section and have a slightly smaller diameter clamp for the negative post.
6   Clean the threads of the solenoid or ground connection with a wire brush to remove rust and corrosion. Apply a light coat of battery terminal corrosion inhibitor, or petroleum jelly, to the threads to prevent future corrosion.
7   Attach the cable to the solenoid or ground connection and tighten the mounting nut/bolt securely.
8   Before connecting a new cable to the battery, make sure that it reaches the battery post without having to be stretched.
9   Connect the positive cable first, followed by the negative cable.

5   Ignition system - general information

1987 through 1990 four-cylinder engine

These models are equipped with an ignition system consisting of a solid state Ignition Control Module (ICM), an electronic distributor, an Electronic Control Unit (ECU), a specially machined flywheel and a Top Dead Center (TDC) sensor.

The solid state ICM is located in the engine compartment on the right (passenger's) side of the firewall in the engine compartment, consists of a solid state ignition circuit and an integrated ignition coil that can be removed and serviced separately if necessary. The ICM controls ignition timing, using signals from the ECU.

The ECU gets its information regarding TDC, BDC and engine speed from a TDC sensor mounted on the flywheel/driveplate housing. The flywheel has two teeth machined off

every 180-degrees to define a precise point 90-degrees before TDC and BDC.

Carbureted six-cylinder engine

The Solid State Ignition (SSI) system used on these models is made up of the Micro Computer Unit (MCU), located in the passenger compartment, conventional distributor which uses vacuum to control timing and a coil and an ignition control module located on the passenger's side firewall in the engine compartment.

1991 and later four-cylinder and 1991 through 1999 six-cylinder models

All 1991 and later four- and six-cylinder engines use the same ignition system. It consists of an engine computer (located on the driver's side firewall, behind the windshield washer reservoir), a distributor and a coil mounted on the engine block next to the distributor. On 1991 and 1992 models, the engine computer is referred to as the Engine Controller (ECM). On 1993 and later models, it is referred to as the Powertrain Control Module (PCM).

2000 six-cylinder models

The 2000 models are equipped with a distributorless ignition system. The ignition system consists of the battery, ignition coils, spark plugs, camshaft position sensor, crankshaft position sensor and the Powertrain Control Module (PCM). The PCM controls the ignition timing and spark advance characteristics for the engine. The ignition timing is not adjustable.

The ignition system uses a "waste spark" method of spark distribution. The system utilizes three ignition coils in a coil rail assembly. Each coil is paired with the opposite cylinder in the firing order (1-6, 5-2, 3-4) so one cylinder under compression fires simultaneously with its opposing cylinder, where the piston is on the exhaust stroke. Since the cylinder on the exhaust stroke requires very little of the available voltage to fire its plug, most of the voltage is used to fire the plug of the cylinder on the compression stroke. Conventional ignition coils have one end of the secondary winding connected to the engine ground. On a waste spark system, neither end of the secondary winding is grounded - instead one end of the coil's secondary winding is directly attached to the spark plug and the other end is attached to the spark plug of the companion cylinder.

The PCM controls the ignition system by opening and closing the ignition coil ground circuit. The computerized ignition system provides complete control of the ignition timing by determining the optimum timing in response to engine speed, coolant temperature, throttle position and vacuum pressure in the intake manifold. These parameters are relayed to the PCM by the camshaft position sensor, crankshaft position sensor, throttle position sensor and the manifold absolute pressure sensor. The PCM and crankshaft position sensors are very important components of the ignition system. The ignition system will not operate and the engine will not start if the PCM or the crankshaft position sensor are defective. Refer to Chapter 6 for additional information on the various sensors.

6   Ignition system - check

All except 2000 six-cylinder models

Refer to illustration 6.1

Warning: *Because of the high voltage generated by the ignition system, extreme care should be taken when this check is performed.*

1   If the engine turns over but won't start, disconnect the spark plug wire from any spark plug and attach it to a calibrated ignition tester (available at most auto parts stores). Connect the clip on the tester to a bolt or metal bracket on the engine **(see illustration)**. If you're unable to obtain a calibrated ignition tester, remove the wire from one of the spark plugs and, using an insulated tool, hold the end of the wire about 1/4-inch from a good ground.

2   Crank the engine and watch the end of the tester or spark plug to see if bright blue, well-defined sparks occur. If you're not using a calibrated tester, have an assistant crank the engine for you.

3   If sparks occur, sufficient voltage is reaching the plug to fire it (repeat the check at the remaining plug wires to verify that the distributor cap and rotor are OK). However, the plugs themselves might be fouled, so remove and check them as described in Chapter 1.

4   If no sparks or intermittent sparks occur, remove the distributor cap and check the cap and rotor as described in Chapter 1. If moisture is present, dry out the cap and rotor, then reinstall the cap and repeat the spark test.

5   If there's still no spark, detach the coil secondary wire from the distributor cap and hook it up to the tester (reattach the plug wire to the spark plug), then repeat the spark check. Again, if you don't have a tester, hold the end of the wire about 1/4-inch from a good ground.

6   If sparks now occur, the distributor cap, rotor or plug wire(s) may be defective.

7   If no sparks occur, check the primary wire connections at the coil to make sure they're clean and tight. Check for voltage at the coil. Make any necessary repairs, then repeat the check again.

8   If there's still no spark, the coil-to-cap wire may be bad (check the resistance with an ohmmeter and compare it to Specifications). If a known good wire doesn't make any difference in the test results, the ignition coil may be defective.

2000 six-cylinder models

Refer to illustration 6.14

Caution: *Because of the ignition system design on these six-cylinder models, a special set of spark plug wires must be obtained or fabricated before the ignition system check can be performed. A test set can be fabricated from bulk spark plug wire and terminals available at most auto parts stores. As an alternative, individual jumper wires can be used to ground the spark plug terminals not being tested. Whichever method you choose, make sure all the spark plug terminals are either connected to a spark plug or grounded to the engine block before cranking the engine or damage to the ignition coils may result.*

9   Disable the fuel system by removing the fuel pump relay from the power distribution center (see Chapter 12).

10   Remove the bolts retaining the ignition coil rail (see section 7). Carefully detach the coil rail from the spark plug, turn the coil rail over and place it in a secure location. Do not disconnect the electrical connector from the ignition coil rail.

11   Attach a calibrated ignition system tester (available at most auto parts stores) to one of the spark plug boots. Using a heavy gauge jumper wire, connect the clip on the

tester to the bolt or bare metal bracket on the engine. Connect the remaining ignition coil spark plug terminals to the spark plugs or ground them to the engine. Crank the engine and watch the end of the tester to see if a bright blue, well-defined spark occurs (weak spark, or intermittent spark could also be an indication of problems).

12   If a spark occurs, sufficient voltage is reaching the plug to fire it (repeat the check at the remaining spark plug terminals to verify that the ignition coils are good). If the ignition system is operating properly the problem lies elsewhere; i.e. a mechanical or fuel system problem. However, the spark pugs may be fouled, so remove and check them as described in Chapter 1.

13   If a spark occurs at one or more of the coils, remove the ignition coil rail and measure the primary resistance of the ignition coils (see Section 7). Check the spring inside each spark plug boot for corrosion or damage. Replace the ignition coil rail if defective.

14   If no spark occurs at all coils, disconnect the electrical connector from the coil rail and check for battery voltage to the ignition coil rail from the auto shut-down relay and power distribution center. Attach a 12 volt test light or voltmeter to a good engine ground point and check for power at the dark green/orange wire terminal of the ignition coil rail harness connector **(see illustration)**. Battery voltage should be available with the ignition key on. If there is no battery voltage present at the coil rail connector, check the auto shut-down relay (see Chapter 12) and circuits between the power distribution center and ignition coil rail (don't forget to check the fuses). Also check the auto shut-down relay control circuit from the relay to the PCM for continuity.

15   If the previous checks are correct, check for a trigger signal from the Powertrain Control Module. Attach a test light to the dark green/orange wire terminal and one of the other terminals of the coil rail harness connector. Crank the engine. The test light should blink with the engine cranking if a trigger signal is present. Check for a trigger signal between the dark green/orange wire terminal and each of the other terminals in the

CAV	CIRCUIT	FUNCTION
1	K91 16TN/RD	COIL DRIVER NO. 1
2	A142 16DG/OR	AUTOMATIC SHUT DOWN RELAY OUTPUT
3	K92 16TN/PK	COIL DRIVER NO. 2
4	K93 16TN/OR	COIL DRIVER NO. 3

6.14 Ignition coil rail electrical connector terminal identification (harness side) - 2000 six-cylinder engine

7.2a The ignition coil on 1987 through 1990 fuel-injected models is located on the right (passenger's) side of the firewall in the engine compartment - when removing the coil, unscrew the mounting bracket bolts (arrows)

connector. If a trigger signal is present at the coil rail connector, the Powertrain Control Module and the crankshaft position sensor are functioning properly. If a trigger signal is not present at the coil terminals, check the crankshaft position sensor (see Chapter 6). If the crankshaft position sensor is good, have the PCM checked by a dealer service department or other qualified repair shop.

7   Ignition coil - check and replacement

Refer to illustrations 7.2a, 7.2b, 7.2c, 7.4a, 7.4b, 7.4c, 7.5a, 7.5b and 7.5c

1991 and later four-cylinder and 1991 through 1999 six-cylinder models

1   Detach the cable from the negative battery terminal.

7.4a On 1987 through 1990 fuel-injected models - to check the coil primary resistance, touch the ohmmeter leads to the positive and negative terminals and compare this reading to the coil primary resistance listed in this Chapter's Specifications Section

7.2b On carbureted six-cylinder models, the coil is mounted next to the distributor - to remove the electrical connector, grasp it securely and pull it straight off the terminals

2   Mark the wires and terminals with pieces of numbered tape, then remove the primary wires and the high-tension cable from the coil **(see illustrations)**. Disconnect the coil mounting bracket, remove the coil/bracket assembly, clean the outer case and check it for cracks and other damage.
3   Clean the coil primary terminals and check the coil tower terminal for corrosion. Clean it with a wire brush if any corrosion is found.
4   Check the coil primary resistance by attaching the leads of an ohmmeter to the positive and negative terminals **(see illustrations)**. Compare your readings to the primary resistance listed in this Chapter's Specifications.
5   Check the coil secondary resistance by hooking one of the ohmmeter leads to the primary terminals and the other to ohmmeter lead to the large center (high-tension) terminal **(see illustrations)**. Compare your readings to the secondary resistance listed in this Chapter's Specifications.
6   If the measured resistances are not as specified, the coil is probably defective and should be replaced with a new one.

7.4b To check the coil primary resistance on carbureted models, touch the leads of an ohmmeter to the positive and negative terminals, then compare the reading with the coil primary resistance in this Chapter's Specifications

7.2c On 1991 and later models, the coil is mounted in front of the distributor

7   For proper ignition system operation, all coil terminals and lead wires should be kept clean and dry.
8   Install the coil in the vehicle and hook up the wires.
9   Attach the cable to the negative battery terminal.

2000 six-cylinder models
Check

10   Remove the ignition coil rail assembly (see Replacement procedure).
11   Clean the three outer cases and check for cracks or other damage. Clean the coil primary terminals and check the springs and spark plug boots for damage. If either the springs or spark plug boots are damaged, the coil rail assembly must be replaced.
12   Check the coil primary resistance. Connect an ohmmeter to terminals no. 2 and 1; 2 and 3; 2 and 4; of the coil connector. Each measurement is the primary resistance of one of the three coils in the coil rail assembly.
13   Compare your measurements to the resistance values in this Chapter's Specifications. If either measured resistance value is not as specified, replace the ignition coil rail assembly. **Note:** *The entire ignition coil rail assembly must be replaced if only one coil is defective.*

7.4c On 1991 and later models, connect the leads of an ohmmeter to the positive and negative primary terminals and compare the reading with the coil primary resistance in this Chapter's Specifications

7.5a To check the coil secondary resistance on 1987 through 1990 fuel-injected models, touch one lead of the ohmmeter to one of the primary terminals and the other lead to the high tension terminal, then compare the reading to the coil secondary resistance listed in this Chapter's Specifications

7.5b On carbureted models, check the coil secondary resistance by touching one lead of the ohmmeter to one of the primary terminals and the other lead to the high tension terminal; compare this reading to the coil secondary resistance listed in this Chapter's Specifications

7.5c To check the coil secondary resistance on 1991 and later models, touch one lead of the ohmmeter to one of the primary terminals and the other lead to the high tension terminal, then compare the reading to the coil secondary resistance listed in this Chapter's Specifications

Replacement

Refer to illustrations 7.14 and 7.16

Note: *The ignition coil rail assembly consists of the three ignition coils, spark plug boots, springs, electrical connector and internal wiring. None of the components are serviced separately. The entire assembly is removed and replaced as a unit.*

14   Remove the ignition coil rail assembly mounting bolts **(see illustration)**.

15   Carefully work the spark plug boots off the spark plugs by alternately prying at one end of the coil rail, then the other. If difficulty is encountered, twist the spark plug boots with a spark plug boot removal tool to loosen the seal.

16   Position the coil rail to access the electrical connection. Disconnect the electrical connector from the coil rail by first pushing the slide tab up, then press the release lock and pull the connector off **(see illustration)**.

17   Remove the ignition coil rail assembly.

18   When installing the ignition coil rail, position all of the spark plug boots over the spark plugs and press the ignition coil rail down until the boots are completely seated.

19   Install the mounting bolts and tighten them in stages until secure.

20   Connect the electrical connector and slide the tab down until locked in place.

8   Ignition control module - check and replacement (1990 and earlier four-cylinder models and carbureted six-cylinder models)

Check

1   You need an approved ignition control module tester (Tester J-24642E or equivalent) to test the ignition control modules used with any of the vehicles covered by this manual. Without this equipment, module testing is beyond the scope of the home mechanic. If you have access to the necessary tool, the instructions for testing the module are provided by the manufacturer.

FRONT

7.14 Ignition coil rail installation details - 2000 six-cylinder models

1   Coil rail
2   Mounting bolts (1 of 4)
3   Ignition coils
4   Electrical connector

7.16 Ignition coil rail electrical connector details - 2000 six-cylinder models

1   Valve cover
2   Ignition coil rail
3   Slide tab
4   Release lock
5   Electrical connector

9.5 Exploded view of the distributor assembly used on carbureted models

1   Pin
2   Gear
3   Washer
4   Distributor body
5   Vacuum advance mechanism
6   Wick
7   Washer
8   Pickup coil
9   Pickup coil retainer
10 Trigger wheel
11 Pin
12 Rotor
13 Cap

Replacement

Four-cylinder models

2   Remove the ignition coil (see Section 7).
3   Remove the two screws that attach the module to the coil frame. Pull off the module.
4   Installation is the reverse of removal.

Six-cylinder models

5   Disconnect the electrical connectors from the module.
6   Remove the mounting screws and remove the module from the firewall.
7   Installation is the reverse of removal.

9   Trigger wheel and/or pickup coil assembly - removal and installation (carbureted models only)

Refer to illustration 9.5

Removal

1   Detach the cable from the negative battery terminal.
2   The following procedure may be easier if

you remove the distributor (see Section 12) but it's not absolutely necessary that you do so.
3   If you do decide to remove the distributor, place it in a bench vise.
4   Remove the distributor cap and rotor (see Chapter 1).
5   Using the trigger wheel puller tool, available at most auto parts stores, remove the trigger wheel **(see illustration)**. Use a flat washer to prevent the puller from contacting the inner shaft. Remove the pin.
6   Remove the pickup coil assembly retainer and washers from the pivot pin on the base plate.
7   Remove the two pickup coil plate screws.
8   Lift the pickup coil assembly from the distributor housing.

Installation

9   Position the pickup coil assembly into the distributor housing.
10 Make sure the pin on the pickup coil assembly fits into the hole in the vacuum advance mechanism link.
11 Install the washers and retainer on the pivot pin to secure the pickup coil assembly to the base plate.
12 Position the wiring harness in the slot in the distributor housing. Install the two pickup coil plate screws and tighten them securely.
13 Install the trigger wheel on the shaft with hand pressure. The long portion of the teeth must face up. When the trigger wheel and slot in the shaft are properly aligned, use a pin punch and a small hammer to tap the pin into the locating groove in the trigger wheel and shaft. If the distributor is not installed in the engine, support the shaft while installing the trigger wheel pin.
14 Install the rotor and the distributor cap.
15 Attach the cable to the negative battery terminal.

10 Vacuum advance mechanism - check and replacement (carbureted models only)

Check

1   Hook up a timing light in accordance with the manufacturer's instructions.
2   Make sure the vacuum hose is attached to the vacuum advance mechanism **(see illustration 9.5)**.
3   Run the engine until it reaches normal operating temperature.
4   With the engine idling, watch the timing marks at the front of the engine with the timing light (see Chapter 1 for more information). **Note:** *The white paint mark on the timing degree scale identifies the specified timing degrees Before Top Dead Center (BTDC) at 1600 rpm; it does not identify TDC.*
5   Slowly increase the engine speed to 2000 rpm, noticing how quickly the ignition timing advances. Disconnect and plug the vacuum hose from the vacuum advance

mechanism. Again, increase the engine speed to 2000 rpm and notice how quickly the ignition timing advances. With the hose connected, the ignition timing should advance more quickly than it does with the hose disconnected. If it doesn't, replace the vacuum advance mechanism. **Note:** *A defective Micro Computer Unit (MCU) can also alter ignition timing.*
6   Unplug and reconnect the hose to the vacuum advance mechanism.

Replacement

7   Detach the cable from the negative battery terminal.
8   Remove the distributor cap and rotor (see Chapter 1).
9   The following procedure is easier if you remove the distributor (see Section 12), but it's not absolutely necessary that you do so.
10 If you do decide to remove the distributor, place it in a bench vise.
11 Remove the pickup coil (see Section 9).
12 Remove the vacuum hose and attaching screws from the vacuum advance mechanism **(see illustration 9.5)**. Tilt the vacuum advance mechanism to disengage the link from the pickup coil pin, which protrudes through the distributor housing. If necessary, loosen the base plate screws to get more clearance. Lift the vacuum advance mechanism out of the distributor housing.
13 To calibrate a new vacuum advance mechanism:

a) *Insert an appropriately sized Allen wrench into the vacuum hose tube of the old vacuum advance mechanism; count the number of clockwise turns necessary to bottom the adjusting screw.*
b) *Turn the adjusting screw of the replacement vacuum advance mechanism clockwise to bottom it, then turn it counterclockwise the same number of turns you counted above.*

14 Install the advance mechanism on the distributor housing. Make sure the link is engaged on the pin of the pickup coil.
15 Install and tighten the vacuum advance mechanism attaching screws. If you loosened the base plate screws, tighten them too.
16 Install the pickup coil (see Section 9).
17 Install the distributor (see Section 12).
18 Install the distributor cap and rotor (see Chapter 1).
19 Attach the cable to the negative battery terminal.
20 Check the ignition timing and adjust it, if necessary (see Chapter 1).
21 Attach the vacuum hose to the vacuum advance mechanism.

11 Centrifugal advance mechanism - check and replacement (carbureted models only)

1   Detach the vacuum hose from the vacuum advance mechanism and plug it **(see illustration 9.5)**.

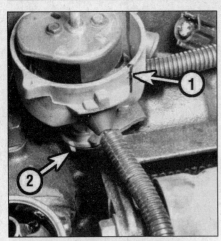

12.6 Before loosening the distributor hold-down bolt, make a mark on the edge of the distributor base directly below, and in line with, the rotor tip (1), then mark the distributor base and the engine block (2) to ensure that the distributor is installed correctly

2   Hook up a timing light and tachometer in accordance with the manufacturer's instructions.
3   Start the engine and, with the engine idling, watch the timing marks at the front of the engine with the timing light (see Chapter 1 for more information).
4   Slowly increase engine speed to 2000 rpm. Timing should advance smoothly as engine speed increases. If it advances unevenly, the centrifugal advance mechanism is faulty. Replace the distributor (see Section 12). You will need to switch the following parts to the replacement distributor:

a) *Cap and rotor (see Chapter 1).*
b) *Trigger wheel and/or pickup coil assembly (see Section 9).*
c) *Vacuum advance mechanism (see Section 10).*

12   Distributor - removal and installation (all except 2000 six-cylinder models)

Refer to illustrations 12.6, 12.10a, 12.10b, 12.10c, 12.11a, 12.11b, 12.11c, 12.11d, 12.12a, 12.12b, 12.12c, 12.14a and 12.14b

Removal

1   Detach the cable from the negative battery terminal.
2   Detach the primary lead from the coil.
3   Disconnect all electrical wires from the distributor. If the wires don't unplug at the distributor, follow the wires as they exit the distributor to find the connector.
4   Look for a raised "1" on the distributor cap. This marks the location for the number one cylinder spark plug wire terminal. If the cap does not have a mark for the number one

12.10a To seat the distributor on a 1987 through 1994 four-cylinder engine, use a screwdriver to rotate the oil pump gear so the slot is slightly past the three o'clock position . . .

terminal, locate the number one spark plug and trace the wire back to its corresponding terminal on the cap.
5   Remove the distributor cap (see Chapter 1) and turn the engine over until the rotor is pointing toward the number one spark plug terminal (see locating TDC procedure in Chapter 2).
6   Make a mark on the edge of the distributor base directly below the rotor tip and in line with it (if the rotor on your engine has more than one tip, use the center one for reference). Also, mark the distributor base and the engine block to ensure that the distributor is installed correctly **(see illustration)**.
7   Remove the distributor hold down bolt and clamp, then pull the distributor straight up to remove it. **Caution:** *DO NOT turn the crankshaft while the distributor is out of the engine, or the alignment marks will be useless.*

Installation

Note: *If the crankshaft has been moved while the distributor is out, the number one piston must be repositioned at TDC. This can be done by feeling for compression pressure at the number one plug hole as the crankshaft is turned. Once compression is felt, align the ignition timing zero mark with the pointer.*
8   Insert the distributor into the engine in exactly the same relationship to the block that it was in when removed.
9   To mesh the helical gears on the camshaft and the distributor, it may be necessary to turn the rotor slightly. Recheck the alignment marks between the distributor base and the block to verify that the distributor is in the same position it was in before removal. Also check the rotor to see if it's aligned with the mark you made on the edge of the distributor base.

Seating the distributor

Note: *If you have difficulty seating the distributor on the engine block, use the appropriate Step (10, 11 or 12 below) for the type of engine you have. If the distributor seats properly, with the flange flush with the engine block, proceed to Step 13.*

12.10b . . . then, with the distributor cap removed, install the distributor with the rotor pointing toward the five o'clock position

12.10c When the 1987 through 1994 four-cylinder distributor is completely and correctly seated (engaged), the rotor should be at the six o'clock position

10   If you have difficulty getting the distributor to seat properly on a 1987 through 1994 four-cylinder engine, use the following procedure:

a) *Make sure the number one piston is at TDC (see Chapter 2).*
b) *Working over the right side (passenger) fender, look into the hole in the engine block where the distributor mounts. You should see the oil pump gear slot* **(see illustration)**. *Put a screwdriver into the slot and rotate the oil pump gear so the gear slot is slightly past the three o'clock position.*
c) *With the distributor cap removed, install the distributor with the rotor pointing to the five o'clock position* **(see illustration)**.
d) *With the distributor fully engaged in its correct location, the rotor should be pointing to the six o'clock position* **(see illustration)**.
e) *If the distributor is still not installed correctly, repeat this procedure.*

11   If you are having difficulty getting the distributor to seat properly on a 1995 four-cylinder engine, use the following procedure:

a) *Make sure the number one cylinder is at TDC (see Chapter 2).*

12.11a To seat the distributor on a 1995 four-cylinder engine, use a screwdriver to rotate the oil pump gear so the slot is at the ten o'clock position . . .

10 O'CLOCK POSITION

FRONT ➡

OIL PUMP SLOT

1 O'CLOCK POSITION

BASE SLOT

FRONT ➡

DISTRIBUTOR BASE

12.11c Visually line up the distributor with the centerline of the base slot in the one o'clock position

12.11b . . . then rotate the distributor shaft and install a 3/16-inch drift pin punch tool through the correct alignment hole in the plastic ring and into the mating hole in the distributor housing

DISTRIBUTOR HOUSING (TOP VIEW)

PULSE RING

4.0L 6-CYLINDER ENGINE ALIGN. HOLE

2.5L 4-CYLINDER ENGINE ALIGN. HOLE

PLASTIC RING

MATING ACCESS HOLE IN DISTRIBUTOR HOUSING

DISTRIBUTOR BASE SLOT

FRONT ➡

DISTRIBUTOR BASE

CLAMP BOLT MOUNTING HOLE (ON ENGINE)

12.11d When the distributor is installed correctly, the centerline of the base slot will be aligned with the clamp bolt hole on the engine

b) *Look into the hole in the engine block where the distributor mounts. You should see the oil pump gear slot* **(see illustration)**. *Put a screwdriver into the hole and rotate the oil pump gear so the gear slot is slightly before the ten o'clock position.*

c) *The pulse ring must be locked in place to hold the rotor in the number one cylinder firing position during installation. Lift the camshaft position sensor straight up and out of the distributor. Rotate the distributor shaft and install a 3/16 inch drift pin punch tool through the correct alignment hole in the plastic ring and into the mating hole in the distributor housing* **(see illustration)**. *This will prevent the distributor shaft and rotor from rotating during installation.*

d) *Install the rotor onto the shaft.*

e) *Visually line up the distributor with the centerline of the base slot in the one o'clock position* **(see illustration)**.

f) *Install the distributor. It will rotate clockwise during installation and when the distributor is fully installed the centerline of the base slot will be aligned with the clamp bolt hole on the engine* **(see illustration)**. *The rotor should also be pointing to slightly past (clockwise of) the three o'clock position.*

g) *If the distributor is still not installed correctly, repeat this procedure.*

12   If you have difficulty getting the distributor to seat properly on a carbureted six-cylinder engine, use the following procedure:

a) *Make sure the number one piston is at TDC (see Chapter 2).*

b) *Look into the hole in the engine block where the distributor mounts. You should see the oil pump gear slot. Put a screwdriver into the slot and rotate the oil pump gear so the rotor will be lined up with the number 1 terminal when the distributor is inserted.*

c) *If the distributor is still not installed correctly, repeat this procedure.*

13   If you have difficulty getting the distributor to seat properly on a fuel-injected six-cylinder engine, use the following procedure:

a) *Look into the hole in the engine block where the distributor mounts. You should see the oil pump gear shaft* **(see illustration)**. *Put a screwdriver into the slot in the oil pump gear shaft and rotate the shaft until the slot is slightly past the 11 o'clock position.*

b) *If you removed it, Install the rotor.*

c) *Without engaging the distributor gear with the camshaft gear in the engine, position the distributor in the hole in the engine block. Be sure the distributor gasket is installed.*

d) *Visually line up the hold-down ear of the distributor housing with the hold-down clamp bolt hole* **(see illustration)**.

e) *Turn the rotor to the four o'clock position* **(see illustration)**.

FRONT OF ENGINE

11 O'CLOCK

OIL PUMP GEAR SHAFT

12.13a To seal the distributor on a 1987 through 1994 six-cylinder engine, use a screwdriver to turn the oil pump gear shaft until the slot is slightly past the 11 o'clock position . . .

HOLD-DOWN EAR

FRONT

HOLD-DOWN CLAMP BOLT HOLE

12.13b . . . visually line up the hold-down ear of the distributor housing with the hold-down clamp bolt hole . . .

12.13c ... turn the rotor to the four o'clock position, then slide the distributor down into the block until it seats

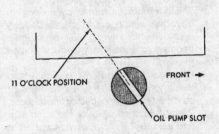

12.14a To seat the distributor on a 1995 inline six-cylinder engine, use a screwdriver to rotate the oil pump gear so the slot is at the eleven o'clock position

12.14b When the distributor is installed correctly, the centerline of the base slot will be aligned with the clamp bolt hole on the engine

f) Slide the distributor down into the engine block until it seats. Keep the hold-down ear aligned to the hole in the block.

g) The rotor should be in the five o'clock position with the trailing edge of the rotor blade lined up with the mark you scribed on the distributor housing prior to removal (the number one spark plug wire post location).

h) If the distributor still won't seat properly, repeat this procedure.

14 If you are having difficulty getting the distributor to seat properly on a fuel-injected 1995 inline six-cylinder engine, use the following procedure:

a) Make sure the number one cylinder is at TDC (see Chapter 2).

b) Look into the hole in the engine block where the distributor mounts. You should see the oil pump gear slot (see illustration). Put a screwdriver into the hole and rotate the oil pump gear so the gear slot is slightly before the eleven o'clock position.

c) The pulse ring must be locked in place to hold the rotor in the number one cylinder firing position during installation. Lift the camshaft position sensor straight up and out of the distributor. Rotate the distributor shaft and install a 3/16 inch drift pin punch tool through the correct alignment hole in the plastic ring and into the mating hole in the distributor housing (see illustration 12.11b). This will prevent the distributor shaft and rotor from rotating during installation.

d) Install the rotor onto the shaft.

e) Visually line up the distributor with the centerline of the base slot in the one o'clock position (see illustration 12.11c).

f) Install the distributor. It will rotate clockwise during installation and when the distributor is fully installed the centerline of the base slot will be aligned with the clamp bolt hole on the engine (see illustration). The rotor should also be pointing to slightly past (clockwise of) the five o'clock position.

g) If the distributor is still not installed correctly, repeat this procedure.

15 Place the hold-down clamp in position and loosely install the bolt.

16 On 1995 four-cylinder and inline 6-cylinder models, remove the pin punch tool from the distributor. Install the camshaft position sensor onto the distributor and align the wiring harness grommet with the notch in the distributor. Install the rotor.

17 Attach the electrical wires to the distributor.

18 Reattach the spark plug wires to the plugs (if removed).

19 Connect the cable to the negative terminal of the battery.

20 Check the ignition timing (see Chapter 1) and tighten the distributor hold-down bolt securely.

13 Stator - replacement (1991 and later, except 2000 six-cylinder models)

Refer to illustrations 13.4, 13.6 and 13.7
Note: *The stator is also referred to as the camshaft position sensor on early models. Refer to Chapter 6 for camshaft position sensor information relating to 2000 six-cylinder models.*

1 Remove the distributor from the engine (see Section 12).

2 Remove the distributor cap and rotor (see Chapter 1).

3 Secure the distributor shaft gear in a bench vise. Wrap a rag around the shaft to prevent damage from the vise jaws.

4 Use a small punch and hammer to drive out the retaining pin, then remove the distributor gear from the shaft (see illustration).

5 Remove the distributor shaft from the distributor housing.

6 On 1991 through 1994 models, perform the following:

a) Mark the location of the stator (see illustration) so you can return it to the same location during reassembly.

13.4 Use a small punch and hammer to drive out the retaining pin, then remove the distributor gear from the shaft

13.6 After marking the position of the stator assembly, remove the retaining screw, push the grommet through the distributor housing and remove the stator (1991 through 1994)

b) Remove the stator retaining screw (see illustration 13.6).

c) Remove the stator harness (see illustration 13.6) by pushing the grommet through the distributor housing. Remove the stator assembly.

7 On 1995 and later models, except 2000 six-cylinder models, lift the stator (camshaft

13.7 Lift the stator (camshaft position sensor) assembly from the distributor housing

position sensor) from the distributor housing (see illustration).

8   Installation is the reverse of removal.

14   Charging system - general information and precautions

The charging system includes the alternator, an internal voltage regulator, a charge indicator, the battery, a fusible link and the wiring between all the components. The charging system supplies electrical power for the ignition system, the lights, the radio, etc. The alternator is driven by a drivebelt at the front of the engine.

The purpose of the voltage regulator is to limit the alternator's voltage to a preset value. This prevents power surges, circuit overloads, etc., during peak voltage output.

The fusible link is a short length of insulated wire integral with the engine compartment wiring harness. Production fusible links are identified by the flag color. See Chapter 12 for additional information regarding fusible links.

The charging system doesn't ordinarily require periodic maintenance. However, the drivebelt, battery, battery cables and connections should be inspected at the intervals outlined in Chapter 1.

The dashboard warning light should come on when the ignition key is turned to Start, then go off immediately. If it remains on, there is a malfunction in the charging system (see Section 15). Some vehicles are also equipped with a voltmeter. If the voltmeter indicates abnormally high or low voltage, check the charging system (see Section 15).

Be very careful when making electrical circuit connections to a vehicle equipped with an alternator and note the following:

a) *When reconnecting wires to the alternator from the battery, be sure to note the polarity.*

b) *Before using arc welding equipment to repair any part of the vehicle, disconnect the wires from the alternator and the battery terminals.*

c) *Never start the engine with a battery charger connected.*

d) *Always disconnect both battery leads before using a battery charger.*

e) *The alternator is turned by an engine drivebelt which could cause serious injury if your hands, hair or clothes become entangled in it with the engine running.*

f) *Because the alternator is connected directly to the battery, it could arc or cause a fire if overloaded or shorted out.*

g) *Wrap a plastic bag over the alternator and secure it with rubberbands before steam cleaning the engine.*

15   Charging system - check

Refer to illustration 15.5

1   If a malfunction occurs in the charging circuit, don't automatically assume that the alternator is causing the problem. First check the following items:

a) *Check the drivebelt tension and condition (see Chapter 1). Replace it if it's worn or deteriorated.*

b) *Make sure the alternator mounting and adjustment bolts are tight.*

c) *Inspect the alternator wiring harness and the connectors at the alternator and voltage regulator. They must be in good condition and tight.*

d) *Check the fusible link (if equipped) located between the starter solenoid and the alternator. If it's burned, determine the cause, repair the circuit and replace the link (the vehicle won't start and/or the accessories won't work if the fusible link blows). Sometimes a fusible link may look good, but still be bad. If in doubt, remove it and check for continuity with an ohmmeter or test light.*

e) *Start the engine and check the alternator for abnormal noises (a shrieking or squealing sound indicates a bad bearing).*

f) *Check the specific gravity of the battery electrolyte. If it's low, charge the battery (doesn't apply to maintenance free batteries).*

g) *Make sure the battery is fully charged (one bad cell in a battery can cause overcharging by the alternator).*

h) *Disconnect the battery cables (negative first, then positive). Inspect the battery posts and the cable clamps for corrosion. Clean them thoroughly if necessary (see Chapter 1). Reconnect the cable to the negative terminal.*

i) *With the key off, connect a test light between the negative battery post and the disconnected negative cable clamp.*

 1) *If the test light does not come on, reattach the clamp and proceed to the next step.*

 2) *If the test light comes on, there is a short (drain) in the electrical system of the vehicle. The short must be repaired before the charging system can be checked.*

15.5 To seat the Delco alternator, locate the test hole in the back, ground that tab that's located inside the hole by inserting a screwdriver blade into the hole and touching the tab and the case at the same time

 3) *Disconnect the alternator wiring harness.*
  (a) *If the light goes out, the alternator is bad.*
  (b) *If the light stays on, pull each fuse until the light goes out (this will tell you which component is shorted).*

2   Using a voltmeter, check the battery voltage with the engine off. If should be approximately 12-volts.

3   Start the engine and check the battery voltage again. It should now be approximately 14-to-15 volts.

4   On Delco alternators, locate the test hole in the back of the alternator. **Note:** *If there is no test hole, the vehicle is equipped with a newer CS type alternator. Further testing of this type of alternator must be done by a dealer service department or automotive electrical shop. Nippondenso alternators (used on later models) have no test hole.*

5   Ground the tab that is located inside the hole by inserting a screwdriver blade into the hole and touching the tab and the case at the same time **(see illustration)**. **Caution:** *Do not run the engine with the tab grounded any longer than necessary to obtain a voltmeter reading. If the alternator is charging, it is running unregulated during the test. This condition may overload the electrical system and cause damage to the components.*

6   The reading on the voltmeter should be 15-volts or higher with the tab in the test hole grounded.

7   If the voltmeter indicates low battery voltage, the alternator is faulty and should be replaced with a new one (see Section 16).

8   If the voltage reading is 15-volts or higher and a no charge condition is present, the regulator or field circuit is the problem. Remove the alternator (see Section 16) and have it checked further by an auto electric shop.

16.2 To remove the alternator, detach the electrical connectors (arrows) from below. . .

16.3a . . . loosen the alternator adjustment bolt . . .

16.3b . . . and remove the alternator pivot bolt from below

16 Alternator - removal and installation

Refer to illustrations 16.2, 16.3a and 16.3b

1   Detach the cable from the negative terminal of the battery.
2   Detach the electrical connectors from the alternator **(see illustration)**.
3   Loosen the alternator adjustment and pivot bolts and detach the drivebelt **(see illustrations)**.
4   Remove the adjustment and pivot bolts and separate the alternator from the engine.
5   If you are replacing the alternator, take the old one with you when purchasing a replacement unit. Make sure the new/rebuilt unit looks identical to the old alternator. Look at the terminals - they should be the same in number, size and location as the terminals on the old alternator. Finally, look at the identification numbers - they will be stamped into the housing or printed on a tag attached to the housing. Make sure the numbers are the same on both alternators.
6   Many new/rebuilt alternators DO NOT have a pulley installed, so you may have to switch the pulley from the old unit to the new/rebuilt one. When buying an alternator, find out the shop's policy regarding pulleys - some shops will perform this service free of charge.

17.2 Mark the front and rear end frame housings with a scribe or paint mark before separating them

7   Installation is the reverse of removal.
8   After the alternator is installed, adjust the drivebelt tension (see Chapter 1).
9   Check the charging voltage to verify proper operation of the alternator (see Section 15).

17 Alternator brushes - replacement

Refer to illustrations 17.2 17.4a, 17.4b, 17.5, 17.6, 17.7, 17.8 and 17.11

1   Remove the alternator from the vehicle (see Section 16).

17.4a Carefully separate the drive end frame and the rectifier end frame

Delco alternator

Note: *The following procedure applies only to SI type alternators. CS types have riveted housings and cannot be disassembled.*
2   Scribe or paint marks on the front and rear end frame housings of the alternator to facilitate reassembly **(see illustration)**.
3   Remove the four through-bolts holding the front and rear end frames together.
4   Separate the drive end frame from the rectifier end frame **(see illustrations)**.
5   Remove the bolts holding the stator to the rear end frame and separate the stator from the end frame **(see illustration)**.

17.4b Inside a typical Delco alternator

1   *Brush holder*
2   *Paper clip (holding the brushes in place)*
3   *Regulator*
4   *Resistor (not all models)*
5   *Diode trio*
6   *Rectifier bridge*

17.5 After removing the bolts holding the stator assembly to the end frame, remove the stator

17.6 Remove the nuts attaching the diode trio to the rectifier bridge and remove the trio

17.7 After removing the screws that attach the regulator, brush holder and the resistor (if equipped) to the end frame, remove the regulator

17.8 Slip the brush retainer off the brush holder and remove the brushes (arrow)

17.11 To hold the brushes in place during reassembly, insert a paper clip through the hole in the rear end frame nearest rotor shaft

17.12 To replace the brushes on Nippondenso alternators, remove the B+ terminal nut, washer and insulator (arrow)

17.13 Remove the Nippondenso alternator rear cover attaching nuts (arrows) and remove the cover

6   Remove the nuts attaching the diode trio to the rectifier bridge and remove the trio **(see illustration)**.
7   Remove the screws attaching the resistor (not used on all models) and regulator and brush holder to the end frame and remove

the regulator **(see illustration)**.
8   Remove the brushes from the brush holder by slipping the brush retainer off the holder **(see illustration)**.
9   Remove the springs from the brush holder.

10   Installation is the reverse of the removal procedure, but be sure to note the following:
11   When installing the brushes in the brush holder, install the brush closest to the end frame first. Slip a paper clip through the rear of the end frame to hold the brush, then insert the second brush and push the paper clip in to hold both brushes while reassembly is completed **(see illustration)**. The paper clip should not be removed until the front and rear end frames have been bolted together.

Nippondenso alternator

Refer to illustrations 17.12, 17.13, 17.14a, 17.14b, 17.15 and 17.16

12   With the alternator removed from the vehicle (see Section 16), remove the B+ insulator nut and insulator **(see illustration)**.
13   Remove the rear cover attaching nuts and remove the rear cover **(see illustration)**.
14   Remove the brush holder attaching screws and lift the brush holder from the alternator **(see illustrations)**.
15   Before installing the new brush holder assembly, check for continuity between each

17.14a Remove the brush holder attaching nuts (arrows) . . .

17.14b . . . and remove the brush holder assembly (Nippondenso alternator)

17.15 Using an ohmmeter, check for continuity between each brush and appropriate field terminal (if there's no continuity, switch one of the leads to the other field terminal or brush)

17.16 Depress the brushes with your index finger as you slide the brush holder into place

20.3 Before unbolting the starter motor assembly, detach the wires (arrows) from the solenoid (or from the starter motor itself, on some models) - be sure the battery is disconnected

brush and the appropriate field terminal **(see illustration)**.

16   To install the brush holder assembly, use your finger to depress the brushes **(see illustration)**, then slide the holder over the commutator slip rings and screw it into place.

17   Installation is otherwise the reverse of removal. When installing the B+ insulator, be sure to align the guide tang with the hole in the rear cover.

18   Starting system - general information and precautions

The sole function of the starting system is to turn over the engine quickly enough to allow it to start.

The starting system consists of the battery, the starter motor, the starter solenoid, a remote starter relay (on some models) and the wires connecting them. A number of different starter motors - including Bosch, Mitsubishi and Motorcraft - are used on the vehicles covered by this manual. If you replace the starter motor, be sure to take the old starter with you to the parts department to make sure you get the right replacement. The solenoid is mounted directly on the starter motor or, on Motorcraft units, is a separate component located in the engine compartment.

The solenoid/starter motor assembly is installed on the lower part of the engine, next to the transmission bellhousing.

When the ignition key is turned to the Start position, the starter solenoid is actuated through the starter control circuit. The starter solenoid then connects the battery to the starter. The battery supplies the electrical energy to the starter motor, which does the actual work of cranking the engine.

The starter on a vehicle equipped with an automatic transmission can only be operated when the transmission selector lever is in Park or Neutral.

Always observe the following precautions when working on the starting system:

a) *Excessive cranking of the starter motor can overheat it and cause serious damage. Never operate the starter motor for more than 15 seconds at a time without pausing to allow it to cool for at least two minutes.*

b) *The starter is connected directly to the battery and could arc or cause a fire if mishandled, overloaded or shorted out.*

c) *Always detach the cable from the negative terminal of the battery before working on the starting system.*

19   Starter motor - testing in vehicle

Note: *Before diagnosing starter problems, make sure the battery is fully charged.*

1   If the starter motor does not operate at all when the switch is turned to Start, make sure the shift lever is in Neutral or Park (automatic transmission).

2   Make sure that the battery is charged and that all cables, both at the battery and starter solenoid terminals, are clean and secure.

3   If the starter motor spins but the engine is not cranking, the overrunning clutch in the starter motor is slipping and the starter motor must be replaced.

4   If, when the switch is actuated, the starter motor does not operate at all but the solenoid clicks, then the problem lies with either the battery, the starter relay (if equipped), the main solenoid contacts or the starter motor itself (or the engine is seized).

5   If the solenoid plunger cannot be heard when the switch is actuated, the battery is bad, the fusible link is burned (the circuit is open) or the solenoid itself is defective.

6   To check the solenoid, connect a jumper lead between the battery (+) and the ignition switch wire terminal (the small terminal) on the solenoid. If the starter motor now operates, the solenoid is OK and the problem is in the ignition switch, neutral start switch or the wiring.

7   If the starter motor still does not oper-

ate, remove the starter/solenoid assembly for disassembly, testing and repair.

8   If the starter motor cranks the engine at an abnormally slow speed, first make sure that the battery is charged and that all terminal connections are tight. If the engine is partially seized, or has the wrong viscosity oil in it, it will crank slowly.

9   Run the engine until normal operating temperature is reached, then disconnect the coil wire from the distributor cap and ground it.

10   Connect a voltmeter positive lead to the positive battery post and connect the negative lead to the negative post.

11   Crank the engine and take the voltmeter readings as soon as a steady figure is indicated. Do not allow the starter motor to turn for more than 15 seconds at a time. A reading of 9-volts or more, with the starter motor turning at normal cranking speed, is normal. If the reading is 9-volts or more but the cranking speed is slow, the motor is faulty. If the reading is less than 9-volts and the cranking speed is slow, the solenoid contacts are probably burned, the starter motor is bad, the battery is discharged or there is a bad connection.

20   Starter motor - removal and installation

Refer to illustrations 20.3, 20.4a, 20.4b and 20.4c

Note: *On some vehicles, it may be necessary to remove the exhaust pipe(s) or frame cross-member to gain access to the starter motor. In extreme cases it may even be necessary to unbolt the mounts and raise the engine slightly to get the starter out.*

1   Detach the cable from the negative terminal of the battery.

2   Raise the vehicle and support it securely on jackstands.

3   Clearly label, then disconnect the wires from the terminals on the starter motor and solenoid (if mounted on the starter) **(see illustration)**.

20.4a The starter lower mounting bolt (six-cylinder model shown)

20.4b The starter upper mounting bolt (six-cylinder engine) - view is from the front, looking toward the rear

20.4c On some four-cylinder engines, the starter is held in place by E-12 Torx-head bolts (arrows) which will require a special socket

21.3 Before removing the solenoid from the starter motor, detach the starter motor terminal strap (arrow) - Mitsubishi starter shown

21.4 To detach the solenoid from the starter motor, remove the solenoid attaching screws (arrows) from the front of the starter solenoid mount (Mitsubishi starter shown) - Bosch starters only have one screw

21.7 If you have a Motorcraft starter solenoid, it's located near the battery - to remove it, detach the wires and remove the mounting bracket bolts - be sure the battery is disconnected!

4   Remove the mounting bolts **(see illustrations)** and detach the starter.
5   Installation is the reverse of removal.

21 Starter solenoid - removal and installation

1   Disconnect the cable from the negative terminal of the battery.

All solenoids except Motorcraft

Refer to illustrations 21.3 and 21.4
2   Remove the starter motor (see Section 20).

3   Disconnect the strap from the solenoid to the starter motor terminal **(see illustration)**.
4   Remove the screws which secure the solenoid to the starter motor **(see illustration)**.
5   On some models it may be necessary to twist the solenoid in a clockwise direction to disengage the flange from the starter body.
6   Installation is the reverse of removal.

Motorcraft solenoid

Refer to illustration 21.7
7   Locate the solenoid - it's mounted in the engine compartment near the battery **(see illustration)**. Detach the electrical wires from the starter solenoid terminals. Label them to assure proper reassembly.
8   Remove the solenoid mounting bracket bolts and detach the solenoid. 9
Installation is the reverse of removal.

Chapter 6
Emissions control systems

Contents

1   General Information

Refer to illustration 1.6

To prevent pollution of the atmosphere from incompletely burned and evaporating gases, and to maintain good driveability and fuel economy, a number of emission control systems are incorporated. The principal systems are:

Positive Crankcase Ventilation (PCV) system
Closed Crankcase Ventilation (CCV) system
Evaporative emissions control system
Thermostatically controlled Air Cleaner (TAC) system
Exhaust Gas Recirculation (EGR) system
Catalytic converter
Computerized Emissions Control (CEC) system

The sections in this Chapter include descriptions, checking procedures within the scope of the home mechanic and component replacement procedures (when possible) for each of the systems listed above.

Before assuming an emissions control system is malfunctioning, check the fuel and ignition systems carefully. The diagnosis of some emission control devices requires specialized tools, equipment and training. If checking and servicing becomes too difficult or if a procedure is beyond your ability, consult a dealer service department or other qualified shop. Remember, the most frequent cause of emissions problems is simply a loose or broken vacuum hose or wire, so always check the hose and wiring connections first.

This doesn't mean, however, that emission control systems are particularly difficult to maintain and repair. You can quickly and easily perform many checks and do most of the regular maintenance at home with common tune-up and hand tools. **Note:** *Because of a Federally-mandated extended warranty which covers the emission control system components, check with your dealer about warranty coverage before working on any emissions-related systems. Once the warranty has expired, you may wish to perform some of the component checks and/or replacement procedures in this Chapter to save money.*

Pay close attention to any special precautions outlined in this Chapter. It should be noted that the illustrations of the various systems may not exactly match the system installed on your vehicle because of changes made by the manufacturer during production or from year-to-year.

The Vehicle Emissions Control Information (VECI) label is located in the engine compartment **(see illustration)**. This label contains important emissions specifications and adjustment information. When servicing the engine or emissions systems, the VECI label in your particular vehicle should always be checked for up-to-date information.

2   Crankcase ventilation systems

Positive Crankcase Ventilation (PCV) system (earlier models)

Refer to illustrations 2.1a and 2.1b

1   The Positive Crankcase Ventilation (PCV) system **(see illustrations)** reduces hydrocarbon emissions by scavenging crankcase vapors. It does this by circulating fresh air from the air cleaner through the crankcase, where it mixes with blow-by gases and is rerouted through a PCV valve to the intake manifold.

2   The main components of the PCV system are the PCV valve, a fresh air filtered inlet and the vacuum hoses connecting these two components with the engine. 4.2L six-cylinder engines also have a PCV shut-off solenoid to shut off the flow of crankcase vapors to the intake manifold under certain operating conditions.

1.6 A typical Vehicle Emissions Control Information (VECI) label (1990 four-cylinder engine shown)

2.1a Positive Crankcase Ventilation (PCV) system (four-cylinder engine)

2.1b Positive Crankcase Ventilation (PCV) system (4.2L six-cylinder engine)

2.5a Closed Crankcase Ventilation (CCV) system (four-cylinder engine)

2.5b Close Crankcase Ventilation (CCV) system (4.0L six-cylinder engine)

3   To maintain idle quality, the PCV valve restricts the flow when the intake manifold vacuum is high. If abnormal operating conditions (such as piston ring problems) arise, the system is designed to allow excessive amounts of blow-by gases to flow back through the crankcase vent tube into the air cleaner to be consumed by normal combustion.

4   Checking and replacement of the PCV valve and filter is covered in Chapter 1.

Closed Crankcase Ventilation (CCV) system (later models)

Refer to illustrations 2.5a and 2.5b

5   Later fuel-injected models are equipped with a Closed Crankcase Ventilation (CCV) system **(see illustrations)**. The CCV system performs the same function as a conventional PCV system but does not use a vacuum controlled valve.

6   A molded vacuum tube connects manifold vacuum to a grommet on the front of the valve cover (four-cylinder engine) or top rear of the cover (4.0L six-cylinder engine). The grommet contains a calibrated orifice that meters the amount of crankcase vapors drawn out of the engine. A fresh air supply hose from the air cleaner is connected to the rear of the valve cover (four-cylinder engine) or the top front of the cover (4.0L six-cylinder engine). When the engine is operating, fresh air enters the engine and mixes with the crankcase vapors. Manifold vacuum draws the vapor/air mixture through the calibrated orifice and into the intake manifold. The vapors are consumed during combustion.

3   Evaporative emissions control system

Refer to illustrations 3.3, 3.6a, 3.6b, 3.6c, 3.6d and 3.8

General description

1   This system is designed to trap and store fuel that evaporates from the fuel system that would normally enter the atmosphere in the form of hydrocarbon (HC) emissions.

2   The system is very simple and consists of a charcoal-filled canister, canister purge valve (and canister purge solenoid on some models), a combination rollover/pressure relief valve and connecting lines and hoses.

3   When the pressure in the fuel tank exceeds 3 psi (caused by fuel evaporation), a pressure relief/rollover valve opens, preventing excessive pressure build-up in the tank and allowing the fuel vapors to flow to an evaporative canister containing charcoal that absorbs the fuel vapors **(see illustration)**. On carbureted models, the carburetor float bowl is also vented to the evaporative canister to allow vapors from the float bowl to flow to the canister. When the engine is started (cold), the charcoal continues to absorb and store fuel vapor. As the engine warms up, the stored vapors are routed to the intake manifold or air cleaner and combustion chambers where they are burned during normal engine operation.

4   A canister purge valve controls when the

3.3 A typical evaporative emissions charcoal-filtered canister - the arrow points to the purge valve

stored vapors are allowed to flow to the intake manifold or air cleaner. This valve is actuated by intake manifold vacuum. On some models, system purging is not com-

3.6a A typical emissions control system vacuum schematic (1987 through 1989 four-cylinder engine)

3.6b A typical emissions control system vacuum schematic (4.2L six-cylinder engine)

puter controlled and a coolant temperature switch in line between the intake manifold (or air cleaner) and canister purge valve assures that purging occurs only when coolant temperature is above 70-degrees F. On some models, the computer controls a solenoid that's in line between the intake manifold (or air cleaner) and purge valve. This solenoid serves the same function as the coolant temperature switch.

5   The relief valve, which is mounted in the fuel filler cap, opens to vent excessive pressure or vacuum in the fuel tank.

Checking

6   See Chapter 1 for information regarding routine maintenance of the canister. Check hoses and lines for misrouting, cracks, deterioration and other damage (see illustrations). Check the fuel tank filler gasket for deforma-

tion and other damage. The most common symptom of a problem with this system is a fuel odor under the hood, which is most often caused by a damaged canister or hoses.

7   To check the purge valve, unplug the upper vacuum hose from the valve (see illustration 3.3) and connect a hand vacuum pump in its place. Also unplug the purge hose leading to the intake manifold or air cleaner and attach a short piece of vacuum

3.6c A typical emissions control system vacuum schematic (1990 and later four-cylinder engine)

3.6d A typical emissions control system vacuum
schematic (4.0L six-cylinder engine)

hose in its place. When vacuum is applied
with the vacuum pump, you should be able to
blow through the length of vacuum hose
attached to the purge hose port. When no
vacuum is applied, you should not be able to
blow through the hose.

8   To check the purge solenoid (models so
equipped) **(see illustration)**, unplug the electrical connector from the solenoid and apply
battery voltage to the terminals using two
jumper wires. You should hear a click if the
solenoid is operating properly. **Caution:**
*Don't leave the jumper wires connected to
the solenoid any longer than necessary to
perform this check.*

**3.8 A typical evaporative emissions
system purge solenoid - on some models
(like the one shown here) the solenoid
also controls vacuum to the EGR valve**

4   Thermostatically controlled Air Cleaner (TAC) system (carburetor and TBI-equipped models through 1990)

Refer to illustration 4.1

General description

1   The Thermostatic Air Cleaner (TAC) provides heated intake air during warmup, then
maintains the inlet air temperature within
a 70-degrees F to 105-degrees F operating
range by mixing warm and cool air. This
allows leaner fuel/air mixture settings for the
carburetor or throttle body, which reduces
emissions and improves driveability **(see
illustration)**.

2   The TAC system is comprised of the following major components:

a) A heat shroud that partially encloses the
     exhaust manifold.
b) A heated air tube.
c) A special air cleaner assembly equipped
     with a bi-metal temperature sensor.
d) A time delay valve.
e) A check valve.
f) A vacuum motor.
g) A heat duct valve assembly.

3   A vacuum motor, which operates a heat
duct valve in the air cleaner, etc. maintains a
balance between two fresh air inlets - one hot
and one cold - and is actuated by the intake
manifold vacuum.

4   When the engine temperature is cold,
warm air radiating off the exhaust manifold is

**4.1 A typical thermostatically controlled
air cleaner (six-cylinder engine shown,
four-cylinder engine similar)**

1   *Air cleaner cover*
2   *PCV valve filter*
3   *Bi-metal temperature sensor*
4   *Check valve*
5   *Vacuum motor*
6   *Heated air tube*
7   *Ambient body (cold) air duct*
8   *Time delay valve*
9   *Trap door assembly (not on all models)*
10   *Trap door time delay valve (not on all
     models)*

routed, by a shroud which fits over the manifold, up through a heated air tube and into the air cleaner. This provides warm air for the carburetor or TBI, resulting in better driveability and faster warmup. As the temperature inside the air cleaner rises, the heat duct valve is gradually closed by the vacuum motor (which, in turn is controlled by a bi-metal temperature sensor inside the air cleaner) and the air cleaner draws air through a cold (ambient) air duct instead. The result is a consistent intake air temperature.

5   On some models, a trap door system opens in a similar manner to close off the air cleaner from the outside air when the engine is inoperative.

Checking

General operation

Note: *Make sure the engine is cold before beginning this test.*

6   Always check the vacuum source and the integrity of all vacuum hoses between the source and the vacuum motor before beginning the following test. Do not proceed until all cracked and broken hoses have been replaced.

7   Apply the parking brake and block the wheels.

8   Detach the flexible duct (if equipped) from the air cleaner snorkel (see Chapter 4).

9   With the engine off, observe the heat duct valve inside the air cleaner snorkel. It should be fully open to cold air. If it isn't, it might be binding or sticking. Make sure it's not rusted in an open or closed position by attempting top move it by hand. If it's rusted, it can usually be freed by cleaning and oiling the hinge. If it fails to work properly after servicing, replace it.

10   Start the engine. Note the position of the heat duct valve. Now it should be fully closed to incoming cold air.

11   Have an assistant rapidly depress and release the accelerator 1/2 to 3/4 of its travel. The heat duct valve should briefly remain stationary, then move to the cold air position, then back to the heated air position.

12   Loosely attach the flexible duct to the air cleaner and warm the engine to normal operating temperature. Remove the flexible duct and observe the heat duct valve. It should be either fully open or at a mixture position (half open) that provides the correct temperature for the inlet air to the carburetor or TBI.

13   Stop the engine and connect the flexible duct to the air cleaner.

14   If the heat duct valve does not function as described above, look for a mechanical bind in the linkage and disconnected vacuum hoses or air leaks at the vacuum motor, bi-metal sensor, time delay valve, check valve, intake manifold or vacuum hoses.

15   If the heat duct valve manually operates freely and you cannot find any hose disconnections or leaks, attach a hose from an intake manifold vacuum source directly to the vacuum motor and start the engine.

   a)   *If the heat duct valve closes, either the*

thermal switch, time delay valve or check valve is defective.

   b)   *If the heat duct valve does not close, replace the vacuum motor.*

Bi-metal temperature sensor

16   Detach the two vacuum hoses from the sensor.

17   If necessary, remove the sensor (see replacement procedure below) and cool it below 40-degrees F in a freezer.

18   Attach a vacuum pump to one of the sensor's vacuum fittings and a vacuum gauge to the other fitting.

19   Apply 14 in-Hg. vacuum to the sensor.

20   With the sensor at a temperature below 40-degrees F, the gauge should indicate a vacuum. Disconnect the vacuum pump momentarily to relieve the vacuum.

21   Warm the sensor above 55-degrees F and again attempt to apply vacuum. There should not be steady vacuum reading on the gauge.

22   Replace the sensor if it's defective.

Component replacement

Note: *Before replacing the following components, check on parts availability. On some models the components can only be replaced with a complete air cleaner assembly.*

Heat duct valve vacuum motor

23   Remove the air cleaner (see Chapter 4)

24   Clearly label, then detach the vacuum hose from the heat duct valve vacuum motor.

25   Drill out the rivet which secures the heat duct valve vacuum motor to the air cleaner snorkel.

26   Lift the motor and tilt it to one side to detach the motor linkage from the heat duct valve assembly. Remove the motor.

27   Installation is the reverse of removal. If you don't have a rivet tool, you'll need a self-tapping sheet-metal screw of the correct diameter to attach the vacuum motor to the snorkel. Make sure the rivet (or the screw) does not interfere with the movement of the duct valve.

Bi-metal temperature sensor

28   Remove the air cleaner (see Chapter 4).

29   Detach the two vacuum hoses from the sensor.

30   Pry up the tabs on the sensor retaining clip. Remove the clip, gasket and sensor from the air cleaner. Before removing the sensor, note its position in relation to the air cleaner to ensure proper reassembly.

31   Installation is the reverse of removal. Be sure to use a new gasket.

Trap door vacuum motor

32   Remove the air cleaner (see Chapter 4).

33   Clearly label, then detach the vacuum hoses from the heat duct valve motor, bi-metal sensor and the trap door vacuum motor.

34   Drill out the rivet which secures the trap door vacuum motor to the bracket.

35   Lift the vacuum motor from the bracket

and tilt it to one side to clear the door arm. Remove the motor.

36   Installation is the reverse of removal. If you don't have a rivet tool, you'll need a self-tapping sheet-metal screw of the correct diameter to attach the vacuum motor to the bracket. Make sure the rivet (or the screw) does not interfere with the movement of the trap door.

---

5   Pulse air system

General description

Refer to illustration 5.5

1   The Pulse Air system, used on earlier models, uses the alternating pressure and vacuum pulsation created in the exhaust system to draw air into the exhaust system. This additional air aids in further burning of exhaust gasses in the exhaust system, resulting in lower emissions. Air is supplied from the filtered side of the air cleaner through a hose to the air control valve, which is controlled by the computer. When opened by the air switch solenoid, the air valve allows air to flow to the air injection check valve, through which it enters the exhaust system. The following explains the components of the system:

   a)   *The air injection check valve is a reed valve that is opened and closed by the vacuum and pressure exhaust pulsations. During vacuum pulsations, atmospheric pressure opens the check valve and forces air into the exhaust system.*

   b)   *The air control valve controls the supply of filtered air routed to the air injection check valve. The valve is opened and closed by the air switch solenoid.*

   c)   *The air switch solenoid controls the air control valve by switching vacuum to the air control valve on and off during varying operating conditions. The solenoid is controlled by the computer.*

   d)   *Vacuum is stored in the vacuum storage reservoir until it's released by the air switch solenoid.*

   e)   *Depending on operating conditions, the computer switches the air injection point to and from the exhaust manifold and catalytic converter. The computer does this by energizing and de-energizing the air switch solenoids.*

Checking

2   Because of the complexity of the Pulse Air system, it is difficult to diagnose a malfunctioning system at home. However, if you suspect the system is malfunctioning, a simple inspection is as follows:

3   Inspect all hoses, vacuum lines and wires. Be sure they are in good condition and all connections are clean and tight.

4   If there is still a malfunction in the system take the vehicle to a dealer service department or a certified emission control repair shop for testing.

Component replacement

5   To replace Pulse Air system components, refer to the accompanying exploded view of the Pulse Air system **(see illustration)**.

6   Exhaust Gas Recirculation (EGR) system (1987 through 1990 models)

Caution: *Do not operate the engine (other than temporarily for testing) with any EGR system components disconnected or not operating as designed. Doing so can lead to severe engine damage from detonation.*

General description

Refer to illustration 6.2

1   This system recirculates a portion of the exhaust gases into the intake manifold to reduce the combustion temperatures and thus decrease the amount of oxides of nitrogen (NOx) in the exhaust.

2   The main component in the system is the EGR valve. The EGR valve is a vacuum-controlled device which regulates the amount of exhaust gas bled into the intake. Some six-cylinder engines use a backpressure transducer (normally mounted near the EGR valve) **(see illustration)**. The backpressure transducer measures the amount of exhaust gas backpressure on the exhaust side of the EGR valve and varies the strength of the vacuum signal to the EGR valve based on backpressure. The transducer uses this signal to provide the correct amount of recirculated exhaust gas under various conditions.

3   The EGR valves on later four-cylinder and all 4.0L six-cylinder engines use an EGR solenoid. The EGR solenoid is controlled by the computer. When energized by the computer, the solenoid closes and prevents vacuum from reaching the EGR valve. When it's not energized, the solenoid is open and vacuum is applied to the EGR valve. The computer monitors engine coolant temperature and other operating conditions to determine when EGR operation is desired. On many four-cylinder engines, one solenoid controls vacuum to both the EGR valve and the canister purge valve **(see illustration 3.8)**.

4   EGR systems on earlier four-cylinder and all 4.2L six-cylinder engines are not computer controlled. They use a Coolant Temperature Override (CTO) valve and a Thermal Vacuum Switch (TVS). The CTO restricts vacuum flow to the EGR valve when coolant temperature is below about 115-degrees F. The TVS, located in the air cleaner, restricts vacuum flow to the EGR valve when intake air temperature is below about 50-degrees F.

5   Common engine problems associated with the EGR system are rough idling, stalling at idle, rough engine performance during light throttle application and stalling during deceleration. Keep in mind that changes in exhaust system backpressure (caused by

5.5 An exploded view of a typical Pulse Air System

1	Air cleaner	
2	Air cleaner-to-downstream air control valve vacuum hose	
3	Air cleaner-to-upstream air control valve vacuum hose	
4	Upstream vacuum hose	
5	Upstream air control valve	
6	Downstream air control valve	
7	Upstream check valve hose	
8	Downstream vacuum hose	
9	Downstream check valve hose	
10	Upstream check valve	
11	Downstream check valve	
12	Downstream tube-to-converter	
13	Upstream tube-to-exhaust pipe	
A	Air switch solenoid (upstream)	
B	Air switch solenoid (downstream)	
C	Control wires from computer (downstream)	
D	Control wires from computer (upstream)	
E	Vacuum storage reservoir	

6.2 A typical EGR valve and vacuum transducer on a six-cylinder engine (4.0L six-cylinder shown)

6.7 Location of the EGR valve on four-cylinder models - when checking the valve, remove the vacuum hose and connect a hand vacuum pump

6.20 A typical CTO valve - it is normally threaded into the intake manifold

1   *Inlet port (to a ported vacuum source)*
2   *Outlet port (to the TVS)*

blockage or leaks) can cause the EGR system to malfunction, sometimes resulting in driveability problems.

Checking

Warning: *Use extreme caution when the engine is running. Do not stand in line with the engine cooling fan. Keep your hands away from the pulleys, belts or fan. Do not wear loose clothing.*

General

Refer to illustration 6.7

6   With the engine at normal operating temperature, the parking brake set and the wheels blocked, have an assistant raise the engine speed to approximately 1500 rpm while you watch the EGR valve stem. It should move, indicating the EGR valve is opening. If it does not open, the EGR valve is not receiving vacuum or the EGR valve is malfunctioning.

7   Disconnect the vacuum hose from the EGR valve and connect a hand vacuum pump in its place **(see the accompanying illustration or illustration 6.2)**. With the engine idling, apply about 15 in-Hg of vacuum. The valve should open and the engine should run roughly or stall.

a) *If the valve holds vacuum and opens, but the engine does not run roughly or stall, the EGR valve and/or passages (in the intake manifold) are clogged or the EGR tube is corroded, damaged or clogged. Remove the components and clean or replace them as necessary.*

b) *If the valve does not hold vacuum, the valve diaphragm is ruptured. Replace the valve.*

c) *If the valve holds vacuum but does not open, the valve is stuck. Replace it.*

EGR solenoid

8   Apply the parking brake and block the wheels.

9   Warm the engine to normal operating temperature and perform the following checks with the engine idling.

10   Check the vacuum to the solenoid (it should be 15 in-Hg minimum). If vacuum is low or non-existent, check for kinks, twists or loose connections of the vacuum hoses and lines.

11   If the vacuum is OK, reconnect the vacuum line to the input port and connect a vacuum gauge to the solenoid output port.

12   If vacuum reads zero, go to the next step. If the gauge is reading a vacuum, have the solenoid and the ECU checked by the dealer service department or other qualified shop.

13   Disconnect the electrical connector at the solenoid. There should now be vacuum at the output port. If not, replace the EGR valve solenoid.

Backpressure transducer

14   Disconnect the vacuum output, input and backpressure lines. Remove the transducer.

15   Plug the output port, connect a hand-operated vacuum pump to the input port.

16   Apply 1 to 2 psi of air pressure to the backpressure port with a hand-operated air pump.

17   Using the hand-operated vacuum pump, apply 12 in-Hg of vacuum.

18   The transducer must be replaced if it does not hold a vacuum.

Coolant Temperature Override (CTO) valve

Refer to illustration 6.20

19   Inspect vacuum hoses for air leaks, correct routing and loose connections.

20   Disconnect the outlet hose from the CTO (leading to the TVS) and connect a vacuum gauge to the outlet port on the CTO **(see illustration)**.

21   Start the engine and run at approximately 1500 rpm (engine cold). No vacuum should be present.

22   Replace the CTO valve if vacuum is indicated.

23   Run the engine until coolant temperature reaches or exceeds 115-degrees F.

24   With the engine rpm at 1500, vacuum should be indicated. If not, replace the CTO valve.

Thermal Vacuum Switch (TVS)

25   The TVS is located in the air cleaner. Cool the TVS to approximately 40-degrees F (it may be necessary to remove the switch and refrigerate it), disconnect the vacuum hose from the TVS inner port and connect a hand-operated vacuum pump in its place.

26   Apply vacuum to the TVS. The TVS check valve should maintain a vacuum. If not, replace the TVS.

27   Start the engine. When air cleaner intake air temperature is above 50-degrees F, vacuum should not remain. Replace the TVS if vacuum is maintained.

Component replacement

EGR valve and (if equipped) transducer

28   Locate the EGR valve on the intake manifold **(see illustration 6.2 or 6.7)**.

29   Remove the air cleaner assembly or the air horn assembly from the throttle body as needed for access (see Chapter 4).

30   Detach the vacuum hose from the EGR valve or EGR valve vacuum transducer.

31   Remove the two EGR valve mounting bolts.

32   Remove the EGR valve, the old gasket and restrictor plate (if so equipped). Discard the old gasket.

33   Clean the gasket mating surfaces of the intake manifold and the EGR valve (if you're not installing a new one). Use a gasket scraper, then clean the surfaces with lacquer thinner or acetone.

34   Clean all exhaust passages in the intake manifold to insure a free flow.

35   Installation is the reverse of removal. Be sure to use a new gasket.

Coolant Temperature Override (CTO) valve

Warning: *Never remove the radiator cap until the engine has cooled completely (at least five hours after the engine has been run).*

36   Drain the coolant (see Chapter 1).

37   Detach the vacuum hoses, making sure all hoses are marked for easier installation.

38   Using an open-end wrench, remove the CTO valve from the intake manifold.

39   Clean the threaded of hole in the intake manifold to remove corrosion and old sealant.

40   Use Teflon tape on the threads of the new CTO valve.

41   Installation is the reverse of the removal.

42   Fill the cooling system (see Chapter 1).

Thermal Vacuum Switch (TVS)

43   Remove the air cleaner.

44   Detach and label the vacuum hoses from the TVS.

6.48 EGR tube removal (four-cylinder engine)

6.55 Typical six-cylinder engine EGR tube installation details (4.0L six-cylinder engine shown, 4.2L six-cylinder engine similar)

45 Detach the retaining clip(s) attaching the TVS to the air cleaner.
46 Remove the TVS from the air cleaner.
47 Installation is the reverse of the removal.

EGR tube (four-cylinder engine)

Refer to illustration 6.48

48 Remove the EGR tube-to-exhaust manifold bolts **(see illustration)**.
49 Using a flare-nut wrench (if available), unscrew the EGR tube nut at the intake manifold.
50 Remove the tube and discard the gasket.
51 Clean the gasket mating surface with a scraper, then wipe it with a rag soaked in lacquer thinner or acetone.
52 Install the EGR tube. Install the EGR tube line nut to the intake manifold first.
53 Connect the EGR tube to the exhaust manifold. Be sure to use a new gasket.

EGR tube (six-cylinder engine)

Refer to illustration 6.55

54 To remove the EGR tube, it may be necessary to loosen the exhaust manifold mounting bolts (see Chapter 2 Part B).
55 Using a flare-nut wrench (if available), loosen the EGR tube line nuts at the intake and exhaust manifolds **(see illustration)**.
56 Remove the EGR tube.
57 Install the EGR tube, but don't tighten the line nuts at this time.
58 Tighten the intake manifold line nut first.
59 Tighten the exhaust manifold line nut next.
60 If loosened, tighten the exhaust manifold bolts to the torque listed in the Specifications in Chapter 2, Part B.

7   Catalytic converter

Note: *Because of a Federally mandated extended warranty which covers emissions-related components such as the catalytic converter, check with a dealer service department before replacing the converter at your own expense.*

General description

1   The catalytic converter is an emissions control device added to the exhaust system to reduce pollutants from the exhaust gas stream. Two types of converters are used. Your vehicle may be equipped with either of the two. The conventional oxidation catalyst reduces the levels of hydrocarbon (HC) and carbon monoxide (CO). The three-way catalyst lowers the levels of oxides of nitrogen (NOx) as well as HC and CO.

Checking

2   The test equipment for a catalytic converter is expensive and highly sophisticated. If you suspect that the converter on your vehicle is malfunctioning, take it to a dealer or authorized emissions inspection facility for diagnosis and repair.
3   Whenever the vehicle is raised for servicing of underbody components, check the converter for leaks, corrosion, dents and other damage. Check the welds/flange blots that attach the front and rear ends of the converter to the exhaust system. If damage is discovered, the converter should be replaced.
4   Although catalytic converters don't break too often, they do become plugged. The easiest way to check for a restricted converter is to use a vacuum gauge to diagnose the effect of a blocked exhaust on intake vacuum.

a) Open the throttle until the engine speed is about 2000 rpm.
b) Release the throttle quickly.
c) If there is no restriction, the gauge will quickly drop to not more than 2 in-Hg or more above its normal reading.
d) If the gauge does not show 5 in-Hg or more above its normal reading, or seems to momentarily hover around its highest reading for a moment before it returns, the exhaust system, or the converter, is plugged (or an exhaust pipe is bent or dented, or the core inside the muffler has shifted).

Component replacement

5   Refer to the information on exhaust system component replacement in Chapter 4.

8   Computerized Emission Control (CEC) systems

These vehicles are equipped with a computer to monitor and control engine functions. The computer goes by various names on the models covered by this manual:

a) Micro Computer Unit (MCU) (1987 through 1989 models)
b) Electronic Control Unit (ECU) (1990 and 1991 models)
c) Single Board Engine Controller (SBEC) (1990 and 1991 models)
d) Single Board Engine Controller II (SBEC II) (1992 and later models)
e) Powertrain Control Module (PCM) (1993 and later models). These systems monitor various engine operating conditions and adjust the air/fuel mixture, ignition timing, engine idle speed, etc. to promote better fuel economy, improve driveability and reduce exhaust emissions.

Each of the systems used on the various models covered by this manual includes a computer and many information sensors and output actuators. The information sensors inform the computer of the vehicle's current operating parameters, the computer compares this information to its "map" (which tells what these parameters should be), and, if the information does not match the map, the computer sends signals to the output actuators to alter engine operation to match the map. Information sensors are discussed in Section 10 of this Chapter. Output actuators include the following:

a) Carburetor mixture control solenoid or fuel injector(s) (see Chapter 4)
b) EGR/evaporative emissions solenoid(s) (see Sections 3 and 6).
c) Ignition control module (see Chapter 5).

Self-diagnostic codes

Code	Probable cause	Code	Probable cause
11	Ignition	33	Air conditioning clutch relay
13	Manifold Absolute Pressure (MAP) sensor vacuum	41	Alternator field
14	Manifold Absolute Pressure (MAP) sensor electrical	42	Automatic shutdown relay
		44	Battery temperature sensor
15	Distance sensor or circuit	46	Battery over voltage
17	Engine running too cool	47	Battery under voltage
21	Oxygen sensor or circuit	51	Oxygen sensor – lean condition indicated
22	Coolant temperature sensor or circuit	52	Oxygen sensor – rich condition indicated
23	MAT sensor or circuit	53	Internal engine controller fault
24	Throttle Position Sensor (TPS) sensor or circuit	54	Distributor sync pickup
25	Automatic Idle Speed (AIS) circuit	55	End of Code Output
27	Fuel injector control	62	Emissions Maintenance Reminder (EMR) mileage accumulator
31	EVAP solenoid or circuit	63	Controller failure EEPROM write denied

Trouble code chart - 1991 through 1995 models

d) Pulse air switch solenoids (see Section 5).
e) Automatic Idle Speed (AIS) motor or idle stepper motor (see Chapter 4).
f) Fuel pump relay (see Chapter 4).

Complete diagnosis of the computerized emission control system is beyond the scope the home mechanic. Fortunately, all of these systems are protected by a Federally mandated extended warranty (5 years/50,000 miles, or whichever comes first, at the time this manual was written). This warranty covers all emissions control components (EGR, PCV, CCV, Pulse Air, evaporative control systems, information sensors, the catalytic converter, etc.). It also covers emissions related parts like the carburetor, certain fuel injection components, exhaust manifold and major ignition system components (the distributor, ignition wires and coil, spark plugs, etc.). Contact a dealer service department for further details regarding the coverage for your vehicle; he is obligated by Federal law to provide you with a detailed list of the emission related parts on your vehicle which are protected by the Federal warranty.

If your vehicle is out of warranty and you suspect a problem with the computerized emissions control system, the next two Sections in this Chapter are designed to help you diagnose the system. If you are uncertain what the problem is after using these two Sections, take the vehicle to a dealer service department or other qualified shop that has the special equipment and expertise to diagnose these systems completely.

9 Self-diagnostic codes (1991 and later models) - description and code retrieving

Refer to illustration 9.2
Note: *The diagnostic trouble codes on all models can be extracted from the Powertrain Control Module (PCM) using a specialized SCAN tool. On 1991 THROUGH 1997 models only, the PCM can be placed in the diagnostic mode and the trouble codes flashed on the Check Engine light. On 1998 and later models, have the vehicle diagnosed by a dealer service department or other qualified automotive repair facility if the proper SCAN tool is not available.*

1   The PCM will illuminate the CHECK ENGINE light (also known as the Malfunction Indicator Lamp) on the dash if it recognizes a fault in the system. The light will remain illuminated until the problem is repaired and the code is cleared or the PCM does not detect any malfunction for several consecutive drive cycles.
2   The diagnostic codes for the On Board Diagnostic (OBD) system can be extracted from the PCM using a SCAN tool on all models **(see illustration)**. On 1991 through 1997

9.2 Scanners like the Actron Scantool and the AutoXray XP240 are powerful diagnostic aids - programmed with comprehensive diagnostic information, they can tell you just about anything you want to know about your engine management system

Check Engine Light Flash Code	Generic Scan Tool Code	DRB Scan Tool Display	Description of Diagnostic Trouble Code
12			Battery power to PCM was disconnected
54	P0340	No Cam Signal at PCM	No camshaft signal detected during engine cranking.
53	P0601	Internal Controller Failure	PCM Internal fault condition detected.
47	P0162	Charging System Voltage Too Low	Battery voltage sense input below target charging during engine operation. Also, no significant change detected in battery voltage during active test of generator output circuit.
46	P1594	Charging System Voltage Too High	Battery voltage sense input above target charging voltage during engine operation.
42	P1388	Auto Shutdown Relay Control Circuit	An open or shorted condition detected in the auto shutdown relay circuit.
41	P0622	Generator Field Not Switching Properly	An open or shorted condition detected in the generator field control circuit.
37	P0743	Torque Converter Clutch Soleniod/Trans Relay Circuits	An open or shorted condition detected in the torque converter part throttle unlock solenoid control circuit (3 speed auto RH trans. only).
35	P1491	Rad Fan Control Relay Circuit	An open or shorted condition detected in the low speed radiator fan relay control circuit (2.5L only).
34	P1595	Speed Control Solenoid Circuits	An open or shorted condition detected in the Speed Control vacuum or vent solenoid circuits.
33	P0645	A/C Clutch Relay Circuit	An open or shorted condition detected in the A/C clutch relay circuit.
31	P0443	EVAP Purge Solenoid Circuit	An open or shorted condition detected in the duty cycle purge solenoid circuit.
27	P0203 or P0202 or P0201	Injector #3 Control Circuit Injector #2 Control Circuit Injector #1 Control Circuit	Injector #3 output driver does not respond properly to the control signal. Injector #2 output driver does not respond properly to the control signal. Injector #1 output driver does not respond properly to the control signal.
25	P0505	Idle Air Control Motor Circuits	A shorted or open condition detected in one or more of the idle air control motor circuits.
24	P0122 or P0123	Throttle Position Sensor Voltage Low Throttle Position Sensor Voltage High	Throttle position sensor input below the minimum acceptable voltage Throttle position sensor input above the maximum acceptable voltage.
22	P0117	ECT Sensor Voltage Too Low	Engine coolant temperature sensor input below minimum acceptable voltage.

Trouble code chart - 1997 and later models

Check Engine Light Flash Code	Generic Scan Tool Code	DRB Scan Tool Display	Description of Diagnostic Trouble Code
22	or P0118	ECT Sensor Voltage Too High	Engine coolant temperature sensor input above maximum acceptable voltage.
17	1281	Engine Is Cold Too Long	Engine did not reach operating temperature within acceptable limits.
14	P0107 or P0108	MAP Sensor Voltage Too Low MAP Sensor Voltage Too High	MAP sensor input below minimum acceptable voltage. MAP sensor input above maximum acceptable voltage.
13	P1297	No Change in MAP From Start to Run	No difference recognized between the engine MAP reading and the barometric (atmospheric) pressure reading from start-up.
11	P0320	No Crank Reference Signal at PCM	No crank reference signal detected during engine cranking.
	P0351	Ignition Coil #1 Primary Circuit	Peak primary circuit current not achieved with maximum dwell time.
42	P1389	No ASD Relay Output Voltage at PCM	An Open condition Detected In The ASD Relay Output Circuit.
63	P1696	PCM Failure EEPROM Write Denied	Unsuccessful attempt to write to an EEPROM location by the PCM.
37	P0753	Trans 3-4 Shift Sol/Trans Relay Circuits	Current state of output port for the solenoid is different from expected state.
23	P0112 or P0113	Intake Air Temp Sensor Voltage Low Intake Air Temp Sensor Voltage High	Intake air temperature sensor input below the maximum acceptable voltage. Intake air temperature sensor input above the minimum acceptable voltage.
27	P0204	Injector #4 Control Circuit	Injector #4 output driver does not respond properly to the control signal.
21	P0132	Left Upstream O2S Shorted to Voltage	Oxygen sensor input voltage maintained above the normal operating range.
	P0154	O2 2/1 Signal Inactive	No signal at O2 2/1 sensor
	P0152	O2 2/1 Shorted High	Oxygen sensor input voltage sustained above the normal operating range.
53	PO600	PCM Failure SPI Communications	PCM internal fault condition detected
27	P0205 or P0206	Injector #5 Control Circuit Injector #6 Control Circuit	Injector #5 output driver does not respond properly to the control signal. Injector #6 output driver does not respond properly to the control signal.
45	P0712 or	Trans Temp Sensor Voltage Too Low	Voltage less than 1.55 volts.

Trouble code chart - 1997 and later models (continued)

Check Engine Light Flash Code	Generic Scan Tool Code	DRB Scan Tool Display	Description of Diagnostic Trouble Code
45	P0713	Trans Temp Sensor Voltage Too High	Voltage greater than 3.76 volts.
27	P0207	Injector #7 Control Circuit	Injector #7 output driver does not respond properly to the control signal.
	or		
	P0208	Injector #8 Control Circuit	Injector #8 output driver does not respond properly to the control signal.
77	P1683	SPD CTRL PWR RLY; or S/C 12V Driver CKT	Malfuntion detected with power feed to speed control servo solenoids
34	P1596	MUX S/C Switch High	Speed control switch input above the maximum acceptable voltage.
	or		
	P1597	MUX S/C Switch Low	Speed control switch input below the minimum acceptable voltage.
42	P1282	Fuel Pump Relay Control Circuit	An open or shorted condition detected in the fuel pump relay control circuit.
21	P0133 or P0152	O2 1/1 Slow Response	Oxygen sensor response slower than minimum required switching frequency.
	or		
	P0135	O2 1/1 Heater Circuit	Upstream oxygen sensor heating element circuit malfunction
	P0139	O2 1/1 Slow Response	Oxygen sensor response slower than minimum required switching frequency.
	P0141	O2 1/2 Heater Circuit	Oxygen sensor heating element circuit malfunction.
43	P0300	Multiple Cylinder Mis-fire	Misfire detected in multiple cylinders.
	or		
	P0301	Cylinder #1 Mis-fire	Misfire detected in cylinder #1.
	or		
	P0302	Cylinder #2 Mis-fire	Misfire detected in cylinder #2.
	or		
	P0303	Cylinder #3 Mis-fire	Misfire detected in cylinder #3.
	or		
	P0304	Cylinder #4 Mis-fire	Misfire detected in cylinder #4.
72	P0420	Catalyst 1/1 Effic	Catalyst efficiency below required level.
31	P0441	Incorrect Purge Flow	Insufficient or excessive vapor flow detected during evaporative emission system operation.
37	P1899	P/N Switch Stuck in Park or in Gear	Incorrect input state detected for the Park/Neutral switch, auto. trans. only.
	P0551	Pwr Steering Sw Perf	Power steering high pressure seen at high speed (2.5L only).
52	P0172	Left Bank or Fuel System Rich	A rich air/fuel mixture has been indicated by an abnormally lean correction factor.
51	P0171	Right Rear (or just) Fuel System Lean	A lean air/fuel mixture has been indicated by an abnormally rich correction factor.

Trouble code chart - 1997 and later models (continued)

Check Engine Light Flash Code	Generic Scan Tool Code	DRB Scan Tool Display	Description of Diagnostic Trouble Code
	P0175	Fuel System 2/1 Rich	A rich air/fuel mixture has been indicated by an abnormally lean correction factor.
	P0174	Fuel System 2/1 Lean	A lean air/fuel mixture has been indicated by an abnormally lean correction factor.
	P0153	O2 2/1 Slow Response	Oxygen sensor response slower than minimum required switching frequency.
	P0159	O2 2/1 Slow Response	Oxygen sensor response slower than minimum required switching frequency.
	P0155	O2 2/1 Heater circuit	Oxygen sensor heater element malfunction.
	P0161	O2 2/1 Heater circuit	Oxygen sensor heater element malfunction.
21	P0138	Left Bank Downstream or Downstream and Pre-Catalyst O2S Shorted to Voltage	Oxygen sensor input voltage maintained above the normal operating range.
	P0158	O2 2/2 Shorted High	Oxygen sensor input voltage maintained above the normal operating range.
17	P0125	Closed Loop Temp Not Reached	Engine does not reach 20°F within 5 minutes with a vehicle speed signal.
24	P0121	TPS Voltage Does Not Agree With MAP	TPS signal does not correlate to MAP sensor
14	P1296	No 5 Volts To MAP Sensor	5 Volt output to MAP sensor open.
25	P1294	Target Idle Not Reached	Actual idle speed does not equal target idle speed.
37	P1756 or P1757	Governor Pressure Not Equal to Target @ 15-20 PSI Governor Pressure Above 3 PSI In Gear With 0 MPH	Governor sensor input not between 10 and 25 psi when requested. Governor pressure greater than 3 psi when requested to be 0 psi.
37	P0740	Torq Conv Clu, No RPM Drop At Lockup	Relationship between engine speed and vehicle speed indicates no torque converter clutch engagement (auto. trans. only).
42	P0462 or P0463 or P0460	Fuel Level Sending Unit Volts Too Low Fuel Level Sending Unit Volts Too High Fuel Level Unit No Change Over Miles	Open circuit between PCM and fuel gauge sending unit. Circuit shorted to voltage between PCM and fuel gauge sending unit. No movement of fuel level sender detected.
44	P1493 or P1492	Ambient/Batt Temp Sen VoltsToo Low Ambient/Batt Temp Sensor VoltsToo High	Battery temperature sensor input voltage below an acceptable range. Battery temperature sensor input voltage above an acceptable range.

Trouble code chart - 1997 and later models (continued)

Check Engine Light Flash Code	Generic Scan Tool Code	DRB Scan Tool Display	Description of Diagnostic Trouble Code
21	P0131 or P0137	Left Bank and Upstream O2S Shorted to Ground	O2 sensor voltage too low, tested after cold start.
		Downstream, Left Bank Downstream and Pre-Catalyst O2S Shorted to Ground	O2 sensor voltage too low, tested after cold start.
11	P1391	Intermittent Loss of CMP or CKP	Intermittent loss of either camshaft or crankshaft position sensor
31	P0442 or P0455	Evap Leak Monitor Small Leak Detected	A small leak has been detected by the leak detection monitor
		Evap Leak Monitor Large Leak Detected	The leak detection monitor is unable to pressurize Evap system, indicating a large leak.
45	P0711	Trans Temp Sensor, No Rise After Start	Sump temp did not rise more than 16°F within 10 minutes when starting temp is below 40°F or sump temp is above 260°F with coolant below 100°F.
37	P0783	3-4 Shift Sol, No RPM Drop @ 3-4 Shift	The ratio of engine rpm/output shaft speed did not change beyond on the minimum required.
15	P0720	Low Ouput Spd Sensor RPM Above 15 mph	Output shaft speed is less than 60 rpm with vehicle speed above 15 mph.
45	P1764 or P1763 or P1762	Governor Pessure Sensor Volts Too Low	Voltage less than .10 volts.
		Governor Pressure Sensor Volts Too HI	Voltage greater than 4.89 volts.
		Governor Press Sen Offset Volts Too Lo or High	Sensor input greater or less than calibration for 3 consecutive Neutral/Park occurances.
37	P0748	Governor Pressure Sol Control/Trans Relay Circuits	Current state of solenoid output port is different than expected.
37	P1765	Trans 12 Volt Supply Relay Ctrl Circuit	Current state of solenoid output port is different than expeted.
43	P0305 or P0306 or P0307 or P0308	Cylinder #5 Mis-fire	Misfire detected in cylinder #5.
		Cylinder #6 Mis-fire	Misfire detected in cylinder #6.
		Cylinder #7 Mis-fire	Misfire detected in cylinder #7.
		Cylinder #8 Mis-fire	Misfire detected in cylinder #8.
	P0432	Catalyst 2/1 EFFIC	Catalyst 2/1 efficiency below required level
	P0151	O2 2/1 Voltage Low	Oxygen sensor input voltage maintained below normal operating range.

Trouble code chart - 1997 and later models (continued)

Check Engine Light Flash Code	Generic Scan Tool Code	DRB Scan Tool Display	Description of Diagnostic Trouble Code
	P0157	O2 2/1 Voltage Low	Oxygen sensor input voltage maintained below normal operating range.
31	P1495 or P1494	Leak Detection Pump Solenoid Circuit	Leak detection pump solenoid circuit fault (open or short)
		Leak detection pump SW or mechanical fault	Leak detection pump switch does not respond to input.
11	P1398	Mis-fire Adaptive Numerator at Limit	CKP sensor target windows have too much variation
31	P1486	Evap leak monitor pinched hose found	Plug or pinch detected between purge solenoid and fuel tank
45	P0751	O/D Switch Pressed (LO) More Than 5 Min	Overdrive Off switch input too low for more than 5 minutes.
	P0147	O2 1/3 Heater Circuit	Oxygen sensor heater element malfunction.
21	P0133 or P1195	Cat Mon slow O2 1/1	A slow switching oxygen sensor has been detected in bank 1/1 during catalyst monitor test.
	P0153 or P1196	Cat Mon slow O2 2/1	A slow switching oxygen sensor has been detected in bank 2/1 during catalyst monitor test.
	P0129 or P1197	Cat Mon slow O2 1/2	A slow switching oxygen sensor has been detected in bank 1/2 during catalyst monitor test.
15		No vehicle speed sensor signal	No Vehicle speed sensor signal detected during driving conditions.

Trouble code chart - 1997 and later models (continued)

models only, the system can be accessed to flash the trouble codes on the CHECK ENGINE light. To extract the diagnostic trouble codes on 1991 through 1997 models using this method, proceed as follows:

a) *Without starting the engine, turn the ignition key ON, OFF, ON, OFF and finally ON. The CHECK ENGINE light on the dash will begin to flash.*

b) *If any trouble codes are stored in the PCM memory, the CHECK ENGINE light will flash the number of the first digit, pause and flash the number of the second digit. For example: Code 23, air temperature sensor circuit would be indicated by two flashes, pause three flashes. A long pause will appear between individual codes if more than one code is present. Carefully observe the flashes and record the exact code number(s) onto paper.*

c) *After the stored codes have been indicated (or if everything in the self diagnosis system is functioning properly), the CHECK ENGINE light will flash a Code 55. Refer to the accompanying charts for trouble code identification.*

d) *If the ignition key is turned OFF during the code extraction process and possibly turned back ON, the self diagnostic*

system will automatically invalidate the procedure. Restart the procedure to extract the codes. **Note:** *The self diagnostic system cannot be accessed with the engine running.*

3   The preferred code extraction method requires a special SCAN tool that is programmed to interface with the OBD system by plugging into the diagnostic connector. When used, the SCAN tool has the ability to diagnose in-depth driveability problems and it allows freeze frame data to be retrieved from the PCM stored memory. Freeze frame data is an OBD II PCM feature that records all related sensor and actuator activity on the PCM data stream whenever an engine control or emissions fault is detected and a trouble code is set. This ability to look at the circuit conditions and values when the malfunction occurs provides a valuable tool when trying to diagnose intermittent driveability problems. If the tool is not available and intermittent driveability problems exist, have the vehicle checked at a dealer service department or other qualified repair shop. **Note:** *The SCAN tool trouble code designation is referred to as a P0 or P1 code. Refer to the "Generic Scan Tool Code" column of the trouble code chart for the code identification.*

Clearing diagnostic trouble codes

Note: *Always clear the codes from the PCM before starting the engine after a new electronic emission control component is installed onto the engine. The PCM stores the operating parameters of each sensor. The PCM may set a trouble code if a new sensor is allowed to operate before the parameters from the old sensor have been erased.*

1991 through 1995 models

4   On these models the trouble codes can be erased by disconnecting the cable from the negative terminal of the battery for at least 15 seconds. Certain driveability problems may be encountered for a while after doing this, as the computer must "relearn" its operating parameters.

1997 and later models

5   After the system has been repaired, the codes must be cleared from the PCM memory using a SCAN tool. **Caution:** *Do not disconnect the battery from the vehicle in an attempt to clear the codes. If necessary, have the codes cleared by a dealer service department or other qualified repair facility.*

10.2 An oxygen sensor located in the exhaust manifold (arrow)

10 Information sensors

1   Information sensors inform the computer of the engine's current operating conditions so adjustments (air/fuel mixture, ignition timing, idle speed, etc.) can be made to achieve lower emissions and improved fuel economy. For more information on the computerized emissions control system, see Section 8. **Note:** *Because of a Federally mandated extended warranty which covers emissions-related components such as the information sensors, check with a dealer service department before replacing the sensors at your own expense.*

Oxygen sensor

Refer to illustration 10.2

2   The Oxygen (O2) sensor is located in the exhaust manifold or exhaust down pipe **(see illustration)**. It provides a variable voltage signal (about 0 to 1 volt) to the computer, based on the oxygen content in the exhaust. The computer uses this information to determine whether or not the fuel/air mixture needs to be altered by adjusting the pulse width of the fuel injectors or the carburetor mixture control solenoid.

3   Checking the oxygen sensor is beyond the scope of the home mechanic. Take the vehicle to a dealer service department or other qualified shop for diagnosis. Replacement of the oxygen sensor is covered in Chapter 1.

Knock sensor

General information

Refer to illustration 10.4

4   A knock sensor **(see illustration)** is used on some models. The knock sensor on four-cylinder and 4.0L six-cylinder engines is on the left side of the engine block, above the oil pan. On 4.2L six-cylinder engines, it's in the intake manifold in front of the carburetor. The sensor is a piezoelectric crystal transducer that indicates detonation (knock) during engine operation. Electrical voltage from the sensor to the computer retards the ignition advance to eliminate detonation (knock).

Replacement

Note: *Checking the knock sensor is beyond the scope of the home mechanic. Take the vehicle to a dealer service department or other qualified shop for diagnosis.*

5   If necessary for access to the sensor, raise the front of the vehicle and support it securely on jackstands.

6   Disconnect the knock sensor electrical connector.

7   Carefully unscrew the sensor.

8   Clean the threaded hole of any corrosion and old sealant. Use Teflon tape on the threads of the new sensor.

9   Install the new knock sensor into the engine block or intake manifold. Torque it to 89 in-lbs. This torque is critical for the proper operation of the knock sensor.

10   Connect the electrical connector to the sensor.

11   Lower the vehicle.

Coolant Temperature Sensor (CTS)

General information

Refer to illustration 10.12

12   The CTS is a device that monitors the coolant temperature. It is normally mounted in the thermostat housing **(see illustration)**.

As the coolant temperature changes, the resistance of the sensor changes, providing a varying input voltage to the computer. The computer uses information from the CTS to adjust fuel/air mixture, ignition timing and control EGR valve operation.

Replacement

Warning: *Wait until the engine is completely cool (at least five hours after it has been run) before replacing the CTS.*

Note: *Checking the CTS is beyond the scope of the home mechanic. Take the vehicle to a dealer service department or other qualified shop for diagnosis.*

13   Prepare the new sensor by wrapping the threads with Teflon tape or applying a non-hardening thread sealant. Open the radiator cap to release any residual pressure. Squeeze the upper radiator hose and reinstall the cap (this will create a slight vacuum in the cooling system, which will minimize coolant loss).

14   Disconnect the electrical connector from the sensor. Place rags around the sensor to prevent spilling coolant. Unscrew the old sensor and immediately install the new one, tightening it securely. Plug in the electrical connector. Check the coolant level and add some, if necessary (see Chapter 1).

Manifold Absolute Pressure (MAP) sensor

General information

Refer to illustrations 10.15a and 10.15b

15   On early models, the MAP sensor is located on the firewall, near the valve cover **(see illustration)**. It is connected electrically to the computer and to the throttle body by a vacuum hose. On later models, the MAP sensor is attached directly to the throttle body **(see illustration)** or to the rear of the intake manifold (2.4L four-cylinder models). The MAP sensor reads load (pressure) changes in the intake manifold. This causes electrical resistance changes in the MAP sensor, resulting in changing input voltage to the computer. The computer uses this information (input voltage) to vary the air/fuel mixture.

10.4 The knock sensor (arrow) is located on the engine block or on the intake manifold, near the carburetor (as shown here)

10.12 The coolant Temperature Sensor (CTS) is normally mounted in the thermostat housing

10.15a The manifold Absolute Pressure (MAP) sensor is mounted on the firewall (early models)

10.15b The Manifold Absolute Pressure (MAP) sensor is mounted to the side of the throttle body (later six-cylinder model shown)

1   Throttle body
2   MAP sensor
3   L-shaped rubber fitting
4   Mounting screws

10.30 The Manifold Air Temperature (MAT) sensor (arrow) is mounted in the intake manifold (four-cylinder engine shown)

Checking

Early models

16   Inspect the vacuum hose connections from the throttle body to the MAP sensor. Replace a cracked or broken hose with a new one.

17   Disconnect the vacuum hose from the MAP sensor and connect a hand vacuum pump. Apply vacuum. The sensor should hold vacuum. If it does not, replace the sensor.

18   Further testing should be referred to a dealer service department or other qualified shop.

Later models

19   Check that the electrical connector is firmly connected to the MAP sensor **(see illustration 10.15b)**. Also check that the L-shaped fitting from the MAP sensor to the throttle body is securely connected.

Replacement

Early models

20   Disconnect the electrical connector from the MAP sensor.

21   Detach the vacuum hose from the MAP sensor.

22   Remove the two mounting nuts.

23   Remove the MAP sensor from the firewall.

24   Installation is the reverse of removal.

Later models

25   Detach the air filter intake tube from the throttle body.

26   Remove the two mounting screws.

27   Detach the MAP sensor from the throttle body. Slide the rubber L-shaped fitting from the throttle body.

28   Remove the L-shaped fitting from the MAP sensor.

29   Installation is the reverse or removal.

Manifold Air Temperature (MAT) sensor

General information

Refer to illustration 10.30

30   The MAT sensor is installed in the intake

manifold **(see illustration)**. Its sensor element extended into the air stream. The sensor resistance changes as the air stream temperature changes, sending a varied input voltage to the computer. The computer uses this information to alter the fuel/air mixture.

Replacement

Note: *Checking the MAT sensor is beyond the scope of the home mechanic. Take the vehicle to a dealer service department or other qualified shop for diagnosis.*

31   Remove the air cleaner (if necessary).

32   Disconnect the electrical connector from the MAT sensor.

33   Using a flare-nut wrench (if available), remove the MAT sensor from the intake manifold.

34   Clean the threaded hole to remove any corrosion or old sealant.

35   Use Teflon tape on the threads of the new MAT sensor.

36   Installation is the reverse of removal.

Throttle Position Sensor (TPS)

37   The throttle position sensor, which is

mounted on the side of the carburetor or throttle body and connected directly to the throttle shaft, senses throttle movement and position, then transmits an electrical signal to the computer. This signal enables the computer to determine when the throttle is closed, in its normal cruise condition or wide open.

38   Checking the TPS is beyond the scope of the home mechanic. Take the vehicle to a dealer service department or other qualified shop for diagnosis. To replace the TPS, see Chapter 4.

Crankshaft Position Sensor (CKP)

General information

Refer to illustration 10.39

39   The CKP, used on later fuel-injected models, is attached to the transmission bellhousing **(see illustration)**. The CKP detects teeth on the flywheel as they pass the sensor during engine operation and provides the computer with information concerning engine speed and crankshaft angle. This information is used to advance or retard ignition timing and fuel injection.

Checking

40   Disconnect the CKP electrical connector from the main wiring harness.

10.39 The Crankshaft Position Sensor (CKP) is mounted in the transmission bellhousing (four-cylinder engine shown, six-cylinder engine similar)

10.47 Distance sensor installation details

10.50 Camshaft position sensor installation details - 2000 six cylinder models

1   Oil filter
2   Camshaft position sensor
3   Clamp bolt
4   Oil pump drive clamp
5   Camshaft position sensor mounting bolts
6   Electrical connector

41   Connect an ohmmeter across terminals A and B (marked on the connector). The reading should be 200 ± 75 ohms (engine at normal operating temperature).
42   If the readings are not to specification, replace the CKP.

Replacement

43   Disconnect the electrical connector from the CKP.
44   Detach the CKP by removing the two bolts.
45   Installation is the reverse of removal.

Distance sensor

Refer to illustration 10.47

46   Some models are equipped with a distance sensor (instead of a speedometer cable) that sends a pulsating voltage signal to the computer that the computer converts to miles per hour.
47   To replace the distance sensor (located at the rear of the transfer case), raise the vehicle, support it securely on jackstands, disconnect the electrical connector from the sensor and unscrew it from the speedometer adapter **(see illustration)**. Installation is the reverse of removal.

Camshaft position sensor (2000 six-cylinder models)

General information

48   The camshaft position sensor, in conjunction with the crankshaft position sensor, determines the timing for the fuel injection on each cylinder. The camshaft position sensor is a Hall-Effect device. The sensor is located on top of the oil pump drive and is triggered by a pulse ring. It replaces the distributor assembly used on earlier models.

Replacement

Refer to illustrations 10.50 and 10.52
Note: *The camshaft position sensor is located on top of the oil pump drive assembly. It is possible to replace the camshaft position sensor without removing the oil pump drive assembly. If the oil pump drive assembly must be removed, the mounting flange must be precisely marked in relation to the engine block or it will be necessary to reset the cam-*

shaft position sensor with a scan tool.
49   Disconnect the electrical connector from the camshaft position sensor.
50   If removing the sensor only, remove the two mounting bolts and remove the sensor from the oil pump drive **(see illustration)**. Install the new sensor, tighten the bolts securely and connect the electrical connector.
51   If removing the oil pump drive assembly, position the number one cylinder at TDC on the compression stroke (see Chapter 2B).
52   Remove the sensor (see Step 50). Insert an appropriate size alignment pin (such as a drill bit) through the holes in the sensor base and pulse ring **(see illustration)**. If the holes do not align, rotate the crankshaft until they do.
53   Mark the position of the oil pump drive mounting flange base to the engine block to ensure the oil pump drive can be re-installed in exactly the same position as originally installed.
54   Remove the oil pump drive hold-down bolt and withdraw the oil pump drive assembly. Remove and discard the O-ring.
55   If the crankshaft has been moved while the oil pump drive is out, the number one piston must be repositioned at TDC. This can be done by feeling for compression pressure at the number one spark plug hole as the crankshaft is rotated. Once compression is felt, continue rotating the crankshaft until the mark on the crankshaft damper is aligned with the zero or TDC mark on the timing indicator (see Chapter 2B).
56   Turn the pulse ring until the hole in the pulse ring aligns with the hole in the housing and install the alignment pin through the holes **(see illustration 10.52)**. Install a new O-ring on the oil pump drive assembly.
57   Insert the oil pump drive into the engine block and align the marks made in Step 53. Because of the helical-cut drive gear, the assembly will rotate clockwise as the gears engage. Be sure to compensate by starting the installation with the drive gear assembly positioned counterclockwise from the desired finished position. Installing the oil pump drive

assembly is very similar to installing a distributor, see Chapter 5 for additional information, if necessary. The oil pump drive must be installed in the same position as originally installed before removal. When properly installed, a line drawn through the center of the camshaft position sensor and electrical connector should be parallel with the centerline of the engine. **Note:** *If the alignment marks are lost or poor driveability symptoms appear after installing the oil pump drive, take the vehicle to a dealer service department or other properly equipped repair facility and have the fuel system synchronization reset with a scan tool.*
58   Install the oil pump drive hold-down clamp and tighten the bolt to 17 ft-lbs.
59   The remainder of installation is the reverse of removal.

10.52 Before removing the camshaft position sensor on a 2000 six-cylinder model, position the engine with the number one cylinder at TDC and install an appropriate size alignment pin through the hole in the base of the pulse ring

1   Pulse ring
2   Alignment pin
3   Oil pump driveshaft assembly

Chapter 7 Part A
Manual transmission

Contents

Specifications

Lubricant type.. See chapter 1

Torque specifications **Ft-lbs** (unless otherwise indicated)

Clutch housing-to-engine bolts
3/8-inch diameter bolts	27
7/16-inch diameter bolts	43
M12 metric bolts	55

Shift lever cover (or tower) bolts
AX 4/5, 15 transmission	13
BA 10/5 transmission	17
NV3550 transmission	75 in-lbs

1   General information

All vehicles covered in this manual come equipped with either a four or five-speed manual transmission or an automatic transmission. All information on the manual transmission is included in this Part of Chapter 7. Information on the automatic transmission can be found in Part B of this Chapter. Information on the transfer case can be found in Part C of this Chapter.

Due to the complexity, unavailability of replacement parts and the special tools necessary, internal repair by the home mechanic is not recommended. The information in this Chapter is limited to general information and removal and installation of the transmission.

Depending on the expense involved in having a faulty transmission overhauled, it may be a good idea to replace the unit with either a new or rebuilt one. Your local dealer or transmission repair shop should be able to supply you with information concerning cost, availability and exchange policy. Regardless of how you decide to remedy a transmission problem, you can still save a lot of money by removing and installing the unit yourself.

2   Manual transmission shift lever - removal and installation

Refer to illustrations 2.4, 2.7a and 2.7b

AX 4/5 or 15 transmission

1   Place the transmission into first or third gear.
2   Raise the vehicle and support it securely on jackstands.
3   Support the engine with a floor jack. Place a block of wood between the jack and the engine oil pan.
4   Remove the crossmember **(see illustration)**.
5   Lower the transmission/transfer case, but no more than three inches.
6   Reach around the right side of the transmission/transfer case and remove the dust boot from the shift tower and slide it up.

2.4 Crossmember installation details

1   Crossmember-to-frame nuts
2   Transmission mount nuts

2.7a Press down on the retainer and turn it counterclockwise

2.7b The lugs (arrow) inside the shift tower engage with the slots in the retainer

3.1 Pry on the transmission/transfer case with a pry bar or a large screwdriver to check for excessive looseness

7   Press down on the retainer and turn it counterclockwise to release it **(see illustrations)**. Remove the shift lever from the shift tower.
8   Installation is the reverse of removal.

BA 10/5 transmission

9   Remove the shift knob and locknuts from the shift lever.
10   Remove the screws from the shift lever boot retainer.
11   Remove the shift lever dust boot.
12   Detach the shaft retainer plate. Don't remove the stub shaft from the lever. **Note:** *Some BA 10/5 transmission shift levers may be held in place with a snap-ring instead of a retainer plate.*
13   Installation is the reverse of removal.

NV3550 transmission

14   Shift the transmission into first or third gear.
15   Remove the center console and shift boot
16   Install nuts on two M6 x 1.0 bolts and thread the bolts into the threaded holes at the base of the shift lever.
17   Tighten the nuts equally until the shift lever loosens on the shift tower stub shaft.
18   Remove the shift lever from the shift tower.

3   Transmission mount - check and replacement

Refer to illustration 3.1

1   Insert a large screwdriver or pry bar into the space between the transfer case and the crossmember **(see illustration)**. Try to pry the transmission/transfer case up slightly.
2   The transmission/transfer case should not move away from the insulator much at all. If it does, replace it.
3   To replace the mount, remove the nuts attaching it to the crossmember and the bolts attaching it to the transmission/transfer case **(see illustration 2.4)**.
4   Raise the transmission/transfer case slightly with a jack and remove the mount, noting which holes are used in the crossmember for proper alignment during installation.

5   Installation is the reverse of the removal. Be sure to tighten the nuts/bolts securely.

4   Manual transmission - removal and installation

Refer to illustrations 4.7, 4.8 and 4.10

Removal

Note: *The transmission and transfer case are removed as a single unit.*
1   Disconnect the negative cable from the battery.

2   Working inside the vehicle, remove the shift lever (see Section 2).
3   Raise the vehicle and support it securely on jackstands.
4   Disconnect the speedometer cable and electrical connectors from the transmission. If equipped, remove the crankshaft position sensor (see Chapter 6). On 1993 and earlier models, disconnect the clutch hydraulic line from the release cylinder (see Chapter 8). On 1994 models, unbolt the release cylinder from the transmission - there's no need to disconnect the hydraulic line.

4.7 AX 4/5 transmission/transfer case with the crossmember removed

1	*Clutch bleed fitting*	5	*Transfer case shift linkage*
2	*Clutch hydraulic line*	6	*Transfer case*
3	*AX 4/5 manual transmission*	7	*Speedometer cable*
4	*Transmission/transfer case mount*		

4.8 When removing the transmission/ transfer case, it's a good idea to use a transmission jack equipped with safety chains

4.10 Move the transmission/transfer case toward the rear until the input shaft clears the clutch

5   Remove the driveshafts (see Chapter 8). Use a plastic bag to cover the transfer case openings to prevent lubricant loss and contamination.

6   Support the engine by placing a jack (with a block of wood as an insulator) under the engine oil pan. The engine should remain supported at all times while the transmission is out of the vehicle.

7   Remove the nuts and bolts from the crossmember **(see illustration 2.4)**, lower the crossmember and remove it from the vehicle **(see illustration)**.

8   Support the transmission with a jack -

preferably a special jack made for this purpose. Safety chains will help steady the transmission on the jack **(see illustration)**. **Warning:** *The assembly is very heavy and awkward to remove - a transmission jack equipped with safety chains is highly recommended.*

9   Remove the bolts securing the transmission bellhousing to the engine.

10   Make a final check that all wires and hoses have been disconnected from the transmission and then move the transmission and jack toward the rear of the vehicle until the transmission input shaft is clear of the clutch pressure plate. Keep the transmission level as this is done **(see illustration)**.

11   Once the input shaft is clear, lower the transmission/transfer case and remove it from under the vehicle. **Caution:** *Do not depress the clutch pedal while the transmission is out of the vehicle.*

12   The clutch components can be inspected at this time by removing the clutch from the engine (see Chapter 8). In most cases, new clutch components should be routinely installed if the transmission is removed.

Installation

13   If removed, install the clutch components (see Chapter 8).

14   With the transmission/transfer case secured to the jack as on removal, raise the transmission/transfer case into position, then carefully slide it forward, engaging the input shaft with the clutch plate hub. DO NOT use excessive force to install the transmission / transfer case. If the input shaft does not slide into place, readjust the angle of the transmission so it is level and/or turn the input shaft so the splines engage properly with the clutch.

15   Install the bellhousing bolts, tightening them to the torque listed in this Chapter's Specifications.

16   Install the crossmember support. Tighten the fasteners securely.

17   Remove the jack supporting the engine.

18   Install the various items removed previously, referring to Chapter 8 for the installation of the driveshaft.

19   Make a final check that all wires, hoses and the speedometer cable have been connected and that the transmission has been filled with lubricant to the proper level (see Chapter 1). Lower the vehicle.

20   Working inside the vehicle, install the shift lever (see Section 3) and the transfer case shift linkage (see Chapter 7, Part C).

21   Connect the negative battery cable. Road test the vehicle for proper operation and check for leakage.

5.4a AX 4/5 manual transmission subassemblies - exploded view

1   *Shift lever*
2   *Shift lever retainer*
3   *Restrict pins*
4   *Front bearing retainer*
5   *Clutch housing*
6   *Snap-ring*
7   *Back-up light switch*
8   *Intermediate plate*
9   *Adapter housing*
10   *Adapter screw plug*
11   *Output shaft*
12   *Reverse idler gear*
13   *Input shaft*
14   *Counter gear*
15   *Straight screw plug*
16   *Spring*
17   *Locking ball*

5.4b AX 4/5 manual transmission output shaft - countershaft and synchronizer - exploded view

1   Output shaft
2   Snap-ring
3   Snap-ring
4   Fifth gear
5   Rear bearing retainer
6   Synchronizer ring fourth gear
7   Input shaft
8   Counter gear
9   Counter rear bearing
10 Snap-ring
11 Spacer
12 Needle roller bearing fifth gear
13 Counter fifth gear
14 Hub sleeve no. 3
15 Synchronizer ring fifth gear
16 Gear spline piece no. 5

5   Manual transmission overhaul - general information

Refer to illustrations 5.4a, 5.4b, 5.4c, 5.4d, 5.4e and 5.4f

Note: *The manufacturer doesn't provide exploded view drawings of the NV3550 transmission.*

Overhauling a manual transmission is a difficult job for the do-it-yourselfer. It involves the disassembly and reassembly of many small parts. Numerous clearances must be precisely measured and, if necessary, changed with select fit spacers and snap-rings. As a result, if transmission problems arise, it can be removed and installed by a competent do-it-yourselfer, but overhaul should be left to a transmission repair shop. Rebuilt transmissions may be available - check with your dealer parts department and auto parts stores. At any rate, the time and money involved in an overhaul is almost sure to exceed the cost of a rebuilt unit.

Nevertheless, it's not impossible for an inexperienced mechanic to rebuild a transmission if the special tools are available and the job is done in a deliberate step-by-step manner so nothing is overlooked.

The tools necessary for an overhaul include internal and external snap-ring pliers, a bearing puller, a slide hammer, a set of pin punches, a dial indicator and possibly a hydraulic press. In addition, a large, sturdy workbench and a vise or transmission stand will be required.

During disassembly of the transmission, make careful notes of how each piece comes off, where it fits in relation to other pieces and what holds it in place. Exploded views are included **(see illustrations)** to show where the parts go - but actually noting how they are installed when you remove the parts will make it much easier to get the transmission back together.

Before taking the transmission apart for repair, it will help if you have some idea what area of the transmission is malfunctioning. Certain problems can be closely tied to specific areas in the transmission, which can make component examination and replacement easier. Refer to the *Troubleshooting* section at the front of this manual for information regarding possible sources of trouble.

5.4c AX 4/5 manual transmission output shaft - exploded view

1   Rear bearing
2   Inner race
3   First gear needle roller bearing
4   First gear
5   First gear synchronizer ring
6   Hub sleeve no. 1
7   Second gear synchronizer ring
8   Second gear
9   Second gear needle roller bearing
10 Output shaft
11 Third gear
12 Third gear synchronizer ring
13 Hub sleeve no. 2
14 Snap-ring

5.4d AX 4/5 manual transmission shift components - exploded view

1   Shift lever shaft
2   Shift lever housing
3   Reverse restrict pin
4   Shift fork shaft no. 2
5   Shift fork no. 2
6   Shift fork no. 1
7   Shift fork shaft no. 1
8   Shift fork shaft no. 3
9   Shift fork shaft no. 4
10   Reverse shift arm bracket
11   Shift fork no. 3
12   Reverse shift arm and fork
13   Shift fork shaft no. 5
14   Reverse shift head

1	Fifth gear	48	Thrust washer
2	Fifth gear roller bearing	49	Endplay shim
3	Fifth gear	50	Intermediate shaft roller bearing race
4	Fifth gear snap-ring	51	Oil seal
5	Reverse gear nut	52	Rear case
6	Washer (not used in all models)	53	Fifth gear roller bearing race
7	Reverse gear	54	Snap-ring
8	Rear bearing retainer	55	Intermediate shaft roller bearing
9	Rear bearing race	56	Alignment dowels
10	Rear bearing	57	First-second lock spring and ball
11	Rear bearing shim	58	Roll pin
12	Shim washer	59	Idler shaft
13	First gear bearing	60	Reverse idler gear
14	Bearing spacer	61	Roll pin
15	First gear	62	Fifth-reverse shift fork
16	First-second synchronizer hub	63	Fifth-reverse shift rail
17	Synchronizer hub	64	First-second shift rail
18	Second gear housing	65	Roll pin
19	Second gear	66	first-second shift fork
20	Mainshaft	67	Roll pin
21	Third gear bearing	68	Third-fourth shift fork
22	Third gear	69	Third-fourth shift rail lock pin
23	Third-fourth synchronizer	70	Third-fourth shift rail
24	Synchronizer hub	71	Detent plug
25	Spring washer	72	First-second detent spring
26	Lock ring	73	First-second detent ball
27	Pilot bearing shims	74	Interlock ball
28	Pilot bearing	75	Lock finger
29	Pilot bearing race	76	Back-up light switch and washer
30	Input shaft	77	Alignment dowels
31	Front bearing	78	Front case - left half
32	Front bearing race	79	Detent plug
33	Front bearing shims	80	Fifth-reverse detent spring
34	Front bearing retainer	81	Fifth-reverse detent ball
35	Oil seal	82	Front case - right half
36	Mounting studs	83	Intermediate case
37	Bearing race	84	Fill plug and washer
38	Cluster front bearing	85	Drain plug and washer
39	Front bearing race	86	Access plug
40	Cluster gear		

41	Cluster rear	45	Fifth gear synchronizer
42	Bearing race	46	Fifth intermediate rear
43	Intermediate shaft	47	Fifth intermediate bear bearing
44	Synchronizer hub		

5.4e BA 10/15 manual transmission - exploded view

5.4f AX15 output shaft - exploded view

Chapter 7 Part B
Automatic transmission

Contents

Specifications

Torque specifications

	Ft-lbs (unless otherwise indicated)
Front band adjusting screw	
With adapter	36 in-lbs
Without adapter	72 in-lbs
Rear band adjusting screw	72 in-lbs
Bellhousing-to-engine bolts	
10 mm bolts	25
12 mm bolts	42
Neutral start switch	24
Torque converter-to-driveplate bolts	40
Transmission pan bolts	See Chapter 1

1 General information

All vehicles covered in this manual come equipped with either a four or five-speed manual transmission or a three-speed automatic transmission. Information on the automatic transmission is included in this Part of Chapter 7. Information on the manual transmission can be found in Part A of this Chapter, and information on the transfer case can be found in Part C of this Chapter.

Due to the complexity of the automatic transmission and the need for specialized equipment to perform most service operations, this Chapter contains only general diagnosis, routine maintenance, adjustment and removal and installation procedures.

If the transmission requires major repair work, it should be left to a dealer service department or an automotive or transmission repair shop. You can, however, remove and install the transmission yourself and save the expense, even if the repair work is done by a transmission shop.

2 Diagnosis - general

Note: *Automatic transmission malfunctions may be caused by five general conditions: poor engine performance, improper adjust-ments, incorrect fluid level, hydraulic malfunctions or mechanical malfunctions. Diagnosis of these problems should always begin with a check of the easily repaired items: fluid level and condition (see Chapter 1), shift linkage adjustment and throttle linkage adjustment. Next, perform a road test to determine if the problem has been corrected or if more diagnosis is necessary. If the problem persists after the preliminary tests and corrections are completed, additional diagnosis should be done by a dealer service department or transmission repair shop. Refer to the Troubleshooting section at the front of this manual for information on symptoms of transmission problems.*

Preliminary checks

1   Drive the vehicle to warm the transmission to normal operating temperature.
2   Check the fluid level as described in Chapter 1:

a) *If the fluid level is unusually low, add enough fluid to bring the level within the designated area of the dipstick, then check for external leaks (see below).*

b) *If the fluid is foaming, drain it and refill the transmission, then check for coolant in the fluid or a high fluid level.*

c) *If the fluid level is abnormally high, drain off the excess, then check the drained fluid for contamination by coolant. The presence of engine coolant in the automatic transmission fluid indicates that a failure has occurred in the internal radiator walls that separate the coolant from the transmission fluid (see Chapter 3).*

3   Check the engine idle speed. **Note:** *If the engine is malfunctioning, do not proceed with the preliminary checks until it has been repaired and runs normally.*

4   Check the Throttle Valve (TV) linkage or cable for freedom of movement. Adjust it if necessary (see Section 4). **Note:** *The TV linkage/cable may function properly when the engine is shut off and cold, but it may malfunction once the engine is hot. Check it cold and at normal engine operating temperature.*

5   Inspect the shift control linkage (see Section 3). Make sure that it's properly adjusted and that the linkage operates smoothly.

Fluid leak diagnosis

6   Most fluid leaks are easy to locate visually. Repair usually consists of replacing a seal or gasket. If a leak is difficult to find, the following procedure may help.

7   Identify the fluid. Make sure it's transmission fluid and not engine oil or brake fluid (automatic transmission fluid is a deep red color).

8   Try to pinpoint the source of the leak. Drive the vehicle several miles, then park it

3.4 Shift linkage details

4.2a Throttle Valve (TV) linkage details

over a large sheet of cardboard. After a minute or two, you should be able to locate the leak by determining the source of the fluid dripping onto the cardboard.
9   Make a careful visual inspection of the suspected component and the area immediately around it. Pay particular attention to gasket mating surfaces. A mirror is often helpful for finding leaks in areas that are hard to see.
10   If the leak still cannot be found, clean the suspected area thoroughly with a degreaser or solvent, then dry it.
11   Drive the vehicle for several miles at normal operating temperature and varying speeds. After driving the vehicle, visually inspect the suspected component again.
12   Once the leak has been located, the cause must be determined before it can be properly repaired. If a gasket is replaced but the sealing flange is bent, the new gasket will not stop the leak. The bent flange must be straightened.
13   Before attempting to repair a leak, check to make sure that the following conditions are corrected or they may cause another leak. **Note:** *Some of the following conditions cannot be fixed without highly specialized tools and expertise. Such problems must be referred to a transmission repair shop or a dealer service department.*

Gasket leaks

14   Check the pan periodically. Make sure the bolts are tight, no bolts are missing, the gasket is in good condition and the pan is flat (dents in the pan may indicate damage to the valve body inside).
15   If the pan gasket is leaking, the fluid level or the fluid pressure may be too high, the vent may be plugged, the pan bolts may be too tight, the pan sealing flange may be warped, the sealing surface of the transmission housing may be damaged, the gasket may be damaged or the transmission casting may be cracked or porous. If sealant instead of gasket material has been used to form a seal between the pan and the transmission housing, it may be the wrong sealant.

Seal leaks

16   If a transmission seal is leaking, the fluid level or pressure may be too high, the vent may be plugged, the seal bore may be damaged, the seal itself may be damaged or improperly installed, the surface of the shaft protruding through the seal may be damaged or a loose bearing may be causing excessive shaft movement.
17   Make sure the dipstick tube seal is in good condition and the tube is properly seated. Periodically check the area around the speedometer gear or sensor for leakage. If transmission fluid is evident, check the O-ring for damage.

Case leaks

18   If the case itself appears to be leaking, the casting is porous and will have to be repaired or replaced.
19   Make sure the oil cooler hose fittings are tight and in good condition.

Fluid comes out vent pipe or fill tube

20   If this condition occurs, the transmission is overfilled, there is coolant in the fluid, the case is porous, the dipstick is incorrect, the vent is plugged or the drain back holes are plugged.

---

3   Shift linkage - check and adjustment

Refer to illustration 3.4

Check

1   Firmly apply the parking brake and try to momentarily operate the starter in each shift lever position. The starter should operate in Park and Neutral only. If the starter operates in any position other than Park or Neutral, adjust the shift linkage (see below). If, after adjustment, the starter still operates in positions other than Park or Neutral, the neutral start switch is defective or in need of adjustment (see Section 6).

Adjustment

2   Place the shift lever in Park. Raise the vehicle and support it securely on jackstands.
3   Check the condition of the shift rods, bellcrank and the brackets. Replace any worn or damaged parts. Do not adjust worn or damaged parts.
4   Loosen the trunnion lock bolt so that the bellcrank and shift rod slides freely **(see illustration)**.
5   Be sure the shift lever on the transmission is all the way to the rear, in the last detent. This is the Park position.
6   Make sure the park lock is engaged by trying to rotate the driveshaft. The driveshaft will not rotate if the park lock is functioning properly.
7   When properly adjusted, there should be no lash in the shift linkage. Push up on the bellcrank while pulling down on the shift rod. Tighten the lock bolt while holding the shift rod and bellcrank.
8   Lower the vehicle.
9   With the parking brake firmly applied, make sure the engine starts only in Park and Neutral. If the linkage is adjusted properly, but the starter operates in positions other than Park or Neutral, check the neutral start switch (see Section 6).
10   Check the steering wheel lock to make sure it operates smoothly.

---

4   Throttle Valve (TV) linkage/cable - adjustment

1   The Throttle Valve (TV) linkage or cable can be adjusted to correct harsh, delayed or erratic shifting and lack of kickdown.

TV linkage

Refer to illustrations 4.2a, 4.2b and 4.6
2   Remove the TV control rod spring **(see illustration)**. Use the spring to hold the adjusting link against the nylon stop, in the forward position **(see illustration)**.
3   Block the choke open and set the throttle off the fast idle cam. On models equipped

4.2b The Throttle Valve (TV) spring is used to hold the adjusting link against the nylon stop

1   *Spring*
2   *Link*
3   *Nylon stop*
4   *Bolt (clamp/retainer)*
5   *Throttle Valve (TV) control rod*
6   *Clamp*

with a throttle-operated solenoid valve, turn the ignition switch on (to energize the solenoid), and open the throttle half way to lock it. Return the throttle to the idle position.
4   Raise the vehicle and support it securely with jackstands.
5   Loosen the retainer and clamp bolts on the TV linkage adjusting link **(see illustration 4.2b)**.
6   Use a spare spring to hold the transmission TV lever all the way forward, against the stop **(see illustration)**. Hook the spring to the bellhousing boss.
7   Push on the end of the link to eliminate any lash, pull the clamp to the rear so the bolt bottoms in the rear of the rod slot. Tighten the clamp bolt. Pull the TV control rod to the rear until the rod bolt bottoms in the front rod slot and tighten the retainer bolt.
8   Install the TV control rod spring, remove the extra spring from the transmission lever and lower the vehicle.

TV cable

Refer to illustrations 4.9a and 4.9b
9   With the ignition switch in the Off position, retract the cable adjuster by depressing the button, then pushing the conduit in **(see illustrations)**.

4.9b TV cable adjuster details

4.6 Use a spare spring to hold the Throttle Valve (TV) lever forward

A   Lever
B   Spring
C   Casting on bellhousing

10   Rotate the throttle lever on the throttle body to the wide-open position.
11   Hold the throttle lever open and allow the cable conduit to extend all the way, which automatically adjusts the cable. Once the conduit is fully extended, release the adjuster button.
12   Depress the accelerator pedal to the floor and have an assistant check to make sure the throttle lever on the throttle body moves to the full-throttle position and doesn't bind.

5   Bands - adjustment

Refer to illustrations 5.5 and 5.8
1   The transmission bands should be adjusted at the specified intervals or when the upshifts or downshifts become consistently harsh and/or erratic.
2   Raise the vehicle and support it securely on jackstands.

Front band

3   The front band adjusting screw is located

5.5 An adapter extension and inch-pound torque wrench are required to adjust the front transmission band

4.9a The TV cable adjuster is located along the valve cover, near the throttle body

on the left side of the transmission, just above the Throttle Valve (TV) control levers.
4   Loosen the adjusting screw locknut and back it off five turns. Check the adjusting screw to make sure it turns freely in the case, lubricating it if necessary.
5   Using an inch-pound torque wrench, an adapter extension and a 5/16-inch socket, tighten the adjusting screw to the torque listed in this Chapter's Specifications **(see illustration)**. If the adapter tool is not used, the alternate torque must be used.
6   Back the screw off 2-1/2 turns.
7   Tighten the adjusting screw locknut securely while holding the screw with a socket or wrench so it does not rotate.

Rear band

8   The rear band adjusting screw is accessible after removing the oil pan **(see illustration)**. Consequently, it's very convenient to make this adjustment at the time of the transmission fluid filter change (see Chapter 1).
9   Remove the transmission oil pan.
10   Loosen the adjusting screw lock nut.
11   Tighten the adjusting screw with an inch-pound torque wrench and a 1/4-inch socket to the torque listed in this Chapter's Specifications.
12   Back out the adjusting screw four full turns. Install the locknut, hold the screw with a

5.8 The rear band adjusting screw is accessible after removing the transmission oil pan

6.2 The neutral start switch screws into the housing and contacts the internal shaft lever (transmission oil pan removed for clarity)

socket or wrench so it can't turn and tighten the locknut securely.

13   Install the transmission oil pan (see Chapter 1) and lower the vehicle.

14   Refill the transmission with transmission fluid to the proper level (see Chapter 1).

6   Neutral start switch - check and replacement

Refer to illustration 6.2

1   The neutral start and back-up light switches are combined into one unit. The switch has three terminals with the neutral switch being the center one. A ground for the starter solenoid circuit is provided through the shift lever in only the Neutral and Park positions.

2   Raise the vehicle and place it securely on jackstands. Detach the electrical connector from the Neutral start switch **(see illustration)** and test the switch for continuity. Continuity should exist between the center terminal and transmission case only when the shift lever is in Neutral and Park. If the switch appears to be faulty, check the shift linkage (see Section 3) before replacing the switch.

3   Prior to replacing the switch, place a container under it to catch the transmission fluid.

4   Remove the switch and allow the fluid to drain into the container.

5   Place the shift lever in Park or Neutral and check the lever finger position, lever and shaft alignment with the switch opening.

6   Install the switch and seal, tighten the switch to the torque listed in this Chapter's Specifications.

7   Test the switch for continuity and plug in the connector.

8   Lower the vehicle and check the transmission fluid level (see Chapter 1), adding specified fluid as necessary.

7   Automatic transmission - removal and installation

Refer to illustration 7.9

Removal

1   Disconnect the negative cable from the battery.

2   Disconnect the upper bracket of the transmission filler tube.

3   Raise the vehicle and support it securely on jackstands.

4   Drain the transmission fluid (see Chapter 1), then reinstall the pan.

5   Drain the transfer case fluid (see Chapter 1).

6   Remove the torque converter cover.

7   Remove the transmission filler tube.

8   Remove the starter motor (see Chapter 5).

9   Mark the relationship of the torque converter to the driveplate so they can be installed in the same position **(see illustration)**.

10   Remove the torque converter-to-driveplate nuts. Turn the crankshaft for access to each nut. Turn the crankshaft in a clockwise direction only (as viewed from the front).

11   Remove the driveshafts (see Chapter 8).

12   Disconnect the speedometer cable.

13   Detach the electrical connectors from the transmission. If equipped, remove the crankshaft position sensor (see Chapter 6).

14   Disconnect the TV linkage or cable (see Section 4).

15   Disconnect the shift linkage and the transfer case linkage (see Section 3).

16   Support the engine with a jack. Use a block of wood under the oil pan to spread the load.

17   Support the transmission/transfer case with a jack - preferably a jack made for this purpose. Safety chains will help steady the transmission/transfer case on the jack.

18   Unbolt the transmission mount from the crossmember. Remove the crossmember-to-frame bolts.

19   Raise the transmission enough to allow removal of the crossmember.

20   Remove the bolts securing the transmission to the engine.

21   Lower the transmission slightly and disconnect and plug the transmission fluid cooler lines.

22   Move the transmission/transfer case to the rear to disengage it from the engine block dowel pins and make sure the torque converter is detached from the driveplate. Secure the torque converter to the transmission so it won't fall out during removal (a pair of locking pliers clamped onto the bellhousing will work).

Installation

23   Prior to installation, rotate the torque converter back and forth to make sure the converter hub is securely engaged in the pump.

24   With the transmission/transfer case secured to the jack, raise it into position. Be sure to keep it level so the torque converter

7.9 Make alignment marks on the driveplate and the torque converter

does not slide forward.

25   Align the holes in the bellhousing with the dowels on the engine block, then push the transmission assembly forward into position until it rests against the block. If it won't go all the way, find out why it isn't - don't force it or use the bolts to draw the transmission to the engine.

26   Install the bellhousing bolts. Tighten the bolts to the torque listed in this Chapter's Specifications.

27   Turn the torque converter to line up the threaded holes with the holes in the driveplate. The alignment mark on the torque converter and the driveplate made in Step 9 must line up.

28   Install the torque converter-to-driveplate bolts. Tighten them to the torque listed in this Chapter's Specifications.

29   Connect the transmission cooler lines.

30   Install the transmission/transfer case crossmember and tighten the fasteners securely.

31   Remove the jacks supporting the transmission/transfer case and the engine.

32   Install the dipstick tube.

33   Install the starter motor (see Chapter 5).

34   Connect the shift linkage, TV linkage or cable and transfer case shift linkage.

35   Plug in the transmission electrical connectors.

36   Install the torque converter cover.

37   Install the driveshafts (see Chapter 8).

38   Connect the speedometer cable.

39   Adjust the shift linkage and TV linkage/cable (see Sections 3 and 4).

40   Lower the vehicle.

41   Fill the transmission with the specified fluid (see Chapter 1), run the engine and check for fluid leaks.

8   Brake transmission shift interlock cable - removal, installation and adjustment

Warning: *Some models covered by this manual are equipped with airbags. Always disable the airbag system when working in the vicinity of airbag system components (see Chapter 12).*

8.1 Details of the brake transmission shift interlock system (later models)

Removal and installation

Refer to illustrations 8.1 and 8.5

1   Later models are equipped with a brake transmission shift interlock cable, which prevents the transmission from being shifted out of Park or Neutral unless the brake pedal is depressed. Here's how it works: When you depress the brake pedal, a switch down at the pedal closes the circuit to a solenoid that releases the park/brake interlock cable **(see illustration)**. If you don't depress the brake pedal, the solenoid locks the park/brake interlock cable, which prevents the shift lever from being moved. This safety system is virtually trouble-free. However, the following procedure is included in the event that the cable should ever break, or should you have to disconnect it in order to service something else.

2   Remove the steering column lower shroud **(see illustration 18.11a in Chapter 12)**, remove the headlight switch knob and shaft (see Section 13 in Chapter 12) and the steering column opening cover **(see illustration 24.8 in Chapter 11)**.

3   Remove the cable tie that secures the brake transmission shift interlock cable to the steering column. The cable tie is located in front of the solenoid **(see illustration 8.1)**.

4   Unplug the electrical connector from the solenoid.

5   With the ignition key in the unlocked position, disengage the lock tab which connects the end of the cable to the steering column **(see illustration)** and detach the cable from the steering column.

6   Remove the center console assembly (see Chapter 11).

7   Disconnect the cable eyelet from the bellcrank on the shift lever.

8   Disconnect the cable from the shift lever bracket.

9   Remove the cable.

10   Installation is the reverse of removal. Be sure to adjust the cable before installing the center console.

Adjustment

Refer to illustration 8.12

11   Shift the transmission into Park. If you have just installed or replaced the cable, the center console and gear position indicator trim panel should still be off. If they're not, remove them now (see Chapter 11).

12   Pull up the cable lock button **(see illustration)** to release the park/brake interlock cable.

8.5 With the ignition key in the unlocked position, disengage the lock tab which connects the end of the cable to the steering column and detach the cable from the steering column

8.12 To release the park/brake interlock cable, pull up on the cable lock button

13   Turn the ignition switch to the LOCK position.

14   Using a suitable spacer, create a one-millimeter gap between the shifter pawl and the top of the shift gate.

15   Pull the cable forward, then release the cable and press down the cable lock button until it snaps into place.

16   Check your adjustment as follows:

a)   *Verify that you cannot press in the release button in the shift handle (floor shift) or move the release lever (column shift).*

b)   *Turn the ignition switch to the RUN position.*

c)   *Verify that you cannot shift out of PARK unless the brake pedal is applied.*

d)   *With the transmission shift lever out of PARK, release the brake pedal and the release button or release lever, then shift through all the gears. Verify that the ignition key doesn't go to the LOCK position.*

e)   *Verify that the shift lever can be returned to the PARK position without having to apply the brake.*

f)   *Move the shift lever back to the PARK position and verify that when the ignition key is turned to the LOCK position, the shift lever cannot be moved out of PARK.*

g)   *If the system operates as described, the adjustment is correct. If it doesn't, readjust the cable.*

17   Install the center console.

Chapter 7 Part C
Transfer case

Contents

Specifications

Torque specifications
	Ft-lbs (unless otherwise indicated)
Transfer case-to-transmission fasteners	26
Speedometer cable adapter/vehicle speed sensor clamp bolt	90-110 in-lbs
Vehicle speed sensor-to-adapter retaining screw	15-27 in-lbs

1 General information

The transfer case is a device which passes power from the engine and transmission to the front and rear driveshafts.

Four transfer cases are used on these models: New Process (NP) 207, NP 231, NP 242 and New Venture (NV) 231. All four units are the same part-time design with three operating ranges: 2WD high, 4WD high and 4WD low. The 4WD modes should only be engaged on unpaved surfaces, as the transfer case is undifferentiated.

2 Shift linkage - adjustment

Refer to illustrations 2.1a, 2.1b, 2.2 and 2.4
Warning: *Some models covered by this manual are equipped with airbags. Always disable the airbag system when working in the vicinity*

2.1b Transfer case shift linkage - exploded view

2.1a Transfer case shift levers and boots - exploded view

2.2 Pull the shift lever back and insert a shim between the lever and the shift gate - secure the lever in this position with wire

---

of airbag system components (see Chapter 12).

1   Remove the shift lever boot for access to the lever (see illustrations).

2   Position the shift lever as far to the rear as possible (4L position) and insert a 1/8-inch drill bit between the shift lever and the shift gate (see illustration). Secure the shifter with wire and the drill bit with tape.

3   Raise the vehicle and support it securely on jackstands.

4   Under the vehicle, loosen the shift linage trunnion lock bolt and make sure the shift rod fits freely in the trunnion and shift lever (see illustration). Tighten the bolt securely.

5   Lower the vehicle, remove the shim and reinstall any components which were removed.

3   Oil seals - replacement

1   Oil leaks frequently occur due to wear of the extension housing oil seal and/or the speedometer drive gear (or distance sensor) oil seal and O-ring. Replacement of these seals is relatively easy, since the repairs can usually be performed without removing the transmission or transfer case from the vehicle.

Extension housing oil seal

Refer to illustration 3.6

2   The extension housing oil seal is located at the extreme rear of the transfer case, where the rear driveshaft is attached. If leakage at the seal is suspected, raise the vehicle and support it securely on jackstands. If the seal is leaking, lubricant will be built up on the front of the driveshaft and may be dripping from the rear of the transfer case.

3   Refer to Chapter 8 for the removal of the driveshaft.

4   Using a soft-faced hammer, carefully tap the dust shield (if equipped) to the rear and remove it. Be careful not to distort it.

5   Using a screwdriver or pry bar, carefully pry the oil seal out of the rear of the transmission or transfer case. Do not damage the splines on the output shaft.

6   If the oil seal cannot be removed with a screwdriver or pry bar, a special oil seal removal tool (available at auto parts stores) will be required (see illustration).

7   Using a large section of pipe or a very large deep socket as a drift, install the new oil seal. Drive it into the bore squarely and make sure it's completely seated.

8   Reinstall the dust shield by carefully tap-

2.4 Loosen the lock bolt on the trunnion and adjust the rod so it fits freely in the trunnion and shift lever

3.6 Removing the oil seal using a special tool

3.9a Location of the speedometer cable and drive gear housing on the transfer case (distance sensor similar)

ITEM	TORQUE	
A	2-3 N•m	(15-27 in. lbs.)
B	10-12 N•m	(90-110 in. lbs.)

3.9b An exploded view of the vehicle speed sensor and adapter assembly used on later models

3.11 Mark the relationship between the speedometer adapter housing (or vehicle speed sensor) and the transfer case - the adapter is offset and must be installed in the same relationship

ping it into place. Lubricate the splines of the transmission output shaft and the outside of the driveshaft yoke with lightweight grease, then install the driveshaft (see Chapter 8). Be carefully not to damage the lip of the seal.

Speedometer cable /vehicle speed sensor O-ring/oil seal

Refer to illustrations 3.9a, 3.9b, 3.14a, 3.14b and 3.15

Note: *Later models do not have a speedometer cable. They use a vehicle speed sensor instead.*

9   The speedometer cable and drive gear (or vehicle speed sensor) housing is located on the back of the transfer case **(see illustrations)**. Look for transmission oil around the cable housing to determine if the seal and O-ring are leaking.

10   Disconnect the speedometer cable (or unplug the electrical connector from the vehicle speed sensor).

11   Mark the relationship of the speedometer adapter to the transfer case **(see illustration)**.

12   Remove the hold-down bolt and withdraw the adapter.

13   On models with a vehicle speed sensor, remove the speed sensor retaining screw and separate the sensor from the adapter, then remove the speedometer pinion from the adapter **(see illustration 3.9b)**.

14   Remove and discard the old O-rings. On models with a speedometer cable, there is an O-ring on the outside of the adapter and

3.14a Use a small screwdriver to remove the O-ring from the groove . . .

3.14b . . . then lift the adapter seal from the inside of the housing

there's a seal inside the adapter housing **(see illustrations)**. On models with a vehicle speed sensor, there's an O-ring on the outside of the adapter and there's another O-ring on the vehicle speed sensor **(see illustration 3.9b)**. Before installing the new O-ring(s)/seal, coat them with clean transmission fluid.

15   On models with a vehicle speed sensor, install the sensor in the adapter and tighten the sensor screw to the torque listed in this Chapter's Specifications. On these models, count the number of teeth on the speedometer pinion, jot down this figure, then install the pinion in the adapter. Note the index number on the adapter body **(see illustration)**. These numbers will correspond to the number of teeth on the pinion. Lubricate the pinion teeth with transmission fluid.

16   Install the adapter/speed sensor assembly in the transfer case and, on models with a speedometer cable, align the marks you made in Step 11, then install the hold-down clamp and bolt and tighten the bolt to the torque listed in this Chapter's Specifications.

17   On models with a vehicle speed sensor, rotate the adapter until the correct (corresponding to the number of pinion teeth) range numbers are at the 6 o'clock position. Install the hold-down clamp and bolt and tighten the bolt to the torque listed in this

Chapter's Specifications.
18   Reconnect the speedometer cable or plug in the electrical connector.

4   Transfer case - removal and installation

Note: *The transmission/transfer case are removed together, as an assembly. See Part A Section 7 for the manual transmission/transfer case and Part B Section 7 for the automatic transmission/transfer case.*

Removal

1   Once the transmission/transfer case is out of the vehicle remove the nuts securing the transmission to the transfer case, then separate the two.

Installation

2   Installation is the reverse of removal. Be sure to tighten the transfer case-to-transmission nuts to the torque listed in this Chapter's Specifications. **Caution:** *DO NOT use excessive force to install the transfer case to the transmission - if the input shaft does not slide place, readjust the angle so it is level and/or turn the input shaft so the splines engage properly with the transmission.*

5   Transfer case overhaul - general information

Refer to illustrations 5.4a and 5.4b

Overhauling a transfer case is a difficult job for the do-it-yourselfer. It involves the disassembly and reassembly of many small parts. Numerous clearances must be precisely measured and, if necessary, changed with select fit spacers and snap-rings. As a result, if transfer case problems arise, it can be removed and installed by a competent do-it-yourselfer, but overhaul should be left to a transmission repair shop. Rebuilt transfer cases may be available - check with your dealer parts department and auto parts stores. At any rate, time and money involved in an overhaul is almost sure to exceed the cost of a rebuilt unit.

Nevertheless, it's not impossible for an inexperienced mechanic to rebuild a transfer case if the special tools are available and the job is done in a deliberate step-by-step manner so nothing is overlooked.

The tools necessary for an overhaul include internal and external snap-ring pliers, a bearing puller, a slide hammer, a set of pin punches, a dial indicator and possibly a hydraulic press. In addition, a large, sturdy workbench and vise or transmission stand will be required.

During disassembly of the transfer case, make careful notes of how each piece comes off, where it fits in relation to other pieces and what holds it in place. Exploded views are included **(see illustrations)** to show where the parts go - but actually noting how they are installed when you remove the parts will make it much easier to get the transfer case back together.

Before taking the transfer case apart for repair, it will help if you have some idea what area of the transfer case is malfunctioning. Certain problems can be closely tied to specific areas in the transfer case, which can make component examination and replacement easier.

3.15 On models with a vehicle speed sensor, make sure that the correct range numbers (corresponding to the number of pinion teeth) are at the 6 o'clock position

5.4a The NP 231 transfer case - exploded view

1	Front yoke nut, seal, washer, yoke and oil seal	18	Synchronizer sleeve	36	Extension housing
2	Shift detent plug, spring and pin	19	Synchronizer stop ring	37	Bushing
3	Front retainer and seal	20	Snap-ring	38	Oil seal
4	Front case	21	Output shaft front bearing	39	Oil pick-up screen
5	Vacuum switch and seal	22	Output shaft (front)	40	Tube connector
6	Vent assembly	23	Drive sprocket	41	Oil pick-up tube
7	Input gear bearing and snap-ring	24	Drive chain	42	Pick-up tube 0-ring
8	Low range gear snap-ring	25	Drive sprocket bearings	43	Magnet
9	Input gear retainer	26	Output shaft rear bearing	44	Range lever nut and washer
10	Low range gear thrust washers	27	Mainshaft	45	Ranger lever
11	Input gear	28	Oil seal	46	0-ring and seal
12	Input gear pilot bearing	29	Oil pump assembly	47	Sector
13	Low range gear	30	Rear bearing	48	Mode spring
14	Range fork shift hub	31	Snap-ring	49	Mode fork
15	Synchronizer hub snap-ring	32	Rear case	50	Mode fork inserts
16	Synchronizer hub springs	33	Fill plug and gasket	51	Range fork inserts
17	Synchronizer hub and inserts	34	Drain plug and gasket	52	Range fork bushings
		35	Rear retainer	53	Range fork

5.4b The NP 242 transfer case - exploded view

1	Front bearing retainer and seal	20	Drain/fill plug	39	Mainshaft bearing rollers
2	Front case	21	Rear bearing retainer	40	Drive sprocket
3	Shift sector	22	Extension housing	41	Drive chain
4	Low range fork inserts	23	Bushing and oil seal	42	Snap-ring
5	Shift rail	24	Vacuum switch	43	Oil pump seal
6	Shift bracket	25	Magnet	44	Oil pump
7	Slider bracket	26	Thrust ring	45	Rear bearing and snap-ring
8	Bushing and spring	27	Snap-ring	46	Front output shaft rear bearing
9	Mode fork and inserts	28	Shift sleeve	47	Snap-ring
10	Bushing	29	Low range gear	48	Driven sprocket
11	Fork spring	30	Pilot bushing (input gear/mainshaft)	49	Front output shaft
12	Bushing	31	Front output shaft front bearing and	50	Mainshaft bearing spacers
13	Vent tube assembly		snap-ring	51	Shift lever washer and nut
14	Input gear bearing and snap-ring	32	Intermediate clutch shaft	52	Shift lever
15	Low range gear snap-ring	34	Snap-ring	53	Sector 0-ring and seal
16	Retainer, low range gear	35	Mainshaft	54	Detent pin, spring and plug
17	Thrust washer, low range gear	36	Different assembly	55	Seal plug
18	Input gear	37	Oil pump tube 0-ring	56	Front yoke nut, seal, washer, yoke
19	Rear case	38	Oil pump pick-up tube and screen		slinger and oil seal

Chapter 8
Clutch and drivetrain

Contents

Specifications

Clutch
Fluid type .... See Chapter 1

Torque specifications
Ft-lbs (unless otherwise indicated)

Clutch
Clutch master cylinder nuts or bolts	
1987 through 1995	19
1996 through 1999	28
2000	200 in-lbs
Pressure plate-to-flywheel bolts	
Four-cylinder engine	23
Six-cylinder engine	40

Drivetrain
Driveshaft U-joint strap bolts	14
Front differential pinion shaft nut	210
Rear axle pinion shaft lock bolt	14
Front axle shift motor housing bolts	108 in-lbs
Front axleshaft hub nut	175
Front hub assembly-to-steering knuckle bolts	75
Brake backing plate nuts	32
Rear axle U-bolt nuts	44 to 59

1 General information

The information in this Chapter deals with the components from the rear of the engine to the drive wheels, except for the transmission and transfer case, which are dealt with in the previous Chapter. For the purposes of this Chapter, these components are grouped into three categories; clutch, driveshaft and axles. Separate Sections within this Chapter offer general descriptions and checking procedures for components in each of the three groups.

Since nearly all the procedures covered in this Chapter involve working under the vehicle, make sure it's securely supported on sturdy jackstands or on a hoist where the vehicle can be easily raised and lowered.

2 Clutch - description and check

Refer to illustrations 2.1a and 2.1b

1 All vehicles with a manual transmission use a single dry plate, diaphragm spring type clutch **(see illustrations)**. The clutch disc has a splined hub which allows it to slide along the splines of the transmission input shaft. The clutch and pressure plate are held in

2.1a An exploded view of the clutch assembly (four-cylinder models through 1993)

2.1b An exploded view of the clutch assembly (six-cylinder models through 1993)

c) *To check for complete clutch release, run the engine (with the parking brake applied to prevent movement) and hold the clutch pedal approximately 1/2-inch from the floor. Shift the transmission between 1st gear and Reverse several times. If the shift is rough, component failure is indicated.*

d) *Visually inspect the pivot bushing at the top of the clutch pedal to make sure there is no binding or excessive play.*

3   Clutch components - removal, inspection and installation

Warning: *Dust produced by clutch wear and deposited on clutch components is hazardous to your health. DO NOT blow it out with compressed air and DO NOT inhale it. DO NOT use gasoline or petroleum-based solvents to remove the dust. Brake system cleaner should be used to flush the dust into a drain pan. After the clutch components are wiped clean with a rag, dispose of the contaminated rags and cleaner in a covered, marked container.*

Removal

Refer to illustration 3.4

1   Access to the clutch components is normally accomplished by removing the transmission, leaving the engine in the vehicle. If, of course, the engine is being removed for major overhaul, then check the clutch for wear and replace worn components as necessary. However, the relatively low cost of the clutch components compared to the time and trouble spent gaining access to them warrants their replacement anytime the engine or transmission is removed, unless they are new or in near perfect condition. The following procedures are based on the assumption the engine will stay in place.

2   Referring to Chapter 7 Part A, remove the transmission from the vehicle. Support the engine while the transmission is out. Preferably, an engine hoist should be used to support it from above. However, if a jack is used underneath the engine, make sure a piece of wood is positioned between the jack and oil pan to spread the load. **Caution:** *The pick-up for the oil pump is very close to the bottom of the oil pan. If the pan is bent or distorted in any way, engine oil starvation could occur.*

3   To support the clutch disc during removal, install a clutch alignment tool through the clutch disc hub.

4   Carefully inspect the flywheel and pressure plate for indexing marks. The marks are usually an X, an O or a white letter. If they cannot be found, scribe marks yourself so the pressure plate and the flywheel will be in the same alignment during installation **(see illustration)**.

5   Turning each bolt a little at a time, loosen the pressure plate-to-flywheel bolts. Work in a criss-cross pattern until all spring

contact by spring pressure exerted by the diaphragm in the pressure plate.

2   The clutch release mechanism is operated by hydraulic pressure. The hydraulic release system consists of the clutch pedal, a master cylinder and fluid reservoir and the interconnecting hydraulic line. On 1987 through 1993 models, the hydraulic release bearing (combination release bearing/slave cylinder assembly) is mounted inside the clutch housing. On 1994 and later models, the slave cylinder is mounted outside the clutch housing and the release bearing and release lever are mounted inside the clutch housing.

3   When pressure is applied to the clutch pedal to release the clutch, hydraulic pressure is exerted against the release bearing through the clutch hydraulic line. The bearing pushes against the fingers of the diaphragm spring of the pressure plate assembly, releasing the clutch plate.

4   Terminology can be a problem when discussing the clutch components because commonly used terms may be different from those used by the manufacturer. For exam-

ple, the driven plate is also called the clutch plate or disc, the clutch release bearing is sometimes called a throwout bearing or a concentric bearing, and so on.

5   Other than to replace components with obvious damage, some preliminary checks should be performed to diagnose clutch problems.

a) *The first check should be of the fluid level in the clutch master cylinder. If the fluid level is low, add fluid as necessary and inspect the hydraulic system for leaks. If the master cylinder reservoir has run dry, bleed the system as described in Section 8 and retest the clutch operation.*

b) *To check "clutch spin down time," run the engine at normal idle speed with the transmission in Neutral (clutch pedal up - engaged). Disengage the clutch (pedal down), wait several seconds and shift the transmission into Reverse. No grinding noise should be heard. A grinding noise would most likely indicate a problem in the pressure plate or the clutch disc (assuming the transmission is in good condition).*

3.4 Mark the relationship of the pressure plate to the flywheel (arrow) (in case you are going to reuse the same pressure plate)

3.7 Check the surface of the flywheel for cracks, hot spots (dark colored areas) and other obvious defects; resurfacing by a machine shop will correct minor defects - the surface on this flywheel is in fairly good condition; however, resurfacing is always a good idea

3.9 The clutch disc (typical)

1 **Lining** - *will wear down in use*
2 **Rivets** - *secure the lining and will damage the pressure plate or flywheel surface if allowed to contact it*
3 **Marks** - *"Flywheel side" or something similar*

NORMAL FINGER WEAR

EXCESSIVE WEAR

EXCESSIVE FINGER WEAR

BROKEN OR BENT FINGERS

3.11 Replace the pressure plate if excessive wear of damage is noted

pressure is relieved. Then hold the pressure plate securely and completely remove the bolts, followed by the pressure plate and clutch disc.

Inspection

Refer to illustrations 3.7, 3.9 and 3.11

6   Ordinarily, when a problem occurs in the clutch, it can be attributed to wear of the clutch driven plate assembly (clutch disc). However, all components should be inspected at this time.

7   Inspect the flywheel for cracks, heat checking, grooves and other obvious defects **(see illustration)**. If the imperfections are slight, a machine shop can machine the surface flat and smooth, which is highly recommended regardless of the surface appearance. Refer to Chapter 2 for the flywheel removal and installation procedure.

8   Inspect the pilot bearing (see Section 5).

9   Inspect the lining on the clutch disc. There should be at least 1/16-inch of lining above the rivet heads. Check for loose rivets, distortion, cracks, broken springs and other obvious damage **(see illustration)**. As mentioned above, ordinarily the clutch disc is routinely replaced, so if in doubt about the condition, replace it with a new one.

10   Check the condition of the release bear-

ing following the procedure in Section 4.

11   Check the machined surfaces and the diaphragm spring fingers of the pressure plate **(see illustration)**. If the surface is grooved or otherwise damaged, replace the pressure plate. Also check for obvious damage, distortion, cracking, etc. Light glazing can be removed with medium grit emery cloth. If a new pressure plate is required, new and factory-rebuilt units are available.

Installation

Refer to illustration 3.13

12   Before installation, clean the flywheel and pressure plate machined surfaces with lacquer thinner or acetone. It's important that no oil or grease is on these surfaces or the lining of the clutch disc. Handle the parts only with clean hands.

13   Position the clutch disc and pressure plate against the flywheel with the clutch held in place with an alignment tool **(see illustration)**. Make sure it's installed properly (most replacement clutch plates will be marked *"flywheel side"* or something similar - if not marked, install the clutch disc with the damper springs toward the transmission).

14   Tighten the pressure plate-to-flywheel bolts only finger tight, working around the pressure plate.

15   Center the clutch disc by ensuring the alignment tool extends through the splined hub and into the pilot bearing in the crankshaft. Wiggle the tool up, down or side-to-side as needed to bottom the tool in the pilot bearing. Tighten the pressure plate-to-flywheel bolts a little at a time, working in a criss-cross pattern to prevent distorting the cover. After all of the bolts are snug, tighten them to the specified torque. Remove the alignment tool.

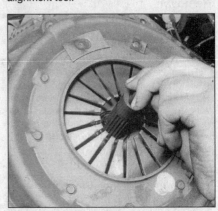

3.13 Center the clutch disc in the pressure plate with an alignment tool before the bolts are tightened

**4.2 Remove the bolts (arrows), then slide the insulator plate
and rubber insulator back on the lines (six-cylinder shown;
on four-cylinder models, the bleeder line is on the
other side of the transmission)**

**4.3 Remove the hydraulic release bearing retaining nut - be sure
to use a new nut upon installation**

16   Using high-temperature grease, lubricate the inner groove of the release bearing (see Section 4). Also place grease on the transmission input shaft bearing retainer.

17   Install the clutch release bearing as described in Section 4.

18   Install the transmission and all components removed previously. Tighten all fasteners to the proper torque specifications.

4   Clutch release bearing - removal, inspection and installation

Warning: *Dust produced by clutch wear and deposited on clutch components is hazardous to your health. DO NOT blow it out with compressed air and DO NOT inhale it. DO NOT use gasoline or petroleum-based solvents to remove the dust. Brake system cleaner should be used to flush the dust into a drain pan. After the clutch components are wiped clean with a rag, dispose of the contaminated rags and cleaner in a covered, marked container.*

1987 through 1993 models
Removal
Refer to illustrations 4.2 and 4.3

1   Following the appropriate procedure outlined in Chapter 7, remove the transmission.

2   Unbolt the insulator plate from the clutch housing and slide the plate and rubber insulator off the lines **(see illustration)**.

3   Remove the pressed metal retaining nut from the base of the hydraulic release bearing **(see illustration)** and slide the release bearing assembly off the transmission input shaft bearing retainer.

Inspection
4   Hold the center portion of the bearing stationary and rotate the outer portion while applying pressure. If the bearing doesn't turn smoothly or if it's noisy, replace it with a new one. Wipe the bearing with a clean rag and

inspect it for damage and wear. Don't immerse the bearing in solvent - it is sealed for life and immersion would ruin it.

5   Hydraulic release bearings must also be checked for fluid leakage where the rubber seal meets the cylinder housing. If any leakage is evident, replace the entire assembly.

Installation
6   Installation is the reverse of the removal procedure, with a couple of points which must be noted.

7   Install a new pressed metal retaining nut. **Note:** *When new, the hydraulic release bearing is retained in the compressed position by nylon straps - they are designed to break the first time the clutch pedal is depressed, so there is no need to remove them.*

8   Install the transmission (see Chapter 7).

9   Connect the hydraulic line and bleed the system as described in Section 7.

1994 and later models
Removal
Refer to illustration 4.11

10   Following the procedure outlined in Chapter 7A, remove the transmission.

11   Disconnect the release bearing from the release lever and slide the release bearing off the transmission input shaft **(see illustration)**.

Inspection
12   Hold the center portion of the release bearing stationary and rotate the outer portion while applying pressure. If the bearing doesn't turn smoothly or if it's noisy, replace it with a new one. Wipe the bearing with a clean rag and inspect it for damage and wear. Don't immerse the bearing in solvent - it is sealed for life and immersion would ruin it.

13   Inspect the release fork and fork pivot. Make sure the fork pivot is secure in the clutch housing and that it isn't bent or damaged.

Installation
14   Installation is the reverse of the removal procedure, with a couple of points that must be noted.

15   Fill the inner groove of the release bearing with high-temperature grease. Also apply a light coat of the same grease to the input shaft splines and to the face of the release bearing where it contacts the pressure plate diaphragm fingers.

16   Lightly lubricate the clutch release bearing where it contacts the release lever with the same grease.

17   Install the transmission (see Chapter 7A).

18   Bleed the system as described in Section 7.

**4.11 Disconnect the retaining clip securing
the release lever, disconnect the release
lever and slide the release bearing off the
transmission input shaft (1994 models)**

5.9 If you don't have an internal puller and slide hammer, pack the recess behind the pilot bearing with heavy grease and force it out hydraulically with a steel rod slightly smaller than the bore in the bearing - when the hammer strikes the rod, the bearing will pop out of the crankshaft

5   Pilot bearing - inspection and replacement

Refer to illustrations 5.9, 5.10a and 5.10b

1   The clutch pilot bearing is a needle roller type bearing which is pressed into the rear of the crankshaft. Its primary purpose is to support the front of the transmission input shaft. The pilot bearing should be inspected whenever the clutch components are removed from the engine. Due to its inaccessibility, if you are in doubt as to its condition, replace it with a new one. **Note:** *If the engine has been removed from the vehicle, disregard the following steps which do not apply.*
2   Remove the transmission (refer to Chapter 7 Part A).
3   Remove the clutch components (see Section 3).
4   Inspect the bore of the pilot bearing for any excessive wear, scoring, lack of grease, dryness or obvious damage. If any of these conditions are noted, the bearing should be replaced. A flashlight will be helpful to direct light into the recess.
5   Removal can be accomplished with a special internal puller and slide hammer, but an alternative method also works very well.
6   Find a solid steel bar which is slightly smaller in diameter than the bearing. Alternatives to a solid bar would be a wood dowel or a socket with a bolt fixed in place to make it solid.
7   Check the bar for fit - it should just slip into the bearing with very little clearance.
8   Pack the bearing and the area behind it (in the crankshaft recess) with heavy grease. Pack it tightly to eliminate as much air as possible.
9   Insert the bar into the bearing bore and strike the bar sharply with a hammer which will force the grease to the back side of the bearing and push it out **(see illustration)**. Remove the bearing and clean all grease from the crankshaft recess.

5.10a The pilot bearing incorporates an O-ring seal which cannot be replaced separately (if any indication that the seal is leaking, or if the bearing is dry, replace it) - the bearing must be installed with the seal towards the transmission

10   To install the new bearing, pack the inside of the bearing and lightly lubricate the outside surface with wheel bearing grease. Drive the bearing into the recess with a bushing driver or an appropriately-sized socket. The seal must face out and the bearing must go in perfectly straight **(see illustrations)**.
11   Install the clutch components, transmission and all other components removed previously, tightening all fasteners properly.

6   Clutch master cylinder - removal, overhaul and installation

Note: *Before beginning this procedure, contact local parts stores and dealer service departments concerning the purchase of a rebuild kit or a new master cylinder. Availability and cost of the necessary parts may dictate whether the cylinder is rebuilt or replaced with a new one. If it's decided to rebuild the cylinder, inspect the bore as described in Step 12 before purchasing parts.*

6.3 To avoid rounding off the corners of the fitting nut (left arrow) for the clutch fluid line at the clutch master cylinder, use a flare nut wrench when loosening it; the upper mounting bolt and lower mounting nut (right arrows) are also visible in this photo - you can remove the lower nut now, but the upper nut has to be removed from under the dash

5.10b Tap in the bearing with a bushing driver or a socket

1987 through 1993 models
Removal

Refer to illustrations 6.3, 6.5 and 6.6

1   A pair of support rods are bolted into the engine compartment between the firewall and the front cross member. Loosen the locknut at the front of the left (driver's side) support rod and swing the rod to the side. Although you can remove the clutch master cylinder without removing this support rod, you can't remove the reservoir cap to drain the clutch fluid or to refill the reservoir when you're done.
2   Remove the clutch master cylinder reservoir cap, and, using a suction gun or large syringe, suck out as much fluid as possible.
3   Disconnect the hydraulic line **(see illustration)** from the clutch master cylinder, using a flare nut wrench, if available.
4   Remove the master cylinder mounting nuts. **Note:** *On some models, the lower nut faces forward and the upper nut faces to the rear (i.e. the bolt head faces forward); on these models, remove the upper nut from under the dash.*
5   Working under the dash, disconnect the pushrod from the clutch pedal. It is retained by a cotter pin, plastic washer and spring washer **(see illustration)**.

6.5 Remove the cotter pin (arrow), plastic washer and spring washer, then disconnect the pushrod from the clutch pedal pin

6.6 An exploded view of the clutch master cylinder assembly (note how the upper mounting nut faces to the rear of the unit)

6.10 Push on the pushrod and remove the snap-ring with a pair of snap-ring pliers

6.11 Pull the plunger assembly from the bore of the clutch master cylinder

6.14a Pry the retainer tab out with a small screwdriver to release the valve stem

6.14b Exploded view of the clutch master cylinder components

1	Pushrod	7	Reservoir	13	Plunger spring
2	Dust boot	8	Retaining clamp	14	Valve stem retainer
3	Snap-ring	9	Stern tip seal	15	Plunger rear seal
4	Washer	10	Valve stem	16	Plunger front seal
5	Master cylinder body	11	Retainer spring	17	Plunger
6	Reservoir cap	12	Spring retainer	18	Valve stem assembly

6   Also from under the dash, remove the master cylinder upper mounting nut, if it faces to the rear **(see illustration)**. Rather than attempt to loosen the nut from this position, it is much easier to simply hold the nut while an assistant unscrews the bolt from the engine side of the firewall.

7   Pull the cylinder out of the hole in the firewall. Be careful not to let any of the fluid drip onto the vehicle's paint, as it will damage it.

Overhaul

Refer to illustrations 6.10, 6.11, 6.14a and 6.14b

8   On models with a removable reservoir, detach the reservoir from the cylinder body by loosening the clamp.

9   Mount the cylinder in a vise, with the vise jaws clamping on the mounting flange. It's a good idea to line the jaws of the vise with wood or rags to prevent damage to the

flange surface.

10   Pry the dust boot from the cylinder. Push in on the pushrod to depress the plunger, then remove the snap-ring with a pair of snap-ring pliers **(see illustration)**. Remove the pushrod and boot. Discard the snap-ring.

11   Pull the plunger assembly from the bore **(see illustration)**. If it's hard to pull out, remove the cylinder from the vise, turn it so the flanged end is down and tap it sharply against a block of wood.

12   Inspect the bore of the cylinder for scratches, score marks, pitting and ridges. The surface must be smooth to the touch. If the bore isn't perfectly smooth, the master cylinder must be replaced with a new or factory rebuilt unit.

13   If the cylinder will be rebuilt, use the

parts contained in the rebuild kit and follow any specific instructions which accompany the kit. Wash all parts to be re-used with brake cleaner or clean brake fluid. DO NOT use petroleum-based solvents.

14   Compress the spring and, using a small screwdriver, pry up on the valve stem retainer tab to release the retainer, spring and valve stem assembly **(see illustrations)**.

15   Remove the plunger, then remove and discard the seals from the plunger.

16   Separate the spring retainer and the valve stem assembly from the plunger spring.

17   Remove the valve stem from the spring retainer. Remove the stem tip seal and spring washer from the stem. Discard the seal.

18   Install the new plunger seals on the plunger, making sure the lips of the seals face the small end of the plunger.

19   Install the new valve stem tip seal and spring washer onto the valve stem. The shoulder of the stem tip seal must fit into the undercut at the end of the stem.

20   Place the spring retainer on the valve stem and over the spring washer, making sure the large end of the retainer is facing the seal end of the valve stem.

21   Slide the stem and spring retainer assembly into place on the plunger spring.

22   Holding the plunger in one hand, compress the spring against the plunger and guide the valve stem into the hole in the retainer. When the end of the stem passes through the hole, bend the tab on the retainer in to lock the stem and retainer to the plunger.

23   Lubricate the cylinder bore and plunger assembly with clean brake fluid. Install the assembly in the cylinder bore.

24   Place a new seal, snap-ring and dust boot on the pushrod. Lubricate the end of the pushrod, the seal and the lips of the dust boot with the grease provided in the rebuild kit. Install the pushrod, depress the plunger and seat the snap-ring in its groove.

25   Slide the pushrod seal (not shown in illustration 6.14b) and dust boot up against the end of the cylinder and stretch the boot over the cylinder body.

Installation

26   Position the cylinder against the firewall and install the lower mounting nut, but don't tighten it fully yet.

27   Connect the hydraulic line to the cylinder, tightening the fitting by hand only. Since the cylinder is still loose, it can be wiggled around slightly to make it easier to align the fitting threads.

28   If the upper mounting nut faces to the rear, install the upper mounting bolt, again using an assistant to tighten the bolt while the nut is held stationary.

29   Connect the pushrod to the clutch pedal, install the washers and a new cotter pin.

30   Tighten the lower mounting nut.

31   Tighten the hydraulic line fitting securely.

32   Install the fluid reservoir if it was previously removed.

33   Fill the reservoir with brake fluid conforming to DOT 3 specifications and bleed the system as described in Section 8.

1994 and later models

Note: *The clutch master cylinder, slave cylinder and connecting hydraulic line are serviced as an assembly. None of these components can be serviced separately, and all fittings are sealed. If any one of the components is faulty, the entire assembly must be replaced.*

Removal

34   Raise the vehicle and place it securely on jackstands.

35   Remove the slave cylinder mounting nuts. Move the slave cylinder away from the clutch housing.

36   Disengage the hydraulic line from the body clips.

37   Lower the vehicle.

38   Make sure the master cylinder filler cap is secure.

39   Remove the lower master cylinder mounting nut. **Note:** *The upper nut must be removed from under the dash.*

40   Working under the dash, disconnect the pushrod from the clutch pedal. It is retained by a metal clip.

41   Also working under the dash, remove the master cylinder upper mounting nut that faces to the rear. Rather than attempting to loosen the nut from this position, it is much easier to simply hold the nut while an assistant unscrews the bolt from the engine side of the firewall.

42   Carefully pull the release/master cylinder assembly up and out of the engine compartment. Be careful not to let any of the fluid drip onto the vehicle's paint, as it will be damaged.

Installation

43   Carefully work the release/master cylinder assembly down and onto the engine compartment, working it past the engine and clutch housing.

44   Position the master cylinder against the firewall and install the lower mounting nut, but don't tighten it fully yet.

45   Install the upper mounting bolt, again using an assistant to tighten the bolt while the nut is held stationary.

46   Connect the pushrod to the clutch pedal and install the metal clip.

47   Tighten the lower mounting nut securely.

48   Raise the vehicle and place it securely on jackstands.

49   Insert the slave cylinder pushrod through the clutch opening and into the release lever. Be sure the cap on the end of the rod is securely engaged onto the lever, then install the mounting nuts. Tighten the nuts securely.

50   Attach the hydraulic line onto the body clips.

51   Lower the vehicle.

7   Clutch hydraulic system - bleeding

Refer to illustration 7.4

1   The hydraulic system should be bled to remove all air whenever any part of the system has been removed or if the fluid level has fallen so low that air has been drawn into the master cylinder. The procedure is very similar to bleeding a brake system.

2   Fill the master cylinder with new brake fluid conforming to DOT 3 specifications. **Caution:** *Don't re-use any of the fluid coming from the system during the bleeding opera-*

tion. Also, don't use fluid which has been inside an open container for an extended period of time.

3   Raise the vehicle and place it securely on jackstands to gain access to the release cylinder (or bleeder screw), which is located on the side of the clutch housing.

4   Remove the dust cap which fits over the bleeder screw **(see illustration)** and push a length of plastic hose over the screw. Place the other end of the hose in a clear container with about two inches of brake fluid. The hose end must be in the fluid at the bottom of the container.

5   Have an assistant depress the clutch pedal and hold it. Open the bleeder screw on the transmission, allowing fluid to flow through the hose. Close the bleeder screw when the flow of bubbles or old fluid ceases. Once closed, have your assistant release the pedal. **Note:** *The bleeder screw used on four-cylinder models is on the right side of the transmission; the bleeder screw used on six-cylinder models is on the left side of the transmission, right above the fitting for the clutch hydraulic line (see the transmission removal and installation procedure in Chapter 7 Part A).*

6   Continue this process until all air is evacuated from the system, indicated by a solid stream of fluid being ejected from the bleeder screw each time with no air bubbles in the hose or container. Keep a close watch on the fluid level inside the master cylinder - if the level drops too low, air will be sucked back into the system and the process will have to be started all over again.

7   Lower the vehicle. Top off the fluid level and check carefully for proper operation before placing the vehicle in normal service.

7.4 The bleeder screw is located on the right (passenger's) side of the transmission housing on four-cylinder models; on six-cylinder models, it's on the left side, immediately above the fitting for the clutch hydraulic line (see illustration 4.7 in the Transmission removal and installation procedure in Chapter 7)

8.1 Front axle assembly

8.3a Front driveshaft assembly

8.3b Rear driveshaft assembly

8.5a Typical Dana Model 35 axle assembly (pre-1990 unit shown; 1990 and later axles use a C-clip to connect the inner end of axleshafts to differential

9.5b The axle build date and manufacturer's number are stamped on the passenger's side axle tube near the housing cover; the axle assembly part number and ratio are on a tag attached to the left side of the housing cover

8   Axles, axleshafts, differentials and driveshafts - general information

Refer to illustrations 8.1, 8.3a, 8.3b, 8.5a and 8.5b

The models covered by this manual are equipped with Jeep's "Command-Trac" front axle (see illustration), which uses a two-piece (outer and intermediate) axleshaft in the right axle tube. The outer splines of the left axleshaft and the right (outer) axleshafts mesh with splines in the wheel hub. The front axleshafts have single cardan universal joints at their outer ends to allow the front wheels to turn left or right while transmitting torque.

The inner end of the intermediate shaft is connected to the differential side gear by a snap-ring. When you select four-wheel drive operation by shifting the transfer case lever into one of the 4WD ranges, the two shafts are coupled together by a shift collar which engages matching splines located on the end of each axleshaft. The shift collar is controlled by a vacuum shift motor and shift fork, which are mounted on the right axle tube where the shift collar is located between the intermedi-

ate and outer axleshafts. When you select two-wheel drive, the vacuum shift motor and shift fork move the shift collar out of engagement with the two axleshaft splines. During two-wheel drive operation, the disengaged differential free-wheels instead of turning the ring gear, pinion and front driveshaft, saving unnecessary wear on these components.

The front driveshaft (see illustration) is equipped with single cardan universal joints at both ends and a slip yoke at its front end (the end which connects to the yoke at the drive pinion gear shaft). The rear driveshaft (see illustration) also has single cardan universal joints at both ends. The rear driveshaft also has a slip yoke on its front end (the end that connects it to the transfer case output shaft yoke). Slip yokes and single cardan universal joints are equipped with "Zerk" type grease fittings; they should be lubricated at the recommended intervals (see Chapter 1).

The front and rear driveshafts are finely balanced by the manufacturer during assembly. If you remove or disassemble a driveshaft, carefully mark the relationship of the parts to ensure that you reassemble them so they're in the same relationship to each other as they were prior to disassembly. If you don't, the driveshafts can vibrate excessively.

The Model 35 rear axle (see illustration) has "semi-floating" axleshafts supported on their outer ends by the rear wheel bearings. The axle assembly is held in alignment to the body by the suspension leaf springs. The axle build date and manufacturer's number are stamped on right (passenger's side) axle tube near the housing cover; the axle assembly part number and ratio are on a tag attached to the left side of the housing cover (see illustration).

The rear axle is equipped with a standard or an optional Trac-Lok (limited slip) differential. Trac-Lok differentials transfer torque from one wheel to the other if traction is lost and the wheel begins to spin.

Because of the complexity and critical nature of the differential adjustments, as well as the special equipment needed to perform the operations, disassembly of the differential should be done by a dealer service department or other repair shop.

9   Driveline inspection

1   Raise the rear of the vehicle and support it securely on jackstands.

2   Crawl under the vehicle and visually inspect the driveshaft. Look for any dents or cracks in the tubing. If any are found, the driveshaft must be replaced.

3   Check for any oil leakage at the front and rear of the driveshaft. Leakage where the driveshaft enters the transmission or transfer case indicates a defective rear transmission or transfer case seal. Leakage where the driveshaft enters the differential indicates a defective pinion seal. For these repair operations refer to Chapter 7 and Section 14, respectively.

4   While under the vehicle, have an assistant turn the rear wheel so the driveshaft will rotate. As it does, make sure the universal joints are operating properly without binding, noise or looseness.

5   The universal joint can also be checked with the driveshaft motionless, by gripping your hands on either side of the joint and attempting to twist the joint. Any movement

10.3 Before removing the bolts, mark the relationship of the driveshaft yoke to the differential pinion shaft yoke - to prevent the driveshaft from turning when loosening the flange bolts, insert a screwdriver through the yoke

10.12 On the rear U-joint of the front driveshaft, mark the relationship of the U-joint flange to the transfer case companion flange - when removing the bolts, insert a screwdriver through the U-joint to prevent the driveshaft from turning

11.2 A pair of needle-nose pliers can be used to remove the universal joint snap-rings

at all in the joint is a sign of considerable wear. Lifting up on the shaft will also indicate movement in the universal joints.

6   Finally, check the driveshaft mounting bolts at the ends to make sure they are tight.

7   The above driveshaft checks should be repeated on the front driveshaft. In addition, check for grease leakage around the sleeve yoke, indicating failure of the yoke seal.

8   Check for leakage where the driveshafts connect to the transfer case and front differential. Leakage indicates worn oil seals.

9   Also check for leakage at the ends of the axle housings (at the drum brake backing plates), which would indicate a defective axle seal.

10   Driveshafts - removal and installation

Note: *Whenever a driveshaft is removed, new U-joint straps should be used during installation.*

1   Disconnect the negative cable from the battery. Place the transmission and transfer case in Neutral with the parking brake off.

2   Raise the vehicle and support it securely on jackstands.

Rear driveshaft

Refer to illustration 10.3

3   To ensure that the driveshaft maintains its balance, it must be reinstalled in the same position. Using a scribe, white paint or a hammer and punch, place alignment marks on the yokes at the drive pinion gear shaft and at the rear of the driveshaft **(see illustration)**.

4   Remove the rear universal joint bolts and straps **(see illustration 10.3)**. Turn the driveshaft (or tires) as necessary to bring the bolts into the most accessible position.

5   Tape the bearing caps to the spider to

prevent the caps from coming off during removal.

6   Lower the rear of the driveshaft and then slide the slip yoke at the front out of the transmission or transfer case.

7   To prevent loss of fluid and protect against contamination while the driveshaft is out, wrap a plastic bag over the transmission or transfer case housing and hold it in place with a rubber band.

8   Remove the plastic bag from the transfer case and wipe the area clean. Inspect the oil seal carefully. Procedures for replacement of this seal can be found in Chapter 7.

9   Slide the slip yoke at the front of the driveshaft into the transfer case.

10   Raise the rear of the driveshaft into position, checking to be sure the marks are in alignment. If not, turn the rear wheels to match the pinion flange and the driveshaft.

11   Remove the tape securing the bearing caps and install new straps and bolts. Tighten the bolts to the torque listed in this Chapter's Specifications.

11.4 To press the universal joint out of the driveshaft yoke, set it up in a vise with the small socket pushing the joint and bearing cap into the large socket

Front driveshaft

Refer to illustration 10.12

12   Using white paint, chalk or a scribe, mark the relationship of the rear universal joint flange to the transfer case companion flange **(see illustration)**. Also mark the relationship of the front U-joint to the pinion shaft yoke at the front differential.

13   Remove the strap bolts from the front U-joint. Unbolt the rear U-joint flange from the transfer case companion flange **(see illustration 10.12)** and remove the shaft from the vehicle. Tape the bearing caps to the spider to prevent the caps from falling off.

14   Installation is the reverse of the removal procedure. Be sure to tighten the fasteners to the torque listed in this Chapter's Specifications.

11   Universal joints - replacement

Refer to illustrations 11.2, 11.4 and 11.9

Note: *A press or large vise will be required for this procedure. It may be a good idea to take the driveshaft to a repair or machine shop where the universal joints can be replaced for you, normally at a reasonable charge.*

1   Remove the driveshaft as outlined in the previous Section.

2   Using a small pair of pliers, remove the snap-rings from the spider **(see illustration)**.

3   Supporting the driveshaft, place it in position on either an arbor press or on a workbench equipped with a vise.

4   Place a piece of pipe or a large socket with the same inside diameter over one of the bearing caps. Position a socket which is of slightly smaller diameter than the cap on the opposite bearing cap **(see illustration)** and use the vise or press to force the cap out (inside the pipe or large socket), stopping just before it comes completely out of the yoke. Use the vise or large pliers to work the cap the rest of the way out.

5   Transfer the sockets to the other side and press the opposite bearing cap out in the same manner.

11.9 If the snap-ring will not seat in the groove, strike the yoke with a hammer - this will relieve tension that has set up in the yoke, and slightly spring the yoke ears (this should also be done if the joint feels tight when assembled)

12.6a Mark the relationship of the pinion shaft to the pinion shaft yoke

12.6b Hold the pinion shaft yoke in place and loosen the nut

6   Pack the new universal joint bearings with grease. Ordinarily, specific instructions for lubrication will be included with the universal joint servicing kit and should be followed carefully.

7   Position the spider in the yoke and partially install one bearing cap in the yoke. If the replacement spider is equipped with a grease fitting, be sure it's offset in the proper direction (toward the driveshaft).

8   Start the spider into the bearing cap and then partially install the other cap. Align the spider and press the bearing caps into position, being careful not to damage the dust seals.

9   Install the snap-rings. If difficulty is encountered in seating the snap-rings, strike the driveshaft yoke sharply with a hammer. This will spring the yoke ears slightly and allow the snap-rings to seat in the groove **(see illustration)**.

10   Install the grease fitting and fill the joint with grease. Be careful not to overfill the joint, as this could blow out the grease seals.

11   Install the driveshaft. Tighten the flange bolts to the specified torque.

12   Pinion oil seal - replacement

Refer to illustrations 12.6a and 12.6b

Note: *The following procedure applies to both front and rear differentials.*

1   A pinion shaft oil seal failure results in the leakage of differential gear lubricant past the seal and onto the driveshaft yoke or flange. The seal is replaceable without removing or disassembling the differential.

2   Loosen the front or rear wheel lug nuts, raise the vehicle and place it on jackstands.

3   Remove the front or rear wheels. If you're replacing the rear differential pinion seal, also remove the rear brake drums. **Note:** *The wheels must be removed before you can obtain an accurate reading of the*

amount of torque required to turn the pinion.

4   Disconnect the driveshaft from the pinion shaft yoke (see Section 10).

5   Using a torque wrench, slowly turn the pinion shaft nut and measure the torque required to turn the pinion.

6   Mark the relationship of the pinion shaft to the pinion shaft yoke **(see illustration)**. Hold the pinion shaft yoke with a large pair of adjustable pliers, then remove the nut **(see illustration)**.

7   Remove the pinion shaft yoke from the shaft, using a puller if necessary.

8   After noting what the visible side of the oil seal looks like, carefully pry it out of the differential with a screwdriver or pry bar. Be careful not to damage the splines on the pinion shaft.

9   Lubricate the new seal lip with multi-purpose grease or differential lubricant and carefully install it in position in the differential. Using a seal driver or a short section of pipe of the proper diameter and a hammer, carefully drive the seal into place.

10   Clean the sealing lip contact surface of the pinion shaft yoke. Apply a thin coat of multi-purpose grease to the seal contact surface and the shaft spines and, using a soft-faced hammer, tap the pinion shaft yoke onto the shaft, making sure the match-marks line up.

11   Coat the threads of a new pinion shaft nut with multi-purpose grease and, using the holder to hold the flange, tighten the nut just enough to eliminate all end-play in the pinion shaft.

12   Turn the pinion shaft yoke several times to seat the bearing.

13   Using a torque wrench, see how much torque is required to turn the pinion shaft. The desired preload is the previously recorded torque value plus five inch-pounds. If the preload is less than desired, retighten the nut in small increments until the desired preload is reached. If the maximum torque (add five inch-pounds to the torque required to loosen the nut on disassembly) is reached before the preload figure is obtained, the bearing spacer must be replaced by a repair shop. **Note:** *Do not back-off the pinion nut to*

reduce the preload. After the preload is properly adjusted, proceed to the next Step.

14   Connect the driveshaft to the pinion shaft yoke (see Section 10).

15   Install the brake drums, if you're working on the rear pinion seal, and the wheels, lower the vehicle to the ground and tighten the lug nuts to the torque listed in the Chapter 1 Specifications.

16   Test drive the vehicle and check around the differential pinion shaft yoke for evidence of leakage.

13   Front axle hub and bearings - removal, service and installation

Refer to illustrations 13.4a, 13.4b and 13.4c

Removal

1   Pry the hubcap from the wheel, remove the cotter pin and nut lock then loosen the axle hub nut.

2   Loosen the front wheel lug nuts, raise the front of the vehicle and support it securely on jackstands. Remove the wheel.

3   Remove the disc brake caliper and disc (see Chapter 9).

4   Remove the axle hub nut. Unbolt the hub assembly from the steering knuckle and pull it out of the knuckle bore **(see illustrations)**. If the axle sticks in the hub splines, try tapping it loose with a dead blow hammer. If that doesn't work, push it out of the hub with a puller.

Service

5   On early models the hub bearings may be serviced, but due to the special tools and expertise required to separate and reassemble the hub and bearings, this job should be left to a dealer service department or repair shop. On later models, the hub and bearing assembly must be replaced as an assembly. Check with a parts specialist to determine parts availability for your model.

Installation

6   Using sandpaper or emery cloth, clean the opening in the steering knuckle to remove

13.4a An exploded view of the front axle hub and bearing assembly

1	Cotter pin	10	Bearing carrier
2	Nut retainer	11	Inner bearing race
3	Nut	12	Inner bearing
4	Washer	13	Inner bearing seal
5	Brake disc	14	Carrier seal
6	Hub	15	Disc brake splash shield
7	Outer bearing seal	16	Axleshaft dust slinger
8	Outer bearing	17	Bearing carrier bolts
9	Outer bearing race	18	Axleshaft

any rust or dirt that may be present. Lubricate the axleshaft splines with wheel bearing grease. Smear the opening in the steering knuckle with wheel bearing grease and install the hub assembly, tightening the bolts to the specified torque.

7   Install the washer and hub nut, tightening the nut securely. Install the brake disc and caliper (see Chapter 9), mount the wheel and lower the vehicle. Tighten the lug nuts to the torque listed in the Chapter 1 Specifications.

14   Front axleshafts - removal, overhaul and installation

Removal
Left or right outer axleshaft
Refer to illustration 14.4

1   Following the procedure described in Section 13, remove the front axle hub and bearing assembly.
2   Remove the disc brake splash shield **(see illustration 13.4a).**

13.4b Remove the three bolts (arrows) (front bolt not visible in this photo) that secure the hub assembly to the steering knuckle - a twelve-point socket will be necessary

3   If equipped with a shift motor and the right side axle is being removed, follow the procedure described in Section 15 and remove the front axle shift motor.
4   Slide the axle straight out of the axle housing **(see illustration)**.

Right side intermediate axleshaft (models with shift motor)
Refer to illustration 14.7

5   Remove the right side outer axleshaft (see above Steps).
6   Remove the differential cover (see the differential lubricant changing procedure in Chapter 1).
7   Remove the intermediate shaft retaining clip in the differential case **(see illustration)**.
8   Slide the intermediate shaft out of the axle housing.
9   Tighten the axle hub nut to the specified torque and install the nut lock and a new cotter pin. Install the hubcap.

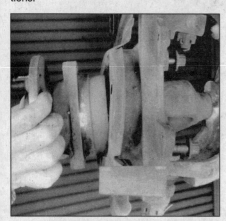

13.4c Carefully pull the hub assembly out of the steering knuckle

14.4 Once the hub and bearing assembly has been removed, the axleshaft can be pulled straight out of the housing

RETAINING CLIP

14.7 The right side intermediate axleshaft is held in the differential by a retaining clip

14.10a   Exploded view of the front axleshaft U-joint assembly

14.10b   Push the snap-rings out of the groove in the U-joint bearings with a small screwdriver

U-joint overhaul

Refer to illustrations 14.10a and 14.10b

10   Follow the U-joint replacement procedure in Section 11, but note that the snap-rings are inboard of the yoke ears and fit into grooves in the bearing caps **(see illustration)**. They are removed by driving them out with a screwdriver **(see illustration)**.

Installation

11   Installation is the reverse of the removal procedure. If the intermediate axleshaft was removed, use a new gasket on the differential cover and fill the differential housing with the specified type of gear lubricant (see Chapter 1). If the front axle shift motor was removed, lubricate the axleshaft splines, shift collar and fork with wheel bearing grease.

15   Front axle shift motor - check, removal and installation

1   Raise the front of the vehicle and support it securely on jackstands.

Check

2   Disconnect the vacuum line from the shift motor and connect a hand-held vacuum pump to the front port of the motor.

3   Apply vacuum to the motor and rotate the right front wheel to ensure that the axle is fully disengaged. The shift motor should hold vacuum for at least 30 seconds. If it leaks, replace it.

4   If the motor holds vacuum, connect the vacuum pump to the rear port on the shift motor. Plug the other ports and apply vacuum once again. It should hold vacuum for 30 seconds also. If not, replace the motor.

5   With vacuum still applied, remove the plug from the port where the vacuum line to the transfer case connects. Check for vacuum. If vacuum is not present, continue on to the next step.

6   Rotate the right front wheel to ensure that the axle has shifted completely. If it hasn't, remove the shift motor and check for freeness of the sliding shift collar.

7   Inspect the vacuum harness from the shift motor to the transfer case for kinks, cracks and other signs of damage. Check the vacuum harness connectors for a good, tight fit on the vacuum ports.

Removal

Refer to illustrations 15.8, 15.10a and 15.10b

8   Unplug the vacuum harness from the shift motor **(see illustration)**.

9   Remove the shift motor housing bolts and lift the shift motor housing, motor and fork from the axle housing. Remove all traces of old gasket material.

10   Mark the relationship of the shift fork to the housing to return it to its original position upon reassembly **(see illustration)**. Rotate the shift motor and remove the shift fork and motor retaining snap-rings **(see illustration)** by pushing them down with two screwdrivers. Pull the motor out of the housing.

Installation

11   Remove the O-ring from the shift motor and install a new one if the same motor is to be reinstalled.

12   Slide the shift motor into the housing and install the shift fork, lining up the previously applied match-marks. Install the snap-rings, making sure they are completely seated in their grooves.

13   Liberally coat the shift collar and axleshaft splines with wheel bearing grease. Engage the shift fork with the shift collar and set the assembly into position on the axle housing. Be sure to use a new gasket. Install the bolts and tighten them to the specified torque.

14   Connect the vacuum harness and check the front differential lubricant level (see Chapter 1).

16   Front axle assembly - removal and installation

1   Loosen the front wheel lug nuts, raise the front of the vehicle and support it securely on jackstands positioned under the frame rails. Remove the front wheels.

2   Unbolt the front brake calipers and hang them out of the way with pieces of wire - don't let the calipers hang by the brake hose (see Chapter 9).

15.8   Unplug the vacuum harness connectors (right three arrows), then remove the four bolts that retain the shift motor housing (left four arrows)

15.10a   Mark the relationship of the shift fork to the housing so it will be reinstalled correctly

15.10b Remove the shift fork and motor retaining snap-ring (arrow is pointing to fork retaining snap-ring) and slide the motor out of the housing

17.1 On models with the bearing pressed on the axleshaft, the axle is retained by a retaining plate bolted to the brake backing plate

3   Remove the caliper brackets and brake discs (see Chapter 9).
4   Disconnect the vacuum harness from the front axle shift motor (see Section 15).
5   Mark the relationship of the front drive-shaft to the front differential pinion shaft yoke, then disconnect the driveshaft from the yoke (see Section 10). On 1987 through 1995 models, discard the U-joint straps.
6   Disconnect the drag link (at the right side of the tie-rod), steering damper and track bar; disconnect the shock absorbers; loosen the stabilizer bar links at the stabilizer bar and disconnect the stabilizer bar links from the axle (see Chapter 10).
7   On 1987 through 1995 models, loosen the nuts and bolts that attach the spring rear eyes to the frame brackets; loosen the nuts and bolts that attach the front of the springs to the shackles (see Chapter 10).
8   On 1997 and later models, unbolt the upper and lower suspension arms from the axle (see Chapter 10).
9   Position a hydraulic jack under the differential. If two jacks are available, place one under the right side axle tube to balance the assembly. Raise the jack high enough to

relieve the axle weight from the springs, then remove the spring shackle nuts and bolts and lower the front of the springs to the floor (see Chapter 10).
10   Remove the axle with the floor jack.
11   Installation is the reverse of the removal procedure. On 1987 through 1995 models, be sure to use new U-joint straps and tighten the bolts of the torque listed in this Chapter's Specifications. Be sure to tighten to the suspension fasteners to the torque values listed in the Chapter 10 Specifications.

17   Rear axleshaft and bearing assembly - removal and installation

Refer to illustration 17.1
1   Loosen the wheel lug nuts, raise the rear of the vehicle and support it securely on jackstands. Remove the wheel. Remove the brake drum. **Note:** *Two types of axleshaft retaining methods are used on the models covered by this manual. On the first type, the axle bearing is pressed on the axleshaft and*

the axleshaft is retained in the tube by a bearing retaining plate **(see illustration)**. *On the second type, the axle bearing is pressed into the axle tube and the axleshaft is retained by C-clip locks in the differential. To determine which type you have, remove the brake drum and inspect the end of the axle tube behind the axleshaft flange. If a bearing retaining plate is visible, the axle bearing is pressed on the axleshaft. Models equipped with C-clips are not equipped with a bearing retaining plate, the end of the axle tube and the axleshaft seal will be visible.*

Models with a bearing retainer
Removal
Refer to illustrations 17.2, 17.3, 17.5a and 17.5b
2   Remove the nuts attaching the bearing retainer (and brake backing plate) to the axle tube flange **(see illustration)**.
3   Connect a slide hammer and adapter to the axle flange and pull the axleshaft assembly from the axle housing **(see illustration)**.
4   If the bearing must be replaced, take the assembly to a dealer service department or a

17.2 Unscrew the four brake backing plate nuts using a socket on an extension passing through the hole in the axle flange

17.3 Pull the axle from the housing using a slide hammer and axle flange adapter

17.5a Remove the inner axle seal from the housing using a slide hammer and internal puller jaw attachment

17.5b Lubricate the seal lip, then drive the seal into position with an installation tool or a piece of pipe with an outside diameter slightly smaller than the outside diameter of the seal

repair shop to have the old bearing and outer seal removed and new ones installed. If a new bearing is installed, be sure to also replace the inner seal (see next Step).

5   If the brake backing plate shows evidence of leaking differential lubricant, the inner axleshaft seal should be replaced. Remove the seal using the slide hammer with an internal puller jaw attachment **(see illustration)**. Install the new seal using a seal driver or piece of pipe **(see illustration)**.

Installation

6   Wipe the bearing bore in the axle housing clean. Pack the bearing with wheel bearing grease and apply a thin coat of grease to the outer surface of the bearing.

7   Smear the lips of the inner seal with grease, then guide the axleshaft straight into the axle housing, being careful not to damage the seal.

8   Install the retaining nuts for the brake backing plate and bearing retainer, and tighten them to the torque listed in this Chapter's Specifications. Slide the brake drum over the axle flange.

9   Install the wheel and lug nuts, tightening the lug nuts securely. Lower the vehicle and tighten the lug nuts to the torque listed in the Chapter 1 Specifications.

Models with a C-clip

Removal

Refer to illustrations 17.12a, 17.12b, 17.13 and 17.17

10   Clean away all foreign material from the area where the differential housing cover mates with the differential housing.

11   Loosen the differential housing cover bolts and drain the differential lubricant from the housing (see Chapter 1). Remove the housing cover.

12   Rotate an axleshaft until you can see the lock bolt for the differential pinion shaft. Remove the lock bolt and the pinion shaft from the differential carrier **(see illustrations)**. Caution: *Don't turn the wheels or the carrier after the shaft has been removed, or the spider gears might fall out.*

13   Push in on the axleshaft (toward the differential) and remove the axleshaft C-clip lock from its recessed groove in the axleshaft **(see illustration)**. If you need a screwdriver to pry it up far enough to pull it out, make sure you don't damage the gear teeth.

14   Slide the axleshaft out of the axle tube. Use care to prevent damage to the axleshaft bearing and seal, which will remain in the axle tube.

15   Inspect the bearing contact surface on the axleshaft. It should be a dull gray in appearance and may even appear to be slightly dented. But if you see signs of brinelling, pitting and spalling, the axleshaft AND the bearing must be replaced.

17.12a Rotate the axleshaft until you can see the lock bolt for the differential pinion shaft and remove the lock bolt . . .

17.12b . . . and then carefully remove the pinion shaft from the differential carrier (don't turn the wheels or the carrier after the shaft has been removed, or the spider gears might fall out)

17.13 Push in the axle flange, remove the C-clip lock from the inner end of the axleshaft

16   Even if there are no signs of extreme bearing/axleshaft wear, the brake backing plate may be leaking differential lubricant. If it is, replace the outer axleshaft seal by prying it out of the axle tube with a small pry bar or a large screwdriver.

17   If you're going to install a new bearing, you can remove the seal at the same time as the bearing, provided you use Bearing Removal Tool Set 6310, or a similar setup **(see illustration)**. Use the adapter tool with the smallest "foot" from the removal tool set. Thread the adapter onto the threaded rod. With the foot parallel to the adapter bracket, insert it through the bearing bore and pivot it 90-degrees (i.e. pivot it perpendicular to the bracket) with a suitable device. Position the guide against the axleshaft tube and turn the nut against the guide plate to remove the bearing.

Installation

Refer to illustration 17.20

18   Thoroughly wipe clean the axleshaft bearing bore in the axle tube.

19   Position the new axleshaft bearing on the "pilot" of your bearing installation tool. Insert the axleshaft bearing into the axle tube bore (make sure the bearing isn't cocked in the bore). Gently tap the driver handle until the bearing is seated firmly against the shoulder in the axle tube. **Caution:** *Don't use the new axleshaft seal to seat the bearing in the axle tube bore; this could damage the seal and cause lubricant to leak from the axle tube.*

20   Install the new seal using a special seal installation seal driver, available at most auto parts stores **(see illustration)**, or a suitably sized section of pipe. When the installation tool contacts the axle tube "face," the seal will be positioned at the proper depth in the bore.

21   Wipe the bearing bore in the axle housing clean. Pack the bearing with wheel bearing grease and apply a thin coat of grease to the outer surface of the bearing.

22   Lubricate the bearing bore and the seal lip, then guide the axleshaft straight into the axle tube and engage its splines with the splines in the differential side gear. Make sure you don't damage the axleshaft seal lip.

23   Push in on the axleshaft and install the C-clip lock in the recessed groove on the inner end of the axleshaft. To seat the C-clip lock into the counterbore in the differential side gear, pull the axleshaft out.

24   Insert the pinion shaft into the differential carrier, through the thrust washers and the pinion gears. Align the hole in the shaft with the lock bolt hole in the carrier, install the lock bolt and tighten it to the torque listed in this Chapter's Specifications.

25   Install the differential housing cover (see Chapter 1).

26   Install the brake drum (see Chapter 9).

27   Install the wheel and lug nuts. Tighten the lug nuts securely. Lower the vehicle and

17.17 An exploded view of a special bearing removal tool, with which you can remove the axleshaft bearing and seal simultaneously

17.20 You can install the new seal using a special seal installation tool, or a suitably sized section of pipe - when the installation tool contacts the axle tube "face," the seal is positioned at the proper depth in the bore

tighten the lug nuts to the torque listed in the Chapter 1 Specifications.

28   Refill the differential housing with the specified lubricant (see Chapter 1).

29   Test drive the vehicle to make sure the brakes and axle are operating properly. If the vehicle has Trac-Lok (i.e. a limited slip differential), make 10 to 12 slow, figure-eight turns to ensure that the new lubricant is pumped through the clutch discs.

18   Rear axle assembly - removal and installation

1   Loosen the rear wheel lug nuts, raise the vehicle and support it securely on jackstands placed underneath the frame rails, either adjacent to or slightly in front of the rear spring front eyes.

2   Remove the wheels.

3   Disconnect the driveshaft from the differential pinion shaft yoke and hang the rear of the driveshaft from the underbody with a piece of wire (see Section 10).

4   Unbolt the rear track bar from the axle tube (see Chapter 10).

5   Disconnect the axle vent tube from its fitting.

6   Disconnect the parking brake cables from the equalizer (see Chapter 9).

7   Support the rear axle assembly with a floor jack placed under the differential.

8   Disconnect the shock absorbers from the axle (see Chapter 10).

9   Disconnect the flexible brake hose from the floorpan fitting. Plug the end of the hose or wrap a plastic bag tightly around it to prevent excessive fluid loss and contamination.

10   Loosen, but don't remove, the bolts that attach the spring eyes to the frame brackets and shackles (see Chapter 10).

11   Remove the U-bolt nuts from the leaf spring tie plates (see Chapter 10).

12   Raise the rear axle assembly slightly, then unbolt the springs from the shackles (see Chapter 10) and lower the rear ends of the springs to the floor (only on models with the axle housing mounted above the spring).

13   Lower the jack and move the axle assembly out from under the vehicle.

14   Installation is the reverse of the removal procedure. Be sure to tighten the U-bolt nuts and the U-joint strap bolts to the torque values listed in the Chapter 10 Specifications.

Notes

Chapter 9 Brakes

Contents

Specifications

General

Brake fluid type	See Chapter 1

Disc brakes

Disc minimum thickness*
1989 and earlier models	0.815 inch
1990 models	0.940 inch
1991 models	0.890 inch
1992 and later models	Stamped or cast into disc

Disc runout (maximum)
1989 and earlier models	0.004 inch
1990 and 1991 models	0.005 inch
1992 through 2002 models	0.003 inch
2003 and later models	0.004 inch
Thickness variation	0.0005 inch
Brake pad minimum thickness	See Chapter 1

Refer to the marks cast or stamped into the disc (they supercede information printed here)

Drum brakes

Drum maximum diameter (refinish limit)
1989 and earlier models	10.060 inch
1990 and 1991 models	9.050 inch
1992 and later models	Stamped or cast into drum

Refer to the marks cast or stamped into the disc (they supercede information printed here)

Torque specifications
Ft-lbs (unless otherwise indicated)

Power brake booster pushrod nuts (pre-1991 models)
Inner nut	25
Outer nut	75 in-lbs
Power brake booster mounting nuts	25 to 29
Master cylinder mounting nuts	18
1996 and earlier models	15
1997 and later models	13 to 18

Caliper mounting pins
1987 through 1989 models	25 to 35
1990 and later models	132 in-lbs
Wheel cylinder mounting bolts	84 in-lbs
Wheel lug nuts	See Chapter 1
Wheel speed sensor mounting bolt	90 in-lbs

1 General information

Refer to illustration 2.1

The vehicles covered by this manual are equipped with hydraulically operated front and rear brake systems. The front brakes are ventilated discs; the rear brakes are either drums (models through 2002) or solid discs (2003 and later models). Both the front and rear brakes are self-adjusting. The front and rear disc brakes automatically compensate for pad wear, while the rear drum brakes incorporate an adjustment mechanism, which is activated as the brakes are applied when the vehicle is stopped in reverse. Anti-lock brakes are optional on most models.

Hydraulic circuits

The hydraulic system consists of two separate circuits; if a leak or failure occurs in one hydraulic circuit, the other circuit will remain operative. The master cylinder has separate reservoirs for each circuit. A visual warning of circuit failure or air in the system is given by a warning light activated by dis-

1.2 Schematic of the brake hydraulic system

1   *Master cylinder*
2   *Combination valve*
3   *Disc brake caliper*
4   *Wheel cylinder*

2.5a   If you've got a pre-1990 model, use a large C-clamp to push the piston back into the caliper bore - note that one end of the clamp is on the flat area on the backside of the caliper and the other end (screw end) is pressing against the outer brake pad

placement of the piston in the pressure differential switch portion of the combination valve (on non-ABS systems) from its normal "in balance" position.

Master cylinder/reservoir assembly

The master cylinder used on all models is an aluminum type with a nylon reservoir. It is not rebuildable. If found to be defective, it must be replaced. (The reservoir grommets are replaceable, however).

Combination valve

The combination valve, used on non-ABS models, performs two functions. A proportioning valve controls front-to-rear brake action during rapid stops.

A brake pressure differential switch continuously compares the front and rear brake pressures. If a failure occurs somewhere in the system, a red warning light on the instrument cluster comes on. Once a failure has occurred, the warning light remains on until the system has been repaired.

On ABS-equipped vehicles, the ABS unit performs the functions of the combination valve.

Power brake booster

A dual-diaphragm, vacuum-operated power brake booster, mounted between the firewall and the master cylinder, utilizes engine manifold vacuum and atmospheric pressure to provide assistance to the hydraulic brake system.

Anti-lock Brake System (ABS)

Some later models have an Anti-lock Braking System (ABS) that aids vehicle stability during heavy braking or on wet or uneven surfaces.

Parking brake

The parking brake system consists of a lever between the front seats, the cables connecting this lever to the rear brakes, an equalizer for balancing the tension of the two

rear cables, and the parking brake shoes. On all models with rear drums, the parking brake system utilizes the brake shoes themselves. On 2003 and later models with rear discs, small parking brake shoes are housed inside the rear disc assemblies.

Service

After completing any operation involving disassembly of any part of the brake system, always test drive the vehicle to check for proper braking performance before resuming normal driving. When testing the brakes, perform the tests on a clean, dry flat surface. Conditions other than these can lead to inaccurate test results.

Test the brakes at various speeds with both light and heavy pedal pressure. The vehicle should stop evenly without pulling to one side or the other. Avoid locking the brakes because this slides the tires and diminishes braking efficiency and control of the vehicle.

Tires, vehicle load and front-end alignment are factors which also affect braking performance.

2   Disc brake pads (front and rear) - replacement

Refer to illustrations 2.5a, 2.5b, 2.6, 2.7a through 2.7j and 2.8a through 2.8k
Warning: *Disc brake pads must be replaced on both front wheels at the same time - never replace the pads on only one wheel. Also, the dust created by the brake system is harmful to your health. Never blow it out with compressed air and don't inhale any of it. An approved filtering mask should be worn when working on the brakes. Do not, under any circumstances, use petroleum-based solvents to clean brake parts. Use brake system cleaner or clean brake fluid only!*
Note: *When servicing the disc brakes, use only high quality, nationally recognized name brand pads.*

1   Remove the cover from the brake fluid reservoir.

2   Loosen the wheel lug nuts, raise the front of the vehicle and support it securely on jackstands.

3   Remove the front wheels. Work on one brake assembly at a time, using the assembled brake for reference if necessary.

4   Inspect the brake disc carefully as outlined in Section 4. If machining is necessary, follow the information in that Section to remove the disc, at which time the pads can be removed from the calipers as well.

5   Push the piston back into the bore to provide room for the new brake pads. A C-clamp can be used to accomplish this on pre-1990 models **(see illustration)**; on 1990 and later models, use a screwdriver to lever the piston into its bore **(see illustration)**. As the piston is depressed to the bottom of the caliper bore, the fluid in the master cylinder will rise. Make sure it doesn't overflow. If necessary, siphon off some of the fluid.

6   Before removing the caliper, wash off all traces of brake dust with brake system cleaner **(see illustration)**.

7   If you're replacing the brake pads on a 1990 or later model, proceed to the next step. To replace the brake pads on a pre-1990 model, **see illustrations 2.7a through 2.7j**. Don't skip any steps - follow the instructions, in the exact sequence shown, in the caption under each illustration.

8   To replace the brake pads on a 1990 or later model, **see illustrations 2.8a through 2.8k**. Don't skip any steps - follow the instructions, in the exact sequence shown, in the caption under each illustration.

9   When reinstalling the caliper, be sure to tighten the mounting pins to the torque listed in this Chapter's Specification. After the job has been completed, firmly depress the brake pedal a few times to bring the pads into contact with the disc.

10   Check for fluid leakage and make sure the brakes operate normally before driving in traffic.

2.5b A C-clamp is hard to use on the calipers used on 1990 and later models; use a screwdriver to lever the piston back into the caliper bore

2.6 Before removing the caliper, wash off all traces of brake dust with brake system cleaner

2.7a Using an Allen wrench, unscrew the two caliper mounting pins (arrows) - do not disconnect the brake hose banjo bolt (center arrow) unless you're removing the caliper to overhaul it (pre-1990 models)

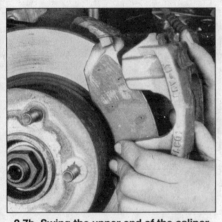

2.7b Swing the upper end of the caliper out of the anchor plate, then remove the caliper completely. Take this opportunity to check for fluid leakage around the caliper piston boot, which would indicate the need to overhaul the calipers (pre-1990 models)

2.7c Once the caliper is removed from the anchor plate, hang it from the coil spring with a piece of wire - DON'T let it hang by the brake hose

2.7d Pry down the lower anti-rattle clip and remove the outer brake pad (pre-1990 models)

2.7e Pull the anti-rattle clips away from the pad with your index fingers and force the inner brake pads out with your thumbs (pre-1990 models)

2.7f Before installing the brake pads, clean the sliding surfaces on the caliper and anchor plate and apply a thin coat of high-temperature grease to the anchor plate in the area shown (pre-1990 models)

2.7g Position the anti-rattle clips on the anchor plate and install the inner brake pad (pre-1990 models)

2.7h Place the lower end of the outer pad on the anchor plate and push it down against the anti-rattle clip, the lift up on the upper anti-rattle clip and swing the pad into position (pre-1990 models)

2.7i Engage the notch in the lower end of the caliper with the anchor plate, then rotate it over the pads (pre-1990 models)

2.7j Lubricate the mounting pins with high-temperature grease, push them into the caliper and tighten them to the torque listed in this Chapter's Specifications (pre-1990 models)

2.8a On 1990 and later models, remove the caliper pins (upper and lower arrows) with a 12-point box wrench - do NOT remove the brake hose banjo bolt (middle arrow) unless you are removing the caliper for overhaul

2.8b Slide the caliper assembly off the disc (1990 and later models)

2.8c Grasp the caliper between your hands like this and pull the inner pad off with your fingers (1990 and later models)

2.8d Pry off the outer pad with a screwdriver (1990 and later models)

2.8e Inspect the rubber dust boots (arrows) for the caliper pins and replace them if they're torn or damaged, then lubricate the caliper pins with high temperature grease (1990 and later models)

2.8f When you install the inner brake pad, make sure the retaining clips on the back of the pad are pushed into the hole in the caliper piston as far as they'll go (i.e., the back of the pad is seated firmly against the piston) (1990 and later models)

3   Disc brake caliper - removal, overhaul and installation

Warning: *Dust created by the brake system is harmful to your health. Never blow it out with compressed air and don't inhale any of it. An approved filtering mask should be worn when working on the brakes. Do not, under any circumstances, use petroleum-based solvents to clean brake parts. Use brake system cleaner or clean brake fluid only!*

Note: *If an overhaul is indicated (usually because of fluid leakage) explore all options before beginning the job. New and factory rebuilt calipers are available on an exchange basis, which makes this job quite easy. If it's decided to rebuild the calipers, make sure a rebuild kit is available before proceeding. Always rebuild the calipers in pairs - never rebuild just one of them.*

Removal

1   Remove the cover from the brake fluid reservoir, siphon off two thirds of the fluid into a container and discard it.

2   Loosen the wheel lug nuts, raise the front of the vehicle and support it securely on jackstands. Remove the front wheels.

3   Bottom the piston in the caliper bore **(see illustrations 2.5a or 2.5b)**.

4   **Note:** *Do not remove the brake hose from the caliper if you are only removing the caliper. Remove the brake hose banjo bolt and detach the hose (see illustrations 2.7a and 2.8a). Have a rag handy to catch spilled fluid and wrap a plastic bag tightly around the end of the hose to prevent fluid loss and contamination.*

5   Unscrew the two caliper pins and detach the caliper from the vehicle (refer to Section 2 if necessary).

Overhaul

Refer to illustrations 3.7, 3.8a, 3.8b, 3.9, 3.10, 3.15 and 3.16

6   Clean the exterior of the caliper with brake cleaner or clean brake fluid. Never use gasoline, kerosene or petroleum-based cleaning solvents. Place the caliper on a clean workbench.

7   Position a wooden block or several shop rags in the caliper as a pad, then use compressed air to remove the piston from the caliper **(see illustration)**. Use only enough air pressure to ease the piston out of the bore. If the piston is blown out, even with the cushion in place, it may be damaged. **Warning:** *Never place your fingers in front of the piston in an attempt to catch or protect it when applying compressed air, as serious injury could occur.*

8   Carefully pry the dust boot out of the caliper bore **(see illustrations)**.

2.8g When you install the outer brake pad, make sure the retaining clip on the back of the pad is pushed all the way down onto the caliper . . .

2.8h . . . and the locating lugs (arrows in previous photos) are aligned with their respective holes (arrows in this photo) in the caliper (1990 and later models)

2.8i Before installing the caliper, lubricate the sliding surfaces (upper arrows) on the lower edges of the brake pads and on the steering knuckle (lower arrow) with high temperature grease (1990 and later models)

2.8j When you install the caliper and pad assembly back onto the brake disc rotor, make sure you don't damage the new pads, and make sure the bushings (arrow points to lower bushing, upper bushing not visible in this photo) don't snag on the steering knuckle and tear (view shown is from underneath looking straight up) (1990 and later models)

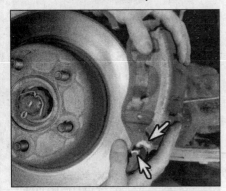

2.8k Make sure the notches in the lower edges of the brake pads (upper arrow) are properly seated onto the sliding surface of the steering knuckle (lower arrow) (1990 and later models)

3.7 With the caliper padded to catch the piston, use compressed air to force the piston out of its bore - make sure your hands or fingers are not between the piston and caliper frame!

3.8a Carefully pry the dust boot out of the caliper

3.8b Exploded view of the disc brake caliper

3.9 The piston seal should be removed with a plastic or wooden tool to avoid damage to the bore and seal groove (a pencil will do the job)

3.10 Grab the ends of the mounting pin bushings with needle-nose pliers and, using a twisting motion, push them through the caliper ears

9   Using a wood or plastic tool, remove the piston seal from the groove in the caliper bore **(see illustration)**. Metal tools may cause bore damage.

10   Remove the caliper bleeder screw, then remove and discard the mounting pin bushings **(see illustration)**. Discard all rubber parts.

11   Clean the remaining parts with brake system cleaner or clean brake fluid, then blow them dry with compressed air.

12   Carefully examine the piston for nicks and burrs and loss of plating. If surface defects are present, the parts must be replaced.

13   Check the caliper bore in a similar way. Light polishing with crocus cloth is permissible to remove light corrosion and stains. Discard the caliper pins if they're corroded or damaged.

14   When assembling the caliper, lubricate the piston bore and seal with clean brake fluid. Position the seal in the caliper bore groove.

15   Lubricate the piston with clean brake fluid, install it squarely in the bore and apply pressure to bottom it in the caliper **(see illustration)**.

16   Stretch the dust boot over the groove in the piston, then carefully seat it in the caliper bore **(see illustration)**.

17   Install the bleeder screw.

18   Install new inner and outer mounting pin bushings.

Installation

Refer to illustration 3.22

19   Inspect the caliper pins for excessive corrosion. Replace them if necessary.

20   Clean the sliding surfaces of the caliper and the anchor plate.

21   Install the caliper (see Section 2).

22   Install the brake hose and banjo bolt. Be sure to use new copper sealing washers **(see illustration)**. Tighten the bolt to the torque listed in this Chapter's Specifications.

23   If the brake hose was disconnected, be sure to bleed the brakes (see Section 10).

24   Install the wheels and lower the vehicle. Tighten the wheel lug nuts to the torque listed in this Chapter's Specifications.

3.15 When installing the piston, make sure it doesn't become cocked in the caliper bore while pushing it down

3.16 If the correct seal driver tool isn't available, a drift punch can be used to tap around the circumference until the dust boot is seated

25   After the job has been completed, firmly depress the brake pedal a few times to bring the pads into contact with the disc.

26   Check brake operation before driving the vehicle in traffic.

4   Brake disc - inspection, removal and installation

Refer to illustrations 4.4a, 4.4b, 4.5a and 4.5b

Inspection

1   Loosen the wheel lug nuts, raise the vehicle and support it securely on jackstands. Remove the wheel.

2   Remove the brake caliper as described in Section 3. It's not necessary to disconnect the brake hose. After removing the caliper mounting pins, suspend the caliper out of the way with a piece of wire as shown in **illustration 2.7c**. Don't let the caliper hang by the hose and don't stretch or twist the hose. Reinstall two of the lug nuts to hold the disc in place.

3.22 Be sure to use NEW copper sealing washers on both sides of the banjo fitting when reattaching the brake hose (earlier style caliper shown, later style similar, except banjo fitting is on back instead of front of caliper)

4.4a Use a dial indicator to check disc runout - if the reading exceeds the specified allowable runout limit, the disc will have to be machined or replaced

4.4b Using a swirling motion, remove the glaze from the disc surface with sandpaper or emery cloth

4.5a The minimum thickness is cast into the inside of the disc

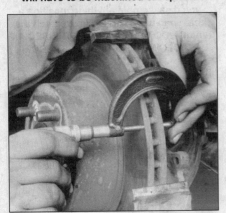

4.5b Use a micrometer to measure disc thickness at several points

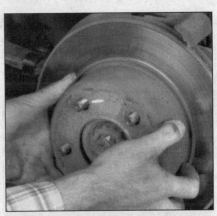

4.6 When removing the disc from the hub, make sure you don't damage the threads on the wheel studs

3   Visually check the disc surface for score marks and other damage. Light scratches and shallow grooves are normal after use and may not always be detrimental to brake operation, but deep score marks - over 0.015-inch (0.38 mm) - require disc removal and refinishing by an automotive machine shop. Be sure to check both sides of the disc. If pulsating has been noticed during application of the brakes, suspect disc runout. Be sure to check the wheel bearings to make sure they're properly adjusted.

4   To check disc runout, place a dial indicator at a point about 1/2-inch from the outer edge of the disc **(see illustration)**. Set the indicator to zero and turn the disc. The indicator reading should not exceed the specified allowable runout limit. If it does, the disc should be refinished by an automotive machine shop. **Note:** *Professionals recommend resurfacing of brake discs regardless of the dial indicator reading (to produce a smooth, flat surface that will eliminate brake pedal pulsations and other undesirable symptoms related to questionable discs). At the very least, if you elect not to have the discs resurfaced, deglaze them with sandpaper or emery cloth (use a swirling motion to ensure a nondirectional finish)* **(see illustration)**.

5   The disc must not be machined to a thickness less than the specified minimum

refinish thickness. The minimum (or discard) thickness is cast into the inside of the disc **(see illustration)**. The disc thickness can be checked with a micrometer **(see illustration)**.

Removal

Refer to illustration 4.6

6   Remove the two lug nuts that were installed to hold the disc in place, then slide the disc off the hub **(see illustration)**.

Installation

7   Place the disc over the wheel studs on the hub.

8   Install the caliper and brake pad assembly over the disc and position it on the steering knuckle (refer to Section 2 for the caliper installation procedure, if necessary). Tighten the caliper mounting pins to the specified torque.

9   Install the wheel, then lower the vehicle to the ground. Depress the brake pedal a few times to bring the brake pads into contact with the disc. Bleeding of the system will not be necessary unless the brake hose was disconnected from the caliper. Check the operation of the brakes carefully before placing the vehicle into normal service.

5   Drum brake shoes - replacement

Refer to illustrations 5.5a through 5.5y, 5.6a through 5.6ee, 5.7, 5.9a and 5.9b

Warning: *Drum brake shoes must be replaced on both wheels at the same time - never replace the shoes on only one wheel. Also, the dust created by the brake system is harmful to your health. Never blow it out with compressed air and don't inhale any of it. An approved filtering mask should be worn when working on the brakes. Do not, under any circumstances, use petroleum-based solvents to clean brake parts. Use brake system cleaner or clean brake fluid only!*

Caution: *Whenever the brake shoes are replaced, the retracting and hold-down springs should also be replaced. Due to the continuous heating/cooling cycle that the springs are subjected to, they lose their ten-*

sion over a period of time and may allow the shoes to drag on the drum and wear at a much faster rate than normal. When replacing the rear brake shoes, use only high quality nationally recognized brand name parts.

1   Loosen the wheel lug nuts, raise the rear of the vehicle and support it securely on jackstands. Block the front wheels to keep the vehicle from rolling.

2   Release the parking brake.

3   Remove the wheel. **Note:** *All four rear brake shoes must be replaced at the same time, but to avoid mixing up parts, work on only one brake assembly at a time.*

4   Remove the rear drums. If either brake drum is difficult to pull off the axle and shoe assembly, make sure the parking brake is completely released, then apply some penetrating oil at the hub-to-drum joint. Allow the oil to soak in and try to pull off the drum. If you still can't pull it off, retract the brake shoes **(see illustration 5.5e)**.

5   If you're replacing the rear brake shoes on a 1990 or later model, go to Step 6. If you're replacing the rear brake shoes on a pre-1990 model, follow **illustrations 5.5a through 5.5y**. Don't skip around - follow the instructions, in the sequence shown, in the captions accompanying the illustration.

5.5a An exploded view of the left rear brake assembly on pre-1990 models

5.5b Wash off the brake assembly with brake cleaner and allow it to dry before you disassemble anything (position a drain pan under the brake to catch the runoff) - DO NOT USE COMPRESSED AIR TO BLOW THE BRAKE DUST FROM THE PARTS!

5.5c Pull out on the adjuster lever and turn the star wheel to retract the brake shoes (pre-1990 models)

5.5d Pull back on the self-adjuster cable and push the adjusting lever toward the rear, unhooking it from the secondary brake shoe (pre-1990 models)

5.5e Remove the primary and secondary shoe retracting springs - the spring removal tool shown here can be purchased at most auto parts stores and greatly simplifies this step (pre-1990 models)

5.5f Remove the self-adjuster cable and anchor pin plate from the anchor pin (pre-1990 models)

5.5g Remove the secondary shoe retracting spring and cable guide from the secondary shoe (pre-1990 models)

5.5h Remove the primary shoe hold-down spring and pin . . .

5.5i . . . then lift the primary shoe and adjusting screw from the backing plate (pre-1990 models)

5.5j Remove the parking brake link (pre-1990 models)

5.5 k Remove the secondary shoe hold-down spring and pin, then lift the shoe from the backing plate - pry the parking brake lever retaining clip off the pivot pin . . .

5.5l . . . then separate the lever from the secondary shoe - be careful not to lose the spring washer (pre-1990 models)

5.5m Lubricate the brake shoe contact areas (arrows) with high temperature grease (pre-1990 models)

5.5n Attach the new shoe to the parking brake lever, install the spring washer and retaining clip on the pivot pin, then crimp the clip closed with a pair of pliers (pre-1990 models)

5.5o Install the secondary shoe and hold-down spring to the backing plate, then position the end of the parking brake link into the notch (arrow) (pre-1990 models)

5.5p Lubricate the adjusting screw with high temperature multi-purpose grease (pre-1990 models)

5.5q Place the primary shoe against the backing plate, then install the hold-down spring - make sure the parking brake strut and wheel cylinder pushrods engage in the brake shoe slots (pre-1990 models)

5.5r Install the anchor pin plate . . .

5.5 s . . . and the self-adjuster cable (pre-1990 models)

5.5t Hook the end of the secondary shoe retractor spring through the cable guide and into the hole in the shoe, then stretch the spring over the anchor pin (pre-1990 models)

5.5u Install the primary shoe retractor spring – the tool shown here is available at most auto parts stores and makes this step much easier and safer (pre-1990 models)

5.5v Hook the adjuster lever spring into the hole at the bottom of the primary shoe (pre-1990 models)

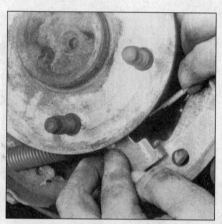

5.5w Hook the adjuster lever spring and cable into the adjuster lever and pull the cable down and to the rear, inserting the hook on the lever into the hole in the secondary shoe (pre-1990 models)

5.5x Wiggle the assembly to ensure the shoes are centered on the backing plate (pre-1990 models)

5.5y This is what the rear drum brake assembly should look like on pre-1990 models when you're done (left side shown)

RIGHT REAR BRAKE ASSEMBLY

ADJUSTER LEVER SPRING

TRAILING SHOE

CYLINDER-TO-SUPPORT SEAL

HOLDDOWN PINS

HOLDDOWN SPRING AND RETAINERS

ACCESS PLUGS

ADJUSTER CABLE

PARK BRAKE LEVER

ADJUSTER LEVER

SHOE SPRING

SUPPORT PLATE

CABLE GUIDE

CABLE HOLE PLUG

PIN

PARK BRAKE STRUT AND SPRING

SHOE RETURN SPRINGS

SHOE GUIDE PLATE

ADJUSTER SCREW ASSEMBLY

LEADING SHOE

HOLDDOWN SPRING AND RETAINERS

5.6a An exploded view of the right rear brake assembly on 1990 and later models

5.6b Wash off the brake assembly with brake cleaner and allow it to dry before you disassemble anything (position a drain pan under the brake to catch the runoff) - DO NOT USE COMPRESSED AIR TO BLOW THE BRAKE DUST FROM THE PARTS!

5.6c Pry the adjuster lever up and off the star wheel on the adjuster screw and turn the star wheel to retract the brake shoes (1990 and later models)

5.6d Unhook the adjuster cable from its hole (arrow) in the adjuster lever and let it hang out of the way (1990 and later models)

5.6e Unhook the adjuster lever spring from the adjuster lever (before you remove it, make sure you have a clear mental image of how it looks when it's correctly installed on the pivot pin for the parking brake lever, with its lower end hooked around the front edge of the adjuster lever and its other, unhooked end pressing against the inside circumference of the trailing shoe) (1990 and later models)

5.6f Remove the adjuster lever (1990 and later models)

5.6g Remove the return spring (1990 and later models)

5.6h Unhook the primary and secondary return spring from the anchor pin with a brake spring tool (1990 and later models)

5.6l Unhook the lower end of the primary return spring from the leading shoe and disconnect the metal loop on the upper end of the adjuster cable from the anchor pin (arrow) (1990 and later models)

5.6j Remove the shoe guide plate from the anchor pin (1990 and later models)

5.6k Remove the lower end of the secondary return spring from the trailing shoe (1990 and later models)

5.6l Remove the cable guide (1990 and later models)

5.6m Depress the retainer for the hold-down spring on the leading shoe and give it a slight twist to release it from the hold-down pin . . .

5.6n . . . then remove the spring and retainer from the leading shoe (it's a good idea to remove the hold-down pin by pulling it out from the back side of the brake backing plate to ensure you don't lose it) - now remove the retainer, hold-down spring and pin from the trailing shoe in the same fashion (1990 and later models)

5.6o Disengage the notch in the front end of the parking brake strut from its corresponding notch in the leading shoe and remove the strut and spring (1990 and later models)

5.6p Spread the leading and trailing shoes apart and remove them from the brake support plate with the spring and adjuster screw assembly still attached (you can disconnect and remove the spring and adjuster screw assembly first, but the shoes will fall off; by keeping everything together this way during removal, you can see how the spring and adjuster fit between the two shoes) (1990 and later models)

5.6q Disengage the parking brake lever from the back side of the trailing shoe (if you need to detach the parking brake cable from the parking brake lever, see Section 13) (1990 and later models)

5.6r Lubricate the brake support plate with high temperature grease at the indicated (shaded) areas (1990 and later models)

5.6s Lubricate the adjusting screw threads with high temperature multi-purpose grease (see illustration 5.5p), install the adjuster screw and spring between the new leading and trailing shoes as shown and install the shoe assembly back onto the support plate (1990 and later models)

5.6t When you install the parking brake strut between the two shoes, make sure the notch in the rear end of the strut seats properly into its corresponding notch in the trailing shoe (arrow) (1990 and later models)

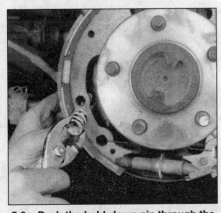

5.6u Push the hold-down pin through the brake support plate from the back side of the plate, install the hold-down spring and retainer, depress the retainer, give it a little twist and release spring pressure - now tug on the retainer and make sure it doesn't pop loose from the flanged head on the hold-down pin (1990 and later models)

5.6v Install the hold-down pin, spring and retainer for the trailing shoe in exactly the same way you just installed the hold-down spring assembly for the leading shoe, then check it to make sure it's properly installed (1990 and later models)

5.6w Engage the hooked end closer to the coiled part of the front return spring with its hole (arrow) in the leading shoe - engage the hooked end closer to the coiled part of the rear return spring into its hole in the adjuster cable guide and install the cable guide onto the trailing shoe (1990 and later models)

5.6x Install the shoe guide plate and the upper end of the adjuster onto the anchor pin (1990 and later models)

5.6y Install the hooked end that's farther away from the coiled part of the front return spring to the anchor pin with a brake spring installation tool (1990 and later models)

5.6z Install the hooked end that's farther away from the coiled part of the rear return spring to the anchor pin with a brake spring installation tool (1990 and later models)

5.6aa Route the lower end of the adjuster cable into its groove in the cable guide (1990 and later models)

5.6bb Install the adjuster lever spring on the pivot for the parking brake lever - make sure it's installed exactly the way it was before, with the loop in the spring (arrow) facing up, the hooked end facing forward and down, and the straight end facing to the rear and up against the inside circumference of the trailing shoe (1990 and later models)

5.6cc Install the adjuster lever onto the pivot for the parking brake lever, then engage the hooked end of the adjuster lever spring over the forward end of the lever with a small screwdriver (1990 and later models)

5.6dd Hook the lower end of the adjuster cable over its corresponding notch (arrow) in the adjuster lever (1990 and later models)

5.6ee The rear brake assembly should look like this when you're done! (1990 and later models)

5.7 The maximum allowable drum diameter is cast into the drum

5.9a To adjust the brakes, remove the rubber plug from the adjustment hole in the backing plate, lift the adjuster lever off the star wheel on the adjuster screw with a narrow screwdriver and, using a brake adjuster tool or another screwdriver . . .

6   If you're replacing the rear brake shoes on a 1990 or later model, follow **illustrations 5.6a through 5.6ee**. Don't skip around - follow the instructions, in the sequence shown, in the captions accompanying the illustrations.

7   Before reinstalling the drum, check it for cracks, score marks, deep scratches and hard spots, which will appear as small discolored areas. If the hard spots can't be removed with fine emery cloth, or if any of the other conditions listed above exist, take the drum to an automotive machine shop to have it turned. **Note:** *Professionals recommend resurfacing the drums whenever a brake job is done. Resurfacing will eliminate the possibility of out-of-round drums. If the drums are worn so much that they can't be resurfaced without exceeding the maximum allowable diameter (stamped into the drum)* **(see illustration)**, *then new ones will be required. At the very least, if you elect not to have the*
drums resurfaced, remove the glazing from the surface with medium-grit emery cloth using a swirling motion.

8   Once the new shoes are in place, install the drums on the axle flanges.

9   Remove the rubber plugs from the brake backing plates. Pull the lever off the adjusting star wheel with one narrow screwdriver and turn the adjusting wheel with a brake adjuster tool (or another screwdriver), moving the shoes away from the drum **(see illustrations)**. Turn the star wheel until the brakes drag slightly as the drum is turned, then turn the wheel in the opposite direction until the drum turns freely again. **Note:** *You must keep the adjuster lever off the star wheel while you're turning it or it won't turn.*

10   Repeat this adjustment on the opposite wheel and install the backing plate plugs.

11   Mount the wheel, install the lug nuts, then lower the vehicle. Tighten the lug nuts to the torque listed in the Chapter 1 Specifications.

5.9b ... turn the adjuster wheel in the direction shown until the shoes drag on the brake drum, then turn the wheel in the opposite direction until the drum turns freely again; make sure you keep the adjuster lever off the star wheel while you're turning the wheel (drum removed for clarity in this photo)

12 Make a number of forward and reverse stops to allow the brakes to self-adjust themselves.

13 Check brake operation before driving the vehicle in traffic.

6 Wheel cylinder - removal, overhaul and installation

Note: *If an overhaul is indicated (usually because of fluid leakage or sticky operation) explore all options before beginning the job. New wheel cylinders are available, which makes this job quite easy. If it's decided to rebuild the wheel cylinder, make sure that a rebuild kit is available before proceeding. Never overhaul only one wheel cylinder - always rebuild both of them at the same time.*

Removal

Refer to illustration 6.4

1 Raise the rear of the vehicle and support

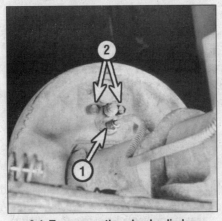

6.4 To remove the wheel cylinder, disconnect the brake line fitting (1), then remove the two wheel cylinder mounting bolts (2)

it securely on jackstands. Block the front wheels to keep the vehicle from rolling.

2 Remove the brake shoe assembly (see Section 5).

3 Remove all dirt and foreign material from around the wheel cylinder.

4 Completely loosen the brake line fitting **(see illustration)**. Don't pull the brake line away from the wheel cylinder.

5 Remove the wheel cylinder mounting bolts **(see illustration 6.4)**.

6 Detach the wheel cylinder from the brake backing plate and place it on a clean workbench. Immediately plug the brake line to prevent fluid loss and contamination. **Note:** *If the brake shoe linings are contaminated with brake fluid, install new brake shoes.*

Overhaul

Refer to illustration 6.7

7 Remove the bleeder screw, piston cups, pistons, boots and expander assembly from the wheel cylinder body **(see illustration)**.

8 Clean the wheel cylinder with brake fluid or brake system cleaner. **Warning:** *Do not,*

under any circumstances, use petroleum based solvents to clean brake parts!

9 Use compressed air to remove excess fluid from the wheel cylinder and to blow out the passages.

10 Check the cylinder bore for corrosion and score marks. Crocus cloth can be used to remove light corrosion and stains, but the cylinder must be replaced with a new one if the defects cannot be removed· easily, or if the bore is scored.

11 Lubricate the new cups with brake fluid.

12 Assemble the wheel cylinder components. Make sure the recessed sides of the cups face in.

Installation

13 Place the wheel cylinder in position and install the bolts.

14 Connect the brake line and tighten the fitting. Install the brake shoe assembly.

15 Bleed the brakes (see Section 10).

16 Check brake operation before driving the vehicle in traffic.

7 Master cylinder - removal, overhaul and installation

Note: *Before you decide to overhaul the master cylinder, compare the cost of a new or factory rebuilt unit versus the cost of a rebuild kit.*

Removal

Refer to illustrations 7.2 and 7.4

1 Place rags under the brake line fittings and prepare caps or plastic bags to cover the ends of the lines once they are disconnected. **Caution:** *Brake fluid will damage paint. Cover all body parts and be careful not to spill fluid during this procedure.*

2 Loosen the threaded fittings **(see illustration)** that connect the brake lines to the master cylinder. To prevent rounding off the flats on these nuts, a flare-nut wrench, which wraps around the nut, should be used.

6.7 Exploded view of a typical wheel cylinder

1 *Piston and boot*
2 *Wheel cylinder body*
3 *Piston cups*
4 *Expander assembly*
5 *Bleeder screw*

7.2 To disconnect the brake lines from the master cylinder, unscrew these threaded fittings (arrows) – use a flare nut wrench if you have one, to prevent rounding off the corners of the nuts

7.4 To detach the master cylinder assembly from the brake booster, remove these nuts (arrows)

7.7 Use a Phillips head screwdriver to push the primary piston into the cylinder, then remove the snap-ring with a pair of snap-ring pliers

7.8 Remove the primary piston assembly from the cylinder

7.9 Eject the secondary piston assembly by applying compressed air to the secondary brake line port (while doing this, cover the opening in the cylinder with a piece of wood to serve as a shield - only apply enough air to ease the piston out!)

7.13 Assembled view of the secondary piston - note that the lips of the seals face away from each other

3   Pull the brake lines away from the master cylinder slightly and plug the ends to prevent contamination.

4   Remove the two master cylinder mounting nuts **(see illustration)** and remove the master cylinder from the vehicle.

5   Remove the reservoir cover, then discard any fluid remaining in the reservoir.

Overhaul

Refer to illustrations 7.7, 7.8, 7.9 and 7.13

6   Mount the master cylinder in a vise with the vise jaws clamping on the mounting flange.

7   Remove the primary piston snap-ring by depressing the piston and extracting the ring with a pair of snap-ring pliers **(see illustration)**.

8   Remove the primary piston assembly from the cylinder bore **(see illustration)**. Discard it, since it can only be serviced as an assembly.

9   Reinstall the reservoir cover and remove the secondary piston assembly from the cylinder bore by applying compressed air to the secondary brake line port **(see illustration)**.

10   Inspect the cylinder bore for corrosion and damage. If any corrosion or damage is

found, replace the master cylinder body with a new one, as abrasives cannot be used on the bore.

11   Remove the seals, O-ring, piston spring and seal retainer from the secondary piston. Discard them.

12   Clean the master cylinder body and secondary piston with clean brake fluid or brake cleaner.

13   Assemble the O-rings, seals, piston spring and seal retainer to the secondary piston **(see illustration)**. Make sure the seal lips face away from each other.

14   Lubricate the cylinder bore and primary and secondary piston assemblies with clean brake fluid. Install the secondary piston assembly into the cylinder.

15   Install the primary piston assembly in the cylinder bore, depress it and install the snap-ring.

16   Inspect the reservoir cover and diaphragm for cracks and deformation. Replace it if it's damaged in any way.

17   **Note:** *Whenever the master cylinder is removed, the complete hydraulic system must be bled. The time required to bleed the system can be reduced if the master cylinder is filled with fluid and bench bled (see Steps 18 through 22 below) before it's installed on the vehicle.*

18   Insert threaded plugs of the correct size into the cylinder outlet holes and fill the reservoirs with brake fluid. The master cylinder should be supported in such a manner that brake fluid will not spill during the bench bleeding procedure.

19   Loosen one plug at a time, starting with the rear outlet port first, and push the piston assembly into the bore to force air from the master cylinder. To prevent air from being drawn back into the cylinder, the appropriate plug must be replaced before allowing the piston to return to its original position.

20   Stroke the piston three or four times for each outlet to ensure that all air has been expelled.

21   Since high pressure is not involved in the bench bleeding procedure, an alternative to the removal and replacement of the plugs with each stroke of the piston assembly is available. Before pushing in on the piston assembly, remove one of the plugs completely. Before releasing the piston, however, instead of replacing the plug, simply put your finger tightly over the hole to keep air from being drawn back into the master cylinder. Wait several seconds for the brake fluid to be drawn from the reservoir to the piston bore, then repeat the procedure. When you push down on the piston it will force your finger off the hole, allowing the air inside to be expelled. When only brake fluid is being ejected from the hole, replace the plug and go on to the other port.

22   Refill the master cylinder reservoir and install the diaphragm and cover assembly.

Installation

23   Carefully install the master cylinder by reversing the removal steps, then bleed the brakes (see Section 10).

8.1 To test the pressure differential switch, unplug the electrical connector (upper arrow); to remove the combination valve, loosen the four threaded fittings (lower arrows) with a flare-nut wrench and detach the hydraulic lines

8   Combination valve - check and replacement

Check

Refer to illustration 8.1

1   Disconnect the wire connector from the pressure differential switch **(see illustration)**. **Note:** *When unplugging the connector, squeeze the side lock releases, moving the inside tabs away from the switch, then pull up. Pliers may be used as an aid if necessary.*
2   Using a jumper wire, connect the switch wire to a good ground, such as the engine block.
3   Turn the ignition key to the On position. The warning light in the instrument panel should light.
4   If the warning light does not light, either the bulb is burned out or the electrical circuit is defective. Replace the bulb (see Chapter 12) or repair the electrical circuit as necessary.
5   When the warning light functions correctly, turn the ignition switch off, disconnect the jumper wire and reconnect the wire to the switch terminal.
6   Make sure the master cylinder reservoirs are full, then attach a bleeder hose to one of the rear wheel bleeder valves and immerse the other end of the hose in a container partially filled with clean brake fluid.
7   Turn on the ignition switch.
8   Open the bleeder valve while a helper applies moderate pressure to the brake pedal. The brake warning light on the instrument panel should light.
9   Close the bleeder valve before the helper releases the brake pedal.
10   Reapply the brake pedal with moderate to heavy pressure. The brake warning light should go out.
11   Attach the bleeder hose to one of the front brake bleeder valves and repeat Steps 8 through 10. The warning light should react in the same manner as in Steps 8 and 10.
12   Turn off the ignition switch.
13   If the warning light did not come on in Steps 8 and 11, but does light when a jumper is connected to ground, the warning light switch portion of the combination valve is defective and the combination valve must be replaced (the components of the combination valve are not individually serviceable).

Replacement

14   Place a container under the combination valve and protect all painted surfaces with newspapers or rags.
15   To disconnect the hydraulic lines from the combination valve, use a flare-nut wrench to loosen the threaded fittings at the valve **(see illustration 8.1)**. Plug the lines to prevent further loss of fluid and to protect the lines from contamination.
16   Disconnect the electrical connector from the pressure differential switch.
17   Remove the bolt holding the valve to the mounting bracket and remove the valve from the vehicle.
18   Installation is the reverse of the removal procedure.
19   Bleed the entire brake system.

9   Brake hoses and lines - inspection and replacement

Inspection

Refer to illustrations 9.1a and 9.1b

1   About every six months, with the vehicle raised and supported securely on jackstands, the rubber hoses **(see illustrations)** which connect the steel brake lines with the front and rear brake assemblies should be inspected for cracks, chafing of the outer cover, leaks, blisters and other damage.

9.1a Typical brake hoses, lines and fixtures (pre-1990 models)

9.1b Typical brake hoses, lines and fixtures
(1990 and later models)

These are important and vulnerable parts of the brake system and inspection should be complete. A light and mirror will be helpful for a thorough check. If a hose exhibits any of the above conditions, replace it with a new one.

Replacement

Front brake hose

Refer to illustrations 9.2a and 9.2b

2   Disconnect the brake line from the hose fitting, being careful not to bend the frame bracket or brake line **(see illustrations)**. Use a flare nut wrench, if you have one, to protect the corners of the fitting from becoming rounded off.

3   Detach the integral hose bracket from the frame (you'll need a Torx drive socket of the correct size to remove the bracket bolts on some vehicles).

4   Remove the inlet fitting bolt from the brake caliper **(see illustration 2.7a or 2.8a)** and separate the hose from the caliper. Discard the sealing washers.

5   To install the hose, first attach it to the caliper, using new sealing washers on both sides of the fitting. Tighten the inlet fitting bolt to the torque listed in this Chapter's Specifications.

6   Without twisting the hose, screw the brake line threaded fitting into the hose fitting, but don't tighten it yet.

7   Install the bolt which attaches the integral hose bracket to the frame and tighten it securely.

8   Tighten the brake line threaded fitting securely.

9   When the brake hose installation is complete, there should be no kinks in the hose. Make sure the hose doesn't contact any part of the suspension. Check this by turning the wheels to the extreme left and right positions. If the hose makes contact, remove it and correct the installation as necessary. Bleed the system (see Section 10).

Rear brake hose

Refer to illustrations 9.10a, 9.10b and 9.12

10   Using a back-up wrench, disconnect the hose at the frame bracket **(see illustrations)**, being careful not to bend the bracket or steel lines.

11   Remove the U-clip with a pair of pliers

9.2a Typical front brake line/hose fitting - inside wheel well, between metal brake line and flexible brake hose (note the Torx type bolt used to affix integral bracket to the body)

9.2b To disconnect a metal brake line from a rubber front brake hose, unscrew the threaded fitting and pull the metal line out of the fitting for the hose - to remove the hose, disconnect the hose, disconnect the banjo bolt at the caliper end, then remove the Torx bolt

9.10a Typical rear brake line/hose fitting - on bracket welded to inside of frame rail, between metal brake line and flexible brake hose

9.10b To disconnect a metal brake line from a rubber rear brake hose, put a back-up wrench on the rubber hose fitting to prevent it from turning, loosen the threaded fitting on the metal brake line, them remove the U-clip with a pair of pliers

and separate the female fitting from the bracket.

12   Disconnect the brake hose at the junction block **(see illustration)**, then unbolt and remove the hose.

13   Attach the hose to the junction block and tighten the fitting securely. Without twisting the hose, install the female end of the hose in the frame bracket.

14   Install the U-clip retaining the female end to the bracket.

15   Using a back-up wrench, attach the steel line fittings to the female fittings. Again, be careful not to bend the bracket or steel line.

16   Make sure the hose installation did not loosen the frame bracket. Tighten the bracket if necessary.

17   Fill the master cylinder reservoir and bleed the system (refer to Section 11).

Metal brake lines

18   When replacing brake lines be sure to use the correct parts. Don't use copper tubing for any brake system components. Purchase steel brake lines from a dealer or auto parts store.

19   Prefabricated brake line, with the tube ends already flared and fittings installed, is available at auto parts stores and dealers. These lines are also bent to the proper shapes.

20   When installing the new line, make sure it's securely supported in the brackets and has plenty of clearance between moving or hot components.

21   After installation, check the master

9.12 Disconnect the two hydraulic lines at the junction block, then unbolt and remove the hose

cylinder fluid level and add fluid as necessary. Bleed the brake system as outlined in the next Section and test the brakes carefully before driving the vehicle in traffic.

10   Brake system bleeding

Refer to illustration 10.8

Warning: *Wear eye protection when bleeding the brake system. If the fluid comes in contact with your eyes, immediately rinse them with water and seek medical attention.*

Note: *Bleeding the hydraulic system is necessary to remove any air that manages to find its way into the system when it's been opened during removal and installation of a hose, line, caliper or master cylinder.*

1   It will probably be necessary to bleed the system at all four brakes if air has entered the system due to low fluid level, or if the brake lines have been disconnected at the master cylinder.

2   If a brake line was disconnected only at a wheel, then only that caliper or wheel cylinder must be bled.

3   If a brake line is disconnected at a fitting located between the master cylinder and any of the brakes, that part of the system served by the disconnected line must be bled.

4   Remove any residual vacuum from the brake power booster by applying the brake several times with the engine off.

5   Remove the master cylinder reservoir cover and fill the reservoir with brake fluid. Reinstall the cover. **Note:** *Check the fluid level often during the bleeding operation and add fluid as necessary to prevent the fluid level from falling low enough to allow air bubbles into the master cylinder.*

6   Have an assistant on hand, as well as a supply of new brake fluid, a clear container partially filled with clean brake fluid, a length of 3/16-inch plastic, rubber or vinyl hose to fit over the bleeder valve and a wrench to open and close the bleeder valve.

7   Beginning at the right rear wheel, loosen the bleeder valve slightly, then tighten it to a

10.8 When bleeding the brakes, a hose is connected to the bleeder valve at the caliper or wheel cylinder and then submerged in brake fluid. Air will be seen as bubbles in the tube and container. All air must be expelled before moving to the next wheel.

point where it is snug but can still be loosened quickly and easily.

8   Place one end of the hose over the bleeder valve and submerge the other end in brake fluid in the container **(see illustration)**.

9   Have the assistant pump the brakes slowly a few times to get pressure in the system, then hold the pedal firmly depressed.

10   While the pedal is held depressed, open the bleeder valve just enough to allow a flow of fluid to leave the valve. Watch for air bubbles to exit the submerged end of the tube. When the fluid flow slows after a couple of seconds, close the valve and have your assistant release the pedal.

11   Repeat Steps 9 and 10 until no more air is seen leaving the tube, then tighten the bleeder valve and proceed to the left rear wheel, the right front wheel and the left front wheel, in that order, and perform the same procedure. Be sure to check the fluid in the master cylinder reservoir frequently.

12   Never use old brake fluid. It contains moisture which will deteriorate the brake system components.

13   Refill the master cylinder with fluid at the end of the operation.

14   Check the operation of the brakes. The pedal should feel solid when depressed, with no sponginess. If necessary, repeat the entire process. **Warning:** *Do not operate the vehicle if you are in doubt about the effectiveness of the brake system.*

11   Power brake booster - check, removal and installation

Operating check

Refer to illustration 11.2

1   Depress the brake pedal several times with the engine off and make sure that there is no change in the pedal reserve distance.

11.2 Push down on the brake pedal, then start the engine - the brake pedal should go down slightly, indicating normal booster operation

11.3 With the engine turned off, the pedal should gradually rise with each pump if the booster is functioning properly

11.9a Unplug the electrical connector from the brake light switch (arrow) - if the vehicle is a pre-1991 model, remove the two booster pushrod nuts (arrows) and slide out the pushrod bolt; BE SURE TO NOTE WHICH SIDE OF THE BOLT IS INSERTED FROM - YOU MUST INSERT IT FROM THE SAME DIRECTION DURING REASSEMBLY OR THE BRAKE PEDAL COULD BIND

11.9b On 1991 and later models, the booster pushrod is secured to the brake pedal assembly with a retaining clip instead of nuts (note that the pushrod is attached to the left side of the pedal on manual transmission models and the right side on automatic transmission models)

11.10a These four bolts attach the brake booster bracket to the firewall, but you have to remove the nuts for these bolts from inside the vehicle, up under the dash

11.10b Brake booster installation details (typical)

2   Depress the pedal and start the engine. If the pedal goes down slightly, operation is normal **(see illustration)**.

Airtightness check

Refer to illustration 11.3

3   Start the engine and turn it off after one or two minutes. Depress the brake pedal several times slowly. If the pedal goes down farther the first time but gradually rises after the second or third depression, the booster is airtight **(see illustration)**.

4   Depress the brake pedal while the engine is running, then stop the engine with the pedal depressed. If there is no change in the pedal reserve travel after holding the pedal for 30 seconds, the booster is airtight.

Removal

Refer to illustrations 11.9a, 11.9b, 11.10a and 11.10b

5   Power brake booster units should not be disassembled. They require special tools not normally found in most service stations or shops. They are fairly complex and because

of their critical relationship to brake performance it is best to replace a defective booster unit with a new or rebuilt one.

6   To remove the booster, first unbolt the brake master cylinder from the booster (see Section 7) and carefully pull it forward.

7   Disconnect the hose leading from the engine to the booster. Be careful not to damage the hose when removing it from the booster fitting.

8   Locate the pushrod connecting the booster to the brake pedal, underneath the dash.

9   Unplug the brake light switch wire connector **(see illustration)** and, on pre-1991 models, remove the pushrod bolt nuts and pull out the bolt. Discard the bolt and nuts. On 1991 and later models, the pushrod is attached to a small stud on the brake pedal and secured to the stud with a retaining clip. Remove this clip **(see illustration)**.

10   Remove the four nuts holding the brake booster to the firewall **(see illustrations)**. You may need a light to see these nuts - they're located fairly high up the firewall, under the dash.

12.4 To adjust the parking brake cables, apply the parking brake, loosen the equalizer locknut (1) and - holding the equalizer rod with a pair of locking pliers to prevent it from turning - turn the adjuster nut (2) until the cable tension is fairly taut; when you're satisfied that the cable tension is correct, tighten the locknut; if you're replacing either rear cable, you'll have to compress the cable housing retainer tangs (arrows) to free the cable from the bracket

11   Slide the booster straight out from the firewall until the bolts clear the holes and remove the booster assembly, bracket and spacer gasket(s).
12   Detach the old booster assembly from the mounting bracket and install the bracket onto the new booster unit. Tighten the mounting nuts securely.

Installation

13   Installation procedures are basically the reverse of those for removal. Don't forget to reinstall the spacer gasket(s) between the booster mounting bracket and the firewall. Tighten the pushrod nuts, booster mounting nuts and the master cylinder mounting nuts to the torque listed in this Chapter's Specifications. **Warning:** *On pre-1991 models, when you install the bolt that attaches the booster pushrod to the brake pedal, insert it from the*

13.5 Compress the retainer tangs to free the cable and housing from the frame bracket

13.3 To disconnect the cable end from the parking brake lever, pull back on the return spring and maneuver the cable out of the slot in the lever

same side as it was originally installed (usually from the right side on manual transmission models and from the left side on automatic transmission models). And make sure the bolt passes through the brake pedal first, THEN the pushrod on these models.

12   Parking brake - adjustment

Refer to illustration 12.4
1   The adjustment of the parking brake, often overlooked or put off by many motorists, is actually a fairly critical adjustment. If the parking brake cables are too slack, the brake won't hold the vehicle on an incline - if they're too tight, the brakes may drag, causing them to wear prematurely. Another detrimental side effect of a tightly adjusted parking brake cable is the restriction of the automatic adjuster assembly on the rear drum brakes, which will not allow them to function properly.
2   The first step in adjusting slack parking brake cables is to ensure the correct adjustment of the rear drum brakes. This can be accomplished by making a series of forward and reverse stops, which will bring the brake shoes into proper relationship with the brake drums.
3   Fully apply and release the parking brake four or five times, then set the parking brake lever or pedal to the fifth notch.
4   Raise the rear of the vehicle and support it securely on jackstands. While holding the equalizer rod with a pair of locking pliers, loosen the equalizer locknut and turn the equalizer adjuster nut **(see illustration)** until the cables are fairly taut.
5   Release the parking brake and apply it, making sure it travels five to seven clicks. If it travels too far, tighten the adjuster nut a little more. If the travel is less than five clicks, the locknut will have to be loosened.
6   After the parking brake has been properly adjusted, tighten the locknut, then place the handle or pedal in the released position and rotate the rear wheels, making sure the

13.4 Compress the retainer tangs (arrows) to free the cable and housing from the brake support plate

brakes don't drag.
7   Lower the vehicle and test the operation of the parking brake on an incline.

13   Parking brake cables - replacement

Refer to illustrations 13.3, 13.4 and 13.5
1   Release the parking brake. Loosen the rear wheel lug nuts, raise the rear of the vehicle and support it securely on jackstands.
2   Remove the rear wheel and brake drum (or caliper and disc). Loosen the equalizer nut fully **(see illustration 12.4)**.
3   On drum-brake models, following the procedure in Section 5, remove the brake shoes, then disconnect the parking brake cable end from the parking brake lever **(see illustration)**.
4   Compress the cable housing retainer tangs at the brake support plate **(see illustration)** and push the cable and housing through the backing plate or bracket. On disc-brake models, unhook the cable end from the actuator lever.
5   Compress the cable housing retainer tang at the bracket on the frame **(see illustration)** and pry the housing out of the frame bracket, then compress the cable housing retainer tang at the bracket right behind the equalizer and slide the forward end of the cable out of its slot in the equalizer **(see illustration 12.4)**.
6   Installation is the reverse of the removal procedure. Be sure to adjust the parking brake as described in Section 12.

14   Brake light switch - replacement

Refer to illustrations 14.2a and 14.2b
1   Disconnect the cable from the negative terminal of the battery.
2   From under the dash, unplug the brake light switch electrical connector and remove the pushrod bolt (pre-1991 models) or the retaining clip (1991 and later models) (see Section 11). Remove the brake light switch,

noting the positions of the bushings, spacers and sleeves **(see illustrations)**.

3   Lubricate the switch bushings, spacers and sleeves with a light coat of multi-purpose grease and position the switch against the brake pedal. Install the pushrod bolt and nuts or retaining clip (see Section 11). On pre-1991 models, be sure to tighten the nuts to the torque listed in this Chapter's Specifications.

4   Plug in the electrical connector and reconnect the battery.

5   On pre-1991 models, the switch is not adjustable. On 1991 and later models, it is adjustable.

6   To check the switch adjustment on 1991 and later models, move the brake pedal forward by hand and watch the switch plunger. It should be fully extended at the point at which pedal freeplay is taken up and brake application begins. A clearance of about 1/8-inch should exist between the plunger and the pedal at this point.

7   If the plunger-to-pedal clearance is correct and the brake lights are operating, no adjustment is necessary. If the plunger doesn't fully extend and the clearance between the pedal and switch barrel is insufficient, adjust the switch.

8   To adjust the switch, grasp the brake pedal and pull it to the rear as far as possible. The switch plunger barrel will "ratchet" to the rear in its retaining clip to the correct position. Measure the plunger-to-pedal clearance to make sure it's correct and verify that the brake lights are still operating correctly. **Warning:** *Make SURE the brake pedal returns to its fully released position after adjustment. The switch can interfere with full pedal return if it's too far forward, resulting in dragging brakes caused by partial brake application.*

15   Anti-lock Brake System (ABS) - general information

Description

Some 1994 models have an Anti-lock Brake System (ABS) designed to maintain vehicle maneuverability, directional stability and optimum deceleration under severe braking conditions on most road surfaces. It does so by monitoring the rotational speed of all four wheels and controlling the brake line pressure to all four wheels during braking. This prevents the wheels from locking up prematurely during hard braking.

Components

Pump

The pump, which is driven by an electric motor, provides high-pressure brake fluid to the hydraulic assembly, where it is stored in the hydraulic bladder accumulator.

Hydraulic assembly

The integral hydraulic assembly includes a booster/master cylinder, modulator, hydraulic bladder accumulator and fluid reservoir. Basically, the assembly regulates

14.2a An exploded view of the non-adjustable brake light switch assembly on pre-1991 models

14.2b An exploded view of the adjustable brake light switch assembly used on 1991 and later models

hydraulic pressure (stored in the accumulator) to meet the demands of the braking system. The hydraulic assembly is located on the fenderwell on the driver's side of the vehicle.

Electronic control unit

The electronic control unit is mounted to the right of the steering column under the dash and is the "brain" for the system. The function of the control unit is to accept and process information received from the wheel speed sensors to control the hydraulic line pressure, avoiding wheel lock up. The control unit also constantly monitors the system, even under normal driving conditions, to find faults with the system.

If a problem develops within the system, the Brake Warning light will glow on the dashboard. A diagnostic code will also be stored, which, when retrieved by a service technician, will indicate the problem area or component.

Wheel speed sensors

A speed sensor is mounted at each wheel. The speed sensors send signals to the electronic control unit, indicating wheel rotational speed.

Diagnosis and repair

If the Brake Warning light on the dashboard comes on and stays on, make sure the parking brake is not applied and there's no problem with the brake hydraulic system. If neither of these is the cause the ABS system is probably malfunctioning. Although a spe-

cial electronic tester is necessary to properly diagnose the system, the home mechanic can perform a few preliminary checks before taking the vehicle to a dealer service department which is equipped with this tester.

a) *Make sure the brakes, calipers and wheel cylinders are in good condition.*
b) *Check the electrical connectors at the electronic control unit.*
c) *Check the fuses.*
d) *Follow the wiring harness to the speed sensors and brake light switch and make sure all connections are secure and the wiring isn't damaged.*

If the above preliminary checks don't rectify the problem, the vehicle should be diagnosed by a dealer service department.

16   Parking brake shoes (rear disc brakes) - replacement

Refer to illustrations 16.4 and 16.5a through 16.5o

Warning: *Dust created by the brake system is harmful to your health. Never blow it out with compressed air and don't inhale any of it. An approved filtering mask should be worn when*

16.4 Pull the cable up as shown, then place a punch or screwdriver in the hole

16.5a Pushing on the pin from the backing plate side with your finger, pry the front hold-down clip loose, then pull the pin out

16.5b Remove the rear hold-down clip and pin the same way

working on the brakes. Do not, under any circumstances, use petroleum-based solvents to clean brake parts. Use brake system cleaner only!

1   Loosen the wheel lug nuts, release the parking brake, raise the rear of the vehicle and support it securely on jackstands. Block the front wheels to keep the vehicle from rolling. Remove the rear wheels.

2   Remove the rear brake calipers (don't disconnect the hoses). Hang them with a length of wire.

3   Remove the wheel stud clips and slide the rear brake discs off the studs. **Note:** If the brake disc cannot be easily pulled off the axle and shoe assembly, make sure that the parking

brake is completely released, then apply some penetrating oil at the hub-to-disc joint. Allow the oil to soak in and try to pull the disc off.

4   Remove the center console (see Chapter 11). Pull the parking brake cable up **(see illustration)**. Move the spring until the two tabs pass each other and then insert a screwdriver into the side hole. Release the tension on the spring.

16.5c Disengage the lower spring from the parking brake shoes

16.5d Remove the adjuster

16.5e Disengage the upper spring from the rear parking brake shoe

16.5f Remove both parking brake shoes

16.5g Here's how the shoes, springs and adjuster go together

16.5h Holding them together with the upper spring, install the new shoes

16.5i Spread the upper ends of the shoes apart and engage them with the anchor as shown

16.5j Install the adjuster

16.5k Make sure the adjuster is engaged with the shoes as shown

16.5l Install the lower spring

16.5m Make sure the coils of the lower spring are facing down, away from the adjuster

5   Clean the parking brake shoe assembly with brake system cleaner then follow the accompanying illustrations **(16.5a through 16.5o)** for the parking brake shoe replacement procedure. Be sure to stay in order and read the caption under each illustration. **Note:** *All four parking brake shoes must be replaced at the same time, but to avoid mixing up parts, work on only one brake assembly at a time.*

6   Before installing the disc, check the parking brake surfaces of the disc for cracks, score marks, deep scratches and hard spots, which will appear as small discolored areas. If any of the above listed conditions cannot be removed with sandpaper or emery cloth, the disc must be replaced.

7   The remainder of installation is the reverse of removal.

8   Check brake operation before driving in traffic.

9   To increase the effectiveness of the new parking brake shoes, make one stop from about 25 mph using only light force on the parking brake. Make sure that you are not in traffic while you do this and that it is otherwise safe.

16.5n Install the rear pin and hold-down clip as shown, with the head of the pin firmly seated into the lower, smaller part of the hole in the clip

16.5o Install the front pin and hold-down clip the same way

Chapter 10
Suspension and steering systems

Contents

Specifications

Torque Specifications

Front suspension (1995 and earlier models) — Ft-lbs (unless otherwise indicated)

Leaf spring
- Spring eye-to-shackle bolt nuts — 95
- Spring eye-to-frame bracket bolt nuts — 105
- Tie plate U-bolt nuts — 90

Shock absorber
- Upper nut — 45
- Lower eye bolt nut — 45

Stabilizer bar
- Stabilizer bar-to-link bolt nut — 45
- Stabilizer bar-to-frame bracket nuts — 30
- Stabilizer bar link-to-tie plate nut — 45

Track bar
- Axle bracket nut
  - 1987 through 1993 — 74
  - 1994 — 125
  - 1995 — 105
- Frame bracket nut
  - 1987 through 1994 — 125
  - 1995 — 105
- Steering knuckle-to-axle balljoint stud nuts — 100

Front suspension (1997 and later models)

Shock absorber
- Upper nut — 17
- Lower nuts — 21

Stabilizer bar
- Stabilizer bushing clamp bolts — 40
- Stabilizer bar link upper nut — 45
- Stabilizer bar link lower bolt — 70

Suspension arm bolts and nuts
- Upper arm (both ends) — 55
- Lower arm
  - Axle bracket nut — 85
  - Frame bracket nut — 130

Track bar
- Ball stud-to-frame bracket nut — 65
- Bolt/nut at axle housing bracket — 55

Steering knuckle balljoint nuts
- Upper — 75
- Lower — 80

Torque Specifications

Ft-lbs (unless otherwise indicated)

Rear suspension (1995 and earlier models)
Leaf spring
Spring-to-shackle bolt nuts	95
Spring-to-frame bracket bolt nuts	105
Tie plate U-bolt nuts	90
Shock absorber nuts	44
Track bar nuts	125

Rear suspension (1997 and later models)
Shock absorber
Upper bolts	23
Lower nut	74
Stabilizer bar	
Stabilizer-to-link nut	40
Stabilizer bushing clamp bolts	40
Suspension arm bolts and nuts	
Upper arm (both ends)	55
Lower arm (both ends)	130
Track bar	
Track bar-to-frame bracket bolt/nut	74
Track bar-to-axle tube bracket bolt/nut	74

Steering
Airbag module arming screw (1995 models)	10 to 15 in-lbs
Airbag module-to-steering wheel	
Nuts (1995 models)	100 in-lbs
Screws (1997 and later models)	90 in-lbs
Steering wheel nut	
1995 and earlier	25
1997 and later	40
Intermediate shaft pinch bolt nuts	33
Steering gear mounting bolts	
1995 and earlier	65
1997 and later	70
Pitman arm-to-Pitman arm shaft nut	185
Drag link-to-Pitman arm nut	60
Drag link clamp bolt nuts	36
Drag link-to-tie rod nut	35
Steering damper locknut	30
Tie-rod-to-steering knuckle nuts	35
Tie-rod adjustment sleeve clamp bolt nut	14
Steering damper-to-tie-rod nut	53
Steering damper-to-axle bracket bolt	55
Wheel lug nuts	See Chapter 1

1   General information

Refer to illustrations 1.1, 1.2, 1.3a and 1.3b

The front suspension on 1987 through 1995 models **(see illustration)** consists of a solid front axle, suspended by two semi-elliptic, multi-leaf springs and a pair of hydraulic shock absorbers. The leaf springs are attached to the axle by U-bolts and tie plates which are positioned by spring saddles welded to the axle tubes. The rear end of each spring is attached to a frame bracket with a bolts and nut; the front end of each spring is attached to a pair of shackle plates with a nut and bolt. A rubber bushing, pressed into the ends of the springs, acts as an insulator between the spring and the bolt. Clips are bolted to the springs to align the leafs with each other and keep them together. A stabilizer bar reduces body roll and a track bar prevents lateral movement.

The rear suspension on 1987 through 1995 models **(see illustration)** is virtually identical to the front: It also uses a solid rear axle, two semi-elliptic, multi-leaf springs and a pair of shock absorbers. The springs are attached to the axle and the frame in identical fashion to the front setup. Again, a track bar prevents lateral movement. However, no stabilizer bar is employed at the rear.

On 1997 and later models, the front axle is suspended by a pair of shock absorbers and two coil springs. Four control arms allow the axle to move vertically; a track bar prevents lateral movement. A stabilizer bar controls body roll. Each steering knuckle is positioned by a pair of balljoints pressed into the upper and lower ends of a yoke welded to the end of the axle. The rear suspension on 1997 and later models is virtually identical to the front suspension.

Inspect the leaf springs periodically. Look for broken and shifted leafs, loose and missing clips and broken center bolts. The rubber bushings pressed into the "eyes" (rolled ends) of the spring leafs will gradually loosen up; eventually, they'll loosen up enough to allow some movement to occur between rubber and metal. This is usually accompanied by a squeaking noise. At first, this noise can be eliminated by simply tightening the spring attaching bolts (don't exceed the torque specification). However, if the noise persists even after you've tightened a bushing bolt, suspect an excessively loose bushing in a spring eye, a misaligned bushing (not centered in the spring eye) or misalignment of the springs caused by damaged suspension components. If any of these symptoms develop, you'll have to replace the bushing(s) and/or repair or replace any damaged suspension components.

Steering is either manual or power-assisted. An intermediate shaft connects the steering column to a recirculating-ball type steering gearbox. The steering gear transmits turning motion through a pitman arm to a drag link attached to a tie rod. The ends of

1.1 Front suspension and steering components (1987 through 1995 models)

1	Drag link end	7	Leaf spring shackles	12	Tie rod
2	Stabilizer bar clamp	8	Pitman arm	13	Front axle assembly
3	Stabilizer bar	9	Leaf spring	14	Steering damper
4	Drag link	10	Tie rod adjustment sleeve	15	Shift motor
5	Track bar	11	Leaf spring bracket and	16	Shock absorber
6	Steering gear		U-bolts		

17 Stabilizer bar-to-leaf spring bracket connecting link
18 Steering knuckle
19 Lower balljoint

1.2 Rear suspension components (1987 through 1995 models)

1	Leaf spring shackle	3	Track bar	5	Shock absorber
2	Leaf spring	4	Rear axle assembly	6	Leaf spring bracket and U-bolts

1.3a Front suspension and steering components (1997 and later 4WD models)

1	Stabilizer bar	7	Track bar	12	Lower yoke-to-steering knuckle balljoint
2	Stabilizer bar link	8	Lower suspension arm (upper arms		(upper balljoints not visible in this photo)
3	Coil spring		not visible in this photo)	13	Axleshaft CV joint
4	Adjuster tube for right tie-rod	9	Differential	14	Left tie-rod end
5	Drag link	10	Axle tube	15	Adjuster tube for left tie-rod
6	Steering damper	11	Axle tube yoke	16	Tie-rod

1.3b Rear suspension components (1997 and later models; 4WD model shown; 2WD models similar)

1	Shock absorber	4	Axle tube	7	Lower suspension arm (upper arms
2	Coil spring	5	Differential		not visible in this photo)
3	Track bar	6	Stabilizer bar		

2.2a Remove the cotter pins from the bolts that attach the stabilizer bar to the links, remove the nuts and disconnect the ends of the bar from the links (left stabilizer bar-to-link bolt and nut shown, right similar)

2.2b If the stabilizer bar proves difficult to separate from the links at either end, remove this nut and washer, and disconnect the link(s) from the leaf spring tie plate(s) (left link shown, right similar)

2.3a To detach the stabilizer bar from the vehicle, remove these two bolts (arrows) from the left bracket

2.5 An exploded view of the stabilizer bar, a bracket and a link (right end shown)

the tie rod are connected to the steering knuckles. All steering linkage connections - pitman arm to drag link, drag link to tie rod and tie rod to steering knuckles - are balljoints. The steering knuckles themselves are also attached to the axle with upper and lower balljoints. A steering damper between the frame and the tie rod reduces "bump steer" (the slight turning of a wheel away from its normal direction of travel as it moves through its suspension travel).

When working on the suspension or steering system components, you'll often run into fasteners which seem impossible to loosen. That's because they're continually subjected to water, road grime, mud, etc., and can become rusted or "frozen," making them extremely difficult to remove. To loosen stubborn fasteners, use plenty of penetrating oil and allow it to soak in for a while.

Sometimes a sharp blow with a hammer and punch is effective in breaking the bond between the nut and the bolt threads, but make sure the punch doesn't slip off the fastener and ruin the threads. Heating a frozen fastener with a torch sometimes helps too, but we don't recommend this method because of the danger of starting a fire. Long breaker bars or "cheater" (extension) pipes increase your leverage, but they can also break off bolts and ball studs if too much force is applied. And never use a cheater pipe on a ratchet. If you do, the extra leverage provided by the cheater could damage the ratcheting mechanism. Sometimes, it's easier to break loose a frozen fastener if you first turn the nut or bolt in the tightening (clockwise) direction. Nuts are also easier to remove if you clean the exposed threads of bolts and ball studs with a wire brush. Cleaning up the threads also protects them from damage during removal of a rusted or frozen nut. Always discard fasteners that require drastic measures to unscrew and replace them with new fasteners during reassembly.

Always inspect steering and suspension fasteners any time they're loosened or

2.3b . . . then detach the right bracket bolts (arrows) and remove the bar and brackets; while the bar is off the vehicle, pull the rubber bushings off the bar and inspect them for hardness, cracks or other damage - replace them if they are hard, cracked or otherwise deformed

removed. If necessary, replace them with new parts with the same part number or of original equipment quality and design. For your safety, observe all torque values listed in this Chapter's Specifications to ensure that suspension and steering assemblies don't come apart. Never attempt to heat or straighten any suspension or steering components. Instead, replace any bent or damaged part with a new one.

Most of the procedures in this Chapter involve jacking up the vehicle and working partly or totally underneath it, so get a good pair of jackstands and use them to support the vehicle any time it's elevated. It's also helpful to have a hydraulic floor jack to lift the vehicle; floor jacks are also handy for supporting components such as axle assemblies during certain procedures. **Warning:** *Never, under any circumstances, rely on a jack as the sole means of support while working on or under the vehicle.*

2   Stabilizer bar and bushings - removal and installation

1   Apply the parking brake. Raise the front of the vehicle and support it securely on jackstands.

1987 through 1995 models

Refer to illustrations 2.2a, 2.2b, 2.3a, 2.3b and 2.5

2   Remove the cotter pins **(see illustration)** from the stabilizer bar-to-link bolts, then remove the stabilizer bar-to-link nuts. If the bolts are difficult to remove, disconnect the lower ends of the links from the leaf spring tie plates **(see illustration)**.

3   Remove the stabilizer bar bracket bolts **(see illustrations)** and detach the bar from the vehicle.

4   Pull the brackets off the stabilizer bar and inspect the bushings for cracks, hardness and other signs of deterioration. If the bushings are damaged, replace them.

5   Position the stabilizer bar bushings on the bar **(see illustration)**.

6   Push the brackets over the bushings and raise the bar up to the frame. Install the bracket bolts but don't tighten them completely at this time.

2.10 To disconnect the stabilizer bar from the axle, remove the upper link nut; it's not necessary to remove the lower link nut and bolt unless you're planning to replace the link itself (1997 and later models)

2.11 To disconnect the stabilizer bar from the frame, remove the bushing clamp bolts (arrows); inspect the rubber bushings and replace them if they're hard, cracked or otherwise deformed (1997 and later models)

3.2 To detach the upper end of the shock absorber from the vehicle, remove the upper nut (arrow), washer and rubber grommet (1987 through 1995 models)

3.3a To detach the lower end of the shock absorber from the axle, remove this bolt and nut (arrows) (1987 through 1995 models)

3.3b Front shock absorber mounting details (1997 and later models)

3.4 Front shock absorber mounting details - note the relationship of the retainers (washers) and rubber grommets - up top, there are two rubber grommets because one goes below the body, the other above it (1987 through 1995 models)

7   Install the stabilizer bar-to-link nuts, washers, spacers and rubber bushings and tighten the nuts securely. Install a new cotter pin in each bolt.

8   If you disconnected the lower ends of the links from the leaf spring tie plates, reattach them and tighten the nuts securely.

9   Tighten the bracket bolts securely.

1997 and later models

Refer to illustrations 2.10 and 2.11

10   Remove the stabilizer bar-to-link nuts **(see illustration)**. If it is necessary to remove the links, simply unbolt them from the axle brackets.

11   Remove the retaining bolts from the stabilizer bar bushing clamps **(see illustration)** and detach the bar from the vehicle.

12   Pull the bushings off the stabilizer bar and inspect them for cracks, hardness and other signs of deterioration. If the bushings are damaged, replace them. Inspect the bushings in the lower ends of the links, replacing them if necessary.

13   Position the stabilizer bar bushings on the bar.

14   Push the brackets over the bushings and raise the bar up to the frame. Install the bracket bolts but don't tighten them completely at this time.

15   Install the stabilizer bar-to-link nuts, washers, spacers and rubber bushings, tightening the nuts to the torque listed in this

Chapter's Specifications.

16   Tighten the bracket bolts to the torque listed in this Chapter's Specifications.

3   Front shock absorbers - removal and installation

Removal

Refer to illustrations 3.2, 3.3a and 3.3b

1   Loosen the wheel lug nuts, raise the vehicle and support it securely on jackstands. Apply the parking brake. Remove the wheel.

2   Remove the upper shock absorber stem nut **(see illustration)**. Use an open end wrench to keep the stem from turning. If the nut won't loosen because of rust, squirt some penetrating oil on the stem threads and allow it to soak in for awhile. It may be necessary to keep the stem from turning with a pair of locking pliers, since the flats provided for a wrench are quite small.

3   Remove the lower shock mounting nut and bolt **(see illustrations)** and pull the shock absorber out from the wheel well. Remove the washers and the rubber grommets from the top of the shock absorber.

Installation

Refer to illustration 3.4

4   Extend the new shock absorber as far as possible. Position a new washer and rubber grommet **(see illustration)** on the stem

4.3 To remove a rear shock, remove this bolt (arrow), both washers and the nut (not visible in this photo) . . .

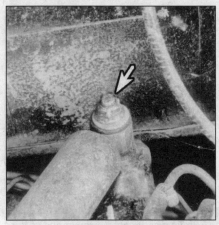

4.4a . . . then remove the upper mounting nut (arrow) and washer from the upper mounting stud and slide the upper shock eye off the stud (1987 through 1995 models)

4.4b Rear shock absorber mounting details (1997 and later models)

5.2a To disconnect the upper end of the front track bar from the frame bracket, remove this nut and bolt (arrows)

and guide the shock up into the upper mount.
5   Install the upper rubber grommet and washer and wiggle the stem back-and-forth to ensure the grommets are centered in the mount. Tighten the stem nut securely.
6   Install the lower mounting bolts and nuts and tighten them securely.

---

4   Rear shock absorbers - removal and installation

Refer to illustrations 4.3, 4.4a, 4.4b and 4.5
1   Raise the rear of the vehicle and support it securely on jackstands.
2   Support the rear axle assembly with a floor jack placed under the differential. Raise the jack just enough to take the spring pressure off the shock absorbers (the shock absorbers limit down travel of the suspension).
3   Remove the shock absorber lower retaining nut, washers and bolt **(see illustration)**.
4   Remove the upper mounting nut and washer **(see illustration)** and slide the shock off the upper mounting stud.
5   Installation is the reverse of the removal procedure **(see illustration)**. Be sure to place

4.5 Rear shock absorber mounting details - be sure to place a washer on each side of the lower shock eye during installation (1987 through 1995 models)

a washer on either side of the eye at the lower end of the shock and tighten the nuts to the torque listed in this Chapter's Specifications.

---

5   Track bar - removal and installation

Refer to illustrations 5.2a, 5.2b, 5.2c, 5.3a and 5.3b
Note: *This procedure applies to the front and rear track bars.*
1   Raise the front of the vehicle and support it securely on jackstands.
2   Remove the retaining nut and bolt from the frame rail bracket **(see illustrations)**.

5.2b Front track bar mounting details (1997 and later models)

5.2c To disconnect the upper end of the rear track bar from the frame bracket, remove this nut and bolt (arrows)

5.3a To disconnect the lower end of the front track bar from the front axle bracket, remove this nut (not visible in this photo) and bolt (arrow)

5.3b To disconnect the lower end of the rear track bar from the rear axle bracket, remove this nut (arrow) and bolt

6.3 If you're removing a front leaf spring, remove the stabilizer bar link nut (left arrow), then remove these four nuts (right arrows) and the tie plate

6.4 If you're removing a rear leaf spring, remove the lower shock eye nut and bolt (top and upper center arrows), then remove the four remaining nuts (arrows) and the tie plate

6.6a If you're removing a front leaf spring, remove this nut and bolt (arrows) from the shackle at the front crossmember

6.6b If you're removing a rear leaf spring, remove this nut and bolt (arrows) from the shackle at the rear crossmember

3   Remove the bolt and nut **(see illustrations)** from the axle bracket end of the bar and remove the bar from the vehicle.
4   Installation is the reverse of the removal procedure. Be sure to tighten the fasteners to the torque listed in this Chapter's Specifications.

---

6   Leaf springs and bushings (1987 through 1995 models) - removal and installation

Note: *This procedure applies to front and rear leaf spring assemblies. It also applies to both ends of each axle, but we recommend that you do one side at a time, to keep the axle under control and so you'll have one side to use as a "guide" to reassembly.*

Bushing check

1   All models are equipped with silent block type rubber bushings which are pressed into the spring eyes. The bushings should be inspected for cracks, damage and looseness

indicating excessive wear. To check for wear, jack up the frame until the weight is removed from the spring bushing. Pry the spring eye up-and-down to check for movement. If there is considerable movement, the bushing is worn and should be replaced.

Spring removal

Refer to illustrations 6.3, 6.4, 6.6a, 6.6b, 6.7a and 6.7b

2   Loosen the front or rear wheel lug nuts, raise the front or rear of the vehicle and support it securely on jackstands. Remove the wheel. Support the front or rear axle assembly with a floor jack positioned underneath the differential. Raise the axle just enough to take the axle weight off the spring.
3   If you're removing a front leaf spring, remove the stabilizer bar link nut at the spring tie plate **(see illustration)**.
4   If you're removing a rear leaf spring, disconnect the rear shock absorber from the axle tube bracket **(see illustration)**.
5   Unscrew the U-bolt nuts, the spring tie plate and the U-bolts from the axle **(see illustrations 6.3 and 6.4)**.
6   Remove the spring-to-shackle bolt **(see illustrations)**.

7   Remove the spring eye-to-frame bracket bolt **(see illustrations)** and remove the spring from the vehicle.

Bushing replacement

Refer to illustration 6.13

8   The bushings are of two different sizes and tools can be fabricated from threaded rod for pressing them out. For small diameter bushings, cut an eight inch length of 3/8-inch diameter threaded rod and, for the large diameter bushings, cut an eleven-inch length of 1/2-inch diameter threaded rod.
9   Insert the threaded rod through the bushing.
10   Place a socket over one end of the rod with the open end toward the bushing to serve as a driver. The socket must be large enough to bear against the bushing outer sleeve and small enough to pass through the spring eye.
11   Install a flat washer and hex nut on the rod behind the socket.
12   On the opposite end of the threaded rod, install a piece of pipe to serve as a receiver. The inside diameter of the pipe must be large enough to accommodate the bushing while still seating against the spring eye

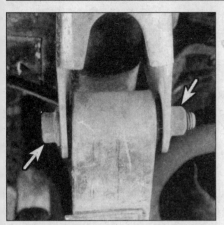

6.7a If you're removing a front leaf spring, remove this nut and bolt (arrows) from the frame bracket

6.7b If you're removing a rear leaf spring, remove this nut and bolt (arrows) from the frame bracket

6.13 A threaded rod and two approximately-sized sockets can be used to remove and install the spring eye bushings

surface. It must also be long enough to accept the entire bushing.

13 Secure the pipe section on the rod with a flat washer and nut **(see illustration)**. The washer must be large enough to properly support the pipe.

14 Tighten the nuts finger tight to align the components. The socket must be positioned in the spring eye and aligned with the bushing and the pipe must butt against the eye surface so the bushing can pass through it.

15 Press the bushing out of the spring eye by tightening the nut at the socket end of the rod.

16 Remove the bushing and tool from the spring eye.

17 Install the new bushing on the threaded rod and assemble and align the tools as previously described.

18 Line up the bushing with the spring eye and press the new bushing into position.

19 Loosen the nuts and check to make sure the bushing is centered in the spring eye with the ends of the bushing flush with or slightly below the sides of the eye. If necessary, reinstall the tools and adjust the bushing position.

Spring installation

20 Installation is the reverse of the removal procedure. Be sure to tighten the spring mounting bolts and the spring tie plate U-bolt nuts to the torque listed in this Chapter's Specifications. **Note:** *The vehicle must be standing at normal ride height before tightening the front and rear mounting bolts.*

7 Suspension arms (1997 and later models) - removal and installation

Note: *Remove and install only one suspension arm at a time to avoid the possibility of the axle housing shifting out of position, which would make reassembly much more difficult. If it is absolutely necessary to remove more than one at a time, support the axle with a floor jack.*

7.2 Front suspension arm mounting details (1997 and later models)

Front suspension arms

1 Raise the front of the vehicle and support it securely on jackstands.

Upper arm

Refer to illustration 7.2

2 Remove the nut and bolt securing the upper suspension arm to the axle housing bracket **(see illustration)**.

3 Remove the bolt and nut connecting the upper suspension arm to the frame bracket and remove the arm from the vehicle.

4 Check the arm for distortion and cracks. If the arm is damaged, replace it.

5 Inspect the bushing in the axle housing (upper arm only) for cracking, hardness and general deterioration. If it is in need of replacement, take the arm to a dealer service department or an automotive machine shop to have it replaced.

6 Installation is the reverse of removal. Be sure to tighten the fasteners to the torque listed in this Chapter's Specifications. **Note:** *The fasteners should be tightened after the vehicle has been lowered.*

Lower arm

Refer to illustration 7.7

7 Paint or scribe alignment marks on the cam adjusters and suspension arm to insure

7.7 Before disconnecting the lower suspension arm from the axle housing bracket, mark the relationship of the cam adjuster to the suspension arm, then remove the nut and pull out the bolt (1997 and later models)

proper reassembly **(see illustration)**.

8 Remove the lower suspension arm nut, the cam and the cam bolt from the bracket on the axle housing.

9 Remove the nut and bolt from the frame rail bracket **(see illustration 7.2)** and remove the lower suspension arm.

10 Installation is the reverse of removal. Be sure to re-align the marks you made between the cam adjuster and the suspension arm and tighten the fasteners to the torque listed in this Chapter's Specifications. **Note:** *The fasteners should be tightened after the vehicle has been lowered.*

Rear suspension arms

11 Raise the rear of the vehicle and support it securely on jackstands.

Upper arm

Refer to illustrations 7.12a and 7.12b

12 Remove the nut and bolt securing the

7.12a Rear suspension arm-to-axle mounting details (1997 and later models)

7.12b Rear suspension arm-to-frame mounting details (1997 and later models)

9.2 To remove the horn pad, pull it straight off with both hands - don't use a screwdriver or any other tool to pry the pad off; it's unnecessary and you'll damage or scratch something

upper suspension arm to the axle housing bracket **(see illustrations)**.

13   Remove the nut and bolt connecting the upper suspension arm to the frame rail bracket and remove the arm from the vehicle.

14   Check the arm for distortion and cracks. Inspect the bushings for tears and cracks. If the arm or either bushing is damaged, replace the arm.

15   Installation is the reverse of removal. Be sure to tighten all fasteners to the torque listed in this Chapter's Specifications.

Lower arm

16   Remove the nut and bolt connecting the lower suspension arm to the axle bracket **(see illustration 7.12a)**.

17   Remove the nut and bolt connecting the lower suspension arm to the frame rail bracket **(see illustration 7.12b)** and remove the lower suspension arm.

18   Installation is the reverse of removal. Be sure to tighten the fasteners to the torque listed in this Chapter's Specifications. **Note:** *The fasteners should be tightened after the vehicle has been lowered.*

8   Coil spring (1997 and later models) - removal and installation

Note: *This procedure applies to the front and rear coil springs.*

1   Loosen the front wheel lug nuts, raise the front of the vehicle and support it securely on jackstands. Remove the wheels.

2   Mark and disconnect the front driveshaft from the front differential pinion shaft yoke (see Chapter 8), then hang the driveshaft out of the way with a piece of wire.

3   Support the axle assembly with either a floor jack under the differential or, preferably, two jacks, one at each end of the axle (the latter option provides better balance). Unbolt the lower suspension arms from the axle (see Section 7).

4   Unbolt the stabilizer bar links and the

shock absorbers at the front axle housing (see Sections 2 and 3, or Sections 2 and 4).

5   Disconnect the track bar at the axle bracket (see Section 5).

6   If you're servicing a front coil spring, separate the drag link from the Pitman arm (see Section 12).

7   Slowly lower the axle assembly until the coil springs are fully extended. If you are using only one jack, have an assistant support the right side of the axle as it's lowered. Remove the spring from the vehicle.

8   Check the spring for deep nicks and corrosion, which will cause premature failure of the spring. Replace the spring if these or any other questionable conditions are evident.

9   Position the coil spring on the axle housing, place the spring retainer over the bottom coil of the spring and tighten the spring retainer bolt securely.

10   Raise the axle up into position and connect the lower suspension arms to the axle housing (see Section 5). Tighten the fasteners to the specified torque.

11   If you're servicing a front coil spring, connect the drag link to the Pitman arm (see Section 12).

12   Connect the track bar to its bracket on the axle (see Section 5).

13   Connect the stabilizer bar links and the shock absorbers to the front axle housing (see Sections 2 and 3, or Sections 2 and 4).

14   Connect the front driveshaft to the differential pinion shaft yoke (see Chapter 8).

15   Install the wheels and lug nuts and lower the vehicle. Tighten the lug nuts to the torque listed in the Chapter 1 Specifications.

9   Steering wheel - removal and installation

Models without an airbag

Refer to illustrations 9.2, 9.3a, 9.3b and 9.4

1   Disconnect the cable from the negative terminal of the battery.

2   Detach the horn pad from the steering wheel and disconnect the wires to the horn switch **(see illustration)**.

3   Remove the steering wheel retaining nut, then mark the relationship of the steering shaft to the hub (if marks don't already exist or don't line up) to simplify installation and ensure steering wheel alignment **(see illustration)**. Remove the three screws and detach the horn contact components **(see illustration)**.

4   Use a puller to detach the steering wheel from the shaft **(see illustration)**. Don't hammer on the shaft to dislodge the steering wheel.

5   To install the wheel, align the mark on the steering wheel hub with the mark on the shaft and slip the wheel onto the shaft. Install the nut and tighten it to the specified torque.

6   Connect the horn wire and install the horn pad.

7   Connect the negative battery cable.

Models with an airbag

Refer to illustrations 9.10 and 9.11

8   If you're working on a 1995 model, roll down the driver's side window.

9   Disconnect the cable from the negative terminal of the battery. Wait at least two minutes before proceeding (this will disable the airbag system on 1997 and later models; proceed to the next Step for the airbag disarming procedure on 1995 models).

10   If you're working on a 1995, pry off the small cover from the top of the steering wheel hub. Get out of the vehicle, reach into the vehicle and, using an 8 mm socket, unscrew the arming screw until it stops (it should protrude approximately one inch from the surface of the steering wheel trim) **(see illustration)**. The airbag is now disarmed.

11   Remove the airbag module fasteners from the backside of the steering wheel. Lift the airbag module away from the wheel and, on 1997 and later models, unplug the electrical connectors from the module **(see the**

9.3a Remove the steering wheel retaining nut

9.3b An exploded view of the steering wheel assembly

WASHER
EXTENSION
CONTACT PIN
RETAINING NUT
INSULATOR
CANCELING CAM
FLEX-PLATE
RECEIVER
HORN BUTTON
BUSHING

9.4 You may be able to separate the steering wheel from the steering shaft by hand, but if the splines are frozen, remove the wheel from the shaft with a puller - DO NOT HAMMER ON THE SHAFT!

accompanying illustration and illustration 9.10). Set the module aside in an isolated location. **Warning:** *Carry the module with the trim side facing away from your body, and set it down with the trim side facing up.*

12   Perform Steps 3 and 4 of this Section.

13   To install the wheel, refer to Step 5. **Warning:** *If the clockspring for the airbag system was inadvertently turned, refer to Chapter 12, Section 24, for the centering procedure (1997 and later models only).* Be sure to carefully thread the wiring harness for the cruise control, airbag (1997 and later models) and horn through the proper openings in the steering wheel.

14   Position the airbag module over the steering wheel, plug in the electrical connectors and install the module. Tighten the module fasteners to the torque listed in this Chapter's Specifications.

15   If you're working on a 1995 model, close the door and, reaching through the window, screw in the arming screw, tightening it to the torque listed in this Chapter's Specifications.

16   Connect the negative battery cable.

AIRBAG MODULE
NUT
ARMING SCREW COVER
ARMING SCREW
NUT
SPEED CONTROL SWITCH/TRIM BAR
SPEED CONTROL SWITCH CONNECTOR
SCREW

9.10 Airbag module and steering wheel details - 1995 models

FWD
SCREW
STEERING WHEEL
DRIVER'S AIRBAG MODULE
CLOCKSPRING
AIRBAG WIRE
HORN SWITCH WIRE

9.11 Airbag module and steering wheel details - 1997 and later models

10.2 Using white paint, mark the relationship of the upper and lower universal joints to the steering shaft and steering gear input shaft, respectively; then remove the upper pinch bolt (arrow) and lower pinch bolt (not shown, but identical)

10 Intermediate shaft - removal and installation

Refer to illustrations 10.2 and 10.3
Warning: *On 1997 and later models, make sure the steering shaft is not turned while the intermediate shaft is removed or you could damage the airbag system. To prevent the shaft from turning, position the wheels pointing straight ahead, thread the seat belt through the steering wheel and fasten it into its latch. If the steering wheel is inadvertently turned, remove the steering wheel and center the clockspring (see Chapter 12).*

1   Turn the front wheels to the straight ahead position.
2   Using white paint, mark the relationship of the upper universal joint to the steering shaft and the lower universal joint to the

10.3 An exploded view of the intermediate shaft assembly

steering gear input shaft **(see illustration)**.
3   Remove the upper and lower universal-joint pinch bolts **(see illustration)**. Some designs require the steering gear to be loosened (bolts removed) and repositioned to allow shaft removal (see Section 11).
4   Pry the intermediate shaft out of the steering shaft universal joint with a large screwdriver, then pull the shaft from the steering gearbox.
5   Installation is the reverse of the removal procedure. Be sure to align the marks and tighten the pinch bolts to the torque listed in this Chapter's Specifications.

11 Steering gear - removal and installation

Warning: *On 1997 and later models, make sure the steering shaft is not turned while the steering gear is removed or you could damage the airbag system. To prevent the shaft from turning, position the wheels pointing straight ahead, thread the seat belt through the steering wheel and fasten it into its latch.*

If the steering wheel is inadvertently turned, remove the steering wheel and center the clockspring (see Chapter 12).

Removal

Refer to illustrations 11.2, 11.4a, 11.4b, 11.5 and 11.6
1   Raise the front of the vehicle and support it securely on jackstands. Apply the parking brake.
2   Place a drain pan under the steering gear (power steering only). Disconnect the hoses/lines **(see illustration)** and cap the ends to prevent excessive fluid loss and contamination. If available, use a flare-nut wrench to disconnect the hoses/lines.
3   Mark the relationship of the intermediate shaft lower universal joint to the steering gear input shaft. Remove the intermediate shaft lower pinch bolt (see Section 10).
4   Remove the Pitman arm nut and washer **(see illustration)**. Mark the relationship of the Pitman arm to the shaft so it can be installed in the same position **(see illustration)**.
5   Separate the Pitman arm from the shaft with a two-jaw puller **(see illustration)**.
6   Support the steering gear and remove the mounting bolts **(see illustration)**. Lower the unit, separate the intermediate shaft from the steering gear input shaft and remove the steering gear from the vehicle.

Installation

7   Raise the steering gear into position and connect the intermediate shaft, aligning the marks.
8   Install the steering gear mounting bolts and washers and tighten them to the torque listed in this Chapter's Specifications.
9   Slide the Pitman arm onto the shaft. Make sure the marks are aligned. Install the washer and nut and tighten the nut to the specified torque.
10   Install the intermediate shaft lower pinch bolt and tighten it to the torque listed in this

11.2 An exploded view of the power steering lines and hoses

11.4a Remove the Pitman arm nut (arrow) and washer . . .

11.4b . . . then, before removing the Pitman arm, mark its relationship to the steering gear shaft

11.5 Use a two-jaw puller to separate the Pitman arm from the steering gear shaft

Chapter's Specifications.

11   Connect the power steering hoses/lines to the steering gear and fill the power steering pump reservoir with the recommended fluid (see Chapter 1).

12   Lower the vehicle and bleed the steering system (see Section 14).

12   Steering linkage - inspection, removal and installation

Caution: *DO NOT use a "pickle fork" type balljoint separator - it may damage the balljoint seals.*

Inspection

Refer to illustration 12.1

1   The steering linkage **(see illustration)** connects the steering gear to the front wheels and keeps the wheels in proper relation to each other. The linkage consists of the Pitman

11.6 An exploded view of the steering gear assembly

12.1 An exploded view of the steering linkage assembly

12.6a Remove the cotter pin from the castellated nut which retains the drag link ball stud to the tie-rod (shown) and loosen - but don't remove - the nut, remove the cotter pin and loosen the nut on the ball stud that retains the other end of the drag link to the pitman arm (not shown) . . .

12.6b . . . then attach a puller to each ball stud, separate the ball studs from the pitman arm (shown) and the tie-rod (not shown) and remove the drag link

12.7 If the drag link or tie-rod ends must be replaced, measure the distance from the end of the drag link/tie-rod end to the center of the ball stud so the new drag link/tie-rod end can be set to this dimension

12.10 Remove the cotter pin from the castellated nut that attaches the steering damper ball stud to the tie rod, loosen the nut, install a two-jaw puller (see illustration 12.6b) and separate the steering damper from the tie rod

12.11 Remove the nut and bolt (arrow) from the frame bracket and remove the steering damper

arm, fastened to the steering gear shaft, which moves the drag link back and forth. This back and-forth motion is transmitted to the tie rod, which itself moves back-and-forth to turn the steering knuckle. The tie-rod is connected to the steering knuckles with a pair of balljoints. The right balljoint is an integral part of the right end of the tie rod. The left tie-rod end is clamped to the left end of the tie-rod with a threaded adjustable sleeve. Used with the tie-rod and the drag link, this adjustment sleeve provides toe adjustment and steering wheel alignment. A steering damper, connected between the frame and the tie-rod, reduces shimmy and unwanted forces to the steering gear. All critical connections - pitman-arm-to-drag link, drag link-to-tie-rod, tie-rod-to-steering knuckle, steering damper-to-tie-rod - use balljoints.

2   Set the wheels in the straight ahead position and lock the steering wheel.

3   Raise one side of the vehicle until the tire is approximately 1-inch off the ground.

4   Mount a dial indicator with the needle resting on the outside edge of the wheel. Grasp the front and rear of the tire and, using light pressure, wiggle the wheel back-and-forth and note the dial indicator reading. The gauge reading should be less than 0.108-inch. If the play in the steering system is more than specified, inspect each steering linkage pivot point and ball stud for looseness and replace parts if necessary.

5   Raise the vehicle and support it on jackstands. Check for torn ball stud boots, frozen joints and bent or damaged linkage components.

Removal and installation

Drag link

Refer to illustrations 12.6a, 12.6b and 12.7

6   Remove the cotter pins **(see illustration)** from the castellated nuts, loosen the nuts, separate the ball studs from both ends of the drag link with a two-jaw puller (see

illustration) and remove the drag link. **Note:** *If only one drag link end needs replacing, separate the ballstud at that end only.*

7   If either drag link end must be replaced, measure the distance from the end of the drag link to the center of the ball stud and record it **(see illustration)**. Loosen the clamp bolt and unscrew the drag link end. The number of threads showing on the inner and outer drag link ends should be equal within three threads. Don't tighten the clamps yet.

8   Installation is the reverse of removal. When you install the drag link, insert the drag link ends into the pitman arm and the tie-rod until they're fully seated. Install the castellated nuts and tighten them to the torque listed in this Chapter's Specifications. Install new cotter pins. You may have to tighten the nuts slightly to align a slot in the nut with the hole in each ball stud.

9   Tighten the clamp nuts to the torque listed in this Chapter's Specifications.

Steering damper

Refer to illustrations 12.10 and 12.11

10   Remove the cotter pin from the castel-

lated nut that attaches the steering damper ball stud to the tie rod **(see illustration)**, loosen the nut, install a two-jaw puller and separate the steering damper from the tie rod.

11   Remove the nut and bolt **(see illustration)** from the frame bracket and remove the steering damper.

12   If the balljoint on the end of the damper shaft must be replaced, replace the entire steering damper assembly.

13   Installation is the reverse of removal. Tighten the nuts to the torque listed in this Chapter's Specifications.

Tie-rod

Note: *If only the left tie-rod end needs replacing, ignore Step 15, separate only the left tie-rod end in Step 16, then proceed to Step 18.*

14   Loosen the wheel lug nuts, raise the vehicle and support it securely on jackstands. Apply the parking brake. Remove the wheels.

15   Remove the cotter pin and castellated nut that connect the steering damper to the tie-rod and disconnect the steering damper from the tie rod (see Steps 10 and 11).

13.2 To disconnect the tie-rod from the steering knuckle, remove the cotter pin from the castellated nut, loosen - but don't remove - the nut (to prevent the parts from separating violently), install a small two-jaw puller and press the ball stud out of the knuckle

13.8b If you're installing a new steering knuckle on a pre-1990 model, remove the anchor plate bolts (arrows), remove the anchor plate and install it on the new knuckle

16   Remove the cotter pins and loosen, but do not remove, the castellated nuts from the ball studs on each end of the tie-rod. Using a two-jaw puller, loosen the right tie-rod balljoint and the left tie-rod end from the steering knuckle **(see illustration 7.2)** and the drag link ball stud from the tie-rod (see Step 6). Remove the castellated nuts. Pull the drag link ball stud from the tie rod, pull the right tie-rod balljoint and the left tie-rod end from the steering knuckles, and remove the tie rod.

17   If the right tie-rod balljoint must be replaced, replace the entire tie-rod.

18   If the left tie-rod end must be replaced, measure the distance from the end of the tie-rod to the center of the ball stud and record it **(see illustration 12.7)**. Loosen the adjustment sleeve clamp and unscrew the tie-rod end.

19   Lubricate the threaded portion of the left tie-rod end with chassis grease. Screw the new tie-rod end into the adjuster tube and

13.5 To remove the steering knuckle, remove the cotter pins, loosen the castellated nuts on the upper and lower balls studs (arrows) and strike the top of the knuckle with a hammer

13.9 On pre-1990 models, the split ring seat must be screwed in to a depth of 0.206 inch, measured from the spindle boss to the flats of the seat; you can make this measurement with a depth micrometer, or a vernier caliper (as shown here)

adjust the distance from the tube to the ball stud to the previously measured dimension. Don't tighten the clamp yet.

20   To install the tie-rod, insert the balljoint studs into the steering knuckles until they're seated. Install the nuts and tighten them to the torque listed in this Chapter's Specifications. If a ball stud spins when attempting to tighten the nut, force it into the tapered hole with a large pair of pliers.

21   Install new cotter pins. If necessary, tighten the nuts slightly to align a slot in each nut with a hole in its respective ball stud.

22   Tighten the clamp nuts to the torque listed in this Chapter's Specifications.

23   Install the wheel and lug nuts, lower the vehicle and tighten the lug nuts to the torque specified in Chapter 1. Drive the vehicle to an alignment shop to have the front end alignment checked and, if necessary, adjusted.

Pitman arm

24   See Section 11 for this procedure.

13.8a Cutaway of the split-ring seat used to adjust height of lower balljoint (which determines amount of vertical freeplay of steering knuckle) on steering knuckles used on pre-1990 models

13   Steering knuckle - removal and installation

Removal

Refer to illustrations 13.2 and 13.5

1   Loosen the wheel lug nuts, raise the vehicle and support it securely on jackstands. Remove the wheel.

2   Disconnect the tie-rod end from the steering knuckle **(see illustration)**.

3   Remove the disc brake caliper and disc (see Chapter 9).

4   Remove the front axle hub and bearing assembly and remove the axleshaft (see Chapter 8).

5   Remove the cotter pins and loosen the castellated nuts on the balljoint studs **(see illustration)**.

6   Using a large hammer, tap the steering knuckle at the top to separate it from the balljoint studs.

7   Carefully check the steering knuckle for cracks, especially around the steering arm and spindle mounting area. Check for elongated balljoint stud holes. Replace the steering knuckle if any of these conditions are found.

Installation

Refer to illustrations 13.8a, 13.8b and 13.9

8   If you're replacing the steering knuckle on a 1990 or later model, proceed to Step 10; if you're replacing the steering knuckle on a pre-1990 model, unscrew the split ring seat **(see illustration)** from the lower mount and transfer it to the new knuckle. Also remove the disc anchor plate from the old knuckle **(see illustration)**.

9   Measure the depth of the split ring seat in the knuckle using a depth micrometer or vernier caliper **(see illustration)**. Screw the split ring seat in or out to attain the proper depth of 0.206 inch.

15.2 Before you remove the power steering pump mounting bolts, unplug the power steering pressure switch (A), and disconnect the high pressure line (B) and the return hose (C) (this unit has an integral reservoir - some models use a remote reservoir bolted to the radiator, as shown in illustration 11.2)

15.3a Front power steering pump mounting bolts

15.3b Rear power steering pump mounting bolts

10   Position the steering knuckle on the axle housing, inserting the balljoint studs into the holes in the knuckle. Install the nuts and tighten them to the torque listed in this Chapter's Specifications. Remember to use new cotter pins.

11   Install the axleshaft (see Chapter 8).

12   Install the front axle hub and bearing assembly (see Chapter 8).

13   If you removed the disc anchor plate from a pre-1990 steering knuckle, install it on the new knuckle and tighten the bolts to the torque listed in Chapter 9.

14   Install the brake disc and caliper (see Chapter 9).

15   Connect the tie-rod to the steering knuckle and tighten the nut to the torque listed in this Chapter's Specifications. Install a new cotter pin.

16   Install the wheel and lug nuts. Lower the vehicle and tighten the lug nuts to the torque listed in the Chapter 1 Specifications.

14 Balljoints - replacement

The balljoints are a press fit in the front axle housing, which necessitates the use of a special tool to remove and install them. Since the tool is not normally available to the home mechanic, it is recommended that the vehicle be taken to a dealer service department or other qualified repair shop to have the balljoints replaced.

15 Power steering pump - removal and installation

Refer to illustration 15.2, 15.3a, 15.3b, 15.4, 15.5 and 15.6

Removal

1   Loosen the pump drivebelt and slip the

15.4 This special tool, designed for removing power steering pump pulleys, is available at most auto parts stores

belt over the pulley (see Chapter 1).

2   Unplug the power steering pressure switch **(see illustration)**. Using a suction gun, suck out as much power steering fluid from the reservoir as possible. Position a drain pan under the pump and disconnect the high pressure line and fluid return hose. It may be necessary to remove the air cleaner housing for access to the return hose (if so, see Chapter 4). Cap the ends of the lines to prevent excessive fluid leakage and the entry of contaminants. **Note:** *This is a good time to inspect and, if necessary, replace the power steering hoses/lines* **(see illustration 11.2)**.

3   Remove the front and rear pump mounting bolts **(see illustrations)**, then lift the pump from the engine.

4   If it is necessary to remove the pulley from the pump, first measure how far the pump shaft protrudes from the face of the pulley hub. Remove the pulley from the shaft with a special power steering pump pulley removal tool **(see illustration)**. This tool can be purchased at most auto parts stores.

Installation

5   A special pulley installation tool is available for pressing the pulley back onto the

15.5 To install the pulley on the shaft, use a long bolt with the same thread pitch as the internal threads of the power steering pump shaft, a nut, washer and a socket that's the same diameter as the pulley hub

pump shaft, but an alternate tool can be fabricated from a long bolt, nut, washer and a socket of the same diameter as the pulley hub **(see illustration)**. Push the pulley onto the shaft until the shaft protrudes from the hub the previously recorded amount.

6   Installation of the power steering pump is the reverse of the removal procedure **(see illustration)**. Be sure to bleed the power steering system following the procedure in Section 14.

16 Power steering system - bleeding

1   Following any operation in which the power steering fluid lines have been disconnected, the power steering system must be bled to remove all air and obtain proper steering performance.

2   With the front wheels in the straight ahead position, check the power steering fluid level and, if low, add fluid until it reaches the Cold (C) mark on the dipstick.

3   Start the engine and allow it to run at fast idle. Recheck the fluid level and add more if necessary to reach the Cold (C) mark on the dipstick.

P/S PUMP WITH REMOTE RESERVOIR

P/S PUMP WITH INTEGRAL RESERVOIR

REAR PUMP ATTACHING BOLTS

PUMP MOUNTING BRACKET

PIVOT BOLT

ADJUSTMENT BRACKET

ADJUSTMENT SLOT LOCKNUT

REAR ENGINE MOUNT BRACKET

ADJUSTMENT BOLT COLLAR

PUMP PULLEY

ADJUSTMENT BRACKET TO REAR BRACKET BOLTS

DRIVE BELT ADJUSTMENT BOLT

15.6 An exploded view of a typical late-model power steering pump/reservoir assembly (some models use a remote reservoir as shown in illustration 11.2)

4   Bleed the system by turning the wheels from side-to-side, without hitting the stops. This will work the air out of the system. Keep the reservoir full of fluid as this is done.

5   When the air is worked out of the system, return the wheels to the straight ahead position and leave the vehicle running for several more minutes before shutting it off.

6   Road test the vehicle to be sure the steering system is functioning normally and noise free.

7   Recheck the fluid level to be sure it is up to the Hot (H) mark on the dipstick while the engine is at normal operating temperature. Add fluid if necessary (see Chapter 1).

17   Wheels and tires - general information

Refer to illustration 17.1

All vehicles covered by this manual are equipped with metric-sized fiberglass or steel belted radial tires **(see illustration)**. Use of other size or type of tires may affect the ride and handling of the vehicle. Don't mix different types of tires, such as radials and bias belted, on the same vehicle as handling may be seriously affected. It's recommended that tires be replaced in pairs on the same axle,

METRIC TIRE SIZES

P 185 / 80 R 13

TIRE TYPE
P-PASSENGER
T-TEMPORARY
C-COMMERCIAL

ASPECT RATIO
(SECTION HEIGHT)
―――――――――
(SECTION WIDTH)

RIM DIAMETER
(INCHES)
13
14
15

SECTION WIDTH
(MILLIMETERS)
185
195
205
ETC

70
75
80

CONSTRUCTION TYPE
R-RADIAL
B-BIAS - BELTED
D-DIAGONAL (BIAS)

SECTION WIDTH

SECTION HEIGHT

17.1 Metric tire size code

but if only one tire is being replaced, be sure it's the same size, structure and tread design as the other.

Because tire pressure has a substantial effect on handling and wear, the pressure on all tires should be checked at least once a month or before any extended trips (see Chapter 1).

Wheels must be replaced if they are bent, dented, leak air, have elongated bolt holes, are heavily rusted, out of vertical symmetry or if the lug nuts won't stay tight. Wheel repairs that use welding or peening are not recommended.

Tire and wheel balance is important to the overall handling, braking and performance of the vehicle. Unbalanced wheels can adversely affect handling and ride characteristics as well as tire life. Whenever a tire is installed on a wheel, the tire and wheel should be balanced by a shop with the proper equipment.

18   Front end alignment - general information

Refer to illustration 18.3

A front end alignment refers to the adjustments made to the front wheels so they are in proper angular relationship to the suspension and the ground. Front wheels that are out of proper alignment not only affect steering control, but also increase tire wear. The only front end adjustments possible on these vehicles are caster and toe-in.

Getting the proper front wheel alignment is a very exacting process, one in which complicated and expensive machines are necessary to perform the job properly. Because of this, you should have a technician with the proper equipment perform these tasks. We will, however, use this space to give you a basic idea of what is involved with front end alignment so you can better understand the process and deal intelligently with the shop that does the work.

Toe-in is the turning in of the front wheels **(see illustration)**. The purpose of a toe specification is to ensure parallel rolling of the front wheels. In a vehicle with zero toe-in, the distance between the front edges of the wheels will be the same as the distance between the rear edges of the wheels. The actual amount of toe-in is normally only a fraction of an inch. Toe-in adjustment is controlled by the tie-rod end position on the tie-rod. Incorrect toe-in will cause the tires to wear improperly by making them scrub against the road surface.

Caster is the tilting of the top of the front steering axis from the vertical **(see illustration)**. A tilt toward the rear is positive caster

CAMBER ANGLE (FRONT VIEW)

18.3 Front end alignment details

A minus B = C (degrees camber)
D = Degrees caster
E minus F = toe-in (measured in inches)
G - toe-in (expressed in degrees)

CASTER ANGLE (SIDE VIEW)

TOE-IN (TOP VIEW)

and a tilt toward the front is negative caster. On 1995 and earlier models this angle is adjusted by installing tapered shims between the front axle pads and the leaf spring brackets. On 1997 and later models it's adjusted by an adjusting cam at the axle-end of each lower control arm.

Camber (the tilting of the front wheels from vertical when viewed from the front of the vehicle) is factory present at 0-degree and cannot be adjusted. If the camber angle isn't correct, the components causing the problem must be replaced. NEVER ATTEMPT TO ADJUST THE CAMBER ANGLE BY HEATING OR BENDING THE AXLE OR ANY OTHER SUSPENSION COMPONENT!

Chapter 11 Body

Contents

1 General information

The vehicles covered in this manual have a separate frame and body.

As with other parts of the vehicle, proper maintenance of body components plays an important part in preserving the vehicle's market value. It's far less costly to handle small problems before they grow into larger ones. Information in this Chapter will tell you all you need to know to keep seals sealing, body panels aligned and general appearance up to par.

Major body components which are particularly vulnerable in accidents are removable. These include the hood, fenders, grille and doors. It's often cheaper and less time consuming to replace an entire panel than it is to attempt a restoration of the old one. However, this must be decided on a case-by-case basis.

2 Body - maintenance

1   The condition of your vehicle's body is very important, because the resale value depends a great deal on it. It's much more difficult to repair a neglected or damaged body than it is to repair mechanical components. The hidden areas of the body, such as the wheel wells, the frame and the engine compartment, are equally important, although they don't require as frequent attention as the rest of the body.

2   Once a year, or every 12,000 miles, it's a good idea to have the underside of the body steam cleaned. All traces of dirt and oil will be removed and the area can then be inspected carefully for rust, damaged brake lines, frayed electrical wires, damaged cables and other problems. The front suspension components should be greased after completion of this job.

3   At the same time, clean the engine and the engine compartment with a steam cleaner or water soluble degreaser.

4   The wheel wells should be given close attention, since undercoating can peel away and stones and dirt thrown up by the tires can cause the paint to chip and flake, allowing rust to set in. If rust is found, clean down to the bare metal and apply an anti-rust paint.

5   The body should be washed about once a week. Wet the vehicle thoroughly to soften the dirt, then wash it down with a soft sponge and plenty of clean soapy water. If the surplus dirt is not washed off very carefully, it can wear down the paint.

6   Spots of tar or asphalt thrown up from the road should be removed with a cloth soaked in solvent.

7   Once every six months, wax the body and chrome trim. If a chrome cleaner is used to remove rust from any of the vehicle's plated parts, remember that the cleaner also removes part of the chrome, so use it sparingly.

3 Vinyl trim - maintenance

Don't clean vinyl trim with detergents, caustic soap or petroleum-based cleaners. Plain soap and water works just fine, with a soft brush to clean dirt that may be ingrained. Wash the vinyl as frequently as the rest of the vehicle.

After cleaning, application of a high quality rubber and vinyl protectant will help prevent oxidation and cracks. The protectant can also be applied to weatherstripping, vacuum lines and rubber hoses, which often fail as a result of chemical degradation, and to the tires.

4 Upholstery and carpets - maintenance

1   Every three months remove the carpets or mats and clean the interior of the vehicle (more frequently if necessary). Vacuum the upholstery and carpets to remove loose dirt and dust.

2   Leather upholstery requires special care. Stains should be removed with warm water and a very mild soap solution. Use a clean, damp cloth to remove the soap, then wipe again with a dry cloth. Never use alcohol, gasoline, nail polish remover or thinner to clean leather upholstery.

3   After cleaning, regularly treat leather upholstery with a leather wax. Never use car wax on leather upholstery.

4   In areas where the interior of the vehicle is subject to bright sunlight, cover leather seats with a sheet if the vehicle is to be left out for any length of time.

5 Body repair - minor damage

See photo sequence

Repair of minor scratches

1   If the scratch is superficial and does not penetrate to the metal of the body, repair is very simple. Lightly rub the scratched area with a fine rubbing compound to remove loose paint and built up wax. Rinse the area with clean water.

2   Apply touch-up paint to the scratch, using a small brush. Continue to apply thin layers of paint until the surface of the paint in the scratch is level with the surrounding paint. Allow the new paint at least two weeks to harden, then blend it into the surrounding

These photos illustrate a method of repairing simple dents. They are intended to supplement *Body repair - minor damage* in this Chapter and should not be used as the sole instructions for body repair on these vehicles.

1 If you can't access the backside of the body panel to hammer out the dent, pull it out with a slide-hammer-type dent puller. In the deepest portion of the dent or along the crease line, drill or punch hole(s) at least one inch apart . . .

2 . . . then screw the slide-hammer into the hole and operate it. Tap with a hammer near the edge of the dent to help 'pop' the metal back to its original shape. When you're finished, the dent area should be close to its original contour and about 1/8-inch below the surface of the surrounding metal

3 Using coarse-grit sandpaper, remove the paint down to the bare metal. Hand sanding works fine, but the disc sander shown here makes the job faster. Use finer (about 320-grit) sandpaper to feather-edge the paint at least one inch around the dent area

4 When the paint is removed, touch will probably be more helpful than sight for telling if the metal is straight. Hammer down the high spots or raise the low spots as necessary. Clean the repair area with wax/silicone remover

5 Following label instructions, mix up a batch of plastic filler and hardener. The ratio of filler to hardener is critical, and, if you mix it incorrectly, it will either not cure properly or cure too quickly (you won't have time to file and sand it into shape)

6 Working quickly so the filler doesn't harden, use a plastic applicator to press the body filler firmly into the metal, assuring it bonds completely. Work the filler until it matches the original contour and is slightly above the surrounding metal

7 Let the filler harden until you can just dent it with your fingernail. Use a body file or Surform tool (shown here) to rough-shape the filler

8 Use coarse-grit sandpaper and a sanding board or block to work the filler down until it's smooth and even. Work down to finer grits of sandpaper - always using a board or block - ending up with 360 or 400 grit

9 You shouldn't be able to feel any ridge at the transition from the filler to the bare metal or from the bare metal to the old paint. As soon as the repair is flat and uniform, remove the dust and mask off the adjacent panels or trim pieces

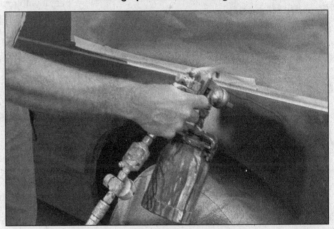

10 Apply several layers of primer to the area. Don't spray the primer on too heavy, so it sags or runs, and make sure each coat is dry before you spray on the next one. A professional-type spray gun is being used here, but aerosol spray primer is available inexpensively from auto parts stores

11 The primer will help reveal imperfections or scratches. Fill these with glazing compound. Follow the label instructions and sand it with 360 or 400-grit sandpaper until it's smooth. Repeat the glazing, sanding and respraying until the primer reveals a perfectly smooth surface

12 Finish sand the primer with very fine sandpaper (400 or 600-grit) to remove the primer overspray. Clean the area with water and allow it to dry. Use a tack rag to remove any dust, then apply the finish coat. Don't attempt to rub out or wax the repair area until the paint has dried completely (at least two weeks)

paint by rubbing with a very fine rubbing compound. Finally, apply a coat of wax to the scratch area.

3   If the scratch has penetrated the paint and exposed the metal of the body, causing the metal to rust, a different repair technique is required. Remove all loose rust from the bottom of the scratch with a pocket knife, then apply rust inhibiting paint to prevent the formation of rust in the future. Using a rubber or nylon applicator, coat the scratched area with glaze-type filler. If required, the filler can be mixed with thinner to provide a very thin paste, which is ideal for filling narrow scratches. Before the glaze filler in the scratch hardens, wrap a piece of smooth cotton cloth around the tip of a finger. Dip the cloth in thinner and then quickly wipe it along the surface of the scratch. This will ensure that the surface of the filler is slightly hollow. The scratch can now be painted over as described earlier in this section.

Repair of dents

4   When repairing dents, the first job is to pull the dent out until the affected area is as close as possible to its original shape. There is no point in trying to restore the original shape completely as the metal in the damaged area will have stretched on impact and cannot be restored to its original contours. It is better to bring the level of the dent up to a point which is about 1/8-inch below the level of the surrounding metal. In cases where the dent is very shallow, it is not worth trying to pull it out at all.

5   If the back side of the dent is accessible, it can be hammered out gently from behind using a soft-face hammer. While doing this, hold a block of wood firmly against the opposite side of the metal to absorb the hammer blows and prevent the metal from being stretched.

6   If the dent is in a section of the body which has double layers, or some other factor makes it inaccessible from behind, a different technique is required. Drill several small holes through the metal inside the damaged area, particularly in the deeper sections. Screw long, self tapping screws into the holes just enough for them to get a good grip in the metal. Now the dent can be pulled out by pulling on the protruding heads of the screws with locking pliers.

7   The next stage of repair is the removal of paint from the damaged area and from an inch or so of the surrounding metal. This is easily done with a wire brush or sanding disk in a drill motor, although it can be done just as effectively by hand with sandpaper. To complete the preparation for filling, score the surface of the bare metal with a screwdriver or the tang of a file or drill small holes in the affected area. This will provide a good grip for the filler material. To complete the repair, see the Section on filling and painting.

Repair of rust holes or gashes

8   Remove all paint from the affected area and from an inch or so of the surrounding

metal using a sanding disk or wire brush mounted in a drill motor. If these are not available, a few sheets of sandpaper will do the job just as effectively.

9   With the paint removed, you will be able to determine the severity of the corrosion and decide whether to replace the whole panel, if possible, or repair the affected area. New body panels are not as expensive as most people think and it is often quicker to install a new panel than to repair large areas of rust.

10   Remove all trim pieces from the affected area except those which will act as a guide to the original shape of the damaged body, such as headlight shells, etc. Using metal snips or a hacksaw blade, remove all loose metal and any other metal that is badly affected by rust. Hammer the edges of the hole inward to create a slight depression for the filler material.

11   Wire brush the affected area to remove the powdery rust from the surface of the metal. If the back of the rusted area is accessible, treat it with rust inhibiting paint.

12   Before filling is done, block the hole in some way. This can be done with sheet metal riveted or screwed into place, or by stuffing the hole with wire mesh.

13   Once the hole is blocked off, the affected area can be filled and painted. See the following subsection on filling and painting.

Filling and painting

14   Many types of body fillers are available, but generally speaking, body repair kits which contain filler paste and a tube of resin hardener are best for this type of repair work. A wide, flexible plastic or nylon applicator will be necessary for imparting a smooth and contoured finish to the surface of the filler material. Mix up a small amount of filler on a clean piece of wood or cardboard (use the hardener sparingly). Follow the manufacturer's instructions on the package, otherwise the filler will set incorrectly.

15   Using the applicator, apply the filler paste to the prepared area. Draw the applicator across the surface of the filler to achieve the desired contour and to level the filler surface. As soon as a contour that approximates the original one is achieved, stop working the paste. If you continue, the paste will begin to stick to the applicator. Continue to add thin layers of paste at 20-minute intervals until the level of the filler is just above the surrounding metal.

16   Once the filler has hardened, the excess can be removed with a body file. From then on, progressively finer grades of sandpaper should be used, starting with a 180-grit paper and finishing with 600-grit wet-or-dry paper. Always wrap the sandpaper around a flat rubber or wooden block, otherwise the surface of the filler will not be completely flat. During the sanding of the filler surface, the wet-or-dry paper should be periodically rinsed in water. This will ensure that a very smooth finish is produced in the final stage.

17   At this point, the repair area should be surrounded by a ring of bare metal, which in turn should be encircled by the finely feath-

ered edge of good paint. Rinse the repair area with clean water until all of the dust produced by the sanding operation is gone.

18   Spray the entire area with a light coat of primer. This will reveal any imperfections in the surface of the filler. Repair the imperfections with fresh filler paste or glaze filler and once more smooth the surface with sandpaper. Repeat this spray-and-repair procedure until you are satisfied that the surface of the filler and the feathered edge of the paint are perfect. Rinse the area with clean water and allow it to dry completely.

19   The repair area is now ready for painting. Spray painting must be carried out in a warm, dry, windless and dust free atmosphere. These conditions can be created if you have access to a large indoor work area, but if you are forced to work in the open, you will have to pick the day very carefully. If you are working indoors, dousing the floor in the work area with water will help settle the dust which would otherwise be in the air. If the repair area is confined to one body panel, mask off the surrounding panels. This will help minimize the effects of a slight mismatch in paint color. Trim pieces such as chrome strips, door handles, etc., will also need to be masked off or removed. Use masking tape and several thicknesses of newspaper for the masking operations.

20   Before spraying, shake the paint can thoroughly, then spray a test area until the spray painting technique is mastered. Cover the repair area with a thick coat of primer. The thickness should be built up using several thin layers of primer rather than one thick one. Using 600-grit wet-or-dry sandpaper, rub down the surface of the primer until it is very smooth. While doing this, the work area should be thoroughly rinsed with water and the wet-or-dry sandpaper periodically rinsed as well. Allow the primer to dry before spraying additional coats.

21   Spray on the top coat, again building up the thickness by using several thin layers of paint. Begin spraying in the center of the repair area and then, using a circular motion, work out until the whole repair area and about two inches of the surrounding original paint is covered. Remove all masking material 10 to 15 minutes after spraying on the final coat of paint. Allow the new paint at least two weeks to harden, then use a very fine rubbing compound to blend the edges of the new paint into the existing paint. Finally, apply a coat of wax.

6   Body repair - major damage

1   Major damage must be repaired by an auto body shop specifically equipped to perform major repairs. These shops have the specialized equipment required to do the job properly.

2   If the damage is extensive, the body must be checked for proper alignment or the vehicle's handling characteristics may be adversely affected and other components

9.4 Loosen the nuts (arrow) and detach the support rods

9.3 Typical radiator grille and panel details (1987 through 1995 models)

may wear at an accelerated rate.

3   Due to the fact that all of the major body components (hood, fenders, etc.) are separate and replaceable units, any seriously damaged components should be replaced rather than repaired. Sometimes the components can be found in a wrecking yard that specializes in used vehicle components, often at considerable savings over the cost of new parts.

7   Hinges and locks - maintenance

Once every 3000 miles, or every three months, the hinges and latch assemblies on the doors, hood, liftgate and tailgate should be given a few drops of light oil or lock lubricant. The door latch strikers should also be lubricated with a thin coat of grease to reduce wear and ensure free movement. Lubricate the door and liftgate locks with spray-on graphite lubricant.

8   Fixed glass - replacement

Replacement of the windshield and fixed glass requires the use of special fast-setting adhesive/caulk materials and some specialized tools and techniques. These operations should be left to a dealer service department or a shop specializing in glass work.

9   Radiator grille panel - removal and installation

Warning: *The air conditioning system is under high pressure. Do not loosen any hose fittings or remove any components until the system has been discharged. Air conditioning refrigerant should be properly discharged into an EPA-approved recovery/recycling unit by a*

dealer service department or an automotive air conditioning repair facility. Always wear eye protection when disconnecting air conditioning system fittings.

1987 through 1995 models

Refer to illustrations 9.3 and 9.4
1   On air conditioned models, take the vehicle to a properly equipped shop and have the air conditioning discharged before beginning work.
2   Remove the attaching bolts and detach the radiator and shroud from the grille panel (see Chapter 3).
3   Remove the bolts attaching the grille panel to the crossmember and fenders **(see illustration)**.
4   Loosen the support rod nuts, detach the rod, then lift the grille panel up and tilt it forward, then disconnect the wiring harness **(see illustration)**.
5   With air conditioning disconnected (see Step 1), disconnect the high pressure hose from the sight glass and cap it.
6   Remove grille panel from the vehicle.
7   Installation is the reverse of removal.

1997 and later models

Refer to illustration 9.19
8   If the vehicle is air-conditioned, have the air conditioning system evacuated before proceeding.
9   Remove the front crossmember cover.
10   Remove the crossmember valance cover.
11   Remove the cooling system reservoir.
12   Remove the bolts that secure the radiator and shroud to the grille panel.
13   If the vehicle is air-conditioned, disconnect the high-pressure and low-pressure lines at the quick-disconnect fittings. Cap the lines to prevent contamination.
14   Remove the bolts radiator support rod-to-grille panel bolts.

9.19 When installing the grille panel on 1997 and later models, make sure that the bumpers are correctly aligned

15   Unplug the electrical connectors for the headlights, turn signals, side markers and horns.
16   Remove the fender-to-grille panel bolts.
17   Remove the grille-to-frame mount bolt.
18   Detach the grille from the vehicle.
19   Installation is the reverse of removal. When placing the grille in position, make sure that the rubber support bumpers **(see illustration)** are aligned.

10   Hood - removal, installation and adjustment

Refer to illustrations 10.3 and 10.5
Note: *The hood is heavy and somewhat awkward to remove and install - at least two people should perform this procedure.*

Removal and installation

1   Use blankets or pads to cover the cowl area of the body and the fenders. This will protect the body and paint as the hood is lifted off.
2   Disconnect any cables or wire harnesses which will interfere with removal. Disconnect the windshield washer nozzles. Disconnect the ground strap.

3　Close the hood and scribe alignment marks around the hinge with a grease pencil (so the marks can be cleaned off later) to ensure proper alignment during installation **(see illustration)**.

4　Using a #40 Torx head bit, remove the hinge-to-hood bolts, then lift the hinges up out of the way.

5　Lift off the hood **(see illustration)**.

6　Installation is the reverse of removal. Be sure to line up the hinges with the grease pencil marks and tighten the hinge-to-hood bolts securely.

Adjustment

7　Fore-and-aft and side-to-side adjustment of the hood is done by moving the hood in relation to the hinge plate after loosening the bolts.

8　Loosen the bolts and move the hood into correct alignment. Move it only a little at a time. Tighten the hood bolts, then open and close the hood to check the alignment.

11　Windshield assembly - removal and installation

Refer to illustrations 11.2, 11.3a, 11.3b, 11.4a and 11.4b

1　Remove the windshield wiper assemblies. First mark the position of each wiper arm on the wiper pivot shaft to ensure correct reassembly. Next, insert an ice-pick-type tool through the hole that's just above the pivot shaft on the wiper arm. Grasp the wiper arm at the pivot shaft and pull off the assembly.

2　Detach the convertible or hardtop from the windshield frame. The hardtop can be propped up out of the way on wood blocks after loosening the attaching bolts **(see illustration)**.

3　On 1987 through 1995 models, remove the windshield retainers **(see illustration)**. On 1997 and later models, remove the pivot screw closest to the hinge pivot point **(see illustration)** and tilt the windshield forward.

10.3　Use a grease pencil to mark the hood hinge location - the marks can be easily cleaned later

10.5　Typical hood components (1987 through 1995 models; later models similar)

11.2　Use wood blocks to prop up the hardtop

11.3a　A Torx tool will be required to remove the windshield retaining bolts

11.3b　Windshield hinge installation details (1997 and later models)

11.4a Windshield and frame details (1987 through 1995 models)

11.4b Windshield and frame details (1997 and later models)

4   Remove the hinge screws and lift the windshield frame assembly off the vehicle **(see illustrations)**.
5   Installation is the reverse of removal.

12 Front fender - removal and installation

1987 through 1995 models

Refer to illustrations 12.3 and 12.4
1   Release the hood hold-down.
2   Detach the sidemarker lamp and disconnect the radio antenna (see Chapter 12).
3   Remove the bolts from the front edge of the fender **(see illustration)**.
4   Remove the rear support and fender-to-body bolts **(see illustration)**.
5   Detach the fender from the vehicle.
6   Installation is the reverse of removal.

12.3 The front fender bolts are easily accessible

12.4 Front fenders - exploded view

12.18 Body side molding installation details (1997 and later models)

12.8 Fender flare mounting details (1997 and later models)

1997 and later models

Front fender flare

Refer to illustration 12.8

7   Remove the side marker lamp (see Chapter 12).

8   Remove the flare-to-fender retaining screws **(see illustration)**.

9   Detach the flare from the front fender.

10 Installation is the reverse of removal. Make sure that the surface between the fender and the flare is clean before reattaching the flare.

Front fender

Left

Refer to illustrations 12.18 and 12.19

11 Disconnect the cable from the negative battery cable.

12 Remove the windshield washer reservoir.

13 Remove the horns (see Chapter 12).

14 Remove the EVAP canister (see Chapter 6).

15 Unbolt the Anti-lock Brake System (ABS) hydraulic control unit (HCU) from the support tray (see Chapter 9). Do NOT disconnect the hydraulic lines from the HCU; simply remove the bolts attaching the HCU to the support tray. Support the HCU by securing it to the firewall with some wire. Remove the HCU support tray.

16 Detach the forward wiring harness clips from the fender. Detach the headlight connector. Thread the wire harness for the fog lamp (if equipped), the parking light and the side marker light through the access hole in the fender well.

17 Remove the fender flare, if equipped (see Steps 7 through 9 above).

18 Remove the body side molding, if equipped, as follows: Remove the bolts from

the underside of the body molding **(see illustration)**. Lift up the molding to disengage it from the molding support. (If it's necessary to remove the molding support, you'll have to drill out and discard the rivets. Use new rivets when installing the molding support.)

19 Remove the fender-to-body bolts, the fender-to-HCU tray support bracket bolts and the fender-to-grille bolts **(see illustration)**.

20 Installation is the reverse of removal. To install the body side molding correctly, put the upper edge of the molding over the upper edge of the molding support and slide it down.

Right

21 Remove the battery (see Chapter 5).

22 Remove the air cleaner housing (see Chapter 4).

23 Remove the bolts that attach the Power Distribution Center (PDC) to the fender (see Chapter 12). Detach the PDC wire harness clips from the battery tray and from the fender. Move the PDC and support it from the firewall with a piece of wire.

24 Detach the air conditioning high pressure line retainer from the fender.

25 Detach the forward wiring harness clips from the fender.

26 Remove the battery tray.

27 Detach the connector for the battery temperature sensor.

28 Disconnect the vacuum line from the reservoir located under the battery tray reinforcement bracket.

29 Thread the wire harness for the fog lamp (if equipped), the parking light and the side marker light through the access hole in the fender well.

30 Remove the fender flare, if equipped (see Steps 7 through 9).

31 Remove the body side molding, if equipped (see Step 18 above).

32 Remove the fender-to-body bolts, the fender-to-battery tray support bracket bolts and the fender-to-grille bolts **(see illustration 12.19)**.

33 Installation is the reverse of removal. To install the body side molding correctly, put the upper edge of the molding over the upper edge of the molding support and slide it down.

12.19 Front fender mounting details (1997 and later models)

13 Bumpers - removal and installation

1987 through 1995 models

Refer to illustrations 13.3a and 13.3b

1   Disconnect any wiring or other components that would interfere with bumper removal.

2   Support the bumper with a jack or jackstand. Alternatively, have an assistant support the bumper as the bolts are removed.

3   Remove the bolts that secure the bumper mounting brackets to the frame, then detach the bumper **(see illustrations)**.

4   Installation is the reverse of removal.

5   Tighten the retaining bolts securely.

6   Install any components that were removed.

1997 and later models

Refer to illustrations 13.7a and 13.7b

7   The bumpers on these models are equipped with extensions **(see illustrations)** which can be replaced without removing the bumpers.

8   Removing and installing the bumpers is otherwise similar to the procedure for earlier models (see Steps 1 through 6).

13.3a Front bumper details

14 Door - removal, installation and adjustment

Refer to illustrations 14.1, 14.3 and 14.4

1   Remove the door trim panel (see Section 17). Disconnect any wire harness connectors and push them through the door opening so they won't interfere with door removal. Detach the door return strap **(see illustration)**.

2   Place a jack or jackstand under the door or have an assistant on hand to support it when the hinge bolts are removed. **Note:** *If a*

13.3b The rear bumper is welded to the frame, but the bumperette bolts (arrows) are easily accessible

jack or jackstand is used, place a rag between it and the door to protect the door's painted surfaces.

Convertible

3   Scribe around the lower door hinge with a grease pencil (so the marks can removed later), then remove the bolts with a Torx head tool **(see illustration)**.

4   Remove the upper door hinge pin nut, extract the pin and lift the door off the vehicle **(see illustration)**.

13.7a Front bumper extension mounting details (1997 and later models)

13.7b Rear bumper extension mounting details (1997 and later models)

14.1 Partially close the door and lift the return strap off the pin

14.3 After marking the hinge location with a grease pencil, remove the bolts (arrows) with a Torx-head tool

14.4 Remove the nut (arrow) and pull the hinge pin out

Hardtop

5   Remove the hinge pin nuts, extract the pins and remove the door from the vehicle (**see illustration 14.4**).

All models

6   Installation is the reverse of removal. Tighten the hinge-to-door bolts and hinge nuts securely.

7   Following installation of the door, check the alignment and adjust it if necessary as follows:

a) *Forward-and-backward adjustments are made by loosening the lower door hinge-to-body bolts.*

b) *Forward-and-backward and up-and-down adjustments can be made by loosening the hinge-to-door bolts*

c) *The door lock striker can also be adjusted in-and-out.*

15.3 Unplug the wiper motor connections and remove the wiper arm

15 Liftgate - removal, installation and adjustment (hardtop models only)

Refer to illustrations 15.3, 15.6 and 15.9

1   Open the liftgate and cover the upper body area around the opening with pads or cloths to protect the painted surfaces when the liftgate is removed.

2   Unplug the dome lamp and defroster electrical connector from the liftgate wiring harness.

3   Remove the rear wiper motor cover and unplug the electrical harness and washer hose. Remove the wiper arm by pulling the tab away from the pivot shaft and pulling the arm off the shaft (**see illustration**).

4   Scribe around the hinge flanges with a grease pencil so the liftgate can be easily adjusted when installed.

5   While an assistant supports the liftgate, pry off the clips and detach the support cylinders.

6   Remove the hinge bolts and detach the liftgate from the vehicle (**see illustration**).

7   Installation is the reverse of removal.

15.6 Remove the retaining clips, detach the support cylinders, then remove the bolts and lift the liftgate off

Tighten the hinge bolts securely.

8   After installation, close the liftgate and make sure it's in proper alignment with the surrounding body panels.

9   The engagement of the liftgate can be adjusted by removing the screws and the striker and adding or removing shims underneath to raise or lower it (**see illustration**). If you add or remove shims, tighten the striker screws to the specified torque.

16 Tailgate - removal and installation

Refer to illustrations 16.1a, 16.1b, 16.1c, 16.2, 16.4a and 16.4b

Removal

1   On 1987 through 1995 models, open the tailgate and remove the check rod cover (**see illustration**). Use pliers to remove the check

15.9 Liftgate latch striker details

16.1a Remove the check rod cover screws (arrows) (1987 through 1995 models)

16.1b Remove the check rod spacer . . .

16.1c . . . and squeeze the rod to detach it from the bracket

16.2   Center high-mounted stoplight contact cover installation details (1997 and later models)

rod spacer, the squeeze the check rod and detach it from the bracket **(see illustrations)**. Remove the check rod and plastic shield from the tailgate.

2   On 1997 and later models, remove the spare tire, open the tailgate and remove the contact cover for the center high-mounted stoplight **(see illustration)**. Unplug the electrical connectors for the center high-mounted stoplight and disengage the wire harness from the tailgate.

3   Close the tailgate and scribe around the body hinge with a grease pencil.

4   Use a Torx-head tool to remove the hinge bolts, then release the latch and lift the tailgate from the vehicle **(see illustration)**.

Installation

5   Place the tailgate in the closed position, with the latch engaged. Place the hinge in the marked position and install the bolts. Tighten the bolts securely.

6   Install the check rod and cover.

17   Door trim panel - removal and installation

Refer to illustrations 17.4a, 17.4b, 17.5a and 17.5b

1   Disconnect the negative cable from

16.4a   After marking the hinge position, remove the bolt with a Torx-head tool

the battery.

2   Remove the armrest and door handle assemblies.

3   On hardtop models, remove the Allen head screw and detach the window regulator handle.

4   On convertible top models, unzip the plastic window, then push down and pull up sharply to detach the window assembly from

16.4b   Tailgate hinge assembly mounting details (1997 and later models)

the door **(see illustration)**. Rotate the window grommets and lift them out of the door panel **(see illustration)**.

5   Insert a flat, forked tool or a padded screwdriver between the trim panel and the door and disengage the plastic clip **(see illustration)**. Work around the outer edge until the panel is free. On convertible models, insert screwdriver into the grommet holes

17.4a   Convertible door details

17.4b   Rotate the window grommets and lift them out of the door

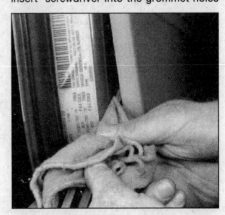

17.5a   A flat, forked tool or a screwdriver padded with a rag makes the job of prying the panel retainers loose much easier

17.5b On convertible models, work through the window retainer grommet holes to pry the upper door trim clips loose

and detach the upper door panel clips **(see illustration)**.

6   For access to the inner door on hardtop models, carefully peel back the plastic watershield.

7   Once all of the clips are disengaged, detach the trim panel, unplug any wire harness connectors and remove the trim panel from the vehicle.

8   Prior to installation of the door panel, be sure to reinstall any retainers in the panel which may have come out during the removal procedure and remain in the door itself.

9   Plug in the wire harness connectors and place the panel in position in the door. Press the door panel into place until the clips are seated and install the handle and armrest assemblies. Install the manual regulator window crank (if equipped).

18   Door latch, lock cylinder and handle - removal and installation

Refer to illustrations 18.3a, 18.3b, 18.6 and 18.7

1   Remove the door trim panel and watershield (see Section 17).

2   On hardtop models, remove the door window glass (see Section 23).

18.6 Push the retaining clip off the lock cylinder housing to release it from the door

18.3a Convertible top door details

18.3b Hardtop model door latch details

Door latch

3   Remove the three door latch retaining screws from the end of the door, disconnect the links, then remove the latch **(see illustrations)**.

4   Installation is the reverse of removal. Tighten the door latch retaining screws securely.

Lock cylinder

5   Disconnect the link from the lock cylinder.

6   Use pliers to slide the retaining clip off and remove the lock cylinder from the door **(see illustration)**. Installation is the reverse of removal.

Handle

7   Remove the retaining nuts, pull the handle out, detach the control rod and remove the handle from the door **(see illustration)**.

8   Installation is the reverse of removal. Tighten the retaining screws securely.

18.7 Hardtop door handle details

19.1 Typical tailgate latch assembly - exploded view

A	Cover screw	E	Latch-to-tailgate screw
B	Cover	F	Latch rod
C	Lock cylinder rod	G	Handle
D	Latch mechanism	H	Handle screw

J	Latch housing
K	Gasket

19 Tailgate latch, lock cylinder and handle - removal and installation

Refer to illustrations 19.1, 19.2 and 19.3

1   Open the tailgate, remove the screws and detach the latch cover **(see illustration)**.

2   Remove the clip and detach the latch rod **(see illustration)**.

3   Remove the latch retaining screws, disconnect the lock cylinder rod, remove the retaining clip and detach the lock cylinder **(see illustration)**.

4   Remove the latch handle screws, disengage the handle from the latch, then remove the latch mechanism.

5   Installation is the reverse of removal.

20 Hardtop - removal and installation

Refer to illustration 20.2

1   Remove the hardtop-to-windshield frame screw.

2   Remove the hardtop-to-body bolts and

19.2 Detach the clip and disconnect the latch rod

19.3 Remove the E-clip, detach the lever, then remove the lock cylinder

20.2 Hardtop details

21.1a Detach the snaps at the front corners . . .

21.1b . . . then disconnect the upper door frame

21.2 After unzipping the windows, detach the interior snap

21.3 Release the spreader bar tension by pulling it down

washers **(see illustration)**.

3   Unplug any electrical connectors that would interfere with removal.

4   With the help of an assistant, lift the hard top off the vehicle, taking care not to damage the foam sealer used between the top and body.

5   Installation is the reverse of removal.

21   Convertible top - removal and installation

Refer to illustrations 21.1a, 21.1b, 21.2, 21.3, 21.5, 21.6, 21.7 and 21.8

1   Detach the snaps at the front corner of the top, disconnect the upper frame and unsnap the fasteners, then remove the door windows **(see illustrations)**.

2   Unzip the front and rear side curtain zippers, unsnap the interior tab and pull the bot-

tom edges out of the channel, then slide the front edge of the side curtain down and remove it **(see illustration)**.

3   Pull the spreader bar down to release the tension **(see illustration)**.

4   Open the tailgate and unzip the top and side zippers on the rear curtains.

5   Push the bottom of the rear support bows forward about two-inches out of the side rail notch **(see illustration)**.

6   Detach the top from the drip rails and from the retainer along the upper end of the windshield frame **(see illustration)**.

7   Fold the top back at the front support bow **(see illustration)**.

8   Slide drip rail lock forward, pull it off the lockpin on the windshield frame, then slide the whole assembly to the rear so the bottom of the rear support bows move forward and fold under the bows and drip rails **(see illustration)**.

21.5 Push the rear support bows forward out
of the side rail notch

21.6 Detach the top from the drip
rail and windshield frame

9   Slide the front support bow out of the
side rail, then remove the convertible top
assembly from the vehicle.
10   Installation is the reverse of removal.

22 Center console and bezel - removal and installation

1987 through 1995 models

Refer to illustration 22.3

1   Disconnect the negative cable at the
battery.
2   Open the console door for access.
3   Remove the retaining screws (**see illustration**).
4   Detach the console and lift it from the
vehicle.
5   Installation is the reverse of removal.

1997 and later models

Warning: *Some models covered by this manual are equipped with airbags. Always disable
the airbag system when working in the vicinity
of airbag system components (see Chapter 12).*

Center console

Refer to illustrations 22.11a and 22.11b

6   Move the seats to the full rearward position. Place the passenger seat in the fully
reclining position.
7   On vehicles with an automatic transmission, grasp the shift handle firmly and yank it
upward to remove it from the shift lever.
8   On vehicles with an automatic transmission, use a small flat-bladed screwdriver to
pry up the gear position indicator trim panel.
9   On vehicles with a manual transmission,
pry up the shift boot.
10   On vehicles with a mini console, remove
the trim disc from the bottom of the cup
holder.

21.7 Fold the top back to the first bow

21.8 Slide the top assembly to the rear
so the bottom of the bows move
forward and fold under

22.3 Console - exploded view

22.11a Mini console mounting details (1997 and later models)

22.11b Full console mounting details (1997 and later models)

11   Remove the console retaining bolts **(see illustrations)**.

12   Shift the transfer case to the 4L position and engage the parking brake.

13   Lift up the console, rotate it if necessary, and remove it through the passenger door.

Center bezel

Refer to illustration 22.15

14   Remove the instrument panel top cover (see Step 28 in Section 24).

15   Remove the ash tray. Remove the screw in the back of the ash tray that attaches the center bezel to the lower instrument panel **(see illustration)**.

16   Remove the two screws that attach the center bezel to the top of the instrument panel.

17   Using a wide, flat-bladed tool, carefully pry the lower edge of the center bezel away from the instrument panel.

18   Lift up the lower edge of the center bezel to release the four snap clip retainers that secure it to the instrument panel.

19   Remove the center bezel.

20   Installation is the reverse of removal.

23   Door window glass - removal and installation (hardtop models only)

Refer to illustration 23.3

1   Remove the door trim panel and watershield (see Section 17).

2   Lower the window glass.

1987 through 1995 models

Vent glass

3   Remove the division channel upper screw and the lower adjustment screw **(see illustration)**.

4   Detach the front three inches of weatherstripping from the upper door frame, then remove the division channel and tilt the glass out of the frame.

5   Installation is the reverse of removal.

Window glass

6   Remove the glass channel stop bumper **(see illustration 23.3)**.

7   Remove the screws attaching the window regulator arm guide to the glass, then remove the guide assembly **(see illustration 23.3)**.

22.15 Center bezel mounting details (1997 and later models)

23.3 Door glass components (1987 through 1995 models)

8   Lower the glass to the bottom of the door, then remove the vent glass division channel screws. Pull out about three inches of weatherstripping from the upper door frame, then remove the division channel.

9   Raise the glass and tilt it toward the hinge side of the door, then detach it from the rear channel. Remove the glass by pulling it up and out of the door.

10   Installation is the reverse of removal. The amount of effort required to raise and lower the window glass can be adjusted by moving the lower end of the division channel fore-and-aft before tightening the lower adjustment screw.

1997 and later models

Refer to illustrations 23.13a and 23.13b

11   Pull the door glass run channel from the door sail.

12   Roll the glass all the way down.

13   Remove the door sail panel screws and remove the sail **(see illustrations)**.

14   Roll up the glass 1/4-turn to access the regulator arm guide.

15   Remove the screws that attach the regulator arm guide to the glass.

16   Lift the glass upward while tilting it inward, then remove it from the door.

17   Installation is the reverse of removal.

24   Instrument panel - removal and installation

1995 and earlier models

Refer to illustrations 24.2a, 24.2b and 24.3

1   Disconnect the negative battery cable.

2   Remove the screws from the instrument panel **(see illustrations)**.

3   Once the screws have been removed, grasp the individual panel pieces and pull out sharply at the top to detach them from the dash **(see illustration)**.

4   Installation is the reverse of removal.

23.13a Remove the door sail panel screws . . .

23.13b . . . then pry the sail panel loose with a small stick (1997 and later models)

24.2a Remove the two lower instrument panel screws under the steering column with a Phillips screwdriver

24.2b The upper and lower instrument panel screws run the length of the dash

24.3 After removing the attaching screws, pull the bezel parts out sharply to detach them from the dash

24.8 Remove these two screws from the cover for the steering
column opening and remove the cover (1997 and later models)

24.10 To remove the knee blocker, remove these four screws
(1997 and later models)

1997 and later models

Refer to illustrations 24.8, 24.10, 24.20, 24.24a, 24.24b, 24.27, 24.28 and 24.30
Warning: *Some models covered by this manual are equipped with airbags. Always disable the airbag system when working in the vicinity of airbag system components (see Chapter 12).*

5   Disconnect the cable from the negative battery terminal.

6   If the vehicle is equipped with a tilt steering column, raise the column to its highest position.

7   Remove the headlight switch knob and shaft (see Section 13 in Chapter 12).

8   Remove the two screws that retain the cover for the steering column opening **(see illustration)**.

9   Pull the steering column opening cover straight back as far back as it will go. Work the lower edge of the cover rearward to disengage the hooks on the lower edge of the cover from the pivots on the lower edge of the instrument panel. Remove the cover.

10   Remove the four screws that attach the knee blocker to the instrument panel **(see illustration)**. Remove the knee blocker.

11   Insert the key in the ignition switch and turn the key to the On position.

12   Insert a pin punch (or a small screwdriver) through the access hole in the lower steering column cover, then depress the retainer tang in the key lock cylinder and pull the lock cylinder out of the ignition switch lock housing (see Section 18 in Chapter 12).

13   Remove the three screws that attach the lower steering column cover to the upper column cover **(see illustration 18.11a in Chapter 12)**.

14   If the vehicle is equipped with a tilt steering column, lower the column to its lowest position. If the vehicle is equipped with a non-tilt steering column, loosen the two nuts that attach the upper steering column bracket to the steering column support bracket studs on the dash panel, then lower the column enough to remove the upper steering column cover.

15   Remove the upper and lower steering column covers.

16   If the vehicle is equipped with a tilt steering column, disconnect the tilt mechanism control cable from the tilt lever to facilitate access to the steering column electrical connectors.

17   Unplug the electrical connectors to the multi-function switch, wiper/washer switch, ignition switch, anti-theft system, etc.

18   Detach the steering column wiring harness retainer from the steering column.

19   It's not absolutely necessary to remove the steering wheel in order to remove the steering column, but it is recommended since it reduces the chance of damaging the airbag system. (If you prefer to separate the airbag, steering wheel and steering column/steering shaft into three components, refer to Chapter 12 for instructions on disabling and removing the airbag and refer to Chapter 10 for steering wheel removal.) If you opt to leave the steering wheel installed, it's critical that the steering wheel not be allowed to move in relation to the steering column. The steering wheel must remain indexed to the steering column because of the "clockspring" under the steering wheel. The clockspring, which is part of the driver's side airbag circuit, carries current from the main harness to the steering wheel-mounted airbag, in the event of an accident. Using cable ties, immobilize the steering wheel and the steering column so that they cannot be moved in relation to one another. **Warning:** *Failure to prevent steering wheel rotation can damage the clockspring, which can cause the airbag system to fail.*

20   Remove the pinch bolt from the upper half of the steering shaft coupler **(see illustration)**.

21   Remove the four nuts that attach the steering column mounts to the steering column support bracket. Lower the steering column mounts off the support bracket studs and remove the column/steering wheel assembly. **Warning:** *If the steering wheel is*

still installed, do NOT lay the steering column/steering wheel assembly on the airbag.

22   Reach through the steering column opening and clearly label and unplug all electrical connectors.

23   Disconnect the heater/air conditioning temperature control cable from the blend-air door lever.

24   Release the glove box latch and open the glove box door. On 1997 models, support the glove box door with one hand, reach inside the glove box, depress the tab **(see illustration)**, then pull the door open until the tab clears the glove box opening. On 1998 and later models, support the glove box door with one hand, grasp the check strap as close to the glove box door as possible and slide the rolled end of the check strap out of the edge of the door **(see illustration)**.

25   Lower the glove box door and disengage the hooks on the lower edge of the glove box door from the slots on the instrument panel. Remove the glove box.

26   Reach through the glove box opening and clearly label and unplug all electrical connectors.

27   Remove the two nuts that attach the lower side of the passenger side airbag module bracket to the studs on the dash panel **(see illustration)**.

28   The instrument panel top cover uses five equally spaced snap clip retainers to attach the top cover to the instrument panel. Using a suitable tool with a wide, flat blade, carefully pry up the instrument panel top cover from the instrument panel **(see illustration)**.

29   It's not absolutely necessary to remove the instrument cluster from the instrument panel, but if you're planning to replace the instrument panel, now would be a good time to remove the instrument cluster bezel and the cluster (see Section 20 in Chapter 12). The instrument panel is also lighter (and therefore easier to maneuver) with the cluster removed.

30   Remove the three instrument panel-to-door hinge pillar screws **(see illustration)**

STEERING COLUMN

COUPLER

24.20 Steering column mounting details (1997 and later models)

RETAINING TAB

GLOVE BOX

24.24a On 1997 models, support the glove box door with one hand, reach inside the glove box, depress the tab and pull the door open until the tab clears the glove box opening (1997 and later models)

GLOVE BOX DOOR AND BIN

SCREW

CHECK STRAP

LOCK CYLINDER

LATCH AND HANDLE

24.24b On 1998 and later models, support the glove box door with one hand, grasp the check strap as close to the glove box door as possible and slide the rolled end of the check strap out of the edge of the door (1997 and later models)

GRAB HANDLE

LOWER AIRBAG BRACKET

NUT

GLOVE BOX OPENING

24.27 Remove the two nuts that attach the lower side of the passenger side airbag module bracket to the studs on the dash panel (1997 and later models)

INSTRUMENT PANEL TOP COVER

FWD

24.28 To separate the instrument panel top cover from the instrument panel, pry it off with a suitable wide, flat-bladed tool (1997 and later models)

STUDS

NUT

SCREW

24.30 The instrument panel is attached to the door hinge pillar by three screws at each end and to the dash panel studs by four nuts across the top (1997 and later models)

25.1a The front bucket seat frame bolts to the floor

25.1b Typical rear bench seat details

that attach each end of the instrument panel to the door hinge pillars.

31 Remove the four nuts that attach the top of the instrument panel to the dash panel studs.

32 Using an assistant, lift the instrument panel out of the vehicle.

33 Installation is the reverse of removal. Be sure to torque the steering column fasteners to 17 ft-lbs, and the intermediate shaft cou-

pler bolt to 36 ft-lbs.

25 Seats - removal and installation

Refer to illustrations 25.1a and 25.1b

1 Remove the retaining bolts and lift the seats from the vehicle **(see illustrations).**

2 Installation is the reverse of removal.

Tighten the retaining bolts.

Chapter 12
Chassis electrical system

Contents

Specifications

Torque specifications

Airbag module retaining nuts (1995 models)	100 in-lbs
Airbag module retaining screws (1997 and later models)	
Driver's side	90 in-lbs
Passenger side	105 in-lbs

1   General information

The electrical system is a 12–volt, negative ground type. Power for the lights and all electrical accessories is supplied by a lead/acid-type battery which is charged by the alternator.

This Chapter covers repair and service procedures for the various electrical components not associated with the engine. Information on the battery, alternator, distributor and starter motor can be found in Chapter 5.

It should be noted that when portions of the electrical system are serviced, the negative battery cable should be disconnected from the battery to prevent electrical shorts and/or fires.

2   Electrical troubleshooting - general information

A typical electrical circuit consists of an electrical component, any switches, relays, motors, fuses, fusible links or circuit breakers related to that component and the wiring and connectors that link the component to both the battery and the chassis. To help you pinpoint an electrical circuit problem, wiring diagrams are included at the end of this book.

Before tackling any troublesome electrical circuit, first study the appropriate wiring diagrams to get a complete understanding of what makes up that individual circuit. Trouble spots, for instance, can often be narrowed down by noting if other components related to the circuit are operating properly. If several components or circuits fail at one time, chances are the problem is in a fuse or ground connection, because several circuits are often routed through the same fuse and ground connections.

Electrical problems usually stem from simple causes, such as loose or corroded connections, a blown fuse, a melted fusible link or a bad relay. Visually inspect the condition of all fuses, wires and connections in a problem circuit before troubleshooting it.

If testing instruments are going to be utilized, use the diagrams to plan ahead of time where you will make the necessary connections in order to accurately pinpoint the trouble spot.

The basic tools needed for electrical troubleshooting include a circuit tester or voltmeter (a 12–volt bulb with a set of test leads can also be used), a continuity tester, which includes a bulb, battery and set of test leads, and a jumper wire, preferably with a circuit breaker incorporated, which can be used to bypass electrical components. Before attempting to locate a problem with test instruments, use the wiring diagram(s) to decide where to make the connections.

Voltage checks

Voltage checks should be performed if a circuit is not functioning properly. Connect one lead of a circuit tester to either the negative battery terminal or a known good ground. Connect the other lead to a connector in the circuit being tested, preferably nearest to the battery or fuse. If the bulb of the tester lights, voltage is present, which means that the part of the circuit between the connector and the battery is problem free. Continue checking the rest of the circuit in the same fashion. When you reach a point at which no voltage is present, the problem lies between that point and the last test point with voltage. Most of the time the problem can be traced to a loose connection. **Note:** *Keep in mind that some circuits receive voltage only when the ignition key is in the Accessory or Run position.*

3.1 The fuse block is located under the left side of the instrument panel, next to the parking brake mechanism - turn signal and hazard flashers are located at the top (arrows)

Finding a short

One method of finding shorts in a circuit is to remove the fuse and connect a test light or voltmeter in its place to the fuse terminals. There should be no voltage present in the circuit. Move the wiring harness from side-to-side while watching the test light. If the bulb goes on, there is a short to ground somewhere in that area, probably where the insulation has rubbed through. The same test can be performed on each component in the circuit, even a switch.

Ground check

Perform a ground test to check whether a component is properly grounded. Disconnect the battery and connect one lead of a self-powered test light, known as a continuity tester, to a known good ground. Connect the other lead to the wire or ground connection being tested. If the bulb goes on, the ground is good. If the bulb does not go on, the ground is not good.

Continuity check

A continuity check is done to determine if there are any breaks in a circuit - if it is passing electricity properly. With the circuit off (no power in the circuit), a self-powered continuity tester can be used to check the circuit. Connect the test leads to both ends of the circuit (or to the "power" end and a good ground), and if the test light comes on the circuit is passing current properly. If the light doesn't come on, there is a break somewhere in the circuit. The same procedure can be used to test a switch, by connecting the continuity tester to the switch terminals. With the switch turned On, the test light should come on.

Finding an open circuit

When diagnosing possible open circuits, it is often difficult to locate them by sight because oxidation or terminal misalignment are hidden by the connectors. Merely wiggling a connector on a sensor or in the wiring harness may correct the open circuit condition. Remember this when an open circuit is

indicated when troubleshooting a circuit. Intermittent problems may also be caused by oxidized or loose connections.

Electrical troubleshooting is simple if you keep in mind that all electrical circuits are basically electricity running from the battery, through the wires, switches, relays, fuses and fusible links to each electrical component (light bulb, motor, etc.) and to ground, from which it is passed back to the battery.

Any electrical problem is an interruption in the flow of electricity to and from the battery.

3   Fuses - general information

Refer to illustrations 3.1 and 3.3

The electrical circuits of the vehicle are protected by a combination of fuses, circuit breakers and fusible links. The fuse block is located under the instrument panel on the left side of the dashboard **(see illustration)**.

Each of the fuses is designed to protect a specific circuit, and the various circuits are identified on the fuse panel itself.

Miniaturized fuses are employed in the fuse block. These compact fuses, with blade terminal design, allow fingertip removal and replacement. If an electrical component fails, always check the fuse first. The easiest way to check fuses is with a test light. Check for power at the exposed terminal tips of each fuse. If power is present on one side of the fuse but not the other, the fuse is blown. A blown fuse can also be confirmed by visually inspecting it **(see illustration)**.

Be sure to replace blown fuses with the correct type. Fuses of different ratings are physically interchangeable, but only fuses of the proper rating should be used. Replacing a fuse with one of a higher or lower value than specified is not recommended. Each electri-

cal circuit needs a specific amount of protection. The amperage value of each fuse is molded into the fuse body.

If the replacement fuse immediately fails, don't replace it again until the cause of the problem is isolated and corrected. In most cases, the cause will be a short circuit in the wiring caused by a broken or deteriorated wire.

4   Fusible links - general information

Refer to illustrations 4.2, 4.3, 4.4 and 4.5

Some circuits are protected by fusible links. The links are used in circuits which are not ordinarily fused, such as the ignition circuit.

Later models are equipped with a Power Distribution Center (PDC) located next to the battery **(see illustration)**. The PDC uses maxi fuses instead of fusible links. These maxi fuses are checked visually, just like standard fuses **(see illustration)**.

Although the fusible links appear to be a heavier gauge than the wire they are protect-

3.3 When a fuse blows, the element between the terminals melts - the fuse on the left is blown, the fuse on the right is good

4.2 The Power Distribution Center is located in the engine compartment, next to the battery

OK   NOT
            OK

MAXI FUSES

**4.3 Like standard fuses, the maxi fuses
can be checked visually**

FUSIBLE LINK CHART		
Wire Gauge	Color Code	Color
12 Ga.	BK	Black
14 Ga.	RD	Red
16 Ga.	DB	Dark Blue
18 Ga.	GY	Gray
20 Ga.	OR	Orange
30 Ga.	LG	Light Green

**4.4 Always replace
a burned-out fusible
link with one of the
same color code**

ing, the appearance is due to the thick insulation. All fusible links are several wire gauges smaller than the wire they are designed to protect. The fusible links are color coded and a link should always be replaced with one of the same color (**see illustration**).

Fusible links cannot be repaired, but a new link of the same size wire can be put in its place. The procedure is as follows:

a) *Disconnect the negative cable from the battery.*

b) *Disconnect the fusible link from the wiring harness.*

c) *Cut the damaged fusible link out of the wiring just behind the connector.*

d) *Strip the insulation back approximately 1-inch (**see illustration**).*

e) *Position the connector on the new fusible link and twist or crimp it into place.*

f) *Use rosin core solder at each end of the new link to obtain a good solder joint.*

g) *Use plenty of electrical tape around the soldered joint. No wires should be exposed.*

h) *Connect the battery ground cable. Test the circuit for proper operation.*

5 Circuit breakers - general information

Circuit breakers protect components such as wipers and headlights. Some circuit breakers are located in the fuse box.

On some models the circuit breaker resets itself automatically, so an electrical overload in a circuit breaker protected system will cause the circuit to fail momentarily, then come back on. If the circuit does not

**4.5 Fusible link
repair details**

come back on, check it immediately. Once the condition is corrected, the circuit breaker will resume its normal function.

6 Relays - general information

Refer to illustrations 6.2a and 6.2b

Several electrical accessories and components on the vehicle use relays to transmit electrical signals to components. Most models are also equipped with an Auto Shutdown (ASD) relay that is designed to shut off power to the fuel and ignition systems under certain conditions. If a relay is defective, that component will not operate properly.

On early models, the various relays are grouped together in several locations (**see illustration**). On later models, the relays are all contained within the power distribution center located under the hood (**see illustration**).

If a faulty relay is suspected, it can be removed and tested by a dealer service department or repair shop. Defective relays must be replaced as a unit.

7 Turn signal and hazard flashers - check and replacement

1987 through 1995 models
Turn signal flasher

1 The turn signal flasher, a small canister-shaped unit located in the fuse block, flashes the turn signals (**see illustration 3.1**).

2 When the flasher unit is functioning properly, an audible click can be heard during its operation. If the turn signals fail on one side or the other and the flasher unit does not make its characteristic clicking sound, a faulty turn signal bulb is indicated.

**6.2a On early models, various relays (arrow) are located
next to the battery**

**6.2b On later models,
the relays are contained
within the power
distribution center**

1 *Power distribution center*
2 *Latches*
3 *Cover*
4 *Right side front fender*

FWD

7.15 Combination flasher unit installation details (1997 model shown)

8.2 Use a screwdriver to detach the headlight connector

8.3 Remove four screws and lift the headlight bezel off

8.4 Remove the four headlight retainer screws (arrows)

8.5a Detach the retainer . . .

3   If both turn signals fail to blink, the problem may be due to a blown fuse, a faulty flasher unit, a broken switch or a loose or open connection. If a quick check of the fuse box indicates that the turn signal fuse has blown, check the wiring for a short before installing a new fuse.
4   To replace the flasher, simply pull it out of the fuse block.
5   Make sure that the replacement unit is identical to the original. Compare the old one to the new one before installing it.
6   Installation is the reverse of removal.

Hazard flasher

7   The hazard flasher, a small canister-shaped unit located in the fuse block **(see illustration 3.1)**, flashes all four turn signals simultaneously when activated.
8   The hazard flasher is checked in a fashion similar to the turn signal flasher (see Steps 2 and 3).
9   To replace the hazard flasher, pull it out of the fuse block.
10   Make sure the replacement unit is identical to the one it replaces. Compare the old one to the new one before installing it.
11   Installation is the reverse of removal.

1997 and later models

Refer to illustration 7.15
12   On these models, the turn signal flasher

and hazard flasher are combined into a single unit.
13   Disconnect the cable from the negative battery cable.
14   Remove the knee blocker from the instrument panel (see Section 24 in Chapter 11).
15   Reach through the right side of the steering column opening in the instrument panel and unscrew the combination flasher bracket from the upper steering column mounting bracket (to the right of the steering column) **(see illustration)**.
16   Lower the combination flasher and mounting bracket slightly, then disconnect the combination flasher from the wiring harness connector.
17   Remove the combination flasher and mounting bracket as a single assembly. Don't bother to separate the old flasher unit from the bracket. The new flasher comes with a new bracket.
18   Installation is the reverse of removal.

---

8   Headlights - removal and installation

1987 through 1995 models

Refer to illustrations 8.2, 8.3, 8.4, 8.5a and 8.5b
1   Disconnect the negative cable from the battery.

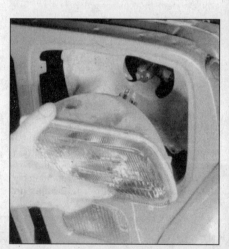

8.5b . . . then lower the headlight from the opening

2   Detach the electrical connector from the headlight **(see illustration)**.
3   Remove the four screws and detach the headlight bezel **(see illustration)**.
4   Remove the retainer screws, taking care not to disturb the adjusting screws **(see illustration)**.
5   Detach the retainer and remove the headlight **(see illustrations)**.
6   Place the headlight in position and

8.9 To remove the headlight bezel, remove the bezel retaining screws (1997 and later models)

8.10 To remove the headlight retaining ring, remove the retaining ring screws (1997 and later models)

9.1a Headlight adjusting screw locations (1987 through 1995 models)

install the retainer and screws. Tighten the screws securely.

7   Place the bezel in position and install the retaining screws.

8   Plug in the electrical connector and reconnect the battery cable.

1997 and later models

Refer to illustrations 8.9 and 8.10

9   Remove the headlight bezel screws and detach the headlight bezel **(see illustration)**.

10   Remove the headlight retaining ring screws **(see illustration)**. Remove the headlight retaining ring.

11   Pull out the headlight and unplug the electrical connector from the light. Remove the headlight.

12   Installation is the reverse of removal.

13   When you're done, check and, if necessary, adjust the headlight beam (see Section 9).

9   Headlights - adjustment

Refer to illustration 9.1

Note: The headlights must be aimed correctly. If adjusted incorrectly they could blind the driver of an oncoming vehicle and cause a serious accident or seriously reduce your ability to see the road. The headlights should be checked for proper aim every 12 months and any time a new headlight is installed or front end body work is performed. It should be emphasized that the following procedure is only an interim step which will provide temporary adjustment until the headlights can be adjusted by a properly equipped shop.

1   Headlights have two spring loaded adjusting screws, one on the top controlling up-and-down movement and one on the side controlling left-and-right movement accessible from the back of the headlights, in the engine compartment **(see illustration)**.

2   There are several methods of adjusting the headlights. The simplest method requires

a blank wall 25 feet in front of the vehicle and a level floor **(see illustration)**.

3   Position masking tape vertically on the wall in reference to the vehicle centerline and the centerlines of both headlights.

4   Position a horizontal tape line in reference to the centerline of all the headlights. **Note:** It may be easier to position the tape on the wall with the vehicle parked only a few inches away.

5   Adjustment should be made with the vehicle sitting level, the gas tank half-full and no unusually heavy load in the vehicle.

6   Starting with the low beam adjustment, position the high intensity zone so it is two inches below the horizontal line and two inches to the side of the headlight vertical line away from oncoming traffic. Adjustment is made by turning the top adjusting screw clockwise to raise the beam and counterclockwise to lower the beam. The adjusting screw on the side should be used in the same manner to move the beam left or right.

7   With the high beams on, the high intensity zone should be vertically centered with the exact center just below the horizontal line. **Note:** It may not be possible to position the headlight aim exactly for both high and low beams. If a compromise must be made, keep in mind that the low beams are the most used and have the greatest effect on driver safety.

8   Have the headlights adjusted by a dealer service department or service station at the earliest opportunity.

10   Bulb replacement

Refer to illustrations 10.1a, 10.1b, 10.1c, 10.2, 10.3a, 10.3b and 10.4

Warning: Some models covered by this manual are equipped with airbags. Always disable the airbag system when working in the vicinity of airbag system components (see Section 24).

1   The lenses of many lights are held in place by screws, which makes it a simple

9.1b Headlight adjusting screw locations (1997 and later models)

1   Vertical   2   Horizontal

9.2 Headlight aiming details

10.1a The front parking light bulbs are accessible after removing the screws (arrows) and lens . . .

10.1b . . . as are the taillight bulbs . . .

10.1c . . . and the center high-mount stop light bulb (1997 and later models)

10.2 To replace a fog light bulb, remove the reflector from the housing, pull out the bulb retainer and remove the bulb from the retainer (1997 and later models)

10.3a Turn the parking light bulb holder to align the tabs, then withdraw it from the bezel housing - push the bulb in and turn it counterclockwise to remove it

10.3b The tail light bulb is also removed by turning it counterclockwise and withdrawing it

procedure to gain access to the bulbs **(see illustrations)**. On some lights the lenses are held in place by clips. The lenses can be removed either by unsnapping them or by using a small screwdriver to pry them off.

2   To replace a fog light bulb, remove the reflector-to-fog light housing screws, pull the reflector assembly out of the housing **(see illustration)**, squeeze the bulb retainer together, pull it out of the reflector and remove the bulb from the retainer. Installation is the reverse of removal.

3   Several types of bulbs are used. Some are removed by pushing in and turning them counterclockwise **(see illustrations)**. Others can simply be unclipped from the terminals or pulled straight out of the socket.

4   To gain access to the instrument panel lights, the instrument cluster will have to be removed first (see Section 18) **(see illustration)**.

11   Radio and speakers - removal and installation

Warning: *Some models covered by this manual are equipped with airbags. Always disable the airbag system when working in the vicinity of airbag system components (see Section 24).*

Radio

Refer to illustrations 11.4

1   Disconnect the negative cable at the battery.

2   On 1987 through 1995 models, remove the instrument panel (see Chapter 11). On 1997 and later models, remove the center bezel (see Section 22 in Chapter 11).

3   Remove the radio retaining screws.

4   Slide the radio out and support it, dis-

10.4 After removing the instrument cluster, simply pull the bulbs out to remove them

connect the ground cable, antenna and electrical connectors, then remove the assembly from the instrument panel **(see illustration)**.

5   Installation is the reverse of removal.

Speakers

1987 through 1995 models

Passenger side

6   Reach up behind the right side of the instrument panel and remove the four nuts retaining the speaker in place.

11.4 Support the radio and unplug the electrical connector and antenna cable

11.10 The parking brake assembly will have to be unbolted and moved out of the way for access to the driver side speaker

11.14 Speaker mounting details (1997 and later models)

12.2 Unscrew the antenna mast with a small wrench

12.6 Remove the screws and pull the cable out through the holes in the body

7   Detach the speaker and pull it out for access to the electrical connector. Unplug the connector and remove the speaker.

8   Installation is the reverse of removal.

Driver side

Refer to illustration 11.10

9   In the engine compartment, remove the nuts from the two parking brake assembly studs which project through the firewall.

10   In the passenger compartment, remove the bolt holding the parking brake assembly to the instrument panel, then lower the assembly out of the way **(see illustration)**.

11   With the speaker now accessible, remove the retaining nuts.

12   Unplug the connector and remove the speaker.

13   Installation is the reverse of removal. On Hardtop models, make sure to install the ground wire when installing the parking brake assembly bolt.

1997 and later models

Instrument panel speakers

Refer to illustration 11.14

14   Remove the two speaker bezel-to-instrument panel screws **(see illustration)**.

15   Using a wide, flat-bladed tool, carefully pry the upper and lower edges of the speaker bezel off the instrument panel to release the two snap clip retainers that attach the bezel to the instrument panel. Remove the speaker bezel from the instrument panel.

16   Remove the foam rubber speaker baffle from the speaker **(see illustration 11.14)**.

17   Remove the four screws that attach the speaker to the instrument panel. Pull out the speaker, unplug the electrical connector from the speaker and remove the speaker.

18   Installation is the reverse of removal.

Sound bar speakers

19   Remove the four screws that attach the speaker grille and speaker to the sound bar. Lower the speaker and grille and unplug the electrical connector from the speaker. Remove the speaker and grille.

20   Installation is the reverse of removal.

12   Antenna - removal and installation

Warning: *Some models covered by this manual are equipped with airbags. Always disable the airbag system when working in the vicinity of airbag system components (see Section 24).*

Antenna mast

Refer to illustration 12.2

1   The antenna mast can be unscrewed and replaced with a new one in the event it is damaged, following the procedure below. Follow the procedure beginning with Step 4 to replace the antenna and cable as an assembly.

2   Use a small wrench to unscrew the mast **(see illustration)**.

3   Install the new antenna mast finger tight and tighten it securely with the wrench.

Antenna and cable

Refer to illustration 12.6

4   Disconnect the negative cable at the battery.

5   Remove the radio and disconnect the antenna cable (see Section 11). Connect a string or wire to the radio end of the cable.

6   Remove the antenna pad and mast assembly and pull the cable out through the hole in the body **(see illustration)**. **Note:** *On 1997 and later models, the antenna mast must be unscrewed and the cover removed from the base for access to the base screws.*

7   Connect the string or wire to the new cable and pull it into the passenger compartment.

8   Install the antenna pad and mast assembly.
9   Connect the cable to the radio, then install the radio.
10   Connect the battery negative cable.

13   Headlight switch and dash illumination rheostat - removal and installation

Refer to illustrations 13.4a and 13.4b
Warning: *Some models covered by this manual are equipped with airbags. Always disable the airbag system when working in the vicinity of airbag system components (see Section 24).*

1987 through 1995 models

1   Disconnect the negative cable at the battery.
2   Remove the instrument cluster bezel (see Chapter 11).
3   Remove the instrument cluster indicator bezel (see Section 18).
4   Remove the switch or rheostat screws, pull the switch or rheostat assembly out, then unplug the electrical connector **(see illustrations)**.
5   Plug in the new switch or rheostat securely, then place it in position and install the screws. The remainder of installation is the reverse of removal.

1997 and later models

Refer to illustration 13.10
6   Disconnect the cable from the negative battery terminal.
7   Pull out the headlight switch control knob to the ON position.
8   Reach up under the instrument panel to the left of the steering column and push the headlight switch retainer button **(see illustration 13.10)**. While holding the button down, pull out the headlight switch control knob and shaft.
9   Remove the steering column cover and knee blocker (see Section 24 in Chapter 11).

13.4a After removing the screws, grasp the switch securely and unplug it from the electrical connector

10   Remove the spanner nut that attaches the headlight switch to the instrument panel **(see illustration)**.
11   Separate the headlight switch from the instrument panel and unplug the electrical connector. Remove the switch.
12   Installation is the reverse of removal.

14   Headlight dimmer switch - (1987 through 1995 models) removal and installation

Refer to illustration 14.7
Warning: *Some models covered by this manual are equipped with airbags. Always disable the airbag system when working in the vicinity of airbag system components (see Section 24).*
1   Disconnect the negative battery cable.
2   Remove the instrument cluster bezel (see Chapter 11).
3   On air-conditioned models, remove the attaching screws and detach the evaporator housing and bracket from the instrument panel for access to the switch.
4   Tape the switch actuating rod to the steering column to prevent disengagement.

13.4b The dash illumination rheostat is removed in the same way as the headlight switch - unplug it from the connector and remove the screws

5   Remove the two bolts, detach the rod, unplug the electrical connector and lower the switch from the steering column.
6   Engage the new switch with the rod and place it in position, then install the mounting bolts finger-tight.
7   Remove the securing tape from the rod, then insert a 3/32-inch drill bit into the adjustment hole **(see illustration)**. Push the switch toward the steering wheel to take up the slack in the actuator control rod, then tighten the bolts securely.
8   Remove the drill bit, plug in the connector and install any components which were removed.
9   Connect the battery cable.

15   Turn signal/hazard warning switch (1987 through 1995 models) - removal and installation

Refer to illustrations 15.3, 15.4, 15.5, 15.7 and 15.8
Warning: *Some models covered by this manual are equipped with airbags. Always disable*

13.10 Headlight switch mounting details (1997 and later models)

14.7 Dimmer switch adjustment details

15.3 Turn signal electrical connector

15.4 The retaining ring can be removed with a screwdriver after depressing the lock plate with a special tool

the airbag system when working in the vicinity of airbag system components (see Section 24).

1   The turn signal/hazard switch is located at the top end of the steering column and is operated by the multi-function control stalk.

2   Disconnect the negative battery cable, then remove the steering wheel (see Chapter 10).

3   Unplug the turn signal electrical connector (see illustration). Wrap tape around the connector to prevent snagging when the harness is pulled up out of the column. Remove the plastic harness cover by pulling it up and off the weld nuts, then sliding it off the harness.

4   Depress the lock plate using a special tool, available at most auto parts stores, then use a small screwdriver to pry out the retaining ring (see illustration).

5   Remove the lock plate, canceling cam and upper bearing spring (see illustration).

6   Remove the hazard switch knob.

7   Remove the turn signal actuator arm screw (see illustration).

8   Remove the turn signal switch attaching screws (see illustration).

9   Remove the instrument cluster bezel (see Chapter 11).

10   Remove the steering column attaching nuts and bolts, then lower the column.

11   Lift the switch out and guide the wiring harness up through the steering column opening.

12   Installation is the reverse of removal. After installation, it may be necessary to adjust the dimmer switch (see Section 14).

16   Windshield wiper/washer switch (1987 through 1995 models) - check and replacement

Refer to illustrations 16.4a, 16.4b, 16.4c, 16.6, 16.9, 16.10, 16.12 and 16.14

Warning: *Some models covered by this manual are equipped with airbags. Always disable*

15.5 With the lock plate removed, the canceling cam and spring can be lifted off

15.7 Use a Phillips screwdriver to remove the multi-function actuator screw

15.8 Turn signal switch attaching screws

the airbag system when working in the vicinity of airbag system components (see Section 24).

1   These models are equipped with a multi-function lever located on the left side of the steering column which controls the wiper/washer, turn signal and dimmer switches. The wipers are two-speed with an optional intermittent feature.

Check

2   Disconnect the negative cable from the battery.

3   Unplug the electrical connector from the switch.

4   Use an ohmmeter or self-powered test light to check for continuity between the switch terminals at the electrical connector with the switch in the indicated positions (see illustrations).

5   Replace the wiper/washer switch if the continuity is not as specified.

Replacement

6   Unplug the electrical connector and tape it flat against the harness (see illustration).

7   Remove the turn signal switch as described in Section 15, except that it won't be necessary to pull the connector out of the column, only to pull it up far enough for access to the housing screws.

8   Remove the ignition lock cylinder (see Section 21).

9   Bend the end of a straightened paper clip into a hook, insert it into the loop of the key warning buzzer switch, then lift the switch out (see illustration).

10   Remove the four screws or bolts and lift the housing and shroud assembly off the column (see illustration).

11   Remove the wiper/washer switch actuating lever by pulling it straight out.

12   Remove the switch cover, then remove the pivot screw and detach the wiper/washer switch (see illustration).

13   Install the new switch and cover.

14   Push on the dimmer switch rod to make sure it's connected. Place the housing and shroud assembly in position on the steering column with the lock pin forward of the slot in the lock rack, then position the first tooth with the most forward gear of the lock rack (see illustration).

15   Install the screws and carefully mate the housing and shroud assembly.

16.4a Wiper/washer connector terminal details

A   *Delay - dark green (intermittent only)*
B   *Washer - pink*
C   *High - violet*
D   *Ignition - white*
E   *Low/park - grey*
F   *Off/park - yellow*
G   *Delay - brown (intermittent only*

SWITCH POSITION	TERMINALS	ZERO OHMS
Off	E and F	Yes
	All Others	No
Lo	D and E	Yes
	All Others	No
Hi	C and D	Yes
	All Others	No
Wash	B and D	Yes
	D and E	Yes
	All Others	No

16.4b Two-speed wiper switch check chart - ohmmeter readings should be as specified in the three switch positions

SWITCH POSITION	TERMINALS	ZERO OHMS
Off	E and F	Yes
	All Others	No
Lo	D and E	Yes
	All Others	No
Hi	C and D	Yes
	All Others	No
Wash/Mist	B and D	Yes
	D and E	Yes
	All Others	No
Delay	A and G	152-480K ohms

16.4c Intermittent wiper switch check chart - ohmmeter should be as specified in each switch position

16.6 Unplug the connector at the bottom of the steering column and wrap it with tape, as shown

16.9 With the key in the On position, hook a piece of wire (a straightened paper clip works well) under the spring retainer and remove the key buzzer switch

16.10 The housing and shroud assembly is held in place by four attaching screws or bolts

16   Install the key and lock cylinder assembly and make sure the lock pin extends fully when the key is in the lock position (see illustration 16.14).

17   Installation is the reverse of removal.

17 Multi-function switch (1997 and later models) - removal and installation

1997 through 2000 models

Refer to illustrations 17.8a and 17.8b

Warning: *Some models covered by this manual are equipped with airbags. Always disable the airbag system when working in the vicinity of airbag system components (see Section 24).*

1   On these models, the headlight dimmer, turn signal and hazard flasher and windshield wiper/washer switches are integrated into one switch assembly on the steering column. This switch is known as a multi-function switch.

2   Disconnect the cable from the negative battery terminal and then wait at least two minutes before proceeding.

3   Remove the knee blocker (see Section 24 in Chapter 11).

4   Place the tilt column, if equipped, in the fully raised position.

5   Insert a small screwdriver or pin punch through the access hole in the lower steering column cover and push in the ignition key lock cylinder retaining tumbler (see Section 18). While depressing the retaining tumbler, pull the ignition lock cylinder and key out of the ignition lock housing.

6   Remove the three screws that attach the lower steering column cover to the upper cover.

7   On vehicles with a non-tilt steering column, loosen the two nuts that secure the column upper mounting bracket to the dash panel steering column bracket studs. Lower the column far enough to remove the upper steering column cover.

8   Remove the three screws (two on the top of and one on the side of the switch water shield) that attach the switch water shield and

16.12 Remove the wiper/washer switch cover and pivot screw

bracket to the steering column (see illustrations).

9   Carefully pull the lower mounting tab on the switch water shield bracket away from the steering column far enough to clear the screw boss below the multi-function switch lever.

16.14 Make sure the dimmer switch rod is secure by pushing on it and that the nylon spring retainer is forward of the lock rack

17.8a To detach the switch water shield and bracket from the steering column, remove the two screws (arrows) on the top of the switch shield . . .

17.8b . . . and the screw (arrow) on the bottom of the bracket (1997 through 2000 models)

10   Remove the water shield and bracket and the multi-function switch from the steering column and unplug the electrical connectors. (On vehicles equipped with a tilt steering column, lifting up on the tilt release lever will provide extra clearance for switch removal.)

11   Carefully remove the water shield by pulling it off over the hazard warning switch knob and the multi-function switch lever. This left half of the multi-function switch includes the headlight dimmer switch and the hazard warning flasher and turn signal switch.

12   To remove the windshield wiper and washer switch (the right half of the multi-function switch), carefully pull the windshield wiper and washer switch up and away from the right side of the steering column and unplug the electrical connector from the switch.

13   Installation is the reverse of removal.

2001 and later models

14   The multi-function switch consists of a main body that fits over the top of the steering column and two stalks. One stalk is on the left of the column and controls the lighting functions such as the headlights and interior lights; the other is on the right of the column and controls the front and rear wiper and washer systems.

15   The switch can be removed and taken to the dealer for diagnosis if necessary.

16   Disconnect the cable from the negative terminal of the battery.

17   On vehicles with tilt steering columns, lower the column as much as possible and allow the tilt lever to remain in the released position.

18   Remove the steering column covers (see Chapter 11).

19   Disconnect both electrical connectors from the switch.

20   Grasp the switch and pull it upward while wiggling it gently to release it from the locating tabs.

21   Installation is the reverse of the removal procedure.

---

18 Ignition lock cylinder - removal and installation

Warning: *Some models covered by this manual are equipped with airbags. Always disable the airbag system when working in the vicinity of airbag system components (see Section 24).*

1987 through 1995 models

Refer to illustration 18.5

1   Disconnect the negative cable from the battery.

2   Remove the turn signal/hazard warning switches (see Section 15).

3   Remove the ignition key lamp assembly.

4   Place the lock cylinder in the On position.

5   On 1990 and earlier models, remove the retaining screw and withdraw the cylinder from the steering column (**see illustration**). On 1991 and later models, insert a thin screwdriver in the slot adjacent to the screw

18.5 Remove the screw and pull the lock cylinder out (1990 and earlier models)

and press against the spring latch to remove the cylinder.

6   Insert the lock cylinder into position and install the screw (1990 and earlier models only). Tighten the screw securely.

7   Installation is the reverse of removal.

1997 through 2000 models

Refer to illustrations 18.11a and 18.11b

8   Disconnect the negative battery cable and wait at least two minutes before proceeding.

9   If the vehicle is equipped with an automatic transmission, put the shift lever in the PARK position.

10   Turn the key to the ON position.

11   Insert a small screwdriver or pin punch through the access hole in the lower steering column cover (**see illustration**) and depress the release tang (**see illustration**) on the bottom of the key lock cylinder. While pushing up on the release tang, pull out the key lock cylinder.

12   Installation is the reverse of removal. Be sure to push in the key lock cylinder until it snaps into place.

2001 and later models

Note: *On later models, if the key is difficult to turn, the problem may not be in the switch or lock cylinder. On automatic transmission vehicles with floor console-mounted shifters, the shifter interlock cable may be out of adjustment. If it is defective inside the steering column, the steering column must be replaced. On manual transmission vehicles, the small button behind the key cylinder may be defective. If it is defective, the steering column must be replaced.*

13   Put the key into the lock cylinder.

14   On vehicles equipped with an automatic transmission, place the shifter in Park.

15   Remove the steering column covers.

16   Turn the key to the On position.

17   Push a small punch or a similar tool into the hole in the bottom of the switch.

18   Pull out on the key while pushing in on the punch. The cylinder will slide out with the key.

18.11a To release the ignition key lock cylinder, insert a pin punch through the access hole in the lower steering column cover, depress the release tang in the lock cylinder and pull out the cylinder; to remove the lower steering column cover, remove these three screws (1997 and later models)

---

19   To install a new cylinder, first put the key into it. Turn it to the On position.

20   Line the cylinder up in the correct "On" orientation with the housing and slide it in. It will snap into place.

21   Turn the key to the Lock position.

22   The remainder of installation is the reverse of removal.

---

19 Ignition switch - check and replacement

Warning: *Some models covered by this manual are equipped with airbags. Always disable the airbag system when working in the vicinity of airbag system components (see Section 24).*

1987 through 1995 models

Refer to illustrations 19.4a and 19.4b

1   Disconnect the negative cable from the battery.

2   The ignition switch is located on the steering column and is actuated by a rod attached to the key lock cylinder.

18.11b Release tang location on ignition key lock cylinder (1997 and later models)

POSITION	CIRCUIT	
START	I-1, B-1 & S	CONNECTED
	G-1, G-2	GROUNDED
ON	I-1 & B-1	CONNECTED
	A & B-2	CONNECTED
	I-3 & B-3	CONNECTED
OFF	OPEN	
OFF-LOCK	OPEN	
ACC.	A & B-2	CONNECTED

19.4a Terminal details and schematic diagram of the ignition switch

Check

3   Remove the switch (see Steps 6 through 9).
4   Use an ohmmeter or self-powered test light and the accompanying illustration and check chart to check for continuity between the switch terminals **(see illustrations).**
5   If the switch does not have correct continuity, replace it.

Replacement

6   Disconnect the negative cable from the battery.
7   Insert the key into the lock cylinder and turn it to the Off-Lock position.
8   On models so equipped, remove the intermittent wiper module.
9   Unplug the electrical connector, remove the bolts, then detach the switch from the actuator rod and lower it from the steering column.
10   Installation is the reverse of removal. Move the switch slider to the Accessory position. On standard steering columns, this is all the way to the left (steering wheel side), on tilt columns, all the way to the right (away from the steering wheel). As the switch is engaged to the actuator rod, push the switch down the steering column to remove any slack from the rod before fully tightening the bolts.

1997 through 2000 models

Refer to illustrations 19.14, 19.15 and 19.16
11   Remove the ignition key lock cylinder

19.4b Ignition switch continuity chart - continuity should be as specified in each switch position

(see Section 18).
12   Remove the lower steering column cover screws **(see illustration 18.11a)** and remove the cover.
13   Unplug the two electrical connectors from the ignition switch.
14   Remove the ignition switch retaining screw **(see illustration).** (The screw is a tamper-proof Torx type.)
15   Using a small screwdriver, depress the locking tab **(see illustration)** and remove the ignition switch from the steering column.
16   Installation is the reverse of removal. Before installing the switch, rotate the slot in the switch to the ON position **(see illustration).**

2001 and later models

Refer to illustrations 19.20, 19.21 and 19.22
17   Remove the ignition key lock cylinder.
18   Remove the multi-function switch.

19.16 Before installing the switch, be sure to rotate the slot in the switch to the ON position (1997 and later models)

19.20 Location of the tamper-proof Torx screw

19.14 Remove the ignition switch retaining screw (the tamper-proof Torx type) (1997 and later models)

19.15 Using a small screwdriver, depress the lock tab and remove the ignition switch from the steering column (1997 and later models)

19   Disconnect the wiring from the switch.
20   Use a tamper-proof Torx screwdriver to remove the screw securing the switch **(see illustration).** These special screwdrivers are available at tool dealers and some auto supply stores.
21   Release the switch from the lock tabs by pulling it straight out **(see illustration).**

19.21 The switch is pulled straight out to release it

19.22 This is the switch turned to the ON position (it must be in this position before it can be installed)

22   To install the switch, first turn it to the On position **(see illustration)**.
23   The remainder of installation is the reverse of removal.

20   Instrument cluster - removal and installation

Warning: *Some models covered by this manual are equipped with airbags. Always disable the airbag system when working in the vicinity of airbag system components (see Section 24).*

1987 through 1995 models

Refer to illustrations 20.3, 20.4, 20.5a and 20.5b

1   Disconnect the negative cable from the battery.
2   Remove the instrument cluster bezel (see Chapter 11).
3   On 1991 and earlier models, remove the retaining screws and detach the indicator bezel **(see illustration)**.
4   Remove the cluster and switch panel screws and pull the cluster out far enough for access to the electrical and speedometer connectors **(see illustration)**. On some models it may be necessary to disconnect the

20.3 Remove the screws and detach the indicator bezel

speedometer cable at the transmission or cruise control adapter to provide sufficient slack so the cluster can be pulled out (see Section 19).
5   Unplug the connectors, detach the speedometer cable (later models) and remove the cluster **(see illustrations)**.
6   Installation is the reverse of removal.

1997 and later models

Refer to illustrations 20.11a, 20.11b and 20.12

7   Disconnect the negative battery cable and wait at least two minutes before proceeding.
8   Remove the headlight switch knob and shaft (see Section 13).
9   Remove the two screws that retain the cover for the steering column opening **(see illustration 24.8 in Chapter 11)**. Pull the steering column opening cover straight back as far back as it will go. Work the lower edge of the cover rearward to disengage the hooks on the lower edge of the cover from the pivots on the lower edge of the instrument panel. Remove the cover.
10   The instrument panel top cover uses five equally-spaced snap clip retainers to attach the top cover to the instrument panel. Using a suitable tool with a wide, flat blade, carefully pry up the instrument panel top cover from

20.4 Cluster and switch panel screw locations

20.5a On later models, the speedometer is part of the cluster and you'll have to disconnect the speedometer cable by squeezing the release lever as shown here

the instrument panel **(see illustration 24.28 in Chapter 11)**.
11   Remove the two screws that attach the lower edge of the cluster to the instrument panel and remove the three screws that attach the upper edge of the cluster to the instrument panel **(see illustrations)**. Pull off the cluster bezel and remove it from the instrument panel.
12   Remove the four screws that attach the instrument cluster to the instrument panel **(see illustration)**.

20.5b Pull the cluster out and detach the electrical connector

20.11a To detach the instrument cluster bezel, remove these two screws from the lower edge of the cluster . . .

20.11b . . . and remove these three screws from the upper edge (1997 and later models)

20.12 To detach the instrument cluster from the instrument panel, remove the four retaining screws (1997 and later models)

13   Pull the instrument cluster back and disconnect it from the two "self-docking" electrical connectors.

14   Installation is the reverse of removal. (The two self-docking connectors are rigidly mounted and are aligned with their corresponding connector halves in the back of the cluster. When the cluster is placed in position and pushed back into place, it will automatically plug into the connectors.)

21   Speedometer cable (1987 through 1995 models) - removal and installation

Refer to illustration 21.2

Warning: *Some models covered by this manual are equipped with airbags. Always disable the airbag system when working in the vicinity of airbag system components (see Section 24).*

1   Disconnect the negative cable from the battery.

2   Disconnect the speedometer cable from the transmission/transfer case or cruise control adapter **(see illustrations).**

3   Detach the cable from the routing clips in the engine compartment and pull the cable up to provide enough slack to allow disconnection from the speedometer.

21.2 Unscrew the collar and pull the speedometer cable out of the cruise control adapter (shown) or transmission housing

4   Remove the instrument cluster screws, pull the cluster out and disconnect the speedometer cable from the back of the cluster **(see illustration 18.5a).**

5   Remove the cable from the vehicle.

6   Prior to installation, lubricate the speedometer end of the cable with spray-on speedometer cable lubricant (available at auto parts stores).

7   Installation is the reverse of removal.

22   Windshield wiper motor - removal and installation

1987 through 1995 models

Refer to illustrations 22.2, 22.3, 22.4, 22.5, 22.9 and 22.11

Removal

1   Disconnect the negative cable from the battery.

2   Use a pencil or marking pen to mark the

22.2 After marking the position, grasp the wiper arm, insert a punch or ice pick in the release clip hole and pull the arm assembly off the spindle

arm-to-spindle relationship, remove the windshield wiper arms **(see illustration).**

3   Remove the hold-down bolts at the corners and fold the windshield forward, out of the way. Remove the wiper motor screws or bolts **(see illustration).**

4   Use a screwdriver to disconnect the wiper linkage drive arm **(see illustration).**

5   Grasp the motor securely, lift it out through the access hole and detach the drive arm by prying it off the pivot (DO NOT remove the pivot nut) **(see illustration).**

6   On models with intermittent wipers, remove the two screws and detach the wiper module from the instrument panel.

7   Reach up under the instrument panel in the passengers compartment and unplug the motor electrical connector, then remove the wiper motor from the vehicle.

Installation

8   Insert the wiring harness through the access hole and plug it in. Install the intermittent wiper module.

22.3 Wiper motor bolt location (arrows)

22.4 Pry the wiper linkage drive arm off with a screwdriver

22.5 Pry the drive arm off the pivot with a screwdriver - DO NOT remove the nut

9   Turn the wiper motor on to cycle it to the Park position, shut if off, then connect the wiper linkage drive arm to the motor **(see illustration)**.
10   Lower the motor and arm assembly into position and install the screws/bolts. Tighten the screws/bolts securely.
11   Connect the drive arm to the pivot shaft **(see illustration)**.
12   The remainder of installation is the reverse of removal.

1997 and later models

Front motor

Refer to illustrations 22.13 and 22.19

13   Remove the screw that attaches the center of the cowl plenum cover/grille panel to the cowl plenum **(see illustration)**.
14   Open and support the hood.
15   Peel the ends of the cowl-to-hood seal away from the metal flange where the dash panel and cowl plenum panel meet. Pull back the seal far enough to access the screws that secure the outer ends of the cowl plenum cover/grille panel to the cowl plenum panel.
16   Remove the screw that attaches each outer end of the cowl plenum cover/grille panel to the cowl plenum panel.
17   Remove the cowl plenum cover/grille panel. Be careful not to damage the paint around the pivot openings of the panel.
18   Reach into the cowl plenum and unplug the wiper motor electrical connector.
19   Remove the three wiper module mounting bracket screws **(see illustration)**.
20   Remove the wiper module from the cowl plenum as a unit.
21   Release the retainer that secures the wiper motor electrical harness to the wiper module bracket.
22   Turn over the wiper module and remove the nut that attaches the wiper linkage crank arm to the wiper motor output shaft.

22.9 Use large pliers to press the drive arm onto the shaft

23   Remove the three screws that attach the wiper motor to the wiper module mounting bracket.
24   Installation is the reverse of removal.

Rear motor

Refer to illustration 22.25

25   From the outside of the liftgate glass, remove the rear wiper motor output shaft nut and bezel **(see illustration)**.
26   From the outside of the liftgate glass, remove the rear wiper motor output shaft rubber gasket.
27   From the inside of the liftgate glass, remove the three screws that attach the rear wiper motor cover to the motor.
28   Disconnect the electrical connector from the motor.
29   Loosen - but don't remove - the right liftgate glass hinge nut.
30   From the inside of the liftgate glass, carefully separate the wiper motor from the liftgate glass until the output shaft clears the hole in the glass.
31   Move the motor to the right until the

22.11 Press the drive arm evenly onto the wiper motor shaft using two pairs of pliers

slotted hole in the motor mounting bracket clears the grommet under the right liftgate glass hinge nut.
32   Remove the rear wiper motor.
33   Installation is the reverse of removal.

23   Cruise control system - description and check

The cruise control system maintains vehicle speed with a vacuum actuated servo motor located in the engine compartment, which is connected to the throttle linkage by a cable. The system consists of the servo motor, clutch switch, brake switch, control switches, a relay and associated vacuum hoses.

Because of the complexity of the cruise control system and the special tools and techniques required for diagnosis, repair should be left to a dealer service department or a repair shop. However, it is possible for the home mechanic to make simple checks of the wiring and vacuum connections for minor faults which can be easily repaired.

22.13 Cowl plenum cover/grille panel mounting details (1997 and later models)

22.19 Front windshield wiper motor mounting details (1997 and later models)

22.25 Rear windshield wiper motor mounting details (1997 and later models)

24.4 Airbag module and steering wheel details - 1995 models

These include:

a) *Inspect the cruise control actuating switches for broken wires and loose connections.*

b) *Check the cruise control fuse.*

c) *The cruise control system is operated by vacuum so it's critical that all vacuum switches, hoses and connections are secure. Check the hoses in the engine compartment for tight connections, cracks and obvious vacuum leaks.*

24 Airbag system (1995 and later models) - general information

1   1995 and later models are equipped with a Supplemental Restraint System (SRS), more commonly known as airbags. This system is designed to protect the driver and, on 1997 and later models, the front seat passenger, from serious injury in the event of a head-on or frontal collision. It consists of an airbag module in the center of the steering wheel, and, on 1997 and later models, the right side of the instrument panel. 1995 models have a self-contained system, in which the impact sensor is housed within the airbag module on the steering wheel. The system on 1997 and later models utilizes a control module (which contains an impact sensor) mounted on the forward part of the transmission tunnel, under the heater/air conditioner floor duct, a "clock-spring" under the steering wheel which can transmit current to the driver's side airbag module regardless of steering wheel position, and a passenger's side airbag module mounted above he glove box.

2   Whenever working in the vicinity of any airbag system components it is important to disable the system to prevent accidental deployment of the airbag(s), which could cause personal injury.

1995 models

Disarming the system

Refer to illustration 24.4

3   Roll down the driver's side window.

4   Pry off the small cover from the top of the steering wheel hub. Get out of the vehicle and close the door, then using an 8 mm socket, reach in and unscrew the arming screw until it stops (it should protrude approximately one inch from the surface of the steering wheel trim) **(see illustration)**. The airbag is now disarmed.

Arming the system

5   Reach through the driver's window and turn the arming screw until it is seated (tighten it to approximately 15 in-lbs). Install the arming screw cover on the steering wheel hub.

Airbag module removal and installation

6   Disarm the airbag system as described earlier in this Section.

7   Removal of the driver's side airbag is covered in Chapter 10, Section 9.

1997 and later models

Disarming the system

8   Turn the ignition switch to the Off position. Disconnect the cable from the negative terminal of the battery. Make sure the battery cable cannot accidentally come into contact with the battery terminal.

9   Wait at least two minutes for the back-up power supply to be depleted before beginning work.

Arming the system

10   Make sure the ignition switch to the Off position.

11   Connect the cable to the negative terminal of the battery.

12   Turn the ignition switch to the On position. Confirm that the airbag warning light glows for 6 to 8 seconds, then goes out, indicating the system is functioning properly.

Centering the clockspring

13   If the airbag system clockspring becomes uncentered (during steering wheel removal, for example), it must be centered to prevent it from breaking.

14   With the steering wheel removed, turn the clockspring rotor clockwise until it stops (don't apply too much force) **(see illustrations)**.

24.14a Airbag module, steering wheel and clockspring details - 1997 and later models

15   Turn the clockspring rotor counterclockwise about 2-1/2 turns; the flats on the rotor
should be horizontal and the arrow on the
rotor should be pointing straight up. Also, the
wiring harness should be positioned at the
bottom; if it isn't, turn the clockspring an
additional 1/2 turn.

16   Install the steering wheel following the
procedure described in Chapter 10.

Airbag module removal and installation

Driver's side

17   Disarm the airbag system as described
earlier in this Section.

18   Removal of the driver's side airbag is
covered in Chapter 10, Section 9.

Passenger side

Refer to illustration 24.21

19   Disarm the airbag system as described
earlier in this Section.

20   Remove the instrument panel (see
Chapter 11).

21   Prop the instrument panel up on its side.
Remove the three nuts that attach the airbag
module to the instrument panel **(see illustration)**.

22   Remove the airbag module.

23   Installation is the reverse of removal. Be
sure to tighten the airbag module retaining
screws to the torque listed in this Chapter's
Specifications.

25   Wiring diagrams - general information

Refer to illustration 25.4

Since it isn't possible to include all
wiring diagrams for every year covered by
this manual, the following diagrams are those
that are typical and most commonly needed.

Prior to troubleshooting any circuits,
check the fuse and circuit breakers (if
equipped) to make sure they're in good condition. Make sure the battery is properly
charged and check the cable connections
(see Chapter 1).

When checking a circuit, make sure that
all connectors are clean, with no broken or
loose terminals. When unplugging a connector, do not pull on the wires. Pull only on the
connector housings themselves.

Refer to the accompanying chart for the
wire color codes applicable to your vehicle
(see illustration).

**24.14b When properly centered,
the airbag clockspring will be
positioned like this, with the
arrow on the rotor pointing
straight up, the flats in the center
of the rotor will be horizontal,
and the wiring harness will be
positioned at the bottom**

**24.21 To detach the
passenger side airbag
module from the
instrument panel,
remove these three nuts**

**25.4 Wiring diagram
color codes**

COLOR CODE	COLOR	STANDARD TRACER COLOR	COLOR CODE	COLOR	STANDARD TRACER CODE
BL	BLUE	WT	OR	ORANGE	BK
BK	BLACK	WT	PK	PINK	BK OR WT
BR	BROWN	WT	RD	RED	WT
DB	DARK BLUE	WT	TN	TAN	WT
DG	DARK GREEN	WT	VT	VIOLET	WT
GY	GRAY	BK	WT	WHITE	BK
LB	LIGHT BLUE	BK	YL	YELLOW	BK
LG	LIGHT GREEN	BK	*	WITH TRACER	

Symbol	Description	Symbol	Description
+	POSITIVE	CONNECTOR	CONNECTOR
−	NEGATIVE	MALE CONNECTOR	MALE CONNECTOR
	GROUND	FEMALE CONNECTOR	FEMALE CONNECTOR
	FUSE	MULTIPLE CONNECTOR	MULTIPLE CONNECTOR
	CIRCUIT BREAKER	DENOTES WIRE CONTINUES ELSEWHERE	DENOTES WIRE CONTINUES ELSEWHERE
	CAPACITOR	SPLICE	SPLICE
Ω	OHMS	SPLICE IDENTIFICATION	SPLICE IDENTIFICATION
	RESISTOR	OPTIONAL WIRING WITH / WIRING WITHOUT	
	VARIABLE RESISTOR	THERMAL ELEMENT (BI-METAL STRIP)	
	SERIES RESISTOR	"Y" WINDINGS	
	COIL	"DELTA" WINDINGS	
	STEP UP COIL	88:88	DIGITAL READOUT
	OPEN CONTACT	SINGLE FILAMENT LAMP	
	CLOSED CONTACT	DUAL FILAMENT LAMP	
	CLOSED SWITCH	L.E.D.-LIGHT EMITTING DIODE	
	OPEN SWITCH	THERMISTOR	
	CLOSED GANGED SWITCH	GAUGE	
	OPEN GANGED SWITCH	TIMER	TIMER
	TWO POLE SINGLE THROW SWITCH	MOTOR	
	PRESSURE SWITCH	ARMATURE AND BRUSHES	
	SOLENOID SWITCH	DENOTES WIRE GOES THROUGH GROMMET	
	MERCURY SWITCH	DENOTES WIRE GOES THROUGH 40 WAY DISCONNECT	
	DIODE OR RECTIFIER	STRG COLUMN	DENOTES WIRE GOES THROUGH 11 WAY STEERING COLUMN CONNECTOR
	BY-DIRECTIONAL ZENER DIODE		

Wiring diagram legend

Typical 2.5L engine fuel injection system wiring diagram (2 of 3) (1987 through 1995 models)

Typical 2.5L engine fuel injection system wiring diagram (1 of 3) (1987 through 1995 models)

Typical starting system wiring diagram (1987 through 1995 models)

Typical 2.5L engine fuel injection system wiring diagram (3 of 3) (1987 through 1995 models)

Typical charging system wiring diagram (1987 through 1995 models)

Typical ignition switch wiring diagram (1987 through 1995 models)

Typical front end lighting wiring diagram (1987 through 1995 models)

Typical 4.0L engine fuel injection system wiring diagram (1987 through 1995 models)

Typical headlight switch wiring diagram (1987 through 1995 models)

Typical instrument panel lighting wiring diagram (1987 through 1995 models)

Typical Stop/turn and hazard flasher system wiring diagram (1987 through 1995 models)

Typical standard windshield washer/wiper system wiring diagram (1987 through 1995 models)

Typical emission maintenance reminder wiring diagram (1987 through 1995 models)

Typical intermittent windshield washer/wiper system wiring diagram (1987 through 1995 models)

Typical rear washer/wiper system wiring diagram (1987 through 1995 models)

Typical backup lamp/neutral safety switch wiring diagram (1987 through 1995 models)

Typical heater system wiring diagram (1987 through 1995 models)

Typical air conditioning system wiring diagram (1987 through 1995 models)

Typical rear lighting wiring diagram (1987 through 1995 models)

Typical starting system circuit (1997 and later models)

Typical charging system circuit (1997 and later models)

Typical front lighting circuit (1997 and later models) (2 of 5)

Typical front lighting circuit (1997 and later models) (1 of 5)

Typical front lighting circuit (1997 and later models) (4 of 5)

Typical front lighting circuit (1997 and later models) (3 of 5)

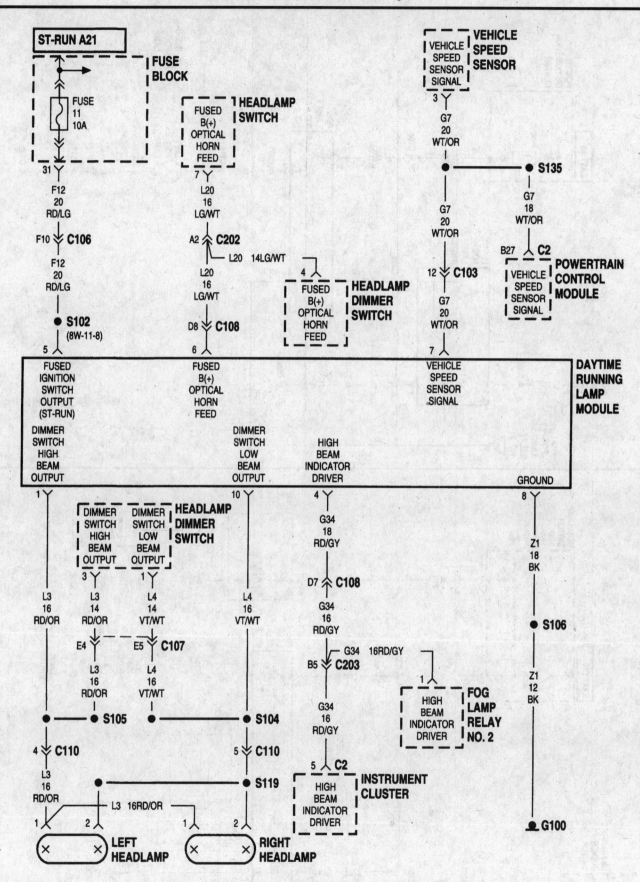

Typical front lighting circuit (1997 and later models) (5 of 5)

Typical rear lighting circuit (1997 and later models) (1 of 3)

Typical rear lighting circuit (1997 and later models) (3 of 3)

Typical rear lighting circuit (1997 and later models) (2 of 3)

Typical turn signal circuit (1997 and later models) (1 of 2)

Typical turn signal circuit (1997 and later models) (2 of 2)

Typical windshield wiper and washer circuit (1997 and later models) (2 of 3)

Typical windshield wiper and washer circuit (1997 and later models) (1 of 3)

Typical windshield wiper and washer circuit (1997 and later models) (3 of 3)

Typical air conditioning and heater circuit (1997 and later models) (1 of 2)

Typical air conditioning and heater circuit (1997 and later models) (2 of 2)

Typical interior lighting circuit (1997 and later models) (1 of 4)

Typical interior lighting circuit (1997 and later models) (2 of 4)

Typical interior lighting circuit (1997 and later models) (4 of 4)

Typical interior lighting circuit (1997 and later models) (3 of 4)

Typical audio system circuit (1997 and later models) (1 of 2)

Typical audio system circuit (1997 and later models) (2 of 2)

Typical fuel and ignition system circuit (1997 and later models) (1 of 14)

Typical fuel and ignition system circuit (1997 and later models) (2 of 14)

Typical fuel and ignition system circuit (1997 and later models) (3 of 14)

Typical fuel and ignition system circuit (1997 and later models) (4 of 14)

Typical fuel and ignition system circuit (1997 and later models) (5 of 14)

Typical fuel and ignition system circuit (1997 and later models) (7 of 14)

Typical fuel and ignition system circuit (1997 and later models) (6 of 14)

Typical fuel and ignition system circuit (1997 and later models) (9 of 14)

Typical fuel and ignition system circuit (1997 and later models) (8 of 14)

Typical fuel and ignition system circuit (1997 and later models) (10 of 14)

Typical fuel and ignition system circuit (1997 and later models) (11 of 14)

Typical fuel and ignition system circuit (1997 and later models) (12 of 14)

Typical fuel and ignition system circuit (1997 and later models) (13 of 14)

Typical instrument circuit (1997 and later models) (1 of 8)

Typical fuel and ignition system circuit (1997 and later models) (14 of 14)

Typical instrument circuit (1997 and later models) (2 of 8)

Typical instrument circuit (1997 and later models) (3 of 8)

Typical instrument circuit (1997 and later models) (4 of 8)

Typical instrument circuit (1997 and later models) (5 of 8)

Typical instrument circuit (1997 and later models) (6 of 8)

Typical instrument circuit (1997 and later models) (8 of 8)

Typical instrument circuit (1997 and later models) (7 of 8)

Index

Haynes Automotive Manuals

NOTE: If you do not see a listing for your vehicle, consult your local Haynes dealer for the latest product information.

HAYNES XTREME CUSTOMIZING
11101 Sport Compact Customizing
11102 Sport Compact Performance
11110 In-car Entertainment
11150 Sport Utility Vehicle Customizing
11213 Acura
11255 GM Full-size Pick-ups
11314 Ford Focus
11315 Full-size Ford Pick-ups
11373 Honda Civic

ACURA
12020 Integra '86 thru '89 & Legend '86 thru '90
12021 Integra '90 thru '93 & Legend '91 thru '95

AMC
Jeep CJ - see JEEP (50020)
14020 Mid-size models '70 thru '83
14025 (Renault) Alliance & Encore '83 thru '87

AUDI
15020 4000 all models '80 thru '87
15025 5000 all models '77 thru '83
15026 5000 all models '84 thru '88

AUSTIN-HEALEY
Sprite - see MG Midget (66015)

BMW
18020 3/5 Series not including diesel or all-wheel drive models '82 thru '92
18021 3-Series incl. Z3 models '92 thru '98
18022 3-Series, E46 chassis '99 thru '05, Z4 models '03 thru '05
18025 320i all 4 cyl models '75 thru '83
18050 1500 thru 2002 except Turbo '59 thru '77

BUICK
19010 Buick Century '97 thru '05
Century (front-wheel drive) - see GM (38005)
19020 Buick, Oldsmobile & Pontiac Full-size (Front-wheel drive) '85 thru '05
Buick Electra, LeSabre and Park Avenue; Oldsmobile Delta 88 Royale, Ninety Eight and Regency; Pontiac Bonneville
19025 Buick Oldsmobile & Pontiac Full-size (Rear wheel drive)
Buick Estate '70 thru '90, Electra '70 thru '84, LeSabre '70 thru '85, Limited '74 thru '79
Oldsmobile Custom Cruiser '70 thru '90, Delta 88 '70 thru '85, Ninety-eight '70 thru '84
Pontiac Bonneville '70 thru '81, Catalina '70 thru '81, Grandville '70 thru '75, Parisienne '83 thru '86
19030 Mid-size Regal & Century all rear-drive models with V6, V8 and Turbo '74 thru '87
Regal - see GENERAL MOTORS (38010)
Riviera - see GENERAL MOTORS (38030)
Roadmaster - see CHEVROLET (24046)
Skyhawk - see GENERAL MOTORS (38015)
Skylark - see GM (38020, 38025)
Somerset - see GENERAL MOTORS (38025)

CADILLAC
21030 Cadillac Rear Wheel Drive all gasoline models '70 thru '93
Cimarron - see GENERAL MOTORS (38015)
DeVille - see GM (38031 & 38032)
Eldorado - see GM (38030 & 38031)
Fleetwood - see GM (38031)
Seville - see GM (38030, 38031 & 38032)

CHEVROLET
24010 Astro & GMC Safari Mini-vans '85 thru '03
24015 Camaro V8 all models '70 thru '81
24016 Camaro all models '82 thru '92
24017 Camaro & Firebird '93 thru '02
Cavalier - see GENERAL MOTORS (38016)
Celebrity - see GENERAL MOTORS (38005)
24020 Chevelle, Malibu & El Camino '69 thru '87
24024 Chevette & Pontiac T1000 '76 thru '87
Citation - see GENERAL MOTORS (38020)
24027 Colorado & GMC Canyon '04 thru '06
24032 Corsica/Beretta all models '87 thru '96
24040 Corvette all V8 models '68 thru '82
24041 Corvette all models '84 thru '96
10305 Chevrolet Engine Overhaul Manual
24045 Full-size Sedans Caprice, Impala, Biscayne, Bel Air & Wagons '69 thru '90
24046 Impala SS & Caprice and Buick Roadmaster '91 thru '96
Impala - see LUMINA (24048)
Lumina '90 thru '94 - see GM (38010)
Lumina APV - see GM (38035)
24048 Lumina & Monte Carlo '95 thru '05

24050 Luv Pick-up all 2WD & 4WD '72 thru '82
Malibu '97 thru '00 - see GM (38026)
24055 Monte Carlo all models '70 thru '88
Monte Carlo '95 thru '01 - see LUMINA (24048)
24059 Nova all V8 models '69 thru '79
24060 Nova and Geo Prizm '85 thru '92
24064 Pick-ups '67 thru '87 - Chevrolet & GMC, all V8 & in-line 6 cyl, 2WD & 4WD '67 thru '87; Suburbans, Blazers & Jimmys '67 thru '91
24065 Pick-ups '88 thru '98 - Chevrolet & GMC, full-size pick-ups '88 thru '98, C/K Classic '99 & '00, Blazer & Jimmy '92 thru '94; Suburban '92 thru '99; Tahoe & Yukon '95 thru '99
24066 Pick-ups '99 thru '06 - Chevrolet Silverado & GMC Sierra '99 thru '06, Suburban/Tahoe/Yukon/Yukon XL/Avalanche '00 thru '06
24070 S-10 & S-15 Pick-ups '82 thru '93, Blazer & Jimmy '83 thru '94
24071 S-10 & Sonoma Pick-ups '94 thru '04, Blazer & Jimmy '95 thru '04, Hombre '96 thru '01
24072 Chevrolet TrailBlazer & TrailBlazer EXT, GMC Envoy & Envoy XL, Oldsmobile Bravada '02 thru '06
24075 Sprint '85 thru '88 & Geo Metro '89 thru '01
24080 Vans - Chevrolet & GMC '68 thru '96
24081 Chevrolet Express & GMC Savana Full-size Vans '96 thru '05

CHRYSLER
25015 Chrysler Cirrus, Dodge Stratus, Plymouth Breeze '95 thru '00
10310 Chrysler Engine Overhaul Manual
25020 Full-size Front-Wheel Drive '88 thru '93
K-Cars - see DODGE Aries (30008)
Laser - see DODGE Daytona (30030)
25025 Chrysler LHS, Concorde, New Yorker, Dodge Intrepid, Eagle Vision, '93 thru '97
25026 Chrysler LHS, Concorde, 300M, Dodge Intrepid, '98 thru '03
25027 Chrysler 300, Dodge Charger & Magnum '05 thru '07
25030 Chrysler & Plymouth Mid-size front wheel drive '82 thru '95
Rear-wheel Drive - see Dodge (30050)
25035 PT Cruiser all models '01 thru '03
25040 Chrysler Sebring, Dodge Avenger '95 thru '05
Dodge Stratus '01 thru 05

DATSUN
28005 200SX all models '80 thru '83
28007 B-210 all models '73 thru '78
28009 210 all models '79 thru '82
28012 240Z, 260Z & 280Z Coupe '70 thru '78
28014 280ZX Coupe & 2+2 '79 thru '83
300ZX - see NISSAN (72010)
28018 510 & PL521 Pick-up '68 thru '73
28020 510 all models '78 thru '81
28022 620 Series Pick-up all models '73 thru '79
720 Series Pick-up - see NISSAN (72030)
28025 810/Maxima all gasoline models, '77 thru '84

DODGE
400 & 600 - see CHRYSLER (25030)
30008 Aries & Plymouth Reliant '81 thru '89
30010 Caravan & Plymouth Voyager '84 thru '95
30011 Caravan & Plymouth Voyager '96 thru '02
30012 Challenger/Plymouth Saporro '78 thru '83
30013 Caravan, Chrysler Voyager, Town & Country '03 thru '06
30016 Colt & Plymouth Champ '78 thru '87
30020 Dakota Pick-ups all models '87 thru '96
30021 Durango '98 & '99, Dakota '97 thru '99
30022 Dodge Durango models '00 thru '03
Dodge Dakota models '00 thru '04
30023 Dodge Durango '04 thru '06, Dakota '05 and '06
30025 Dart, Demon, Plymouth Barracuda, Duster & Valiant 6 cyl models '67 thru '76
30030 Daytona & Chrysler Laser '84 thru '89
Intrepid - see CHRYSLER (25025, 25026)
30034 Neon all models '95 thru '99
30035 Omni & Plymouth Horizon '78 thru '90
30036 Dodge and Plymouth Neon '00 thru '05
30040 Pick-ups all full-size models '74 thru '93
30041 Pick-ups all full-size models '94 thru '01
30042 Dodge Full-size Pick-ups '02 thru '05
30045 Ram 50/D50 Pick-ups & Raider and Plymouth Arrow Pick-ups '79 thru '93
30050 Dodge/Plymouth/Chrysler RWD '71 thru '89
30055 Shadow & Plymouth Sundance '87 thru '94
30060 Spirit & Plymouth Acclaim '89 thru '95
30065 Vans - Dodge & Plymouth '71 thru '03

EAGLE
Talon - see MITSUBISHI (68030, 68031)
Vision - see CHRYSLER (25025)

FIAT
34010 124 Sport Coupe & Spider '68 thru '78
34025 X1/9 all models '74 thru '80

FORD
10355 Ford Automatic Transmission Overhaul
36004 Aerostar Mini-vans all models '86 thru '97
36006 Contour & Mercury Mystique '95 thru '00
36008 Courier Pick-up all models '72 thru '82
36012 Crown Victoria & Mercury Grand Marquis '88 thru '06
10320 Ford Engine Overhaul Manual
36016 Escort/Mercury Lynx all models '81 thru '90
36020 Escort/Mercury Tracer '91 thru '00
36022 Ford Escape & Mazda Tribute '01 thru '03
36024 Explorer & Mazda Navajo '91 thru '01
36025 Ford Explorer & Mercury Mountaineer '02 thru '06
36028 Fairmont & Mercury Zephyr '78 thru '83
36030 Festiva & Aspire '88 thru '97
36032 Fiesta all models '77 thru '80
36034 Focus all models '00 thru '05
36036 Ford & Mercury Full-size '75 thru '87
36044 Ford & Mercury Mid-size '75 thru '86
36048 Mustang V8 all models '64-1/2 thru '73
36049 Mustang II 4 cyl, V6 & V8 models '74 thru '78
36050 Mustang & Mercury Capri all models Mustang, '79 thru '93; Capri, '79 thru '86
36051 Mustang all models '94 thru '04
36052 Mustang '05 thru '07
36054 Pick-ups & Bronco '73 thru '79
36058 Pick-ups & Bronco '80 thru '96
36059 F-150 & Expedition '97 thru '03, F-250 '97 thru '99 & Lincoln Navigator '98 thru '02
36060 Super Duty Pick-ups, Excursion '99 thru '06
36061 F-150 full-size '04 thru '06
36062 Pinto & Mercury Bobcat '75 thru '80
36066 Probe all models '89 thru '92
36070 Ranger/Bronco II gasoline models '83 thru '92
36071 Ranger '93 thru '05 & Mazda Pick-ups '94 thru '05
36074 Taurus & Mercury Sable '86 thru '95
36075 Taurus & Mercury Sable '96 thru '05
36078 Tempo & Mercury Topaz '84 thru '94
36082 Thunderbird/Mercury Cougar '83 thru '88
36086 Thunderbird/Mercury Cougar '89 and '97
36090 Vans all V8 Econoline models '69 thru '91
36094 Vans full size '92 thru '05
36097 Windstar Mini-van '95 thru '03

GENERAL MOTORS
10360 GM Automatic Transmission Overhaul
38005 Buick Century, Chevrolet Celebrity, Oldsmobile Cutlass Ciera & Pontiac 6000 all models '82 thru '96
38010 Buick Regal, Chevrolet Lumina, Oldsmobile Cutlass Supreme & Pontiac Grand Prix (FWD) '88 thru '05
38015 Buick Skyhawk, Cadillac Cimarron, Chevrolet Cavalier, Oldsmobile Firenza & Pontiac J-2000 & Sunbird '82 thru '94
38016 Chevrolet Cavalier & Pontiac Sunfire '95 thru '04
38017 Chevrolet Cobalt & Pontiac G5 '05 thru '07
38020 Buick Skylark, Chevrolet Citation, Olds Omega, Pontiac Phoenix '80 thru '85
38025 Buick Skylark & Somerset, Oldsmobile Achieva & Calais and Pontiac Grand Am all models '85 thru '98
38026 Chevrolet Malibu, Olds Alero & Cutlass, Pontiac Grand Am '97 thru '03
38027 Chevrolet Malibu '04 thru '07
38030 Cadillac Eldorado '71 thru '85, Seville '80 thru '85, Oldsmobile Toronado '71 thru '85, Buick Riviera '79 thru '85
38031 Cadillac Eldorado & Seville '86 thru '91, DeVille '86 thru '93, Fleetwood & Olds Toronado '86 thru '92, Buick Riviera '86 thru '93
38032 Cadillac DeVille '94 thru '05 & Seville '92 thru '04
38035 Chevrolet Lumina APV, Olds Silhouette & Pontiac Trans Sport all models '90 thru '96
38036 Chevrolet Venture, Olds Silhouette, Pontiac Trans Sport & Montana '97 thru '05
General Motors Full-size Rear-wheel Drive - see BUICK (19025)

GEO
Metro - see CHEVROLET Sprint (24075)
Prizm - '85 thru '92 see CHEVY (24060), '93 thru '02 see TOYOTA Corolla (92036)

(Continued on other side)

Haynes North America, Inc., 861 Lawrence Drive, Newbury Park, CA 91320-1514 • (805) 498-6703

Haynes Automotive Manuals (continued)

NOTE: If you do not see a listing for your vehicle, consult your local Haynes dealer for the latest product information.

40030 Storm all models '90 thru '93
Tracker - *see SUZUKI Samurai (90010)*

GMC
Vans & Pick-ups - *see CHEVROLET*

HONDA
42010 Accord CVCC all models '76 thru '83
42011 Accord all models '84 thru '89
42012 Accord all models '90 thru '93
42013 Accord all models '94 thru '97
42014 Accord all models '98 thru '02
42015 Honda Accord models '03 thru '05
42020 Civic 1200 all models '73 thru '79
42021 Civic 1300 & 1500 CVCC '80 thru '83
42022 Civic 1500 CVCC all models '75 thru '79
42023 Civic all models '84 thru '91
42024 Civic & del Sol '92 thru '95
42025 Civic '96 thru '00, CR-V '97 thru '01, Acura Integra '94 thru '00
42026 Civic '01 thru '04, CR-V '02 thru '04
42035 Honda Odyssey all models '99 thru '04
42037 Honda Pilot '03 thru '07, Acura MDX '01 thru '07
42040 Prelude CVCC all models '79 thru '89

HYUNDAI
43010 Elantra all models '96 thru '01
43015 Excel & Accent all models '86 thru '98

ISUZU
Hombre - *see CHEVROLET S-10 (24071)*
47017 Rodeo '91 thru '02; Amigo '89 thru '94 and '98 thru '02; Honda Passport '95 thru '02
47020 Trooper & Pick-up '81 thru '93

JAGUAR
49010 XJ6 all 6 cyl models '68 thru '86
49011 XJ6 all models '88 thru '94
49015 XJ12 & XJS all 12 cyl models '72 thru '85

JEEP
50010 Cherokee, Comanche & Wagoneer Limited all models '84 thru '01
50020 CJ all models '49 thru '86
50025 Grand Cherokee all models '93 thru '04
50029 Grand Wagoneer & Pick-up '72 thru '91 Grand Wagoneer '84 thru '91, Cherokee & Wagoneer '72 thru '83, Pick-up '72 thru '88
50030 Wrangler all models '87 thru '03
50035 Liberty '02 thru '04

KIA
54070 Sephia '94 thru '01, Spectra '00 thru '04

LEXUS
ES 300 - *see TOYOTA Camry (92007)*

LINCOLN
Navigator - *see FORD Pick-up (36059)*
59010 Rear-Wheel Drive all models '70 thru '05

MAZDA
61010 GLC Hatchback (rear-wheel drive) '77 thru '83
61011 GLC (front-wheel drive) '81 thru '85
61015 323 & Protegé '90 thru '00
61016 MX-5 Miata '90 thru '97
61020 MPV all models '89 thru '94
Navajo - *see Ford Explorer (36024)*
61030 Pick-ups '72 thru '93
Pick-ups '94 thru '00 - *see Ford Ranger (36071)*
61035 RX-7 all models '79 thru '85
61036 RX-7 all models '86 thru '91
61040 626 (rear-wheel drive) all models '79 thru '82
61041 626/MX-6 (front-wheel drive) '83 thru '92
61042 626 '93 thru '01, MX-6/Ford Probe '93 thru '01

MERCEDES-BENZ
63012 123 Series Diesel '76 thru '85
63015 190 Series four-cyl gas models, '84 thru '88
63020 230/250/280 6 cyl sohc models '68 thru '72
63025 280 123 Series gasoline models '77 thru '81
63030 350 & 450 all models '71 thru '80

MERCURY
64200 Villager & Nissan Quest '93 thru '01
All other titles, see FORD Listing.

MG
66010 MGB Roadster & GT Coupe '62 thru '80
66015 MG Midget, Austin Healey Sprite '58 thru '80

MITSUBISHI
68020 Cordia, Tredia, Galant, Precis & Mirage '83 thru '93

68030 Eclipse, Eagle Talon & Ply. Laser '90 thru '94
68031 Eclipse '95 thru '01, Eagle Talon '95 thru '98
68035 Mitsubishi Galant '94 thru '03
68040 Pick-up '83 thru '96 & Montero '83 thru '93

NISSAN
72010 300ZX all models including Turbo '84 thru '89
72015 Altima all models '93 thru '04
72020 Maxima all models '85 thru '92
72021 Maxima all models '93 thru '04
72030 Pick-ups '80 thru '97 Pathfinder '87 thru '95
72031 Frontier Pick-up '98 thru '04, Xterra '00 thru '04, Pathfinder '96 thru '04
72040 Pulsar all models '83 thru '86
Quest - *see MERCURY Villager (64200)*
72050 Sentra all models '82 thru '94
72051 Sentra & 200SX all models '95 thru '04
72060 Stanza all models '82 thru '90

OLDSMOBILE
73015 Cutlass V6 & V8 gas models '74 thru '88
For other OLDSMOBILE titles, see BUICK, CHEVROLET or GENERAL MOTORS listing.

PLYMOUTH
For PLYMOUTH titles, see DODGE listing.

PONTIAC
79008 Fiero all models '84 thru '88
79018 Firebird V8 models except Turbo '70 thru '81
79019 Firebird all models '82 thru '92
79040 Mid-size Rear-wheel Drive '70 thru '87
For other PONTIAC titles, see BUICK, CHEVROLET or GENERAL MOTORS listing.

PORSCHE
80020 911 except Turbo & Carrera 4 '65 thru '89
80025 914 all 4 cyl models '69 thru '76
80030 924 all models including Turbo '76 thru '82
80035 944 all models including Turbo '83 thru '89

RENAULT
Alliance & Encore - *see AMC (14020)*

SAAB
84010 900 all models including Turbo '79 thru '88

SATURN
87010 Saturn all models '91 thru '02
87011 Saturn Ion '03 thru '07
87020 Saturn all L-series models '00 thru '04

SUBARU
89002 1100, 1300, 1400 & 1600 '71 thru '79
89003 1600 & 1800 2WD & 4WD '80 thru '94
89100 Legacy all models '90 thru '99
89101 Legacy & Forester '00 thru '06

SUZUKI
90010 Samurai/Sidekick & Geo Tracker '86 thru '01

TOYOTA
92005 Camry all models '83 thru '91
92006 Camry all models '92 thru '96
92007 Camry, Avalon, Solara, Lexus ES 300 '97 thru '01
92008 Toyota Camry, Avalon and Solara and Lexus ES 300/330 all models '02 thru '05
92015 Celica Rear Wheel Drive '71 thru '85
92020 Celica Front Wheel Drive '86 thru '99
92025 Celica Supra all models '79 thru '92
92030 Corolla all models '75 thru '79
92032 Corolla all rear wheel drive models '80 thru '87
92035 Corolla all front wheel drive models '84 thru '92
92036 Corolla & Geo Prizm '93 thru '02
92037 Corolla models '03 thru '05
92040 Corolla Tercel all models '80 thru '82
92045 Corona all models '74 thru '82
92050 Cressida all models '78 thru '82
92055 Land Cruiser FJ40, 43, 45, 55 '68 thru '82
92056 Land Cruiser FJ60, 62, 80, FZJ80 '80 thru '96
92065 MR2 all models '85 thru '87
92070 Pick-up all models '69 thru '78
92075 Pick-up all models '79 thru '95
92076 Tacoma '95 thru '04, 4Runner '96 thru '02, & T100 '93 thru '98
92078 Tundra '00 thru '05 & Sequoia '01 thru '05
92080 Previa all models '91 thru '95
92081 Prius all models '01 thru '08
92082 RAV4 all models '96 thru '05
92085 Tercel all models '87 thru '94
92090 Toyota Sienna all models '98 thru '02
92095 Highlander & Lexus RX-330 '99 thru '06

TRIUMPH
94007 Spitfire all models '62 thru '81
94010 TR7 all models '75 thru '81

VW
96008 Beetle & Karmann Ghia '54 thru '79
96009 New Beetle '98 thru '05
96016 Rabbit, Jetta, Scirocco & Pick-up gas models '75 thru '92 & Convertible '80 thru '92
96017 Golf, GTI & Jetta '93 thru '98 & Cabrio '95 thru '98
96018 Golf, GTI, Jetta & Cabrio '99 thru '02
96020 Rabbit, Jetta & Pick-up diesel '77 thru '84
96023 Passat '98 thru '01, Audi A4 '96 thru '01
96030 Transporter 1600 all models '68 thru '79
96035 Transporter 1700, 1800 & 2000 '72 thru '79
96040 Type 3 1500 & 1600 all models '63 thru '73
96045 Vanagon all air-cooled models '80 thru '83

VOLVO
97010 120, 130 Series & 1800 Sports '61 thru '73
97015 140 Series all models '66 thru '74
97020 240 Series all models '76 thru '93
97040 740 & 760 Series all models '82 thru '88
97050 850 Series all models '93 thru '97

TECHBOOK MANUALS
10205 Automotive Computer Codes
10206 OBD-II & Electronic Engine Management Systems
10210 Automotive Emissions Control Manual
10215 Fuel Injection Manual, 1978 thru 1985
10220 Fuel Injection Manual, 1986 thru 1999
10225 Holley Carburetor Manual
10230 Rochester Carburetor Manual
10240 Weber/Zenith/Stromberg/SU Carburetors
10305 Chevrolet Engine Overhaul Manual
10310 Chrysler Engine Overhaul Manual
10320 Ford Engine Overhaul Manual
10330 GM and Ford Diesel Engine Repair Manual
10333 Building Engine Power Manual
10340 Small Engine Repair Manual, 5 HP & Less
10341 Small Engine Repair Manual, 5.5 - 20 HP
10345 Suspension, Steering & Driveline Manual
10355 Ford Automatic Transmission Overhaul
10360 GM Automatic Transmission Overhaul
10405 Automotive Body Repair & Painting
10410 Automotive Brake Manual
10411 Automotive Anti-lock Brake (ABS) Systems
10415 Automotive Detailing Manual
10420 Automotive Electrical Manual
10425 Automotive Heating & Air Conditioning
10430 Automotive Reference Manual & Dictionary
10435 Automotive Tools Manual
10440 Used Car Buying Guide
10445 Welding Manual
10450 ATV Basics
10452 Scooters, Automatic Transmission 50cc to 250cc

SPANISH MANUALS
98903 Reparación de Carrocería & Pintura
98904 Carburadores para los modelos Holley & Rochester
98905 Códigos Automotrices de la Computadora
98910 Frenos Automotriz
98913 Electricidad Automotriz
98915 Inyección de Combustible 1986 al 1999
99040 Chevrolet & GMC Camionetas '67 al '87 Incluye Suburban, Blazer & Jimmy '67 al '91
99041 Chevrolet & GMC Camionetas '88 al '98 Incluye Suburban '92 al '98, Blazer & Jimmy '92 al '94, Tahoe y Yukon '95 al '98
99042 Chevrolet & GMC Camionetas Cerradas '68 al '95
99055 Dodge Caravan & Plymouth Voyager '84 al '95
99075 Ford Camionetas y Bronco '80 al '94
99077 Ford Camionetas Cerradas '69 al '91
99088 Ford Modelos de Tamaño Mediano '75 al '86
99091 Ford Taurus & Mercury Sable '86 al '95
99095 GM Modelos de Tamaño Grande '70 al '90
99100 GM Modelos de Tamaño Mediano '70 al '88
99106 Jeep Cherokee, Wagoneer & Comanche '84 al '00
99110 Nissan Camioneta '80 al '96, Pathfinder '87 al '95
99118 Nissan Sentra '82 al '94
99125 Toyota Camionetas y 4Runner '79 al '95

Over 100 Haynes motorcycle manuals also available

10-07